Normans
Byzantines

PENGUIN BOOKS

A HISTORY OF VENICE

John Julius Norwich was born in 1929. He was educated at Upper
Canada College, Toronto, at Eton, at the University of Strasbourg
and, after a spell of National Service in the Navy, at New College,
Oxford, where he took a degree in French and Russian. In 1952 he
joined the Foreign Service, where he remained for twelve years,
serving at the embassies in Belgrade and Beirut and with the British
Delegation to the Disarmament Conference at Geneva. In 1964 he
resigned from the service in order to write.

His many and varied publications include two books on the medieval
Norman Kingdom in Sicily, *The Normans in the South* and *The
Kingdom in the Sun*, which are published by Penguin in one volume
entitled *The Normans in Sicily*; two travel books, *Mount Athos* (with
Reresby Sitwell) and *Sahara*; *The Architecture of Southern England*;
Glyndebourne; two anthologies of poetry and prose, *Christmas
Crackers* and *More Christmas Crackers*; and *A History of Venice*,
originally published in two volumes. He is also the author of a three-
volume history of the Byzantine Empire: *Byzantium: The Early
Centuries*, *Byzantium: The Apogee* and *Byzantium: The Decline
and Fall*. Many of his books are published by Penguin. In addition he
has written and presented some thirty historical documentaries for
television, and is a regular lecturer on Venice and numerous other
subjects.

Lord Norwich is chairman of the Venice in Peril Fund, Co-chairman
of the World Monuments Fund and a former member of the
Executive Committee of the National Trust. He is a Fellow of the
Royal Society of Literature, the Royal Geographical Society and
the Society of Antiquaries, and a Commendatore of the Ordine al
Merito della Repubblica Italiana. He was made a CVO in 1993.

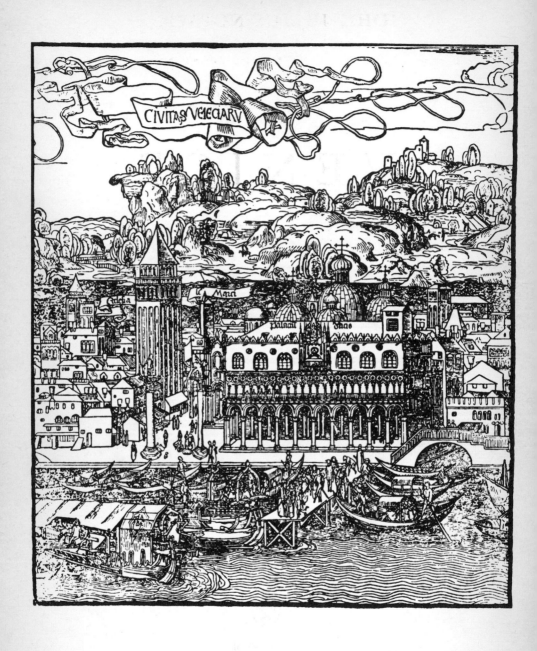

JOHN JULIUS NORWICH

A History of

VENICE

Penguin Books

PENGUIN BOOKS

Published by the Penguin Group
Penguin Books Ltd, 27 Wrights Lane, London W8 5TZ, England
Penguin Putnam Inc., 375 Hudson Street, New York, New York 10014, USA
Penguin Books Australia Ltd, Ringwood, Victoria, Australia
Penguin Books Canada Ltd, 10 Alcorn Avenue, Toronto, Ontario, Canada M4V 3B2
Penguin Books (NZ) Ltd, Private Bag 102902, NSMC, Auckland, New Zealand

Penguin Books Ltd, Registered Offices: Harmondsworth, Middlesex, England

First published by Allen Lane in two volumes:
Venice, the Rise to Empire 1977, and *Venice, the Greatness and the Fall* 1981
Published by Allen Lane in one volume: *A History of Venice* 1982
Published in Penguin Books 1983
7 9 10 8

Printed in England by Clays Ltd, St Ives plc
Set in Monophoto Garamond

The author and publishers are grateful to the following for permission
to use photographs: B.B.C. Hulton Picture Library for the frontispiece
and nos. 50, 51; Bodleian Library, Oxford, for nos. 14, 28; Osvaldo
Böhm, Venice, for nos. 1, 3, 6, 7, 8, 9, 10, 11, 13, 15, 16, 17, 20, 22, 23,
25, 26; the Trustees of the British Museum for nos. 12, 41, 48, 49, 53,
59; Courtauld Institute of Art for nos. 4, 5, 24, 27, 29, 30; the Italian
Tourist Office for no. 2; Mansell Collection for nos. 18, 19, 21, 31, 32,
33, 34, 35, 36, 37, 38, 39, 42, 43, 44, 45, 46, 47, 54, 55, 56, 58; the
National Gallery, London, for no. 57; The Trustees of the National
Maritime Museum for nos. 40, 52.

For Jason
and in memory of the grandfather
he never knew who loved Venice
and should have written this book

Contents

CONTENTS

PART THREE *A Power in Europe*

PART FOUR *Decline and Fall*

Illustrations

Maps

Central and Eastern Mediterranean

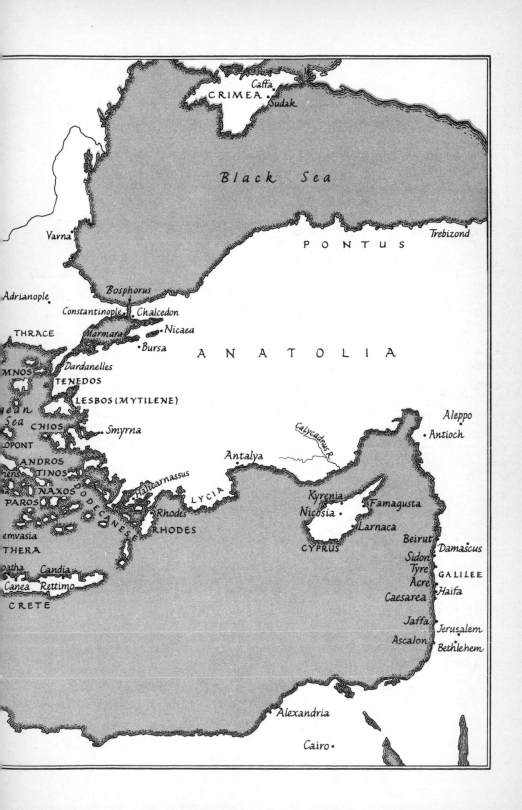

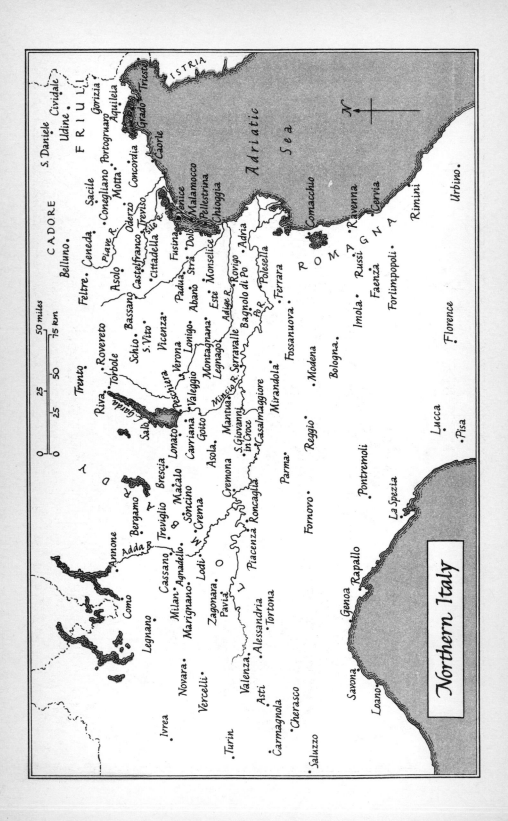

Northern Italy

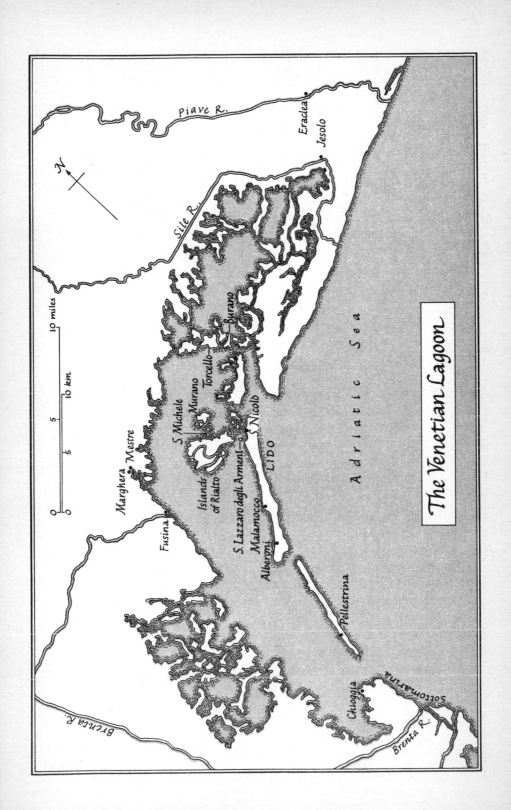

The Venetian Lagoon

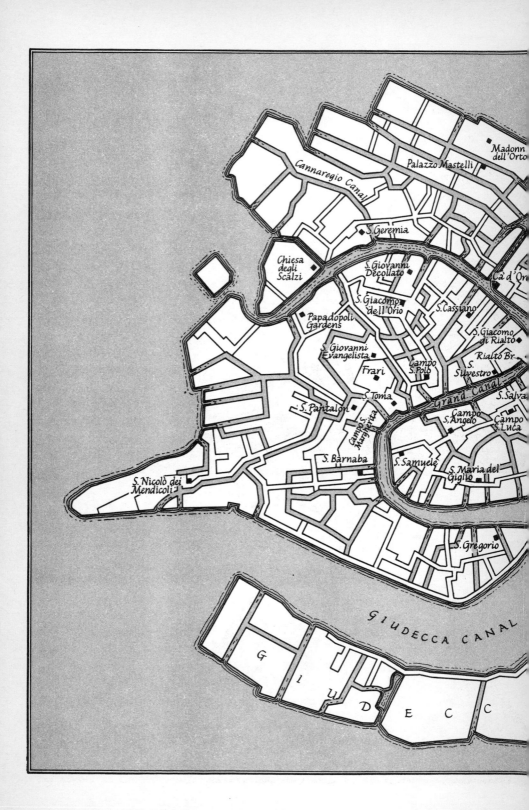

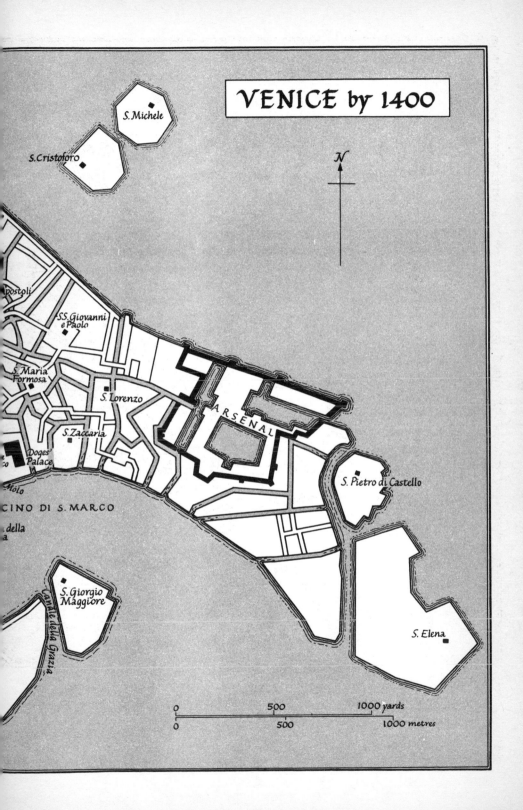

VENICE by 1400

S. Michele

S. Cristoforo

N

postoli

SS. Giovanni
e Paolo

S. Maria
Formosa

S. Lorenzo

ARSENAL

S. Zaccaria

Doges
Palace

S. Pietro di Castello

Molo

CINO DI S. MARCO

della
a

S. Giorgio
Maggiore

Canale della Grazia

S. Elena

0   500   1000 yards
0   500   1000 metres

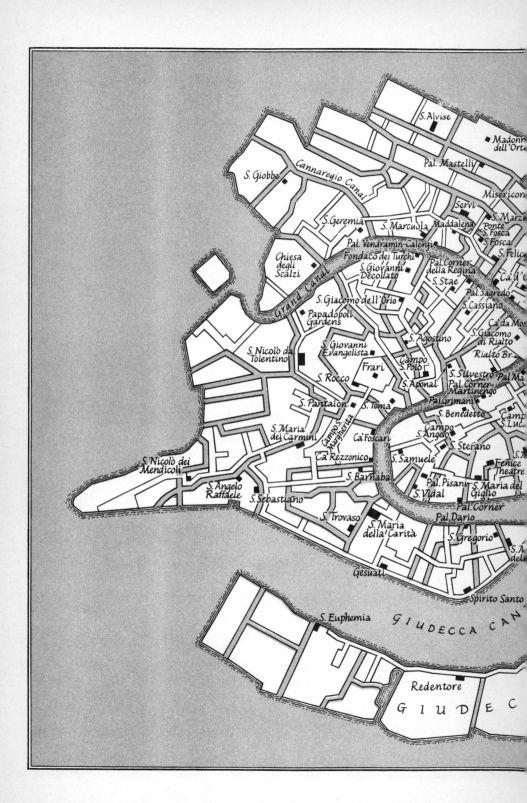

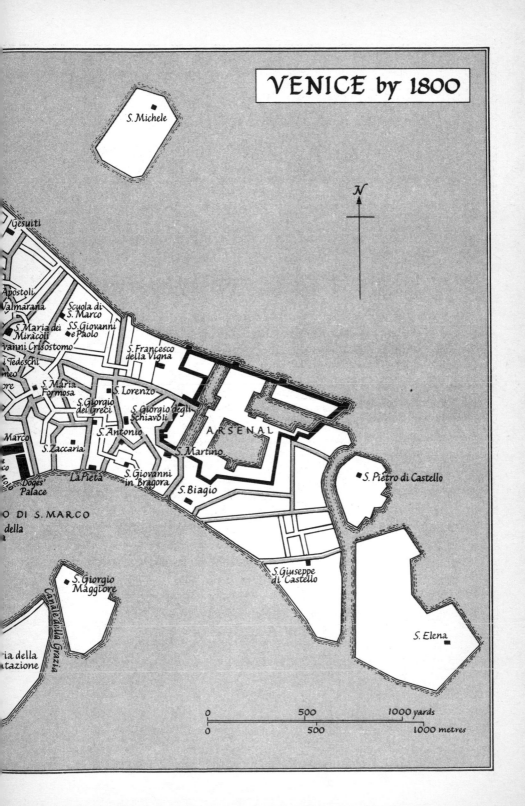

VENICE by 1800

N

S. Michele

Gesuiti

Apostoli
Valmarana

Scuola di
S. Marco

S. Maria dei
Miracoli

SS. Giovanni
e Paolo

vanni Crisostomo

S. Francesco
della Vigna

i Tedeschi

neo

ore

S. Maria
Formosa

S. Lorenzo

S. Giorgio
dei Greci

S. Giorgio degli
Schiavoli

Marco

S. Antonio

ARSENAL

S. Zaccaria

S. Martino

S. Pietro di Castello

o

Doges'
Palace

La Pietà

S. Giovanni
in Bragora

S. Biagio

O DI S. MARCO

della

S. Giuseppe
di Castello

S. Giorgio
Maggiore

Canale della Grazia

S. Elena

ria della
tazione

| 0 | | 500 | | 1000 yards |
| 0 | | 500 | | 1000 metres |

Joe Links

Acknowledgements

During the shamefully long time that I have been working on this book, I have received help and encouragement from many friends, both English and Venetian. Some debts, however, must be individually acknowledged, and my particular thanks must go to Mollie Philipps, for her unflagging – and invaluable – work on the bibliography and illustrations; to Joe Links, himself the author of one of the most delightful books on Venice ever written, for the loan of books and for his eagle-eyed scrutiny of the proofs; to Peter Lathrop Lauritzen for the bottomless erudition with which he cleared up several knotty problems on the spot; to Jean Curtis and Euphan Scott for their patient typing and retyping of an almost indecipherable manuscript; to Barbara Reynolds for allowing me to use her translation of the Ariosto epigraph to Chapter 2; to Douglas and Sarah Matthews for the index; to Marilyn Perry, Philip Longworth, and the late John Benn. My only regret is that readers of this one-volume edition will not have a chance of seeing the lovely jackets designed by my wife Anne for the two separate volumes of the original English edition.

Almost every word in the pages which follow was written in the Reading Room of the London Library, my debt to which – as to every member of its superb staff – can only be recorded, never measured.

Introduction

First experiences should be short and intense. When my parents took me to
Venice in the summer of 1946, we stayed only a few hours; but I can still feel –
not remember, *feel* – the impact it made on my sixteen-year-old brain. With
his usual blend of firmness and commonsense, my father limited to two the
buildings we actually entered: the Basilica of St Mark and Harry's Bar. For
the rest of the time, wandering on foot or drifting gently in a gondola, I
subconsciously absorbed the first essential Venetian lesson – a lesson, incidentally, that poor Ruskin, beavering away at his crockets and cusps round
the Doges' Palace, never learnt: that in Venice, more than anywhere else,
the whole is greater than the sum of the parts. However majestic the churches,
however magnificent the *palazzi*, however dazzling the pictures, the ultimate
masterpiece remains Venice itself. Interiors, even the great golden mystery
of St Mark's, are but details. The relation of Piazza and Piazzetta, the sublime setting of S. Giorgio Maggiore at precisely the right angle to the Molo,
the play of light at a canal's curve, the slap of water against the hull of a
gondola, the all-pervading smell of the sea – for let there be no mistake
about it, except when the wind is blowing across from Mestre and Marghera,
Venice is the sweetest-smelling city in Europe – these are the first things to
be experienced and understood. There will be time for Titian and Tintoretto
later. Even Carpaccio must wait his turn.

As we wandered and drifted, my father talked about Venetian history,
and I learned that Venice was not just the most beautiful city that I had ever
seen; she had also been an independent republic for over 1,000 years – longer
than the period separating us from the Norman Conquest – during much of
which she had been mistress of the Mediterranean, the principal crossroads

xxi

between East and West, the richest and most prosperous commercial centre of the civilized world. He told me how the sea had protected her, not only in her first stormy beginnings but all through her history, making her the only city in Italy never to have been invaded, ravaged or destroyed – never, that is, until Napoleon, the self-styled 'Attila of the Venetian State', in a single sustained outburst of vindictive malice, put an end to the Most Serene Republic forever. Her unique system of government, my father admitted, was stern, occasionally even harsh; but he believed that it had a better record of fairness and justice than any other in Europe, and that it had been much maligned by historians. For that very reason, one of these days, he intended to write a history of Venice himself and set the record straight.

We departed, that first day, just as dusk was falling and the lights were coming on along the Grand Canal; I have never left any city with such bitter regret. But the next year we were back again, for longer; I began to explore on my own, and discovered what I now know to be one of the major pleasures of life: that of walking through Venice at night. By eleven, the streets are virtually deserted by all but the cats; the lighting, limited to the occasional ordinary electric bulb, is perfect; the silence is broken only by one's own footsteps and the occasional ripple of unseen water. On those walks, now nearly thirty years ago, I fell in love with the city. I have walked it, and loved it, ever since.

My father died on New Year's Day, 1954. Although he left a considerable collection of books on Venice and a few pages of notes, his long-projected history remained unwritten. The need for it, however, seems to me to be greater now even than it was in his day. More and more publicity is rightly given to the city's desperate struggle for survival; and yet, despite a plethora of admirable guide-books, descriptive essays, surveys of art and architecture and historical studies of individual periods, I know of only one (and that all too short) consecutive general history of the Republic written in English in the twentieth century. In the nineteenth, admittedly, there were several; but all of these, to my possibly jaundiced eye, tend to veer between the inaccurate and the unreadable – or, indeed, as often as not, to combine the two.

This book, then, is an attempt to fill the gap – to tell the whole story of Venice, from her misty beginnings to that sad day for Europe when Doge Lodovico Manin slowly removed his ducal cap and gave it to his secretary, murmuring that he would not be needing it again. The task has not been easy. One of the most intractable problems with which the historian of Venice has to contend is that which stems from the instinctive horror, amounting at times to a phobia, shown by the Republic to the faintest suggestion of the cult of personality. Sooner or later, anyone tackling the subject

Latin
Casanova
Carmagnola

finds himself looking wistfully across to the *terra firma* and that superb, swaggering pageant of Medici and Malatesta, Visconti and della Scala, Sforza and Borgia and Gonzaga. The echoing names of Venice, by contrast, evoke *palazzi* more often than people, and it is hard to find much human interest in the decrees and deliberations of the faceless Council of Ten.

Another difficulty has been the constant temptation to digress; to talk more about painting and sculpture, music and architecture, costumes, customs and social life – particularly the social life of the eighteenth century, which attained a level of sophisticated artificiality equalled only, perhaps, by the military life of three hundred years before. (Casanova and Carmagnola – who was more out of touch with reality? Which figure was the more tragic – or, for that matter, the more ultimately ridiculous?) This temptation I have tried so far as possible to resist – though I am conscious of having been less than entirely successful, particularly where architecture is concerned. Books on such subjects are plentiful nowadays, expertly written and profusely illustrated; and the present work is quite long enough as it is.

It would have been a good deal longer still but for the fact that in the history of Venice there always seems to be too much happening or too little. The early years, when the primary sources are few and all too often contradictory, can be quickly covered; but, as the Republic increases in importance, so the picture becomes more and more complex. The period extending from the thirteenth century, which began with the Latin capture of Constantinople and the foundation of Venice's commercial Empire, to the sixteenth with its long and miserable story of French intervention in Italy, leading to that agonizing moment when Venice saw virtually the whole of civilized Europe ranged against her – that period is so packed with incident, so crammed with complication, that there were moments when I doubted whether my work would ever be done, or whether anyone would read it if it were. Then, suddenly, the pace slackens. To readers who may raise their eyebrows when they find fewer pages given to a century in the later part of this book than were allotted to a decade in the central section, and who thereby deduce with relief that the author is running out of steam, I can only point out that all political historians of the Republic, of whatever nationality and at whatever period they were writing, have been suspected of the same. The simple fact is that in the seventeenth century, by comparison with its predecessors, relatively little happened in the political life of the Republic, and in the eighteenth – at least until the end – even less; but for which happy circumstance I should have several more years' work still ahead of me.

And yet, though the problems have been great, far greater have been the compensations. The sheer individuality of the place, for one thing. For

INTRODUCTION

Venice, alone of all the still-great cities of Italy, was born and brought up Greek. It is no accident that she possesses the greatest Byzantine church in the world that is still used for Christian worship, and a Patriarch to preside in it. Long after she shed her dependence on Constantinople, she continued to turn her back on Italy and to look resolutely eastward; the nightmare tangle of medieval Italian politics, of Guelf and Ghibelline, Emperor and Pope, feudal baron and civic commune – none of this was for her. And by the time she did at last condescend to carve out a mainland empire, her character was fixed in its own unique and quirkish mould.

Secondly, there is the unchanging quality of the city itself. Protected by the waters of her lagoon throughout her independent history from all foreign invaders except the last – and, in the present century, from the more insidious menace of the motor car – Venice still maintains essentially the same appearance that she presented to the world not only in the days of Canaletto but even in those of Carpaccio and Gentile Bellini. This apparent triumph over time would be an extraordinary phenomenon in any city; when the city happens to be the most beautiful in the world, the phenomenon becomes a miracle. It is also a particular blessing for the historian since it enables him to conjure up, in his own imagination at any rate, a far clearer and livelier vision of his subject at earlier periods than would have been possible anywhere else in Europe.

But this is not a work of imagination, and I have tried to keep mine firmly in check. Nor, on the other hand, is it a work of profound scholarship; the sheer time span has forced me to keep the narrative moving ahead at all costs, and there has been little opportunity for detailed analysis. The one luxury I have allowed myself has been the occasional reference to buildings and monuments still standing in Venice today which have a direct bearing on the events described. For the rest, my only aim has been to tell the story as concisely and coherently as possible; my only regret that the task of doing so has fallen to me rather than to my father, who would have done it so much more brilliantly, a quarter of a century ago.

Il n'est pas rare de voir de grandes émigrations de peuples inonder un pays, en changer la face et ouvrir pour l'histoire une ère nouvelle; mais qu'une poignée de fugitifs, jetée sur un banc de sable de quelques cents toises de largeur, y fonde un état sans territoire; qu'une nombreuse population vienne couvrir cette plage mouvante, où il ne se trouve ni végétation, ni eau potable, ni matériaux, ni même de l'espace pour bâtir; que de l'industrie nécessaire pour subsister, et pour affermir le sol sous leurs pas, ils arrivent jusqu'à présenter aux nations modernes le premier exemple d'un gouvernement régulier, jusqu'à faire sortir d'un marais des flottes sans cesse renaissantes, pour aller renverser un grand empire, et recueillir les richesses de l'Orient; qu'on voit ces fugitifs tenir la balance politique de l'Italie, dominer sur les mers, réduire toutes les nations à la condition de tributaires, enfin rendre impuissants tous les efforts de l'Europe liguée contre eux: c'est là sans doute un développement de l'intelligence humaine qui mérite d'être observé.

DARU, *Histoire de la République de Venise*

PART ONE

The Barbarian Invasions
to the Fourth Crusade

QUESTION: *Quid est mare?*
ANSWER: *Refugium in periculis.*

Alcuin's Catechism

I

Beginnings

[to 727]

A few in fear
Flying away from him, whose boast it was
That the grass grew not where his horse had trod,
Gave birth to Venice. Like the water-fowl,
They built their nests above the ocean waves;
And where the sands were shifting, as the wind
Blew from the north or south – where they that came
Had to make sure the ground they stood upon,
Rose, like an exhalation from the deep,
A vast metropolis, with glistening spires,
With theatres, basilicas adorned;
A scene of light and glory, a dominion,
That has endured the longest among men.

Samuel Rogers

The origins of Venice encircle her still. No great city has managed to preserve, in its immediate surroundings, so much of the atmosphere and environment which gave it birth. The traveller approaching Venice, whether by sea as she should be approached, or by land across the causeway, or even by air, gazes out on the same flat, desolate expanse of water and reed and marsh that the first Venetians chose for their own; and is struck, more forcibly every time, not just by the improbability but by the sheer foolhardiness of their enterprise. It is a curious world, this world of the Venetian lagoon; some 200 square miles of salt water, much of it shallow enough for a man to wade through waist-deep, but criss-crossed with deeper channels along which Venetian shipping has for centuries made its way to the open sea; studded with shoals formed by the silt which the Brenta, Sile and other, grander streams like the Po and the Adige have brought down from the Alps; scored with endless lines of posts and piles driven into its sandy bed to mark invisible but important features – lobster pots and fishing-grounds, wrecks and cables, moorings, shallows, and recommended routes to be followed by the *vaporetti* that ply to and fro between the city and the outlying islands. In any season, under any light,

Lombardy

it appears strangely devoid of colour; the water is not deep enough to take on either the rich, velvety blue of the central Mediterranean or that astringent green that characterizes much of the Adriatic. And yet, especially on autumn evenings when the days are drawing in and the surface glistens like oil under a low, misty sun, it can be beautiful – so beautiful that one is surprised that the great Venetian painters, seduced as always by the splendour of their city, took so little interest in their less immediate surroundings. How differently the Dutch would have reacted! But then the Venetian school was essentially joyous; the lagoon, for all its beauty, can be quite unutterably sad. Who in their senses, one wonders, would leave the fertile plains of Lombardy to build a settlement – let alone a city – among these marshy, malarial wastes, on little islets of sand and couchgrass, the playthings of current and tide?

This is a question to which there can be only one answer, since there is only one motive strong enough to induce so apparently irrational a step – fear. The first builders of Venice were frightened men. Where they originally came from is immaterial; Illyria probably, though there is a tradition as old as Homer himself that they were of Anatolian stock, and had fled westward after the fall of Troy. However that may be, by about A.D. 400, when the history of Venice begins, they were living prosperous, cultivated lives in a chain of splendid cities of the Roman Empire like Padua and Altino, Concordia and Aquileia, strung out along the northern and north-western shores of the Adriatic, looking to the lagoon for their supplies of salt and fresh fish but for very little else.

So, doubtless, they would have continued, given half a chance. But then, in the early years of the fifth century, the barbarians swept down. The Goths came first under their leader Alaric, falling on Aquileia in 402, pillaging and burning their way through the rich provinces of Istria and Venetia, sending a tremor of shock and foreboding down the whole length of Italy. The populations of the towns and villages fled before them, seeking a refuge at once unenviable and inaccessible, where their enemies would have neither the incentive nor the ability to follow them. Thus it was that the wisest came to the islands of the lagoon. There, they believed, these savages from landlocked central Europe, lacking both ships and knowledge of the sea, would – with any luck – ignore them, turning their attention instead to the richer and far more tempting prizes on the mainland. They were right. As further surges of invaders followed during the next few years, rolling in an intermittent avalanche down the peninsula, so more and more fugitives found their way through the channels and shoals to safety. In 410 Alaric sacked Rome; and eleven years later the

4

city of Venice was formally brought into being – at the stroke of noon on Friday 25 March 421.

So, at least, runs the old and venerable Venetian tradition. Unfortunately the document on which it is based, connecting the foundation with a visit by three consuls sent out from Padua to establish a trading-post on the islands of the Rialto, is a good deal more plausible than it is authentic. Such a mission may well have landed on the islands; it may even, as the document goes on to assert, have celebrated the event by raising up a church dedicated to St James.[1] But certainly the Paduans made little or no attempt to follow up this early attempt at colonial expansion, while the date given with such formidable exactitude seems rather too early for any independent initiative on the part of the islanders themselves. In the first half of the century at least, few of them yet saw themselves as permanent residents. When each wave of barbarians had passed, the majority would return to their homes – or what was left of them – and try to resume their old mainland lives. It was only later that their descendants came to understand that this was not to be.

For the Goths were merely the beginning. In 452 they were followed by a new scourge, fiercer and far more cruel – Attila the Hun, advancing remorselessly over North Italy, leaving a trail of devastation and destruction behind him. He too attacked Aquileia, which defended itself heroically for three months until its besiegers, unaccustomed to such resistance, were minded to give up the attempt and pass on to some easier victim. But one day Attila, on a tour of the walls, looked up and noticed a flight of young storks heading away from the city with their young. 'He seized,' – the quotation from Gibbon is irresistible – 'with the ready penetration of a statesman, this trifling incident which chance had offered to superstition', and pointed it out to his soldiers as a sure sign that Aquileia was doomed. Thus encouraged, they renewed their efforts; and a day or two later the ninth greatest metropolis in the Roman Empire was little more than an empty shell.

In the years that followed, more and more towns and villages and homesteads suffered a similar fate; and the flow of refugees increased. Many continued to return to the mainland when the danger had passed but there were many others who, finding their new lives more congenial than they had expected, made up their minds to stay. Thus, as conditions

---

1. It is this legend that lies at the root of the claim of the church of S. Giacomo di Rialto to be the oldest in Venice. The present building, however, goes back no further than the end of the eleventh century (see p. 82, n. 1).

on the mainland deteriorated, the island communities grew and began to prosper; and in 466 their respective representatives met together at Grado to work out a rudimentary system of self-government, through tribunes elected annually by each of them. It was a loose association at this stage, and one that was not even confined to the little archipelago which we now know as Venice; Grado itself lies on its own lagoon due south of Aquileia, some sixty miles away. But that distant assembly marks, more accurately than anything else, the beginning of the slow constitutional process from which the Most Serene Republic was ultimately to evolve.

Self-government, to be sure, is not the same as independence; yet the geographical isolation of these early Venetians did enable them to hold themselves politically aloof from the successive upheavals by which Italy was now being shaken. Even the fall of the Roman Empire of the West and the dethronement of its last Emperor, the callow young Romulus Augustulus, by the barbarian Odoacer caused few ripples out in the lagoons. And when Odoacer was in his turn overthrown by Theodoric the Ostrogoth, even Theodoric may have been a little unsure how far he could presume on Venetian obedience. A letter, addressed in the year 523 to 'the maritime tribunes' from his capital at Ravenna by his praetorian prefect Cassiodorus, certainly seems somewhat fulsome for what must have been after all a fairly routine piece of government business. 'The Istrian harvests of wine and oil', writes Cassiodorus,

have this year been particularly abundant, and orders have been given for their safe transport to Ravenna. Pray show your devotion, therefore, by bringing them hither with all speed. For you possess many vessels in the region . . . and you will be, in a sense, sailing through your native country. Besides your other blessings, there is open to you a way which is ever free of danger; for when the winds rage and the sea is closed against you, you may sail up the pleasantest of rivers. Your ships need fear no angry gusts, since they may continually hug the shore. Often, with their hulls invisible, they seem to be moving across the fields. Sometimes you pull them with ropes, at others men help them along with their feet . . .

For you live like sea birds, with your homes dispersed, like the Cyclades, across the surface of the water. The solidity of the earth on which they rest is secured only by osier and wattle; yet you do not hesitate to oppose so frail a bulwark to the wildness of the sea. Your people have one great wealth – the fish which suffices for them all. Among you there is no difference between rich and poor; your food is the same, your houses are all alike. Envy, which rules the rest of the world, is unknown to you. All your energies are spent on your salt-fields; in them indeed lies your prosperity, and your power to purchase those things which you have not. For though there may be men who have little need of gold, yet none live who desire not salt.

Be diligent, therefore, to repair your boats – which, like horses, you keep tied up at the doors of your dwellings – and make haste to depart . . .[1]

Even when allowances are made for Cassiodorus's naturally florid style, the impression he leaves is unmistakable: though these strange water-people could be extremely useful to the central government, they must be handled with care. Yet the real value of his letter lies in the picture that it gives – the earliest that has come down to us – of life in the lagoons.[2] It shows, too, that the twin pillars on which the future greatness of Venice was to be based – commerce and sea power – were even then firmly in position. Already those early settlers had trade in their blood. The salt that they gathered from their shallow pans was not only a valuable commodity in itself; it could also be used to preserve the fish and game that they netted with almost equal ease from the waters and marshes around them. By the middle of the sixth century the flat-bottomed Venetian trading barge was a common sight along the rivers of north and central Italy.

A rudimentary navy, too, was taking shape. In Theodoric's day, so far as we can tell, it was called upon mainly for the occasional transportation of essential supplies to Ravenna; but the peace that Theodoric had brought to the peninsula did not long survive his death. Though his original invasion had been carried out under Byzantine auspices, his subsequent rule had been absolute; he had brooked no interference, from Constantinople or anywhere else. Under him, Italy was no longer in any real sense part of the Eastern Empire. To make matters worse, he and his subjects after him had continued zealously to uphold their Arian beliefs. Arianism – according to which Christ was not truly divine, but merely a creation of God the Father and therefore inferior to Him – had long since been condemned as heresy; unfortunately, however, it had been preached by the first Christian missionaries with whom most of the barbarians had come in contact, and it was still openly professed by nearly all the tribes of Europe. Theodoric himself was a tolerant man, who protected all shades of religious belief and had decreed particularly severe penalties for anti-semitism; but the faith of his people made them fair

1. *Variarum*, Book XII, Letter 24.
2. For a more recent, but inevitably less authentic, attempt to recreate the atmosphere of sixth-century Venice, it is interesting to compare d'Annunzio's violently chauvinistic play *La Nave*, set in Venice in A.D. 552.

game for Byzantine ambitions. Thus it was, in 535, that the Emperor Justinian launched his great campaign for the reconquest of his Italian heritage, entrusting the task to his most gifted general, Belisarius.

Once again the people of the lagoons remained, so far as they were able to remain, on the sidelines; but once again their ships were in urgent demand, this time for less peaceful purposes. In 539 Belisarius and his army reached the walls of Ravenna. The Venetians were requested to hold their harbours ready for any Greek ships that might arrive with reinforcements, sending all their own available smaller vessels to assist in the blockade of the capital.

Ravenna fell; Italy became imperial once again; and though many years were to pass before peace returned to the whole peninsula, the old Roman provinces of Venetia and Istria, territorially unchanged, readily submitted to their new Greek masters. To their inhabitants this was no hardship. Day-to-day administration continued as before in the hands of their own elected tribunes; their relations with the imperial authorities were distant but cordial. In 551 we find them helping Belisarius's successor, the septuagenarian eunuch Narses, by bringing a contingent of Lombard mercenaries by sea to Ravenna after they had been cut off by floods. In return, Narses is said to have built two churches on the islands of Rialto. One, which bore the names of Sts Geminianus and Menna – a curious twinning of a bishop of Modena and an obscure Phrygian martyr – probably stood in what is now the middle of St Mark's Square; the other, occupying the site of the present chapel of St Isidore in the basilica itself, was dedicated to Venice's first tutelary saint, St Theodore of Amasea, who can still be seen with his dragon-crocodile on the western column of the Piazzetta.

Twice in twelve years the Venetians had come to the aid of Constantinople, with a fleet that was now beyond doubt the most powerful in the Adriatic. They may well therefore have been treated with some special consideration by the imperial Exarch at Ravenna and his provincial governor, the *magister militum*; and something of the kind is certainly suggested by the *Altino Chronicle*, a gloriously ungrammatical hotch-potch of fact and legend put together in the twelfth century which remains, for better or worse, one of our principal sources for these early years. It tells a slightly garbled story of how, after the death of Justinian in 565 had brought about Narses' disgrace and dismissal, his successor Longinus paid an official visit to the lagoon. The Venetians' address to him on this occasion is worth quoting:

The Lord, who is our help and protection, has preserved us that we may live in these watery marshes, in our huts of wood and wattle. For this new Venice which we have raised in the lagoons has become a mighty habitation for us, so that we fear no invasion or seizure by any of the Kings or Princes of this world, nor even by the Emperor himself . . . unless they come by sea, and therein lies our strength.

Despite the implied defiance of these words, Longinus seems to have been given an enthusiastic enough reception, 'with bells and flutes and cytherns and other instruments of music, loud enough to drown the very thunder of heaven'. Later, Venetian ambassadors accompanied him to Constantinople and returned with the first formal agreement to be concluded between Venice and Byzantium according to which, in return for their loyalty and service when required, the settlements were assured of military protection and trading privileges throughout the Empire.

The *Altino Chronicle* claims that Longinus deliberately refrained from demanding any formal oath of submission, and for the next thousand years patriotic local opinion was staunchly to maintain that Venice was never entirely subject to Byzantium. The words quoted above – transcribed, let it be remembered, after an interval of some six centuries – are another reflection of this attitude; it is only in the past hundred years or so that Byzantine scholars have looked hard and mercilessly at the contemporary evidence and have established beyond question that the early Venetians, whether or not they enjoyed special privileges, remained subjects of the Empire in the fullest sense of the term, just as surely as their less fortunate neighbours on the mainland. Independence did not miraculously descend on them at their city's birth; like their democratic institutions, it was to grow, slowly and organically, over the years – which may be why it lasted so long.

Eunuchs, as everybody knows, are dangerous people to cross; and the dismissal of Narses, if tradition is to be believed, had far greater consequences for Venice – and indeed for all Italy – than the clarification of her political status. The old man had served his Emperor well. At an age when he might have expected a comfortable retirement he had been fighting one desperate campaign after another, up and down the whole length of the peninsula. Even after his final defeat of the Ostrogoths among the foothills of Vesuvius in 553, his task was not done. He had at once embarked on a programme of reorganization and reconstruction – on which he was still engaged, twelve years later at the age of eighty-seven, when the blow fell. As a crowning insult after his dismissal, the Empress

Sophia sent him a golden distaff and invited him, since he was no true man, to go and spin in the apartments of her women. 'I will spin her such a skein,' Narses is said to have muttered, 'that she shall not find the end of it in her lifetime'; at once he sent off messengers, laden with all the fruits of the Mediterranean, to the Lombard King Alboin in what is now Hungary, inviting him to lead his people down to the land which brought forth such abundance.

Alboin accepted, and in 568 the Lombards invaded Italy in the last, and the most lasting, of the barbarian invasions. Once again the long trains of refugees made their way from the mainland cities to the settlements in the lagoons; but now there was a difference. No longer did they come as individual frightened men and women, intending to remain in their self-inflicted exile only until better times returned. They had lost their faith in those better times. They had had enough of the bloodshed and the rapine and the wanton destruction that grew worse with every new visitation of this human plague. Now they arrived *en masse*, whole communities together, led by their bishops bearing the sacred relics which, enshrined in the churches that they were to build in their new homes, would provide a symbolic continuity with their former lives – the one tangible link between the past and present.

The early histories are rich in the stories and legends connected with these new migrations as, during the next seventy years, Lombard power spread over Italy. The *Altino Chronicle* records, for example, how Bishop Paul of that city heard a voice from heaven commanding him to climb to the top of a nearby tower and look at the stars; and how those stars showed him – presumably by the paths made by their reflections on the water – the island to which he must lead his flock. They settled in Torcello, naming it after the 'little tower' the bishop had climbed. Similarly, with episcopal if not always divine guidance, the people of Aquileia – now laid waste for the third time in 150 years – found their way to Grado, those of Concordia to Caorle, those of Padua to Malamocco. Finally in 639, in the reign of the Emperor Heraclius, the Lombards captured Oderzo – whose inhabitants, together with the Greek provincial administration, fled to the already existing settlement of Cittanova at the mouth of the Piave. Oderzo had been the last imperial foothold in mainland Venetia. Henceforth, apart from an isolated corner of the Istrian peninsula, the once-great province was reduced to the settlements on the lagoon. Its provincial capital was Cittanova, now renamed Heraclea in honour of the Emperor; but Torcello seems to have been considered as of at least equal importance and it was there, in that same year of 639 that a basilica was erected in honour of the Virgin, with Heraclius himself as its patron. The document recording its foundation still exists, and even identifies the Byzantine officials concerned – Isaac, Exarch of Ravenna, and Maurice, his *magister militum*; so indeed does the church itself, now known as the cathedral of S. Maria Assunta.[1]

But for the later history of the Republic the most important of these flights from Lombard domination was also one of the first – that from Aquileia to Grado. The see of Aquileia had traditionally been founded by St Mark himself, in consequence of which its metropolitan Archbishop – later to bear the title of Patriarch – was supreme in the lagoons, occupying a place in the Italian hierarchy second only to that of the Pope of Rome. At the time of which we are speaking, however, this honour was more theoretical than real, since the Archbishop Paulinus had led his followers not only away from heresy (the Lombards being Arian to a man) but also, almost simultaneously, into schism. The historical and theological reasons for his break with Rome – the Schism of the Three Chapters, as it is generally called – need not detain us here. What is significant for our purposes is the fact that, ecclesiastically speaking, Venice was born schismatic; and though the Metropolitan of Grado was to return to the Roman fold in 608 the schism continued, in the person of a rival Archbishop at old Aquileia, for nearly another century – during which each persisted in his denunciation of the other as an impostor and reciprocal anathemas thundered backwards and forwards between the two. At last the dispute was settled, but the old unity was gone. Aquileia and Grado continued independently of each other as separate sees, the first with authority over the old mainland territories of the province, the second covering Istria and the lagoons. Their mutual jealousies were to poison Venice's relations with the mainland, both political and religious, for generations to come; but it was the Patriarch of Grado who occupied the ancient episcopal throne in which St Mark had once sat, now re-erected in the great church built there by Paulinus and his followers soon after their arrival. That church still stands. It is dedicated, surprisingly, not to the Evangelist but to St Euphemia, the leader of an obscure group of local virgins martyred at Aquileia soon after his departure; but it begins the association of St Mark with Venice which was merely to be confirmed when his body was brought from Alexandria some 250 years later.

1. The cathedral was rebuilt in 864 and again in 1008; and it is this latter structure that we see today. The superb mosaics are slightly later, dating from the twelfth and thirteenth centuries. Owing to the ever-shifting contours of the Adriatic coast, Heraclea has now disappeared, virtually without trace. It probably stood not on the site of the present village that bears its name, but a few miles to the south-east, near Cortelazzo.

With this sudden new influx of permanent settlers Venice began to develop fast; but she was not yet, in any sense of the word, a city. Despite the two churches built by Narses, the islands of Rialto which comprise the Venice we know today were, in the sixth and seventh centuries, still largely uninhabited. At this stage the future Republic was nothing more than a loose association of island communities, dotted about over a wide area and with little effective unity except that which was imposed by its Byzantine overlords. Even its Latin name, and the one invariably used by its inhabitants, was a plural – *Venetiae*[1] – and it still had no real nucleus. Heraclea was the seat of the Byzantine governor, Grado that of the Patriarch; neither amounted to more than a large village. More prosperous than either was Torcello, whose superiority as a commercial centre was recognized but, with the passage of time, increasingly resented by her neighbours. As the individual settlements grew, such stresses and strains were probably inevitable; the Venetians of the seventh century seem to have preserved little enough of that prelapsarian innocence that had so struck Cassiodorus in the sixth. The old-established tribunes and the more recently arrived bishops tended always to contest one another's authority, while differences between one community and the next were more and more liable to lead to open fighting which the Byzantine authorities were powerless to control. The imperial presence at Heraclea prevented the Venetians themselves from producing a leader who might have given them the cohesion they needed; and there is no telling how long this unsatisfactory state of affairs might have continued but for the events of the year 726, when Byzantine Italy underwent the crisis that was ultimately to bring about its downfall.

This crisis had begun when the Byzantine Emperor Leo III ordered the destruction of all icons and holy images throughout his dominions. The effect of his decree was immediate and shattering. Everywhere men rose in wrath; the monasteries, in particular, were outraged. In the eastern provinces of the Empire, where the cult of icons had reached such proportions that they frequently served as godparents at baptisms, a puritan reaction had been inevitable and Leo had found some measure of support; but in the more moderate West, which had done nothing to deserve them, the new laws were rejected with indignation. The imperial province in

---

1. It would be pleasant, but by no means easy, to accept the traditional theory about the origin of the name. Sansovino – the scholar-son of the architect, whose *Venetia, città nobilissima et singolare, descritta in XIII libri*, published in 1581, remains one of the greatest works on the city ever penned – states it thus: 'It is held by some that this word VENETIA signifies *VENI ETIAM*, that is, Come again, and again, for however oft you come, you will always see new things, and new beauties.'

Italy, enthusiastically encouraged by Pope Gregory II, turned against its masters. Paul, Exarch of Ravenna, was assassinated, his provincial governors put to flight. Throughout the Exarchate the rebellious garrisons – all of whom had been recruited locally – chose their own commanders and asserted their independence. In the lagoon communities, their choice fell on a certain Ursus, or Orso, from Heraclea, who was placed at the head of the former provincial administration and given the title of *Dux*.

There was nothing especially remarkable about this last development; the same thing was happening almost simultaneously in many other insurgent towns. What distinguishes Venice from the rest is the fact that Orso's appointment inaugurated a tradition which was to continue, unbroken, for over a thousand years; and that his title, transformed by the rough Venetian dialect into *Doge*, was to pass down through 117 successors before the Republic's end.

One of the most infuriating aspects of early Venetian history is the regularity with which truth and legend pursue separate courses. This is a tendency of which the reader will already be only too well aware; and if he happens to have read any of the standard English works on the subject he will also know that the above account of the way the Doges began is by no means that which has been generally accepted in the past. If you believe that Venice was born in freedom you cannot at the same time accept the theory of a revolt against a foreign oppressor. According, therefore, to the authorized version, a general assembly of all the people of the lagoons had been summoned to Heraclea in 697 by the Patriarch of Grado. Pointing out that their internal conflicts were putting the whole future of the state in jeopardy, he had proposed that the Venetians should elect a single ruler in place of the twelve tribunes. Their choice had fallen on a certain Paoluccio Anafesto who, as their first Doge, shortly afterwards concluded a treaty of friendship with the Lombard King Liutprand.

As a story, this sounds perfectly probable. It certainly commands the respect due to age, since it goes back at least as far as the beginning of the eleventh century, to John the Deacon, putative author of the earliest history of Venice that we possess. And in every list of Doges, there, sure enough, is Paoluccio's name at the head; we even have an imaginary portrait of him to start off the long series around the walls of the *Sala del Maggior Consiglio* of their palace. Unfortunately, he never existed; not at least as a Doge, nor even as a Venetian. Nor was there ever any treaty with Liutprand. All we learn from the original sources is that a certain *dux* Paulicius, with Marcellus, his *magister militum*, was responsible for fixing the Venetian boundary-line near Heraclea and that this line was later accepted by the Lombards. Venetia being as we now know a Byzantine province at that time, the obvious and indeed the only legitimate conclusion to be drawn from this is that the mysterious Paulicius was none other than Paul, Exarch of Ravenna from 723 until his murder by the rebels in 727 – the very year, incidentally, to which John the Deacon ascribes the death of Paoluccio. As an imperial viceroy his authority would have been indispensable for any frontier delimitation, as would that of the provincial governor Marcellus – who, by a similar triumph of wishful thinking, has gone down in history as the city's second Doge. It is the historians of Venice, just as much as her architects, who have sunk their foundations into shifting sands.

2

Emergence

[727–811]

Lor mostra appresso un giovene Pipino
Che con sua gente par che tutto copra
Dalle Fornaci al lito pelestino;
E faccia con gran spesa e con lung' opra
Il ponte a Malamocco; e che vicino
Giunga a Rialto, e vi combatta sopra.
Poi fuggir sembra, e che i suoi lasci sotto
L'acque, che 'l ponte il vento e 'l mar gli han rotto.

Pepin the Younger he moves on to show,
Who with his army seems to cover all
The region from the outlet of the Po
As far as Pellestrina's littoral;
Who builds a pontoon bridge at Malamocco;
Whose troops attack Rialto, but to fall
Into the depths of the lagoon and drown
When wind and water wash the structure down.

Ariosto, *Orlando Furioso*
Canto XXXIII (Tr. Barbara Reynolds)

Byzantine Italy's insurrection against her Greek masters did not last long. Pope Gregory, who had provided the moral leadership, himself had no wish to see the power of the Lombard heretics further strengthened; it soon became clear that the provisions of the iconoclast decree neither would nor could be seriously enforced in the West; and as tempers cooled there seemed to emerge a general feeling that so long as the newly established democratic institutions could still be maintained in the individual cities, these would be well advised to continue as before in at least nominal adherence to the Empire. Thus it comes as no surprise to learn that within a few years of the uprising Doge Orso was granted the imperial title of *Hypatos*, or Consul – a distinction of which he seems to have been so proud that his descendants came to surname themselves *Ipato*. Whatever developments might have occurred in the political sphere, Venice's institutional and emotional links with Constantinople clearly remained unbroken. And Orso was only the first of many Doges who were to puff themselves up with Byzantine honorifics; resonant appellations like *patricius*, *proedrus* or *spatharius* appear regularly and, one sometimes suspects, indiscriminately up to the tenth century and even later. Before long the Doge's dress was to be modelled on that of the Exarch, and even on that of the Emperor himself; the ducal ceremonial was deliberately to reflect the imperial usages; Sunday prayers in St Mark's were to echo the Greek liturgy current in St Sophia. Many a Byzantine maiden was to be shipped off to the West, into the arms of a Venetian bridegroom; many a Venetian was to send his son eastward to finish his education in Constantinople.

Politically, however, the Empire's grip on Venice had been loosened. To be sure, the Greeks did not relinquish it without a struggle; but it was by now clear that Byzantine power in North Italy was dying. When in 742, after a short interregnum, Orso's son Teodato – or Deusdedit, as he is sometimes rather pedantically called – was elected second Doge of Venice, simultaneously transferring his seat of government from imperial Heraclea to the more central and republican Malamocco,[1] he found himself for all practical purposes a sovereign ruler.

Ravenna finally fell in 751, and though the vacuum left in the lagoons was more apparent than real, the Lombards might have been expected to move into Venice to fill it. Fortunately, Liutprand's successor King Aistulf had more pressing problems on his mind. In that very same year, beyond the Alps, the young Pepin – son of Charles Martel – had deposed the Merovingian King Childeric and seized the Frankish throne. Almost at once, at the invitation of Pope Stephen III, he had crossed into Italy and twice, in quick succession, had smashed the Lombard armies. Henceforth, though the greater part of his conquests was bestowed on Stephen – leading to the foundation of the Papal State and the temporal power of the Pope – the Franks were to be the controlling force in North Italy. Yet once again Venice was spared. The region of the lagoons had not formed part of the territorial redistribution; the Franks were in no hurry to extend their power any further around the Adriatic; and it was not till sixty years after the fall of the Exarchate that the Venetians were at last obliged to defend their young Republic by force of arms.

This is not, however, to say that the second half of the eighth century

1. Old Malamocco did not occupy the same site as the present village, but further across the Lido on the eastern shore. It was swept away by the sea in 1105 (see p. 82).

promised to be very much more peaceful for them than the first half had been. Venice might have found a form of government that suited her; but she had not yet achieved either internal stability or cohesion. The various settlements were still at loggerheads and even within the individual communities, seething as they were with family feuds and factional strife, flash-point was never far away. Like his father, Doge Teodato came to a violent end – being deposed and blinded by his successor who, scarcely a year later, suffered a similar fate. The fourth Doge lasted a little longer; but after eight years, becoming resentful of the two tribunes who were now elected every year to prevent the abuse of the ducal power, he too was eliminated.

With the election of Maurizio Galbaio in 764, the situation began to improve. A well-born Heraclean, claiming descent from the Emperor Galba,[1] he represented a return to the old pro-Byzantine tradition. His enemies, both the stauncher republicans and those who believed the best hopes for Venetian prosperity to lie in close association with the rising Kingdom of the Franks, would probably have branded him a reactionary; and their suspicions would have been confirmed when, in 778, he associated his son Giovanni with him in the dogeship. For the embryonic Republic, this step was as dangerous as it was unprecedented. Teodato Ipato, it was true, had succeeded his father, but his succession had not been immediate and in any case had been sanctioned by the popular vote. The elevation of Giovanni Galbaio, on the other hand, meant that he would automatically assume full powers on Maurizio's death without his subjects' approval – without, indeed, their being even consulted. To the republicans at least, the fact that the old Doge had taken the trouble to seek and obtain the consent of the Emperor in Constantinople is unlikely to have been much consolation.

It was a bad augury for the future; and the wonder is not only that Maurizio managed to carry out his intention but that in 796 Giovanni was permitted in his turn to associate his own son with him, thereby pushing Venice one step further along the road to a hereditary monarchy. The most likely explanation lies in the fact that the average Venetian was tired of bloodshed, and longed for a system by which one ruler might quietly succeed another with the minimum disruption of everyday life – and, of course, of trade. There was nothing new in this; smoothness of succession has always been one of the most telling arguments in favour of the hereditary principle and, for many nations of the world, has amply

---

1. The Galbaio family later assumed the name of Querini, in which guise it was to play a leading part in later centuries.

justified it in practice. But it was not for the Venetians, as events were soon to show.

The first of the Galbaii, reactionary or not, did much to deserve their confidence. For eleven years he ruled them strongly and well. As their prosperity increased and their numbers grew they began to spread themselves, moving out to various islands in the lagoon which, for one reason or another, the earlier settlers had tended to ignore. The Rialtine group in particular, lying about half-way between the outer line of sand-banks and the mainland shore, had remained almost deserted since the days of Narses. Muddy rather than sandy, difficult of access owing to the surrounding shallows, low-lying and thus susceptible to floods when the *acqua alta*, or high water, came surging in from the Adriatic, these islands had never before seemed a particularly tempting site for intensive colonization. But they were central, and to those who were revolted by the endless bickering and squabbling of the older communities they offered a chance of peace and a fresh start. And so, during the eighth century, building there suddenly began in earnest. At first it seems to have been concentrated at the eastern end, on the little island of Olivolo on which the Trojans, fleeing westward after the destruction of their city, were reputed to have built a fortress and which was consequently later to be known as Castello. It was here in about 775 that Doge Maurizio founded a new bishopric, and transformed a small church bearing the names of St Bacchus and St Sergius into a cathedral dedicated to St Peter.[1]

That same year the old Doge died and his son, as had been expected, gathered all the reins of power into his own hands. Alas, Giovanni Galbaio possessed little of his father's flair: he proved quite unable to deal with the developing situation in the rest of Italy, where the Franks were rapidly consolidating their position and presenting an ever-growing threat to the Republic's independence. Pepin was dead, and had been succeeded by his son Charles – Charlemagne – who had spent much of the previous fifteen years in Italy. During that time he had conceived a cordial dislike of the Venetians whom he suspected, with good reason, of making huge profits out of the slave trade, and he had already on one occasion appealed to the Pope to take active measures against them. The Pope for his part had, since Pepin's defeat of the Lombards, found

1. Another legend attributed the choice of the site to St Peter himself, appearing miraculously to the Bishop of Heraclea and indicating 'the place where he had seen a herd of oxen and sheep feeding together'. S. Pietro di Castello has since been rebuilt several times, most recently in 1598, in a rather unsuccessful pastiche of Palladio. It continued to be the cathedral church of Venice throughout the lifetime of the Republic. Only in 1807 did it yield the title to St Mark's, which till then had technically been nothing but the chapel of the Doges' Palace (see pp. 29–30).

himself master of a considerable section of the Italian peninsula; to defend and preserve it, however, he was utterly dependent on the Kingdom of the Franks. His pro-Frankish policies were naturally supported by the large majority of the Latin clergy; and so it had come about that to the two traditional factions which had already long existed in Venice – those which, at the risk of over-simplification, could be described as the pro-Byzantine at Heraclea and the republican at Malamocco – there had now grown up a third, containing a strong clerical element, which stood for the Frankish alliance.

All through the closing years of the century this third party continued to gain in strength; and it received still further impetus when, on Christmas Day 800, Charlemagne was crowned by the Pope as Emperor of the West. Under the leadership of the Patriarch of Grado – who had for some time shown himself openly rebellious towards the central authority on Malamocco – it now began seriously to threaten the security of the state. Doge Giovanni, who had by now followed his father's example and associated his son, another Maurizio, with him on the ducal throne, was fully aware of the danger; and in an effort to curb the Patriarch's influence within the Church he had recently appointed a young Greek called Christopher to the new see of Olivolo. Unfortunately, Christopher could not take up his duties without prior consecration by the Patriarch; and this ceremony, less because of the bishop's age – which was just sixteen – than because of his prematurely pronounced anti-Frankish tendencies, His Beatitude obstinately refused to perform. The Doge's reply was to send his son with a squadron of ships to Grado. The Patriarch was seized and dragged up to the top of his palace tower from which, already badly wounded, he was hurled to the ground.

Political assassinations seldom achieve the purpose for which they are intended. Horror at the crime spread far beyond Grado, where for generations to come men were to claim that they could still see the bloodstains on the paving beneath the tower; and Maurizio was hardly home before news arrived that the murdered Patriarch's nephew, Fortunatus, had been elected in his stead. More bitterly opposed to the regime of the Galbaii than even his uncle had been, Fortunatus had immediately escaped to Frankish territory; meanwhile other, secular leaders of the opposition, fearing like him that recent events in Grado might prove a prelude to a reign of terror in Venice itself, removed themselves simultaneously to Treviso where, under the leadership of a former tribune named Obelerio degli Antenori, they settled down to plot the two Doges' overthrow. In 804 they succeeded. A popular rising deposed the Galbaii, who were lucky to get away with their lives; young Bishop Christopher followed them into exile; and Obelerio returned in triumph to Venice, where he was at once raised to the supreme power.

But if the Venetians thought that this last *coup* would bring an end to their problems, they were soon disillusioned. Obelerio lost no time in elevating his brother Beato to share his throne, and the new tandem soon proved almost indistinguishable from the old. Internal unrest grew worse than ever. The upheavals of the past two years had aroused still fiercer passions which in their turn had brought about new scores to settle, new insults to be avenged. The age-long feud between Heraclea and Mala-mocco blazed up again and continued until the former was attacked and reduced to ashes. Before many months had passed it looked as though the two hapless rulers would go the way of their predecessors. But now there reappeared on the scene the Patriarch Fortunatus, fresh from the court of Charlemagne, with an offer. If Obelerio would reinstate him, making open avowal of Frankish sovereignty over Venice and the lagoons, the Doge and his brother could rely on the protection of the Western Empire.

Although Obelerio and his brother had led the opposition to the pro-Byzantine Galbaii, their hostility had been more personal than political and they had never shown any particular sympathy for the Franks. Now, however, they had little choice. Thus, on Christmas Day 805 at Aachen, the rulers of Venice did homage to Charlemagne as Emperor of the West – Obelerio even going so far as to choose for himself from among the ladies of the court a Frankish bride, who returned with him to take her place as the first *dogaressa* known to history.

The news of Venice's treachery – for so, understandably, it was considered – was received with deep displeasure at Constantinople. The Byzantines, who had always justifiably considered themselves the rightful inheritors of the Roman Empire, had not yet completely recovered from the shock of Charlemagne's coronation. When, two years later, the reigning Empress Zoë had not immediately rejected his proposal of marriage, they had lost no time in deposing her and banishing her, somewhat inappropriately, to the island of Lesbos; and the new Emperor Nicephorus, though he soon came to accept the Western Empire as a fact of life, was by no means disposed to submit to this still more recent blow to his sovereignty without protest. In 809 a Byzantine squadron sailed up the Dalmatian coast and anchored in the lagoon.

It was received coldly. The admiral's attempts at negotiations were frustrated and envenomed at every turn until at last, losing patience, he was somehow persuaded to attack – not Venice itself, but a Frankish flotilla based at Comacchio, some forty miles to the south. It proved stronger than he had thought. A few days later he retired, beaten and humiliated, to his base at Cephalonia.

In Venice now the situation was as confused as ever it had been. The renewed hostility between the two rival Empires was reflected in a fresh upsurge of party strife. Obelerio and Beato, who had now raised yet a third brother, Valentino, to share their ducal dignity, played their last card. Invoking the agreement of 805, they sent messengers to Charlemagne's son Pepin, now King of Italy at Ravenna, inviting him to occupy Venice and to garrison the entire province. And Pepin accepted. By the terms of the treaty he had little option; he might, nevertheless, have taken the trouble to find out for himself just what his reception was likely to be.

Pepin's expedition, hastily and inadequately prepared, set out from Ravenna early in 810. He found the Venetians ready for him, but not in the sense that he had been led to expect. The people of the lagoons, faced at last with a common danger, had forgotten their internal differences. The explanations and protests of their three Doges they simply ignored; the brothers were traitors, but there would be time to deal with them afterwards. Entrusting the defence of the Republic to one of the older settlers of Rialto, a certain Agnello Participazio,[1] they blocked the channels, removed all buoys and markers, and prepared to face the enemy with everything they had.

Although Pepin met with furious resistance from the moment his army entered Venetian territory, he had little difficulty in making himself master of Chioggia and Pellestrina, at the southern end of the lagoon. But at the Malamocco channel, dividing the island of Pellestrina from that of Malamocco (now better known as the Lido) he was brought to a halt. Of what happened next, there has come down to us a lively account by, of all people, the Byzantine Emperor Constantine VII Porphyrogenitus, in a treatise on imperial administration which he wrote for his son in the middle of the tenth century. Though not quite contemporary, it is probably as reliable as any other source we possess.

The Venetians, seeing King Pepin coming against them with his army and intending to ship his cavalry over to the island of Malamaucus . . . blocked up the passage with a barricade of projecting stakes. So the people of King Pepin, being rendered helpless – for they could not cross elsewhere – encamped on the mainland opposite for six months, fighting with them every day. And the

---

1. His name is also found in the alternative version of Particiaco. Later, in the tenth century, the family changed it altogether to Badoer, in which form it still exists.

Venetians went on ship-board, and took up a position behind the stakes they had fixed, but Pepin stood with his people on the sea shore. And the Venetians fought with arrows and other missiles, preventing them from crossing over to the island. So King Pepin, at a loss, appealed to the Venetians saying 'Ye are under my hand and my providence, since ye belong to my land and my dominions.' But the Venetians answered him, 'We will be the servants of the Roman Emperor,[1] and never shall be thine.'

In other directions, Pepin's armies continued to advance. Grado fell, and so, probably, did those old enemies Heraclea – what was left of it – and Jesolo. But the Malamoccans, their women and children evacuated to Rialto, showed no signs of weakening; the legend runs how one day, hearing that Pepin was determined to starve them out, they showed him the futility of his hopes by bombarding his army with bread. Meanwhile spring had turned to summer, and the fever-ridden shores of the *lidi* began to take their toll of the invaders. Rumours spread, too, that a huge Byzantine fleet was already sailing to Venice's relief. Pepin knew that he had failed, and gave the order to withdraw. The state of his own health may have influenced his decision, for within a few weeks he was dead.

It has been fashionable, in recent years, to accuse the Venetians of having exaggerated the importance of their victory; and indeed, gazing at the two gigantic paintings by Vicentino which commemorate it in the *Sala dello Scrutinio* of the Doges' Palace, one can hardly argue that the theme has been underplayed. It is true that Pepin did not leave until the Venetians, to get rid of him, had agreed to pay an annual tribute, and that this tribute continued to be exacted for well over a century; it is equally true that even though he failed in his most important object, he extended his authority all around the lagoon and well beyond it. But the conquered towns were not to remain in Frankish hands for long; and in any case the significance of the year 810 far exceeds that of any individual political or military event. More than once in the past, the lagoon settlers had asserted their right to exist as an independent entity; in that year, for the first time, they fought for it and proved it. And in doing so they also proved something else – that whatever the rivalries and jealousies of those early times, in a moment of real crisis they were capable of seeing themselves not as men of Malamocco or Chioggia, of Jesolo or Pellestrina, but as Venetians. Pepin had marched against a group of bickering communities; he had been defeated by a united people.

And now, as if in search of some visible sign of their reconciliation, the

---

1. i.e. the Emperor at Constantinople, whose subjects continued to call themselves Ῥωμαῖοι – Romans.

eyes of that people turned towards Rialto and its little cluster of islands that had never been embroiled in the squabbles of their neighbours – that had, on the contrary, served as a refuge for citizens of other, unhappier settlements who had fled from the advancing invader just as their ancestors had fled 300 and 400 years before. Malamocco, valiantly as it had defended itself as a community, had failed as a capital. Its last trio of Doges, the Antenori, had been a disaster. It had never acquired that degree of political neutrality that any federal capital must possess. Moreover, as Pepin had shown, it was vulnerable to attack. It had staved off the enemy once, but only after a hard struggle; next time it might not be so lucky. The outer seaboard of the lagoon, along the line of the *lidi* – those long, narrow sandbanks that protected it from the open Adriatic – was now revealed to be no safer than the mainland.

The islands of the Rialtine archipelago – Rialto itself with Dorsoduro, Spinalunga (the present Giudecca), Luprio (the area around S. Giacomo dell' Orio) and Olivolo (now known as Castello) – possessed neither of these disadvantages. More and more did they appear as a haven of moderation, toleration and good sense in a sea of bitterness and hatred. From their position in the centre of the lagoon, almost impossible of access to those who were unfamiliar with the shoals and shallows that surrounded them, they were superbly placed to defy an attacker. After the fall of Grado they possessed in S. Pietro di Castello the only national ecclesiastical centre remaining to the Republic. Their inhabitants, being at once champions of and refugees from practically all shades of political opinion, were collectively impartial. The hero of the hour, that Agnello Participazio who had turned back the forces of the Western Empire, was himself a Rialtine. To Rialto, then, the capital was moved. The three Doges were exiled. In a last-minute attempt to save their throne and their reputations, they had turned their coats and taken up arms against the invaders they had themselves invited; but it was a pathetic ploy, and it had deceived no one. In their place the Venetians elected the only possible candidate – Agnello himself, whose modest house on the Campiello della Cason (near S. Canciano) became the first Doges' Palace in the Venice that we know today.

Theoretically, the province of Venetia was still part of the Byzantine Empire. But it was by this time entirely autonomous, and the imperial government at Constantinople – which could not have done anything about it anyway – was quite content that it should remain so. The important thing now was to obtain recognition of its autonomy in the

West as well. Within a month or two of Pepin's retreat a Byzantine legate arrived in Venice on his way to the Frankish court at Aachen.

The Byzantines, once they had become accustomed to the idea, had found themselves resenting Charlemagne's existence rather less than might have been expected. Subconsciously, perhaps, they understood that for the new, emerging Europe one Emperor was no longer enough. Constantinople might be the theoretical repository of Roman law, civilization and imperial traditions; but in spirit Constantinople was now entirely Greek. Rome, shattered as she was by the barbarians and demoralized by centuries of near-anarchy, was still the focal point of Latin culture; it was Aachen, not Byzantium, that had re-established the *Pax Romana* in the West.

Had Charlemagne been thirty years younger, he might have been less ready to accept the Byzantine proposals; but he was old and tired, more concerned with the division of his Empire between his surviving heirs than with further territorial extensions. He always maintained that his imperial coronation had taken him by surprise. It had certainly embarrassed him, and he had been careful never to suggest any aggressive designs on the Empire of the East. Byzantine recognition of his own imperial title was all he sought; given that, he asked nothing better than friendly relations with his fellow-Emperor Nicephorus, for which the surrender of his tenuous claim to Venice seemed a small enough price to pay.

The treaty between the two Empires that was agreed in the spring of 811 (although, owing to the deaths of both Charlemagne and Nicephorus, it was not ratified till three years later) gave each what it required – at a price. The Franks obtained recognition of their imperial status while, for the Byzantines, Charlemagne's renunciation of all his claims over the province of Venetia meant not only the continuation of their own suzerainty but also the assurance that the leading maritime power in the Adriatic could not be mobilized against them. The gain on each side, however, involved a corresponding concession by the other; only for Venice herself were the benefits unmitigated. Henceforth she was to enjoy all the advantages, partly political but above all cultural and commercial, of being a Byzantine province, without any real diminution of her independence. For many years to come, the Doges might continue, legally speaking, to be officials of Byzantium, loaded with Byzantine honorifics and, on occasion, with Byzantine gold. But they were none the less Venetians, elected by Venetians, and the Eastern Empire was never again seriously to interfere with their affairs. It is always dangerous to press historical comparisons too far, particularly when dealing with institutions remote alike in time and spirit; but if we think of Venice, in her relations with Constantinople, as enjoying for the next two centuries something akin to what we should now call Commonwealth status, perhaps we should not be so very far wrong.

There were other advantages too. The *Pax Nicephori*, as it came to be called, separated Venice from the rest of Italy and so enabled her to escape, just in time, the political upheavals which were soon to change the face of the peninsula and indeed much of western Europe. Thanks to her links with Byzantium she remained virtually untouched by the feudal system, by communal government of the kind that later became the rule in Lombardy and Tuscany, and by the seemingly endless wars of Guelf against Ghibelline that were intermittently to continue, in one form or another, almost as long as the Republic itself. Thus, paradoxically, it was through her very submission to the Empire of the East that her independence was achieved and her future greatness assured.

3

The City Rises Up

[811–900]

'And so Barnabas took Mark, and sailed unto Cyprus.' If as the shores of Asia lessened upon his sight, the spirit of prophecy had entered into the heart of the weak disciple who had turned back when his hand was on the plough, and who had been judged, by the chiefest of Christ's captains, unworthy thenceforward to go forth with him to the work, how wonderful would he have thought it, that by the lion symbol in future ages he was to be represented among men! . . .

Ruskin, *The Stones of Venice*

With peace restored to the lagoon, Doge Agnello was free to turn his attention to a new problem, every bit as challenging as that which he had just surmounted. The islands of Rialto, flat, muddy and often waterlogged, were neither large enough nor firm enough to accommodate the new influx of settlers. If they were to be made into a capital worthy of the growing Republic, they would have to be strengthened, drained and – wherever primitive methods of land reclamation made it possible – enlarged. They must be protected, too, from the sea, against which the outer line of *lidi* provided a not always effective barrier. To undertake these tasks the Doge appointed a commission of three men. Nicolò Ardisonio was to fortify the *lidi*, buttressing them artificially where necessary; Lorenzo Alimpato was entrusted with the digging of canals, the shoring up of islands and the preparation of building sites; while the buildings themselves were made the responsibility of Agnello's close kinsman, Pietro Tradonico.

These buildings were still for the most part modest, two-storey structures, lightly constructed to minimize subsidence and usually thatched with straw. Already, like Venetian houses today, they tended to have two front doors, one giving out on the land – probably with a little patch of garden for vegetables – and the other opening directly on to the water. Wood was still the most popular building material; it was light, easy to transport, abundant – thanks to the pine forests around the lagoon – and cheap. Bricks, so characteristic of later Venetian architecture, were still almost unknown; the mud of the lagoon was too soft and thin. For the more important buildings where wood seemed insufficiently durable or impressive, there remained only one answer – stone, and in particular the hard, white stone of the Istrian peninsula.

But stone presented its own problems, notably that of weight. The only means of establishing a firm enough foundation for it was to drive thousands of wooden piles into the ooze, so close that they touched one another and their sawn-off tops made a virtually unified, solid surface. It was a long and laborious process, but it worked; many houses in Venice today still stand on piles sunk almost 1,000 years ago, and the technique was to be continued well into the twentieth century.[1] In the ninth, however, it was still in its infancy; there were few stone buildings except the churches – and the great palace that Agnello began for himself and his successors near the old church of St Theodore.

Of this first Doges' Palace nothing now remains. Though it occupied the same site as the present one, its appearance must have been very different; heavily battlemented, with corner towers and drawbridges, it was more a fortress than anything else – and no wonder, in view of the Republic's recent history. Architecturally, it cannot have compared with the splendid edifice that was simultaneously rising just behind it to the east. This was the church and convent of S. Zaccaria, designed to receive the mortal remains of the father of John the Baptist, recently presented to Venice in a gesture of friendship and goodwill by the Byzantine Emperor, Leo V the Armenian. Leo may well have gone even further and paid for the whole building himself; he certainly sent architects and craftsmen from Constantinople. Alas, their work too has disappeared. S. Zaccaria, like most of the older churches of Venice, has been rebuilt and restored so often as to be unrecognizable for what it originally was. But its importance in the early history of the Republic was considerable, and there will be more to say of it as we go on.

This initial period of carefully planned construction laid down the lines on which the new capital was to develop and gave it the basic shape it still preserves. Inevitably, however, the Doge had other more immediate problems to contend with – for the gravest of which he was himself

---

1. Even so colossal a structure as Longhena's church of the Salute, built between 1630 and 1687 on the end of Dorsoduro (the firmest, as its name implies, of all the Rialtine islands), rests entirely on such piles – according to one record, 1,156,627 of them.

responsible. Though by far the most enlightened ruler that Venice had yet produced, he too fell into the temptation of trying to make his office hereditary; and since his elder son Giustiniano was away in Constantinople he raised the younger, Giovanni, to share the dogeship with him. Giustiniano returned in wrath and demanded that his brother be deposed – a step which drove Giovanni in his turn into a fury, and shortly afterwards into exile. But these family quarrels, undignified as they were, never seriously threatened the security of the state. The building work went on uninterrupted; and Agnello Participazio can be accounted, more than anyone else, the first architect of modern Venice. It was only sad for him that he did not live to witness what was, perhaps, the most important single event in the spiritual life of the Republic – that which did more than any other to strengthen its ecclesiastical independence and to focus its national pride and which, incidentally, gave the city its most glorious and enduring monument.

One day – so the story goes – when St Mark was travelling from Aquileia to Rome, his ship chanced to put in at the islands of Rialto. There an angel appeared to him and blessed him with the words '*Pax tibi, Marce, evangelista meus. Hic requiescet corpus tuum.*'[1] The historical evidence for this story is, to say the least, uncertain; the prophecy – since St Mark later became Bishop of Alexandria and remained there till he died – would have seemed improbable; but the legend certainly came in very handy when, in 828 or thereabouts, two Venetian merchants returned from Egypt with a corpse which they claimed to be that of the Evangelist, stolen from his Alexandrian tomb. As might be expected, the details of this enterprise vary from one account to the next; the consensus seems, however, to be that the Christian guardians of the shrine, concerned for the future of their church under Saracen rule, were somehow persuaded – or bribed – to cooperate. The shroud was slit up the back, the body removed and the remains of St Claudian, which lay conveniently near at hand, substituted for it. It was then put into a large basket and carried down to the harbour, where a Venetian ship was waiting.[2]

1. 'Peace be unto you, Mark, my evangelist. On this spot shall your body rest.' The first of these sentences must be familiar to all visitors to Venice, since it is inscribed upon the open book that the ubiquitous winged lion of the city holds in his paw. One of the few exceptions is the stone lion outside the Arsenal; the message being thought too conciliatory for so warlike an institution, his book is held defiantly closed.

2. One account asserts that there were no less than ten Venetian vessels in the port of Alexandria at the time. If so, it is a significant indication of the growth of the merchant fleet of the Republic.

By this time the odour of sanctity that issued from the body was becoming so strong that, in the words of one chronicler,[1] 'If all the spices of the world had been gathered together in Alexandria, they could not have so perfumed the city.' Suspicions were understandably aroused, and local officials arrived to search the ship; but the Venetians had covered their prize with quantities of pork, at the first sight of which the officials, pious Muslims to a man, cried '*Kanzir, kanzir!*' – 'Pig, pig!' – and fled in horror. The body was then wrapped in canvas and hoisted up to the yard-arm, where it remained till the vessel was out of harbour. Even now the dangers were not over, for the vessel headed straight for some uncharted reef and would surely have foundered had not St Mark himself roused the sleeping captain and induced him, just in time, to lower his sail. At last, however, it was brought safely to Venice, where its precious cargo was received with appropriate rejoicing.

Now this story – which is admirably depicted, down to the very cries of the customs men, high on the mosaic walls of the present Basilica[2] – is something more than just another of those legends in which early Venetian history is so rich. That a body thought to be that of St Mark was brought to Venice at this time is generally believed to be a historical fact; and it is equally beyond doubt that Giustiniano Participazio – now sole Doge since the death of his father in 827 – instantly commanded that a special chapel should be built for its reception, in the *brolo* or garden separating the church of St Theodore from his own palace. There is a strong possibility, even, that the whole expedition from Alexandria had been undertaken on the secret orders of the Doge. If the Republic were to command respect in the new Europe that was gradually taking shape around it, it needed some special prestige beyond that which wealth or sea power alone could confer; and in the Middle Ages, when politics and religion were still inextricably intertwined, the presence of an important sacred relic endowed a city with a mystique all its own. The body of St Zacharias might be better than nothing, but it was not really enough. That of an Evangelist, on the other hand, would endow Venice with Apostolic patronage and place her on a spiritual level second only to Rome itself, with a claim to ecclesiastical autonomy – further strengthened by the patriarchal status of her bishop – unparalleled in Latin Christendom.

Similarly, there was no reason why a spiritual advantage should not be turned to straightforward political ends; and here again the relic arrived at an opportune moment. Barely a year before, in 827, a synod at Mantua

1. Martino da Canale, Ch. XI.
2. Above the south transept, near the chapel of S. Clemente.

headed by representatives of the Pope and the Western Emperor had proposed the restoration of the old Patriarchate of Aquileia, giving it authority over the see of Grado. Since Aquileia was part of the Western Empire, such a decision might have constituted a serious threat to Venetian independence. Now, with the body of St Mark slammed, as it were, on to the scales in favour of Grado, the Mantuan decision could be safely ignored. Grado remained the metropolitan see to which the Church of Venice, revived and regenerated in the name of the Evangelist, owed its ecclesiastical allegiance.

It might in these circumstances have been expected that Doge Giustiniano would consign the body to the new cathedral at Olivolo. His decision to preserve it instead in an obvious dependency of his own palace deliberately associated it from the outset with the civil rather than with the religious authorities of the state.[1] From that moment on, old St Theodore and his dragon were relegated to the top of a column in the Piazzetta and, for all practical purposes, forgotten. St Mark became the patron of Venice. His lion, its wings outstretched, its forepaw proudly indicating the angelic utterance, was to be emblazoned on banners and bastions, on poops and prows, whenever and wherever the Venetian writ was to run; his name above all others was invoked by the faithful at prayer and by the soldiers and sailors of the Republic as they went into battle.

History records no more shameless example of body-snatching; nor any – unless we include the events associated with the Resurrection – of greater long-term significance. But once the Venetians had the Evangelist safely among them, they adopted him as their own, more whole-heartedly than any other tutelary saint in any other city. As their guardian, over the centuries, they were to work him hard and to try him sorely; but as their patron they were never to fail him in their love and veneration.

And he, for his part, was to serve them well.

The first church of St Mark – smaller and less magnificent than that which now stands on the same site but still, by the standards of the day, a building fit for an Evangelist to dwell in – received its formal consecration

1. It also conferred on the shrine of St Mark a primacy which has never been lost. 'I am aware of no other city of Europe in which its cathedral was not the principal feature. But the principal church in Venice was the chapel attached to the palace of her prince and called the "Chiesa Ducale". The patriarchal church, inconsiderable in size and mean in decoration, stands on the outermost islet of the Venetian group, and its name, as well as its site, are probably unknown to the greater number of travellers passing hastily through the city.' Ruskin, *The Stones of Venice*, I, ix.

only four years later, in 832.[1] By that time Doge Giustiniano, three years in his grave, had been succeeded by his younger brother. He had always despised Giovanni, and from what we can gather from the scant sources available, he was probably right. Had the new Doge not already reigned briefly at his father's side he would never have been chosen; as it was, his fecklessness and general apathy soon became more than his subjects could stand. On 29 June 836, the feast of St Peter and St Paul, just as he was leaving S. Pietro di Castello after mass, he was seized by some of his own subjects and compelled to abdicate. Then, tonsured and forcibly ordained, he was sent to end his days in a monastery at Grado.

One of the main reasons for the Venetians' dissatisfaction with Giovanni Participazio had been his ineffectiveness in dealing with a new menace which was now looming ever larger on the horizon. For some years already, Adriatic trade had been harassed by Slav pirates, slipping out from their lairs in the hidden creeks and inlets of the Dalmatian coast around the mouths of the Narenta[2] and Cetina rivers and falling upon any well-laden merchantman that caught their fancy. Early successes had caused a rapid growth in their numbers, to the point where Venetian captains were becoming chary of putting to sea and Venetian commerce was being threatened with slow strangulation. Nor was Venice the only sufferer; the Western Empire too was beginning to feel the pinch as sea communications with Ravenna, Padua and the other cities of imperial Italy became progressively harder to keep open.

Firm action against these pirates was thus a matter of high priority for any new ruler; and Pietro Tradonico from Jesolo, now raised from his position on the building commission to be the eleventh Doge of Venice, was not a man to shirk his responsibilities. Within three years of his election we find him leading a naval expedition to Dalmatia; and in 840, his hand strengthened by the moderately successful outcome of these operations, he sent an ambassador to the Franks to conclude a treaty with Charlemagne's grandson, the Emperor Lothair. Much of this treaty was a simple confirmation of previous agreements, but it is remarkable for two reasons. First, the original manuscript of it still exists, the oldest Venetian diplomatic document to have been preserved. Secondly, it contains an explicit pledge by the Doge to bear responsibility for the defence of the Adriatic against the Slavs or any other enemy, together with the implicit

1. Though usually described as a basilica, this first church was not built on the basilican plan any more than its successors. Like them, it was almost certainly modelled on the Church of the Holy Apostles at Constantinople – now long since destroyed – and was cruciform, as was the custom for Apostolic churches.

2. Now better known by its Slavonic name of Neretva.

acknowledgement by Lothair of his own naval weakness and Venice's consequent rights over the central Mediterranean.

At about this time, too, another race was giving another Empire still graver cause for concern. In 827 a Byzantine governor of Sicily named Euthymius, in an effort to avoid the consequences of his recent elopement with a local nun, had proclaimed his independence and invited the Aglabi Saracens of North Africa to support him. It was just the opportunity they needed. Landing in strength along the south-west coast they soon got rid of Euthymius, and before their conquest was complete they were already using the island as a springboard from which to attack the Byzantine province of Apulia. There, the Greek garrisons in Bari, Brindisi and Otranto found themselves as helpless against this new enemy as the Franks had been against the Dalmatians. In the past thirty years the Emperors at Constantinople, reassured by their friendship with Venice and the growing Venetian power at sea, had allowed themselves to neglect their own bases in the Adriatic. Even on the Eastern shores, the once formidable strongholds of Durazzo and Cephalonia were no longer able to launch an offensive on any scale. Thus it was that in 840 or thereabouts – at roughly the same time as the Venetian plenipotentiaries were signing their treaty with Lothair – there arrived at Rialto no less a personage than the Patriarch of Constantinople himself, to confer upon the Doge the title of *spatharius* and seek his active help against the Saracen peril.

Tradonico responded at once. The Saracens, he saw, constituted a far more serious threat in the long term than any number of Slav corsairs; it was in the interests of Venice, just as much as of Constantinople, to prevent them from establishing themselves in the narrow waters. The Venetian navy was quickly made ready, and early in 841 sixty of its largest ships, each carrying some 200 men, sailed out of the lagoon to their appointed rendezvous with a Byzantine squadron. The combined fleet then moved on southward, until it came upon the Saracens off the little Calabrian port of Crotone.

Whether the Greek admiral fled at the first engagement – as the Venetians were later indignantly to aver – or whether the fault lay elsewhere, we shall never know; but the Christian defeat was total. The pride of the Venetian navy went to the bottom, the land force which had been disembarked near Taranto was wiped out. The Saracen fleet then advanced unhindered up the Adriatic, sacking Ancona and reaching the very edge of the lagoon before the shoals and currents swirling around the delta of the Po forced it to turn back.

Once again Venice had been saved by her geography; but this time she had no cause to congratulate herself on her good fortune. The sea that she had claimed as her preserve, and that the two great Empires of Europe had recognized as such only a year before, had been openly demonstrated to be nothing of the kind. The very next year was to see the Saracens pressing yet further up the coast, the Venetians powerless as ever to check them. Meanwhile the Narenta pirates, seeing that they had less to fear than they had imagined, grew bolder and still more predatory. It was to be many decades before these twin scourges were finally eliminated and the Adriatic approaches made safe again for Venetian and imperial shipping.

After so complete a débâcle, it was inevitable that Venice's relations with Byzantium should have suffered a sharp deterioration. The old links were still there, but they were becoming more tenuous all the time. With the Empire of the West, on the other hand, once the principle of independence – both political and ecclesiastical – had been properly established, friendship continued to blossom. In 856 Lothair's son and successor, the young Emperor Lewis II, went so far as to pay a state visit to Venice with his Empress. They were met and entertained by the Doge and his son Giovanni – whom, it is hardly necessary to add, he had associated with himself on the ducal throne – at Brondolo, a little to the south of Chioggia; thence they were conveyed with much pomp to Rialto, where they remained three days, in the course of which the Emperor stood godfather to Giovanni's little daughter.

On the domestic front, too, Doge Pietro had his problems. It was now nearly half a century since the Venetian capital had been established on the islands of Rialto; after all that had gone before, it was hardly likely that their comparative freedom from factional strife – one of the principal reasons for their selection – should last for ever. Despite her Adriatic enemies, Venice was now the leading emporium and clearing-house in the Christian Mediterranean. Trade was expanding in all directions; the advantage went to the first to seize it; and in the prevailing atmosphere of commercial ruthlessness and cut-throat competition, new jealousies and resentments were bound to arise. Many of the recent settlers had brought their old animosities with them. For most of his 28-year reign – the longest of any Doge to date – Pietro Tradonico kept the peace with remarkable success; it was only after the death of Giovanni – one of the few associate Doges to justify an institution that was nearly always disastrous – that he found that he could no longer hold the balance between the factions. Perhaps he resorted to repressive measures which his subjects found intolerable, perhaps he showed too much favour towards one group and thereby antagonized another; whatever the reason, a conspiracy took shape, and on 13 September 864 the conspirators struck. It was the eve of the Exaltation of the Cross, a day on which by tradition the Doge attended mass at S. Zaccaria; and as the old man – with well over fifty years' service to the state behind him, he cannot have been far short of eighty – was leaving the church after vespers, he was sprung upon by an armed band and left dead in the square. The ensuing struggle between his attendants and the attackers soon led to a riot; we read that the nuns of the convent attached to the church did not at first dare to venture out to rescue the body. Not until after nightfall could it be brought to safety and given a decent burial.

Meanwhile the servants of the murdered Doge – probably a bodyguard of Croatian slaves – had hurried back to the palace and barricaded themselves in. There, while the street fighting raged throughout the city, they kept up their resistance for several days until they heard that five of the leading conspirators had in their turn met their deaths at the hands of the mob. Only then did peace return sufficiently for a certain Orso, a nobleman whose principal qualification was that he had had no part in the plot, to be elected to the supreme power.

Tradition, unsupported by any firm historical evidence, maintains that this new Doge was of the family of Participazio. Three of his four predecessors had borne this name, and the fourth, Pietro Tradonico, had been closely related by marriage; if, therefore, tradition is to be trusted, we must see the new election as indicating a further drift towards the hereditary principle. But Orso, whether a Participazio or not, showed no disposition to allow the old order of things to continue. Immediately on his accession he launched a radical programme of reform; and his first target was his own authority.

From the beginnings of her independence, Venice had been theoretically a democracy. Not only was the dogeship itself an electoral office, but the Doge was attended by two tribunes whose explicit purpose was to prevent him from abusing it. Furthermore, there had always been provision for what was known as the *arengo*, when all the citizens met in general assembly to vote on major decisions affecting the security of the state. But democracies are unstable institutions; they need constant maintenance if they are to work. In Venice, over the years, the tribunes had declined in importance, the *arenghi* were never called, and public affairs had become the preserve of whatever little clique chanced to surround the Doge of the day. Orso now instituted a system of elected *giudici*, or judges – high state officials, part ministers, part magistrates, who formed the nucleus from which the future ducal *curia* was to grow and provided an effective check on the arbitrary misuse of the supreme power. Meanwhile changes in the structure of local government brought the outlying islands into closer dependence on the central administration.

Having reorganized the governmental machine, Orso next turned his attention to Church affairs. Here, by contrast, he adopted a policy of decentralization. Several of the old bishoprics in and around the lagoon had ceased to exist, or had returned to the cities from which they had been driven by the barbarian invasions; there remained only Grado, Altino and Olivolo, to which the new diocese of Equilo had recently been added, with the result that many outlying areas were falling increasingly under the influence of the Patriarch of Aquileia or other equally undesirable ecclesiastics in the territory of the Western Empire. To counteract this tendency Caorle, Malamocco, Cittanova – the old Heraclea – and Torcello, which heretofore served only as the occasional seat of the Bishop of Altino, were all given sees of their own. Neither the new bishops nor the old were in any way subordinated to the civil power of the Republic; but their very independence increased their loyalty. Within a few years we find all the newly appointed bishops supporting the Doge in one of his periodic disputes with the Patriarch of Grado, and three times in a single year refusing summonses from the Pope himself to attend a synod in Rome to settle the matter.

Another dispute, with the Patriarch of Aquileia this time, was even more satisfactorily handled. This rascally primate seems somehow to have acquired temporal control over a large part of the duchy of Friuli – from which, probably as a result of pique over the new bishoprics, he was conducting his own armed campaign against Venetian merchants. Orso's answer was an economic blockade. The mouths of all rivers passing through Aquileian territory were closed and all exports to and from the city banned. The Patriarch was brought to his knees; and it is worth noting that in the ensuing treaty, while Orso was prepared to accept that the Venetian merchants trading with Aquileia should continue to pay reasonable duties on their goods, he cheerfully stipulated that his own personal trading representatives in the area should be exempt from all taxation. There spoke the authentic voice of Venice. The state might come first, but enlightened self-interest was never very far behind.

Orso's constitutional reforms, far-reaching as they were, did not extend to the problem of nepotism. Like most of his predecessors he had associated his son with him during his lifetime, and on his death in 881 this son,

Giovanni, assumed the throne in smooth and undisputed succession. But Giovanni was himself no longer young and his health was uncertain; after a few years' ineffectual struggle he had to admit himself unequal to his office. His subjects agreed. Constitutionally, yet at the same time showing more determination to be heard than at any previous time in Venetian history, they demanded not his abdication – for they seem to have been genuinely fond of him – but the enthronement at his side of the 45-year-old Pietro Candiano.

Alas, only five months later, on 18 September 887, Pietro was killed while leading an expedition against the Dalmatian pirates, the first Doge to die in battle for the Republic. Reluctantly, old Giovanni took up the reins again until a successor could be found; and this time the people's choice fell on Pietro Tribuno, great-nephew of that ill-fated Doge Tradonico whose murder had caused such havoc in the city a quarter of of a century before.

Pietro Candiano's reign had been brief, bellicose and – at least so far as the Doge himself was concerned – disastrous; that of Pietro Tribuno was to be long and in the main peaceful, with its single emergency ending in Venice's most dazzling military triumph since her victory over Pepin. Tribuno began, auspiciously enough, by renewing the treaty agreements with the Western Empire, first in 888, the year of his accession, and then again in 891. Since Giovanni Participazio had negotiated a similar renewal with the Emperor Charles the Fat as recently as 883, it may be wondered whether so much diplomatic activity was strictly necessary; but at this crucial stage in her political development Venice was still steering a course of extreme delicacy between the two imperial whirlpools, a course on which she was in constant danger of being sucked into one or the other. It was vital for her to seize every opportunity she could of taking her bearings and adjusting her trim. Seldom, in so doing, did she fail to improve her position. Thus, a few years before, a clause had been written into the agreement by which any murderer of a Doge who sought refuge in the Empire should be fined 100 pounds of gold and banished – a mild enough penalty, one would have thought, under the circumstances. In 888 the terms went considerably further: henceforth any Venetian anywhere in imperial Italy would remain under the jurisdiction of the Doge and subject to the laws of Venice rather than to those of the Empire. This provision was directed not only against criminals – extradition, of a kind, had been allowed for since the days of Lothair. Its principal effect was to guarantee to Venetian merchants in Italy the protection of their own law, and thereby to encourage them to extend their operations further and further afield.

Thus, with trade expanding, the economy developing steadily, shipbuilding in full swing, a new iron-founding industry growing fast[1] and the city taking ever more splendid shape as the work of clearance, drainage, reclamation and construction gathered impetus, the last decade of the ninth century proved for the Venetians the happiest and most prosperous of all. Then, in 899, came crisis – with the appearance on the horizon of a new enemy. By this time men might have been forgiven for thinking that the age of the barbarians was past; but the Magyars proved them wrong. Emerging, like so many of their predecessors, from the steppes of Central Asia, they had crossed the Carpathians for the first time only three years before; their savagery and brutality were still unblunted. Several shocked chroniclers of the time go so far as to describe them as cannibals – which, on occasion, they may well have been. Already in 898 they had briefly raided the Veneto, but had withdrawn again before much harm had been done. In the following year, however, they returned in strength and, after an initial reverse, overran the whole Lombard plain. Then they turned towards Venice.

One by one, the cities around the lagoon fell to the Hungarian horde: Cittanova, Fine and Equilo first, then Altino, and the hinterland north and west to Treviso and Padua. Next, swinging south, the Magyars advanced along the *lidi* from Chioggia and Pellestrina up towards Mala-mocco. They reached Albiola without much difficulty, but there – almost exactly where Pepin had come to grief ninety years before – they found Tribuno and his army awaiting them. Coming as they did from the centre of the Asiatic land mass, they had no knowledge or understanding of the sea; the portable coracles which they used for crossing rivers were useless against the Venetian ships. Their defeat was quick and complete. Once again the lagoon had saved the city.

But was even the lagoon enough? Pietro Tribuno did not think so. Some future aggressor, more disciplined and experienced in seamanship, might succeed where the Magyars had failed. Once inside the line of *lidi* he would find the islands of Rialto still largely unprotected. And so the Doge gave orders for the building of a bastion from the castle on the eastern side of Olivolo down to what is now the Riva degli Schiavoni and thence all the way along to S. Maria Zobenigo, and for the manufacture of a great chain of iron which could be stretched across the Grand Canal

---

1. On his accession in 864 Orso Participazio had sent the Byzantine Emperor Basil I a peal of twelve bells cast in a Venetian foundry.

from the church of S. Gregorio on Dorsoduro to the opposite bank.[1]

The chronicler John the Deacon, writing about 100 years after the event, sees the construction of this bulwark as marking the moment when the Rialtine settlement first properly became what he calls a *civitas*. The term is untranslatable; a city, in our sense of the word – although a very small one – had existed there since the days of Doge Agnello and the transfer of the central government. But Pietro Tribuno's wall, and the emergency that brought it into being, gave the citizens a new feeling of cohesion and community that was to have its own importance in the years to come; and one can only hope that the few crumbling remnants of it that still survive at the southern end of the Rio dell' Arsenale will continue to be treated by the authorities of today with the respect that is their due.

1. The precise spot is now occupied by the seventeenth-century Palazzo Gaggia, two buildings to the east of the Palazzo Contarini-Fasan ('Desdemona's house'). It is interesting to note that the churches of S. Maria Zobenigo (del Giglio) and S. Gregorio already existed as landmarks in Venice at this time. They are both still there, though the present structures are of later date: the former – so-called after its founders, the family of Jubanico – now a seventeenth-century building, the latter a fifteenth. A neighbouring *calle* is still called the *Calle del Bastion*.

4

The Adventurer and the Saint

[900–991]

É necessario ad un principe, volendoli mantenere, imparare a potere essere non buono,
ed usarlo o non usarlo secondo la necessità.

A prince who wishes to maintain his position must learn how not to be good,
and make use or not make use of that knowledge as necessary.

Machiavelli, *Il Principe*, Ch. XV

Exalted by her victory over the Hungarians, elevated by her new civic
pride, strengthened and protected by her rapidly rising fortifications,
Venice entered the tenth century in a mood of confidence. Her enemies
were scattered, the two Empires grateful and admiring: trade had never
been better. The future looked bright indeed. Pietro Tribuno continued
to reign wisely and well till 912, when he died and was buried in S.
Zaccaria; and his successor, another Orso Participazio, pursued similarly
peaceable policies with similar success for a further twenty years before
retiring – voluntarily – to the monastery of S. Felice in 932. For the
next forty-four years Venice was to be dominated by one of the most
remarkable families in all her early history – the Candiani.

The first Candiano Doge has already made his all-too-brief appearance
in these pages, dying in action against the Dalmatian pirates in 887. He
was now to be followed by his son, and then – after a brief and wholly
unmemorable hiatus in 939 – by his grandson and great-grandson. All
four, confusingly, were named Pietro; all seem to have been endowed
with more energy than their fellow-men, more aggressiveness, more
self-confidence. All were arrogant and headstrong; one was a national
disaster; none were dull. The second of the line was hardly settled on his
throne before he began a bitter economic blockading war against Istria;
not long after, following a trifling diplomatic incident, he burnt Venice's
neighbour and potential rival, Comacchio, to the ground. The third
sailed twice against the Narenta pirates who had killed his grandfather and
forced them to their knees. And so we come to the fourth; but the wild

and almost incredible career of Pietro Candiano IV cannot be conveniently summed up in a few words; it deserves to be recounted in detail.

His father must have regretted for the rest of his life the decision, only four years after his own accession in 942, to associate young Pietro with him on the ducal throne. From the outset, the boy showed himself a rebel. Whether, as some suggest, he was a corrupt and vicious debauchee or whether, as seems more likely, the rift was fundamentally political is not altogether clear. What is certain is that relations between father and son and their respective factions rapidly deteriorated to the point where open warfare broke out in the streets of the city. Finally the young man was captured, narrowly escaping with his life; it was only thanks to his father's intercession with the judicial authorities that his sentence was commuted to one of perpetual banishment. Thus it was that he was able to enlist as a soldier of fortune under the banners of Guy, Marquis of Ivrea, who in 950 was crowned King of Italy. Away in exile, however, his resentment continued to grow; and a few years later we find him in command of a squadron of corsairs, blockading no less than seven of the Republic's galleys at the mouth of the Po.

Over the centuries, the Venetians had suffered more than most peoples from the effects of piracy. There was no crime that they detested more, none that they were readier to condemn. The old Doge bore his son's shame as long as he could, but a terrible epidemic of plague that struck the city in 959 finally broke his spirit and he died the same year. And then an extraordinary thing happened. The people met together and elected young Pietro in his stead.

If the reasons for the original banishment are hard to analyse, those for this sudden volte-face are harder still. The most probable theory points, quite simply, to another one of those unexpected swings of the political pendulum; Pietro was young, go-ahead and, from what we can deduce, possessed of a certain glamour. A born leader, he was also a Candiano. Finally, there was the practical consideration – and the Venetians were nothing if not practical – that, as past experience had proved, he could be a dangerous thorn in their flesh; it was better to have him on their side than against them. At any rate the decisive votes were cast, and 300 ships were sent down to Ravenna to bring the new Doge back to the lagoon in suitable state.

It was a dark day for Venice when they did so. Though Pietro Candiano no longer had a parent to oppose, he soon proved as resolute as ever in his opposition to all those principles that his father had represented – the old, austere, republican virtues on which the state had been founded and had grown to greatness, the high standards of moral behaviour expected of – if not always evinced by – its leaders, the mistrust of personal pomp and ostentation. Pietro had lived in the sophisticated courts of the mainland; they had given him a taste for luxury, as well as for an autocracy unfettered by the nicely calculated checks and balances with which the Doges of Venice were increasingly hamstrung. He was, however, entirely without the subtlety to see how these controls could be circumvented; and though happy to work constitutionally in matters where he could expect a measure of popular support, in those arising from his insatiable appetite for self-aggrandizement he tried to ride roughshod over the opposition. In Venice, such a man could never last for long.

His energies were not at first entirely misdirected. Within a year or so of his accession he imposed new and severe restrictions on the slave trade, with harsh penalties – physical, financial and even spiritual – for offenders. The traffic was still not altogether forbidden; special provision was made for it to continue where it was necessary 'for the purposes of government'. But the new laws were stringent enough to arouse the potentially dangerous indignation of the Venetian slave traders themselves; and it was probably this consideration that prompted the Doge to draft them not in his name alone but also in those of the Patriarch, bishops and nobles of the city. Whatever the reason for this collective responsibility, it seems to have been taken as a precedent; from this time forward, references to similar councils became increasingly frequent in Venetian legislation.

Pietro's future conduct, however, was a good deal less circumspect. During his exile he had allowed his eye to fall on Waldrada, sister of the Marquis of Tuscany who was at that time one of the richest and most powerful of the Italian princes. He now divorced his Venetian wife, packing her off to end her days in the convent of S. Zaccaria, and brought Waldrada to Venice as his bride – together with an immense dowry of lands in Friuli, the March of Treviso, Adria and the Ferrarese. There was, be it noted, no question of these lands becoming Venetian territory; they were to be the personal property of Pietro. Thus the Venetians suddenly saw, in place of the Doge they thought they had elected, a powerful feudal baron with huge estates on *terra firma* held in vassalage of the Western Emperor – so much for Venice's hard-won independence – living in state like some perfumed princeling of Byzantium, and insulated from his subjects by a bodyguard of foreign mercenaries raised on his mainland dominions.

All this was bad enough; but popular dissatisfaction increased still further when the Doge, who soon after his accession had made his son

Vitale Bishop of Torcello – having had the rival candidate blinded and imprisoned – in 969 procured for him the Patriarchate of Grado. In the past century the Patriarchate had grown steadily in wealth and influence, with the result that the new incumbent found himself second only to his father not just in the hierarchy of the state but also as a landowner, master of nearly all the coast and its hinterland between his see and the Venetian lagoon. Through this he would travel in princely pomp with an extensive retinue, while the local inhabitants came out to do him homage and the monasteries along the way vied with each other in the lavishness of their hospitality.

With the civil and ecclesiastical authority now firmly gathered into his hands, Pietro Candiano was – or seemed to be – all-powerful. Unfortunately, like so many of his otherwise talented family, he never knew when to stop; and when, in the summer of 976, he called on his Venetian subjects to help defend his personal interests in the Ferrarese, the people rose against him. Their first attack on his palace was unsuccessful; the building proved to be too well fortified and the attackers were forced to retire. But now, more determined than ever, they set fire to the neighbouring houses. The timber went up like matchwood in the summer heat, and the flames soon spread to the palace itself

For the events that followed we have the authority of John the Deacon, an authority and perhaps even an eye-witness. Desperate and choking, the Doge with his young wife and infant child tried to escape through the atrium of St Mark's, only to find their passage blocked by a group of nobles. Vainly Pietro pleaded with them, promising satisfaction for all their demands if his and his family's lives could be spared. 'But, affirming him to be a man most wicked [*sceleratissimus*] and deserving of death, they cried out with fearsome voices that he should have no means of escape. And they instantly surrounding him, and setting about him cruelly with the points of their swords, his immortal soul left its bodily prison to seek the haunts of the blessed' – a destination which, from what we know of Pietro Candiano IV, it is unlikely to have found.

Somehow the Dogaressa Waldrada managed to escape with her life; but her baby, run through with a spear, shared the fate of its father. The two bodies were then thrown on to a boat and carted off to the common slaughter-house, where they were rescued only by the intervention of a certain Giovanni Gradenigo, 'a most saintly man', who arranged an obscure but seemlier burial. The convent of S. Zaccaria had now become the traditional resting-place for deceased Doges, but there could be no question of using it on this occasion. Pietro and his child were borne secretly away across the lagoon to the remote abbey of Sant' Ilario, beyond Fusina, while the Venetians, their tempers cooled at last, settled down to rebuild their ravaged city.

Some 300 buildings had been destroyed or badly damaged by the fire, among them St Mark's itself, the Doges' Palace, and the newly completed S. Maria Zobenigo. Of the old church of St Theodore, which dated back to the time when even the churches were built of wood, scarcely a stick remained standing. Venice had got rid of her Doge, but she had paid dearly for her mistake.

Pietro Candiano had been a child of his century – a century which, following the break-up of Charlemagne's Empire in 888, had witnessed the steady political disintegration of Italy. In the north, Lombardy had remained prey to the Magyars for more than fifty years after they had been turned back from the Venetian lagoon. In the south, the Byzantine Empire had shown itself more and more unable to control either the Lombard princelings – who thought of nothing but their own glorification – or the maritime city-republics of Naples, Amalfi and Gaeta, whose loyalties lay in the direction whence the most favourable trade wind happened at the time to be blowing. Between the two, the Papacy presented the most unedifying spectacle of all – under such creatures as John X, strangled in the Castel Sant' Angelo by his mistress's daughter so that she could install her own bastard son by a former Pope in his place; or John XII, who was consecrated at the age of seventeen and during whose reign, according to Gibbon, 'we learn with some surprise that the Lateran Palace was turned into a school for prostitution; and that his rapes of virgins and widows had deterred the female pilgrims from visiting the tomb of St Peter, lest, in the devout act, they should be violated by his successor.'

But if John XII marked the nadir of the papal pornocracy, he was also unwittingly responsible for Italy's deliverance. In 962, defenceless against the encroachments of Berengar II, King of Italy, on his northern borders, he appealed for help to Duke Otto of Saxony who, having recently driven the Hungarians from the Lombard plain, was now the dominant force in North Italy. Otto hurried to Rome, where John – no doubt remembering Pope Leo and Charlemagne – hastily crowned him Emperor. It was the Pope's undoing. His debaucheries were bad enough, but when two years later he also gave signs of insubordination towards the Emperor he had created, the latter promptly summoned a synod and had him deposed. Berengar soon surrendered; Otto was supreme; and the Empire of the West was reborn, to continue in one form or another virtually uninterrupted until the age of Napoleon.

In South Italy the new order had little immediate effect. It would take another 100 years and a Norman conquest to re-establish order there. In the North, however, it brought about a general revulsion against the debauchery and licence of recent years – encouraged, perhaps, by the reflection that the end of the first Christian millennium was fast approaching and with it, as many believed, that of the world itself. This revulsion may well have played its part in the decision taken by the people of Venice to get rid of the fourth Candiano, and is still more likely to have affected them when, on 12 August 976 in the cathedral church of S. Pietro di Castello, they elected his successor.

With Pietro Orseolo I we encounter the only Doge in Venetian history – possibly the only republican head of state anywhere – to have been subsequently canonized. Whether he deserved his halo is open to question; to leave wife, child and heavy political responsibilities at the age of fifty for the peace of a monastic cell would not nowadays be considered much of a qualification for sainthood. From his earliest youth, however, Pietro Orseolo seems to have been a genuine ascetic; and during the two short years of his reign he ruled Venice with a wise and above all a generous hand. He found the Republic in grave financial straits. Candiano's extravagances had emptied the coffers; the Dogaressa Waldrada, who had taken refuge at the German imperial court, was claiming the return of her formidable dowry; meanwhile there was the whole centre of Venice to be rebuilt. So great had been the devastation that Orseolo had been obliged to transfer the seat of government to his own private house, some distance along the Riva beyond the charred remains of the Doges' Palace; and it was from there that he set to work to put the city on its feet again. For the first time, a tithe was imposed upon all Venetians; Waldrada – who, considering everything, was lucky to be alive at all – was paid off in full; while the Doge devoted a great part of his personal fortune – enough, we are told, to yield an annual 8,000 ducats for eighty years – to the rebuilding of the Palace and of the Basilica of St Mark, and to the erection of a new hospital across the Piazzetta, more or less on the site now occupied by the Marciana Library and the eastern end of the Procuratie Nuove.[1]

1. It was as part of his reconstruction of St Mark's that Pietro Orseolo ordered from Constantinople an altar-screen of what Yeats was to describe, 1,000 years later, as 'hammered gold and gold enamelling'. Enlarged and remodelled over the centuries, it is now known as the *Pala d'Oro*.

All too soon, however, there appeared on the scene the faintly sinister figure of a certain Guarinus, otherwise known as Warren, abbot of the monastery of St Michael of Cuxa, a Benedictine foundation near Prades in the French Pyrenees.[1] We cannot be sure how far this man was to blame for the Doge's subsequent action. He may have been deliberately sent as an agent from the Ottonian court where Waldrada, unappeased, had stepped up her diplomatic offensive against Venice with the enthusiastic assistance of her stepson Vitale Candiano, Patriarch of Grado; he may have been just another of those well-meaning but misguided medieval ecclesiastics whose ideal world consisted of one enormous monastery and who spent their lives persuading one public figure after another to retreat into the cloister. Or he may have been neither: Peter Damian, that most uncharitable of saints, attributes the events that followed to the guilty conscience of the Doge himself, whom he accuses of complicity in his predecessor's overthrow and in the destruction of the Palace.[2] On Warren's first visit to Venice in 977, his blandishments, if such there were, had no immediate effect; a year later, however, on the pretext of a pilgrimage to Jerusalem, the abbot was back again – and this time he succeeded. It had been a bad year. Opposition was mounting both inside and outside the city; the tithe was increasingly resented; and although Pietro Orseolo was still spending as much as ever on his own account, he had doubtless come to understand that generosity and popularity are two very different things. He may too have begun to suspect a lack within himself of that last ounce of moral fibre necessary to withstand the pressures by which he was surrounded. On 1 September 978, he took the easy way out and fled. Under the cover of darkness, and accompanied only by his son-in-law Giovanni Morosini and a certain Gradenigo – the same, in all probability, who had retrieved the Candiano corpses two years before – he slipped across the lagoon to Sant' Ilario, where horses were waiting. Having shaved off his beard before his departure he passed unrecognized, and a few weeks later the former Doge was safe in the abbey of his friend. There he lived another nine years, and there his body was preserved until 1732, the year after his canonization, when at the command of Louis XV it was returned to Venice.

1. The monastery was dissolved and destroyed during the French Revolution, and though it has since been resurrected by the Cistercians it retains little of its former glory. There is a reconstruction, containing many of the original capitals, in the Cloisters of the Metropolitan Museum of Art, New York.

2. *Vita Sancti Romualdi*, Ch. V.

The reign of Orseolo's successor, the weak and probably invalid Vitale Candiano,[1] was little more than an interregnum. After only fourteen months in office he too retired to a monastery, leaving the throne to yet another member of his family. Tribuno Memmo, or Menio, was distinguished for his knowledge of horticulture, but for very little else. He was the son-in-law of the murdered Pietro, a fact which did not deter him from proclaiming, on his accession in 979, a general amnesty to all those who fled after the assassination. But if he hoped by this means to restore peace to the lagoon, he was unsuccessful. Venice remained torn by factional strife, with the two principal parties now polarizing themselves each around a leading family and looking respectively to the Eastern and Western Empires for support. On the one side were the Morosini, champions of the old link with Byzantium; on the other the Coloprini, who put their trust in the Empire of the West and its energetic young Emperor, Otto II.

Otto had succeeded his father in 973, at the age of eighteen. For the next seven years he had been busy consolidating his position north of the Alps; then, in December 980, angered and alarmed by the incursions of the Sicilian Muslims in Apulia and Calabria, he headed south into Italy with the object of freeing the peninsula once and for all from Saracen occupation. The fact that the beleaguered provinces were technically part of the Byzantine Empire did not worry him overmuch; his wife Theophano was sister of the two jointly reigning Emperors of Byzantium, Basil II and Constantine VIII, who were far too taken up with problems nearer home to give these distant and to them relatively unimportant possessions the attention they deserved. To begin with, the campaign went well enough; but in the summer of 982, as he was advancing south-westward into Calabria, Otto was surprised by a Saracen force near Stilo. His army was cut to pieces. He himself escaped only by swimming to a passing ship, concealing his identity and later, as the vessel approached Rossano, jumping overboard again and striking out for the shore.

But his determination remained firm; the following June found him at Verona preparing a fresh campaign and, incidentally, renewing the usual treaty of trade and protection with Venice. He did so, probably, in all good faith; but shortly afterwards there arrived at his court a party of Venetians led by Stefano Coloprini, who had killed one of the Morosini faction in the square of S. Pietro di Castello and had been obliged to flee

1. Not to be confused with his namesake, the Patriarch of Grado. His relationship with the other, more famous members of his family is uncertain.

for his life. He had now come to Otto with a proposal. Venice, for all her growing power, still remained dependent on the mainland for her lines of communication and supply. If these were to be cut, she would be brought rapidly to her knees and obliged to accept Coloprini as Doge, who would in return subject the city to imperial suzerainty. The entire Venetian fleet would then be available to Otto for his next campaign against the Saracens.

The prospect of adding this brightest of jewels to his crown was more than the ambitious young Emperor could resist. The treaty he had just renewed was forgotten; instead, he declared an immediate blockade of the Republic. His vassal the Duke of Carinthia was ordered to ensure that the Marches of Verona, Istria and Friuli were closed to Venetian commerce, while the Coloprini and their followers were posted at strategic points along roads and rivers. As autumn turned to winter Venice, still devastated by the conflagration of seven years before, demoralized by civil strife and ruled by an indecisive and vacillating Doge, now found herself faced with the twin threats of famine and an imperial take-over. In one respect the crisis was even greater than in the days when she had met the challenge of Pepin, or later of the Magyars. Then at least she had had the surrounding waters to protect her, with their treacherous shoals and currents that none but her own sailors knew. This time the attackers were themselves Venetians, for whom the lagoon had no secrets. And how many agents and supporters had they left within the city? Panic-stricken, the populace fell upon the houses of those of the Coloprini who had remained behind and razed them to the ground, seizing the women and children as hostages. Then, powerless to do more, they awaited the onslaught.

It never came. Stefano Coloprini suddenly died, and was followed to the grave in December of the same year – 983 – by the Emperor Otto himself, stricken down at the age of twenty-eight by an overdose of medicine (four drachms of aloes) following a fever. His mother Adelaide, who became co-regent in the place of her three-year-old grandson, would probably have liked to carry on the blockade; but the influence of Otto's Byzantine widow Theophano, with whom she shared the regency, was too strong. The best she was able to achieve was an amnesty under which the Coloprini and their fellow rebels were permitted to return to Venice. They would have been better advised to stay away. Their old enemies, the Morosini, had not forgotten their murdered kinsman. They were sworn to vengeance and their memories were long. In 991 they attacked three of the Coloprini just as the latter were boarding a boat outside the newly rebuilt Doges' Palace, ran them through with their swords and hurled them into the water.

It was perhaps not altogether fair to blame Tribuno Memmo for this new outrage. He was certainly related to the Morosini by marriage; and in 982 when Giovanni Morosini, back in Venice after settling his fugitive father-in-law at St Michael of Cuxa and now himself a monk, was looking for land on which to found a Benedictine monastery, the Doge had offered him the little island opposite the palace, known then as the Island of the Cypresses and now as that of S. Giorgio Maggiore. In so far as he took sides at all, therefore, Memmo's sympathies were clear. But he was a gentle, peace-loving man and the last thing he would have wished to see was his city, after nearly a decade of comparative tranquillity, torn asunder yet again by internecine warfare. Blamed, however, he was, attacked and reviled until there was no course open to him but that which had been taken by his two immediate predecessors. He too withdrew to a monastery – S. Zaccaria this time, just behind his former palace – there to end his days in the obscurity he should never have left.[1]

1. Surprisingly enough, this most forgettable of Doges is the earliest to boast a permanent memorial in Venice – even though he had to wait nearly 500 years for it, until Palladio rebuilt the church of S. Giorgio Maggiore in the late sixteenth century. It takes the form of a portrait bust set above a symbolic sarcophagus in a niche on the left-hand side of the façade, in recognition of the fact that it was Memmo to whom, with Giovanni Morosini, the original foundation owed its existence.

5

The Determined Dynasty

[991–1032]

La puissance dépend de l'empire de l'onde;
Le trident de Neptune est le sceptre du monde.

Lemierre

The tenth century had opened in Venice on a note of triumph, with the repulse of the Magyar invaders. It had not, however, fulfilled its early promise. Of the past fifty years, all but two – those covering the brief reign of Pietro Orseolo I – had seen the fate of the Republic entrusted to members, by blood or marriage, of the family of Candiano, whose policies had brought it to the brink of disaster. By their arrogance and ambition – or, as with the last reigning member of their clan Tribuno Memmo, by sheer ineptitude and the inability to give a strong lead in moments of crisis – they had alienated the Empire of the West, largely ignored that of the East, and encouraged dissension at home. As the final decade of the century began, Venice was sick to the heart. A casual visitor might have been impressed by the outward signs of prosperity – the ships in the harbour, the merchandise on the Rialto, the sables and the silks and the spices; but the Republic was no longer feared and respected by her neighbours as once she had been and, as her reputation had waned, so too had her morale. Her own particular form of national pride – that consciousness of being a race apart, springing from a different element, pursuing an individual destiny – which had given courage and cohesion to her founding fathers and impelled their successors to the threshold of greatness seemed to be draining away. Desperately now, Venice needed a strong hand to guide her, to weld her again into a nation, to restore her self-confidence and her self-respect.

And she found it. Old Pietro Orseolo, when he had fled from family and responsibilities thirteen years before, had left behind him a young son, also called Pietro; and it was this son, still only thirty years old, that the Venetians acclaimed in 991 as their new ruler. They could not have made a better choice. Statesman, warrior and diplomatist of genius, Pietro

Orseolo II towers above the other Doges of his day like a giant among pygmies; and from the outset his subjects seem to have recognized his greatness. With his accession, the feuding that had so long poisoned civilized life stopped as suddenly as if it had never happened. It was as though the Venetians had grown up once again into an adult, responsible and gifted people, and now stood ready to follow him on the road to glory.

But for Venice glory meant trade; and the first task of Pietro Orseolo as Doge was to restore friendly and mutually advantageous trading relations with the two Empires. Within a year he had negotiated with Basil II in Constantinople commercial terms more favourable than any that Venice had previously enjoyed. An imperial chrysobul dated March 992 undertook to admit *bona fide* Venetian goods – though not those from other sources carried on Venetian ships – at tariffs far lower than those imposed on foreign merchandise in general. Almost as important, Venetian merchants in Constantinople were henceforth to be directly subject to the Grand Logothete, a high palace official roughly comparable to the Minister of Finance. This spared them the delays and frustrations for which Byzantine bureaucracy was famous and virtually assured them the ear, in emergencies, of the Emperor himself. In return, the Venetian fleet was to be kept ready to transport imperial troops at short notice wherever they might be needed.

With the young Emperor of the West the Doge achieved similar success – perhaps even more, owing to the mutual admiration and affection that rapidly grew up between them. Otto III was an extraordinary child. Born in 980, Emperor at the age of three, he grew up combining the traditional ambitions of his line with a romantic mysticism inherited from his Greek mother, and forever dreaming of a great Byzantinesque theocracy that would embrace Germans, Italians and Slavs alike, with God at its head, and himself and the Pope – in that order – as His twin viceroys. The pursuit of this dream made him still more preoccupied with affairs in Italy than his father had been before him; a young man's hero-worship for the ablest ruler west of Constantinople did the rest. In 996, when Otto crossed the Alps for the first time in his life on the way to his imperial coronation in Rome, he was able to make an impressive demonstration of his friendship. First he compelled two refractory bishops to restore to Venice certain territories that they had wrongfully appropriated for themselves; next he granted the Doge the right to establish Venetian warehouses and trading-stations along the banks of the Piave and the Sile, simultaneously guaranteeing safe conduct and tax exemptions for all Venetians on imperial territory. Most significant of all, he sent personally for Orseolo's third son to join him at Verona, and there stood sponsor to him at his confirmation, bestowing on him his own name, Otto.

Thus, by the end of his fifth year in office, Pietro Orseolo II had assured the commercial prospects of the Republic with the two greatest powers in Christendom. Now more than ever the broad rivers of northern Italy were thronged with Venetian barges, their gunwales sunk almost to the water-line beneath their cargoes of iron and wood, corn and wine, salt and – in spite of everything – slaves; battling their way upstream to the great clearing-houses of Verona, Piacenza or Pavia, whence they would be transported by land across the Apennines to Naples, Amalfi and their neighbours or over the Alps to Germany and northern Europe. Other, heavier vessels would meanwhile beat south-east down the Adriatic, round the Peloponnese, northward again to Constantinople and even, occasionally, the Black Sea. Yet others concentrated on a newer market, still more rapidly expanding: the world of Islam. Heretofore, though there had always been some measure of trade with the Arabs – it was, after all, Venetian merchants who had stolen the body of St Mark from Alexandria – commercial dealings had always been inhibited by such factors as the Saracens' predilection for piracy, Venetian memories of their great attack on the lagoon that had so nearly succeeded 150 years before, and the revulsion still felt by much of western Christendom at the suggestion of any degree of friendly relations with the infidel. Here was yet another attitude that Pietro Orseolo was determined to dispel. Off went his ambassadors to every corner of the Mediterranean where the green banner of the Prophet flew – to Spain and Barbary, Sicily and the Levant; to the courts of Aleppo, Cairo and Damascus, to Cordova, Kairouan and Palermo. Emir after Emir received them with courtesy and accepted their proposals. Agreement after agreement was brought back with pride and satisfaction to the Doge. His imperial neighbours to East and West, ever anxious at the growing Muslim menace in South Italy, might be horrified at his actions and accuse him of treachery to the Faith. But for Pietro, true Venetian that he was, commerce was always preferable to bloodshed – and a good deal more profitable as well.

To the unfettered expansion of Venetian trade, one obstacle only now remained – the Slav pirates of the Dalmatian coast. The last major expedition against them – that led by Pietro Candiano I in 887 – had ended in catastrophe, with the death of the Doge in battle; and though some sixty years later his grandson had managed in part to retrieve the honour of his family and the Republic, the menace was now as great as ever it had been – so great, in fact that throughout the second half of the tenth century Venice had acquired the habit of paying an annual tribute of protection money to ensure the free passage of her ships through the narrow Adriatic waters. But Pietro Orseolo was not a man to submit to blackmail. On his accession he forbade all further payments and, when the next was due, sent six Venetian galleys across to Dalmatia to guard against possible reprisals. Inevitably, a battle followed. The island of Lissa,[1] one of the principal pirate strongholds, fell to the Venetians, who returned joyfully to the lagoon, their vessels crammed to capacity with prisoners of both sexes.

Venice had won the first round, but the pirates were not beaten. Their main concentrations, around the mouths of the Narenta and the Cetina, had not even been affected; and they now turned the full force of their anger against the defenceless inhabitants of the coastal cities. Racially and linguistically, these people had nothing in common with their assailants. The pirates were Croats, a Slav people who had pushed westward from the Carpathians in the sixth and seventh centuries as part of the general Slavonic expansion across the Balkan peninsula, and in the tenth had founded a kingdom of their own. This Croatian Kingdom, however, had never comprised the whole coast of Dalmatia, where the populations of Pola, Zara, Traù and Spalato,[2] and of many other smaller communities along the coast, were the descendants of a Latin-speaking race whose forbears had been citizens of the Roman Empire and who looked upon their Croatian neighbours as barbarian upstarts. These populations, except that of Zara, were all technically subject to Constantinople; their subjection, however, was more theoretical than real. As one historian puts it, 'the name of the Emperor was officially honoured and respected, but he was not obeyed, for he gave no orders'.[3] Knowing only too well, therefore, that help could never be expected from that direction, they appealed to Venice.

If Orseolo needed any further excuse to complete the work he had started, here was the perfect one ready to hand. On 9 May, A.D. 1000 – it

1. Now Vis. Dalmatian place-names present something of a problem, since the classical Latin or Italian versions commonly used by most historians of the period often bear little or no resemblance to their modern Slavonic counterparts. In this book the contemporary Italian names are used throughout, but all modern Slavonic equivalents will be given in footnotes and, in brackets, in the index.
2. Now Pula, Zadar, Trogir and Split.
3. R. Cessi, *Cambridge Medieval History*, Vol. IV, Part I, p. 269.

was Ascension Day – the Doge heard Mass in the cathedral of S. Pietro di Castello, and received from the Bishop of Olivolo a consecrated standard.[1] Thence he proceeded in state to the harbour where the great Venetian fleet lay waiting for him, boarded his flagship and gave the signal to weigh anchor. After a night at Jesolo, the fleet came the next morning to Grado, where the Patriarch – still that same old Vitale Candiano who, after over thirty years in office, seems to have given up political intrigue and settled down as a loyal servant of the Republic – ceremonially greeted them and invested the Doge with relics of St Hermagoras.[2] Finally on 11 May, now spiritually as well as materially equipped for the tasks that lay ahead, the expedition set sail across the Adriatic.

John the Deacon's account of the journey down the Dalmatian coast reads more like the record of a triumphal progress than that of a military campaign. Bishops, barons and city priors welcomed the Venetians at every port of call; civic receptions were held in the Doge's honour; holy relics were brought out for his inspection and adoration. Oaths of fidelity were freely sworn; on occasion young men even rallied, uninvited, to the Venetian colours. At Traù the brother of the Croatian King made voluntary submission, even leaving a hostage in the person of his young son, who was later to receive the Doge's daughter in marriage. It was only when the fleet reached Spalato that Orseolo made direct contact with the enemy, whose leaders came up from the Narenta delta to discuss terms. They were in no position to drive a hard bargain; in return for the Venetian withdrawal they willingly agreed to forgo their annual tribute and to cease their molestation of the Republic's galleys travelling on their lawful occasions.

Unfortunately, however, the Narentines could not speak for all the offshore islands. Curzola[3] proved rather less cooperative and had to be subdued by force, while the men of Lagosta,[4] putting their trust in the almost legendary impregnability of their island fortress, prepared a still more formidable resistance. But the besiegers were equal to the challenge. Advancing under a hail of rocks and stones from the upper ramparts, they soon succeeded in breaching the base of one of the towers – fortunately for them, the one on which Lagosta depended for its water supply.

1. Gfrörer believes that this banner bore, possibly for the first time, the now familiar Venetian emblem of the winged lion with the open book in its paws.

2. The friend and disciple of St Mark, who appointed him first Bishop of Aquileia. He was later beheaded under Nero.

3. Korčula.

4. Lastovo.

And so, writes John the Deacon – who, as Orseolo's friend and most trusted servant, was very probably present:

the enemy, now dejected in spirit, laid down their arms and on bended knees begged nothing more than that they should be delivered from the dreaded peril of death. Therefore the Doge, who was a merciful man, resolved to spare them all, insisting only that their town should be destroyed . . . The Archbishop of Ragusa met him with his clergy, swore allegiance to the Doge and made him many signs of homage[1] . . . Thence, passing once again by the cities through which he had come, he returned in great triumph to Venice.

His subjects greeted him with jubilation, and no wonder. How long the pirates of the Narenta would keep their oath was an open question; but they had at least seen that the Republic was not in a mood to be trifled with, and the fate of Lagosta would not quickly be forgotten. Besides, Venice had now gained a hold over the eastern coast of the Adriatic such as she had never before enjoyed. It was still not technically Venetian territory; the cities and towns of Dalmatia, while swearing their oaths of fidelity and agreeing to pay an annual tribute,[2] had been careful to recall the overall suzerainty of Byzantium, which the Doge in his turn had willingly recognized. But the way was now clear for the opening of warehouses and trading-posts in the principal sea-ports, and for the consequent expansion of trade in the interior of the Balkan peninsula.

Strategically, too, Venice had gained much; henceforth she would have an alternative source of food in an emergency. Although the Rialtine islands were still only partially built over, the patches of productive land remaining on them had long been inadequate to satisfy a rapidly growing population. For her food supplies, Venice was obliged to look to the mainland; hence her consternation during Otto II's landward blockade seventeen years before. In the foreseeable future any such blockade might be a mild inconvenience; it would certainly be no worse. A few ships dispatched across the Adriatic would be back a few days later with all the corn and provisions the city might need. Finally, the pine forests of Curzola and other islands guaranteed a virtually inexhaustible stock of timber for the Venetian shipyards.

And so there was added to the Doge's other honorifics the mellifluous

---

1. This last assertion, it is only fair to state, has been hotly denied by certain historians of Ragusa – now Dubrovnik.

2. From Arbe (Rab), ten pounds of raw silk; from Ossero (Osor) on the island of Cherso (Cres), forty marten skins; from Veglia (Krk), fifteen marten skins and twenty fox skins; from Pola (Pula), 2,000 pounds of oil for the basilica of St Mark. Spalato (Split) undertook to equip two galleys and one barque whenever the Venetians sent a fleet to sea.

title of *Dux Dalmatiae*; and in further commemoration of the expedition
it was decreed that on every succeeding Ascension Day – the anniversary
of the fleet's departure – the Doge, with the Bishop of Olivolo and
the nobles and citizens of Venice, should sail out again by the Lido
port into the open sea for a service of supplication and thanksgiving.
In those early days the service was short and the prayer simple, though
it asked a lot: 'Grant, O Lord, that for us and for all who sail thereon,
the sea may ever be calm and quiet.' The Doge and his suite were then
sprinkled with holy water while the choir chanted the text from the
fifty-first Psalm 'Purge me with hyssop, and I shall be clean'[1] and what
was left of the water was poured into the sea. Later, as the tradition
grew more venerable, so the ceremony grew more elaborate, and included
the casting of a propitiatory golden ring into the waves; thus it was
slowly to become identified with a symbolic marriage to the sea – the
Sposalizio del Mar – a character that it was to retain till the end of the
Republic itself.[2]

For Otto III, the new millennium had had less auspicious beginnings.
In furtherance of his wild politico-mystical ambitions, the young Emperor
had settled in Rome, where he had built himself a magnificent new
palace on the Aventine. Here he lived in a curious combination of
splendour and asceticism, surrounded by a court rigid with Byzantine
ceremonial, eating in majestic solitude off gold plate, then occasionally
shedding his purple dalmatic for a pilgrim's cloak and trudging barefoot
to some distant shrine. But he had retained all his old admiration for
Venice – seeing her, perhaps, as the one place in Italy where Western
practicality and Byzantine mysticism were fused into one – and he hoped,
as ever, to make her the instrument of his Italian policies.

He was disappointed. When an imperial embassy arrived on the Rialto
soon after the Doge's return from Dalmatia with a proposal for joint
operations in North Italy, it met with a firm but polite refusal. Orseolo
understood, better than any Doge before him, how much Venice's
fortunes depended on the sea. Territorial acquisitions on the mainland
had no part in her greatness. He may, on the other hand, have been
rather more interested in another suggestion which was put to John the
Deacon by the Emperor at about the same time: that Otto should pay a

---

1. The text is not quite as surprising as it may appear at first sight. In the Latin Vulgate, the
first word is more accurately translated by *aspergere* – 'sprinkle' – as it is in the New English
Bible. Hyssop branches were used as an aspergent rather than an aperient.
2. See also p. 116.

secret visit to the Doge in Venice 'to hear his wise counsel and for the sake of the love he bore him'.

Unless the Emperor feared an attempt at assassination, his insistence on secrecy is hard to understand. Historians have argued that it was made necessary by the confidential nature of the subjects that he wanted to discuss; but a publicly announced visit would not have prevented privately held discussions and, in any case, both Emperor and Doge were to reveal the fact, if not the details, of the visit within a day or two of Otto's departure. It was admittedly unusual, in those pre-Crusading days, for an Emperor to leave the boundaries of his Empire; there were, however, no particular risks involved. Whatever the reasons, Otto was adamant, and the preparations – which involved John, as the Doge's secret emissary, passing the best part of a year shuttling between the two rulers – were made far longer and more laborious than they would otherwise have been. They were doubtless complicated still further when, in February 1001, the people of Rome rose up in rebellion against the Emperor and drove him from their city.

Otto does not appear to have been unduly discouraged. He celebrated Easter at Ravenna, where John the Deacon was with him to discuss last-minute arrangements. He then gave out that he proposed to spend a few days taking a health cure on the island of Pomposa[1] at the mouth of the Po. Accommodation at the abbey was actually prepared for him, but within a few hours of his arrival he slipped unseen down to the shore where John had a boat waiting and, attended only by a few of his closest associates, sailed off to Venice. After a day and a night in heavy seas he landed during a violent storm on the island of S. Servolo,[2] where Doge Pietro was waiting to greet him. John the Deacon has left us an eye-witness account of what followed. The night, he tells us, was so black that the two could scarcely see each other's faces. It was the Doge – who may not have been in the best of tempers – who began the conversation. 'If you wish to see the monastery of S. Zaccaria,' he remarked to the muffled shape beside him, 'you had better go there at once, so that you may be safely received before dawn within the walls of my palace.' By now Otto and his friends must have been in a state of some exhaustion; but Pietro was merciless. The secrecy had been the Emperor's idea; it was Otto who had involved him in all this inconvenience, subterfuge and

1. The abbey church still stands, together with many of the monastic buildings.
2. S. Servolo is now known to every Venetian as the home of one of the two main lunatic asylums of the city – a function it has fulfilled since 1725, when the Council of Ten set it aside for 'maniacs of noble family in comfortable circumstances'.

embarrassment; it was he, finally, who had dragged him out to this godforsaken island on this cold, stormy night. Very well: he must take the consequences.

There is no indication, in John's chronicle or anywhere else, that Otto was particularly eager to see S. Zaccaria or, even if he were, why his visit there should be so urgent. But he did as he was told. Orseolo did not accompany him. Instead he hurried back to the palace, ostensibly to prepare for the Emperor's reception; in fact, we may devoutly hope, to bed.

This furtive atmosphere was preserved throughout the Emperor's stay. The members of the imperial suite were publicly received by the Doge the next morning, as he emerged from the half-completed basilica of St Mark after Mass. They formally presented their letters of credence as representatives of their master – who, they claimed, had remained for reasons of health in Pomposa – whereupon Pietro Orseolo welcomed them in the name of the Republic, gave orders for their proper accommodation, and then himself slipped away to the remote eastern tower of the palace, where he had secretly installed Otto with a couple of attendants. Even now, John tells us, he took his meals publicly with the others, since 'he could not spend all day with the Emperor for fear of arousing the suspicions of any of his subjects'. If nothing else, it was a good excuse – and it allowed Otto, conspicuously disguised as a poor man, to visit the other churches and monuments in which he professed such an interest.

Some consultations were doubtless held, though no record of them has come down to us. Presents were exchanged, including an ivory throne and footstool for the Emperor; in return, Otto released the Venetians from the obligation to provide him every year with a *pallium* or state robe – a form of tribute which, together with an annual payment of fifty pounds of silver, had been in force since the days of his grand-father, Otto the Great – and, to cement their friendship still further, stood godfather for the second time to one of Pietro's children – on this occasion a new-born baby daughter, whom he personally held at the font. Then, probably not more than two days after his arrival, he slipped out of Venice as quietly as he had come, attended only by John the Deacon and his two personal servants, leaving the rest of his party to take their official departure on the following day.

Once back in Ravenna, however, he immediately announced where he had been; and, obviously by prior arrangement, the Doge made a similar and roughly simultaneous public statement in Venice – which, if John's account is to be believed, was enthusiastically acclaimed by the people.

Again it is not easy to see why; the Venetians dearly loved a show, and the secrecy surrounding the imperial visit had robbed them of a splendid one. But Orseolo's declaration would not have failed to emphasize the effect on the Republic's prestige – to say nothing of his own – of a free decision by the Emperor of the West to leave his dominions for the first time in his life in order to see Venice for himself, to worship at her shrines, admire her beauty and to drink at her fountain of experience and political wisdom. We can only assume that their gratification outweighed their disappointment.

Certainly Venice derived greater benefit from the visit than did Otto. Determined to re-establish himself in Rome, the young Emperor now returned there and prepared to besiege the city. Reinforcements were summoned from Germany; but just as they reached him, and while the Byzantine bride he had so long desired was still on her way from Constantinople, he was struck down by a sudden fever – probably smallpox – and died at the castle of Paterno, near Città Castellana, on 24 January 1002. He was just twenty-two years old. Surprisingly – though in the circumstances fortunately – he had expressed a wish to be buried not in Rome with his father,[1] but in Charlemagne's old capital of Aachen. Thither his body was taken, through hostile Roman territory, by a group of his faithful followers; and there it lies to this day, in the choir of the cathedral.

The death of Otto III did not deflect Pietro Orseolo II from his policy of close friendship with the Empire of the West. When, a month later, the Lombards rose in revolt under Ardoin, Marquess of Ivrea, and crowned him King in defiance of imperial claims, Pietro unhesitatingly backed the legitimate Emperor, Otto's second cousin, Henry II 'the Holy' of Bavaria. He was rewarded before the year's end with a new charter in which he was addressed as 'Doge of Venice and Dalmatia' and all previous privileges were confirmed; and he was also fortunate enough to have other children to whom he could invite an Emperor to stand godfather. The usual arrangements were made, and when Henry paid his first visit to Italy in 1004 the youngest of those sons was there at Verona to meet him. A service of confirmation followed, at which the Emperor acted as sponsor and gave the boy his name. The future of Venetian-imperial relations seemed to be set fair.

It might have been expected that the Doge would have chosen his eldest son rather than his youngest for so signal an honour; but Giovanni

---

1. The tomb of Otto II can still be seen in the crypt of St Peter's. He is the only Western Emperor to have been buried in Rome.

Orseolo was being kept for Byzantium. Pietro had never allowed his *rapprochement* with Otto or Henry to affect his friendship with Basil II. His Dalmatian adventure, if not actually cleared in advance with Constantinople, had certainly found favour with the Emperor of the East, whose rights he had been scrupulously careful to uphold and who was only too happy that Venice should take on the responsibility of policing a region that he was unable to cope with himself. Since then the Doge had acquired even more merit in Byzantine eyes by leading another expedition, smaller but still more valiant, to the relief of the city of Bari. As capital of the so-called Capitanata – the Byzantine province of South Italy which claimed suzerainty over all the land south of a line drawn from Terracina in the west to Termoli on the Adriatic coast – Bari was the largest and most important Greek community in the peninsula. In April 1002, however, it had been attacked by the Saracens and all that summer it lay under siege. Then on 6 September, a Venetian fleet under Orseolo's personal command had forced the blockade, brought provisions to the starving city and, after a three-day battle outside the harbour, had put the aggressors to flight.

The fact that Venice's intervention had been unsolicited – though she had had obvious reasons of her own for wishing to check the expansion of Saracen power in Italy – had further increased the gratitude of the Byzantines; and Orseolo must have seen that now was the moment to consolidate his advantage. Having first associated the nineteen-year-old Giovanni with him on the ducal throne, he sent him off with his younger brother Otto on a state visit to Constantinople, where it was arranged for him to marry the Princess Maria Argyra, niece of the two joint Emperors.[1] The ceremony took place in the imperial chapel, with the Patriarch officiating and the co-Emperors both present to crown the bridal pair in the Eastern fashion – simultaneously bestowing upon them the relics of St Barbara. Magnificent celebrations followed, after which the couple withdrew to a palace which had been put at their disposal. The young Dogaressa was in an advanced state of pregnancy by the time they returned to Venice.

Pietro Orseolo II was now at the climax of his career. By his statesmanship he had raised the Republic to new heights of prosperity and prestige. By his valour he had averted, for many years to come, the two

---

1. Throughout his reign, Basil II, the Bulgar-Slayer, – one of the greatest Emperors in Byzantine history – technically shared the throne with his brother, Constantine VIII. Constantine was, however, a pleasure-loving nonentity who remained in the background, playing virtually no part in political affairs. For the purposes of this history he can be ignored.

principal threats to its security – the Slavs to the east and the Saracens to the south. He had established a Venetian presence – and a modified form of dominion – over the Dalmatian coast. Meanwhile, on a personal level, he had bound his family by bonds of marriage or compaternity to both the Byzantine and the Western Empires and, for the first time in sixty years, has associated a son with him as Doge. But, as his power and reputation grew, so too did the trappings of majesty with which he tended to surround himself. It was not surprising that many Venetians began to wonder whether success was not going to his head and whether he was not secretly planning, as more than one of his predecessors had planned before him, to establish a hereditary monarchy throughout the lagoon.

Then, suddenly, his world collapsed. In the autumn of 1005 a blazing comet appeared in the southern sky, remaining there for three months. Everyone knew it to be a portent; and sure enough early the following year Venice was struck by famine – a famine that the new Dalmatian sources of supply, which had suffered as much as those on the Italian mainland, could do nothing to alleviate. In its wake came plague, carrying off – among many hundreds of more humble citizens – young Giovanni, his Greek wife and their baby son. St Peter Damian, with ill-concealed satisfaction, attributes the Dogaressa's death to divine retribution for her sybaritic oriental ways:

Such was the luxury of her habits that she scorned even to wash herself in common water, obliging her servants instead to collect the dew that fell from the heavens for her to bathe in. Nor did she deign to touch her food with her fingers, but would command her eunuchs to cut it up into small pieces, which she would impale on a certain golden instrument with two prongs and thus carry to her mouth. Her rooms, too, were so heavy with incense and various perfumes that it is nauseating for me to speak of them, nor would my readers readily believe it. But this woman's vanity was hateful to Almighty God; and so, unmistakably, did He take his revenge. For He raised over her the sword of His divine justice, so that her whole body did putrefy and all her limbs began to wither, filling her bedchamber with an unbearable odour such that no one – not a handmaiden, nor even a slave – could withstand this dreadful attack on the nostrils; except for one serving-girl who, with the help of aromatic concoctions, conscientiously remained to do her bidding. And even she could only approach her mistress hurriedly, and then immediately withdraw. So, after a slow decline and agonizing torments, to the joyful relief of her friends she breathed her last.[1]

1. Since Peter Damian does not refer to Maria Argyra by name, nor to the deaths – at the same time and by the same causes – of her husband and son, some authorities have suggested that he may have confused her with another Greek Dogaressa: Theodora, the wife of Doge

Giovanni and his wife died within sixteen days of each other, and were buried at S. Zaccaria in a single tomb. Pietro Orseolo was heart-broken. His dreams for the future vanished. Though not yet fifty, he seems to have lost the desire to live. Perhaps, like his father, he underwent a religious crisis. Unlike old Pietro, however, he did not retire to a monastery. Instead, he raised his third son, Otto, to the dogeship with him, made his will, leaving the bulk of his possessions to the Church and the poor, and then withdrew to a remote wing of the palace, separating himself even from his wife. Less than two years later, in 1008, he died.

Young Otto was still only sixteen. In the circumstances, it is odd that the Venetians should have made no objection when he joined his father on the throne; it is odder still that they should have allowed him to succeed to power without, so far as we know, a single voice being raised against him – the youngest Doge in Venetian history. But in the Middle Ages both men and women matured younger than they do now – for sixteen-year-olds to be given command of armies was by no means unheard of – and Otto Orseolo seems to have been old beyond his years. 'Catholic in faith, calm in purity, strong in justice, eminent in religion, decorous in his manner of life, well-endowed with wealth and possessions, and so filled with all forms of virtue that he was universally considered to be the most fitting successor of his father and grandfather' – thus Andrea Dandolo was to describe him, after a three-century interval which, if a poor guarantee of historical accuracy, at least argues a relatively unprejudiced standpoint.[1] Otto Orseolo had indeed inherited many of his father's characteristics, among them his taste for splendour and his love of power. The new Doge was familiar with the imperial courts of the West and the East, having received his religious confirmation at one and several high honours from the other; and the Magyar princess – daughter of the subsequently canonized King Stephen of Hungary – whom he married shortly after Pietro's death added still more lustre to his position. Like his father, he was quick to build up his image as a magnificent and majestic potentate – so far, at least, as the traditionally austere sensibilities of his subjects permitted.

Domenico Selvo (see p. 69). As Selvo became Doge only in 1071, however, and Peter Damian himself died in February 1072, this theory does not seem very probable. It may well be that Peter did not know about the plague – or if he did that he kept quiet about it, for the very good reason that it would have ruined his story.

1. John the Deacon's chronicle breaks off here, leaving us without any detailed or sustained contemporary record of events.

But for a young man of his ambitions, the outward trappings of power were insufficient. In 1017 the old Patriarch of Grado, Vitale Candiano, died at last, having occupied the patriarchate for as long as anyone could remember – well over half a century; and in his place Otto appointed his own elder brother, Orso. Orso had hitherto been Bishop of Torcello[1], a see which the Doge now passed on to yet another brother, Vitale. He should have known better. The new Patriarch cannot have been more than thirty, the new bishop ten years younger. Inevitably, the former jealousies concerning the Orseoli, the former fears that they were planning to set up some form of hereditary rule, sprang up again, more insistently than before. The dissatisfaction was not yet such as to provoke an uprising, and for a few more years all went smoothly enough; but it did mean that Otto could no longer rely on the goodwill and support of his people when, in 1019, the first serious cloud appeared on the horizon with the appointment of a noble Bavarian, Poppo of Treffen, to the Patriarchate of Aquileia.

History affords no more perfect example of that phenomenon so characteristic of the Middle Ages[2] – the worldly, ambitious warrior-priest. Hardly was he installed before he laid formal claim to the see of Grado as being historically part of his patriarchate, denouncing its legitimate incumbent, Orso, as a fraud and a usurper. His claim found little favour with the Pope, but a good deal more from the anti-Orseolo faction in Venice itself; in 1022–3 we find both the Doge and his brother fleeing the city and taking refuge in Istria. But now it was Poppo's turn to overreach himself. Without papal sanction, he marched into Grado and began systematically sacking the churches and monasteries, sending off their treasures to Aquileia. This was more than the people of Grado or the Venetians themselves could tolerate. There was an immediate reaction in favour of the Orseoli who returned in haste, drove out Poppo and his followers with surprisingly little fuss and resumed their former thrones, Orso in Grado, Otto in the Doges' Palace.

When, in 1024, a synod called in Rome by Pope John XIX dismissed Poppo's claims out of hand and reaffirmed the rights of Grado as an equal and independent see, it must have looked as though the Orseoli had surmounted their difficulties and were once again firmly entrenched in the seats of Venetian power. So they might well have been

---

1. It was during Orso's tenure of the see of Torcello that the present cathedral was built. It still stands today essentially as he left it. (See p. 11n.)

2. At least where western Europe is concerned; in the Orthodox world the tradition has continued up to the present day.

if the Doge had only shown a modicum of sensitivity to popular opinion. But Otto's ambitions were, as always, too strong for him, and two years later a further scandal over Church appointments brought matters finally to a head. His enemies acted quickly and decisively, and this time he had no opportunity to flee. He was seized, shorn of his beard, and dispatched to end his days in Constantinople.

Otto's successor, Pietro Barbolano – but, with that perverseness which characterizes so much of early Venetian nomenclature, more usually known as Centranico – could, at the time of his accession, boast one distinction only: that of having filched, some thirty years before, the relics of St Sabas from Constantinople and deposited them in the church of S. Antonino.[1] For four years he struggled to reunite the city, but his efforts were in vain. The old Orseolo policy of linking their family to the hereditary ruling dynasties of Europe began to pay off. In Constantinople, the Emperor had given an honourable refuge to Otto (his niece's brother-in-law) and had angrily withdrawn the trading privileges granted to old Pietro at the end of the previous century. The new Western Emperor followed suit, while King Stephen of Hungary, determined to avenge his exiled daughter and son-in-law, attacked Dalmatia and annexed a number of the coastal cities.[2] Venice herself remained torn by factions, among which the supporters of the Orseoli, who had remained strong in the city, became even stronger as the new government's problems multiplied and nostalgia for the old days grew. The crisis came in 1032, when Centranico in his turn was compelled to abdicate and Vitale Orseolo, the Bishop of Torcello, hurried off to Constantinople with an invitation to his brother to resume the throne. Meanwhile the third brother Orso, Patriarch of Grado, who like Vitale had managed to ride out the storm, temporarily took the power into his own hands.

All seemed set for a restoration; but Bishop Vitale reached Constantinople to find his brother already gravely ill, and Otto died before he could return to Venice. The Patriarch, who in the intervening months had continued to guide both the religious and the secular destinies of his

1. They were returned 973 years later – in 1965 – by Pope Paul VI at the request of the Orthodox Patriarch, who described movingly how the monks of St Sabas's foundation 'still gathered every evening at the empty tomb' (*The Times*, 18 March 1965).

2. This campaign was probably instigated by his nephew, Otto's son Peter, who was now living in Hungary – where indeed he was eventually to succeed Stephen on the throne. With the casuistry of the age, Peter would have had no difficulty in arguing that his grandfather had conquered Dalmatia for the benefit of the Orseoli, and not for the ungrateful Venetians who had banished them.

city, resigned as soon as the news reached him. An attempt to seize the throne by some obscure offshoot of the family, one Domenico Orseolo, was effortlessly scotched. A modern historian[1] has dismissed him as a *miserabile parodia*; he lasted for a day and a night, then fled to Ravenna.

The days of the Orseoli were passed. They would not return.

1. R. Cessi, *Storia della Repubblica di Venezia.*

6

The Norman Menace

[1032–1095]

These men were brave, and skilled in naval warfare. They were sent forth at the imperial behest, by densely-peopled Venice, a land rich in wealth and in men, where the furthermost gulf of the Adriatic lies under the northern stars. The walls of this nation are surrounded by the sea, and its people cannot visit each others' houses unless they travel by boat. For they dwell ever among the waters, and no nation is more valiant than they in fighting at sea, or in steering their craft over the surface of the waves.

William of Apulia, a contemporary Norman Chronicler

The ignominious attempt by Domenico Orseolo to seize power in Venice proved catastrophic not only for himself but for his family. The Venetians, even those who had supported the restoration of Doge Otto, were shocked by his blatant presumption that the supreme authority in their city had become a perquisite of the Orseolo clan and showed their disgust in the clearest way possible – by conferring the dogeship on Domenico Flabanico, a wealthy silk-merchant who had led the insurrection six years before. Flabanico's known anti-dynastic views, plus the pattern of subsequent Venetian history, have together been responsible for a widely held theory that the new Doge introduced what almost amounted to a revised constitution for the state, according to which the practice of appointing co-regents – and thus in effect successors – was forbidden, and a period of tyranny gave place to one of democratic liberty. One authority[1] has even gone so far as to assert that a special law was passed, ostracizing the entire Orseolo family and debarring it in perpetuity from public office – this despite the fact that the two prelates Orso and Vitale are known to have continued in their respective sees until they died. In fact, such reform as there was resulted from a change not so much of laws but of attitudes. The necessary legislation providing

1. An anonymous annotator of the Ambrosian MS. of Andrea Dandolo's Chronicle – a version which, it is only fair to point out, was described by an eighteenth-century director of the Ambrosian Library in Milan as a *confusa indigestaque farrago*.

for the proper election of Doges and giving adequate powers to the popular assembly already existed. All that was required was the will to implement it. It was this will that Domenico Flabanico possessed and, in a way, personified. And he carried the people with him. During the seven and a half centuries that were to elapse before the Republic came to an end the names of certain leading families recur again and again in the list of Doges; considering that for most of that time Venice was an openly avowed oligarchy, it would be surprising if they did not. But on only two occasions in the whole period do we find the same name appearing twice consecutively; on both of these, the succession is from brother to brother rather than from father to son; and on neither is there any doubt as to the propriety of the election. After the fall of the Orseoli the practice of co-dogeship was never revived, or even indeed attempted.

The eleven-year reign of Domenico Flabanico, then, emerges as something of a milestone in Venetian history. At the same time it seems to have been unusually devoid of incident. The Republic was at peace again, factions were forgotten, and the citizens were able to concentrate on the two things they did best – making money, and enlarging and beautifying their city. This happy state of affairs was, however, rudely interrupted on the Doge's death. During the brief interregnum that followed, the unspeakable Poppo of Aquileia saw another opportunity to subjugate Grado and with the help of his usual army of thugs descended for the second time upon the luckless city, carrying off the few treasures that had somehow eluded him twenty years before. Fortunately Poppo himself died almost immediately afterwards, and his followers hastily fled at the approach of a Venetian fleet under the new Doge, Domenico Contarini; but although his action was formally condemned – and the rights and immunities of Grado confirmed – by the Pope in 1044, the rivalry between the two sees remained a vexed question for many years to come. It would probably have caused still more trouble than it did had not the Patriarchs of Grado, after the death of old Orso in 1045, sensibly decided to establish their principal residence in Venice. Thenceforth their connections with Grado were to grow ever more tenuous; and when in the fifteenth century the Pope officially recognized the transfer, he had little to change but their title.[1]

Apart from the relief of Grado, Doge Contarini's only foreign exploit

1. The first patriarchal palace in Venice stood on the Grand Canal, between the church of S. Silvestro and the Rialto bridge. It can be clearly seen in Carpaccio's *Cure of a Demoniac*, one of the series of paintings depicting the miracles of the Holy Cross, now in the Accademia.

was an expedition in 1062 to Dalmatia.[1] Here, particularly since the intervention of Stephen of Hungary forty years before, the situation was becoming ever more chaotic under the conflicting pressures of Hungarians, Croats and Byzantines. The Venetian recapture of Zara can hardly be said to have put an end to the confusion; but it doubtless reassured the local Latin populations who were feeling increasingly hemmed in, as well as providing a salutary reminder that the Doge did not bear the subsidiary title of Duke of Dalmatia for nothing. On the domestic front, throughout his twenty-eight years of office, Contarini was able to maintain the quiet prosperity inaugurated by his predecessor and to devote much of his time to works of piety – which, in true Venetian style, almost invariably resulted in the glorification of the city at least as much as that of the Almighty Himself. Deciding that old Pietro Orseolo's reconstruction of the fire-ravaged Basilica was no longer worthy of its surroundings, he called for new, more ambitious designs; meanwhile, out on the Lido, there arose a magnificent Benedictine monastery, founded and largely endowed by the Doge and dedicated to St Nicholas of Myra, patron of all who sailed the sea.

The present church of S. Nicolò di Lido is a rather pallid seventeenth-century affair; two splendid Veneto-Byzantine capitals flanking the monastery entrance are almost the only traces of the original structure. It certainly possesses none of the magical beauty of Venice's other (and far older) church with the same dedication, S. Nicolò dei Mendicoli.[2] Over the doorway into the church, however, is a memorial tablet to Contarini recording three military triumphs – the Dalmatian expedition, the recovery of Grado and, finally, the defeat of the Normans in Apulia.[3] The first two come as no surprise; the third is baffling. The Normans were never defeated in Apulia, where their record in the eleventh century is one of a steady succession of victories. Their only encounters with the Venetians were at sea, in the southern Adriatic, first off Durazzo in what is now Albania and later in the Corfu channel; and these took place between ten and fifteen years after Contarini's death. For the sake of his memory it is just as well that they did; for the last and ultimately decisive battle was a disaster for Venice and led to the downfall of his successor, previously one of the most popular Doges in her history.

1. Andrea Dandolo puts it in 1044, but his chronology at this point becomes a little muddled.

2. Recently restored by the British Venice in Peril Fund.

3. The inscription reads: *Domenico Contareno/qui rebellam Dalmatiam compressa foedera domuit/Gradum pulsu Aquileiense recepit/Normannos in Apulia vicit.*

To what, precisely, Domenico Selvo owed his popularity we cannot tell; but we can be sure that it was real enough because there has come down to us, by some lucky chance, a first-hand account of his election written by a parish priest of the church of S. Michele Archangelo, a certain Domenico Tino. It is the earliest eye-witness description of such a ceremony that survives, and it gives us an invaluable glimpse, after the quasi-tyrannies of former years, of the popular will once again in full operation.[1]

The date was 1071, the place – since St Mark's was full of Contarini's workmen – the new monastery church of S. Nicolò on the Lido. Previous Doges, when the basilica had not been available, had been chosen in S. Pietro di Castello; but S. Nicolò was a good deal larger, and its greater capacity was presumably considered to outweigh the difficulties of access. The authorities may indeed have hoped that the choice of so comparatively distant a venue might diminish the numbers of those attending; if so, they were disappointed, since Tino tells us that 'an innumerable multitude of people, virtually all Venice' was present, having sailed across the lagoon *in armatis navibus* – a phrase which suggests that part of the Republic's war fleet was requisitioned for the occasion.

Proceedings began with a High Mass at which, 'to the accompaniment of psalms and litanies', divine inspiration was sought for the choice of a Doge 'who would be both worthy of his nation and acceptable to its people. And now a great shout rose up to the very heavens, and, as with a single voice, all those present cried out, again and again and ever more loudly, the words *Domenicum Silvium volumus et laudamus*.' There could have been no clearer expression of the people's wish; the election was over. A party of the more distinguished citizens then lifted the Doge-elect and bore him, shoulder-high above the cheering crowd, to the quayside; meanwhile the choirs sang the *Kyrie* and *Te Deum*, the bells pealed out from the *campanili* and the oarsmen of the innumerable escorting craft, beating the flat of their blades upon the water, added their own thunderous applause. So it continued all the way back to the city. Selvo, barefoot now and clad only in a simple shift, was led in state to the Basilica where, amid the masons' ladders and scaffolding, he prostrated himself on the newly laid marble pavement, gave thanks, and received his staff of office at the High Altar. At this point – though Tino does not specifically tell us so – he presumably donned the ducal robes for the first time and made a formal procession to the palace, there

1. The complete Latin text can be found in Gallicciolli, *Delle memorie Venete antiche*, Vol. VI, pp. 124–6.

to receive oaths of fidelity from his subjects and to distribute traditional gifts in return.

The reign of Venice's twenty-ninth Doge had begun; but Tino ends his account with a curious detail. 'Without delay,' he writes, 'the Doge gave orders for the restoration and improvement of the doors, seats and tables which had been damaged after the death of Doge Contarini.' Why, one asks, should this have been necessary? There is no evidence of any public disorder after Contarini's death. He was popular with his people; indeed, had he not been, it is hardly likely that Selvo, who had been one of his chief lieutenants, would have been elected with such speed and jubilation. We can only assume that the Venetians had at some moment in the past been ill-advised enough to adopt that barbarous tradition of papal Rome whereby, on the death of the Supreme Pontiff, the Lateran Palace was regularly ransacked by the mob. If so, they certainly abandoned the practice before very long; during future centuries the Doges' Palace was to be attacked on more than one occasion at moments of crisis, but there is no other record of its being broken into as a matter of course. Perhaps, in the eleventh century, the legal position with regard to the ownership of the palace contents on the death of a Doge had not been clearly defined. It soon would be; the days were shortly to come when anyone found guilty of seizure or damage to the property of the Republic would almost certainly spend the rest of a rather short life regretting it.

The first decade of Domenico Selvo's reign was tranquil enough. Soon after his accession he married the Byzantine Princess Theodora Ducas, sister of the reigning Emperor Michael VII, and before long he had restored relations with the Western Empire to a level unknown since the days of the Orseoli, though he narrowly escaped excommunication for himself and an interdict on the entire Republic when the great struggle between the Emperor Henry IV and Pope Gregory VII – better known as Hildebrand – was at its height. For Venice herself, at home and abroad, there was peace; and not till 1081, when the newly crowned Byzantine Emperor Alexius I Comnenus appealed for help against the Norman menace, was that peace disturbed.

The career of the Normans in South Italy and Sicily is one of the great epics of European history. At the time when Alexius made his appeal there were still old men in Apulia who could remember the years when that stream of foot-loose young adventurers had begun to trickle down across the Alps to carve out their fortunes with their swords. Within little more than a generation they had mopped up virtually the entire peninsula south of the Garigliano river; in 1053 they had crushed a numerically far superior army, led by the Pope in person, whom they had subsequently held captive for nine months. Six years later Robert de Hauteville, called Guiscard ('the Crafty'), had been invested by Pope Nicholas II with the Duchies of Apulia, Calabria and Sicily. This last investiture was somewhat premature. The Normans had not yet set foot in Sicily, which was still in Saracen hands. It was to be another thirteen years before Palermo was to surrender to Robert's army, and twenty more before his countrymen were in undisputed possession of the whole island. But even before the fall of the capital, Robert Guiscard's eyes had become fixed on something far beyond his dukedom. He had already begun to meditate the most ambitious undertaking even of his own extraordinary career: a concerted attack on the Byzantine Empire, with Constantinople itself as his final objective. Internal problems with his South Italian dominions prevented him from putting his cherished plan into operation for several years; but by late spring 1081 his invasion fleet was ready to sail. His first target was Durazzo, whence the 800-year-old Via Egnatia ran east across the Balkan peninsula to the imperial capital.

The moment he heard of Robert's landing on imperial territory, the Byzantine Emperor Alexius Comnenus had sent the Doge an urgent appeal for assistance. It was probably unnecessary; the threat to Venice implied by Norman control of the straits of Otranto was every bit as serious as that to the Empire. Certainly Domenico Selvo never hesitated. Giving orders for the immediate preparation of the war fleet, he himself assumed command and soon afterwards was sailing to the attack. Even then, he arrived only just in time. Though themselves delayed by violent storms in which they lost several of their ships, the Normans were already at anchor in the roadstead off Durazzo when the Venetian war galleys bore down upon them.

Robert Guiscard's men fought tenaciously, but their inexperience of sea warfare betrayed them. The Venetians adopted the old Byzantine trick of hoisting manned dinghies to the yard-arms, from which the soldiers could shoot down on the enemy below; it seems too that they had learnt the secret of Greek fire, since a Norman chronicler, Geoffrey Malaterra, writes of how 'they blew that fire, which is called Greek and is not extinguished by water, through submerged pipes, and thus cunningly burned one of our ships under the very waves of the sea.' Against such tactics the Normans were powerless; and it was a reduced and battered fleet that finally beat its way back into harbour.

The Norman army, however, which had disembarked before the battle, was still virtually unimpaired; and after an eight-month siege – during which, at one moment, it inflicted a crushing defeat on a Byzantine force commanded by the Emperor himself – it compelled the city of Durazzo to surrender. Alexius had already sent rich presents to Venice in gratitude for her help; he might have been rather less generous had he known that the fall of the city was due to the treachery of a resident Venetian merchant who arranged for the gates to be opened in return for the hand in marriage of one of Robert Guiscard's daughters.

Thus the first defeat inflicted by Venice on the Norman expeditionary force, crippling as it must have appeared at the time, was soon revealed as only a temporary setback. After the fall of Durazzo the local populations, many of whom felt no particular loyalty to the Byzantines in any case, offered little further resistance to Robert Guiscard's advancing army. Within a few weeks all Illyria had submitted, and soon afterwards the important Macedonian city of Kastoria, half-way across the Balkan peninsula, had followed suit. If Robert had been allowed to keep up his momentum there is little doubt that the next summer would have found him at the gates of Constantinople; and from there it would have been but a short step to his ultimate goal, the throne of the Emperors. It was his misfortune that at this most critical of moments an urgent appeal from the Pope demanded his immediate return.

The story of the capture of Rome by the Emperor Henry IV in the spring of 1084, of Pope Gregory VII's refuge in the Castel Sant' Angelo and of his eventual deliverance by Robert Guiscard, has no place in this book. It is enough here to record that throughout this *annus mirabilis* of Robert's career – when the former penniless brigand had both the Eastern and Western Emperors on the run before him and the greatest of all the medieval Popes in his power – he appears to have been dreaming only of getting back to the Balkans at the earliest possible moment. He had, we are told, sworn on the soul of his father to remain unbathed and unshaven until he could rejoin the army he had left with his son Bohemund at Kastoria; and the occasional reports that reached him in Italy, telling of new counter-offensives by the Byzantines on land and by the Venetians at sea, resulting in massive desertions by his own forces, can only have added to his impatience.

He was back in the autumn, to find the situation even worse than he had expected. A Venetian fleet had recaptured both Durazzo and Corfu; Norman-held territory was once more confined to an offshore island or two and a short strip of coast. But Robert, though now sixty-eight, showed no sign of dismay. Instead, he at once started to plan a new offensive against Corfu. Unfortunately bad weather delayed his ships until November, and when at last they were able to sail the defenders were ready for them. Outside the harbour of Cassiope, in the extreme north-east corner of the island, they were met by a combined Greek and Venetian fleet which inflicted on them a defeat every bit as damaging as that they had suffered off Durazzo the previous year. Still the Guiscard would not admit himself beaten. Three days later he led his navy out yet again – with still more disastrous results. Convinced of their victory, the Venetians sent their fastest pinnaces scudding back up the Adriatic to bring the news to the Rialto.

Throughout his long career, people had tended to underestimate Robert Guiscard; invariably – if they lived at all – they lived to regret it. For the Venetians, it was an understandable mistake; after the two preceding encounters, few of the Norman ships were in a condition to hoist sail, let alone to venture on yet a third battle. But Robert, seeing the pinnaces disappearing over the horizon, recognized his chance. Summoning every vessel he possessed that was still afloat, he flung the broken remnants of his fleet against the unsuspecting enemy galleys in a last desperate onslaught. He had calculated it perfectly. The Venetians were caught utterly unawares, and scarcely had time even to take up a defensive formation before the Normans engaged. To make matters worse their larger ships, having already been emptied of ballast and provisions, rode so high in the water that when in the heat of the battle their entire complement of soldiers and crew all rushed to the same side of the deck, many of them capsized. (So, at least, reports Anna Comnena, the Emperor's daughter, in the remarkable history that she wrote of her father's reign;[1] but it is hard indeed to reconcile with what we know of Venetian seamanship.) Anna assesses the Venetian dead at 13,000, in addition to which she mentions a large number of prisoners – on whose subsequent mutilations at the hands of their captors she dwells with the morbid pleasure that is one of her least attractive characteristics. Finally she invents a fourth action in which she claims that the Venetians had their revenge; but this story must regretfully be dismissed as wishful thinking. There is no trace of it in the Venetian records, nor indeed anywhere else; and if in fact the series of engagements had ended in a triumph for the Republic it is hardly likely that Doge Domenico Selvo would have been deposed and disgraced.

1. *The Alexiad*, Book VI.

There is some doubt as to whether the Doge was in command of the fleet for the last catastrophe. If he was, his fate cannot have been entirely unmerited. But in other respects his policies had not been unsuccessful. The alacrity and enthusiasm with which he had responded to the Byzantine appeal for help had earned Venice the undying gratitude of the Emperor Alexius, who had not been slow in translating it into material form: annual subventions to all the churches in the city, including a special tribute to the treasury of St Mark's – 'the more acceptable', as Gibbon points out, 'as it was the produce of a tax on their rivals of Amalphi' – the grant of anchorages and warehouses along the Golden Horn and finally, in 1082, the extension of former trading privileges till they amounted to full exemption from all taxes and customs duties for Venetian merchants throughout the Empire. The importance of this last concession is almost impossible to exaggerate. Suddenly and at a single stroke, the Venetians found immense territories beckoning them – territories which, for all practical purposes, they could consider as their own. As the great French Byzantinist Charles Diehl put it, 'the Emperor flung open to them the gates of the Orient. On that day Venetian world trade began.'

But the fact remained that, in the short term, Venice had suffered not just a defeat but a humiliation. The cream of her fighting men was lost. Of her nine great galleys – the largest and most heavily armed of all the ships in her war fleet – two were in Norman hands and the other seven at the bottom of the sea, destroyed by an upstart nation with no experience of naval warfare whose own vessels at the time of the conflict had been scarcely able to stay afloat. Meanwhile the Normans were once again in control of the Adriatic approaches. The Venetians could not know that within a few months Robert Guiscard would die of typhoid on the island of Cephalonia, that his similarly stricken army would disintegrate and that the Norman threat would vanish, at least for the time being, as suddenly as it had arisen. For the moment a scapegoat was needed; and that scapegoat could be none other than the Doge himself.

It was all over quite quickly. Selvo seems to have made little or no attempt to defend himself. He was removed from power and packed off to a monastery, and by the end of the year his successor was already enthroned. Probably his spirit was broken, and he was glad enough to go; but it was a sad end to a reign that had begun with such bright promise just thirteen years before.

The historian Andrea Dandolo accuses the new Doge, Vitale Falier, of having 'persuaded the people, by means of promises and bribes, to depose his predecessor'. Perhaps he did; but Dandolo was writing 250 years later and his chronicle is at this point so sketchy and inaccurate that it hardly seems possible to condemn Falier on this testimony alone. An English historian[1] simply notes that 'the ten years of his authority contain little that was eventful and nothing that was unprosperous' – which is probably as good a summing-up as any.

These years, however, did include one great moment in Venetian history – the consecration of the new Basilica of St Mark, which still stands today. Work on this, the third building to occupy the site since the arrival of the Evangelist's remains two and a half centuries before, had been initiated by Doge Contarini and pursued still more enthusiastically by Domenico Selvo – who had even gone so far as to decree, at the outset of his reign, that every Venetian merchantman returning from the East must bring back, as part of its cargo, marbles or fine carvings for the decoration of St Mark's. It was Selvo, too, who had imported artists from Ravenna to begin the mosaic work that is still one of the supreme glories of the Basilica,[2] and we can only hope that, for a day or two during the summer of 1094, he was allowed to leave his cloister for the ceremony of consecration. If so, it may also have been given to him to witness one of the few miracles that the Venetians – a down-to-earth people even then, not normally given to imaginative flights of fancy – like to claim for their own.

After the burning of the original basilica in the great fire of 976 the body of St Mark, so the legend goes, disappeared without trace. It was not thought to have been consumed in the flames; the difficulty was that its precise location had been known to three people only, all of whom had perished before they could pass on their secret. And so, when the new building was at last complete, a three-day fast was declared for the whole city while the Doge, the Patriarch and all the bishops and clergy of the lagoons prayed that the precious relics might be rediscovered. On the third day – it was 25 June – their prayers were answered. Half-way through High Mass there was suddenly heard, from the south transept, the sound of crumbling masonry. All eyes turned to find that part of one of the main supporting piers had fallen away, revealing a hole from which there protruded a human arm. It was immediately recognized as being that of the Evangelist, whose body was now, amid scenes of great jubilation, removed *in toto* from its hiding-place and reburied in the crypt. There it

1. F. C. Hodgson, *The Early History of Venice*.
2. Some at least of the eleventh-century mosaics still exist – notably the portraits of saints in niches flanking the central door leading in from the narthex.

was to remain until 1836, when it was shifted to its present position beneath the high altar.[1]

The consecration of this third and final basilica of St Mark, whether or not accompanied by so signal a mark of divine favour, had an importance which went far beyond the boundaries of the city or the lagoon. Nowhere in the Western world, not in Ravenna or Aachen or even in Rome itself, had so sumptuous a monument been raised to the Christian God – ocular proof not so much of the piety of the Venetians (who were appreciably neither more nor less religious than their neighbours), as of their wealth, of the extent of their commercial Empire, and of the national pride – of a kind still unknown elsewhere in Europe – that was leading them to devote more and more of their private fortunes to the glory and splendour of their city. The lesson cannot have been lost on the Emperor Henry IV when he visited Venice in the summer of 1095, any more than on his numberless fellow-princes who, from the following year and for a century to come, were to pass through the city on their way to and from the East. But before this stream could begin, and indeed within a few weeks of the Emperor's visit, Vitale Falier was dead of the plague. He was buried at Christmas in the Basilica, where his tomb still stands, just inside the outer central doorway on the right, the oldest extant funerary monument in Venice. It was left to his successor to steer the Republic through those critical years of challenge that set the seal on the century – the years of the First Crusade.

1. Two delightful late thirteenth-century mosaics, on the end wall of the south transept, illustrate the discovery. Near by, on the pier just to the left of the Altar of the Sacrament, (Plates 18 and 19) a panel marks the precise place where the miracle occurred.

7

In the Wake of the Crusade

[1095–1130]

Quale ne l'arzanà de' Viniziani
  Bolle l'inverno la tenace pece
  A rimpalmar li legni lor non sani,
Che navicar non ponno; e 'n quelle vece
  Chi fa suo legno novo e chi ristoppa
  Le coste a quel che più viaggi fece;
Chi ribatte da proda e chi da poppa;
  Altri fa remi e altri volge sarte;
  Chi terzeruolo e artimon rintoppa;
Tal, non per foco, ma per divin' arte,
  Bollia là giuso una pegola spessa,
  Che 'nviscava la ripa d'ogni parte.

For as at Venice, in the Arsenal
  In winter-time, they boil the gummy pitch
  To caulk such ships as need an overhaul,
Now that they cannot sail – instead of which
  One builds him a new boat, one toils to plug
  Seams strained by many a voyage, others stitch
Canvas to patch a tattered jib or lug,
  Hammer at the prow, hammer at the stern, or twine
  Ropes, or shave oars, refit and make all snug –
So, not by fire, but by the art divine,
  A thick pitch boiled down there, spattering the brink
  With viscous glue . . .

Dante, *Inferno*, XXI, 7–18
(Tr. Dorothy L. Sayers)

It was on Tuesday 27 November 1095, while Doge Falier lay on his deathbed, that Pope Urban II called upon Western Christendom to march to the rescue of the East. The response was enthusiastic and widespread. By 1 December Count Raymond of Toulouse and many of his lords had declared themselves ready to take the Cross. From Normandy and Flanders, from Denmark, Spain and even Scotland, prince and peasant alike rallied to the call. In Italy too the general reaction was much the same; the people of Bologna actually received a letter from the Pope cautioning them against excess of zeal and reminding them not to leave without the consent of their priests – and, in the case of recently married men, of their wives as well. Further south Robert Guiscard's son Bohemund, now Prince of Taranto, recognized the opportunity he had long been awaiting and raised a small army of his own. Pisa and Genoa, both rapidly gaining in importance as maritime powers, also scented new possibilities for themselves in the East and began to prepare their fleets.

But Venice hung back. Her own Eastern markets were already assured – particularly Egypt, which had become a major clearing-house for spices from India and the southern seas, providing in return a ready market for European timber and metal. Her people were too hardheaded to set much store by emotional outbursts about the salvation of Christendom; war was bad for trade, and the goodwill of the Arabs and the Seljuk Turks – who in the past quarter-century had overrun the greater part of Anatolia – was essential if the caravan routes to Central Asia were to be kept open. The new Doge, Vitale Michiel, preferred to wait, to judge for himself the scale of the enterprise and its prospects of success, before irrevocably committing the Republic. Not till 1097, when the first wave of Crusaders was already marching through Anatolia, did he even begin any serious preparations; and it was only in the late summer of 1099, after the Frankish armies had battered their way into Jerusalem, slaughtering every Muslim in the city and burning all the Jews alive in the main synagogue, that a Venetian fleet of 200 sail filed out through the Lido port.

In command was the Doge's son, Giovanni Michiel, while the spiritual well-being of the expedition was entrusted to Enrico, Bishop of Castello and son of the former Doge Domenico Contarini.[1] Down the Adriatic they went, calling in at the Dalmatian towns to pick up additional men and equipment, around the Peloponnese and so to Rhodes for the winter. There, according to one report, they received urgent representations from the Emperor Alexius, urging them to take no further part in the Crusade and to return home. Alexius had been horrified by the size of the Crusading armies. When he had first appealed to the Pope he had expected individual knights or small companies of trained mercenaries who would submit themselves to his authority and obey his orders; these voracious and utterly undisciplined hordes, some of them religious fanatics, others simple adventurers out for what they could get, had gone through his

1. The name of the see had recently been changed from Olivolo to Castello. It is with Enrico that we encounter this new title for the first time.

dominions like locusts and had totally destroyed that tenuous equilibrium of Christian and infidel on which the survival of his Empire now depended. Nor were they even confining their attacks to the Saracens: that same winter a Pisan fleet had actually been blockading the imperial port of Latakia while Bohemund – who had lost no time in carving out a principality for himself at Antioch – had attacked it simultaneously from the landward side. Considering the long history of Venetian–Byzantine friendship and the favoured treatment enjoyed by the Venetians throughout the Empire, Alexius can hardly have expected them to be guilty of similar conduct; by now, however, he was thoroughly disillusioned with the whole Crusade. If this was what was meant by a Christian alliance, he preferred to carry on alone. Meanwhile he had fought back hard at Latakia and the piratical Pisans had withdrawn, with ill grace, to Rhodes.

Thus, for the first time in their history, the Venetians and the Pisans found themselves face to face. The latter, despite their recent reverse, were in truculent mood; the former, who had watched Pisa's rise to power with misgivings that increased with every passing year, had no intention of allowing these impudent upstarts a share in the rich spoils of the Levant. The battle that followed was long, and costly to both sides. In the end the Venetians made their point; with twenty Pisan ships taken, together with 4,000 prisoners – nearly all of whom were released shortly afterwards – they were able to extract an undertaking from their defeated rival to withdraw altogether from the eastern Mediterranean. Like all such undertakings made under temporary duress, however, it was soon forgotten; and that encounter off the Rhodian shore proved to be only the first round in Venice's struggle with her commercial rivals which was ultimately to be measured not in years but in centuries.[1]

There can be few clearer indications of the spirit in which Venice had embarked on the Crusade than the fact that, six months after her fleet had set out, it had still not struck a single blow for Christendom, nor indeed even reached the Holy Land. As always in her history, Venice put her own interests first; and even now, as winter turned to spring, those interests demanded a few more weeks' delay for the greater glory of the Republic. Shortly before his departure, Bishop Enrico had visited his father's church of S. Nicolò on the Lido and prayed that it might be given to him to bring back the body of its patron from Myra to Venice. Now the city of Myra, St Nicholas's own bishopric and the place of his burial, stands on the mainland of Lycia almost opposite Rhodes. It had

1. There is a painting of this battle, by Vicentino, in the northernmost oval on the ceiling of the Sala dello Scrutinio of the Doges' Palace.

been largely destroyed by the Seljuk Turks, but the great church still stood – as indeed it still does – over the saint's tomb. The Venetians landed, burst in and soon came upon three coffins of cypress wood. In the first two they found the remains of St Theodore and of St Nicholas's uncle; the third, that of the saint himself, was empty. They interrogated the churchwardens, even subjecting them to physical violence in their determination to discover the whereabouts of the body; the unfortunate officials could only stammer that it was no longer in their possession, having been removed some years before by certain merchants from Bari. But the Bishop remained incredulous. Falling to his knees, he prayed loudly for the sacred hiding-place to be revealed. And, sure enough, just as the party was about to leave in disgust, a sudden fragrance in a remote corner of the church led them to another tomb. In it – so the story goes – lay the uncorrupted body of St Nicholas, clutching the palm, still fresh and green, that he had brought back from Jerusalem. All three corpses were triumphantly embarked and the ships, their mission accomplished, set sail at last for Palestine.

After the capture of Jerusalem in July 1099 the Crusading leaders had chosen as their sovereign Godfrey, Duke of Lower Lorraine. Refusing to wear a crown in the city where Christ had worn a crown of thorns, Godfrey had adopted the title of Defender of the Holy Sepulchre, and it was in this capacity that he received, in the middle of June 1100, a report that a large Venetian fleet had put in at Jaffa. The fighting was by no means over; much of the country still lay under Saracen occupation and Godfrey's own naval resources were poor. He hastened down to the coast to welcome the new arrivals, but by the time he reached Jaffa he was far from well. As he had stopped off on his way to attend a banquet given in his honour by his vassal, the Saracen Emir of Caesarea, there were the inevitable rumours of poison. In fact the trouble is more likely to have been typhoid; but at all events Godfrey was barely able to receive the Venetian leaders before being forced to retire in a state of collapse to Jerusalem – leaving his cousin, Count Warner of Gray, to negotiate on his behalf.

The Venetians' terms were hardly redolent of selfless Crusading zeal. In recognition of their assistance they asked free trading rights throughout the Frankish state, a church and a market in every Christian town and, in addition, a third of every other town that they might help to capture in the future. Finally, in return for an annual tribute, they demanded the entire city of Tripoli. Even if all this was granted, they undertook to

remain in the Holy Land on this first visit for only two months, until
15 August.

It was a hard, typically Venetian bargain; and the speed with which
the Franks accepted it shows how desperate they were for naval support.
It was agreed that the first objective should be Acre, and that Haifa
should follow; unfortunately for Crusading plans, however, a strong
north wind delayed the ships near Jaffa, and while they were still there
the news reached them that Godfrey was dead. Here was a problem.
The Frankish leaders were all anxious to be in Jerusalem during the
disputes over the succession and the inheritances that were bound to
ensue. On the other hand, there was now less than a month before the
date fixed by the Venetians for their return; it was unthinkable not to
make use of a fleet whose cooperation had been so dearly bought. Further
discussions accordingly produced a compromise: the assault on Acre
would be postponed; the immediate objective would be Haifa, nearer and
less strongly fortified.

Although Haifa was defended by a small Egyptian garrison, the real
force of its resistance came from the predominantly Jewish population
who, remembering what had happened to their brethren in Jerusalem
less than a year before, fought with a bitter determination to preserve
their city. But the Venetian mangonels and siege machines were too much
for them, and on 25 July – within a week of Godfrey's death – they were
obliged to surrender. Their fears proved to have been fully justified. A
few managed to escape; the majority, Jews and Muslims alike, were
struck down where they stood.

The Venetians themselves are unlikely to have played a leading part in
the massacre. They were not a bloodthirsty people – merchants, not
murderers. The Franks on the other hand had been guilty of this sort
of thing before, not only in Jerusalem but in Galilee as well. The fact
remains that this was a military alliance, and since Michiel, Contarini and
their followers were present it is impossible to absolve the Venetians
altogether from responsibility. Whether they themselves were conscious
of it we cannot say; no mention of any atrocity occurs in the sketchy
Venetian records. Nor is there any indication that they received the
rewards guaranteed to them a month before, though they may have
agreed to defer these until the political crisis was over. Soon after the
fall of Haifa they set sail for home bearing with them, apart from the
trophies and merchandise from the Holy Land, the saintly relics they had
brought from Myra. On their arrival, which was neatly timed for St
Nicholas's Day, they received heroes' welcomes from Doge, clergy and

people, and the reputed body of the saint was reverently interred in Domenico Contarini's church on the Lido.

Did the ceremony have a slightly hollow ring? It should have done, because the luckless churchwardens of Myra had told the truth. Thirteen years before the Venetians arrived there, a group of Apulian merchants had indeed removed St Nicholas's body and had carried it back in triumph to Bari, where work had immediately begun on the basilica bearing his name – now one of the most superb romanesque churches in all Italy. Since the crypt of this glorious building had been consecrated as early as 1089 by Pope Urban himself, and since in the intervening years the great church must have been seen by countless Venetian sailors as it rose higher and ever higher above the city, it seems scarcely conceivable that the Doge and his advisers were unaware of the Bariot claims. As far as we know, however, they made no attempt to discredit them. We can only conclude that the whole thing was one gigantic exercise in self-deception; and that the Venetians, normally so level-headed, were yet perfectly capable of persuading themselves that black was white when the honour and glory and profit – for the financial advantages from the pilgrim traffic were not to be despised – of the Republic demanded that they should. So far as they were concerned, the true corpse of St Nicholas lay in his tomb on the Lido. Several centuries were to pass before the claim was discreetly withdrawn.

The new Doge who ascended the throne when Vitale Michiel died in 1102 is a faintly mysterious figure.[1] Of his origins or previous career we know nothing except that he was another member of the Falier family; nor has anyone ever provided a satisfactory explanation of his Christian name, unique in Venetian and indeed Italian history – Ordelafo. It has been pointed out that Falier is only a Venetian variant of the more usual Faledro, in which form his full name would be virtually a palindrome; perhaps therefore, it can be ascribed merely to some fantastic whim on the part of his parents. In any case there can be no doubt that this was the name by which he was generally known; we find it in several contemporary and near-contemporary documents, and also, in its abbreviated form, identifying his portrait (in Byzantine imperial robes) on the *Pala d'Oro*, Pietro Orseolo's great gold altar-screen in St Mark's which in 1105 Ordelafo had had remodelled and enriched.

---

1. Vitale Michiel's tomb has not survived. Surprisingly enough, however, that of his wife has. She appears to have died shortly before her husband and her tomb is in the atrium of St Mark's, not far from that of Vitale Falier on the other side of the main door.

This work on the *Pala d'Oro* must have been still in progress when
Venice suffered the first of those terrible inundations to which, all through
her history, she has been subject. They are due to a combination of
factors – high tides, heavy rainfall, swollen rivers, strong and persistent
south-easterly winds and other geophysical conditions which only have
recently been understood. Occurring separately, these factors are quite
frequent and cause no particular concern. When they coincide, on the
other hand, they can be almost apocalyptic in their horror, and in January
1106 they coincided catastrophically. We need not necessarily believe the
contemporary accounts of accompanying phenomena – the unseasonable
heat that prostrated man and beast alike, the ominous rumblings from
beneath the lagoon, the fish jumping in terror from the water, the meteors
flashing across the sky; Venetian floods can be dramatic enough without
such trimmings. On this occasion they swept away an entire community.
Of the old town of Malamocco, once the capital of all the lagoon settlements, the outer bastion of defence that had so heroically saved the islands
of Rialto from Pepin 300 years before, not a building remained. The very
land on which it stood crumbled away, and as late as the eighteenth
century the ruins of houses and churches, strewn over the bed of the
lagoon, could still be discerned at low water. The surviving inhabitants
fled, with such of the town's treasures as they had managed to save –
including their prize relic, the head of St Fortunatus – to Chioggia,
whither the old bishopric was shortly afterwards transferred; only much
later did they return to the Lido, to build a new Malamocco on its present,
more protected site further along the island to the west.

Though they too had suffered severely, the people of the Rialto
doubtless congratulated themselves on having escaped the worst of the
deluge; but the terrible year of 1106 had still scarcely begun. Within a
few days a fire broke out in the house of the Zen family in SS. Apostoli,
destroying the greater part of six parishes before it could be brought
under control; and this was followed on 6 April by another, still greater
conflagration which, beginning near S. Lorenzo, wiped out no less than
twenty-four of the city's churches. Some idea of the fury of the flames,
and of the wind which fanned them, can be gained from the fact that at
least one of these fires actually crossed the Grand Canal.[1] At that time,
it must be remembered, many of the smaller churches and almost all the

---

1. It did, however, fortunately spare the beautiful little church of S. Giacomo di Rialto
which had been built a few years before – probably on the site of an earlier church
(see p. 5) – for those using the new market, opened in the adjoining *campo* in 1097. Church
and market-place still look much as they did at that time.

private dwellings in Venice were still built of wood; indeed it was only thanks to their stone and marble construction that the Basilica of St Mark and the Doges' Palace escaped with relatively minor damage. Thenceforth, however, the use of wood for building in all but the poorest quarters was actively discouraged. The fallen churches were rebuilt with the little red bricks known as *altinelle* and the hard white stone from Istria – more expensive perhaps, but infinitely more durable, and to this day the basic materials of Venetian architecture.

The after-effects of these three disasters, following so quickly one upon another, must have kept the Venetians fully occupied for the next year or two; and it was not till 1109 that Doge Ordelafo decided that the time had come for another expedition to the Holy Land, which he would lead himself. Once again, Venetian motives were something short of selflessly idealistic. As the Crusaders gradually consolidated their new dominions in Outremer, so the Christian populations had begun to increase and the markets to expand. But the days were past when Venice could rely on her traditional near-monopoly of the Levant trade. Pisa in particular seemed to have forgotten the promise extracted from her at Rhodes barely ten years before, and was obviously determined to assert herself in the eastern Mediterranean; another rising maritime Republic, Genoa, was not far behind. If Venice were not to be elbowed out altogether, her presence in the area was essential – and it would have to be a presence in strength.

Accordingly a Venetian fleet of some 100 sail left the lagoon in the summer of 1110, arriving in Palestine the following October. Its timing was excellent. King Baldwin I, the former Count of Boulogne who had succeeded Godfrey on the throne of Jerusalem – and who, unlike his predecessor, had felt no qualms about adopting the royal title – was besieging Sidon. Despite the assistance of a strong Scandinavian contingent he was not doing well, and the sudden appearance of the Venetians must have seemed like a godsend. Sidon surrendered on 4 December. Surprisingly, Venice does not seem to have received any land or privileges there; instead, she was granted a section of the city of Acre – in whose capture six years earlier she had played no part at all – together with the use of her own weights and measures and the right to maintain a resident magistrate.

These concessions were accepted with a gratitude somewhat tempered by the knowledge that Genoa and Pisa, both of whom had contributed far more to the early success of the Crusade, had been similarly favoured.

There could be no doubt, however, that Venice had done well out of the expedition, the more so since it was probably one of the vessels taking part that called on the return journey at Constantinople, whence it brought back yet another of those important relics by which the Middle Ages set so much store – the badly bruised body of St Stephen the Proto-martyr. On its arrival in Venice Doge Ordelafo carried it on his own shoulders to the ducal barge and, after heated argument between several rival churches all well aware of its potential value in terms of pilgrim traffic, deposited it in the monastery church of S. Giorgio Maggiore. Thenceforth, for nearly seven centuries until the fall of the Republic, the Doges would lead a torchlight procession to attend vespers in the church on Christmas Night, St Stephen's Eve.[1]

And yet, despite the gains borne home from the East and the promise of more to come, Venice felt herself inadequately equipped for the future. In little over a decade she had put some 300 men-of-war to sea, which was no mean achievement in itself; but if she were fully to exploit the new trading possibilities in the Levant – and hold her own against Pisan and Genoese competition – she would need more, both fighting vessels and merchantmen. An ambitious new shipbuilding programme was called for, and it was now that Doge Ordelafo made his most enduring contribution to the Republic. Hitherto the shipwrights of Venice had been scattered about all over the lagoon, many if not all of them running small private businesses of their own. Under his aegis shipbuilding became a nationalized industry. For its centre he chose two marshy little islands known as the *Zemelle* – 'the twins' in Venetian dialect – at the far end of the Riva to the east of the city; and here, over the next half-century, there grew up that mighty complex of dockyards, foundries, magazines and workshops for carpenters, sailmakers, ropemakers and blacksmiths that Dante described in the *Inferno* and that gave a new word to the English language and many others besides – the Arsenal.[2]

Naturally it would be rather longer before the Arsenal attained that formidable pitch of efficiency in mass production which ultimately enabled it to employ over 16,000 workers – nearly all of them specialists – and, when operating at full capacity, to turn out fully-equipped warships at the rate of one every few hours. Yet within little more than a decade it had transformed the Republic's shipbuilding. Never again would Venice, faced with a sudden emergency, have to rely on whatever vessels in a

1. St Stephen's tomb can still be seen in the north transept, whither it was moved in 1581 from the choir.
2. The word itself comes from the Arabic *Dar Sina'a* – House of Construction.

reasonable state of seaworthiness happened to be on hand. From now on she could plan ahead, undertaking long-term shipbuilding programmes as the situation demanded and state finances allowed. More important still, she could standardize designs and build up stores of spare parts, making it possible to complete even major refits in a fraction of the time that had previously been required. In such conditions too the designs themselves, as well as the techniques, could be revolutionized. It may be no coincidence that the foundation of the Arsenal roughly coincides with the development of rib and plank construction, by which a ship was assembled on a previously erected skeletal framework rather than being built steadily upwards from keel to gunwales; it is certainly true that the beginning of the twelfth century marks the moment when Venice began to design certain vessels primarily for war, and others for trade.

This distinction, however, must not be exaggerated. One of the secrets of Venice's rise to power lay in the fact that she never saw the twin necessities of defence and commerce as altogether separate. Her war captains, then and later, were never averse to trading on the side – a predisposition which meant that many of her military expeditions actually paid for themselves – while her merchant vessels had always to be ready to defend themselves against pirates or, occasionally, competitors. In feudal Europe, where the fighting nobility remained haughtily aloof from trade, such a system would have been unthinkable, but in Venice there was no separate military caste; the nobles were merchants, the merchants noble, and the interests of both were identical. Similarly, the warships produced by the Arsenal were endowed with as much storage space for additional cargoes as could be devised, and the merchantmen given plenty of provision for defence.

Even the Arsenal, however, could not function without raw materials; and the source of the most vital of those materials, timber, was soon seriously threatened. By far the greater part of it came from across the Adriatic, where the thickly wooded islands off the Dalmatian coast furnished an almost inexhaustible supply. The problem was that this territory, as we have seen, had long been coveted by the otherwise landlocked Kingdom of Hungary. Some years previously the Hungarian King Coloman, having annexed the Kingdom of Croatia, had descended upon the coast and captured several of its principal cities – an act of naked aggression which Venice, at that time fully occupied in the East, had been obliged to suffer in silence. Now at last she was able to retaliate. With the help of both Emperors, Henry V – who had visited the city two months before – and Alexius Comnenus, the cities were recovered;

alas, as soon as the conquerors had left for home the Hungarians swept down again. Ordelafo turned about at once and resumed the fight; but not for long. A week or two later, in the summer of 1118, he was killed in battle beneath the walls of Zara.[1]

Doge Ordelafo Falier, in the sixteen years of his reign, had won the deep affection and respect of his people. He had been a born leader of men and, seeing him fall, his followers – who, like all Venetians, hated to fight on land – panicked and fled. The Hungarians pursued them, cutting them down as they ran, and it was only a small proportion of those who had set out so confidently, so short a time before, that returned with the grim news to Venice.

Ordelafo's successor, Domenico Michiel, though present at Zara, had been powerless to prevent the rout. He was no coward; indeed the Altino Chronicle describes him as *vir bellicosus*, and in the years to come he was to give plenty more evidence of his valour. As the grandson of Doge Vitale Michiel and the son of Giovanni, leader of the 1099 expedition to the East, he had been brought up as a patriot, in the firm Venetian tradition of public service. Yet his first act as Doge was to send an embassy to Coloman's son, King Stephen II, to sue for peace. Considering the weakness of his position, the terms he gained were remarkable. Stephen willingly agreed to a five-year truce, during which a large part of the coast, together with the cities and the all-important forests, was allowed to remain in Venetian hands.

This generosity on the part of the Hungarians may to some extent have been due to the news that was trickling in during the summer of 1118 from Palestine. On 2 April, King Baldwin had died. Four months later, on 15 August, the Emperor Alexius Comnenus had followed him to the grave. Meanwhile the Saracens were growing stronger. The future of Christianity in the East looked bleak. Even in the West, the spectacle it presented was hardly edifying. The old struggle between Empire and Papacy showed no sign of being resolved; and when Pope Paschal II had died the previous January, the Emperor Henry V had been so outraged at the choice of his successor Gelasius II that he had nominated an anti-Pope and installed him at the Lateran, driving Gelasius into exile. The example was scarcely edifying; still, this was clearly no time for Christian nations to squabble amongst themselves. The two most powerful states in the central Mediterranean must compose their differences, if only temporarily, for Christ and the common good.

1. See the painting by Aliense in the Sala dello Scrutinio of the Doges' Palace.

Such, at least, seem to have been the arguments of the Doge's ambassadors, and as such King Stephen accepted them. How sincerely they were really believed in Venice is another question. The Venetians had many qualities but, as they had already demonstrated, crusading fervour was not one of them. They were interested in the Crusade only in so far as it opened up new commercial possibilities; it mattered little, if at all, to them whether their trading partners were Christian or Muslim so long as goods were delivered at the right prices and bills paid on time. It was four years more before they were to launch another expedition to the East; and when they did so their motives were, to say the least, mixed.

Not that their help was anything but desperately needed; for by then the Frankish states of Outremer were facing the gravest crisis in their short history. In June 1119 one of their leading princes, Roger of Antioch, had perished with virtually his entire army in a battle appropriately known as the Field of Blood; henceforth, just at the time they needed it most, they were to suffer from an acute shortage of manpower. Their problems were further aggravated by a fleet from Fatimid Egypt, whose ceaseless patrolling of the coast had made regular sea communications almost impossible. King Baldwin II's immediate reaction to the news of the Field of Blood had therefore been to appeal to Venice for help. The new Pope, Calixtus II, had supported him; and before the end of the year a general assembly of all the citizens of Venice had decided – though by no means unanimously – to respond.

Their decision was also influenced by another consideration. For some years now their relations with the Byzantine Empire had been deteriorating. We have seen how, at the time of the First Crusade, they had disregarded the pleas of Alexius Comnenus that they should return home. Even before then, their commercial expansion in the ports of the Aegean and the Black Sea had far exceeded what the Emperor had intended when he had granted special privileges to Domenico Selvo in 1082; and the process had continued until the Empire's own trade was threatened with strangulation. Thus, when Alexius's son John II succeeded to the Byzantine throne in 1118 one of his first acts had been to withdraw these privileges. The Venetians, he gave them to understand, were welcome to continue their normal mercantile activity; from now on, however, they would enjoy only the same treatment as was accorded to their competitors.

The anger with which this news was received on the Rialto was not altogether unjustified. On the assumption that the 1082 treaty would endure, the Venetians had involved themselves in considerable capital outlay; Genoa and Pisa were already giving them cause for concern; and this new blow was more than they were prepared to accept without active protest. The Doge's flagship that sailed out of the lagoon on 8 August 1122 with seventy-one men-of-war and many other smaller vessels in its wake may well have flown the Cross of Christ at its masthead; but it was directed, at least in the first instance, against a Christian and not an infidel enemy.

The fleet's initial objective was no further distant than Corfu, the scene of Venice's humiliation at the hands of Robert Guiscard nearly forty years before. The island had long been an important Byzantine outpost, defended by a strong and determined garrison. The Venetians besieged it for six months to no avail. They would probably have remained still longer had they not been recalled to their crusading vow by a ship sent specially from Palestine with reports of a new disaster: King Baldwin had been taken prisoner. Their presence was required at once if the Latin East was to survive. Reluctantly Doge Michiel gave the order to weigh anchor; but even then he seems to have felt no real urgency. In the course of a leisurely journey eastward he stopped to attack Greek shipping wherever he found it, and – if the Byzantine historian John Cinnamus is to be believed – even turned north into the Aegean, raiding and plundering Lesbos and Chios as well as Rhodes and Cyprus before dropping anchor at the end of May 1123 in the port of Acre.

Now at last the Venetians made amends for their past desultoriness. The Egyptian fleet, they learned, had given up its attempt to blockade Jaffa and had moved south again; it was now lying off Ascalon, the only coastal stronghold, apart from Tyre, still in Muslim hands. That was all the Doge needed to know. He quickly dispatched a flotilla of small ships in pursuit, to lure the Egyptians into battle, while the bulk of his fleet followed just below the horizon. The plan worked beautifully. No sooner had the Egyptians engaged than they found themselves surrounded and overwhelmingly outnumbered. Scarcely a single vessel escaped destruction or capture, the Doge himself winning particular distinction by personally sailing against the flagship of the Fatimid Admiral and sinking it. His victory was more decisive than he knew. Particularly since the loss of Sicily to the Normans at the end of the previous century, Muslim shipwrights had suffered from a chronic shortage of good timber, for which they were obliged to rely on imports from Europe; and when, for strategic reasons, these supplies were cut off[1] – or largely so – they were no longer able to build new vessels or even to keep existing ones in

1. The first such embargo had been ordered by Pietro Candiano IV as early as 960.

good repair. The Venetian victory off Ascalon thus effectively marked the end of Saracen sea power in the eastern Mediterranean.

When Domenico Michiel returned in triumph to Acre – having captured, by way of a bonus, ten fully-laden merchantmen *en route* – there was some hard bargaining to be done. The Franks were determined to make full use of his fleet for the capture of Tyre or Ascalon or both; but the Doge, having proved its worth so conclusively, was in a strong position. Negotiations dragged on for months. They were still in progress at Christmas, when Michiel attended the Nativity celebrations at Bethlehem and was royally entertained in Jerusalem by the Patriarch and other representatives of the captive King. Finally, in the first weeks of 1124, agreement was reached and a treaty signed. Its terms were even more favourable to the Venetians than those agreed in 1100, which Count Godfrey's death had rendered void. In every town of the Kingdom they were granted a street with a church, baths and a bakery, together with exemption from all tolls and customs dues. Their right to the use of their own weights and measures was confirmed, not only for transactions between themselves but for all others as well. Finally, they were promised a third of the cities of Tyre and Ascalon if they helped in their capture.

Now that the Doge knew where he stood, he delayed no longer but sailed northward to Tyre, while the Frankish army marched up simultaneously along the coast. Then as now, Tyre occupied the end of a short and narrow peninsula; its only link with the mainland was an artificial isthmus – hardly more than a causeway – which Alexander the Great had constructed nearly fifteen centuries before. Along this there ran an aqueduct, a lifeline for a city whose own wells and cisterns were quite inadequate for its population. Few places, in short, were more vulnerable to siege. Michiel beached his ships – all except one, which maintained a constant patrol round the seaward approaches – cut the aqueduct and, on 15 February 1124, began the siege.

Despite a steady bombardment from mangonels and catapults, the Tyrians defended their city bravely. The cisterns were full after the winter rains and food stocks were high; there was also a good chance of relief by the Egyptians from the sea or by a land army promised by the Emir of Damascus. But neither came. The Egyptian navy had not yet recovered from its recent defeat, and the Emir dared not march without its support. With the advent of high summer the parched garrison was obliged to capitulate. According to the terms of its surrender, there was no looting; the Christian army marched in on 7 July, and the standard of the King of Jerusalem was hoisted over the main gate, flanked on the two side towers by those of Tripoli and Venice. Michiel accepted his promised third of the city, which was given a Venetian governor, Venetian laws and a magnificent church dedicated to St Mark.

The Venetian overseas empire had begun; it was to endure nearly seven centuries, until the final downfall of the Republic – longer than any other in European history. But the Doge himself remained at Tyre no longer than the few days necessary to see that the Franks were true to their bargain. It was now two years since he had left Venice. Although the expedition had been an unqualified success, it had lasted long enough. One more coastal city remained in infidel hands – Ascalon – and the rewards for assisting in its capture would be considerable. But Ascalon would have to wait – which, for another thirty-nine years, it did. Well pleased with what he had achieved, Michiel returned home with his fleet, stopping only to eject the Hungarians from Spalato and to make a few casual raids on such Byzantine islands as he chanced to pass on the way. With him, it need hardly be noted, went still more relics – the body of St Donatus, brought from Cephalonia and now interred in the exquisite Romanesque church dedicated to him on the island of Murano; that of St Isidore, looted from Chios in circumstances not, perhaps, quite so ideal as those depicted on the wall of his chapel in the north transept of St Mark's; and finally the granite slab on which Christ himself is said to have stood when he preached to the men of Tyre, and which now crowns the altar in the baptistery of the Basilica.

Thus Domenico Michiel was in his turn received with exultation by his subjects, and when in the following year he scored more notable victories against the Hungarians in Dalmatia and the Byzantines in Cephalonia – inducing John Comnenus to restore all the commercial privileges he had withdrawn on his accession – his reputation was assured for ever. In later centuries, indeed, it became almost legendary. Certainly he is the only Doge to be commemorated three times over, by three different painters, in the Sala dello Scrutinio of the Doges' Palace which, with the neighbouring Sala del Maggior Consiglio, can be considered Venice's Hall of Fame;[1] and of the three events there portrayed, only one – the victory over the Egyptian fleet off Ascalon, by Peranda, above the third window on the Piazzetta side – is as historically accurate as even a Renaissance painter might be expected to make it. Further along the same wall there is a picture by Aliense described in the standard guide-

1. The triumphal arch along the end wall contains six small pictures by Lazzarini to the greater glory of the Doge Francesco Morosini, but these all form part of a single design.

book[1] as 'the Doge giving orders for sails and steering gear of the Venetian fleet to be pulled ashore, in order to demonstrate to the allies that the Venetian galleys will not depart until Tyre has been taken'. No chronicler of the time mentions such a gesture; the beaching of ships was normal practice if they were to remain unused for any length of time, and there is no reason to suppose that Michiel had any other idea in mind when he ordered it. The third picture, a small ceiling oval by Bambini, shows the Doge refusing the Crown of Sicily – which he was never offered. His last five years were in fact devoid of any foreign adventures; wisely, he concentrated on affairs within the Republic, where he instituted among other things a rudimentary form of street lighting – making Venice the first city in Europe, with the possible exception of Constantinople, to be regularly and compulsorily lit at night. Already in his day the *ancone* – those little, typically Venetian shrines to the Virgin or parish patron saint at the corners of the canals and principal *calli* – were beginning to appear in profusion; it was Domenico Michiel who, in 1128, arranged that a lamp should be lit in each of them at nightfall, the responsibility for its maintenance devolving on the local parish priest, the cost on the Republic. Then, two years later, after an eleven-year reign, he resigned the dogeship and retired to the monastery of S. Giorgio Maggiore, where he died soon afterwards and where his tomb still stands.

1. Lorenzetti.

8

Between Two Empires

[1130–1172]

Perchè una gente impera e l'altra langue,
Seguendo lo giudicio di costei,
Che è occulta come in erba l'angue.

Therefore some rise to empire, some debase
According to the judgment of her pleasure
Who lieth hidden like a snake in grass.

Dante, *Inferno*, VII, 82
(Tr. J. I. Minchin)

The accession of the thirty-year-old Pietro Polani to the ducal throne left vacant by his father-in-law Domenico Michiel occurred within only a few weeks of two other elevations, far more momentous: of Norman Sicily from the status of a County to that of a Kingdom, and of Count Roger II de Hauteville, Robert Guiscard's nephew, to be its King. In Venetian eyes – indeed, in the eyes of most of Europe – the means by which Roger had achieved this success were not above reproach. A disputed papal election some months before had left two rival candidates, each with an arguably good claim, struggling for the Pontificate; one of them, Innocent II, thanks to the passionate advocacy of St Bernard of Clairvaux, soon had the greater part of Western Christendom behind him; the other, Anacletus, had turned to Roger, who had demanded a royal crown as the price of his support. In the circumstances, it was hardly to be expected that the partisans of Innocent would recognize the new Kingdom – which, moreover, both the Eastern and the Western Empires still claimed for their own; and their reluctance was still further increased by the disturbing speed with which Sicily under the Hautevilles had risen to wealth, prosperity and power. From its position in the dead centre of the Mediterranean the island commanded the trade routes between North and South, East and West, constituting a crossroads and a market-place for three continents; its Byzantine and Islamic past, together with its thriving Greek and Arab populations still living harmoniously together, gave the Sicilian ports a cosmopolitan character that no others could match. In the past two years Roger had absorbed into his own dominions virtually the whole Italian peninsula south of Rome, formerly the property of his feckless and fortunately infertile cousins; and this latest *coup*, by which he was enabled to treat with the princes of Europe as an equal, augured ill for the future.

Nowhere was this alarm more deeply felt than in Venice. Already Sicilian sea power was beginning to rival that of the Republic; and while the bazaars of Palermo and Catania, Messina and Syracuse grew more and more crowded, so dealings on the Rialto had begun, gently but perceptibly, to slacken. To make matters worse, Venetian merchantmen were suffering ever more frequent attacks from Sicilian privateers; by 1135 they could estimate their losses at 40,000 talents. When therefore in that same year a diplomatic delegation from Constantinople called in Venice on its way to the court of the Western Emperor Lothair II in search of financial and naval help for a projected joint expedition against the so-called King of Sicily, Polani not only agreed with enthusiasm but attached to the Byzantine party representatives of his own to lend additional weight to their appeal.

The expedition was duly mounted, and invaded South Italy the following year; but it was military rather than naval and Venice was not in the event asked to participate. This, as it happened, was just as well: despite a few tactical successes, the venture had no lasting effect on Sicilian power or prestige. The old Emperor himself died in December 1137 on his return journey across the Alps; less than eight weeks later the anti-Pope Anacletus followed him to the grave; and in July 1139 Pope Innocent, riding south at the head of an army of his own, was ambushed by Roger and taken prisoner, being released only after he had reluctantly confirmed his captor as the lawful King of Sicily.

The Norman menace was now graver than ever, but for the time being nothing could be done; the new Emperor-elect of the West,[1] Conrad of Hohenstaufen, was too occupied with internal problems in Germany. The papal *curia* had somehow to readjust its policies to the idea that the boisterous new Kingdom on its southern borders was there to stay. In Constantinople John Comnenus remained steadfast in his determination to crush 'the Sicilian usurper'; but in the spring of 1143, while hunting in Cilicia, he accidentally scratched himself with a poisoned arrow and within a few days was dead of septicaemia. In Venice, too,

---

1. Technically, the ruler of the Empire did not become Emperor until he was crowned by the Pope in Rome. This Conrad never managed to achieve; until his death, therefore, he had to content himself with the uncrowned Emperor's title of King of the Romans.

Doge Polani was busy with affairs nearer home. In 1141 the little city of Fano appealed for help against domineering neighbours who threatened to attack her. Never one to let slip a chance to extend her authority, Venice agreed; and the terms of this first treaty ever made between the Republic and another Italian city show as clearly as anything could the position that Venice had now acquired among the populations of the Adriatic coast. Every Venetian henceforth was to enjoy in Fano the same privileges as the native citizens, with a right to Venetian judges in any lawsuit involving both cities. The Fanesi, for their part, were obliged to declare themselves subject allies of the Republic, saving only their fealty – such as it was – to the Western Empire. They were also bound to the payment of an annual tribute, in the form of 1,000 measures of oil for the illumination of St Mark's and 100 for the Doges' Palace.

Two years later there was trouble with the Paduans, who began without warning to divert the course of the Brenta. Their purpose was to shorten the river trip to the lagoon outlets; they little realized what the Venetians knew all too well – that the slightest interference with the geographical system of the lagoon risks upsetting that almost unbelievably delicate balance between land and water which is essential for Venice's survival. Faced with the prospect of vast accumulations of sand forming around Sant' Ilario and the silting up of the existing channels on which they depended, the Venetians lodged a strong protest; and when this was arrogantly rejected they immediately took up arms. The conclusion was inevitable. The Paduans could never hope to match their neighbours in a trial of strength. After a single brief and disastrous confrontation they surrendered, with the promise to pursue their project no further and to repair the damage already done. What, however, is far more important – and indeed the only reason why so trivial an incident is worth mentioning at all in this book – is the fact that in this, the first campaign in her history to be waged entirely on land, Venice engaged mercenaries to do the fighting for her, under the two leading *condottieri* of the day, Guido di Montecchio of Verona[1] commanding the cavalry and Alberto da Bragacurta the infantry. One reason was doubtless the Venetians' lack of experience on an element that always remained foreign to them; they may also, however, have felt the first stirrings of that fear that was later to become an obsession – that any native-born general, returning victorious, might enjoy a prestige and popularity unbecoming a citizen of the Republic, and possibly constituting even a danger to the state. Later centuries, when the *condottieri* were to seize power in city after city

1. The Montecchi are the Montagues of Shakespeare's *Romeo and Juliet*.

until they came to dominate most of North and Central Italy, were to show that such a fear was by no means unjustified.

The Emperor John Comnenus had been succeeded on the throne of Byzantium by his son Manuel, a young man still in his twenties, famous for his dark good looks and possessing none of his father's xenophobic tendencies. His early life had been passed in close contact with the Frankish knights of Outremer, and his admiration for Western institutions had even led him to introduce knightly tournaments to Constantinople – an innovation which, particularly when he took part in them himself, scandalized his older subjects. He was, moreover, an intellectual and a scholar who cannot have failed to be impressed by the reports he had received of the growing brilliance of the court at Palermo which, thanks to Roger's patronage of the arts and sciences, was rapidly becoming the cultural clearing-house of Europe, the one focal point where the leading thinkers of the three great civilizations of the Mediterranean – Latin, Greek and Arab – could meet together for their mutual enlightenment.

Manuel was fully aware of the danger posed by Norman Sicily. But he also knew that with two-thirds of Asia Minor – formerly the main recruiting-ground for Byzantine armies – now occupied by the Seljuk Turks and his western frontier also under constant pressure, his own Empire would have to fight for survival. Had his father been right in his determined hostility to the Sicilian Kingdom? Would it not be wiser to try and make common cause? Soon after his accession he sent an Embassy to Palermo to investigate the possibilities of an alliance, which he hoped might be cemented by the marriage of a Byzantine princess to one of the King's sons.

If these negotiations had succeeded, the consequences for Venice might have been serious indeed, with Roger of Sicily exercising effective control of both sides of the straits of Otranto. But they failed, and Manuel turned instead to the still more important question of his own marriage, to the sister-in-law of the Emperor-elect Conrad, which took place at the beginning of 1146. Just three months afterwards, on Palm Sunday, there followed an event that was to affect the whole civilized world. St Bernard of Clairvaux launched the Second Crusade.

St Bernard's excursions into the political sphere – which, unfortunately, he was throughout his life unable to resist – were almost invariably disastrous; but none ever proved so humiliating a fiasco as this immense expedition, led jointly by Conrad and King Louis VII of France with the purpose of recovering the city of Edessa from the Saracens and consolidating Frankish power in the Levant. Numberless thousands died before they ever reached the Holy Land; those that survived the journey fled after their first and only armed encounter. It is a measure of the paucity of our sources for the Venetian history of the time that we cannot be altogether sure whether Venice participated with a fleet or not. Although one chronicler – Marino Sanudo the elder, writing in the early fourteenth century – tells of the *magnum auxilium* sent by the Republic under the command of Giovanni Polani, the Doge's brother, his report is unsubstantiated by any other historian of the Crusade and can almost certainly be discounted. But the Venetians were not to be left in peace for long. In the first weeks of 1148 they received an urgent appeal from Manuel: a Sicilian fleet had sailed against his Empire.

The commander of this fleet was George of Antioch, a Levantine Greek who had risen from humble origins to be the first holder of Norman Sicily's proudest title – Emir of Emirs, at once the High Admiral[1] and chief minister of the Kingdom. He had first taken Corfu, which had surrendered without a struggle and willingly accepted a Sicilian garrison of 1,000 men. Rounding the Peloponnese and dropping further armed detachments at strategic points along the coast, he had then sailed north again as far as Euboea, raiding and pillaging as he went. A particularly rich haul had been afforded by the ancient city of Thebes, centre of the Byzantine silk manufacture, whence not only bales of damasks and brocades but also a number of highly skilled Jewish workwomen had been seized and carried off to enrich the royal silk factory (which did double duty as a harem) at Palermo. Turning back, he had finally plundered Corinth, his vessels – according to his near contemporary, Nicetas Choniates – 'by now so low in the water that they looked more like merchantmen than the pirate ships they really were'.

Nicetas was right: piracy it was. But it was also something more. King Roger was under no delusions. An attempted alliance between himself and the Byzantine Emperor having proved unworkable, he knew that it was only a question of time before Manuel, probably in conjunction with Venice and the Western Empire, launched a major offensive against him. His own pre-emptive action might precipitate the attack – no bad thing in itself if it caused Manuel to strike before he was ready – but it had at least assured him the possession of chosen strongpoints on the Balkan peninsula and, in Corfu, the principal bridgehead from which any invasion of South Italy might be expected to come.

1. The word *Admiral* is in fact derived, through Norman Sicily, from the Arabic title of *Emir*.

No Venetian ever gave anything for nothing, and Manuel had to grant further extensive trading privileges in Cyprus and Rhodes, as well as in his own capital, before he got what he wanted – the full support of the war fleet of the Republic for six months. Meanwhile he was working desperately to bring his own navy to readiness – some 500 galleys and 1,000 transports, a fitting counterpart to an army of perhaps 20,000 or 25,000 men.

From the outset, this formidable joint force was ill-starred. Though the rendezvous was fixed for April 1148, both sides were grievously delayed – the Greeks by a sudden invasion of the Kumans, a tribe from South Russia who chose this moment to sweep down across the Danube into imperial territory, the Venetians by the death of Doge Polani. It was autumn before the two navies could meet in the southern Adriatic, together to begin the siege of Corfu, and the following spring before the army could join them, accompanied by the Emperor himself in overall command.

The siege, Manuel discovered, on his arrival, was not going well. The citadel in which Roger's garrison was holding out stood on a high crag, towering above the sea and safely beyond the range of Byzantine projectiles. Nicetas reported that the Greeks seemed to be shooting at the very sky itself, while the Sicilians could release deluges of arrows and hailstorms of rocks on to the besiegers. (People wondered, he could not resist adding, how they had taken possession of it so effortlessly the previous year.) More ominous still, perhaps, was the steady worsening of relations between Greeks and Venetians – reaching a climax when the latter occupied a neighbouring islet and set fire to a number of Byzantine vessels lying offshore. They later managed to seize possession of the imperial flagship itself, on which they performed an elaborate charade, making fun of the Emperor's swarthy complexion by dressing up an Ethiopian slave in the imperial vestments and staging a mock coronation on deck in full view of their Greek allies.

Manuel was never to forgive the Venetians this insult. For the moment, however, they were his allies still, and indispensable ones at that. With patience, tact and all the charm for which he was famous, he somehow restored an uneasy harmony; then he himself assumed direct personal command of the siege operations.

Towards the end of the summer Corfu fell – probably through treachery, since Nicetas writes that the garrison commander subsequently entered the imperial service. The Emperor's joy, however, must have been mitigated by the news that George of Antioch had now taken another fleet of forty ships through the Dardanelles and across the Marmara to the very walls of Constantinople. A landing had mercifully been prevented but the Sicilians, undeterred, had sailed on some way up the Bosphorus, pillaging several rich villas along the Asiatic shore, and on their return had even for good measure shot an impudent arrow or two into the gardens of the imperial palace. Nor, once he had recaptured Corfu, was Manuel able to follow up his victory. He was summoned urgently northward to deal with a new insurrection in the Balkans – in which Roger, whose diplomatic tentacles extended far beyond his own shores, may well have been subtly implicated.

So ended the war with Sicily, from which both Venice and Byzantium had expected so much. Apart from the reconquest of a single island captured barely two years before, it had achieved nothing. Sicilian garrisons still remained strung around the Greek coast; King Roger was as secure on his throne and as powerful in Europe and the Mediterranean as ever he had been. Looking back on it in historical perspective, we can now see that the most noteworthy aspect of the war was also perhaps the most unedifying: for in that first sorry fracas between the two so-called allies in the water off Corfu lay the seeds of a deepening hostility between Republic and Empire which were to come to their poisonous fruition, fifty-five years later, in the Fourth Crusade.

When in the spring of 1148 Doge Polani had led his fleet out of the lagoon in response to the Byzantine appeal, the sickness that was to cause his death was already upon him. He had progressed no further than Caorle when he was forced to return, and within a few weeks he was dead. For the next seven years and seven months, Venice was ruled by Domenico Morosini. His family had already played a leading part in Venetian affairs for well over 200 years, and in the centuries to come was to provide the Republic with three other Doges besides Domenico. His reign marked, for his subjects, a happy time. By the end of 1149 peace had been made with the Sicilians; on the maps of the great Arab geographer Abu Abdullah Mohammed al-Edrisi, who spent fifteen years at the court in Palermo and in whose work King Roger took an intense personal interest, the northern Adriatic was clearly labelled *Culfus Venetiarum*, and on Roger's death in 1154 his son and successor William I formally conceded all waters north of a line drawn westward from Ragusa as a Venetian preserve. Despite the Corfu incident relations continued on an ostensibly friendly basis with Byzantium, whose recent trading concessions were beginning to bring in most gratifying returns; while in the Western Empire Conrad's nephew Frederick of Swabia, who succeeded his uncle in 1152, confirmed Venetian privileges without demur. It was no wonder that Morosini's dogeship saw another building boom in the city, marked above all by the completion, 250 years after the sinking of its first foundations, of the campanile of St Mark.

In mainland Italy, on the other hand, the clouds were gathering fast. The 32-year-old Frederick, whose reddish-brown hair and beard were soon to earn him the nickname of Barbarossa, had ascended the throne with one overriding objective. 'My wish,' he confessed frankly to the Pope, 'is to restore to the Roman Empire its ancient greatness and splendour.' It was a conception that left no room for compromise with the Empire of the East, nor with Sicily; least of all with the towns and cities of North Italy, led by Milan, whose spirit of independence, nourished by successive Popes throughout the long years of papal–imperial struggle, was every bit as determined as was Frederick's will to break it. The strength of this spirit, however, seems to have genuinely surprised him when he entered Italy in October 1154, on the way to his imperial coronation. All the cities and major towns sent emissaries to greet him at Roncaglia; but apart from the few who saw in the Empire a chance to shake off Milanese domination, the overwhelming majority left him in no doubt of their resolve to break the old feudal fetters in favour of republican self-government. Frederick for his part was determined to begin as he meant to go on; Milan was at present too strong for him but her little ally Tortona, after a heroic resistance of over two months, was destroyed until not one stone remained on another.

Having thus set what he assumed to be a salutary example, Frederick continued, in the spring of 1155, on his journey southwards to Rome. Predictably, in view of his general arrogance and unwillingness to compromise, his way was not altogether smooth. His first meeting, near Sutri, with the newly-elected Pope Adrian IV – the only Englishman ever to occupy the Throne of St Peter – was exacerbated by his refusal to perform the traditional courtesy of holding the papal stirrup when Adrian dismounted. The Pope retaliated by denying him the Kiss of Peace, and two days were lost before conversations could begin. On this occasion Frederick was persuaded to relent; but when, a day or two later, a delegation from the Roman Senate rode out to greet him and to request the monetary payments and guarantees normally given by Emperors at the time of their coronation, his curt dismissal of them had more serious results. Thanks to brilliant planning by the Pope, he was able to slip unobserved into Rome at dawn on 17 June for a secret coronation, but within hours the city had risen in revolt against him and by nightfall well over 1,000 Roman insurgents and imperial troops were lying dead in the streets or drowned in the Tiber.

Although Venice had sent representatives to make an *acte de présence* at Roncaglia, she had done her utmost to remain aloof from the events that followed. As an independent city-republic that had long since freed herself from imperial control, she could hardly be unsympathetic to the Lombard towns that were now striving to do the same; on the other hand her whole political and economic development had pursued so different a course from theirs that there could be no real emotional identification. Unlike them, she was a world power with a world policy – a policy which involved increasingly delicate diplomatic manoeuvring, not just with the Western Empire but with Byzantium and Norman Sicily, the Papacy and the Crusader states, to say nothing of the Saracens of both North Africa and the Middle East. At this particular moment in her history, with her relations with Manuel Comnenus growing increasingly strained and her Italian markets ever more profitable, she had no wish to antagonize Frederick Barbarossa more than was necessary. When Doge Morosini died in 1156, he left behind him a Republic still uncommitted either way.

His successor, Vitale Michiel II, did his best to steer the same middle path, but it was not long before Frederick's actions in Italy forced him to abandon it. Crossing the Alps again in 1158, at the head of an army far stronger than that which he had brought with him four years before, the Emperor called a second diet at Roncaglia, where his attitude still further enraged the Lombard cities; and though some towns still remained loyal to him, within weeks much of North Italy was in a state of open revolt. Meanwhile a great wave of revulsion against the Empire swept down through the peninsula. What was needed above all was a centre of resistance, some strong power able to focus the aspirations and ideals of those who stood for liberty against domination, republicanism against imperialism, Italian against German. Fortunately for the beleaguered cities, two such powers were near at hand: the Papacy and the Kingdom of Sicily.

Two years before, in 1156, Pope Adrian and King William of Sicily had signed a treaty at Benevento. Since then, working both separately and together, papal and Sicilian diplomatists had achieved a good deal; and in August 1159 representatives from four of the most determined of Frederick's Italian enemies – Milan, Crema, Brescia and Piacenza – met the Pope at Anagni and, in the presence of envoys from King William, swore the initial pact that was to become the nucleus of the great Lombard League. The towns promised to have no dealings with the Empire without first obtaining papal consent, while the Pope in return undertook to excommunicate the Emperor after the customary notice of forty days.

It was Adrian's last political act. He was already a sick man, and on the evening of 1 September 1159 he died of angina. His death gave Frederick Barbarossa an opportunity to sow yet more dissension. Recognizing – rightly – that the next Pope if freely elected would be sure to continue along the lines set by his predecessor, the Emperor now deliberately engineered a schism within the papal curia. Consequently, just as Cardinal Roland of Siena – who, as Adrian's Chancellor, had been the principal architect of his foreign policy – was being enthroned in St Peter's as Pope Alexander III, his colleague Cardinal Octavian of S. Cecilia suddenly seized the papal mantle and put it on himself. Alexander's supporters snatched it back; but Octavian had taken the precaution of bringing with him another, into which he somehow managed to struggle – getting it on back to front in the process. He then made a dash for the throne, sat on it, and proclaimed himself Pope Victor IV. It was hardly an edifying performance; but it worked. Frederick's ambassadors in Rome immediately recognized Victor as the rightful Pontiff. Virtually all the rest of western Europe soon gave its allegiance to Alexander, but the damage was done and the chaotic Italian political scene was further bedevilled, for the next eighteen years, by a disputed Papacy.

Faced with the need to recognize one or the other of the rival Popes, Venice could no longer stand aloof. She was moreover growing seriously alarmed at the way things were going in Lombardy; if Frederick were to continue in his present mood, he was unlikely to show any greater respect for Venetian independence than for that of any other Italian city. So she too declared for Alexander and, by implication, the Lombard rebels. The Emperor's retaliation was swift but ineffectual. Three nearby cities that had remained passively loyal to him – Padua, Verona and Ferrara – were easily persuaded to attack their proud and often domineering neighbour, but were equally easily repulsed. Perhaps their hearts were not really in it; in 1163 we find two of them, Verona and Padua, joined now by Vicenza, actually combining with Venice in an association pledged to yield no more to Barbarossa than their forefathers had yielded to Charlemagne. A subsequent attack on Grado, launched at Frederick's instigation by a German-born Patriarch of Aquileia, was even less successful. A Venetian fleet sped to the rescue and took the Patriarch prisoner with some 700 of his followers, releasing him only after he promised to send the Republic a tribute of a dozen pigs – one for each member of his cathedral chapter – every year on the Wednesday before Lent, in time to be chased by the Venetian populace on the following day (*Giovedì Grasso*) round the Piazza.

To Venice, these two incidents were little more than pinpricks. It was her good fortune that, much as Frederick Barbarossa would have liked to see her humbled at his feet, there were three other objectives on the Italian peninsula which had prior claim to his attention and against which he now marched. One was Ancona where, on territory that in Frederick's eyes formed an integral part of the Western Empire, Manuel Comnenus had some years before established a Byzantine outpost; the second, as always, was Norman Sicily; and the third was Rome, where the Emperor was determined to remove Pope Alexander from his throne and replace him with a new imperial puppet. (Frederick's former protégé, the anti-Pope Victor, had altogether failed to establish himself in the city; in 1164 he had died miserably in Lucca, where for a number of years he had eked out a living on the proceeds of not very successful brigandage and where the local authorities would not even allow him burial within the walls.)

The details of this, the most ambitious of all Frederick's Italian campaigns, need not detain us here. It is enough to say that of his first two objectives he achieved nothing; of the third, all too much. Rome, like the cities of the north, was a commune, with a civic government of its own; and the Romans, who had detested Frederick ever since his first ill-starred coronation visit, fought heroically to keep him out. St Peter's itself, hastily ringed with trenches and converted into a fortress, held out for eight days, but to no avail. The imperial troops burst through the great bronze doors leaving, in the words of a contemporary,[1] the marble pavements of the nave strewn with dead and dying, the high altar itself stained with blood. Alexander was forced into hiding, and on 30 July 1167 Victor's successor, the anti-Pope Paschal, celebrated Mass in the Basilica.

For Frederick, already crowned Emperor but now additionally invested with the golden circlet of a Patrician of Rome – a deliberate insult to the Roman Senate – this was the climax of his career. He could not know that four days later his entire army would be stricken by pestilence. So virulent was the epidemic that he had no course but to order an immediate withdrawal. By the time he regained his imperial headquarters at Pavia he had lost well over 2,000 men, including his Chancellor, Archbishop

1. Otto of St Blaise.

Rainald of Dassel, and many of his most trusted lieutenants and advisers.

It was like some dreadful visitation from the Old Testament – and indeed was considered all over Europe as divine retribution for the desecration of St Peter's and the expulsion of God's Vice-Regent on earth. But Frederick's punishment was not yet over. He was still in Pavia, nursing the remains of his shattered army, when on 1 December no less than fifteen of the leading North Italian cities formed themselves into a Greater Lombard League. It was the supreme gesture of defiance; and such was their contempt for the Emperor that they had not even thought it necessary to wait till he had left Italy before making it.

Of this League Venice was a founder member. She had no land forces to offer, but she pledged her navy to the cause anywhere in the lagoons or in the tributary rivers where navigable. She further agreed to share with her confederates any subsidies that she might receive from Constantinople or Palermo, and to obtain their consent before declaring war or concluding peace with any other state. These undertakings were not, it must be admitted, particularly rigorous. The narrow radius within which the Venetian fleet was bound to defend League interests is surely significant; there was no question of sending it beyond the range of immediate recall if a more serious crisis were to arise elsewhere. It seems clear, nevertheless, that the Republic was now looking again – if not in her commercial policy, then at least in her diplomatic alignments – more and more towards the West. By her adherence to the Lombard League in 1167 she had in fact identified herself with the affairs of mainland Italy more closely than at any former time in the five centuries of her existence.

Meanwhile, relations with Byzantium were growing worse and worse. There were a number of reasons, for which neither party was altogether free of blame. The number of Latins permanently resident in Constantinople at this time has been estimated at not less than 80,000, all enjoying the special privileges that Manuel and his predecessors, in moments of weakness, had been forced to grant. Of these, the Venetians were the most numerous, the most favoured and, in all probability, the most objectionable. Nicetas Choniates, chief of the palace secretariat in Constantinople, complains that their colony had become 'so insolent in its wealth and prosperity as to hold the imperial power in scorn'. He may have been right, up to a point: Venetians were never noted for their humbleness of demeanour and they doubtless gave their Byzantine hosts plenty of cause for complaint. But however much Manuel Comnenus may have been mocked by the Venetian sailors off Corfu no Venetian merchant, whether resident on the Rialto or the Bosphorus, would have dreamt of underestimating him. For some years now, the Republic had watched with misgiving while its chief commercial rivals – Genoa, Pisa and Amalfi – had slowly consolidated their positions in what had once been its own exclusive preserve; and its people were fully aware that this process was part of a deliberate policy by Manuel and his father to reduce Venetian influence. They were worried, too, about recent developments in Dalmatia. Since 1162 they had been at war with Stephen III of Hungary, who in the five succeeding years had managed to capture virtually every coastal city except Zara. Then, in 1167, Manuel Comnenus had entered the lists and gained a decisive victory over Stephen, taking these newly conquered territories for himself. It was an act hardly calculated to endear him to the Venetians; and when shortly afterwards he had the audacity to seek their support in establishing a permanent Byzantine colony at Ancona – with the longer-term objective of reviving the old Exarchate of Ravenna – they had left him in no doubt of their feelings.

It was in this atmosphere of mutual suspicion and resentment that, some time early in 1171, the new Genoese settlement at Galata – the district of Constantinople on the further side of the Golden Horn – was attacked and in large measure destroyed. Who was responsible we shall never know. For Manuel, however, here was precisely the chance that he had been looking for. Casting the blame squarely on the Venetians, on 12 March he gave the order for all citizens of the Republic on Byzantine territory to be placed under immediate arrest, their ships and property confiscated. A few managed to escape in a Byzantine warship, put at their disposal by a Venetian-born captain in the imperial service; but the majority were less lucky. In the capital alone, 10,000 were seized; and when all the prisons had been filled to bursting point, monasteries and convents were requisitioned to accommodate the overspill.

The reaction in Venice can be imagined when the news reached the Rialto. The impression that the attack on the Genoese had been nothing but a pretext was confirmed when the Genoese themselves declared that the Venetians had had nothing to do with the incident; the smoothness with which the operation had been carried out simultaneously across the length and breadth of the Empire showed beyond all doubt that it had been carefully planned in advance; and this reflection served in turn as a bitter reminder of how only two years before, to stamp out rumours that he was contemplating an action of this kind, the Emperor had given the emissaries of the Doge specific guarantees for the security of their countrymen – guarantees which had actually attracted further Venetian capital to the East and so increased the spoils he was now enjoying.

The last of the old ties that had bound Venice to Byzantium were forgotten. Forgotten too were the solemn promises of consultation made less than four years previously to the Lombard League. The Venetians were bent on war. Finance was a problem; for some time the government had been overspending, and Venice had in addition been paying the League heavy annual subsidies. In settlement of debts already incurred, all the revenues of the Rialto had been pledged for the next decade. A forced loan was ordered, for which every citizen would be liable according to his means, and to facilitate its collection the city was divided into the six districts, or *sestieri*, which still exist today: Castello, Cannaregio, Dorsoduro, Santa Croce, S. Polo and S. Marco. There was also a serious shortage of manpower; Venetians living abroad – such of them as were not languishing in Manuel's prisons – were recalled home and expected, if not actually forced, to rally to the colours.

Despite these difficulties, and thanks to the draconian measures he adopted to overcome them, in just over three months Doge Michiel was able to raise and man a fleet of over 120 sail. It was an extraordinary achievement, of which no other state would have been capable; and in September 1171 the Doge led his armada out of the lagoon against the Empire of the East. He stopped at various points in Istria and Dalmatia to pick up such Venetian subjects as he might find, then continued round the Peloponnese to Euboea. There he found ambassadors from Manuel awaiting him. They were in a conciliatory mood. Their master, they assured him, had no wish for war. The Doge had only to send a peace mission to Constantinople; he would then find that all differences could be satisfactorily resolved, and on terms that he would not consider unfavourable.

Vitale Michiel accepted. It was the worst mistake of his life. While his emissaries (who included Enrico Dandolo, later to play so fateful a role in European history) continued their journey to the Bosphorus and spent much of the winter in fruitless discussions with Byzantine officials, he took his fleet on to Chios to await developments. It was there that disaster struck. Plague broke out in the overcrowded ships and spread with terrible speed. By early spring thousands were dead, the survivors so weakened and demoralized through sickness and prolonged inactivity as to be unfit for war or anything else. At this point the ambassadors arrived back from Constantinople. They had been abominably treated, and their mission had proved a total failure. The Emperor obviously had not the faintest intention of changing his attitude; his only purpose had been to gain time, while he improved his own defences.

And so, to top all the Doge's other misfortunes, there was now added a further burden – shame and humiliation for his gullibility in falling into so obvious a trap. He could go no further. His expedition had been disastrous; the flower of Venetian youth lay dead or dying, without having once set eyes on the enemy.[1] The fleet, or what remained of it, was on the brink of open mutiny. His only course now was to return with all speed to Venice and face the wrath of his subjects.

He arrived in the middle of May, 1172, and immediately called a general assembly in the palace to which he reported all that had occurred, defending his own actions and decisions as best he could. He was heard in tight-lipped silence – the more so because, to crown all the other misfortunes he had inflicted upon the Republic, he was now seen to have brought back the plague as well. This final incompetence could not be forgiven. The assembly itself rose up against him; and though outside the palace a mob had gathered and was even now calling for his blood, Vitale Michiel saw that he must flee. Slipping out through a side door, he hurried along the Riva towards the convent of S. Zaccaria.

He never reached it. The way to S. Zaccaria led over the Ponte della Paglia and then, 100 yards or so further along the quay, up a narrow alley known as the Calle delle Rasse. Just as he was about to turn the corner, he was set upon by one of the mob who sprang out from the shadows of a neighbouring house and stabbed him to death.

It is hard not to feel sorry for Vitale Michiel. With the implacable Frederick Barbarossa on one side and the unpredictable Manuel Comnenus on the other, with the north of Italy now unified by the Lombard League and the south by the alliance of Norman Sicily with the greatest of twelfth-century Popes, he had had a far more delicate and difficult course to steer through the shoals of European diplomacy than any of his predecessors. For fifteen of his sixteen years as Doge he had steered it beautifully. Only in his last year, in a moment of crisis and in conditions to which he was utterly unaccustomed, did he take a wrong

1. Among them, so the story goes, perished all the surviving male members of the Giustiniani family – except one, a young monk in the monastery of S. Nicolò di Lido. Rather than allow so distinguished a line to die out, the Pope granted him temporary release from his vows. He left the monastery, married the Doge's daughter and did what was expected of him; then, his posterity assured, he returned to his monastery. His wife waited for the children to grow up; later she too took the veil.

decision. Even so, he can hardly be blamed for the plague – nor even altogether for returning with it to Venice, since to have delayed his homecoming any longer would have provoked certain mutiny.

Not surprisingly, perhaps, there is no monument to his name in Venice today; and yet, until only some thirty years ago, his death was more clearly commemorated – for those who knew the story – than that of any other Venetian. Soon after the murder, when his assassin had been brought to justice and executed, orders were given that the latter's house in the Calle delle Rasse should be razed to the ground, and that no stone building should ever be constructed on that spot. This decree was observed until after the Second World War – which is why all pictures and photographs of the Riva dating from before that time disclose, just beyond the Ponte della Paglia, on one of the most architecturally strategic sites in all Venice, a humble group of old houses of wood and plaster. Only in 1948 were the authorities at last persuaded to set the old tradition aside; and even now, as we glance up at the façade of the Danieli Royal Excelsior Hotel, some of us may wonder whether, in a slightly different and infinitely more disagreeable form, the old curse does not still linger over the spot where Vitale Michiel met his death eight centuries ago.

9

Reconciliation

[1172–1187]

Non combattete mai con la religione . . . perchè questo obbietto ha troppo forza nella mente degl' huomini.

Never fight against religion . . . this concept has too much empire over the minds of men.

Guicciardini

The Venetians did not immediately elect another Doge. They wanted time to think. Their situation was grave in the extreme – there could be no doubt of that. They were now in a state of war with both Empires simultaneously. Their splendid new navy had been reduced to a shadow of what it had been only six months before, many vessels having been deliberately burnt in the Aegean in an effort to contain the plague. Manpower – since none of the prisoners interned in the East had yet been freed – was more than ever a problem, and one which continued to grow as the epidemic claimed increasing numbers of victims in the city and the other communities of the lagoon. The treasury was empty; national bankruptcy could be avoided only by repeating the forced loan of the previous year.[1] Worst of all was the demoralization. Vitale Michiel had been the eighth Doge in the Republic's history to meet a violent death, but the first for over 200 years. Perhaps the Venetians realized the strength of the mass hysteria that had suddenly overcome them, and were conscious of some sort of collective responsibility for the murder. They seem, at any rate, to have felt both shock and shame, a need to examine both their government and themselves.

What, basically, had gone wrong? It was clear that most of the blame, both for the failure of the expedition and for the penury of the state, lay with Michiel; but where were the checks and balances by which his actions should have been controlled? In the general tightening-up of the

1. These state loans – the first of their kind in the world – were soon to become a permanent feature of the Venetian economy, with 4 per cent transferable government bonds offering opportunities for endless speculation on the Rialto.

constitution under Domenico Flabanico the Doge had been provided, as in the early days, with two counsellors; he had moreover been put under an obligation to 'invite' other leading citizens – the *pregadi* – to give additional advice when necessary. With him also lay the right to call the *arengo* of all the people. But Flabanico had been dead for nearly a century and a half; by now the two counsellors had lost much of their authority, the *pregadi* seldom received their 'invitations' and the *arengo*, with the rapid increase of the city's population, was no longer a practical measure. Not only were there too many Venetians to meet together in general assembly as the inhabitants of the early lagoon settlements had done, but there was no way of controlling such large numbers. *Arenghi* had become no more than licensed mobs; recent years had shown all too clearly how little they could be trusted with important decisions of state. As a result they were hardly ever called except when the law specifically demanded them – for the election of a Doge or the declaration of war; and the ducal power was therefore virtually unfettered. There was an urgent necessity to redefine the powers of the three governing elements of the state: Doge, counsellors and people. It was a necessity that led, in 1172 and 1173, to what are arguably the most important constitutional reforms in Venetian history.

The first innovation was an assembly of 480 prominent Venetians, to be nominated by two representatives of each of the six new *sestieri*, and to hold office for one year only. Henceforward this assembly, the *Comitia Majora* – the *Maggior Consiglio*, or, in English, the Great Council – was to be responsible for appointing all the chief officials of the state, including the twelve representatives of the *sestieri*. In practice this meant that after the first year, when these representatives were elected democratically, they and the Great Council, each nominating the other, formed a closed circle which completely excluded the general populace from any say in their composition. The *arengo* was not entirely abolished; but even where it remained mandatory it was, as far as possible, shorn of its effective power. Its most jealously guarded prerogative of all, the election of the Doge, is a case in point. Formerly, as at the accession of Domenico Selvo, the people of Venice had played a very real part in the choice of their leader; their right to do so was one of the corner-stones of the constitution. Henceforth this choice was to be entrusted to eleven special electors, nominated by the Council; the name of the new Doge would simply be announced to the assembled populace as a *fait accompli*. The first attempt to follow this new procedure caused riots, and the objectors were pacified only after a compromise had been agreed upon: the successful candidate must be formally presented to them in St Mark's with the formula 'Here is your Doge, if it please you.' Thus the voice of the people was theoretically preserved; but it was a formality only, and the people knew it.

The next step in the work of reform was to increase the number of the ducal counsellors from two to six. They were to be in constant attendance on the Doge and, since their function was primarily to limit his authority, they must presumably have enjoyed some power of veto over his decisions. They and he together formed an inner council of state, later to be known as the *Signoria* or sometimes the *consiglietto*. As an outer advisory body the *pregadi*, or Senate, remained in being, and their influence also increased – especially in the field of foreign affairs, in which they took most of the important decisions which were subsequently ratified by the Council.

The effect of these measures was, in short, to weaken both the apex and the base of the administrative pyramid while strengthening it in the centre. Venice had taken a few more steps towards the oligarchical form of government that she was to perfect in the following century and to make peculiarly her own. On the other hand it was important that the curtailing of ducal power should not be reflected in any loss of prestige; further additions were accordingly made to the dignities of the Doge and the pomp and ceremonial with which he was surrounded. In future, directly after his election, he was to be carried all round the Piazza on a special circular chair – familiarly called the *pozzetto* from its resemblance to the characteristic well-heads of the city – scattering largesse to the people; thenceforth, whenever he left his palace on state business, he was to be accompanied by a long cortège of nobles, clergy and citizens.

But neither the pomp nor the largesse – limited by subsequent legislation to not less than 100 and not more than 500 ducats – was enough to make up for what had been taken away.

However much the Venetians as a whole may have resented this whittling down of their ancient rights by the new electoral system, nobody seriously questioned the wisdom of the electors when their choice fell on Sebastiano Ziani. The new Doge was highly intelligent, energetic despite his seventy years, and possessed of wide administrative experience. He was also enormously rich. It was just as well. Seeing the Republic on the verge of bankruptcy, he made his first task the restitution of the national finances and, on the advice of the *pregadi*, suspended all payments on the new government bonds. It was a brave decision, but it aroused less resentment than might have been expected. The bondholders were all Venetian citizens; they loved money but they loved Venice more, and this direct appeal to their patriotism met with an immediate response.

There could, however, be no question of continuing the war against Byzantium. Ambassadors set out again for Constantinople to sue for peace and, it was hoped, for the release of all those still in captivity. But their mission was in vain. They found Manuel Comnenus as unyielding as ever. Since what was left of the Venetian fleet was at that moment actively engaged with Frederick Barbarossa's army in the siege of Byzantine-held Ancona, his attitude was not altogether surprising; nevertheless, his rejection of this second overture was to prove a grave mistake, and one which his successors would have bitter cause to regret. Meanwhile it drove the Venetians into the arms of King William II ('the Good') of Sicily, with whom in 1175 they concluded a twenty-year treaty, obtaining commercial terms far more favourable than any that they had previously enjoyed.

And so, under the wise guidance of Sebastiano Ziani, the Republic began to recover. Its material rehabilitation would inevitably take some time; morally, on the other hand, the process was a good deal more rapid – culminating, in the summer of 1177, with an event that focused upon Venice the attention of all Christendom: the reconciliation of Pope Alexander III and Frederick Barbarossa that brought the seventeen-year schism to an end and peace, at last, to Italy. Just over a year before, on 29 May 1176 at Legnano, the Lombard League had inflicted on Barbarossa the most crushing defeat of his career. He had lost much of his army, and had narrowly escaped with his own life; but the disaster had brought him to his senses. After four long Italian campaigns he saw that the Lombard cities were as determined as ever to resist him and, since the formation of their League, well able to do so. Pope Alexander was now recognized almost everywhere – even in much of the Empire itself – as the rightful Pontiff. For Frederick to persist any longer in the policy on which he had already wasted the best years of his life would earn him the derision of Europe.

His ambassadors met the Pope at Anagni to negotiate the terms of the reconciliation. In essence, they were simple enough: on the imperial side, recognition of Alexander, restitution of church possessions and the conclusion of peace with Byzantium, Sicily and the Lombard League; on the papal, confirmation of Frederick's wife as Empress, of his son Henry as King of the Romans and of several distinguished prelates in sees which they originally owed to schismatic anti-Popes. The next question was where the great meeting was to take place. Bologna was suggested, but rejected by Frederick for its Lombard affiliations; finally, after prolonged argument, it was agreed that Pope and Emperor should meet in Venice, on condition that Frederick should not be admitted into the city until Alexander had given his consent.

Politically, no better choice could have been made. To be sure, Venice had been a founder member of the Lombard League. On the other hand her recent troubles with Byzantium had prevented her from playing a very active part in League affairs; at one moment, beneath the walls of Ancona, she had even found herself fighting side by side with the forces of the Western Empire. She possessed a record of independence longer than that of any other North Italian city, and as a great and splendid metropolis she would have no difficulty in accommodating, in the style to which they were accustomed, all the European notables – princes, bishops, ambassadors and representatives from the Lombard towns – who were expected to be present.

On 10 May 1177 the Pope arrived with his *curia*. He was received by the Doge and the Patriarchs of both Grado and Aquileia and, after High Mass in the basilica, was carried in the state barge to the Patriarchal palace at S. Silvestro, which was put at his disposal for as long as he cared to remain. Before his meeting with the Emperor there was much work to be done; during the discussions at Anagni he had had no brief to speak for either Sicily or the League, both of which would have to reach agreement with the imperial plenipotentiaries if the promised Kiss of Peace were to have the significance he intended for it. So now a second round of negotiations began in the Patriarchal chapel. Meanwhile the Emperor, to whom by the terms of the reconciliation Venetian territory was still forbidden, held himself in readiness at Ravenna.

The League representatives in particular proved hard negotiators, and the talks dragged on for the best part of two months. By the beginning of July, however, agreement was in sight and, to speed communications, the Pope agreed to allow Frederick to approach as near as Chioggia, where he could keep in daily touch with developments. Up to this point the Emperor had displayed an exemplary and for him unusual degree of restraint in a situation that he cannot have found anything but deeply humiliating; but at last he began to show signs of losing his patience. In the six years since Venice's break with Byzantium his adherents in the city had multiplied until they constituted quite an influential faction. They now encouraged him to enter it at once, in defiance of the papal veto, and so to force Alexander and the Lombards into granting more favourable terms. Frederick was clearly tempted, but declined to move without the Doge's approval. Ziani, aware that refusal might well provoke an uprising in the Emperor's favour, hesitated; the envoys from the League, in a mixture of anger and apprehension, retired to Treviso. For a moment it looked as if all the careful diplomacy of the past year was to be brought to nothing.

The situation was saved by the Sicilians. The leader of their delegation, Archbishop Romuald of Salerno, ordered his ships to be made ready for a hasty departure hinting that, if he and his mission decided to leave, his master King William would be swift to take revenge for Venice's breach of faith. The Archbishop's meaning was only too clear. In the past two years the already considerable number of Venetian merchants in Palermo, Messina and Catania had enormously increased. There was nothing to prevent William from acting as Manuel Comnenus had acted in 1171. Uncertain no longer, Ziani issued a statement confirming that entry by Frederick Barbarossa into Venice could be permitted only after the papal sanction had been given.

In retrospect, the crisis seems to have provided all the negotiators with a salutary shock. The outstanding details were now quickly settled and on 23 July 1177 agreement was complete. At the Pope's request a Venetian flotilla left for Chioggia and brought Frederick to the Lido, whither a delegation of four cardinals sailed out to greet him. In their presence he solemnly abjured his anti-Pope and made formal acknowledgement of Alexander as rightful Pontiff; they in turn lifted his seventeen-year excommunication. Now at last he could be admitted into Venice. Early next morning the Doge himself arrived at S. Nicolò di Lido, where Frederick had spent the night, with an impressive retinue of nobles and clergy. He personally escorted the Emperor to a barge specially decorated for the occasion, and together they were rowed in state to the Molo.

In Venice itself, meanwhile, the last preparations had been completed. The Venetians' love of pomp and pageantry was already well established; this was one of the greatest days in their history, and they were determined to do justice to the occasion. For days already people had been pouring into the city. Flags were flying, windows dressed. Of the several eye-witness accounts that have survived, perhaps the most vivid and informative is the so-called *De Pace Veneta Relatio*, whose author seems to have been a German churchman. We do not know his name, but he was certainly well placed, both geographically and hieratically, to record what he saw:

At daybreak, the attendants of the Lord Pope hastened to the church of St Mark the Evangelist and closed the central doors of the great portal in front of the church, and thither they brought much timber and deal planks and ladders, and so raised up a lofty and splendid throne. And they also erected two masts of pine wood of wondrous height on each side of the quay, from which hung the standards of St Mark, magnificently embroidered and so large that they touched the ground; for that quay, which is known as the *Marmoreum*, is but a stone's throw from the church. Thither the Pope arrived before the first hour of the day [6 a.m.] and, having heard Mass, soon afterwards ascended to the higher part of his throne to await the arrival of the Emperor. There he sat, with his patriarchs, cardinals, archbishops and bishops innumerable; on his right was the Patriarch of Venice, and on his left that of Aquileia.

And now there came a quarrel between the Archbishop of Milan and the Archbishop of Ravenna as to which should be seen to take precedence; and each strove to sit himself in the third place from that of the Pope, on his right side. But the Pope determined to put an end to their contention, and leaving his own exalted seat descended the steps and placed himself below them. Thus was there no third place to sit in, and neither could sit on his right. Then about the third hour there arrived the Doge's barge, in which was the Emperor, with the Doge and the cardinals that had been sent to him on the previous day; and he was led by seven archbishops and canons of the Church in solemn procession to the papal throne. And when he reached it, he threw off the red cloak he was wearing, and prostrated himself before the Pope, and kissed first his feet and then his knees.[1] But the Pope rose, and taking the head of the Emperor in both his hands he embraced him and kissed him, and made him sit at his right hand, and at last spoke the words 'Son of the Church, be welcome.' Then he took him by the hand and led him into the Basilica. And the bells rang, and the *Te Deum Laudamus* was sung. When the ceremony was done, they both left the church together. The Pope mounted his horse, and the Emperor held his stirrup and then retired to the Doges' Palace. And all this happened on Sunday, the Eve of St James.

And on the same day the Pope sent the Emperor many gold and silver jars filled with food of various kinds. And he sent also a fatted calf, with the words 'It is meet that we should make merry and be glad, for my son was dead, and is alive again; and was lost, and is found.'

For Pope Alexander, the Treaty of Venice marked at once the climax and the culmination of his pontificate. He had had to endure eighteen years of schism and ten of exile from Rome, to say nothing of the implacable hostility of one of the most formidable men ever to wear the crown of the Western Empire; and he had had to wait until he was well into his seventies before receiving his reward. Now, however, that reward had come – nor was it limited to Frederick's recognition of his legitimacy.

1. There is a splendidly anachronistic late sixteenth-century representation of the scene by Zuccari in the north-west corner of the Sala del Maggior Consiglio.

The Emperor had also admitted all the temporal rights of the Papacy over the city of Rome; and the six-year truce that he had concluded with the Lombard League was clearly only a preliminary to his acknowledgement of the independence of the individual Lombard cities. It was the most signal victory ever to have been won by a Pope over imperial pretensions – greater far than the empty triumph at Canossa exactly a century before; and it had been due above all to the wisdom and patience with which Alexander had steered his Church through one of the most troubled periods in her history.

And now that that period was over those qualities remained with him. Neither on the day of his triumph nor at any other time during the Emperor's stay in Venice did Alexander show the slightest inclination to crow over his former enemy. One or two subsequent historians of Venice, like the incorrigibly romantic Martino da Canale writing nearly a century later, have perpetuated the legend of the Pope placing his foot on Frederick's neck, of the Emperor muttering under his breath 'Not to you, but to St Peter' and Alexander replying sharply: 'To me *and* to St Peter.' But this story is told by no contemporary writer and is inconsistent with all the first-hand evidence that has come down to us. The Emperor, too, seems to have behaved impeccably. On the day following the great reconciliation, he tried to carry courtesy even further: having again held the papal stirrup on leaving the Basilica, he would have led Alexander's horse all the way to the point of embarkation if the Pope had not gently restrained him. Did he, one cannot help wondering, remember then the two days spent at Sutri when he had refused to perform the same service for Pope Adrian, on the way to Rome for his coronation twenty-two years before?

The part played by Venice in healing the schism had also been considerable, and her rewards too were correspondingly large. Financially, that memorable summer of 1177 did much to restore her prosperity. The Emperor was the city's guest for eight full weeks, leaving only on 18 September. Pope Alexander remained until mid-October, after a total stay of well over five months. For much of that time Venice was crowded as never before, with her normal floating foreign population of travellers and merchants now swollen to many times its normal size by the greatest princes and prelates of Europe, each bent on outshining his rivals in the splendour of his retinue. One, the Archbishop of Cologne, brought with him a suite of no less than 400 secretaries, chaplains and attendants; the Patriarch of Aquileia boasted 300, as did the Archbishops of Mainz and

Magdeburg. Count Roger of Andria, the second envoy of the King of Sicily, had 330; Duke Leopold of Austria, with a train of only 160, must have cut a sorry figure indeed.

Politically, too, there were benefits. It would have been uncharacteristic of the Venetians to have kept both Emperor and Pope so long in their midst without obtaining anything tangible in return; in fact they concluded special treaties with both. From Frederick Barbarossa they obtained free passage, safe conduct and full exemption from imperial tolls in all parts of the Empire, in return for similar privileges for his own subjects 'as far as Venice but no further' – as clear an acknowledgement as anyone could wish of Venetian supremacy in the Adriatic. Pope Alexander for his part showed his appreciation by granting indulgences to most of the principal churches in the city, and above all by making a final settlement of that age-old struggle between Grado and Aquileia that had brought so much strife and bitterness over the centuries to Venetian ecclesiastical affairs. By its terms the Patriarch of Grado – now permanently resident in Venice – abandoned all claims to the treasures stolen by Poppo of Aquileia a century and a half before, and was granted in return undisputed authority over the communities around the lagoon plus Istria and Dalmatia – where the consequent strengthening of Venice's hold over her subject towns can well be imagined.

There is a Venetian tradition that during his stay Pope Alexander also gave new sacramental significance to the annual Ascension Day ceremony that had been held since A.D. 1000 out in the open sea beyond the Lido port, transforming it from a service of supplication into a symbolic marriage with the Adriatic.[1] Indeed, above one of the doors in the north wall of the Sala del Maggior Consiglio in the Doges' Palace there is a painting by Vicentino of the Pope handing Doge Ziani the ring which he is shortly to cast into the waves. It is sad to have to record that, like the quite fictitious naval battle of Salvore, depicted by Tintoretto's son Domenico immediately to the right, this theory is without foundation. The offering of the golden ring – a symbol, originally, of propitiation pure and simple – was bound to assume matrimonial overtones as the years went by, and it may well have been at about this time that it did so; but though it is reasonably safe to assume that the Pope was present at the 1177 ceremony – Ascension Day falling in that year on 2 June – there is no evidence that he actively participated in it, far less that he radically changed its character.

The greatest gain of all to Venice was in prestige. Throughout that

1. See p. 55.

memorable summer, she was the focus of attention of the whole of Europe – the capital, in a very real sense, of Christendom. Her Doge was playing host to the two leaders of the Western world; his relations with them, if not quite those of an equal, were generally seen to be at least those of a friend and fellow-prince. She had been specifically chosen by both the imperial and the papal negotiators because – to quote once more from the *Relatio* – she was 'subject to God alone . . . a place where the courage and authority of the citizens could preserve peace between the partisans of each side and ensure that no discord or sedition, deliberate or involuntary, should arise'. Admittedly, she only just succeeded; but succeed she did, and in doing so she assumed a new status as a great metropolis and a European power.

The Basilica of St Mark, with the little porphyry lozenge set into the pavement just in front of the central doorway traditionally marking the spot where Frederick Barbarossa abased himself before the Pope, is the only building on the Piazza or the Piazzetta which was already standing in its present form at the time of the events here described. If, however, the general setting for that tremendous ceremony possessed much the same general aspect that it has today, this also is largely due to Doge Sebastiano Ziani. He it was who pulled down the old church of S. Gemin-iano,[1] who bought from the nuns of S. Zaccaria the orchard (known as the *brolo*) which lay between it and the lagoon, who filled in the old Rio Batario – the canal which ran from behind what are now the *Procuratie Vecchie*, across the front of the basilica and past the campanile to the Rio di Zecca next to the public garden – paved the whole thing over in herring-bone brick and gave Venice what we now know as the Piazza S. Marco. He also ordered that all the houses built around it should be linked with arches and colonnades, so that from the start it must have looked very much as it did when Gentile Bellini painted it in 1496 – and, despite the building of the two long lines of the *Procuratie* along the northern and southern sides, it still does today.[2]

Doge Ziani also left his mark on the Doges' Palace and the Piazzetta. The Palace as he found it was in essence that which had been built after

1. See p. 8. It was rebuilt at the far west end of the Piazza, where it stood until Napoleon demolished it for good in 1807 to make way for a ballroom in his new wing of the *Procuratie*.

2. The Bellini picture is that of *The Procession of the Cross in the Piazza S. Marco*, one of the series relating the *Miracles of the Relic of the True Cross* now in the Accademia. (Plate 10) The *Procuratie Vecchie*, to the north, were already begun, though not very far advanced, in Bellini's time. The *Procuratie Nuove*, to the south, were started at the end of the sixteenth century after the demolition of Pietro Orseolo's hospital (see p. 44).

its predecessor had been destroyed during the revolution of 976, with possible additions and embellishments made in the course of repairs after the fire of 1106. Ziani, we are told by Sansovino, 'enlarged it in every direction'; although evidence is sketchy, we can presume that it followed traditional lines and that it looked much like the few Byzantine buildings that still exist along the Grand Canal – the Fondaco dei Turchi for example, or the Palazzi Farsetti and Loredan near the Rialto bridge.

The Piazzetta, meanwhile, was cleared and enlarged just as the Piazza had been. Perhaps as part of the preparations for the arrival of Barbarossa, Pietro Tribuno's old wall was swept away. It had blocked off the approach from the water's edge for nearly 300 years – for the past five of which there had lain alongside it two of the three antique columns that Vitale Michiel had brought back from his ill-starred expedition to the East. (Unlucky as ever, he had lost the third, which had been accidentally dropped overboard during the unloading and still lies in the mud off the Molo.) Several attempts had been made to raise them, all unsuccessful. Now, however, a young Venetian engineer presented himself before the Doge. His real name was Nicolò Staratonio, but he was usually known as Barattieri. This nickname, which suggests in Italian some predilection for card-sharping, may not have been entirely undeserved; we know at any rate that he offered to raise the two columns into position in return for the right to set up public gaming-tables between them. Ziani agreed. Up went the columns, where they stand today, later to be crowned respectively with the Lion of St Mark and St Theodore with his dragon-crocodile. Up, too, went the tables. The Great Council, shortly afterwards, is said to have tried to diminish the value of the concession by designating the same spot for the holding of public executions. From what we know of the temper of the time the attempt may well have had precisely the opposite effect; but Barattieri did not abandon engineering altogether, since we hear of him again building the first Rialto bridge, on pontoons, a few years later.

Statesman, diplomatist and builder, Sebastiano Ziani proved himself also to be a constitutional reformer of rare ability. There is no need to elaborate here on the details of his further reorganization of the administrative machine, the establishment of new offices of state, the additional codification and clarification of the Law; what is more important is the philosophy which lay beneath his whole programme of reform and which tended always to support and strengthen that oligarchic principle that was already the dominant influence in Venetian political thinking. Shortly before his retirement he called a meeting of his chief magistrates, enjoining them *inter alia* to make a point of giving the positions of high-est authority to the wealthiest and most powerful citizens, 'lest, seeing themselves passed over, they grow dissatisfied and are moved to violent action'. This advice was less reactionary than it sounds. Few noble Venetians looked on high office as anything but a responsibility, and often a disagreeable one, severely restrictive of personal liberty and a good deal less profitable than commerce. Civic duties, however, whether to be fulfilled at home or abroad, could not be refused without compelling reasons; from 1185 on, any such refusal actually carried heavy legal penalties.

In a reign that had lasted little more than six years, Sebastiano Ziani had achieved much. But he was already past seventy at the time of his election, and in 1178 he decided to withdraw from public life – retiring, as more than one of his predecessors had done before him, to the mon-astery of S. Giorgio Maggiore. There he died soon afterwards, and was later commemorated, opposite Tribuno Memmo, on the Palladian façade.[1] In his will, he left the rents of certain houses in the Merceria between the Basilica and S. Giuliano to provide food for the prisoners of the state, and other property further along the same street to his monastery, with instructions to supply a dinner every Tuesday for twelve paupers of the city and, for his own family as a lesson in humility, a frugal meal of cheap fish, wine and lentils without oil annually on the feast of St Stephen, before whose tomb a lamp was to be kept perpetually burning.

Shortly before his death, Sebastiano Ziani had made a further change in the existing machinery for the election of a Doge. Instead of the eleven electors nominated directly by the Great Council, it was resolved that the latter should henceforth select only four of its number, and that these should in their turn nominate an electoral team of forty, of whom each should have received at least three votes out of the four and not more than one should come from any single family. The result of this somewhat ungainly procedure – though it was simple enough compared with that of later years – was the election in 1178 of Orio Mastropiero, or Malipiero, an elderly diplomatist who had served on embassies to Palermo and Constantinople and had played a leading part, both as organizer and contributor, in the first state loan of Vitale Michiel. His diplomatic experience, in particular, was to serve him in good stead; for, in the East as in the West, the storm-clouds were gathering again.

On 24 September 1180 the Emperor Manuel Comnenus died after a

1. See p. 48, n.1.

long illness. For the next five years the Byzantine Empire was to be plunged into misery and confusion. Manuel's legitimate heir was his twelve-year-old son Alexius, whose mother, Mary of Antioch, assumed the regency. The first Latin ever to rule in Constantinople – she was the sister of the Norman Prince Bohemund III – Mary openly favoured her Frankish countrymen to the detriment of the Greeks and was consequently detested by her subjects. The first revolt against her failed but the second, in 1182, developed into a full-scale massacre in which virtually all the Westerners in the capital perished, including the women and children and even the sick in the hospitals. The entire Frankish quarter of the city was looted and pillaged in a holocaust compared with which the depredations suffered by the Venetians and Genoese eleven years before must have seemed insignificant indeed. Meanwhile Manuel's cousin Andronicus Comnenus marched on the capital and seized the throne. Mary was strangled, and soon afterwards her young son, who had been compelled to sign his mother's death warrant with his own hand, met his death by the bowstring. He left a fiancée, Agnes – rechristened Anna by the Byzantines – the twelve-year-old daughter of King Louis VII of France. She had arrived in Constantinople some months before, but owing to her extreme youth the wedding had not yet taken place; without further ado Andronicus, now sixty-four, married her and, according to at least one modern authority, consummated the marriage. There followed almost three years of brutality and terror, probably unparalleled in the civilized world until the days of the French Revolution. Then at last, in September 1185, Andronicus was in his turn overthrown and torn to pieces by the mob.

Some time during the previous year, news had reached the Rialto that suggested all too plainly that the brief honeymoon period between Venice and Sicily was nearing its end. King William the Good and his Queen, Joanna of England – the sister of Richard Cœur-de-Lion – were childless and looked like remaining so; next in line to the throne was William's aunt Constance, and she it was whose betrothal was now announced to Henry of Hohenstaufen, son and heir of Frederick Barbarossa. To Venice, as to all her sister-cities of the League, the prospect opened up by such a marriage was appalling. Their success in holding their own for so long against imperial claims was due in large measure to the fact that Frederick had no permanent home in Italy and that by feudal law he could not keep his German forces indefinitely south of the Alps. Henceforth the Emperor would be not merely a titular overlord, but a sovereign ruler in the peninsula.

Little, obviously, could be done while the Byzantine crisis continued; but once Andronicus was out of the way and the docile if ineffectual Isaac II Angelus was installed on the throne of Constantinople the Venetians lost no time. Diplomatic negotiations began in 1186 and a treaty was concluded in the following year. Full compensation was promised for the events of 1171, the Emperor undertaking to defend Venice and all her territories from any attack, whatever its source. In return the Venetians were to provide, on six months' notice, from 40 to 100 galleys, to be equipped in Venetian yards at imperial expense. Three out of every four Venetian residents in Byzantine territory were liable for conscription, to man these vessels under Venetian officers who would however be under the overall command of the imperial admiral. (Since each galley demanded a crew of 140 oarsmen, such figures suggest that some 18,000 Venetian males of military age were still living within the frontiers of the Empire.)

Now Isaac Angelus was a corrupt and feckless ruler – Nicetas Choniates said that he sold government offices like vegetables at a market; but why he decided to entrust his shipbuilding programme to a foreign nation with whom his Empire had been on distinctly hostile terms for the past twenty years – particularly when Constantinople possessed excellent shipyards of its own – is not an easy question to answer. Venice had it both ways. In return for the promise of imperial protection, she was given an effective stranglehold over the entire Byzantine navy. Sixteen years later, when the Empire of the East was to find itself practically defenceless against a Venetian invasion fleet, it would have only itself to blame.

10

The Shameful Glory

[1187–1205]

We can know little (as we care little)
Of the Metropolis: her candled churches,
Her white-gowned pederastic senators,
The cut-throat factions of her Hippodrome,
The eunuchs of her draped saloons . . .

Robert Graves,
The Cuirassiers of the Frontier

The Venetian treaty with Byzantium of 1187 coincided almost exactly
with a major disaster in the East. On 4 July the Saracens under Saladin
shattered the army of Guy of Lusignan, King of Jerusalem, at the battle
of Hattin; and three months later, on 2 October, the Holy City fell. When
the news reached Rome the old Pope, Urban III, died of shock; his
successor, Gregory VIII, lost no time in summoning all Christendom
once again to take the Cross. For Venice, the call came at an opportune
moment. She had recently embarked on one of her periodic campaigns
for the recovery of Zara, which had once more yielded to the blandishments of the King of Hungary; but this time the Hungarian reaction
had been stronger and swifter than expected. The papal injunction for
all Christian powers to unite against the infidel afforded a welcome
chance to withdraw without loss of face.

It was anyway to be expected that the Venetians should respond
enthusiastically to Pope Gregory's appeal. In the general collapse of the
Latin East after Hattin they too had lost much. Tyre, owing to prompt
action by the Sicilian navy and a lucky miscalculation by Saladin, had
remained in Christian hands; but Acre, with its Venetian quarter and
prosperous commercial colony, had surrendered almost at once – together
with Sidon, Beirut and other cities of the coast and hinterland. Doge
Mastropiero accordingly announced a compulsory state loan, the precise
amounts required from leading families being carefully assessed according
to their wealth; and at Easter 1189 the war fleet set sail, carrying an
inchoate and heterogeneous army from all parts of Italy.

In the months that followed, this army was swelled by others – English and French, Danish and Flemish, German and Sicilian. Of the four European sovereigns who had taken the Cross, two died before reaching the Holy Land: young William the Good of Sicily, struck down by illness at thirty-six, and old Frederick Barbarossa, drowned as he was crossing the Calycadnus river in southern Anatolia. But two others were there to lead their subjects into battle: Richard Cœur-de-Lion, already a legend for his courage and chivalry but at heart impetuous, irresponsible and faithless; and Philip Augustus, morose and utterly lacking in charm, but possessed of a wisdom and statesmanship that earned him a place among the best of France's kings while Richard had already proved himself one of England's worst.

The kindest thing that can be said about the Third Crusade is that it was a distinct improvement on the Second. It was better organized and very much better led; it achieved one notable victory when, after a two-year siege, it recaptured Acre; and if the soldiers of the Cross did not always measure up to the superb standards of chivalry set by Saladin – Richard's massacre of nearly 3,000 Saracen prisoners in cold blood after the fall of Acre is a further indelible stain on his reputation – they fought on the whole with courage and occasionally with heroism. Ultimately, however, they failed. Jerusalem remained in Muslim hands. The little Christian Kingdom of Acre might postpone for another century the final dissolution of Outremer; it could do nothing to prevent it.

As for Venice, her part in the Third Crusade – as in the Second – remains something of a mystery. After her impressive beginning, she fades out of the picture. The contemporary chroniclers scarcely give her a mention. Perhaps her contribution was limited to the transport of soldiers and equipment, in which case we may be quietly confident that she received full payment for her services before withdrawing from the fray. The Venetian merchants, certainly, acted smartly enough; they were back in possession of their quarter in Acre within days of the city's surrender. But of that mighty war fleet no more is heard. Doge Mastropiero had answered the papal summons; after that he seems to have felt that nothing more was expected of him. In any case he was not a man for foreign adventures. He preferred to concentrate on improving the judiciary at home, instituting a body of public procurators whose function was to represent the interests of the Republic in all legal proceedings, and establishing special courts for foreigners. It is in his reign, too, that we first hear of the *Quarantia*, or Council of Forty – an executive and judicial body standing half-way between the Great Council and the Doge's inner council, the *Signoria*. Its original purpose seems to have been that of a consultative assembly, like the *pregadi* on a larger scale; subsequently, however, when the latter became a standing commission and thence developed into a permanent Senate, the *Quarantia* became purely judicial.

All these changes were important enough, and Orio Mastropiero's record in the fourteen years of his dogeship is far from negligible. If he still strikes one as being somehow colourless, he is not altogether to blame; for it was his misfortune to fill a gap between the two greatest Doges of the medieval Republic and the two most momentous chapters in its history. Of Sebastiano Ziani and the Peace of Venice the story has already been told; we must now turn to a darker and more shameful triumph: that grim adventure still ludicrously known as the Fourth Crusade, and its architect Enrico Dandolo.

No one knows for certain the age of Enrico Dandolo when, after the death of his predecessor, he was proclaimed Doge of Venice on 1 January 1193. The story goes that he was eighty-five and already stone-blind, but this seems hardly credible when we read of his energy – indeed, his heroism – ten years later, on the walls of Constantinople. More probably, he was in his middle seventies on his accession – which would still make him, at the time of the Fourth Crusade, an octogenarian of several years' standing. A dedicated, almost fanatical patriot, he had spent much of his life in the service of the Republic. We hear of him, for example, in 1171 taking part in Vitale Michiel's Eastern expedition and, in the following year, as one of the Doge's ambassadors on the abortive peace mission to Manuel Comnenus.[1]

Did his loss of sight date from this time? According to his later namesake, the historian Andrea Dandolo, Enrico's arrogance and stubbornness antagonized Manuel to such a point that he actually had him arrested and partially blinded;[2] on the other hand a contemporary and so possibly a more reliable source – an appendix to the Altino Chronicle – reports Doge Ziani as deciding to send his own mission to Constantinople only 'after seeing his predecessor's three ambassadors returned safe and sound'. This passage, combined with what we know of Manuel's character and the absence of any other references to what must have created a major outcry in Venice had it in fact occurred, surely indicates that, although blinding was a regular and recognized punishment in Byzantium, imperial

1. See p. 105.
2. *Cui Henricus Dandulus, pro salute patriae constanter resistens, visu aliqualiter obtenebratus est.*

displeasure cannot be blamed on this occasion. Another theory[1] holds that while in Constantinople Dandolo had been involved in a brawl, in the course of which his eyes had been injured. This too seems on the face of it improbable in view of the Altino testimony; besides, he was not even then in his first youth, but a mature diplomatist of well over forty. Thirty years later, however, the facts are no longer in doubt. Geoffrey de Villehardouin, who knew him well, assures us that 'although his eyes appeared normal, he could not see a hand in front of his face, having lost his sight after a head wound'.[2]

Neither his age nor his blindness, in any case, appears to have had the slightest effect on Dandolo's energies or abilities. Within weeks of his election he had launched a new campaign to recapture Zara; Pisa and Brindisi went to her aid and for several years the Venetians had to fight hard to maintain their power in the Adriatic. The situation was further aggravated when, on Christmas Day 1194, the German Emperor Henry VI assumed the Crown of Sicily in Palermo Cathedral. The Norman-Sicilian Kingdom was effectively at an end.

It was the one eventuality that the Venetians had feared more than any other; and they were not reassured by what they knew of Henry himself. Barbarossa's son possessed all his father's driving determination and strength of will – directing his hatred, however, less against the cities of North Italy than against the Eastern Empire. His aim was, quite simply, to destroy Byzantium, to reunite the old Roman Empire under his own rule, and then to increase it still further by the addition of a great Mediterranean dominion which, after one more decisive Crusade, would include the Holy Land itself. Only a few years before, such a dream might have appeared fantastic, even absurd; but the Comneni were gone, and the family of Angelus who now occupied the throne of Constantinople had proved themselves incapable of effective government. In 1195 the Emperor Isaac II, after ten years of chaos, was dethroned, blinded and imprisoned by his brother Alexius, a weak and unstable megalomaniac, who, though utterly unfitted for responsibility of any kind, had succeeded him under the name of Alexius III.[3] The Holy Land, too, looked ripe for the plucking. Saladin was dead; without his leadership and unifying

1. Runciman, *History of the Crusades*, Vol. III, p. 114.
2. '*Si avoit les iaulç en la teste biaus et si n'en veoit gote, que perdue avoit la veüe par une plaie qu'il ot el chef.*'
3. Nicetas Choniates wrote of him: 'Whatever paper might be presented to the Emperor for his signature, he signed it at once; it was of no concern to him if it contained a meaningless jumble of words, or a request to sail the land or till the sea – or, as the story has it, that Athos should be piled on Olympus.'

influence, the armies of Islam were no longer the formidable adversaries they had been in the past.

In Henry's scheme of things there was obviously no place for an independent maritime republic; and if he had succeeded in his first ambition – as he might well have done – Venice would surely have been one of his victims. Fortunately for the world he did not. In 1197, aged only thirty-two, he died at Messina. A few months later his wife Constance followed him to the grave, leaving their five-year-old son, Frederick, in the care of Pope Innocent III.

With both Empires virtually rudderless and Norman Sicily gone never to return, with Germany embroiled in a civil war over the imperial succession and both England and France similarly – though less violently – occupied with inheritance problems following the death of Cœur-de-Lion in 1199, Pope Innocent found himself without a secular rival in Europe. About Byzantium he had no strong feelings either way; but he too was enthusiastic for a Crusade. The difficulty was to find suitable leaders. The dearth of crowned heads did not worry him; previous experience had shown that kings and princes, by stirring up national rivalries and endless questions of protocol and precedence, were more trouble on such occasions than they were worth. A few great nobles would suit his purpose admirably; and Innocent was still casting round for likely candidates when he received a letter from Count Tibald of Champagne.

One day in September 1197 the effective ruler of Outremer, Henry of Champagne, was reviewing his troops from a window of his palace at Acre when a delegation from the local Pisan colony entered the room behind him. He turned to greet them, and a few moments later thoughtlessly stepped backward. His little dwarf, Scarlet, seized his clothes in an attempt to stop him, but was too late. Together the two crashed to the ground below. Scarlet escaped with a broken leg; Henry was killed.

Two years later his younger brother, Tibald, held a tournament at his castle of Ecri on the Aisne. Because of his youth – he was still only twenty-two – Tibald had not accompanied Henry to the Holy Land; but as the grandson of Louis VII and the nephew of both Philip Augustus and Cœur-de-Lion, he had the Crusades in his blood. He was energetic and ambitious, and possessed of a genuine religious fervour; and when, during the tournament, he and his friends were addressed by the celebrated preacher Fulk of Neuilly who was travelling through France stirring up support for a new expedition to the East, they needed little persuasion. A messenger was sent immediately to Pope Innocent to announce that they had taken the Cross; others hurried off to Tibald's fellow-princes in France, Germany and Flanders to enlist their participation. The response was gratifying; Pope Innocent's prayers had been spectacularly answered.

The principal problem was one of logistics. Richard Cœur-de-Lion, before leaving Palestine, had given it as his opinion that the weakest point of the Muslim East was Egypt, and that it was here that any future expeditions should primarily be directed. This made it clearer than ever that the new army would have to travel by sea, and would need ships in a quantity that could be provided from one source only – the Venetian Republic.

It was in the year 1201, during the first week of Lent, that a party of six knights led by Geoffrey de Villehardouin, Marshal of Champagne, arrived in Venice. At a special meeting of the Great Council they made their request, and eight days later they received their answer. The Republic would provide transport for 4,500 knights with their horses, 9,000 squires and 20,000 foot-soldiers, with food for nine months. The cost would be 84,000 silver marks. In addition Venice would herself provide fifty fully-equipped galleys at her own expense, on condition that she received one half of all the territories conquered.

Fortunately for posterity, Geoffrey has left a full record not only of the Crusade itself but also of these preliminary negotiations. No one was better placed to do so, and few men of his time, one suspects, could have done it better. The Old French in which he writes – in this instance, the *Langue d'Oïl* of the Île de France – is described by a turn-of-the-century English historian as 'one of the most admirable vehicles of expression that the world has seen' and by Gibbon rather more accurately as 'the rude idiom of his age and country'; but his style has clarity and pace, and in his opening pages he gives us an eye-witness account of Venetian demo-cracy – such as it was – in action. Doge Dandolo, it appears, at various times during the deliberations consulted the *Quarantia*, the *pregadi* and the Great Council; but on a matter of such importance an *arengo* was still necessary. 'And so,' writes Geoffrey,

he assembled at least ten thousand men in the church of St Mark, the most beautiful that there is, to hear the Mass and to pray God for His guidance. And after the Mass he summoned the envoys and besought them, that they them-selves should ask of the people the services they required. Geoffrey de Ville-hardouin, Marshal of Champagne, spoke by consent for the others . . . Then the Doge and people raised their hands and cried aloud with a single voice, 'We grant it! We grant it!' And so great was the noise and tumult, that the very earth seemed to tremble underfoot.

On the following day the contracts were concluded. Geoffrey notes in passing that the agreement withheld all mention of Egypt as the immediate objective. He gives no explanation; he and his colleagues were probably afraid – and with good reason, as it turned out – that the news would be unpopular with the rank and file, for whom Jerusalem was the only legitimate goal for a Crusade and who would see no reason to waste time anywhere else. Moreover an Egyptian expedition would necessarily involve a dangerous landing on a hostile coast, as opposed to a quiet anchorage at Christian Acre and an opportunity to recover from the journey before going into battle. The Venetians, for their part, would have been only too happy to cooperate in the deception, for they had another secret of their own: at the very moment that the negotiations were being concluded, their own ambassadors were in Cairo discussing a highly profitable trade agreement with the Sultan's Viceroy, to whom, shortly afterwards, they almost certainly gave a categorical assurance that Venice had no intention of being party to any attack on Egyptian territory.[1]

Such considerations, however, could not be allowed to affect plans for the Crusade, by which still greater prizes might be won; and it was agreed that the Crusaders should all foregather in Venice on St John's Day, 24 June 1202, when the fleet would be ready for them.

Just how Enrico Dandolo proposed to deflect the Franks from their concerted objective we shall never know. He and his agents may have been partly responsible for leaking the true facts about the Crusaders' intentions through the countries of the West; certainly these became public knowledge within a remarkably short time. But if he hoped that the popular reaction to this news would induce the leaders to change their minds he was mistaken. It was the followers who changed theirs. Many, on hearing of their proposed destination, renounced the Crusade altogether; many more decided to make for Palestine regardless, arranging their own transport from Marseilles or the Apulian ports. On the day appointed for the Venetian rendezvous, the army that gathered on the Lido numbered less than one-third of what had been expected.

For those who had arrived as planned the situation was embarrassing in the extreme. Venice had performed her share of the bargain: there lay the fleet, war galleys as well as transports – no Christian man, writes Geoffrey,

1. This allegation cannot be conclusively proved. There is no treaty extant, and though evidence for one is strong there is also a problem of its accurate dating. But most modern historians are convinced; and there would be nothing uncharacteristic in such double-dealing by Venetians at this time. For a more detailed discussion see Hopf, *Geschichte Griechenlands*, I, p. 118, and Hodgson, *Early History of Venice*, pp. 428–34.

had ever seen richer or finer – but sufficient for an army three times the size of that assembled. In their reduced numbers, the Crusaders could not hope to pay the Venetians the money they had promised. When their leader, the Marquis Boniface of Montferrat – Tibald of Champagne having died shortly after his Marshal's return the previous year – arrived in Venice, rather late, he found the whole expedition threatened before it had even set sail. Not only were the Venetians refusing point-blank to allow a single ship to leave port until the money was forthcoming; they were even threatening to cut off provisions to the waiting army, a threat made all the more serious in that the bulk of that army was confined to the Lido, and strictly forbidden to set foot in the city itself. This measure, it should be emphasized, was not intended to be deliberately offensive; it was a normal precaution on such occasions, designed to prevent disturbances of the peace or the spread of infection. But it scarcely improved the atmosphere. Boniface emptied his own coffers, many of the other knights and barons did likewise, and every man in the army was pressed to give all he could; but the total raised, including quantities of gold and silver plate, still fell short by 34,000 marks of what was owing.

For as long as the contributions continued to come in, Dandolo kept the Crusaders in suspense. Then, as soon as he was sure that he had extracted all he could, he came forward with an offer. The city of Zara, he pointed out, had recently fallen into the hands of the King of Hungary. If, before embarking on the Crusade proper, the Franks would agree to assist Venice in its recapture, settlement of their debt could perhaps be postponed. It was a typically cynical proposal, and as soon as he heard of it Pope Innocent sent an urgent message forbidding its acceptance. But the Crusaders, as he later came to understand, had no choice.

There followed another of those ceremonies in the basilica that Enrico Dandolo, despite his years, handled so beautifully. Before a congregation that included all the leading Franks, he addressed his subjects. Geoffrey de Villehardouin, who was there, reports his speech as follows:

'Signors, you are joined with the worthiest people in the world, for the highest enterprise ever undertaken. I myself am old and feeble; I need rest; my body is infirm. But I know that no man can lead you and govern you as I, your Lord, can do. If therefore you will allow me to direct and defend you by taking the Cross, while my son remains in my place to guard the Republic, I am ready to live and die with you and the pilgrims.'

And when they heard him, they cried with one voice, 'We pray God that you will do this thing, and come with us!' . . .

So he came down from the pulpit and moved up to the altar, and knelt there, weeping; and he had the cross sewn on to his great cotton hat, so determined was he that all men should see it.

Thus it came about that on 8 November 1202 the army of the Fourth Crusade set sail from Venice. Its 480 ships, led by the galley of the Doge himself, 'painted vermilion, with a silken vermilion awning spread above, cymbals clashing and four trumpeters sounding from the bows',[1] were, however, bound neither for Egypt nor for Palestine. Just a week later, Zara was taken and sacked. The fighting that broke out almost immediately afterwards between the Franks and Venetians over the division of the spoils scarcely augured well for the future, but peace was eventually restored and the two groups settled themselves in different parts of the city for the winter. Meanwhile the news of what had happened had reached the Pope. Outraged, Innocent at once excommunicated the entire expedition. Though he was later to reconsider, and to restrict his ban to the Venetians only, the Crusade could not be said to have got off to a good start.

Worse, however, was to follow. Early in the new year a messenger arrived with a letter for Boniface from the German King, Philip of Swabia. Now Philip was not only Barbarossa's son, brother to the Emperor Henry VI whose death five years before had left empty the imperial throne of the West; he was also the son-in-law of the deposed Emperor of Byzantium, Isaac Angelus, so that when Isaac's young son, another Alexius, had escaped in 1201 from the prison in which he and his father were being held, Philip's court had been his obvious place of refuge. There he had met Boniface shortly before the latter's departure for Venice, and there it seems likely that the three may have sketched out the plan which Philip now formally proposed in his letter. If the Crusade would escort the young Alexius to Constantinople and enthrone him there in place of his usurper uncle, Alexius in his turn would finance its subsequent conquest of Egypt, supplying in addition 10,000 soldiers of his own and afterwards maintaining 500 knights in the Holy Land at his expense. He would also submit the Church of Constantinople to the authority of Rome.

To Boniface, the scheme had much to recommend it. Apart from what appeared to be the long-term advantages to the Crusade itself and the possibility of paying off the still outstanding debt to Venice, he also saw the possibility of considerable personal gain. And why not? There were, after all, plenty of Crusaders over the past 100 years who had seen no

1. Robert of Clary.

incompatibility in following the Cross and enriching themselves in the process. When he put the idea to Dandolo – to whom, also, it probably came as a less than total surprise – the old Doge accepted it with enthusiasm. He had been in no way chastened by the excommunication; this was not the first time that Venice had defied papal wishes, and it would not be the last. His earlier military and diplomatic experiences had left him with little love for Byzantium; besides, the present Emperor had on his accession made intolerable difficulties over renewing the trading concessions granted by his predecessor. Genoese and Pisan competition was becoming ever more fierce; if Venice were to retain her former hold on the Eastern markets, decisive action would be required. Such action, finally, would involve a welcome postponement of the Egyptian expedition.

The Crusading army proved readier to accept the change of plan than might have been expected. A few refused outright and set off for Palestine on their own; the majority, however, were only too happy to lend themselves to a scheme which promised to strengthen and to enrich the Crusade while also restoring the unity of Christendom. Ever since the great schism, and even before, the Byzantines had been unpopular in the West. They had contributed little or nothing to previous Crusades, during which they were generally believed to have betrayed the Christian cause on several occasions. Young Alexius's offer of active assistance was a welcome change, and not to be despised. Finally, there must have been many among the more materialistically inclined who shared their leader's hope of personal rewards. The average Frank knew practically nothing about Byzantium, but all had been brought up on stories of its immense wealth. And to any medieval army, whether or not it bore the Cross of Christ on its standard, a fabulously rich city meant one thing only – loot.

Young Alexius himself arrived in Zara towards the end of April and a few days later the fleet set sail, stopping at Durazzo and Corfu, in both of which he was acclaimed as the rightful Emperor of the East. On 24 June 1203, a year to the day after the rendezvous in Venice, it dropped anchor off Constantinople. The usurper, Alexius III, had had plenty of warning of its arrival, but had made no serious preparations for his capital's defence; the dockyards had lain idle ever since his idiotic brother had entrusted the whole shipbuilding programme to Venice sixteen years before; and according to Nicetas Choniates – who, as a former imperial secretary, was well placed to know what was going on – he had allowed his principal admiral (who was also his brother-in-law) to sell off the

anchors, sails and rigging of his few remaining vessels, now reduced
to useless hulks and rotting in the inner harbour. His subjects seemed
half-stunned as they gathered on the walls to watch the massive war
fleet as it passed beneath them, beating its way up to the mouth of the
Bosphorus.

But the Crusaders, too, had plenty to stare at. Geoffrey reports:

You may imagine how they gazed, all those who had never before seen
Constantinople. For when they saw those high ramparts and the strong towers
with which it was completely encircled, and the splendid palaces and soaring
churches – so many that but for the evidence of their own eyes they would
never have believed it – and the length and breadth of that city which of all
others is sovereign, they never thought that there could be so rich and powerful
a place in all the world. And mark you that there was not a man so bold that he
did not tremble at the sight; nor was this any wonder, for never since the
creation of the world was there so great an enterprise.

Being in no particular hurry to begin the siege, the invaders first
landed on the Asiatic shore of the straits, near the imperial summer palace
of Chalcedon and the modern Scutari, to replenish their stores. 'The
surrounding land was fair and fertile; sheaves of new-reaped corn stood
in the fields, so that any man might take of it as much as he needed.'
There they easily repulsed a half-hearted attack by a small detachment of
Greek cavalry – it fled at the first charge – and later, with similar lack of
ceremony, dismissed an emissary from the Emperor. If, they told him,
his master were willing to surrender his throne forthwith to his nephew,
they would pray the latter to pardon him and make him a generous
settlement. If not, let him send them no more messengers, but look to
his defence.

Soon after sunrise on the morning of 5 July, they crossed the Bosphorus
and landed below Galata, on the northern side of the Golden Horn.
Being a commercial settlement, largely occupied by foreign trading
communities, Galata was unwalled; its only major fortification was
a single large round tower. This tower, however, was of vital strategic
importance; for in it stood the huge windlass for the raising and lowering of the chain that was used in emergencies to block the entrance
to the Horn.[1] To defend it, a considerable force was drawn up on the
shore, the Emperor himself at its head. Perhaps – though considering
the general demoralization of the Byzantines since the coming of the

1. This original tower no longer stands, having been demolished in 1261. The present
Galata Tower is a fourteenth-century replacement.

Angeli, it is far from certain – they might have done better under different leadership; everyone knew how Alexius had seized the throne, and his character was not one to inspire either love or loyalty. The sight of well over 100 ships, disembarking men, horses and equipment with such speed and precision – for the Venetians were nothing if not efficient – filled them with terror, and scarcely had the first wave of Crusaders lowered their lances for the attack than they turned and fled, the Emperor once again in the lead.

Within the Galata Tower itself, the garrison fought more bravely, holding out for twenty-four hours; but by the following morning it had to surrender. The Venetian sailors unshackled the windlass, and the great iron chain that had stretched over 500 yards across the mouth of the Golden Horn subsided thunderously into the water. The fleet swept in, destroying such few seaworthy Byzantine vessels as it found in the inner harbour. The naval victory was complete.

Constantinople, however, did not give in. Its northern ramparts – those that ran along the shore of the Golden Horn – could not compare in strength or splendour with the tremendous walls on the landward side, erected by the Emperor Theodosius II in the fifth century; but they could still be staunchly defended. Gradually the Greeks began to regain the courage and determination that had heretofore been so conspicuously lacking. In all the 900 years of its existence, their city had not once fallen to a foreign invader. Perhaps, until now, they had never really thought it could. Awake at last to the full extent of the danger that threatened them, they prepared to resist.

The assault, when it came, was directed against the weakest point in the Byzantine defences: the sea frontage of the imperial palace of Blachernae, which occupied the angle formed by the Theodosian land walls and those following the line of the Horn, at the extreme north-west corner of the city. It was launched on the morning of Thursday 17 July, simultaneously from land and sea, with the Venetian ships riding low in the water under the weight of their siege machinery – catapults and mangonels on the forecastles, covered gangplanks and scaling-ladders suspended by rope tackles between the yard-arms. The Frankish army, attacking from land, was initially beaten back by the axe-swinging Englishmen and Danes who for nearly three centuries had formed the Emperor's famous Varangian Guard; it was the Venetians and, to a considerable degree, Enrico Dandolo in person, who decided the day.

The story of the old Doge's courage is told not just by some biased latter-day panegyrist of the Republic, but by Geoffrey de Villehardouin himself. He reports that although the Venetian assault-craft had approached so close inshore that those manning the ladders in the bows were fighting hand-to-hand with the defenders, the Venetian sailors were reluctant to beach the vessels and effect a proper landing.

And here was an extraordinary feat of boldness. For the Duke of Venice, who was an old man and stone blind, stood fully armed on the prow of his galley, with the banner of St Mark before him, and cried out to his men to drive the ship ashore if they valued their skins. And so they did, and ran the galley ashore, and he and they leapt down and planted the banner before him in the ground. And when the other Venetians saw the standard of St Mark and the Doge's galley beached before their own, they were ashamed, and followed him ashore.

As the attack gathered momentum, it soon became clear to the defenders that they had no chance. Before many hours had passed, Dandolo was able to send word to his Frankish allies that no less than twenty-five towers along the wall were already in Venetian hands. By this time his men were pouring into the city itself through breaches in the rampart, setting fire to the wooden houses until the whole Blachernae quarter was ablaze. That evening Alexius III, Emperor of Constantinople, fled secretly from his city, leaving his wife and all his children except a favourite daughter – whom he took with him, together with a few other women, 10,000 pounds of gold and a bag of jewels – to face the future as best they might.

Byzantium, at this gravest crisis in its history, was thus left without an Emperor; and it may seem surprising that, to fill the breach, a hastily convened council of state should have fetched old Isaac Angelus out of his prison and replaced him on the imperial throne. He was even blinder than Dandolo – his brother had taken the precaution of having his eyes put out when deposing him – and he had also proved himself a hopelessly incompetent ruler. He was, however, the legitimate Emperor; and by restoring him the Byzantines doubtless believed that they had removed all grounds for further intervention by the Crusaders. So, in a way, they had; but there remained the question of the promises made by young Alexius to Boniface and Dandolo. These Isaac was now obliged to ratify, agreeing at the same time to make his son co-Emperor with him. Only then did the Franks and Venetians accord him their formal recognition, after which they withdrew to the Galata side of the Golden Horn to await their expected rewards.

On 1 August 1203, Alexius IV was crowned alongside his father and assumed effective power. Immediately he began to regret the offers he had made so rashly at Zara in the spring. The imperial treasury, after his uncle's extravagances, was empty; the new taxes he was forced to introduce were openly resented by his subjects, who knew all too well where their money was going. Meanwhile the clergy – always an important political force in Constantinople – were scandalized when he began to seize and melt down their church plate and furious when they heard of his plans to subordinate them to the Pope of Rome. As autumn gave way to winter his unpopularity steadily grew, and the continued presence of the hated Franks, whose greed appeared insatiable, still further increased the tension. One night a group of them wandering through the city came upon a little mosque which stood in the Saracen quarter, behind the church of St Irene, pillaged it and burnt it to the ground. The flames spread, and for the next forty-eight hours Constantinople was engulfed in the worst fire in its history.

Alexius had been away on a brief and unsuccessful expedition against his fugitive uncle. He returned to find much of his capital in ruins and his subjects in a state of almost open warfare against the foreigners. The situation had clearly reached breaking-point; but when, a few days later, a delegation of three Crusaders and three Venetians came to demand immediate payment of the sum owing to them, there was nothing he could do. According to Villehardouin – who was, as usual, one of the delegates – the party narrowly escaped a lynching on its way to and from the imperial palace. 'And thus,' he writes, 'the war began; and each side did to the other as much harm as it could, both by sea and by land.'

Ironically enough, neither the Crusaders nor the Greeks wanted such a war. The inhabitants of Constantinople had by now one object only in mind: to be rid, once and for all, of these uncivilized thugs who were destroying their beloved city and bleeding them white into the bargain. The Franks, for their part, had not forgotten the reason they had left their homes, and increasingly resented their enforced stay among what they considered an effete and effeminate people when they should have been getting to grips with the infidel. Even if the Greek debt were to be paid in full, they themselves would not benefit materially; it would only enable them to settle their own outstanding account with the Venetians.

The key to the whole impossible affair lay, in short, with Venice – or, more accurately, with Enrico Dandolo. It was open to him at any moment to give his fleet the order to sail. Had he done so, the Crusaders would have been relieved and the Byzantines overjoyed. Formerly, his refusal had always been on the grounds that the Franks would never be able to pay him their debt until they in their turn received the money that Alexius and his father had promised them. In fact, however, that debt was now of relatively little interest to him – scarcely more than was the Crusade itself. His mind was on greater things: the overthrow of the Byzantine Empire and the establishment of a Venetian puppet on the throne of Constantinople.

And so, as prospects of a peaceful settlement receded, Dandolo's advice to his Frankish allies took on a different tone. Nothing more, he pointed out, could be expected of Isaac and Alexius, who had not scrupled to betray the friends to whom they owed their joint crown. If the Crusaders were ever to obtain their due, they would have to take it by force. Their moral justification was complete: the faithless Angeli had no further claim on their loyalties. Once inside the city, with one of their own leaders installed as Emperor, they could pay Venice what they owed her almost without noticing it and still have more than enough to finance the Crusade. This was their opportunity; they should seize it now, for it would not recur.

Within Constantinople too, it was generally agreed that Alexius IV must go; and on 25 January 1204 a great concourse of senators, clergy and people gathered in St Sophia to declare him deposed and elect a successor. During their deliberations – which dragged on inconclusively for three days before fixing on a reluctant nonentity named Nicholas Canabus – the only really effective figure at that moment on the Byzantine stage took the law into his own hands.

Alexius Ducas – nicknamed Murzuphlus on account of his eyebrows, which were black and shaggy and met in the middle – was a nobleman whose family had already produced two Emperors of its own and who now occupied the position of *protovestarius*, which gave him unrestricted access to the imperial apartments. Late at night he burst into where Alexius was sleeping, woke him with the news that his subjects had risen against him and offered him what he claimed was the only chance of escape. Muffling the Emperor in a long cloak, he led him by a side door out of the palace to where a band of fellow-conspirators was waiting. The unhappy youth was then clapped into irons and consigned to a dungeon where, having survived two attempts to poison him, he eventually succumbed to the bowstring. At about the same time his blind father also died; Villehardouin, with that impregnable naivety that characterizes his whole chronicle, attributes his demise to a sudden sickness, brought on at the news of Alexius's fate; it does not seem to have struck him that so convenient a malady might have been artificially induced.[1]

His rivals once eliminated – and Nicholas Canabus having retired with relief into obscurity – Murzuphlus was crowned in St Sophia as Alexius V. Once in control, he immediately began to show those qualities of leadership that his Empire had lacked for so long. For the first time since the Crusaders' arrival, the walls and towers were properly manned, while workmen sweated day and night strengthening them and raising them higher. To the Franks, one thing was plain: there was to be no more negotiation, far less any question of further payments on a debt for which the new Emperor in any case bore no responsibility. An all-out attempt on the city was their only chance; and now that Murzuphlus had revealed himself in his turn as a usurper – and a murderer to boot – they were morally in an even stronger position than if they had moved against Alexius, a legitimate Emperor and their erstwhile ally.

It was exactly what Enrico Dandolo had been saying for months; and from the moment of Murzuphlus's *coup* the old Doge seems to have been recognized, by Venetians and Franks alike, as the leader of the entire expedition. Boniface of Montferrat strove to maintain his influence; with the imperial crown almost within his grasp, it was more than ever vital to him that he should. But his association with the deposed Emperor had been too close, and now that Alexius IV was gone he found himself in some degree discredited. Besides, he had links with the Genoese – and Dandolo knew it.

Early in March there began a series of council meetings in the camp at Galata. They were concerned less with the plan of attack – despite Murzuphlus's work on the defences, its success was apparently considered a foregone conclusion – than with the future administration of the Empire after its conquest. It was agreed that the Crusaders and the Venetians should each appoint six delegates to an electoral committee, and that this should choose the new Emperor. If, as was expected, they decided on a Frank, then the Patriarch should be a Venetian; otherwise vice-versa. The Emperor would receive a quarter of the city and of the Empire, including the two chief palaces – Blachernae on the Golden Horn and the old Boucoleon palace on the Marmara. The remaining three-quarters should be divided equally, half to Venice and half in fief to the Crusading knights. For the Venetian portion, the Doge was specifically

---

1. A fellow Crusader, Robert of Clary, probably came closer to the truth when he wrote '*Si li fist lachier une corde u col, si le fist estranler et sen pere Kyrsaac ausi.*'

absolved from the need to do the Emperor homage. All plunder taken was to be brought to an agreed spot and distributed in similar proportions. Finally, the parties were to undertake not to leave Constantinople for a full year – until March 1205 at the earliest.

The attack began on Friday morning, 9 April. It was to be directed against that same stretch of sea wall facing the Golden Horn where Dandolo and his men had distinguished themselves nine months before. This time, however, it failed. The new, higher walls and towers, no longer accessible from the Venetian mastheads, provided useful platforms from which the Greek catapults could create havoc among the besiegers below. By mid-afternoon the attackers had begun to re-embark their men, horses and equipment and beat their way back to Galata and safety. The next two days were spent in repairing the damage; then, on Monday, the assault was renewed. This time the Venetians lashed their ships together in pairs, thus contriving to throw twice as much weight as before against each tower; soon, too, a strong north wind blew up, driving the vessels far further up the beach below the walls than the oarsmen could ever have done, and allowing the besiegers to work under cover of makeshift shelters stretched from one mast to another. Before long, two of the towers were overwhelmed and occupied. Almost simultaneously, the Crusaders broke open one of the gates in the wall and surged into the city.

Murzuphlus, who had been commanding the defenders with courage and determination, galloped through the streets doing his utmost to rally his men. 'But', writes Nicetas,

they were all swept up in the whirlpool of despair, and had no ears either for his orders or his remonstrances . . . Seeing that his efforts were vain, and fearing to be served up to the Franks as a choice morsel for their table, he took flight, accompanied by Euphrosyne, wife of the Emperor Alexius [III] and her daughter Eudoxia, whom he passionately adored; for he was a great lover of women and had already repudiated two wives in a manner not canonical.

The three sought refuge with the ex-Emperor in Thrace. Meanwhile Murzuphlus duly married Eudoxia and began to gather strength for a counter-offensive.

Once the walls were breached, the carnage was dreadful – so dreadful that even Villehardouin was appalled. Only at nightfall, 'tired of battle and massacre', did the conquerors call a truce and withdraw to camp in one of the great squares of the city. 'That night, a party of the Crusaders, fearing a counter-attack, set fire to the district which lay between themselves and the Greeks . . . and the city began to blaze fiercely, and it burned all that night and all the next day until evening. It was the third fire at Constantinople since the Franks arrived. And there were more houses burnt than there are to be found in the three greatest cities of the Kingdom of France.' After this, such few defenders as had not yet laid down their arms lost the spirit to continue. The next morning the Crusaders awoke to find all resistance at an end.

But for the inhabitants of Constantinople the tragedy had scarcely begun. Not for nothing had the army waited so long outside the world's richest city. Now that it was theirs and that the customary three days' looting was allowed them, they fell on it like locusts. Not since the barbarian invasions some seven centuries before had Europe witnessed such an orgy of brutality and vandalism; never in history had so much beauty, so much superb craftsmanship, been wantonly destroyed in so short a space of time. Among the witnesses – helpless, horrified, almost unable to believe that human beings who called themselves Christians could be capable of such enormities – was Nicetas Choniates:

I know not how to put any order into my account, how to begin, continue, or end. They smashed the holy images, hurled sacred relics of the Martyrs into places I am ashamed to mention, scattering everywhere the body and blood of the Saviour. These heralds of Anti-Christ seized the chalices and the patens, tore out the jewels and used them as drinking cups . . . As for their profanation of the Great Church [St Sophia], it cannot be thought of without horror. They destroyed the high altar, a work of art admired by the entire world, and shared out the pieces among themselves . . . And they brought horses and mules into the Church, the better to carry off the holy vessels and the engraved silver and gold that they had torn from the throne, and the pulpit, and the doors, and the furniture wherever it was to be found: and when some of these beasts slipped and fell, they ran them through with their swords, fouling the Church with their blood and ordure.

A common harlot was enthroned in the Patriarch's chair, to hurl insults at Jesus Christ; and she sang bawdy songs, and danced immodestly in the holy place . . . nor was there mercy shown to virtuous matrons, innocent maids or even virgins consecrated to God . . . In the streets, houses and churches there could be heard only cries and lamentations.

And these men, he continues, carried the Cross on their shoulders, the Cross on which they had sworn to pass through Christian lands without bloodshed, to take arms only against the heathen, and to abstain from the pleasures of the flesh until their holy task was done.

It was Constantinople's darkest hour – perhaps even darker than that, two and a half centuries later, which saw the city's final fall to the Ottoman Sultan. But not all its treasures perished. While the Frenchmen and Flemings abandoned themselves in a frenzy of wholesale destruction, the Venetians kept their heads. They knew beauty when they saw it. They too looted and pillaged and plundered – but they did not destroy. Instead, all that they could lay their hands on they sent back to Venice – beginning with the four great bronze horses which had dominated the Hippodrome since the days of Constantine and which, after a short period in the Arsenal, now stand above the main door of the Basilica of St Mark. The north and south faces of the Basilica are also studded with sculptures and reliefs shipped back at the same time; within, in the north transept, hangs the miraculous icon of the Virgin Nicopoeia – Bringer of Victory – which the Emperors used to carry before them into battle; while the Treasury possesses one of the greatest collections of Byzantine works of art to be found anywhere – a further monument to Venetian rapacity.

After three days of terror, order was restored. As previously arranged, all the spoils – or that part that had not been successfully concealed – were gathered together in three churches, and careful distribution made, a quarter for the Emperor when checked, the remainder to be split equally between Franks and Venetians. As soon as it was done, the Crusaders paid over to Dandolo the 50,000 silver marks they owed. These formalities satisfactorily concluded, both parties applied themselves to the next task, the imperial election.

Boniface of Montferrat, in a desperate attempt to recover his lost prestige and strengthen his own candidacy, had tracked down the Empress Margaret, widow of Isaac Angelus, and married her. He need not have bothered. Enrico Dandolo refused outright to consider him and the choice ultimately fell, thanks to fearsome Venetian pressure, on the easy-going and tractable Count Baldwin of Flanders and Hainault. On 16 May Baldwin received his coronation in St Sophia – the third Emperor to be crowned there in less than a year. And although the newly-appointed Patriarch, the Venetian Tommaso Morosini,[1] had not yet arrived in Constantinople and could not consequently officiate at the ceremony, there can have been few among those present who would have denied that the new Emperor owed his elevation to the Venetian Republic.

---

1. 'Fat as a stuffed pig,' snorted Nicetas later, 'and wearing a robe so tight that it seemed to have been sewn on to his skin.' Though already a monk, Morosini had not taken orders at the time he was selected for the Patriarchate. He was ordained deacon at once, priest a fortnight later, and Bishop the following morning.

In return, Venice had appropriated the best part of the imperial territory for her own. By the terms of her treaty with the Crusaders, she was entitled to three-eighths of the city and the Empire, plus free trade throughout the imperial dominions, from which both Genoa and Pisa were to be rigorously excluded. In Constantinople itself, Dandolo demanded the whole district surrounding St Sophia and the Patriarchate, reaching right down to the shore of the Golden Horn; for the rest, he took for Venice those areas that would reinforce her mastery of the Mediterranean and give her an unbroken chain of ports along the route from the lagoon to the Black Sea – including the western coast of the Greek mainland, the Ionian Islands, all the Peloponnese, Euboea, Naxos and Andros, Gallipoli, the Thracian seaboard, the inland city of Adrianople and finally, after a brief negotiation with Boniface, the all-important island of Crete.

Thus it emerges beyond all doubt that it was the Venetians, rather than the French or Flemings – or even Baldwin himself, who remained little more than a figurehead – who were the real victors of the Fourth Crusade; and that their victory was due, almost entirely, to Enrico Dandolo. From the very first – from that day four years before when the Frankish emissaries had arrived on the Rialto to ask the Republic's help in their holy enterprise – he had turned every development to Venetian advantage. He had regained Zara; he had protected Egypt from attack and so preserved Venice's commercial interests with the Muslim world; he had subtly redirected the Frankish forces towards Constantinople, while leaving the ostensible responsibility for the decision with them. Once there, his courage had largely inspired the first attack; his capacity for intrigue had brought down the Angeli, making essential a second siege and the physical capture of the city; his diplomatic skill had shaped a treaty which gave Venice more than she had dared to hope and laid the foundations for her commercial Empire. Refusing the Byzantine crown for himself – to accept it would have created insuperable constitutional problems at home and might well have destroyed the Republic – and declining even to serve on the electoral commission, he nevertheless knew that his influence over the election (which was held under his auspices, in the old imperial palace that he had temporarily appropriated for himself) would be tantamount to giving Venice a majority and would ensure the success of his own candidate. Finally, while encouraging the Franks to feudalize the Empire – a step which could not fail to create fragmentation and disunity and would prevent its ever becoming strong enough to obstruct Venetian expansion – he had kept Venice herself outside the feudal framework, holding her new dominions not as an imperial fief but by her own right of conquest. For a blind man not far short of ninety it was a remarkable achievement.

Yet even now old Dandolo did not rest. Outside the capital, the Greek subjects of the Empire continued their resistance. Murzuphlus was to cause no further trouble; soon after his marriage he was blinded by his jealous father-in-law, and when a year or two later he was captured by the Franks they brought him back to Constantinople and flung him to his death from a tall column in the centre of the city. But another of Alexius III's sons-in-law set up an Empire in exile at Nicaea, two of the Comneni did the same at Trebizond and, in Epirus, a bastard Angelus proclaimed himself an autonomous Despot. On all sides the erstwhile Crusaders had to fight hard to establish themselves, nowhere more fiercely than in Venice's newly acquired city of Adrianople where, just after Easter, 1205, the Emperor Baldwin fell into the hands of the Bulgars and the old Doge, who had fought determinedly at his side, was left to lead a shattered army back to Constantinople. He is not known to have been wounded; but six weeks later he was dead. His body, rather surprisingly, was not returned to Venice, but was buried in St Sophia – where, in the gallery above the south aisle, his grave may still be seen.

Enrico Dandolo had deserved well of his city; it is a source of still greater surprise that the Venetians never erected a monument to the greatest of all their Doges.[1] But in the wider context of world events, he was a disaster. Though it cannot be said of him that he gave the Crusades a bad name, that is only because the record of those successive forays over the previous century had already emerged as one of the blackest chapters in the history of Christendom. Yet the Fourth Crusade – if indeed it can be so described at all – surpassed even its predecessors in faithlessness and duplicity, brutality and greed. Constantinople, in the twelfth century, had been not just the greatest and wealthiest metropolis of the world, but also the most cultivated both intellectually and artistically and the chief repository of Europe's classical heritage, both Greek and Roman. By its sack, Western civilization suffered a loss greater even than the sack of Rome by the barbarians in the fifth century or the burning of the library of Alexandria by the soldiers of the Prophet in the seventh – perhaps the most catastrophic single loss in all its history.

Politically, too, the damage done was incalculable. Although the Latin rule along the Bosphorus lasted less than sixty years, after which the

---

1. They did, however, commemorate the main episodes of the Fourth Crusade with another of those cycles of paintings in the Doges' Palace, this one running along the south wall of the Sala del Maggior Consiglio.

Greek Empire was to struggle on for nearly two more centuries, that Empire never recovered its strength or any considerable part of its lost dominion. Under firm and forceful leadership – which was not lacking in the century to come – a strong and prosperous Byzantium might have halted the Turkish advance while there was still time. Instead, it was left economically crippled, territorially truncated, powerless to defend itself against the Ottoman tide. There are few greater ironies in history than the fact that the fate of Eastern Christendom should have been sealed – and half Europe condemned to some five hundred years of Muslim rule – by men who fought under the banner of the Cross. Those men were transported, inspired, encouraged and ultimately led by Enrico Dandolo in the name of the Venetian Republic; and, just as Venice derived the major advantage from the tragedy, so she and her magnificent old Doge must accept the major responsibility for the havoc they wrought upon the world.

PART TWO

The Imperial Expansion

Once did she hold the gorgeous East in fee,
And was the safeguard of the West . . .

WORDSWORTH
Ode on the Extinction of
the Venetian Republic

The Latin Empire

[1205–1268]

> . . . her daughters had their dowers
> From spoils of nations, and the exhaustless East
> Pour'd in her lap all gems in sparkling showers:
> In purple was she robed, and of her feast
> Monarchs partook, and deem'd their dignity increased.

Byron, *Childe Harold's Pilgrimage*, IV, ii

When, on 5 August 1205, Sebastiano Ziani's son Pietro was unanimously elected Doge of Venice, the first question that confronted him was one of identity. To the long list of sonorous but mostly empty titles which had gradually become attached to the ducal throne, there had now been added a new one which meant exactly what it said: *Lord of a Quarter and Half a Quarter of the Roman Empire*. Was it any longer possible for a Doge to consider himself – as, in essence, his predecessors had always considered themselves – an Italian prince? Or must he now change his role to that of oriental despot?

It was Venice's good fortune that at this crucial turning-point in her history there emerged to direct her affairs not an ambitious adventurer but a thoughtful, clear-headed man with both feet firmly on the ground. The Zianis were enormously rich – it was popularly rumoured that their wealth was based on a golden cow, discovered by a remote ancestor in his cellar at Altino – and deeply respected in the city, where Pietro was well known for his piety and generosity. In his youth he had been a sailor, and in 1177 he had commanded the flotilla that escorted Frederick Barbarossa from Ravenna to Chioggia. He had also accompanied the Fourth Crusade to Zara and Constantinople; but he does not seem to have stayed very long, since at the time of his election he was already serving as one of the six counsellors to Renier Dandolo, Vice-Doge since his father's departure. Perhaps the bloodshed had sickened him; the Altino Chronicle – a surprisingly reliable source for this particular period – approvingly quotes one of his favourite *dicta*: 'War we can always have if we want it; peace we should zealously seek, and keep when found.'

But for a republic that suddenly and half-unexpectedly acquires a widespread overseas empire at a single swoop, peace tends to prove an elusive amenity. Long before old Dandolo's death it had become clear that the conquered subjects of Byzantium had no intention of accepting the new dispensations without a struggle. Venice might be rich and powerful, but her native-born population was small – nowhere near sufficient to pacify, administer and defend the entire portion that had been allotted to her. She could not look to Constantinople for help; Henry of Flanders, who had succeeded his brother Baldwin as Emperor, was already hard pressed to keep his own dominions in order. Under Ziani's wise guidance, the Venetians therefore made no attempt to take over all their new territories at once. Most of these were entrusted to vassals, usually the younger sons of leading Venetian families who were only too happy to set themselves up as petty princelings in Thrace, Asia Minor and the Aegean archipelago. Only a few of the most strategically important bases – Crete, Durazzo, Corfu and the two ports of Modone and Corone in the Morea – remained under the direct authority of the Republic.

Even these few key outposts were hard enough to control – especially since Venice's recent successes had aroused the furious jealousy of her two principal maritime rivals, Genoa and Pisa. Though both had possessed trading communities in Constantinople, representatives of which had manned the walls of the city alongside the Greeks during the Fourth Crusade, both had been debarred from imperial commerce after the fall of the city[1] and both were determined to prevent Venice from further consolidating her hold on the eastern Mediterranean. In 1206 the self-styled Count of Malta – in reality a Genoese freebooter named Enrico Pescatore – made an armed landing in Crete and, assisted by the local Greek population, captured several strongpoints along the coast. It took two years and two expeditions by the Venetians to dislodge him. To ensure that such a misfortune should not occur again, a certain Giacomo Tiepolo was appointed to Crete with the title of Doge and powers analogous to those of his counterpart in Venice, except that he and his successors were to hold office for two years instead of for life. A sixth of the island was allotted to each of the six *sestieri* of the city; and thus there was founded, in the following year, the Republic's first properly consti-

1. Pisa was in fact readmitted, on sufferance, in 1206; but all Genoese shipping was forbidden until 1218, when Greek and Bulgar pressure on the city called for an end to Venetian–Genoese hostilities.

tuted overseas colony. Even now the native Greeks remained unsubdued. Their lands had been confiscated to make fiefs for their Venetian over-lords, and they bitterly resented the flood of rapacious Latin churchmen who, not content with taking over all ecclesiastical property, even sought to impose the hated Roman rite in place of the traditional Orthodox liturgy. Throughout the century they were to keep up their resistance – as well they might.

But the difficulties in Crete, Corfu and elsewhere were less worrying to Ziani in the long term than those in Constantinople itself. When the city fell to the Crusaders, one of the first tasks of Enrico Dandolo had been to provide for the effective administration of the Venetian districts by the appointment of a governor, the *podestà*; and immediately on his death his compatriots in the city elected one of their number, Marino Zeno, to this office. In Venice, however, where it had always been understood that the *podestà* would be an appointee of the central government, the news of the election was received with some concern, and this was increased by subsequent reports that Zeno had adopted as his own the Doge's new style of 'Lord of a Quarter and Half a Quarter of the Roman Empire', and had even taken to wearing the parti-coloured stockings and scarlet buskins – formerly the prerogative of the Emperor – that Dandolo had worn before him. Could it be that success had already gone to the heads of the Venetians in the Levant, and that they were planning a break-away from the mother-city? A chilly message was dispatched to Zeno: excep-tionally on this occasion, his election would be ratified; but in future every new *podestà* would be sent out from Venice.

According to a long-established Venetian tradition, Doge Ziani at one moment seriously considered the possibility of transferring the capital of the Republic to Constantinople, just as Constantine the Great had done with the Roman Empire nine centuries before. The proposal is said to have been formally discussed in council, its adherents arguing that the focus of Venetian interests had now shifted eastward, that Venice was too far distant from her overseas possessions and that the city was notoriously liable to earthquake and flood;[1] and to have been finally rejected by a single vote, the so-called *Voto della Provvidenza*. But this story is reported only by one or two less reliable chroniclers – the most trustworthy sources for the period do not mention it at all – and although it may well be that some such idea was momentarily put forward, it seems unlikely that it was

1. This last point would have received added force from the memorable earthquake of Christmas Day 1223, which destroyed part of the monastery of S. Giorgio Maggiore and caused the total disappearance of Ammiana and Costanziaca, two small islands in the lagoon.

seriously upheld for very long, still less that it came anywhere near acceptance. One thing only is certain: Venice, by moving her capital to the shores of the Bosphorus, would have sacrificed her security as well as her identity, and would have survived little longer – perhaps even less long – than the pathetic Latin Empire which she did so much to establish. If, despite the probabilities, the 'Providence Vote' were to prove a historical fact, Venetians of all succeeding generations would have had good cause to congratulate themselves on a lucky escape.

By the time Pietro Ziani – now old and sick – resigned early in 1229, to be laid to rest a few weeks later beside his father in S. Giorgio Maggiore, Venice had recovered her political bearings and was back on course. The crucial question had been decided, and the decision was the right one: she would continue as before. She would exploit her new dominions as fully as possible, both politically and commercially, but she would not risk the advantages she already enjoyed by biting off more than she could chew.

Few Venetians can have been more thoroughly convinced of the wisdom of this policy than the new Doge, Giacomo Tiepolo; none, certainly, had better reason to mistrust the promise of Empire. As first Duke of Crete he had had his full share of trouble with the rebellious Greek population – to say nothing of some Venetian adventurers whom he had been ill-advised enough to call to his aid – and had eventually been forced to escape from the island in woman's clothes. His next post had been that of Venetian *podestà* in Constantinople, where he soon saw how rapidly the Crusader Empire was crumbling; in 1219 he had gone so far as to conclude a separate commercial treaty with the Greek Emperor-in-exile at Nicaea, addressing him as 'Emperor of the Romans' – a step which, though it can hardly have endeared him to the Latins, showed a clear political realization of where Venetian interests lay.

His dogeship itself cannot be said to have begun auspiciously. Unlike his predecessor, whose election had been unanimous, he and a rival candidate each polled twenty votes from the forty-strong electoral commission, and the issue had to be decided by lot. It was perhaps to mark his disapproval of the element of chance thus introduced – a sentiment that seems to have been widely shared, since to prevent a recurrence the number of the commissioners was thenceforth increased to forty-one – that old Ziani, lying on his deathbed, refused to receive the new Doge's courtesy call;[1] perhaps, too, it was a sign of general unease that the

1. Andrea Dandolo, who reports the incident, suggests as an additional reason that he

promissione which Tiepolo was obliged to sign on taking office was considerably more detailed, and more restrictive of the ducal power, than that of any Doge before him.

This *promissione*, in effect a sort of coronation oath, had long been a traditional feature of a Doge's accession. In early days it had been a mere formality, usually drafted by the new Doge in person, in which he simply promised to do his duty with impartiality and diligence. Gradually, however, the *promissioni* had become longer and more precise; and that which was now presented to Giacomo Tiepolo – and used as a model for a whole stream of his successors – reads almost like a legal contract. In it the Doge swears to renounce all claims on the revenue of the state – the only exception being his salary (payable quarterly), his share of the tribute from certain Istrian and Dalmatian towns, and certain specified quantities of apples, cherries and crabs from Lombardy and Treviso. He undertakes to contribute to public loans, to respect state secrets, and to enter into no communication with Pope, Emperor, or any other prince without prior permission of his Council, to whom all incoming letters from such potentates must immediately be shown. Firm measures are built in against corruption: the Doge may accept no presents except stipulated quantities of food and wine – not more than one animal or ten brace of birds at a time – and even those are forbidden if the donors have favours to ask; suppliants may offer him only such token gifts as rose-water, leaves, flowers, scented herbs or balsam. Nor is he to make any appointments of associates or successors to the dogeship.

In retrospect, the *promissione* of Giacomo Tiepolo emerges as another significant step in the long process by which the Doge of Venice was slowly reduced over the centuries from autocrat to figurehead. That process had begun at least as early as the days of Domenico Flabanico in the eleventh century, and had continued with the reforms following the assassination of Vitale Michiel. And it was not yet finished. Tiepolo himself was to institute further controls, including a board of five so-called Correctors, charged with the task of drafting each new *promissione* and helped by a trio of Inquisitors who, after careful examination of the late Doge's record, would inform the Correctors of any signs of autocratic or other undesirable tendencies; the latter would then adjust the new *promissione* accordingly. Venice, as usual, was taking no chances.

---

was of doubtful origins – *propter genus suum*. This seems odd, in view of the fact that the name of Tiepolo was one of the oldest in Venice, already known in the seventh century, and furthermore that the two Doges' wives were sisters, both daughters of Tancred of Lecce, the illegitimate and ill-starred King of Sicily.

However cynical Giacomo Tiepolo may have felt about Venice's overseas Empire, he soon found himself faced with far greater problems nearer home. They were caused by the new Emperor of the West, Henry VI's son, Frederick II of Hohenstaufen. This extraordinary figure – perhaps the most remarkable European ruler between Charlemagne and Napoleon – had received his imperial coronation in Rome in 1220. It was, perhaps, the last favour he would ever receive from a Pope; the remaining thirty years of his life were to be taken up with an unremitting struggle against the Papacy and the Italian cities of the reconstituted Lombard League, over which, like his father and grandfather before him, he was determined to re-establish control. Of this new association, founded as recently as 1198, Venice was not a member. Her neutrality, so triumphantly demonstrated by Barbarossa's submission to Pope Alexander twenty-one years before, had stood her in good stead and had been consolidated by the long imperial interregnum following Henry VI's death as well as by her own recent preoccupation with affairs in the East. Now that the storm was blowing up again she was resolved to remain, as far as possible, aloof.

It was in an effort to dispel this aloofness and to win the Republic over to his own side that Frederick visited Venice early in 1233. One would love to know more of his reactions to what he saw. From his maternal grandfather, Roger II of Sicily, and his childhood in cosmopolitan Palermo he had acquired an intellectual curiosity and a familiarity with five European languages and cultures – to say nothing of the Arabic with which he had personally beguiled the Emir of Jerusalem into restoring all the principal shrines to Christian hands – that had made him one of the most civilized men of his age and had already earned him the title of *Stupor Mundi*, Wonder of the World. In Venice, which had now taken the place of Palermo as Europe's foremost bridge, artistic and cultural as well as commercial, between East and West, he must have found much of that same multi-racial, polyglot atmosphere that had done so much to shape his life; while his love of magnificence and display – the exotic menagerie with which he habitually travelled was a source of perpetual amazement to his subjects – would have responded in full measure to the most splendid and most beautiful city he had ever seen.

It is perhaps rather more open to question whether the intellectual accomplishments of Giacomo Tiepolo and those other Venetian notables with whom he came in contact during his short stay proved equally stimulating to the ruler in whose court the sonnet was invented and who could hold his own with the foremost scientists and philosophers of his day. Frederick certainly directed upon them the full power of his formidable personality, backing it up by a confirmation of all the Republic's former privileges in the Empire and several new concessions in Apulia and Sicily. In return he received a splinter from the True Cross – but very little else. He may have made a tactical mistake in commissioning a new imperial crown from a Venetian goldsmith – an incident which caused much heart-searching among the authorities, who finally allowed the work to go forward only on the understanding that it was a strictly private and unofficial transaction. At all events, though perfect cordiality was shown on both sides, Frederick left the city a disappointed man. The Venetians remained, as before, on their guard.

In the years that followed, Venice's relations with the Empire were to deteriorate fast. For all her avowed neutrality, she had no desire to see a strong and probably covetous Frederick on her mainland doorstep. The considerations that had led her to join the first League were still largely valid, and her sympathies could not but be in some degree engaged with the Lombard cities. Before long she was acting as banker for the new League; soon, too, as the fighting grew fiercer, she was offering asylum to the Emperor's enemies. Meanwhile distinguished Venetians were increasingly sought after by the cities to serve as *podestà*. To the modern mind it seems almost inconceivable that these powerful municipalities should regularly and deliberately have appointed foreigners to conduct their affairs; but most of them were too divided – by factional interests and jealousies, ambitions and family feuds – for agreement on any native-born leader to be possible. To such divisions Venice was herself by no means immune; it is a credit to her remarkable gift for self-government that never once in her history was she even tempted to seek a foreign *podestà* of her own.

Still, she must have found the institution useful. Both Padua and Treviso, for example, had Venetians as their *podestà* by 1236, the latter no less a personage than the Doge's son Pietro. In that year it was he who led the city's heroic defence against the besieging army of Frederick II's principal lieutenant in North Italy, the dreaded Ezzelino da Romano, acquiring such a reputation in the process that when the city was forced into surrender in 1237 he was at once invited to occupy the same position in Milan.

The advantage of the *podestà* system, so far as Venice was concerned, was that she could pursue her interests discreetly on the mainland without officially jeopardizing her neutrality. As time went on, however, this neutrality became ever harder to profess, let alone to preserve. Not only was she drawn more and more into the ambit of the Lombard cities; she was also growing anxious at the continued imperial successes – particularly that of Cortenuova in 1237, where Pietro Tiepolo was taken prisoner and paraded in triumph on an elephant, or the still more ominous occasion in the following year when Ezzelino's army reached the very shores of the lagoon and destroyed the convent of S. Ilario at Fusina. Finally, in September 1239, at the instigation of Pope Gregory IX, the Venetians joined perhaps the most surprising alliance in their history – with their two bitterest rivals, Genoa and Pisa. It was even agreed that Venetian and Genoese galleys should fly the standard of the other republic alongside their own.

This arrangement, as might have been expected, did not last long; indeed, apart from a short and rather half-hearted expedition against Frederick's beloved Apulia, the alliance itself resulted in only one significant campaign. This was against the city of Ferrara, which Ezzelino and his other Ghibelline colleague, Salinguerra di Torello, were trying to develop as a commercial rival to Venice. A Venetian fleet – followed, some weeks later, by the Doge in his state barge, the *Bucintoro* – sailed up the Po and blockaded the city; and after five months Salinguerra was at last forced to seek terms. Whether or not, as it was widely alleged, the Venetians seized him during negotiations or whether he gave himself up to them of his own accord is uncertain; though over eighty, he was brought back to Venice and lived there another five years in comfortable captivity, to be honoured on his death with a state funeral and a splendid monument in S. Nicolò on the Lido. His followers in Ferrara were not so lucky; the Guelf faction led by Marquis Azzo VII of Este, which was now able to return from exile, took a merciless revenge. Meanwhile the grants and privileges demanded by Venice and readily granted by Azzo went far beyond any previous demands.

In 1241, at the reputed age of 100, Frederick II's arch-enemy Gregory IX died at last. His successor after a two-year interregnum, Innocent IV,[1] continued his policies; but, at least so far as Venice was concerned, the heat had gone out of the struggle, and the peace treaty she signed with the Emperor in 1245 did little more than confirm the existing state of affairs. To some extent this may have been due to a recrudescence of trouble in Dalmatia which for several years kept the Venetians primarily occupied elsewhere; but the underlying cause was a good deal simpler. Venice had come to realize that the Empire did not after all constitute a direct threat to her sovereignty. Never once did Frederick suggest that the Republic

1. Pope Celestine IV, who in fact succeeded Gregory but who died only eighteen days after his election, can safely be ignored.

owed him any allegiance. In all his written communications with the Doge he always scrupulously avoided referring to the Venetians as *fideles* – that dangerously emotive word, with its arrogant presumption of loyalty, which aroused such wrath among the townsmen of Lombardy. The two short miles of shallow water which separated the islands of Rialto from the mainland had somehow conferred on Venice a special, separate, status; they had saved her not only from conquest, spoliation and destruction but also, and more extraordinarily still, from being looked upon as just another – albeit the richest and most powerful – of the North Italian cities. The acquisition of her overseas Empire in the Levant had still further increased the respect in which she was held. She was no longer a city. She was a nation.

But a nation founded on trade; and that trade, as the Venetians must – at least subconsciously – have realized, owed its phenomenal success not to any territorial expansion but, paradoxically, to the very smallness of the Republic. Here was another benefit conferred by the surrounding lagoon. By virtually confining the Venetians to so restricted a space, it had created in them a unique spirit of cohesion and cooperation – a spirit which showed itself not only at times of national crisis but also, and still more impressively, in the day-to-day handling of their affairs. Among Venice's rich merchant aristocracy everyone knew everyone else, and close acquaintance led to mutual trust of a kind that in other cities seldom extended far outside the family circle. In consequence, the Venetians stood alone in their capacity for quick, efficient business administration. A trading venture, even one that involved immense initial outlay, several years' duration and considerable risk, could be arranged on the Rialto in a matter of hours. It might take the form of a simple partnership between two merchants, or that of a large corporation of the kind needed to finance a full-sized fleet or trans-Asiatic caravan; it might run for an agreed period or, more usually, it might be an *ad hoc* arrangement which would automatically be dissolved when the particular venture was completed. But it would be founded on trust, and it would be inviolable.

This system of easily formed short-term partnerships meant in practice that any Venetian with a little money to invest could have a share in trade. Artisans, widows, the aged, the sick – all could enter into what was known as a *colleganza* with some active but comparatively impecunious young merchant. They would provide two-thirds of the required capital while the merchant would contribute one-third, make the voyage and do all the work. On his return to Venice he was legally bound within one month to present his partner with a complete set of accounts, after which the proceeds would be equally divided. Some small dues might be levied by the state, but in these early days Venetian taxation was low – infinitesimal in comparison with the punitive sums levied by the Byzantines on their own merchants, or by most of the princes of feudal Europe. So profits were high, incentives great, and investment capital increased year by year.

It was the presumed failure of one of these *colleganze* that provided Shakespeare with the basic plot for *The Merchant of Venice*; by the middle of the thirteenth century there was already a considerable Jewish population in the city and its immediate neighbourhood – perhaps 3,000 or more. Many lived at Mestre, on the mainland; others – particularly those who had mercantile dealings with Dalmatia – occupied the island of Spinalunga and were in fact responsible for its change of name to Giudecca. Apart from trade, their principal occupations were, as everywhere in Europe, the lending of money – usury by Venetian citizens being forbidden in the Republic – and the practice of medicine; but apart from certain requirements as to residence there does not appear at this time to have been any legal restriction on their activities – including the exercise of their religion – still less any active persecution. Although at later stages of her history Venice did not always show herself to be more enlightened in her attitude to the Jews than were her European contemporaries, her commercial sense told her from the outset that Jewish capital could be of immense value to her economic growth; and, as usual, her commercial sense was right.

Again and again in Venice's early history we read of Doges suddenly withdrawing from the world and dying only a few weeks or months later. There was certainly no tradition of retirement on grounds of age alone. The Venetians have always been famous for their longevity – to this day their expectation of life comfortably exceeds that of the inhabitants of any other major Italian city – and Enrico Dandolo provides only one example of their still noticeable ability to continue well into their eighth or ninth decades with their energies and vitality almost unimpaired. When a Doge did at last step down from his throne, the speed with which death nearly always followed abdication suggests that he took such a decision only when he knew his life to be ebbing away. For as long as he felt able to govern his people, he did so; but when the task became too much for him, he did not cling to office.

Giacomo Tiepolo was no exception. He retired, not to a monastery like so many of his predecessors but to his own house in the Campo S. Agostino, in the spring of 1249; and he was dead before the autumn. He had served Venice well, in the Levant somehow contriving to hold together the chief elements of her new, dangerously fissile Empire, and in the West serving the interests of her struggling sister-cities (which were also her own) without ever identifying too closely with them or becoming inextricably involved in the strife between Guelf and Ghibelline which was to continue to tear them apart for another century. He had fought the Emperor Frederick – losing two sons in the process – as long and as hard as he felt necessary for the good of the Republic; but no longer and no harder. Meanwhile at home he had continued the work originally begun by Enrico Dandolo fifty years before and in 1242 had produced his celebrated *Statuto*, the most detailed and comprehensive codification of Venetian civil law yet to have appeared.

The other notable appearance in Venice during his reign was that of the two great orders of mendicant friars, the Dominicans and the Franciscans. St Dominic and St Francis had died within five years of each other, in 1221 and 1226 respectively; the results of their labours had been immediate, and by 1230 representatives of both orders had arrived in the city. To each, Doge Tiepolo granted land for a church; to the Dominicans, a marshy expanse to the north of the parish of S. Maria Formosa, to the Franciscans a ruined and long-abandoned abbey close to his own house, across the Grand Canal. By the year of his death, building operations at the two sites were well under way; and although the gigantic churches which were ultimately to rise there – SS. Giovanni e Paolo and S. Maria Gloriosa dei Frari – were not to be completed till the fifteenth century, of the former at least enough had already been constructed for the old Doge to choose it as his burial place.[1]

After four uninspiring years under an elderly pietist named Marin Morosini – who, but for the now inexplicable fact of his selection for the dogeship, would surely have taken his place among the dimmer members of one of the oldest and most brilliant of Venetian families – the election of Renier Zeno early in 1253 seems to have woken the city up again. Zeno had had an eventful, even adventurous, life. He had shown much courage in putting down one of the periodic revolts of Zara in 1242; in the following year, while returning to Venice from the Council of Lyons, he had been taken prisoner by the Count of Savoy. Released by order of the

---

1. The sacristy of SS. Giovanni e Paolo contains a picture by Vicentino of Doge Tiepolo granting the land to the Dominicans. His sarcophagus can still be seen in the arcade on the outer wall of the church, just to the left of the west door.

Emperor, he had then been summoned to the imperial court and forced to justify what Frederick described as Venice's ungrateful policy towards him. Later he had served as *podestà* of Piacenza and, more recently, of Fermo, where he received the news of his election. All this and a good deal more besides we learn from one of the most entertaining (if not always the most reliable) of contemporary chroniclers, Martino da Canale, whose enthusiasm for Zeno occasionally smacks less of the historian than of the publicity agent – which, for all we know, he may have been. Not that the new Doge lacked any talent of his own for self-advertisement; in his irresistible Old French, Martino gives a breathless description of the tournament that was staged to mark his accession. It was held on the Piazza, '*la plus bele place qui soit en tot li monde*':

The pavilions were set up in the square, and all were covered in silken cloth, and the square itself covered in the same manner. And the fine ladies and maidens ascended to the pavilions, and in all the palaces around more ladies appeared at the windows. And Monseigneur the Doge proceeded on foot from the church of St Mark, and all the nobles of Venice with him, and the people thronged the square . . . After him came a company of horsemen all splendidly mounted and richly armed. Then the jousts began, with all the ladies watching. Ah signors, had you been there, you could have seen many a good thrust with a lance . . .

Continually in his chronicle, Martino returns to the theme of Venetian pageantry, recalling the dazzling processions made by the Doge on the great feast-days of the Church, describing with child-like enthusiasm the cloth of gold, the silken banners and the silver trumpets, recreating scene after scene that cries out for a Gentile Bellini or a Carpaccio to capture it – both, alas, still a century and a half away in the future.

But life for Renier Zeno was not just a matter of parading around the Piazza. In 1256 he lent active support to a papal crusade against Ezzelino da Romano, who since Frederick's death had been using the imperial standard as only the most transparent of cloaks for his own personal ambitions. One of the earliest of the great *signori* of North Italy – and certainly the first to maintain his authority for twenty years and more – Ezzelino by his inhuman brutality had earned himself the reputation of an ogre, detested and feared throughout Lombardy, Friuli and the Marches. Thanks to the success of Venice's isolationist policy, he plays only a marginal part in her history: we can spare ourselves the stories of blinded prisoners and mutilated children with which the Pope justified his excommunication, noting only Martino's report of how, when in 1259 Ezzelino was at last hunted down and killed, 'the church bells rang out all over Venice, as they did on the feasts of the saints; and on the night following, the priests climbed to the tops of the bell-towers, where they lit candles and torches, so that the light and the clamour were wondrous to see and to hear'.[1] It was typical of the Venetian attitude, however, that, as Martino points out, these celebrations were occasioned less by the disappearance of a monster and the restoration of peace and security to a terrorized region, than by that of a ruler who had kept back the rents that were legally due to Venetian churches from their properties on the mainland.

But the attention of the Republic was soon turned back from Lombardy to the Levant. On 25 July 1261 a Greek general, Alexius Strategopoulos, launched a surprise attack on Constantinople and captured it, virtually without opposition; on 15 August the Emperor Michael VIII Palaeologus, fifth in that imperial line that had been ruling in exile at Nicaea, re-entered the city; and a month later he and his wife Theodora were crowned anew in St Sophia, now once more consecrated in the Orthodox faith. Byzantium was reborn; the Latin Empire of the East was finished.

For most of the fifty-six years of its existence it had been little more than a bad joke. Surrounded as he was by hostile Greek and Bulgarian states and disloyal Latin ones, maintained largely on gifts from his fellow-monarch St Louis of France and on loans from Venetian bankers who demanded his own son as security, progressively abandoned as more and more of his leading barons and clergy returned to the West – the latter usually taking with them what remained of the church treasure – the last of the Latin Emperors, Baldwin II, had been reduced to stripping the copper from the roofs of his palace and ultimately pawning the city's most precious relic, the Crown of Thorns, to Venetian merchants.[2] He and his Frankish predecessors on the imperial throne had achieved nothing but chaos, spoliation and destruction; their conquest had brought them only poverty and suffering. From the whole sad shambles of the Fourth Crusade and its consequences there had been only one real beneficiary: Venice.

And Venice, likewise, was the one serious loser when the Latin Empire collapsed. The Pope expressed his horror that Constantinople, the second

1. '*Les cloches sonerent par tote Venise, ensi com il sont acostumes de soner as festes des Saints; et la nuit apres, monterent li clers de sor li clochiers, et alumerent cierges et tortis par tos li clochers, et firent si grant luminaire et si grant soner des cloches, que ce fu une grant mervoile de veoir et de oir.*'

2. It was redeemed by St Louis, who subsequently brought it from St Mark's to Paris – where he built the Sainte-Chapelle, the world's most superb reliquary, in its honour. During the French Revolution it was entrusted for safety to the Bishop of Paris and is now to be found, bathetically encased in Second-Empire finery, in the Treasury of Notre Dame.

Rome, should once more have fallen away from the True Faith; St Louis doubtless shed a pious tear for the few remaining relics that would now elude his grasp; but on the Rialto the news meant grave political and financial crisis. For Venice had possessed not only three-eighths of Constantinople itself; her colonies and trading posts were by now scattered all over the Aegean and around the shores of the eastern Mediterranean and the Black Sea. Hitherto they had been satisfactorily protected by a powerful Venetian fleet based in the Golden Horn, but now this vital anchorage was denied them. From Michael Palaeologus they could expect nothing but implacable hostility. His Empire, admittedly, was depleted and impoverished; alone, he would scarcely have constituted a serious rival. But he was not alone. Some months before his triumph he had shrewdly allied himself with the Genoese who, for nearly a century, had been bitterly contesting Venetian supremacy in the Levant. In return for military and financial aid in the reconquest, he had promised them tax and customs concessions and districts of their own in the chief ports of the Empire, including Constantinople itself – all those privileges, in short, that Alexius Comnenus had granted to Venice in 1082 and upon which the Republic's commercial greatness had been founded.

Venetian–Genoese relations, strained at the best of times, had deteriorated still further in recent years, and since 1255 the two Republics had been in a state of open war. There had been three important naval battles off the coast of Palestine, in all of which – thanks in large measure to the courage of the dashing young admiral Lorenzo Tiepolo, son of the former Doge – the Venetians had inflicted crushing defeats on their rivals, expelling them from Acre and capturing an entire fleet of twenty-five galleys sent out from Genoa to their relief. The courage of the Genoese, on this occasion, had not been conspicuous: Martino writes of how one of their supporters from Tyre, a Frenchman named Philippe de Montfort who had himself come to their aid with a troop of cavalry, saw the water full of floundering Genoese sailors and left in disgust, scratching his head and complaining that 'they were good for nothing but brothels, and were like fish-eating birds, flinging themselves into the sea and drowning'.

De Montfort's logic seems as shaky as his ornithology; but his sentiments were clear enough. Genoa's pride had indeed been brought low. From the Genoese church of St Saba at Acre Lorenzo Tiepolo bore home in triumph three short columns, one cylindrical of porphyry and two quadrangular of carved white marble. All three were set up in the Piazzetta, at the south-west corner of the basilica, where they stand to this day.[1] But now the pendulum had swung. It was the Venetians' turn to suffer humiliation, this time in the eyes of the whole civilized world – a humiliation that the simultaneous threat to their commercial Empire can hardly have made easier to bear.

As things turned out, the economic consequences of the reconquest of Constantinople proved somewhat less catastrophic than they had feared. The operation itself had been surprisingly simple. Michael Palaeologus had needed less help from the Genoese than he had expected, and had even managed to avoid direct hostilities with Venice, whose fleet had been providentially absent from the Bosphorus when Strategopoulos had struck. The new Emperor was, moreover, a cautious man; he knew that Venetian naval power was still superior to Genoese, and that still more decisive victories than those at Acre might yet be won. His wisest course lay in playing the two Republics off against each other. He therefore permitted the Venetians to maintain their colony in Constantinople and left them certain minor commercial privileges. In other respects, however, they were made to feel their new position. Their official representative to the Emperor was downgraded from the rank of *podestà* (which was now awarded to the leading Genoese) to that of *bailo*; no longer was he invited as of right to the Emperor's table on the great feasts of the Church. Part of their own quarter of the city was re-allotted to the Genoese colony – now rapidly expanding – which a few years later was to receive in addition the entire district of Galata, across the Golden Horn. Outside the capital, they were forced to stand by, powerless, while their rivals set up trading posts where they themselves had previously enjoyed the monopoly – at Smyrna, on the islands of Chios and Lesbos and, most galling of all, along the coasts of the Black Sea, from which they were henceforth excluded.

Their sense of frustration must have been still further increased by the knowledge that their navy remained supreme. Michael Palaeologus had as yet no fleet worthy of the name, and had the Venetians decided to fight for their lost privileges he would have been incapable of opposing them. But they had their colony in Constantinople to consider; by allowing it to continue in existence, Michael had adroitly provided himself

1. The porphyry column, known as the *Pietra del Bando*, later became the traditional platform from which all Venetian laws were promulgated. In 1902 it performed an even more useful purpose by protecting the corner of the Basilica from the falling *campanile* – suffering considerable damage to itself in the process. To be perfectly honest, there is some doubt about the two square columns, which are not specifically mentioned by any of the contemporary chroniclers. It has been suggested that Tiepolo may have taken them not from St Saba but from the fortified tower called Mongioia which the Genoese had recently completed at Acre. (There is a third column, similar in style, in a corner of the Papadopoli gardens.)

with a pledge for their good behaviour. Clearly, there could be as yet no question of any real diplomatic *rapprochement*; feelings were still running too high. Besides, with the deposed Emperor Baldwin busy canvassing the princes of Europe there might still remain some slender chance of his restoration. For the moment they could only accept the inevitable, and try to make the best of it.

With Genoa, on the other hand, no such considerations applied. The *casus belli* was greater than ever, and the Venetians returned with increased vigour to the attack. The fighting now spread all over the eastern Mediterranean, with countless minor engagements among the Aegean islands and off the coasts of Euboea and the Peloponnese. In one of these engagements, the Genoese were foolish enough to intercept a *carovana* bound for the Rialto – one of the immense convoys that sailed regularly from Levantine ports, bringing to Europe the silks and spices of the East – and escaped destruction only when the Venetian admiral commanding the escort very properly refused to risk the precious cargoes by giving chase. In others they were not so lucky – notably in an encounter off Trapani in western Sicily, in which over 1,100 Genoese sailors jumped overboard and were drowned while another 600, in twenty-seven galleys, were brought back captive to the lagoons.

In Constantinople, meanwhile, the insolence and arrogance of the newly privileged Genoese were making them if anything even more unpopular than the Venetians had been in the past; and, as the news of one Venetian victory after another reached the imperial palace, so Michael's sympathies began to change. He too had a war on his hands, against the remaining petty princelings of the Latin East and the Greek Despots of Epirus, none of whom were willing to return their territories to the restored Empire – an attitude for which they were receiving powerful support from the Pope and from Frederick II's son Manfred of Sicily. Michael was himself in desperate need of money to rebuild both his capital and his shattered fleet; his Genoese alliance, instead of providing it, was involving him in further heavy expenditure – for which he was getting remarkably little in return.

By 1264 Greek ambassadors were in Venice, and in the following year a treaty was drawn up offering the Republic privileges which, if they did not quite equal those that had been lost, represented at least an immense improvement on the existing state of affairs. But the Venetians were in no hurry. The Byzantine East was still in turmoil, and while the future of the Empire remained uncertain there was no point in committing themselves. It was not until 1268 that they finally made up their minds to accept

Michael's offer. Even now they would agree to nothing more than a five-year truce; for that period, however, they promised non-aggression, the withholding of all help to the enemies of the Empire and the liberation of their Greek prisoners in Crete, Modone and Corone, the three principal bases remaining to them in the Aegean. The Emperor undertook in return to respect Venetian settlements both there and elsewhere in the archipelago, and once more to allow Venetian merchants freedom to reside, travel and trade without let or hindrance throughout his dominions. His terms, in fact, could hardly have been more favourable. Two things only were missing: their three-eighths share – though it had gradually become in practice more of a titular claim than a real economic benefit – and the exclusivity that they had formerly enjoyed. For, Michael now stipulated, the Genoese would retain their existing rights. The dangers of the old policy, by which one of the Republics was given full imperial preference at the expense of the other, had now been conclusively demonstrated. Henceforth there would be free competition between them. That way Michael could profit by their rivalry without driving the less favoured party into hostile alliances.

Few short-term truces have had more lasting significance. At a stroke, Venice had effectively re-established her commercial primacy in the Levant and much of that influence which, only seven years previously, she seemed to have lost for ever. Her recovery was in part due to good luck, of which she had certainly received more than her fair share; but it also owed much to the astute diplomatic sense of Doge Zeno and his advisers. When he died within weeks of the treaty's ratification, he left behind him a people that had almost forgotten its recent humiliation, regained its self-respect, and was once more ready to face the future with confidence. In gratitude, and following that tradition of high pomp and sumptuous ceremonial that had marked his reign from the beginning, he was given a funeral as magnificent as only Venice could provide before being laid to rest in the still unfinished church of SS. Giovanni e Paolo. There, in the south-west corner, a part of his tomb is still preserved – a relief of Christ enthroned, with an attendant angel on each hand.

12

The Wages of Arrogance

[1268–1299]

... How woful, that the war-cry of his name should so often reanimate the rage of the soldier, on those very plains where he himself had failed in the courage of the Christian, and so often dye with fruitless blood that very Cypriot Sea, over whose waves, in repentance and shame, he was following the Son of Consolation!

Ruskin, *The Stones of Venice*
(See epigraph to Chapter 3, p. 26)

The first seven decades of the thirteenth century had witnessed the emergence of Venice as a world power. They had seen her extensive possessions in the East first acquired, then developed and consolidated, then lost and finally in large measure regained. More significant by far in the long term, they had seen the eclipse of both Empires, the East and the West. The Byzantine Empire of the Palaeologi, though still with the better part of two centuries to run, would never be more than a frail, struggling shadow of what it had been before the Fourth Crusade. In western Europe, too, the great days of Hohenstaufen imperialism had died with Frederick II in 1250; it was nations – England, France, Spain – not empires (at least in the medieval sense), that were beginning to occupy the forefront of the stage.

For most of those seventy years Venice had been at war. She had had to fight for her new dominions, and to defend them, against Greeks, Genoese, Pisans and Saracens, to say nothing of pirates from every corner of the Mediterranean. Beneath the walls of Zara and of Constantinople, off the shores of Palestine and Pontus, of Crete, Euboea and the Peloponnese, across the waters of the Tyrrhenian and the Adriatic, the Aegean and the Euxine, her galleys had been as fully employed as her merchantmen.

At home, however, life had continued peaceably enough – or nearly. The expansion of trade had brought still greater prosperity; merchandise, wrote Martino da Canale, was pouring in from everywhere like water from fountains, and Venice continued to grow in size and splendour.

The two great churches of the Mendicant Friars rose ever higher; others, springing up in parish after parish, may have yielded to them in size but far surpassed them in opulence. The Grand Canal was already lined with *palazzi* – a few of them, such as the Cà da Mosto or the Fondaco dei Turchi, still standing to this day,[1] their lovely open loggias and arcades testifying to the confidence all Venetians felt in the security of their city at a time when, elsewhere in Europe, castles rather than palaces were still the rule. In 1264 the Piazzetta was paved for the first time, and in the same year a new Rialto bridge was built on wooden piles – the prototype of that painted by Carpaccio in the series of the 'Miracles of the Relic of the True Cross', now in the Accademia. The surface decoration of the Basilica of St Mark, tentatively begun under Domenico Selvo and continued at intervals throughout the twelfth century, gathered momentum with the addition of the glorious mosaics of the atrium and the façade.[2]

Meanwhile, in the constitutional sphere, Giacomo Tiepolo had produced his codification of the laws of the Republic and, with his *promissione*, had brought about a further curtailment of ducal authority. But in the summer of 1268, when the time came to elect a successor to Doge Zeno, there seems to have been a general feeling that this authority might still run out of control and so constitute a threat to the state. Inevitably, the influx of new wealth had brought certain previously unknown and insignificant families to new prominence and power. Between these families and those of the older aristocracy – the so-called *case vecchie* – feuds began once again to develop: feuds familiar enough in earlier centuries, but which the Republic should by then have outgrown. One of them, between the Dandolo and Tiepolo clans, actually led in Zeno's reign to an open brawl in the Piazza, as a result of which a law was hastily passed banning the representation of family emblems or coats of arms on the outside of buildings. The Venetians could not forget their old, almost

1. Both, inevitably, have suffered over the years. Part of the arcading of the Cà da Mosto has been bricked in, and two upper floors added, while the Fondaco has been restored so crudely that one would almost prefer it to look as it did before 1860 (see Plate 13). Other buildings still recognizably of the thirteenth century are the two Donà *palazzi* (on either side of the Madonnetta *traghetto* point) with the Barzizza, a little further on by the S. Silvestro *vaporetto* station; and, on the other side of the Grand Canal, the adjacent Palazzi Farsetti and Loredan, now the offices of the Municipality.

2. Of the latter, all of which are clearly visible in Gentile Bellini's picture in the Accademia (Plate 16), only one alas remains – that on the far left-hand lunette. It represents the *Translation of the Body of St Mark* and provides us with the earliest extant picture of the Basilica itself, at a date soon after the setting up of the horses of Lysippus over the central arch. The four other lunettes, now filled with mediocre work of the seventeenth and eighteenth centuries, stand out in sorry contrast.

pathological fear that one family, one individual even, might somehow gain control of the Republic. They had watched, with a horror not untinged with smugness, the career of Ezzelino da Romano and others of his kind who were even now arising in many less fortunate North Italian cities; and they were fully aware, six centuries and more before Lord Acton, of the effects of absolute power. The new system of election to the dogeship which they now devised must surely rank among the most complicated ever instituted by a civilized state. It strikes the modern mind as ridiculous, and to some extent it was. But it is worth setting down in some detail, if only as an indication of the lengths to which Venice was prepared to go in order to ensure that the supreme office of the state should not fall, either directly or indirectly, into ambitious or unscrupulous hands.

On the day appointed for the election, the youngest member of the Signoria[1] was to pray in St Mark's; then, on leaving the Basilica, he was to stop the first boy he met and take him to the Doges' Palace, where the Great Council, minus those of its members who were under thirty, was to be in full session. This boy, known as the *ballotino*, would have the duty of picking the slips of paper from the urn during the drawing of lots. By the first of such lots, the Council chose thirty of their own number. The second was used to reduce the thirty to nine, and the nine would then vote for forty, each of whom was to receive at least seven nominations. The forty would then be reduced, again by lot, to twelve, whose task was to vote for twenty-five, of whom each this time required nine votes. The twenty-five were in turn reduced to another nine; the nine voted for forty-five, with a minimum of seven votes each, and from these the *ballotino* picked out the names of eleven. The eleven now voted for forty-one – nine or more votes each – and it was these forty-one who were to elect the Doge.[2] They first attended Mass, and individually swore an oath that they would act honestly and uprightly, for the good of the Republic. They were then locked in secret conclave in the Palace, cut off from all contact or communication with the outside world and guarded by a special force of sailors, day and night, until their work was done.

So much for the preliminaries; now the election itself could begin. Each elector wrote the name of his candidate on a paper and dropped it in the urn; the slips were then removed and read, and a list drawn up of

1. The inner council of state (see p. 110).
2. Sir Henry Wotton, James I's ambassador to Venice, was later to maintain that this extraordinary procedure had been invented by a Benedictine monk: 'The whole mysterious frame therein doth much savor of the cloister.'

all the names proposed, regardless of the number of nominations for each. A single slip for each name was now placed in another urn, and one drawn. If the candidate concerned was present, he retired together with any other elector who bore the same surname, and the remainder proceeded to discuss his suitability. He was then called back to answer questions or to defend himself against any accusations. A ballot followed. If he obtained the required twenty-five votes, he was declared Doge; otherwise a second name was drawn, and so on.

With a system so tortuously involved as this, it may seem remarkable that anyone was ever elected at all; but on 23 July 1268, only sixteen days after the death of his predecessor, the vote found its way to Lorenzo Tiepolo. Martino da·Canale, never one to resist describing a good celebration, tells us with relish how the bells of St Mark's rang out and the people flocked to the Basilica, surrounding their new Doge and 'tearing the clothes from his back' – which they seem to have been traditionally permitted to do 'as a sign of his humility and clemency'. Barefoot before the high altar, he took the oath of office and was invested with the banner of St Mark. Then, newly robed and enthroned on the *pozzetto*,[1] he was carried ceremonially round the Piazza, scattering coins as he went, before entering the Doges' Palace and addressing his new subjects. Meanwhile a delegation had hurried off to his house at S. Agostina to inform his wife – the niece of John de Brienne, one of the Latin Emperors in Constantinople – and to escort her to her new home.

'*Deboneire, cortois*, wise, valiant and of excellent parts', enthuses Martino, Lorenzo Tiepolo was 'a name celebrated throughout the world'. Besides his heroism in the Genoese war – still not over – he had spent some time as *podestà* of Fano and could boast a long record of service to the Republic. This record, however, had not prevented him from involving himself in the affray in the Piazza a few years before, and indeed from getting wounded in the course of it; and one of his first non-ceremonial actions as Doge was to send for the leading Dandolos and to make his peace with them. Then the celebrations began in earnest. First the Venetian fleet sailed past the Palace in review, followed by specially decorated ships from Torcello, Murano, Burano and the other island communities of the lagoon. Then, on foot, came a procession of the guilds. Martino's account is too long, and ultimately too tedious, to reproduce in detail; but it is an unrivalled source of information on the commercial life of the city at the time and shows the level of prosperity that had already been reached. The parade was led by the smiths, all crowned with garlands; then came the

1. See p. 110.

skinners, in their richest cloaks of vair and ermine – dress not normally recommended for Venice in late July; the master tailors, all in white with vermilion stars, singing lustily to the accompaniment of their own band; the weavers and quilters, the sandal-makers and mercers, the glass-blowers – already an important group – the makers of gold brocade, and the comb-cutters, bearing great lanterns full of birds, which they released as they passed the Palace. But the first prize for fantasy went to the barbers, led by two mounted knights in full armour and four ladies 'very strangely attired'.[1]

Dismounting before the Doge, they announced themselves. 'Sire, we are two knights errant, who have ridden the world to seek our fortune. After much trouble and labour we have won four fair damsels. If there be any knight at your court who wishes to risk his neck to take these strange ladies from us, we are ready to fight in their defence.' But the Doge replied that they were welcome, and that with God's will they themselves should enjoy their conquests; and that they should be honoured at his court, where no man should gainsay them.

The reign of Lorenzo Tiepolo had begun auspiciously enough; but the Doge never really fulfilled his early promise. With his accession to power, his former good luck seemed to desert him; diplomatically, too, he never quite found his touch. The 1268 harvest was disastrous, and within a few months Venice was stricken by famine. Throughout her history, her lack of agricultural land with her consequent dependence on the importation of grain for her survival had been one of her most serious weaknesses; and now there was revealed another – the jealousy of her neighbours. In vain did she appeal to Padua, Treviso and other towns for supplies, reminding them of the help she had given them during Ezzelino's reign of terror; they refused outright, Padua even going so far as to suspend payment of the annual rents which were payable in corn to Venetian churches and monasteries for their property on *terra firma*. By sending ships further afield, to Sicily and even to Russia, catastrophe was averted; but the Republic's subsequent vengeance was swift and savage. Heavy dues were imposed on all goods passing through Venice to destinations on the mainland; on the pretext that the Adriatic was an integral part of the Venetian heritage, officials were appointed at various ports along the coast to make sure that such goods were not offloaded there instead and to control river traffic along the Po and its tributaries. It was a foolish measure, since it implied a claim that was bound to provoke violent reactions far beyond the cities with which Venice was quarrelling; and

1. '*Aparilles mult estrangement*'.

it led to a three-year war with Bologna which, though it ended inconclusively, did little good to Venetian popularity in North Italy – or indeed
to the Republic's reputation.

Thus, by the time Tiepolo died in August 1275 – to be laid next to his
father in SS. Giovanni e Paolo – his glory had worn distinctly thin. He
had simply not been able to understand that, however much Venice
might consider herself a place apart, exalted and privileged, having nothing
in common either in her history or traditions with her sister cities, in
their eyes she was still one of their own number: richer and more powerful
perhaps, thanks to a mixture of good luck, unscrupulous behaviour and
boundless self-confidence, but in no way essentially superior to themselves and – on land at least – certainly not invincible. In the days when
Barbarossa, Henry VI and Frederick II were making their periodic
descents into Lombardy and the wars between Guelf and Ghibelline were
still at their height, these cities had had other preoccupations; they had
been obliged to steer a course as best they could through the stormy seas
of imperial–papal politics while Venice, protected by her lagoon, could
afford to focus her attentions on the infinitely more attractive East. But
times were changing. As the imperial shadow faded, a new spirit and a
new strength arose within them. Tired of bloodshed, they now looked
for a greater share in the prosperity that Venice had so long enjoyed, and
began to resent the arrogance with which she accepted it as her prerogative and her due.

The eighty-year-old Jacopo Contarini, who was somehow elected to
the dogeship on Tiepolo's death, was – perhaps not surprisingly – no
more sensitive to these developments than his predecessor. By this time
the misguidedness of Venice's policy towards the mainland should have
been self-evident. During the past five years, apart from her unsatisfactory
treaty with Bologna and a five-year truce with Genoa in 1270, the Republic
had been obliged to enter into agreements with at least six other cities,
each of which had involved a grudging modification of her financial –
though not of her territorial – claims. Again in 1274, when at the Council
of Lyons Pope Gregory X[1] recognized Michael Palaeologus as Emperor
and – in return for Michael's acknowledgement of papal primacy and the
apparent healing of the Great Schism – effectively removed any religious
justification for a Latin reconquest of Constantinople, the Pope and 500

1. Gregory had been elected Pope in 1271, after a three-year period during which, thanks
to the machinations of Charles of Anjou, the Papacy had been without an occupant. The
interregnum would have lasted longer if the authorities at Viterbo, where the conclave was
being held, had not taken the somewhat extreme step of removing the roof from the palace in
which the cardinals were assembled.

bishops had also found time to listen to an impassioned diatribe by a delegation from Ancona, protesting against Venetian pretensions.[1] Gregory himself urged a more conciliatory attitude, but in vain. Venice argued that she had been the defender of the Adriatic since the days of antiquity; that it was thanks to her alone that Slavs, Saracens and Normans had successively been driven back; and that Pope Alexander III had in fact invested her with rights over the entire gulf during the Ascension Day ceremony of 1177, when the traditional ring was cast, in his presence, into the waves.

This last claim, in particular, was distinctly shaky; there is no evidence that Pope Alexander had done any such thing.[2] As for the first two, the Anconitans could justly point out that Venice had been acting primarily in her own interests, that they too had done their share of defending, and that anyway neither was a reason to block their free passage up and down their home rivers. The quarrel grew steadily more acrimonious, and in 1277 gave place to open war. The first wave of the Venetian fleet, some twenty-six galleys, left at once for Ancona, but scarcely had they settled down to a siege of the city than a freak summer storm dashed most of them on to the rocks and scattered the remainder for miles up and down the coast. A few days later the second contingent, which had set out all unaware of the disaster, ran straight into the arms of the Anconitans and was captured.

Venice had paid dearly for her arrogance; but she had not yet paid in full. The new German King Rudolf of Habsburg had recently attempted to ingratiate himself with Pope Nicholas III by making him a gift of the territory of Romagna, which included Ancona; so that Venice now found herself embroiled with the Pope as well. Meanwhile, seeing her difficulties, certain discontented factions in Istria and Crete rose simultaneously in revolt. For Jacopo Contarini it was all too much. In March 1280 he resigned – or, perhaps more accurately, he was pensioned off; we know that he was voted an annual 1,500 *piccoli* for the rest of his life which, since he was already eighty-five and bedridden, was not expected to be of long duration.[3]

Contarini's successor, Giovanni Dandolo, is something of a mystery.

1. See Romanin (II, 307), who presumably bases himself on Martino da Canale (p. 682), though I can find no reference to such an intervention in the records of the Council's proceedings.

2. See p. 116.

3. The precise date of his death is unknown; and his tomb, '*in claustro fratrum minorum*' – by which Andrea Dandolo presumably means the Frari – has disappeared.

Despite his distinguished name, the sources reveal nothing of his past history except that he was serving abroad at the time of his election, and his relationship to the great Enrico is equally uncertain.[1] Within a year he had made peace with Ancona. The basic question of Venice's rights in the Adriatic he seems to have left unresolved, presumably in the interests of reaching a quick agreement; but his hands were at last free to tackle the discontents in Istria, now actively supported by the Patriarch of Aquileia – who claimed jurisdiction over the area – and the Count of Gorizia. Once again the Republic got off to a bad start. The Count and Patriarch together had managed to secure the services of a body of German mercenaries, who easily routed the Venetian force that had been sent to subdue a rebellious Trieste; whereat the Triestines, taking over the pursuit, first raided Caorle, capturing the *podestà* and burning his palace, and then advanced as far as Malamocco leaving a trail of devastation behind them.

Not since the days of Pepin, nearly five centuries before, had a hostile naval force approached so close to the city. The Venetians reacted with firmness and speed. The commander of the luckless expedition, Marin Morosini, was flung into prison where he was punished 'in accordance with his misdeeds and as an example to those who should come after him'; plans were announced for mass conscription; a new fleet, considerably larger than the previous one, was dispatched to Trieste. This time all went well. After a fierce resistance the town surrendered, to be followed by most of its neighbours; but it was not until 1285 that the Patriarch could be induced to sign an agreement of understanding with the Republic, and even then the question of his rights in Istria was left unsettled. As a result, hostilities all too soon flared up again, to bedevil Venice militarily, economically and politically for the next twenty years – until, in 1304, all patriarchal claims in the region were surrendered to the Doge in return for an annual payment of 450 marks.

And there were other troubles too. The Kingdom of Sicily, which included virtually all Italy south of Rome, had since 1266 been ruled by Louis IX's brother Charles of Anjou from his capital at Naples. On Easter Monday, 1282, however, a drunken French sergeant in Palermo began importuning a Sicilian woman outside the church of S. Spirito just as vespers were about to begin. He was set upon by her husband and killed;

1. A learned German, basing himself on 'manuscript genealogical lists' in the Museo Correr, concludes that Giovanni was in fact Enrico's great-grandson (Simonsfeld, *Andreas Dandolo und seine Geschichtswerke*, Munich, 1876); but Andrea himself, writing of the eleventh-century seaman Domenico Dandolo, says that he was ancestor of two Doges – Enrico and himself – and mentions neither Giovanni nor indeed Francesco, who was Doge from 1329 to 1339.

the murder led to a riot, the riot to a massacre; 2,000 Frenchmen were dead by morning. The remainder withdrew to the mainland where Charles was still in control, while the Sicilians established King Peter III of Aragon on the throne in Palermo.

In the so-called war of the Sicilian Vespers which now ensued, Venice – although technically she had declared for Charles the previous year – had no desire to take part. It had always been her policy to stay clear of Italian upheavals as far as possible, and her navy was anyway fully engaged in Istria. When therefore Pope Martin IV, who was a Frenchman and consequently a strong champion of Charles, launched a Crusade against Peter in 1284, she refused to join it and expressly forbade her own leading churchmen, the Patriarch of Grado and the Bishop of Castello, to preach it from their pulpits. The result was an interdict, the first – though not the last – that Venice ever suffered, and a decree so solemn that even she dared not disobey.

It is hard, nowadays, to imagine the despondency that settled on a medieval city when it came under the ban of the Church. The bells in the *campanili* fell silent; Mass could no longer be said; services of baptism, marriage and burial were alike prohibited, as were all the religious processions that the Venetians loved. That winter, without the great celebrations of Christmas and Epiphany to enliven it, must have seemed interminable; and with the coming of spring, like some Old Testament visitation of the wrath of God, Venice suffered an earthquake which was in turn followed by disastrous floods. The breakwaters were swept away; houses without number were destroyed, families left homeless and starving. The measures taken for their relief were probably swifter, more generous and more effective than could have been expected in any other European city; but Venice was unable to conceal, from her own people or anyone else, that her fortunes had suddenly and sadly declined.

And yet, surprisingly, it was just at this gloomy moment in her history, while the papal interdict was still in force, that there first appeared, in 1284, one of the most lasting and internationally significant of all Venetian institutions – the golden ducat. The word itself was not new; it had been first given to a silver coin minted by Roger II of Sicily in 1140, and other silver ducats had appeared in Venice in 1202, for the payment of workmen building the fleet for the Fourth Crusade. But Giovanni Dandolo's golden ducat was conceived on quite a different scale from these. His decree stipulated that 'it must be made to the greatest possible fineness, like to the florin [of Florence] *only better*'; and so indeed it must have been, for in no other way could it have maintained, for 513 years until the fall of the Republic, its quality, reputation and value in the market-places of the world.[1]

Giovanni Dandolo reigned nine years. He died on 2 November 1289, leaving his golden memorial behind him – fortunately, since there now remains no other. But however brightly his ducats might shine, they could not blind the eyes of the Venetians to the fact that for the past twenty years nothing seemed to have gone right for them. Militarily they had suffered defeats on land and sea, with serious losses, both in ships and human lives. They had been forced to watch, powerless, while the enemy penetrated to the very confines of the lagoon. Their neighbours, on many of whom they depended for trade, were all in a greater or lesser degree unfriendly. Their chief colony, Crete, was once again in revolt. They had suffered the chilly joylessness – to say nothing of the spiritual dangers – of an interdict, the terrors of earthquake, the misery of flood; and though the ban had been lifted by Pope Martin's successor in 1285 and the devastation wrought by the natural disasters had been largely repaired, there was still little sign of markedly better times ahead. Meanwhile the war with Istria continued to rumble away in the distance.

All states go through such periods of depression; and when they do it is only natural that men should look for a scapegoat. The Venetian populace had already found theirs: the fault, they believed, lay with the new commercial aristocracy, those families who had suddenly acquired wealth and power with the capture of Constantinople and were now using them to push the Republic ever further in the direction of oligarchy, whittling away at the power of the Doge and depriving the man in the street of any say in political life. Pre-eminent among these *parvenus* was the family of Dandolo, of whose two Doges to date the first had been responsible for the appearance of the new order while the second had, it was felt, exemplified all that was most objectionable in it and had led Venice into ever graver tribulations.

It was a view both illogical and unfair; but it was widely enough held to provoke massive demonstrations in the city. Resentful of the loss, by now not only *de facto* but *de jure*, of the one political privilege they had traditionally enjoyed, the people united in a huge effort to make their

1. It later came to be known as a *zecchino* or sequin, a word which originally simply meant that it was fresh from the *zecca*, or mint. The coin has another, documentary, interest: the portraits of successive Doges kneeling before St Mark enable us to trace the changes in their vestments over the centuries, and particularly the evolution of the ducal hat, or *corno*.

voice heard and, thronging the Piazza, demanded that the ducal throne should now be given to the leading member of the one family that stood more than any other for the old, genuinely democratic Venetian order: Doge Lorenzo Tiepolo's son Giacomo.[1]

In many respects this second Giacomo Tiepolo, who could boast a fine military record extending over more than twenty years, might have made an excellent Doge. He had, however, two overwhelming disadvantages. The first, paradoxically, was that he had been the subject of popular demand. If he were now to succeed, even by due process of election, the people would conclude that their manifestations had achieved their object and would further increase their demands for political influence. To the cautious councillors of Venice, this threatened to open the way to mob rule and to the very dangers which the whole intricacy of the electoral system had been specifically designed to avoid. Fortunately, however, there was another objection to Tiepolo's candidature with which his partisans would find it harder to disagree: he was the son and grandson of former Doges. The old traditional fear of hereditary monarchy was reawakened. The fact that his family was venerable and distinguished – one of the *case vecchie* – only increased the potential risk. Three Tiepolo Doges in sixty years would be too much. Giacomo himself seemed to agree. Rather than cause any further dissension, he retired to his villa on the mainland; and shortly afterwards, according to the established process, the 38-year-old Pietro Gradenigo was elected to the vacant throne.

The family of the new Doge belonged, like the Dandolos, to the class of merchant *nouveaux riches*. As his disparaging nickname of Pierazzo suggests, the people mistrusted him; and, as was made abundantly clear by his subsequent actions, from their point of view they were right. But after the withdrawal of their own candidate they had no alternative to put forward; they doubtless noted that the official delegation which was sent to fetch Gradenigo from Capodistria – where he had been serving as *podestà* – had included a representative of the Tiepolos; and, having received the news of his election in stony silence, they grudgingly accepted him as their new ruler.

The change of Doge brought no immediate improvement in Venetian fortunes. Particularly grave was the situation in the Levant, where the Mameluke Sultan of Egypt, Al-Ashraf Khalil, was gathering his forces

1. He may possibly have been Lorenzo's nephew rather than his son: the genealogy is not altogether clear.

for the final offensive against the last survivors of the Crusader states. Tripoli had fallen in 1289, just a few months before Gradenigo's accession; now only Acre remained, with a few dependent towns along the coast. For a century it had been the capital of the Frankish East, the place of refuge for the dispossessed Kings of Jerusalem, the Princes of Galilee and Antioch and other less splendid potentates who, according to a contemporary German chronicler,[1] could be seen still wearing their golden crowns as they walked about the awning-shaded streets. Venice, Pisa, Amalfi and, till its recent eviction, Genoa, each occupied a separate quarter of its own, but the Venetian colony was considerably larger than the rest, Acre being by now the principal point of trans-shipment for its trade with Central Asia and beyond.[2]

When, on Friday 18 May 1291, the Mameluke armies stormed the city of Acre, putting to death virtually all its inhabitants, the blow to Venice was therefore greater than that sustained by any of her commercial rivals. With the obliteration of Outremer – after Acre had fallen the smaller Christian towns could not hope to hold out and quickly suffered the same fate – she had lost at a stroke not only one of her most valuable markets but also an essential entrepôt for her caravans to the further East. To be sure, this latter misfortune was not necessarily permanent; despite energetic attempts by the Pope to launch a new Crusade and his fulminations against any Christian state that dared to have dealings with the infidel, Venice almost immediately entered into discussions with the Sultan, who was later to grant her highly favourable terms. But for the immediate future her Central Asian trade was severely threatened. Everything now depended on the northern route, by way of the Black Sea ports and the Crimea – which brought her face to face once again with her old enemy, Genoa.

Until nearly half-way through the thirteenth century the prevailing political unrest around the shores of the Black Sea had made it a largely unprofitable area for commerce, and Western traders had normally tended to unload at Constantinople; but since 1242, when the Mongols succeeded in unifying the lands of the Western steppes, trading possibilities had vastly improved. After Michael Palaeologus had recovered Constantinople, he had given the Genoese exclusive rights to Black Sea trading; and

1. Herman Corner; see Eckhardt, *Corpus Historicum Medii Aevi*, Vol. II, Col. 942, Leipzig, 1723.

2. Agreeable reminders of the Central Asian trade at this period can be found in the Palazzo Mastelli, on the Campo dei Mori. Set into the wall are late thirteenth-century statues of the three Mastelli brothers, all Levantine merchants (Plate 11), while on the canal side, opposite the church of the Madonna dell'Orto, is a charming stone relief of a heavily-loaded camel.

although seven years later he had allowed the Venetians to return, Genoa – with her ever-growing colony at Galata on the Bosphorus – was still dominant in the area. Under her influence Trebizond supplanted Egypt and the Levant – where the last remnants of the Crusader states were fast disappearing – as the terminal for the Indian spice caravans; while Caffa (the modern Feodosiya) in the Crimea handled the local produce of grain, fish and salt, as well as the furs and slaves from the Russian North. In short, the Venetians found themselves faced with a formidable adversary. An uneasy truce between the two Republics, first signed in 1270 but twice renewed, expired once again in 1291, the year that Acre fell. This time there could be no extension. Genoa was determined to preserve her control, Venice equally resolved to wrest it from her.

Neither side was in a hurry to declare war. For three years preparations continued, Venice entering into an alliance with Pisa, drawing up a register of all able-bodied citizens between seventeen and sixty – who were warned to be ready for instant conscription – and calling upon the richest families of the city to finance the manning and equipment of one, two or even three galleys.[1] Finally, on 7 October 1294, the fleet set sail. Its first engagement, in the far north-east corner of the Mediterranean near the Gulf of Alexandretta, was a catastrophe. The Genoese, seeing that they were outnumbered, adopted the curious tactic of lashing all their ships together to make a single huge floating platform. The almost total loss of manoeuvrability that must have resulted seems to have been outweighed by the fact that they thus exposed a much reduced surface area to their assailants while their crews, able to pass freely from one vessel to the next, could concentrate their strength wherever the fighting was fiercest. The Venetian admiral, Marco Basegio, made the cardinal mistake of underestimating his enemy. Scorning the use of fire-ships, he decided on a direct attack; but the Genoese square did not break, and in the fighting that followed Venice lost twenty-five galleys out of sixty-eight and many of her best men, including Basegio himself.

Genoa was not slow to follow up her advantage. Her navy swooped down on Crete, burning and sacking Canea; then, in 1295, cleverly drawing away the escort of galleys, it utterly destroyed the annual Venetian *carovana* – which, since the fall of Acre and with the Genoese at Galata effectively blocking the Bosphorus, was now loading at the inadequate little ports on the south coast of Asia Minor – in the half-way harbour of Modone. The following year brought still graver news, this time from

1. The only families which were considered rich enough to take on three were the Querini, Contarini, Morosini and Dandolo.

Constantinople. Once again, fighting had broken out between the Venetian and Genoese colonies in the city, in the course of which many Venetians had been massacred. Those who had escaped the slaughter, including the *bailo*, had been immediately arrested by the Emperor Andronicus II – Michael's son, who had clearly inherited all his father's proclivity for casting in his lot with the winning side – and clapped into prison.

This last outrage seemed to snap Venice out of her lethargy. A fleet of forty ships was quickly prepared and dispatched under the command of Rogerio Morosini, nicknamed Malabranca, 'the Evil Claw'. Racing through the Dardanelles and burning every Greek or Genoese ship in sight, he attacked and ravaged Galata. Then, turning up the Golden Horn, he dropped anchor beneath the walls of the imperial palace of Blachernae and destroyed one of the Emperor's galleys laid up on the shore. It was only after Andronicus had paid him a huge indemnity that he returned, with a host of Genoese prisoners, in triumph to the lagoon. At about the same time another Venetian fleet under Giovanni Soranzo burst through the Genoese blockade of the Bosphorus and into the Black Sea, where it seized Caffa and held it against furious attack from the Tartars until the coming of winter at length persuaded it to withdraw.

For three more years the war dragged on, with encounters between the two navies all over the central Mediterranean from Sicily to Cyprus and, in 1298, one more resounding victory for the Genoese off the Dalmatian coast near Curzola.[1] Once again they were numerically weaker, but they had the advantage of the wind and, in Lamba Doria, one of the most brilliant admirals of the age. The Venetian ships were surrounded, and packed so tightly together that a fire breaking out on one of them quickly spread. The crews from Chioggia in particular fought heroically but, when the battle was over, out of the ninety-five Venetian ships that had been involved sixty-five had been taken or sunk. Nine thousand men were killed or wounded, and a further 5,000 borne off captive to Genoa. One at least never arrived: the Venetian admiral, Andrea Dandolo – not to be confused with the historian Doge – is said to have killed himself by beating his head against a mast. Another, more fortunate and more sensible, whiled away his year in a Genoese gaol by dictating to a fellow-prisoner a report of his journeyings in the East – a work later to become celebrated as the *Travels* or *Description of the World*, by Marco Polo.

Despite his extraordinary career, and although he was the author of

1. Korčula.

177

perhaps the most influential travel book ever written, Marco Polo came of a family entirely typical of the Venetian merchant aristocracy of his day. His father, Nicolò Polo, was one of three brothers who were also business partners and of whom at least one, Marco the elder, was resident at Constantinople; but all three seem to have made regular journeys to the Crimea and beyond, for in about 1260 we hear of Nicolò and the third brother, Maffeo, travelling as far east as Bokhara. Here it was that they chanced to meet envoys from the Mongol ruler Kublai Khan, and were persuaded to accompany them back to Kublai's court in what is now Peking.

Unlike his predecessors on the Mongol throne, Kublai Khan was possessed of a remarkably open mind, which he combined with an almost limitless intellectual curiosity. So impressed was he by what the Polo brothers had to tell him about Europe and, in particular, the Christian religion that he decided to send them back to the West as special envoys to Pope Clement IV, with a request that the Pope in his turn should send out a group of educated men to give his people instruction in Christianity and the liberal arts. Back went the brothers, only to find on reaching Acre that Clement had just died, and that no successor had yet been elected. Rather than wait indefinitely at Acre, therefore, they decided to return to Venice.

Had they not done so; had the Pope not died when he did; had they set out again for the East at once as originally planned, it is unlikely that the name of Marco Polo would ever have been heard of. But when Nicolò got home in 1270, after ten years' absence, he found that his wife had died and his son had grown almost to manhood; and when the following year, after the longest interregnum in papal history, the Polos were at last able to fulfil their mission to the new Pope Gregory X – an old personal friend – and embark once again on their long journey back to furthest Asia, they took young Marco with them.

Of the route they followed – through Persia, Oxiana, the Pamirs, Kashgar and the Gobi desert – Marco was later to give the first description ever to reach the West, and indeed virtually the last until the middle of the nineteenth century. It was long and hard, and took four years; at last, however, the Venetians reached Kublai's summer palace at Shangtu. The 21-year-old Marco was an immediate success with the Emperor, who listened enthralled to the stories of his adventures and the wonders he had seen on the journey, and at once took him into the imperial service. Within a short time he was one of the Khan's most trusted officials, travelling the length and breadth of the Empire, governing remote cities and provinces, and carrying out missions to South India and even beyond.

Whether his father and uncle accompanied him on these missions is uncertain. What does seem clear, however, is that Kublai found all three Polos so interesting, or so useful, or both, that for many years he could not be persuaded to let them go. It was only in 1292, when an escort was needed for a Mongol princess who had been promised in marriage to the Persian Khan, that they were at last permitted to leave.

The story of their return after nearly a quarter of a century to the great house in Venice, of their non-recognition by family and friends, and of the subsequent *coup de théâtre* when they suddenly threw back their shabby oriental robes, ripped open the linings and allowed torrents of emeralds, rubies and pearls to cascade over the floor, has become part of the Polo legend. But despite the incredulity with which Marco's stories were received and the exaggeration of which he was accused – earning him the not invariably affectionate nickname of *Milion* because, it was said, he always talked in millions – the book which he dictated to his fellow-prisoner in Genoa is by no means simply the collection of tall stories it was once presumed to be. Many of his descriptions are remarkably accurate; several have been confirmed, after the passage of centuries, by research in Chinese archives. He speaks with authority not only of Kublai's brilliant court at Peking but of his whole Empire, from the far North with its dog-sledges and reindeer to Ceylon, Burma, Siam, Java, Sumatra and Japan – lands unheard of before his time – and even, by hearsay, of the Christian Empire of Abyssinia, of Madagascar and Zanzibar.

Marco Polo died in 1324 and was buried in the church of S. Lorenzo. His sarcophagus was unfortunately lost when the church was rebuilt in 1592; his will, however, has survived in the Marciana Library. There also remain a few vestiges of the old Polo house – including a superb Byzantine archway beneath which Marco must have passed countless times – in a remote corner just behind the church of S. Giovanni Crisostomo, still called, after the greatest and most celebrated of medieval travellers, the *Corte Seconda del Milion*.

After the battle of Curzola the war between Venice and Genoa entered its final phase. There were no more major engagements. A Genoese raiding party managed to attack Malamocco; in retaliation the Venetian Domenico Schiavo, who had already distinguished himself in the attack on Caffa a year or two before, penetrated into the inner harbour of Genoa with three galleys and, as a final insult, actually minted some Venetian coins there before retiring; but both sides were more than ready for peace. In the final reckoning the Venetians had undeniably come off the worse; their reputation in the Mediterranean and beyond had sustained a heavy blow and their self-confidence had been rudely shaken. But despite her splendid victories, Genoa too had suffered much. Though her prestige had never been higher, her total losses had fallen not far short of those of Venice, while her resources from which to make them good were still immeasurably inferior. By contrast the Venetians, tired as they might be, were even now preparing yet another fleet of 100 ships and recruiting teams of Catalan mercenaries to fill the gaps among their cross-bowmen.

The peace treaty, which was eventually signed in May 1299, was negotiated by Matteo Visconti, who had recently come to power in Milan and had offered his services as mediator. It was honourable to both parties; there was no suggestion of victor and vanquished. Nevertheless its terms were unusual – an indication of the narrowness of the distinction still prevailing between legitimate naval warfare and simple freebootery. It was not considered sufficient for the two Republics to pledge their mutual non-aggression; every Venetian captain was individually obliged to swear that he would not attack any Genoese vessel, and vice versa. The Genoese were specifically allowed, however, to go to the defence of any part of the Greek Empire in the event of a Venetian attack. In any war between Genoa and Pisa, the Venetians were to be debarred from Corsica, Sardinia, or any part of the Ligurian coast between Civitavecchia and Nice, always excepting Genoa itself; similarly, if there were fighting in the Adriatic, the Genoese must avoid all ports there except Venice. The treaty was to be ratified not only by the two principals, but also by Padua and Verona on the part of Venice and by Asti and Tortona on the part of Genoa.

The reference to the Greek Empire makes it clear that Venice's quarrel with Andronicus Palaeologus was still unsettled. It was to take another three years, another punitive expedition to Constantinople and the exemplary flogging of Greek prisoners on the decks of the Venetian ships beneath the walls of Blachernae before the Emperor could be brought to terms. And by then Venice herself would be radically, organically, changed.

13

The Oligarchs Triumphant

[1297–1310]

. . . Une ville comme Venise, maîtresse d'un immense et lointain empire, aurait été incapable de le gouverner si elle avait été régie par des institutions démocratiques. Comme l'aristocratie anglaise, à laquelle il ressemble, le patriciat vénétien a donné à la ville de saint Marc des familles où l'art de gouvernement était en quelque sorte héréditaire, et les hommes ont pu changer sans que changeassent les principes et l'esprit politiques. Et c'est pourquoi ce régime oligarchique a conquis en somme le respect et la confiance de ceux qui y furent soumis, par la claire conscience qu'il a donné à tous de son honnêteté et de sa sagesse, par l'ambition qu'il a manifestée de travailler en toute circonstance à la sécurité et à la grandeur de la patrie. Et c'est pourquoi enfin, au XIVe et au XVe siècle, le gouvernement de Venise était probablement un des meilleurs qu'il y eût au monde, et celui qui pouvait le plus utilement servir la cité de saint Marc.

Charles Diehl, *Venise: une République Patricienne*

Matteo Visconti, the self-styled 'Captain-General of Milan' was only one – albeit the most powerful – of the many despots who from about the middle of the thirteenth century had begun to seize control of the cities of North Italy. The Scaligeri were already established in Verona, the Este in Modena and Ferrara; in Mantua, the Gonzaga were poised ready to spring. Tyrants though they might all be in the strict classical sense, their rule was not normally oppressive; more often than not they were popular with their subjects, for whom life was a good deal more peaceful and secure than it had ever been in their fathers' and grandfathers' day.

To the Venetians, however, they were anathema. Again and again we find the Republic strengthening its defences against a similar takeover. The ducal *promissioni* with their ever more stringent measures to prevent nepotism, Renier Zeno's ban on the display of crests or escutcheons, the nightmare rigmarole of the Doge's election, the refusal to consider a third Tiepolo for the vacant throne – all these were symptoms of what, by the turn of the century, had developed into a neurosis. The dangers were in fact greatly exaggerated. Those magnificent autocrats of the mainland had their roots in a tradition which was quite alien to anything Venice had known. They were the products of the highly developed feudal system of western Europe, and of the municipal reaction against it; of the long, grinding contest between Empire and Papacy, Ghibelline and Guelf; and of the quarrels and rivalries that had at once stimulated and bedevilled the rise of the Italian communes.

Venice, on the other hand, was the child of Byzantium, where feudalism – at least until the Fourth Crusade – was unheard of. Not since Charlemagne's treaty with the Emperor Nicephorus had the Western Empire made any serious claim upon her. She was neither Guelf nor Ghibelline. Virtually alone among the major communities of North Italy, she had never been conquered or even invaded. While the rest, when they were not anxiously watching each other, had had to keep their eyes trained northwards to the Emperor beyond the Alps or southwards to the Pope in Rome, Venice had simply turned her back on Italy and looked to the East, to the world that had shaped her beginnings and held the greatest promise for her future. Her political development had thus proceeded on completely different lines from those followed by her sister-cities. They had taken the path of communal government and then, when that had failed, had veered sharply round towards autocracy. She, by contrast, had pursued an unwavering course in a single direction: that of self-perpetuating oligarchy which, when finally achieved, was to govern her – on the whole wisely and well – for almost exactly 500 years until the end came.

At the apex of the political pyramid, the power exercised by the Doge had long been declining. The process had begun with Domenico Flabanico in 1032, when he had put a stop to the practice by which Doges nominated colleagues and successors and had hemmed them round instead with counsellors and *pregadi*; it had continued with the establishment of the Great Council after the assassination of Vitale Michiel in 1172; and, as successive *promissioni* proved, it had not yet ended.[1] At the base of the same pyramid the Venetian populace had as we have already seen lost virtually all its influence and, as recently as 1289, had signally failed to reassert it. Thus the effective basis of the constitution had now become the Great Council, a seat in which was the first step to political power. For those without the advantages of wealth or family

1. A particularly instructive example was provided by the *promissione* of Jacopo Contarini in 1275. The eighty-year-old Doge was obliged to swear, *inter alia*, that he would not take a foreign wife without the consent of the Council, and that neither he nor his sons would buy land outside the Republic or take shares in government loans. Fiefs – presumably in the new Venetian colonies – held by any member of his family were to be given up within a year of his accession. His sons were further explicitly debarred from accepting any state office or employment, apart from those of ambassador or ship's captain.

connections, membership was not easy to obtain. From the start the Council had been self-electing; thus, inevitably over the years, it had grown more and more into a closed society. In 1293, to give but one instance, it included ten Foscari, eleven Morosini and no less than eighteen Contarini. Theoretically, however, and to some degree in practice also, its doors had remained open.

Now, in the last few years of the thirteenth century, Pietro Gradenigo closed them for ever.

Already in 1286, during the dogeship of Giovanni Dandolo, it had been proposed that eligibility for the Council should be restricted to those whose fathers or more distant paternal ancestors had themselves been members. The motion had been rejected by a comfortable majority – including Dandolo himself – and when Gradenigo reopened the question ten years later he met with no greater success. But the young Doge – he was still only forty-five – was renowned for his energy and determination, and on the last day of February, 1297,[1] a new law was proposed and accepted, the most important clause of which required the *Quarantia*[2] to ballot, one by one, on the names of all those who during the previous four years had had a seat in the Great Council, and decreed that all who received twelve or more votes should be members of it until Michaelmas – the normal time for its elections – 1298. When that time came the system was prolonged for a further year and the decree was again renewed in 1299, after which it became the established law of Venice.

For those debarred by these conditions, one loophole remained. Provision was made for three electors, holding office for one year only, whose task would be to submit for election, on the authority and approval of the Doge and his advisers, the names of other candidates not previously eligible. In theory, this provision might be thought to have opened the doors wide again; in fact there is reason to suspect that it was a deliberate attempt by a wily, disingenuous Doge to deceive the opposition. By retaining the power of veto over all new names, he robbed it of much of its force; and in the years that followed he made it clear through the electors that it would be applied in practice only in favour of those who had sat in the Council at some earlier date, or who could prove that a paternal forbear had done so.

These measures did nothing to diminish the size of the Council. On the contrary, as more and more Venetians hastened to prove their eligibility, its numbers – which for many years had been declining from the

1. 1296 according to the contemporary calendar, in which the new year began in March.
2. See p. 123.

original 480 – rapidly increased. Whereas in 1296 it could boast only 210 members, by 1311 there were 1,017 and, by 1340, 1,212. Naturally, not all of these would be present on any one occasion. Venice was small, her foreign interests immense; a considerable proportion of her leading citizens could always be expected to be abroad on diplomatic or commercial business. Nevertheless by 1301 the existing chamber had already become too small[1] and had given place to another, probably half-way down the eastern side of the building.[2] Thus, in the eyes of those responsible for it, the new law probably appeared not so much a restriction as a purification of the body politic; certainly the oligarchy that had so suddenly crystallized could not be described as a narrow one. And yet, for all that, there can be no denying that what has gone down in Venetian history as the *Serrata* – literally, the locking – *del Maggior Consiglio* created, at a stroke, a closed caste in the society of the Republic: a caste with its own inner elite of those who had sat in the Great Council during those four critical years between 1293 and 1297, but which also embraced those whose parentage, or whose own past record, gave them a title to membership. To guard against false claims, the barriers of privilege were raised even higher. In 1315 a list was compiled of all Venetian citizens eligible for election; and from this, in view of the rigid exclusion of all those born out of wedlock or of a non-patrician mother, it was a short step to that great register of noble marriages and births that was later to become famous as the *Libro d'Oro* – the Golden Book.

But what, it might be asked, of the other Venetians, of the immense majority who – though many of them might be rich, intelligent and cultivated – were not qualified to enter this exalted company? Understandably, there was a good deal of initial indignation; but after the passing of a generation or so, when they had had time to accustom themselves to the new dispensation, their resentment was, for the most part at any rate, a good deal less than might have been supposed. There existed – it is impossible to say for how long, since the institution had

---

1. It probably occupied most of the ground floor of the old Palace built by Sebastiano Ziani. According to a surviving document dated 1255, loitering in the neighbouring courtyard was forbidden, and anyone guilty of rowdiness or games-playing outside the windows was liable to be thrown into the water.

2. That which faces the prisons across the narrow Rio di Palazzo, now spanned by the Bridge of Sighs. This addition – which marked the beginning of the transformation of the Doges' Palace from Byzantine to Gothic – did not last long. Much of it disappeared when the Palace was further enlarged some forty years later. The only important features still surviving are the two traceried windows at each side of the south-east corner (See p. 211.)

grown up gradually over the years – a second social order in Venice. This was the class of *cittadini*, the citizens. More humble than their patrician governors, they could none the less take a modest pride in their superiority over the mob – the same sort of pride, perhaps, that St Paul took on being a citizen of the Roman Empire. Later they were to become something distinctly higher, a kind of baronetage roughly akin to the equestrian order in Rome; but even before the *Serrata* they had established their claim to respect. The proof was already there in 1268 when the office of Grand Chancellor had been instituted in Venice, with an explicit proviso that it should always be held by a member of the *cittadini*. It was an office as exalted as its name implies. The Grand Chancellor was the effective head, not only of the ducal chancery but of the entire civil service of the Republic. He wore purple and ranked above Senators, yielding precedence only to the Doge and Signoria and the Procurators of St Mark. Except for the franchise, he enjoyed every prerogative of the nobility. He held his seals for life and when he died was entitled to a funeral of similar splendour to that of the Doge himself.

Other posts, less influential but of considerable importance none the less, were open to *cittadini* and nobility alike; and it was typical of Venetian political wisdom that as time went on the *cittadini* became more and more a bulwark of the oligarchic system, rather than a subversive element outside it – particularly since the so-called *privilegio* of citizenship was not easily accorded. For foreigners seeking it, twenty-five years' residence in Venice or her dominions was the initial requirement; citizenship *de extra*, which allowed its holders full protection outside the boundaries of the Republic, was even harder to obtain. Certain fortunate individuals – craftsmen of rare skills, perhaps, or those who had rendered some signal service – might be rewarded with immediate admission. But by the same token it was the dream of every *cittadino* that, having himself deserved particularly well of the state, he too might similarly slip through the mesh above him and take his place among the nobility.

This is not to say that no voices were raised against Pietro Gradenigo's tremendous step. Some of the new disenfranchised chose, indeed, to rebel – like a certain Marin Bocconio who, as early as the year 1300, conceived a plot to murder the Doge and to overthrow his government. He seems to have been just the sort of man who would most bitterly resent the new dispensations – rich, ambitious, able to call on considerable popular support, but now finding himself permanently debarred from political advancement. Alas, he proved to be a not very gifted conspirator, and the Venetian security police was already an organization to be reckoned with. Bocconio and ten of his colleagues were arrested, and hanged in the usual place – between the two columns in the Piazzetta.[1] His attempt to defend the rights of his fellow-citizens had been a fiasco. It was not, however, the last.

On 31 January 1308, the Marquis Azzo VIII of Este died at Ferrara. For 200 years the house of Este had been one of the most powerful in North Italy. Padua and Verona, Mantua and Modena had all at various times come under its influence, and at Ferrara, through the earlier part of the thirteenth century, it had stoutly defended the Guelf cause against the Ghibelline captain, Salinguerra Torelli. Thus, when the city fell to the Venetians in 1240 and Salinguerra was taken prisoner, the Este had been the obvious choice to take over the effective government; and, although they had ruled virtually as Venetian satraps ever since, they had remained loyal champions of the Guelfs and had given successive Popes cause for complaint.

Azzo's death, however, created a problem. He left no legitimate offspring, only two brothers; but there was a natural son, Fosco, who in turn had a son, Folco; and it was this grandson whom Azzo had named as his heir. No dispensation could have been better calculated to cause trouble. The brothers, furious, disputed the will; Fosco, in an attempt to safeguard his son's inheritance, appealed for help to Venice; Venice dispatched a military force; and from his new seat at Avignon[2] Pope Clement V, determined at all costs to prevent a direct Venetian take-over in Ferrara, resurrected the long-dormant papal claim to suzerainty over the city and decreed in favour of the brothers. In face of this rapid escalation, Fosco lost his nerve. His position in Ferrara had never been strong, and he was certainly not prepared to make a stand against the Pope. Pausing only long enough to install the Venetian militia in the Castel Tedaldo, he fled to Venice, simultaneously ceding to the Republic all his son's claims.

Papal troops now entered Ferrara in their turn; and the legate, Cardinal Pelagrua, sent an embassy to the Doge, demanding the immediate recall of his forces. The Venetians stood firm. They had not sought this sudden

1. See p. 118. The most reliable source (Caresini, quoted by Romanin, III, p. 6) says that they were hanged *turpissime*, which Horatio Brown takes to mean head downwards.

2. The Papacy had removed its seat to Avignon in 1307, and was to remain there for the next seventy years.

armed confrontation, nor had they expected it; but possession of the Castel Tedaldo, commanding as it did the city and the all-important bridge over the Po, afforded them a considerable strategic advantage and they did not feel disposed to give in to threats, from whatever quarter these might come. The legate offered a compromise, whereby Venice might hold the city as a papal fief, in recognition of an annual rent of 20,000 ducats. Still they refused to yield. All rights over Ferrara, they pointed out, had been freely ceded to them by the house of Este. There was no more to be said on the matter.

Cardinal Pelagrua disagreed. On 25 October 1308, he gave the Venetians ten days in which to submit. If they persisted in their attitude, excommunication and interdict would be pronounced on the Republic of Venice, its Doge, his councillors and captains and all those who in defiance of the papal command had given advice or assistance against the forces of the Holy See. All Venetian goods and possessions in Ferrara would be declared confiscate, all commercial treaties annulled, all trade and traffic suspended. Venice – and Chioggia, whose ships had caused particular havoc among the papal transports along the Po – would be subjected to a blockade; such privileges as the Republic had ever been granted by the Pope would be withdrawn.

It was the second time within a quarter of a century that Venice had faced the ban of the Church; but whereas the interdict of 1284 had been largely confined to spiritual sanctions, this new threat affected her whole political and economic life. In its earlier stages, the problem of Ferrara had been entrusted to a special committee of the Great Council, originally twenty in number and later, as the situation deteriorated, increased to forty-five. To meet the present crisis, however, even this was not considered sufficient; the whole Council assembled, several hundred strong. Opinion was sharply divided. Most members of the *case vecchie*, led by Jacopo Querini, pressed for the Republic to capitulate: governments, they pointed out, just as much as individuals, were bound to fear God and to hold in reverence the Vicar of Christ on earth. Besides, Venice had not yet fully recovered, financially or materially, from a long period of wars; this was no moment to embark on yet another, which threatened to be more disastrous than any that had gone before.

Doge Gradenigo, as might have been expected, took the opposite view. The question at issue was political, not spiritual; and politically, the first duty of every man, be he prince or private citizen, was to the state – to increase its dominions, to strengthen its authority, to burnish its glory. Great opportunities occurred seldom; the wise statesman must recognize them and seize them. Here was just such an occasion, by which Venice stood to gain supremacy and security of communications all along the Po. Her rights to Ferrara were unassailable. As for Pope Clement, far away beyond the Alps, he was simply misinformed. Once the true position had been explained to him, it was inconceivable that he would proceed in such a way against the people of Venice, who were loyal sons of the Church and only too anxious to remain so.[1]

The debate was long and angry, and was not confined to the Council Chamber. All the old enmities between the two major factions – on the one side the *case vecchie*, populist, pro-papal, Guelfish, led by the families of Querini and Tiepolo, on the other the oligarchs, champions of territorial expansion, represented by the Gradenigos and the Dandolos – flared up again. Brawls and riots once more became commonplace; citizens went armed about the streets. At last, however, the party of the Doge proved the stronger. Ferrara was Venetian property, and would remain so. A Venetian *podestà* was appointed for the city, and the Ferraresi were granted full rights of Venetian citizenship.

The threatened consequences did not follow at once. Winter had come, and communications with Avignon were tenuous. By the early spring of 1309 it was agreed that a delegation should be sent to Pope Clement to explain 'submissively, but with dignity', the Venetian position. Alas, the decision came too late. The very day after the ambassadors were due to set out, on Maundy Thursday, 27 March, the Pope pronounced his excommunication. Its terms were even more fearsome than had been expected. In addition to the penalties already foreshadowed, the subjects of the Doge were all absolved of their oaths of loyalty to him; they were debarred from giving evidence or making wills; any man might deprive them of their liberty, or even enslave them, without penalty in this world or the next. Finally, all clergy were bound to leave the territory of the Republic within ten days after the expiry of the month's grace that was still allowed in case of a last-minute change of heart.

It says much for the courage of Pietro Gradenigo and those around him that even now Venice did not flinch. Economic and commercial ruin stared her in the face; and, as expected, on the very day that the month's grace expired and the Pope's dreadful sentence came into effect, her enemies and rivals struck. In every corner of Europe and a large

1. The summaries of these speeches are taken, via Romanin, from the Chronicle of Marco Barbaro in the Marciana Library. As Barbaro was writing in the mid-sixteenth century, however, it is more than likely that he is working on the Thucydidean principle, reporting not what was actually said, but the speeches which he himself would have made given the arguments available.

part of Asia, Venetian goods were seized, Venetian assets confiscated, Venetian ships attacked and plundered. In one direction only could Venetian merchantmen still sail out from the Rialto and be assured of a welcome: how the Republic's citizens must have blessed that day in 1297 when in a similar defiance of papal orders they had signed their commercial treaty with the Mameluke Sultan of Egypt, now – since the fall of Acre – controlling the whole Palestinian littoral. It was the one lifeline that the Pope had been powerless to cut.

But already nearly a month before, as soon as the papal Bull had been received by the Doge, the Venetian *podestà* in Ferrara had been ordered to entrench himself in the Castel Tedaldo and to make ready his defences; and when in July the Cardinal Legate proclaimed a Crusade against Venice all the necessary preparations were complete. Florence, Lucca, Ancona and a number of other towns in Tuscany, Lombardy and Romagna, spurred on by jealousy, greed and – one must be fair – perhaps a modicum of filial piety and obedience, hastened to the papal colours and closed in on Ferrara. And the siege began.

From the first, things went badly for the Republic. Her garrison fought with courage but pestilence broke out almost at once, carrying off the *podestà* and increasing numbers of his men. Reinforcements were hurried out, with Marco Querini della Ca' Grande and Giovanni Soranzo smashing through the chain that the papalists had drawn across the Po and forcing their way to the beleaguered citadel. But the enemy forces were too strong, the epidemic grew steadily more virulent, and when the fortress was stormed on 28 August those of the garrison who were still alive lacked the strength to resist. One or two, like Querini, managed to escape; the remainder were blinded or butchered, or both.

Another defeat, another humiliation; yet even now the Venetians did not immediately submit. The war dragged on, half-heartedly – on the Pope's side because of difficulties with Francesco d'Este, one of the brothers whose claims he had upheld; on Venice's because, as we shall soon see, she was occupied with a new crisis at home. Her lesson was still unlearnt. It was to take several more, costlier still, before she was brought to understand the simple truth that her prosperity was founded on trade, and not on territorial aggrandizement. Her strength lay in her unique situation, sea-girt like no other city in the world, secure and inviolable. If, by seeking adventures on *terra firma*, she were to deny herself this one supreme advantage, she could only bring about her own destruction.

As, ultimately, she did.

14

The Conspiracy and the Council

[1310]

Del mille tresento e diese
A mezzo el mese delle ceriese,
Bagiamonte passò el ponte
E per esso fo fatto il consegio di diese.

In one thousand three hundred and ten,
When the cherries were ripening again,
Old Bagiamonte
Passed over the *ponte*
And they founded the Council of Ten.

Old Venetian song, from *Splendor*
Magnificentissimae Urbis Venetiarum,
in Graevius, *Thesaurus Antiquitatum Italiae,* V

By the spring of 1310, Doge Pietro Gradenigo was the most detested man in Venice. The vast majority of his subjects were still smarting over their disenfranchisement; almost all of them held him responsible for the papal interdict, which had not only had a direct impact on the life of every man, woman and child in the Republic but had also brought trade to a virtual standstill. The merchant community in particular, faced with the dual prospect of financial ruin in this world and spiritual damnation in the next, made no secret of their loathing of the man whom they rightly saw as the author of their misfortunes.

To everyone, the news that had reached the lagoon in the last days of the previous August had come as a further shattering blow. Until that moment, there had still been a chance that the Doge's gamble might succeed. Even then, Venice would have been the loser in material terms; possession of Ferrara and mastery of the Po would have availed her little in the face of a multilateral blockade. But at least she would have had something to show for her stand, and her prestige would have remained high. Now even that possibility was gone. The war still continued, and the interdict; but no longer was there any hope of victory. All her sacrifices had been for nothing. Since then, Pietro Gradenigo's enemies had become more vocal. Both inside and outside the Council Chamber, they hammered home their message again and again: how the Doge had betrayed the Republic; how Jacopo Querini and his followers had never ceased to oppose the policies that had brought disgrace and disaster in their wake; how, if Giacomo Tiepolo had been elected as the people had wished, Venice would not now be in her present plight – at war with the Pope, her commercial Empire collapsing about her ears, deprived by a stroke of unparalleled political idiocy of the wise counsel and expertise of many of her most brilliant citizens. The *case vecchie*, who had always enjoyed the support of the people, had once again proved themselves to be far-seeing, clear-thinking and triumphantly right. As for Pietro Gradenigo's reputation for statesmanship – it lay, together with his popularity, at the bottom of the lagoon.

But Gradenigo was still Doge, and still in control. Demonstrations and street fighting, though now more frequent than ever, were ruthlessly put down by his security police, by the *Capi di Contrada*[1] and by the sinisterly-named *Signori di Notte*; and Pietro himself, heedless of public feeling, continued to behave with all his old arrogance. Tempers thus continued to rise, and in the prevailing atmosphere it did not take much to bring them to flash point. The issue that finally did so was in itself relatively insignificant: the proposal to appoint Doimo, Count of Veglia,[2] as one of the six ducal councillors. This was violently opposed by Jacopo Querini, who pointed out that Dalmatian Counts were expressly debarred from all public office except membership of the Great Council and the *pregadi*. His case, relying as it did on the written law of the Republic, was unanswerable; none the less, the appointment was confirmed.

To the Tiepolos, the Querini and their followers, it was the last straw. Fighting broke out again in the Piazza and elsewhere, in the course of which a Tiepolo was gravely wounded by a Dandolo. Civil war seemed imminent, and the government published an emergency decree making it an offence to carry arms. It was a wise measure; unfortunately it had the opposite effect to what was intended. A night or two later, Piero Querini della Ca' Grande, accosted by one of the Signori di Notte and ordered to submit to a search, replied with a violent kick which sent the official sprawling. His followers hurried to his aid, and within minutes the whole quarter was up in arms. Piero was arrested, found guilty and

1. At this time there were thirty *contrade*, or parishes, in Venice; an average of five to each *sestiere*.
2. Now Krk, an island on the Dalmatian coast.

punished. But the matter did not end there. His brother Marco was already nursing a personal grievance against the Doge, who had publicly accused him of cowardice at the time of his escape from Ferrara; and Marco now called a secret meeting of his friends. They readily agreed with him, as he had known they would, that Pietro Gradenigo could no longer be allowed to remain in office; but their first recommendation was, on the face of it, surprising. To lead the conspiracy, they suggested that Querini should summon, from a self-imposed exile on the mainland, his son-in-law Bajamonte Tiepolo.

Though now stigmatized – perhaps not altogether fairly – as one of the blackest villains in the history of Venice, Bajamonte Tiepolo remains a strangely mysterious figure. He was a great-grandson of Bohèmund of Brienne, Prince of the petty Crusader state of Rascia in Bosnia (from whom he seems to have derived his curious Christian name), grandson of Doge Lorenzo and son of that Giacomo who had refused to contest the dogeship with Pietro Gradenigo twenty years before. Of his own background, however, we know little apart from a curious report by Marco Barbaro – writing, it must be remembered, two centuries later – to the effect that in 1300 he had been accused of extortion in the twin Peloponnesian colonies of Modone and Corone. By 1302, with the sum in question still not fully repaid, he had been nominated *podestà* at Nona and a member of the Quarantia, now the supreme judicial body in the state; but the accusation had continued to rankle, and rather than accept these appointments he had retired to his villa at Marocco across the lagoon. Not, in itself, a particularly distinguished record; but there must, one feels, have been more to Bajamonte Tiepolo than this – some quality of character or now-forgotten exploit that made him a well-known, popular and perhaps romantic figure in Venetian eyes. *Il gran cavaliere*, men called him; and when Marco Querini and his fellow-conspirators assembled to plan the overthrow of the Doge, they clearly believed his support to be in some way indispensable to their plans.

Only one voice, at this first meeting, was raised in opposition to the whole idea; that of old Jacopo Querini, who had spent much of his political life fighting Gradenigo and all he stood for but who refused categorically to lend his support to an unconstitutional act of violence. Jacopo, however, was shortly to leave on a government mission to Constantinople; within a few weeks he would be safely out of the way. Meanwhile Bajamonte arrived, and gave himself whole-heartedly to the cause. Political adventurer as he undoubtedly was, he seems to have seen the plot as a means of overthrowing not just Pietro Gradenigo but the whole Venetian constitution, and of establishing himself and his family as despots on the mainland pattern.

The date fixed for the insurrection was Monday 15 June, the Feast of St Vitus. The conspirators had divided themselves into three groups. Two of these, under Bajamonte Tiepolo and Marco Querini respectively, were to assemble on the evening before at the Querini house in S. Polo; thence, at first light, they would cross the Rialto bridge and advance by separate routes to the Piazza and the Doges' Palace. Meanwhile the third group, which had gathered at the little mainland village of Peraga under the leadership of Badoero Badoer,[1] would cross the lagoon at the last moment, wait until the government troops were fully occupied and then, it was hoped, fall on them from the rear.

It was not a particularly imaginative plan, but given the all-important element of surprise it might well have succeeded. Unfortunately, like Marin Bocconio before them, Bajamonte and his friends had underestimated their Doge. A certain Marco Donato who had formerly been a member of the conspiracy suddenly withdrew from it. Whether or not he had been suborned we shall never know; it seems likely enough. Through him, at any rate, Gradenigo was fully informed of the *coup* several days before it was due to take place. This gave him time to summon all his most trusted lieutenants, including the *podestà* of Torcello, Murano and Chioggia, with as many armed men as they could muster; and on the eve of St Vitus they, together with the Signoria, the heads of the Quarantia, the Avogadori, the Signori di Notte and the workmen of the Arsenal who traditionally formed the Doge's personal bodyguard, all secretly assembled in the Palace. Meanwhile, on the Piazza, his Dandolo allies were out in strength.

That night there arose one of those violent summer storms to which Venice has always been subject, whipping up the waters of the lagoon to the point at which Badoer and his party were unable to cross to the city. Had they been able to get a message across to Bajamonte, he might well have postponed the whole operation. But knowing no more of their difficulties than he did of the Doge's own preparations he decided, despite the pouring rain, to proceed as planned. Marco Querini and his son Benedetto consequently set off at the head of the first detachment, galloping[2] through the narrow *calli* to shouts of '*Libertà, e Morte al Doge*

1. The family of Badoer, under its former name of Participazio, was one of the oldest in Venice, with the record number of seven Doges to its credit in the ninth and tenth centuries (see p. 21 n.).

2. At this period, before most of the canal bridges were arched high enough for boats to

Gradenigo!' – which, we are told, were scarcely audible above the howling of the wind – and entering the Piazza half-way along the north side, across what is now the Ponte dei Dai. They fell straight into the arms of the waiting Dandolos. Taken by surprise and heavily outnumbered, there was little they could do. Many of them, including the two Querinis, father and son, were killed; the remainder fled to the nearby Campo S. Luca, where they made a vague attempt to regroup but were again put to flight, even more shamingly, by the confraternity of the *Scuola della Carità* and a few members of the Painters' Guild.

Meanwhile Bajamonte, riding at the head of his company along the Merceria, had paused under the great elder tree which at that time stood by the church of S. Giuliano. Why he did so is uncertain. He may have wished to gather his forces together for the final charge into the Piazza; alternatively and more probably, one of Querini's men may have come back to warn him of the dangers ahead. But warnings were unnecessary, for by now the whole *sestiere* was in an uproar. Clearly, the local populace was not rallying to the insurgents as had been expected. There were no cheers; only insults and imprecations flung from the windows of the barricaded houses. At last Tiepolo advanced to the entrance of the Piazza, where the clock-tower now stands, at which point an old woman tipped a heavy stone mortar out of an upper window. It missed him, but struck his standard-bearer squarely on the head and killed him outright. The sight of his banner, emblazoned with the single word *Libertas*, lying in the mud – for the deluge continued and most of the streets were still unpaved – finally shattered his nerve. Sodden and bedraggled, he and his followers fled back across the Rialto bridge, destroying it behind them.

The insurrection, however, was not quite over. Although Badoer and his group on the mainland were quickly rounded up, brought to Venice and beheaded, Bajamonte managed to entrench himself in his own quarter where, soon afterwards, the survivors of the Querini party joined him. The district was heavily fortified with barricades; the inhabitants of the further side of the Grand Canal, unlike those of S. Marco, were totally loyal to the *case vecchie*; and Doge Gradenigo, despite his victory, could not risk a civil war by launching a direct attack. His terms were generous; and Bajamonte Tiepolo, after an initial show of haughty

---

pass beneath them, horses were common in Venice. In the more populous *calli* they even seem to have constituted something of a traffic problem: from 1291 horsemen riding down the Merceria to the Piazza were required to dismount at S. Salvatore. Horses were normally forbidden in the Piazza itself; they would be left by their owners tied to the little grove of elders by the present clock-tower.

intransigence, capitulated and went off to a four-year exile in Dalmatia
– where, however, he had not the least intention of remaining.

Thus dispassionately described, the rebellion of Bajamonte Tiepolo sounds
almost laughably inept. It was true, as he might have pleaded, that all
occasions had conspired against him. The weather had slowed his progress,
prevented his allies from joining him, and dampened spirits all round.
Marco Donato had betrayed his trust. That halt at S. Giuliano, whatever
its cause, had also lost him valuable minutes, since without it he might
just possibly have arrived on the Piazza in time to save the Querini.
Yet no amount of special pleading could alter or even conceal the fact
that he had failed miserably – and in the process had brought upon
himself, as well as lasting infamy, more than a little ridicule.

In Venice, however, what now appears as an almost trifling incident
was taken very seriously indeed. Had Gradenigo not received advance
warning, the plot might well have succeeded even without the help of
the Badoer contingent; success or failure, it remained a formidable attempt,
not just on the Doge personally, but on the whole fabric of the state – an
attempt, moreover, with which three of the oldest and noblest Venetian
families were identified. Having successfully put out the fire in its early
stages, the government now determined to stamp out such embers as
might continue to smoulder. Bajamonte's sentence had been relatively
light only because they knew the strength of his following and had wisely
decided against making a martyr of him; now that he was safely in exile,
they systematically set about the destruction of his name and reputation.
His house in S. Agostino – better known in the Venetian dialect form of
S. Stin – was torn down within a day or two of his departure until not
one stone was left on another; on its site was raised a so-called Column
of Infamy, bearing the inscription:

> Di Bajamonte fo questo tereno
> E mo per lo so iniquo tradimento
> S'è posto in chomun per l'altrui spavento
> E per mostrar a tutti sempre seno.[1]

The Querini house was to suffer almost as sad a fate. Here the problem
was that Marco and Piero had owned it jointly with a third brother,

---

1. This land was the property of Bajamonte
   And now, through his infamous betrayal,
   Is held by the Commune as a lesson to others.
   So let these words proclaim to all, for ever.

Giovanni, who had played no part in the conspiracy. The government first proposed, therefore, to pull down two-thirds of it only; but difficulties of demarcation arose, and it was finally decided to compensate Giovanni for his share and turn the whole building into a slaughterhouse. Next came a decree calling for the removal or erasure of all existing crests and escutcheons of the two disgraced dynasties – who were, however, permitted to adopt new arms and substitute them for the old. No exceptions were permitted; even the crests beneath the portraits of the two Tiepolo Doges in the Hall of the Great Council were changed, as were those on their tombs at SS. Giovanni e Paolo.

But if these two families – the Badoer were not for some reason penalized in this way – paid a price for their treachery, others were rewarded for theirs. Marco Donato, through whose agency Doge Gradenigo had first learnt of the plot against him, was ennobled and awarded membership of the Great Council in perpetuity for himself and his descendants.[1] Perhaps it was only fitting recognition for one who could claim to have saved the state; yet one reads with greater pleasure of the other beneficiaries. The church of S. Vio – St Vitus, on whose feast-day the uprising occurred – was presented with the stone door-jambs from Bajamonte's house and certain relief decorations from its walls;[2] and it was decreed that on every succeeding St Vitus's Day the Doge should visit it in solemn procession for a thanksgiving mass, followed by an official banquet. Meanwhile the Campo S. Luca, where the remnants of the Querini had been routed, was given a magnificent flagpole from which the *Scuola della Carità* and the Painters' Guild might fly their standards.[3]

And so we come to the last – indeed, the only – heroine in the drama, Giustina (or was it Lucia? – no one is quite sure) Rossi, the old lady who felled Bajamonte's standard-bearer with her mortar. When asked what the Republic could do for her to show its gratitude, she asked two things only: that she and her successors in that house should be allowed to display the banner of Venice from the fateful window on all major feast-days, and that her landlords, the Procurators of St Mark, should never raise her rent. Both requests were granted; and though nowadays on 15 June one may look in vain for a banner in her window, and though the rent of one of the most desirable commercial sites in the city is no

1. Their name is more usually shortened in the Venetian dialect to Donà, in which form it serves partially to identify at least a dozen *palazzi* on the Grand Canal and elsewhere.

2. S. Vio was demolished in 1813, but the decorations (several *paterae* and a cross) were preserved and are now set into the wall of the modern votive chapel that occupies the site, next to the Anglican church of St George.

3. The arms of both institutions and the date, MCCCX, are still visible on its base.

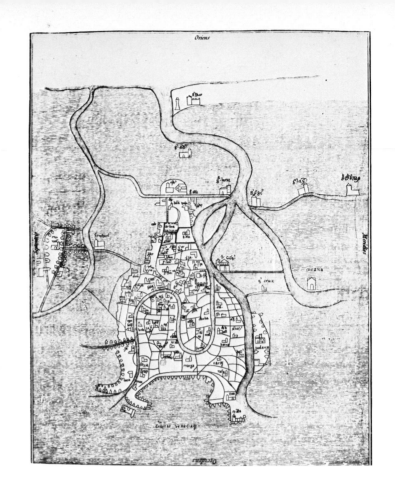

1. One of the earliest surviving maps of Venice, from a twelfth-century manuscript in the Biblioteca Marciana

2. The lion of St Mark, from the column in the Piazzetta. Its origins are uncertain – perhaps Persian (fourth century A.D.) or Chinese, with wings added

3. The apse of the Cathedral of S. Maria Assunta, Torcello.
The mosaics of the Apostles date from *c.* 1100,
that of the Virgin about a century later

4. Torcello. An early eleventh-century Byzantine panel from the screen

5. A detail of the bronze doors of the Basilica of St Mark

6. SS. Maria e Donato, Murano. Late eleventh century

7. The cloister of S. Apollonia, twelfth–thirteenth century.
The only Romanesque cloister in Venice

8. Marble medallion of a Byzantine Emperor (? tenth century) in the Campiello Angaran

9. An arch in the house of Marco Polo, Corte Seconda del Milion. Eleventh–twelfth century

10. A Venetian ship of Marco Polo's time, from the inner right-hand lunette of the façade of St Mark's. The original was replaced in the seventeenth century; it is known only through this detail from Gentile Bellini's *Procession of the Cross in the Piazza S. Marco* in the Accademia

11 (*Right*). A Levantine merchant of the thirteenth century: sculpture in the Campo dei Mori

12. The first golden ducat, 1284, with the name of Doge Giovanni Dandolo, portrayed kneeling before St Mark

13. The Ca' da Mosto, twelfth–thirteenth century. The top two floors are later additions. In the sixteenth–eighteenth centuries it was the Albergo del Leon Bianco, Venice's most celebrated hotel

14. Venice in c. 1400, from a manuscript of that date illustrating the departure of the elder Polos

15. The Basilica of St Mark,
the Doges' Palace behind,
and in the distance
S. Giorgio Maggiore

16. The body of St Mark being carried into the Basilica.
This thirteenth-century mosaic in the extreme left-hand lunette of the
façade is the earliest-known representation of St Mark's
(the bronze horses are already in position)

17. The theft of the body of St Mark. A thirteenth-century mosaic in the Basilica

18. Doge, Patriarch, clergy and people pray
for the relics of the Evangelist to be rediscovered. South transept, St Mark's

19. Their prayers are answered. Mosaics of later thirteenth century

20 (*Below left*). Thirteenth-century carving on a portal, St Mark's

21 (*Below right*). Baptistery, St Mark's. This mid-fourteenth-century mosaic
of Salome provides an invaluable illustration of contemporary Venetian fashion

22 (*Bottom*). The south wall, St Mark's. 'The front of St Mark's became rather
a shrine at which to dedicate the splendour of miscellaneous spoil, than the
organized expression of any fixed architectural law, or religious emotion.' (Ruskin) [?]

23 (*Top*). South front, the Doges' Palace. Fourteenth century

24 (*Above left*). Vettor Pisani – detail from his monument in SS. Giovanni e Paolo

25 (*Above right*). Doge Antonio Venier (1382-1400) by Jacobello dalle Masegne, Museo Correr

26. The tomb of Doge Andrea Dandolo. Baptistery, St Mark's.
'The best existing example of Venetian monumental sculpture'. (Ruskin)

27 (*Right*). The tomb of Doge Michele Morosini, SS. Giovanni e Paolo

28. The Fourth Crusade, from the original manuscript of Geoffrey de Villehardouin

29 (*Above left*). Doge Andrea Contarini (1368–82) from the Caresini Chronicle

30 (*Above right*). Doge Andrea Dandolo (1343–54) from the Caresini Chronicle

longer pegged at fifteen ducats a year, a glance at the upper wall will show that the *vecchia* herself has not been forgotten.[1]

Yet the deepest and most lasting imprint left on Venice by the events of St Vitus's Day 1310 took the form not of a banner, nor of a banquet, nor even of a Column of Infamy, but of an institution – one that was to last as long as the Republic itself, with a name still capable of provoking an occasional shudder of awe: the Council of Ten. It was established on 10 July 1310, by a decree of the Great Council, as a temporary measure only – a sort of Committee of Public Safety, with wide emergency powers to deal with the continuing state of unrest; and the very fact of its foundation, together with the edicts which it issued in the first three weeks of its existence, show more clearly than anything else how tense was the atmosphere in the city during the period immediately following the insurrection. On 12 July, members of the Great Council were permitted to attend armed; on the 19th it was resolved that the doors of the Council Chamber should remain open during sessions; 100 armed men in boats were deputed to patrol the lagoon and canals; a special corps of 200, chosen by the heads of the *sestieri*, were to guard the Piazza, another thirty the Doges' Palace, and ten more were appointed to each of the *contrade* to see that no man passed from one to another after nightfall. Meanwhile each *sestiere* was required to keep 1,500 men permanently under arms; on the sounding of the great tocsin from the campanile of St Mark's, half were to run immediately to the Piazza, while the rest remained to deal with any local uprisings.

When the Council of Ten was first established, its intended life-span was some two and a half months – till Michaelmas, which fell on 29 September. At first its prolongation was for another two months only, but subsequent renewals of its authority were for increasingly long periods, and in 1334 it was made a permanent body. Though its corporate powers were immense, they were subject to characteristically Venetian checks and balances to prevent any individual member's using them for his personal ends. Election – by the Great Council, from lists drawn up by itself and the Signoria respectively – was for a single year, and re-

1. The building that stands on the spot – under the clock-tower where the Merceria gives on to the Piazza – now bears a curious little plaque, erected in 1841, with a representation of the incident in relief; on the pavement below, a tablet of white marble marks the place where the mortar, and presumably the luckless standard-bearer, hit the ground. One of the banners is still preserved in the Museo Correr. I have not been able to discover how long the tent of the *Casa della Grazia del Morter* remained pegged; but a descendant, Nicolò Rossi, won an appeal against its increase a century and a half later, in 1468.

election was forbidden until a further year had passed, during which time any alleged abuses would be carefully investigated. Two members of the same family could never sit simultaneously. Furthermore the Council never allowed itself a single head; there were always three – the *Capi dei Dieci* – serving for a month at a time, a month during which they were forbidden to go out into society lest they should be exposed to bribes or baseless rumours. Finally – the most important point of all and perhaps the one most frequently forgotten – the Ten were powerless by themselves. They acted only in concert with the Doge and his six councillors, bringing their effective number to seventeen. In addition there was always present one of the Avogadori di Comun or state prosecutors, who had no vote but stood ready to advise the members on points of law. The Council met every weekday and seems to have been consistently overworked; its members, however, were unpaid, and venality or corruption was punishable by death.

As this story goes on, there will be a lot more to be said about this remarkable institution and its workings; during these early years many of its most interesting characteristics had not yet fully evolved. From the outset, however, it served two important purposes, which together explain why it so rapidly proved itself indispensable. The first of these was the gathering of intelligence, through a network of spies and undercover agents that was ultimately to spread right across Europe and even beyond. Despite popular legend Venice was never, in the modern sense of the term, a police state; but her intelligence and security services were unequalled. It was just as well. Within less than a year, an agent was reporting from Padua that Bajamonte, having broken the terms of his Dalmatian exile, was back in Lombardy with two of the Querini – one of them a priest – plotting a new rebellion; although in fact he never returned to Venice, this was largely due to the Republic's ability to keep him under continual surveillance and always to remain one jump ahead. But even the Ten could not put a stop to his intriguing – unless it was they who covertly did so in 1329, after which date he is heard of no more.

The second contribution made by the new Council in these first years of its existence was still more vital. The crisis over Ferrara had shown up a serious weakness in the constitution: the lack of any means of reaching a quick decision on a major matter of state and acting upon it with equal dispatch. In their anxiety to avoid the concentration of power, the Venetians had been obliged to accept a loss of executive efficiency that they could ill afford. All important issues had to be ratified by the Great Council which, in the decade since the *Serrata*, had grown steadily until it now numbered about 1,000 members. Inevitably, so unwieldy a body was obliged to delegate, and it was already common practice for it to appoint smaller committees of so-called *savii*, or sages, to handle specific questions. Some of these *savii* were permanent officers with defined responsibilities, not unlike present-day ministers though with rather less authority; indeed, by the middle of the century the *Collegio*, which they formed together with the Doge and his six councillors, had emerged as a fully-fledged cabinet. At this time, however, major questions of policy – to hold Ferrara, for example, in defiance of papal threats – were referred back to the Council in plenary session. It followed that, the graver the situation, the more cumbersome was the apparatus for dealing with it.

With the appearance of the Ten, all this was changed. Acting – as they always did – in conjunction with the Doge and his councillors, their decrees had the same force as those of the Great Council itself. Swift and decisive action once more became a possibility. It is arguable that, so great was the need for this streamlining of the administrative machine, the Council of Ten or something very like it would have been instituted anyway before very long; the fact none the less remains that it was called into being as a direct result of the Tiepoline conspiracy. Bajamonte had failed totally in his object; yet Venice owed him more than she ever admitted, or he ever knew.

15

The Mainland Dominion

[1311–1342]

A che mandarmi il doge tanto piombo? Il tenghi a coprire il campanile di S. Marco.

Why does the Doge send me so much lead? Let him keep it to roof the campanile of St Mark's.

> Mastino della Scala, on receiving letters
> from the Doge bearing leaden seals (*Barbaro Chronicle*)

When Pietro Gradenigo died on 13 August 1311, the prevailing emotion in Venice was one of relief. He had been a strong Doge – too strong, in the view of most of his subjects – but not a wise one. Stubborn and self-willed, mindful of the opinions of others only when considering the best way of imposing his own, he left the Republic in a worse condition than he found it: badly shaken by the Tiepolo plot and its aftermath, its trade reduced to a trickle, the papal interdict still in force. It was no wonder that, as much for fear of hostile demonstrations as on account of the ban of the Church, his body was borne off without ceremony to the abbey of S. Cipriano on Murano and buried there in an unmarked grave.

In their understandable desire that his successor should be as unlike him as possible, the ducal electors first veered too far in the opposite direction, choosing the elderly senator Stefano Giustinian who, rather than accept the greatness thrust upon him, fled to a monastery. Their second choice fell on a certain Marino Zorzi – who was even older – for no better reason than that they chanced to see him as he passed beneath the palace windows, carrying a large sack of bread for distribution to the inmates of the nearby prison. A fifteenth-century historian, Marino Sanudo the younger, explains his election with the words 'He was known as the Saint, since he was so good and so Catholic a man – and he was rich.' After Gradenigo, this was all the Venetians wanted of their Doge: an innocuous figurehead with a respectable if not particularly distinguished diplomatic background, plenty of money and a generous hand with which to dispense it. Zorzi's reputation for piety – he had founded and copiously endowed an orphanage some years before – may, however, have been an additional point in his favour; for any new Doge, the lifting of the interdict would be the first and most important objective.

But Marino Zorzi did not live to achieve it. He died in July 1312, having reigned less than a year. The electors met again, this time with all the windows looking out on to the street pointedly shuttered, and chose Giovanni Soranzo, the conqueror of Caffa during the war with the Genoese fifteen years before.[1] With a dazzling career behind him – as we have seen, he had also distinguished himself at Ferrara, and had subsequently risen to be Chief Procurator of St Mark's – it may well be asked why Soranzo had been passed over in favour of the ineffectual Zorzi the year before; the answer probably lies in the fact that his daughter had married the son of Marco Querini and since the Tiepolo plot had been sharing her husband's exile. At seventy-two, he might also have been considered some way past his prime; but he was to reign for sixteen years, during which Venice slowly returned to her old prosperity. Recovery began in March 1313, when Pope Clement was at last, and with much difficulty, persuaded to lift his ban. The price was high – 90,000 Florentine gold florins, a huge sum for the Republic's depleted coffers, and made more unpalatable still by the Pope's insistence on the specific currency in which it was to be paid. Nevertheless, by dint of a forced loan of 3 per cent on all incomes and the threat to the Florentine bankers in Venice that they would be instantly expelled if they did not change the money at once and at a fair rate, the government met its obligations; and the Pope in return decreed that Venetians might once again circulate freely in Ferrara and carry on their lawful commerce without interference.

It was a capitulation, of course: but to humble oneself before the Pope was somehow less shameful than to do so before a temporal ruler, and for most Venetians it was a small enough price to pay for the resumption of normal economic life and all that stemmed from it. Six months later Zara, which had taken advantage of the Republic's disarray following the Tiepolo plot to stage one of its own periodic rebellions, was successfully brought to heel. Venice was at peace again; trade, once more, had begun to flow; within the next few years treaties were concluded with the Byzantine Empire, with Sicily and Milan, with Bologna, Brescia and

1. See p. 177. Soranzo's conquest of Caffa in 1296 – and the fully-laden Genoese merchantmen which he took as prizes and brought back to Venice – had become something of a legend. It was later commemorated in the ceiling painting by Giulio dal Moro in the *Sala dello Scrutinio* of the Doges' Palace.

Como, with Tunisia, Trebizond and Persia. All this fortunately coincided with the destruction, by the Genoese Benedetto Zaccaria in 1291, of the Moroccan fleet which for years had done its best to close the straits of Gibraltar to Mediterranean shipping. Henceforth the straits were open, and – with Genoa having conveniently entered into a period of comparative eclipse, thanks to a long and acrimonious quarrel with her colony of Pera on the Bosphorus – Venice was able to capture much of the valuable trade with England and Flanders.

Thus, under a wise, moderate and universally respected Doge, morale soared. In the Republic itself new industries arose, with a craftsman being brought to Murano from Germany to teach new techniques in the manufacture of looking-glasses, and a whole colony of silk workers from Lucca who, fleeing from the factional strife that was tearing their own city apart, established themselves in the Calle della Bissa off S. Bartolomeo. Such was the influx of German merchants that by 1318 a special building was necessary to accommodate them all – the first *Fondaco dei Tedeschi*.[1] The paving of streets and *campi* continued apace – doubtless to the consternation of the pigs from the monastery of S. Antonio, who enjoyed free rootling range throughout the city – including that of the main thoroughfare that led from the Piazza to S. Pietro di Castello; fifty new wells were sunk, and huge cisterns constructed for additional storage; another ingenious German was imported to build windmills. Venice also received her first municipal fire service.

At about this time, too, the Arsenal was enlarged – a development made necessary by significant advances in shipbuilding. The mariners' compass had appeared in about 1275, making possible the preparation of charts far more accurate than before. A few more years brought another innovation – the rudder. Until this time the accepted method of steering any large vessel was by means of an oar to one side of the stern, a system which was not only extremely inefficient but which imposed severe limits on size since with large ships it swiftly became unmanageable. The stern rudder, on the other hand, permitted an almost infinite degree of leverage simply by increasing the length of the tiller, and could even have a system of pulleys added if required. The immediate result was bigger ships; and, as these were capable of putting to sea in winter and summer alike, sailoring became for the first time an all-year-round

1. The original *Fondaco dei Tedeschi* was burnt to the ground in 1505; the present building – next to the Rialto bridge, and now the central post office – was completed three years later. The Canal façade was decorated by Giorgione, the side by Titian; traces of their work are said to survive, but I have never found them.

profession and seamanship in its turn underwent a spectacular improvement.

It was probably the opening-up of the English and Flemish trade, more than any other single factor, that led to the introduction in about 1320 of a revolutionary new ship design. Until this time oars had never been used for commercial vessels; they had been kept for warships, where high speeds and manoeuvrability were essential. With the sudden commercial expansion in the years following 1300, however, new considerations had arisen. Now merchantmen too needed to move quickly – and, with more precious cargoes to carry, they demanded increased protection. The answer was found in the merchant galley. It was longer and wider than war galleys, giving it a capacity, even in those early days of its development, of some 150 tons' burden, and in addition to its full complement of sail, was propelled by 200 oarsmen. The expense of maintaining such a crew – who were, incidentally, all free men[1] – was considerable; but it was easily outweighed by the saving of time in every voyage and by the vessel's virtual immunity from piracy, since few pirate ships could match it for speed and, even in the event of a surprise attack, the 200 men could immediately be armed for defence. Thanks to its manoeuvrability, the risk of shipwreck on some rocky coast could also be largely discounted.

Yet the greatest blessing of Giovanni Soranzo's reign, at least as far as the residents of the city were concerned, was peace. After the turbulence of the two previous decades, the Venetians desperately needed a chance to recover – not only materially from their immense losses, but mentally and spiritually from the upheavals they had suffered in every sphere of their daily life. Tempers needed time to cool, animosities to be forgotten, minds and opinions to adjust to changing political conditions in Italy and abroad. Soranzo gave his people just such a breathing space. It is a remarkable testament to a reign of sixteen years that its apparently most exciting single event should have been the birth of three cubs to the pair of lions, a gift of the King of Sicily, that lived in the Doges' Palace. This happy occurrence, which took place at about the hour of matins on Sunday 12 September 1316, is said to have brought flocking to the cage 'almost all the inhabitants of Venice and elsewhere' – crowds even greater, it appears, than those which had been privileged to witness the equally interesting preliminaries three and a half months before

---

1. The crews of these galleys – known as *voluntarie* – were well paid, and allowed to carry goods of their own, free of duty. The practice of using slaves and prisoners in Venetian galleys began only in the mid-sixteenth century.

– and was considered by the Doge to be a matter of such state importance that he had it legally recorded in a sworn affidavit by the official notary.

Another event which in retrospect might be considered to have been of even greater moment – the arrival in 1321 of Dante Alighieri as special emissary from Ravenna – seems to have aroused little or no interest in the city. Admittedly – and infuriatingly – the volume of state archives for that year has been lost; but the extant chronicles and early histories are unenlightening. All we know is that Dante's embassy, which was concerned with the old question of navigation rights along the Po, received a dusty answer; and that when the time came for his return Venice refused to grant him a safe conduct by the most convenient route. He was consequently obliged to make his way back through malarial swampland, as a result of which he caught a fever and died.

But however chilly Doge Soranzo may have been to strangers – and Dante, by his own admission, was not overfond of them himself – he was beloved by his subjects; and it may well have been his popularity as much as anything else that caused the Great Council to make new provision for the magnificence of his successors, increasing their salary and their retinue, commissioning a huge state jewel for festive occasions and a still more magnificent state barge, the *Bucintoro*. Their effective power, on the other hand, remained as restricted as ever; and it is significant that when Soranzo's widowed daughter returned from exile in 1314 she was immediately confined to the convent of S. Maria delle Vergini in a remote corner of Castello. The Doge by tradition made a formal visit there every year; but he could never persuade the Ten to permit her release and she was still a prisoner when he died, aged nearly ninety, on the last day of 1328. His body, girt with his sword and wearing the ceremonial gold shoes of his office, lay in state in the Hall of the Signori di Notte on the south side of the old Palace, looking out over the Molo; from there it was carried into the Basilica where his widow awaited it. After the funeral mass it was placed in the baptistery, in a plain sarcophagus which can still be seen, bearing the Soranzo coat of arms but no name or inscription.

Venetians have always had long memories. It would have taken more than fifteen years of peace and prosperity to make them forget the dark days of the papal interdict; and for their fiftieth Doge they were not slow in choosing Francesco Dandolo, whose patient and skilful advocacy at Avignon had finally induced the Pope to relent. Ruskin writes of how Dandolo 'concealed himself (according to the common tradition) beneath the Pontiff's dining-table; and thence coming out as he sat down to meat, embraced his feet, and obtained, by tearful entreaties, the removal of the terrible sentence'. Unkind historians have suggested that his nickname of *Cane*, 'the Dog', came from the day when he had appeared before His Holiness wearing a collar and chain in token of his humility; in fact, the name had been applied equally to his father before him. It was also borne, with pride, by the man who shortly before Francesco's accession had revealed himself as the Republic's most dangerous enemy.

Though Can Grande della Scala, despot of Verona, was still only thirty-seven years old, he had spent more than half of them extending his dominions and now controlled not just his native city but also Vicenza, Feltre, Belluno – which had made him master of several important Alpine passes – and, since September 1328, Padua. The new Doge thus found himself immediately confronted with the one threat to which Venice was more vulnerable than any other, that of economic blockade; and when in July 1329 the Veronese army captured Treviso, the position became desperate. Three days after his entry into Treviso, Can Grande was carried off by a sudden fever and Venice breathed again; but the respite was short. He was succeeded jointly by his nephews, one of whom, Alberto, was a pleasure-loving nonentity but the other, Mastino, was as ambitious and determined as his uncle. Mastino started as he meant to go on. Transit dues on Venetian goods, heavy tolls on produce bound for the lagoon from *terra firma* irrespective of whether it came from Venetian properties, customs-houses along the Po – the Venetians knew it all, only too well; they had done the same sort of thing themselves. They retaliated sharply, with prohibitive levies of their own on all merchandise passing through Venice to the cities under Mastino's control, but it was an unequal battle and they knew it. Padua, Treviso and the rest could be deprived only of luxuries from the East; they might suffer mild inconvenience, but no real harm. Venice, on the other hand, relied upon the mainland for her staple provisions. During the crisis of 1268 she had somehow managed to find alternative supplies, but since then her population had almost doubled. She was unlikely to be so fortunate again.

If catastrophe were to be averted, it would have to be by force of arms. Even now, in the Great Council, there were plenty of voices raised against such a solution, including that of the Doge himself. It was pointed out that Mastino's military strength would make his ultimate victory almost certain, and that such a victory might well mean the end of the Republic; that Venice for her part possessed no land army and would have to resort to mercenaries, with all the expense and risk that that entailed; and that, as the Ferrara affair had shown, interference in mainland politics always led to disaster. All these arguments were reasonable enough; they were also irrelevant. The fact was that Venice had no choice. She must fight or be destroyed.

She had one point in her favour. The speed of the Scaligeri expansion had caused alarm in other quarters as well. Even while diplomatic negotiations were in progress with potential allies, Mastino was making new enemies. Brescia fell to him in 1332; from the ruling family of Rossi he seized Parma, from the Florentines Lucca. His failures, such as his efforts to wrest Mantua from the Gonzagas or to poison Azzo Visconti of Milan, had made him as hated as his successes. And so an alliance took shape. In Venice itself a hasty census revealed 40,100 able-bodied males between the ages of twenty and sixty.[1] Following the normal custom, these were divided into groups of twelve, from each of which one man – and later, if necessary, a second or a third – would be chosen by lot to join the colours, the remainder sharing his expenses among them; but this time, we are told, many volunteered without waiting for the draw or demanding a wage. Meanwhile various other contingents from Italy, France, Germany and Burgundy – by no means all of whom were mercenaries – assembled some 30,000 strong at Ravenna under the command of Pietro de' Rossi, the most accomplished general of his day, who, as the youngest scion of the family that had ruled in Parma until it was expelled by Mastino, could be trusted to dedicate all his energies and abilities to the task in hand.

In the Basilica on 10 October 1336 Pietro received the banner of St Mark from Doge Dandolo while, both inside and outside the building, the assembled populace cheered him to the echo. A day or two later he and his army had crossed the Brenta into Paduan territory, and on 22 November – St Cecilia's Day – he took the fortress protecting the great saltworks with which Mastino had hoped to break the Venetian monopoly. Then he pressed on to Treviso. These early triumphs persuaded a few more waverers to join the alliance, among them Azzo Visconti, Luigi Gonzaga of Mantua and Obizzo d'Este, whose family had since 1317 been back in power in Ferrara; and in March 1337 a new treaty was signed in Venice, formally establishing a League vowed 'to the destruction and ruin of the brothers Alberto and Mastino, Signori della Scala'. A third

1. This figure is particularly significant in that it enables us to make an informed guess at the total population of the Republic at this time, which cannot have been much less than 200,000.

of its expenses was to be paid by Venice, a third by Florence on the under-standing that Lucca would be restored to her, and a third jointly by the other Lombard cities.

Surrounded by his enemies and finding himself suddenly under attack on several fronts at once, Mastino had no alternative but to sue for peace – sending to Venice as his personal emissary Marsilio di Carrara. It was an extraordinary choice. Marsilio had been despot of Padua until Mastino had seized it from him a few years before; and although he had been allowed to continue as its governor he had since been little more than a puppet of the Scaligeri. His natural resentment had since been increased by a family feud resulting from the seduction – possibly even the rape – of the wife of his cousin Ubertino by Alberto della Scala; now at last he saw the opportunity for revenge. The story is told of how one evening during his Venetian mission he was dining alone with the Doge. He dropped his napkin on the floor, and both men leant down from their chairs to pick it up.

'What would you give me were I to deliver Padua into your hands?' whispered Marsilio.

'The lordship of the city,' replied the Doge.

It was enough. The pact had been made.[1]

At this time Mastino was fiercely defending Padua against the forces of the League; soon, however, a diversionary attack on Brescia by Azzo Visconti called him away, and on 3 August the gates were opened and Pietro de' Rossi entered the city. Alberto della Scala, wenching away as usual in his palace, was captured and sent a prisoner to Venice. His brother fought on a little longer, but to no avail. His empire collapsing around him, he finally capitulated.

The peace treaty was signed on 24 January 1339 (1338, according to the Venetian reckoning).[2] Its terms were remarkably generous. Most surprising of all, the Scaligeri were allowed to retain Lucca – although its outlying lands and fortresses were restored to Florence – and, subject to a moderate payment of restitution to the Rossi, Parma. To Venice went Padua, where the house of Carrara was restored to power under a somewhat nebulous Venetian suzerainty, and the March of Treviso. The western half of the latter she also entrusted to the Carraras; but the region

1. However pleasant it would be to believe that Francesco Dandolo's two greatest diplo-matic triumphs were both achieved not at, but *under* the dinner-table, it should in all fairness be admitted that the best contemporary source for these events, Lorenzo de Monacis, reports the whispered conversation as having taken place while the two were walking under the loggia of the palace.

2. See p. 183n.

directly to the north of Venice, comprising Conegliano, Castelfranco, Sacile, Oderzo and Treviso itself, remained in her direct control.

It was the first time in Venetian history that a large and important area of *terra firma* had been annexed to the territory of the Republic. The immediate advantages were obvious. Provisions of corn and meat were now assured; the danger of blockade was diminished. So important an acquisition, coming as it did on top of the Scaligeri defeat and the elimination of what had seemed a threat to Venice's very survival, had also a profound effect on the national morale. The treaty was celebrated on St Valentine's Day with a grand tournament on the Piazza, and several of the principal allies, including the Carraras, the Gonzagas and the Estes, were admitted into the ranks of the Venetian nobility.

Less immediately apparent were the corresponding disadvantages of Venice's new rôle as a mainland power. Her major problems were those of frontier security. The recent war had greatly strengthened the position of the Visconti of Milan, who were now more powerful than the Scaligeri had ever been. Admittedly they were a good deal further away, and Padua under the Carraras might in other circumstances have served as a buffer state; but since any attack on Carrara territory would have to be considered as an attack on Venice herself, she and Milan were in effect coterminous. She would also have difficulties in future over her land frontier to the north-east, where the Patriarch of Aquileia and his neighbour the Count of Gorizia could always be trusted to stir up trouble whenever they got the chance.

But these problems still seemed far away. For the moment the Venetians applied themselves with energy and enthusiasm to the more immediate challenge presented by their new administrative responsibilities. Their previous experience of ruling an overseas colonial empire had left them few useful precedents for governing in Treviso and the other towns near by. Such places could obviously not be treated as feudal dependencies in the way that the Greek islands had been; nor, equally obviously, could they be run as glorified trading-posts like Modone, Corone, Acre or Negropont. Some new machinery must be devised; and Venice's solution for Treviso – which was to be applied, with minor variations, in most of her other mainland dependencies – was essentially a miniature version of the system that had worked so well in the Republic itself. At its head stood the *podestà* – in the smaller towns he was usually called a *capitano* or a *provveditore* – whose position was closely analogous to that of the Doge and the manner of whose election equally complex. He might be a Venetian nobleman, or a citizen of the town in question.

He too led a life rich in the outward trappings of pomp and splendour, but almost destitute of effective power. Just as the Doge was in reality the servant of the Council of Ten, so the *podestà*'s real master was another, more shadowy official – the Rector, always a Venetian, directly responsible to and in constant touch with the Senate and the Ten. He controlled the police; his was the ultimate responsibility for the entire government, civil and military, of the city or town. Day-to-day legislation, however – local taxation, communications, civic amenities and the rest – was the work of a council of the municipality, corresponding to the Great Council in Venice. In Treviso, this body numbered 300 – a considerable proportion of the educated male population. Thus it was not only an efficient system: it was also, within limits, a democratic one, particularly since Venice's policy was always to allow her subject cities as much individual freedom and independence as was compatible with security. Life under Venetian domination must have been different indeed from that lived under the autocratic despotism of a Scaliger or a Visconti.

Scarcely a year before the death of Francesco Dandolo on the last day of October 1338, the Church of the Frari was finished at last. It had been a century in the building, and its completion was marked by the almost immediate decision to pull it down again and replace it with another, much larger and facing the other way. These two operations seem to have proceeded simultaneously but slowly over the next 100 years, and must have greatly complicated the fufilment of the Doge's wish to be buried in the church. He had, however, left it much of his fortune, and the difficulty was overcome by placing his sarcophagus in the chapter-house – to which, after a long absence vociferously lamented by Ruskin[1], it has now been restored. The painting above it by Paolo Veneziano, depicting the presentation to the Virgin of the Doge and Dogaressa by St Francis and St Elizabeth, is probably the oldest ducal portrait in Venice to be drawn from the life.

On 7 November Bartolomeo Gradenigo was elected in succession. His relationship to Doge Pietro is uncertain; but the choice of any member of the Gradenigo family was a sure sign that the Venetians were beginning to forget the events of thirty and forty years before. Not that the new Doge was likely to emulate his formidable namesake; apart from other considerations, he was already seventy-six. He seems to have been elected, quite deliberately, as a stop-gap. The first candidate proposed, and the obvious one in terms both of ability and popularity,

---

1. *The Stones of Venice*, Vol. III, ii, paras. 58–60.

was another Dandolo, Andrea. But Andrea was still in his early thirties, and unwilling; and there was also the traditional Venetian reluctance to elect two successive Doges from the same family, even if they were no more than distant cousins. How much better, it was felt, for the venerable old Senior Procurator of St Mark's to hold the fort for a while, breaking the sequence and allowing young Dandolo a little longer to mature.

Bartolomeo Gradenigo did just that. He was to reign only three years, but they were not without incident. They saw, first of all, the most terrible flood that Venice had ever suffered in her long, waterlogged history – a disaster which struck her on 15 February 1340 and which she survived only through the fortunate intervention of St Mark, St Nicholas and St George.[1] Two months later there arrived an embassy from Edward III of England, informing the government of the Republic that since the self-styled King Philip of France had declined to settle Anglo-French differences by single combat or by braving ravenous lions – 'who would in no wise harm a true King' – war was inevitable. Edward asked for forty or more galleys for a year, in return for which he offered to pay any sum that the Doge cared to name and also to grant to all Venetians on English soil the same privileges and immunities as were enjoyed by his own subjects. He went on to suggest that the Doge might like to send his two sons to England, where they would be received with every honour due to their rank, including knighthoods. Gradenigo replied that with a Turkish armada of 230 sail already threatening the Eastern Mediterranean Venice could not spare any of her ships to attack a Christian power in the West; none the less, the privileges so generously offered to Venetians in England were gratefully accepted. As for the invitation to his sons, he returned his 'devout and immense thanks' – but they never went.

It was a characteristically Venetian reply; but the Turkish menace was real enough. The whole of Asia Minor was now lost. The Ottoman Sultan Orhan had established his capital in Bursa, only sixty miles or so from Constantinople itself, while the once-glorious Empire of Byzantium, which had never properly recovered from the Fourth Crusade, was under attack from all its neighbours, Christian and Muslim, as well as being divided within itself by violent religious controversies and

---

1. The fisherman on whose boat the three saints took passage across the lagoon on their mission of deliverance was given a ring by St Mark, with instructions to hand it to the Doge. He did so, and a painting by Paris Bordone of this latter event hangs in Room VI of the Accademia.

torn apart by civil war. The imperial treasury was empty; it came as a surprise to no one when in 1343 the Emperor John V Palaeologus was obliged to pawn to Venetian merchants not only all the gold and silver from the Palace but even the imperial crown jewels.[1] If, then, the Turks were to be kept at bay, it was on Venice and to a lesser extent on Genoa that the bulk of the burden would fall, a joint responsibility that made good relations between the two Republics still more important – although, given their continuing bitter rivalry, no easier to achieve.

But for the time being there was peace, with Venice continuing to ride on a wave of commercial prosperity perhaps unparalleled in her history; and, as always when the political and economic situation allowed, the Venetians began once again to enlarge and embellish their capital. Their first foundling hospital was established near the church of S. Francesco della Vigna; a huge state granary was built on the Molo, on the land which now forms the public garden behind the *Procuratie Nuove*; and on the northernmost edge of the city there rose up the great church and convent of the Servi.[2] Far more important than any of these, however, was the reconstruction of the Doges' Palace, a work which began in January 1341 and which was finally to give the building its principal façades, to the south and west, as we know them today.

The centre of Venetian government and administration had already occupied this site, or part of it, since the days of Doge Agnello Partipazio over five centuries before. Since then Doges' Palaces had come and gone; before the work began in 1341 the existing building was essentially that which had been left by Sebastiano Ziani, with the addition of the new Council Chamber that had been built along the eastern side (that which faces the prisons across the narrow Rio di Palazzo, now spanned by the Bridge of Sighs) at the beginning of the century.[3] But this Chamber had already proved to be hopelessly inadequate,

1. At the coronation of John VI Cantacuzenus in 1347, acute observers noted that the jewels in the imperial diadems were all made of glass.

2. None of these buildings has survived. The foundling hospital – known as the *Pietà* from the habit of its founder, Fra Pierazzo of Assisi, of crying '*Pietà, pietà!*' as he went from house to house for contributions – was transferred in the early sixteenth century to the present area of the Pietà where 200 years later, under Antonio Vivaldi, its female inmates constituted the best orchestra in Venice; the granary remained until 1808, when it was pulled down by Napoleon to provide more light for the *Procuratie Nuove* which he had converted into the Royal Palace; and the Servi also was demolished early in the last century. Its ruins were offered for sale, 'ground and all, or stone by stone', to Ruskin in 1852.

3. See p. 184.

and a three-man commission was now appointed to consider whether it should be further enlarged or whether, alternatively, a completely new one should be built in another part of the Palace. Wisely, the commission recommended the latter course; and it was decided that the new Chamber should occupy the major part of the south side of the building at first-floor level.

Although the Doges' Palace is, by any standards, unique, there is one particularly significant respect in which it differs from the corresponding seats of power in the mainland cities of Italy. They are, nearly all of them, dark and threatening reflections of the violence of the age in which they were built. Machiavelli was right when he pointed out that, in Florence, the Palazzo della Signoria was built as a protection for the civic authorities. So, centuries later, was John Addington Symonds when he spoke of Ferrara, 'where the Este's stronghold, moated, drawbridged, and portcullised, casting dense shadow over the water that protects the dungeons, still seems to threaten the public square and overawe the homes of men'. In Venice, by contrast, those for whom the Palace was built had no need for protection and no wish to terrify. Looking at it today, one feels that their instinct must have been to celebrate – to give thanks, with that dazzling fusion of grace, lightness and colour, for the political stability and serenity that they, alone among their neighbours, enjoyed.

The work started in the first days of 1341 under an architect of genius, Pietro Baseggio, and was to continue spasmodically for the next eighty-two years. The first stage, which was confined to the construction of the new Chamber, involved most of the south side and that facing the Piazzetta as far as the seventh column; it must have been more or less complete by July 1365, when Guariento was commissioned to cover the eastern wall with his great fresco of the Crowning of the Virgin in Paradise.[1] The central balcony on the Molo was added, as its inscription proclaims, only in 1404; even then, however, the interior decoration seems to have been unfinished, since it is recorded that the Great Council did not sit for the first time in its new Chamber until 1423. In that year too it was decided to extend the Piazzetta façade to its present length. Thus it was only in 1425 or thereabouts that the building first appeared in all its splendour – just in time, for the Renaissance was already at hand. Another half-century, and that fortunate decision

---

1. This was replaced after the fire by Tintoretto's version. The remains of Guariento's fresco are preserved in another room in the Palace.

would never have been taken; it would have been resolved instead to give the Palace an exterior aspect more in keeping with the contemporary classical taste; and the world's supreme example of secular Gothic architecture would have been lost.[1]

1. The Palace had an even luckier escape in 1577, when Palladio advocated pulling down the whole fire-damaged fabric and replacing it with a new Renaissance building of his own design.

16

Andrea Dandolo and Marin Falier

[1342–1355]

until this hour
What Prince has plotted for his people's freedom?
Or risked a life to liberate his subjects?

Byron, *Marino Faliero*

Rich, noble and popular, Andrea Dandolo was the outstanding Venetian of his generation. In 1333, while still in his early youth, he had been appointed *podestà* of Trieste. Three years later, during the war with the Scaligeri, he had served as *provveditore in campo*, the chief commissariat and finance officer in the field. Since then he had distinguished himself as professor of law at the University of Padua, where he had been the first Venetian to obtain a doctorate. All his life he was to remain a scholar; though he was to die well before he was fifty, he was to leave behind him a collection of the old laws of Venice, an edition of all the treaties made by the Republic with the states of the East (*Liber Albus*) and those of Italy (*Liber Blancus*) and two separate histories in Latin, one of Venice up to his own day and one of the world from its creation until 1280. In short, when Bartolomeo Gradenigo died on 28 December 1342, and was entombed in a sarcophagus that still stands in a niche at the northern end of the atrium of St Mark's, Andrea Dandolo was the obvious candidate to succeed him. Not yet forty, he was, it is true, exceptionally young for a Doge; but the imagined disadvantages of his youth were obviously outweighed by his other qualifications, and his election seemed to carry all the promise of the long, happy and peaceful dogeship he deserved.

The promise, alas, was not fulfilled. His reign began auspiciously enough, when a League that had for some time been projected by the Pope for a combined Crusade against the Turks finally came into being. This comprised the Byzantine Empire, the Kingdom of Cyprus and the Knights Hospitallers in Rhodes, as well as the Papacy and Venice herself, whose fleet of fifteen galleys captured several strategic places

214

on the Anatolian coast, including the city of Smyrna. Smyrna was to remain in Christian hands for the next half-century; but the League itself soon fell apart, ending in characteristically Venetian fashion with a business agreement whereby, in return for an undertaking to defend the Mediterranean for Christendom, the Pope granted Venice the right to all ecclesiastical tithes levied in the Republic for the next three years.

One state in particular was notable by its absence from the League. Genoa had been technically at peace with Venice for the past forty years, but the cut-throat commercial rivalry between the two Republics had grown ever more bitter and their relations had continued, to say the least, strained. As before, the critical area of disagreement was the Crimea. It was here, and above all in the ports of Caffa and Soldaia (now Sudak) that the regular caravans brought the furs and slaves from the Russian North, the bales of silk from Central Asia, the spices from India and the further East; here that the stakes were highest, the competition fiercest, the sharp practices most unscrupulous, the brawls most frequent. In 1344 the situation improved somewhat when, as a result of an attack by the neighbouring Tartar tribesmen on Venetians and Genoese together, the Doge of Genoa – who was none other than Verdi's hero Simone Boccanegra – sent an embassy to Venice proposing an alliance which would include a boycott on Tartar goods; but the Tartars, when they were not actively hostile, were among the most profitable of trading partners, and the agreement was doomed almost before it was signed. The Genoese broke it almost at once; the Venetians, whose record was probably very little better, protested – adding for good measure that the Genoese merchants in Trebizond had unlawfully prevented them from fortifying their own quarter of the city – only to receive a reply to the effect that Trebizond was a Genoese preserve and that the Venetian presence there, and indeed anywhere else around the Black Sea coast, was permitted strictly on sufferance and by courtesy of Genoa. This was not so much an insult as an open challenge to Venice's whole legal and commercial position in the region. War was clearly inevitable; it was postponed only by a disaster in comparison with which even the future of Venetian commerce must have seemed of secondary importance.

Among those valuable if contentious cargoes brought by Venetian and Genoese merchantmen from the Crimea in the first weeks of 1348 were the most fateful quadrupeds in history: the rats that carried the Black Death to Europe. By the end of March Venice was in the grip of the plague, and as spring turned to summer and the heat grew ever more fierce, so the deaths increased until they were estimated at some 600 a day.

A three-man commission, appointed by the Doge to check the spread of the disease, found itself powerless. Special barges were designated to carry the bodies to burial in outlying islands of the lagoon, where it was decreed that they should be covered with not less than five feet of earth; but these measures soon proved inadequate, and despite their daily round of the canals and the all-too-familiar cry of *'Corpi Morti! Corpi Morti!'* from the wretched boatmen, many of the dead continued to lie alone and unburied in the houses. There were virtually no doctors; within the first few weeks almost all of them were dead or fled.[1] Partly to assuage the wrath of heaven by demonstrations of mercy, partly because they could no longer be adequately guarded, debtors and other miscreants were liberated from the prisons; but nothing could prevent the pestilence from running its course. When at last it abated, no less than fifty noble families had been completely wiped out; and Venice had lost three-fifths of her population.

Genoa, meanwhile, had fared little better. It might have been imagined that after such appalling visitations the rivalry between her and Venice would at least temporarily have been forgotten; and the earlier proposal for an alliance against the marauding Tartars was indeed briefly revived. But in 1350 the Genoese seized, apparently without provocation, a number of Venetian vessels as they lay at anchor in the port of Caffa. An embassy sent by Dandolo to Genoa to protest and seek compensation met with the usual rebuff; and the war that had threatened for so long broke out in earnest. The first victory went to Venice, when her fleet under Marco Ruzzini captured and destroyed ten out of fourteen Genoese ships in the harbour of Negropont.[2] But Genoa's revenge was swift: the four of her vessels that escaped sailed for Chios, an island they had recently appropriated from the Byzantines, where by good fortune they found nine more galleys ready for action. Under the command of Filippo Doria all thirteen sped back to Negropont in November, seized it and sacked it, capturing twenty-three Venetian merchantmen in the process.

The loss to Venice of one of her most valuable colonies was great; the humiliation greater still. The local *bailo* was impeached, but acquitted;

1. 'A certain Francesco of Rome was a health officer in Venice for seventeen years. When he retired he received an annuity of twenty-five gold ducats as a reward for staying in Venice during the Black Death . . . When asked why he did not flee with the rest he answered proudly: "I would rather die here than live elsewhere." ' P. S. Ziegler, *The Black Death*, quoting S. d'Irsay, *Annals of Medical History*, Vol. IX, p. 171.

2. Since the entire island – the modern Euboea – was Venetian territory, we must assume that the Genoese commander was still unaware of the outbreak of hostilities and was consequently taken by surprise.

and Ruzzini, who had been away in Crete seeking reinforcements, was made the scapegoat, charged with having delayed his return unnecessarily and deprived of his command. The war, however, was not over; more widespread, fiercer fighting was to come. Mercifully, Venice had potential allies at hand. King Peter of Aragon, eager to lessen Genoa's influence in the western Mediterranean, agreed to provide eighteen fully-armed men-of-war if Venice would pay two-thirds of their upkeep. In Constantinople similarly – so far as his calamitous finances allowed – the Emperor John VI was only too pleased to participate in the humbling of the Genoese, who not only harried his capital continually from their neighbouring colony of Galata (where their annual customs revenue was almost seven times that of Constantinople itself) but seemed to think that they could help themselves to Byzantine islands like Chios and Mitylene whenever they felt like it. On the other hand, he had no wish to drive them out only to see them immediately replaced by Venetians. He readily offered a dozen galleys, armed and manned – of which, however, Venice was once again to pay two-thirds of the cost in return for an undertaking that, in the event of a Venetian victory, Galata should be razed to the ground and the stolen islands returned to him, together with the imperial crown jewels which had now been seven years in pawn.

The diplomatic negotiations that preceded these agreements and the war preparations that followed them were prolonged; the Aragonese treaty was signed only in July 1351, and by the time the allied fleets joined up with each other in the Marmara the season was already too far advanced to allow of any very decisive operations. Each side, however, had entrusted its fortunes to an admiral of outstanding ability – Venice to Nicolò Pisani, and Genoa to yet another member of that brilliant family whose name was to blaze across the city's history for five centuries and more, Paganino Doria; and on 13 February 1352 the opposing fleets faced each other at the mouth of the Bosphorus, under the walls of Galata.

Paganino, guarding his home waters, had the advantage of position and had drawn up his ships in such a way that the attackers could not approach him without dangerously constricting their own line. Pisani saw the trap at once: the sea was rough, the days were short, to attack would be folly. But the Aragonese commander refused to listen. Before Pisani could stop him he cut his cables and bore down upon the Genoese; and the Venetians had no alternative but to follow.

The ensuing battle soon resolved itself into a straight contest between Venice and Genoa. The Byzantines retired almost at once, without engaging the enemy; the Aragonese, after their initial ill-advised heroics, lasted very little longer. It was left to the two most formidable naval powers of the time to fight it out by themselves, and so they did – savagely, with no quarter given on either side. Fire broke out, which the high winds quickly spread through both fleets; still they fought on, far into the night, by the light of their own blazing ships. Finally it was the Venetians, with wind and current both against them, who had to yield. They had lost most of their galleys and some 1,500 of their best fighting men, an appallingly high figure at any time; coming as it did less than four years after the Black Death, it was more catastrophic still. But when the dawn came the Genoese found that their own losses were almost as heavy, to the point where Paganino preferred to conceal them from his fellow-citizens in Galata for fear of causing a general panic. His, certainly, was the victory in the technical sense; but it was a victory that had cost him more dearly than many a defeat. There could be no question of his pursuing the retreating Venetians; nor, when news of the battle reached Genoa, was there any celebration. As the contemporary Genoese chronicler Giorgio Stella remarks, 'I saw no annual com- memoration of this triumph, nor did the Doge visit any church to give thanks, as is the normal custom; perhaps, because so many brave Genoese fell in the fight, the victory of that day is best forgotten.'

Despite their losses during the battle of the Bosphorus, the position of the Genoese in Galata remained as strong as ever; by contrast, that of the Emperor John VI Cantacuzenus became increasingly insecure. His anxieties were now due not only to financial problems and to the enemies by which the Empire was surrounded; there was a growing threat to his throne itself – a throne to which he had no legitimate claim, having usurped it from its rightful occupant, the sixteen-year-old John V Palaeologus, five years before. The latter had not been deposed; Cantacuzenus had preferred to marry him off to his daughter and allow him to continue as titular co-Emperor, though shorn of any real power. As the boy grew older, however, his resentment of his inferior status increased. He soon became the natural focus of opposition to his father- in-law, and by 1352 the Empire was on the brink of civil war. Canta- cuzenus had always detested the Genoese but now, desperate for allies, he could no longer afford politically – let alone economically – to oppose them. In May, with what inner feelings one can well imagine, he signed an agreement granting them a further expansion of their territory at Galata and the right to exclude all comers, including his own Greek subjects, from trade in the Sea of Azov.

For Venice it was a further blow. She managed to offset it in some degree by acquiring from the rival Emperor John Palaeologus the strategically important island of Tenedos, as security for a loan of 20,000 ducats which she was quietly confident that he could never repay; at the same time she recognized that there was no longer anything to be gained by pursuing the Genoese war in Byzantine or Black Sea waters. A further subsidy was sent to the Aragonese – whose continuing support, it was hoped, might be more effectual in the western Mediterranean than it had been in the Levant – and Nicolò Pisani, having triumphantly survived an official inquiry into the Bosphorus action and emerged with his honour unstained, set sail for the new theatre of operations.

The island of Sardinia had for some years been a bone of contention between Genoa and Aragon; and Pisani arrived there to find the Spaniards blockading the port of Alghero and simultaneously preparing to face an attack from a Genoese relief fleet that was even now on the horizon. His arrival was thus perfectly, if fortuitously, timed. The Spanish admiral readily allowed him supreme command and the Genoese were dismayed to discover, instead of the modest force they had expected, a considerable fleet awaiting them. Suddenly, as they approached, the banner of St Mark broke at every Venetian masthead; and their surprise turned to something akin to panic. They defended themselves courageously, above all in the later stages of the battle when the grappling-irons had been brought into service – Pisani had lashed all but ten of his galleys together before the engagement began – and the fighting was hand-to-hand; but they were outnumbered and outmanoeuvred. Forty-one of their ships were taken; only nineteen, including the flagship (on tow) of their humiliated admiral, Antonio Grimaldi, were able to struggle home.

The date was 29 August 1353. Venice's defeat on the Bosphorus eighteen months before had been more than adequately avenged. The news of the battle of La Lojera, as it came to be called, was received in Genoa not so much with despondency as with despair. The whole city went into mourning; men wept for the end of the once-glorious Republic, now doomed to ignominy and servitude. At first, as one reads – in both the Genoese and the Venetian chronicles – of this reaction, it all sounds rather overdone. After all, battles had been lost before; Genoa, like every other state, had had her share of defeats, and Venice had just proved how swift recovery could be. On reflection, however, one begins to understand: this was not just an ordinary wartime reverse. The Genoese knew the probable consequences only too well. Their enemies now controlled the entire Mediterranean, cutting them off not only from the Levant and the Crimea, the principal sources of their wealth, but also from their essential food supplies. The expansion of their city over the past hundred years had made increasing inroads on the narrow fertile strip between the mountains and the sea that constituted the only agricultural land they possessed; thus, like Venice, they had long been dependent on imports, either from overseas or from Lombardy. But Lombardy had for some time been closed to them, all the mountain passes having been blocked by another enemy who also had designs on their territory: Giovanni Visconti, Lord and Archbishop of Milan.

And so, in those late summer days of 1353, Genoa had good reason to mourn. She was in a desperate situation, for which she needed a desperate remedy. Before September was out, she had found one. Of the three evils by which she was threatened – Venice, Milan and starvation – she chose the least. In return for his help and support in continuation of the war, she made voluntary submission to the Archbishop, stipulating only two conditions: that her own laws should remain in force and that the red cross of her patron, St George, should still appear on the standards of her ships above the viper of the Visconti.

The Venetians were, understandably, furious. But they were also frightened. They had been robbed, at the last moment, of the satisfaction of crushing their rival once and for all. Worse, they saw Milan, already too powerful for comfort, now spreading her influence still further. It was inevitable, since Venice herself had become a mainland power with only her Carrara vassals in Padua to separate her from Milanese territory, that she and the Visconti would clash before long; and though it might have been expected that the clash, when it came, would be brought about by the Lombard towns rather than by the Genoese, the situation was none the less serious for that. Hastily she formed a league of mainland states who felt themselves similarly threatened – Montferrat and Ferrara, Verona, Padua, Mantua and Faenza; she even persuaded Charles IV of Bohemia, shortly to become Emperor of the West, to serve as its titular head. All this was achieved within a very short time and, according to the chronicle of Lorenzo de Monacis, 'at almost incredible cost'; but the Visconti could bribe too, and the numbers of the League soon fell away again – Charles himself the richer by 100,000 Venetian ducats – without striking a single blow against either of its enemies.

Archbishop Giovanni, however, was in no hurry to fight. Instead, he dispatched to Venice on a mission of peace the man who, after Dante, was widely celebrated as the greatest poet-diplomat of his time, Francesco Petrarch. Petrarch had already written to Doge Dandolo – a fellow humanist and personal friend – nearly three years before, imploring him to make peace with Genoa in the name of Italian unity. Now he renewed his appeal in the city itself, with all the rhetoric of which he was capable, exhorting the Venetians to extend the hand of friendship to his master and to accept the very favourable terms he was prepared to offer; but, as he later confessed, his journey was useless:

I threw my many words to the winds; and having come full of hope, I returned in sorrow, shame and fear . . . No words of mine, or even of Cicero himself, could have reached ears that were stubbornly stopped, or opened obstinate hearts.[1]

In truth the Venetians were no more impressed by Petrarch than they had been by Dante thirty-three years before. By now they had recovered from the initial shock of the Genoa–Visconti alliance and, as the threat of immediate attack from *terra firma* apparently receded, so their confidence and courage came flooding back. If the Archbishop really wanted peace, it could only be that he did not feel ready for war. They themselves had never been stronger – at least at sea; Visconti or no Visconti, they were resolved to follow up their victory at La Lojera and strike another, possibly decisive, blow at their rival while they could. They were not interested in flowery speeches in the Doge's audience chamber; their attention was focused on the Arsenal.

And rightly, for Genoa had already resumed the war. In the first weeks of 1354 she had sent a light raiding squadron up the Adriatic, where it attacked the islands of Lesina and Curzola[2] on the Dalmatian coast and did considerable damage before making its getaway. As soon as the news reached the lagoon, the Venetians had detailed a squadron of their own to guard the straits of Otranto between the heel of Apulia and Corfu; meanwhile fourteen heavy galleys under Nicolò Pisani had set off in pursuit of the raiders. Failing to find them, Pisani had sailed on to Sardinia, where the Aragonese were still besieging Alghero. It was a fatal mistake. Paganino Doria, back in command of what was left of the Genoese war fleet, saw his chance. With his adversary safely away to the west, he raced to the mouth of the Adriatic, somehow slipping through the newly established Venetian defences. There was

1. *Epistolae de Rebus Familiaribus*, XVIII, 16 (28 May 1354).
2. Hvar and Korčula.

no nonsense now about the coastal islands; sweeping straight up the gulf, he seized and occupied Parenzo on the Istrian coast, barely sixty miles from Venice itself.

At this moment of genuine emergency, the Venetians kept their heads. A Captain-General was appointed, with special powers to take all the measures he thought necessary for the defence of the city; under him were twelve other nobles, each with a work-force of 300 men. There followed a general mobilization of the populace; a special tax was levied, while several prominent citizens armed and equipped additional galleys at their own expense. Finally, a great boom of tree-trunks and iron chains was run across the Lido port between S. Nicolò and Sant' Andrea.

Perhaps the news of these measures – and particularly of the last – was enough to discourage Paganino from advancing further; but it is more likely that he had never really intended to do more than show the world that Genoa was not beaten at sea any more than she was on land, and that she was certainly not frightened, of Venice or of anyone else. If so, he had made his point. He returned down the Adriatic and, once back in the open sea, headed across to the Aegean. Up to this moment there is no record of any attempt by the Venetians to pursue or intercept him; but by now Nicolò Pisani had returned from Sardinia and, guessing that Paganino would sooner or later be sure to put in at the Genoese colony of Chios for revictualling, had set off in the same direction. There, a few weeks later, he found him as expected – only to learn that Doria was expecting another dozen galleys to arrive from home, and had no intention of emerging from harbour until he was ready. At this late season of the year – it was already October – there was little point in waiting for him. Containing his frustration as best he could, Pisani retired disconsolately to winter quarters at Portolungo, in the extreme south-west corner of the Peloponnese, opposite the island of Sapientza.

Paganino Doria, meanwhile, had decided against wintering in Chios. His galleys had arrived, and towards the end of the month he sailed for home. But the wind was against him and he was forced to take shelter, as luck would have it only a mile or two from where the Venetian fleet was lying. While he waited for more favourable weather, his nephew Giovanni – prompted, it appears, more by simple curiosity than by anything else – took a light trireme on a reconnaissance of the Venetian position. He returned to tell his uncle that the enemy was utterly unguarded, and ready for the taking. Paganino did not hesitate. On 4 November he sailed his galleys into Portolungo, catching the Venetians unawares. Most of the crews were ashore; those who had chanced to remain on board could put up no real resistance. 'You would have thought', laments Lorenzo, 'that one side consisted of armed men, the other of defenceless women.' The Venetian fleet numbered fifty-six, including thirty-three galleys. Every one was captured. Of the sailors, the majority escaped to Modone and a number of others were taken prisoner. Some 450, however, were killed – most of them, presumably, in cold blood.

Among those who escaped was Pisani. The fault was not altogether his; he had appointed one of his captains, Nicolò Querini, to guard the harbour entrance with twenty galleys, and it was Querini's dereliction of duty – or, as some said, his treachery – that caused the disaster. But disaster it undoubtedly was: greater far than that of the Bosphorus, greater perhaps than any defeat the Republic had ever suffered in its history. On their return to Venice both Pisani and Querini were called to account, subjected to heavy fines and deprived of their authority; but whereas Querini's deprivation was for six years only, the unfortunate Pisani was sentenced never, on land or sea, to command again.

Death, wrote Petrarch to the Archdeacon of Genoa, was kind to Andrea Dandolo, 'sparing him the sight of his country's bitter anguish and the still more biting letters that I should have written him'. The Doge had in fact died two months before the defeat of Portolungo, on 7 September 1354, and had been laid to rest in a superb Gothic sarcophagus in the baptistery of St Mark's – the last of Venice's rulers to be buried in the Basilica.[1] His death at forty-seven was a double tragedy: for Europe – which lost one of the outstanding humanists and men of letters of the century – and for Venice, since the old man who was now elected to succeed him was within a year to bring disgrace to the dogeship and to end his days on the scaffold.

Marin Falier was a member of one of the oldest noble families of Venice – it had already given two Doges to the Republic – and, at seventy-six, was still leading an active public life as Venetian ambassador to the papal court at Avignon. Until the messengers arrived with the news of his election this post must have been generally looked upon as the culmination of a lifetime spent in distinguished service to the state. As early as 1312 his name appears as one of the electors of Doge Soranzo, and as a member of the Council of Ten on several occasions between

---

1. Ruskin described his tomb, and that of St Isidore in the northern transept, as 'the best existing examples of Venetian monumental sculpture'. Dandolo had been responsible for the mosaics in both the chapel of St Isidore and the baptistery itself, where his own mosaic portrait can be seen above the altar.

1315 and 1327 he had been instrumental in the harrying – and quite possibly in the eventual liquidation – of Bajamonte Tiepolo. He had in his time commanded a fleet in the Black Sea, sat as *savio* on several special commissions and governed as *podestà* in Chioggia, Padua and Treviso; and only two years before his elevation he had been spokesman for the Republic when one of the periodic Hungarian claims to Dalmatia had been referred to the Emperor-elect Charles IV for judgment. On this last occasion Charles had knighted him for his pains, and awarded him the lordship of the Val Mareno in the Alpine foothills. Throughout his career, however, he had been known for his shortness of temper and quickness to take offence; in 1339, while *podestà* of Treviso, he had publicly slapped the face of the local bishop when the latter was late for a procession. As subsequent events were to show, advancing age had done nothing to mellow him.

The chroniclers describe with relish the sinister portents that attended his arrival in Venice. Exceptionally for the first week of October, the city is said to have been shrouded in dense fog, too thick to allow the *Bucintoro*, which had brought him from Chioggia on the last lap of the journey, to approach the Molo. Falier and his suite had to resort to *piatte*, the little flat-bottomed boats that preceded the invention of the gondola; even then they missed the official jetty by the Ponte della Paglia and were eventually put ashore on the Piazzetta, so that the Doge first approached his palace between the two columns – the traditional place of execution for malefactors.

Within a month of his enthronement – and his signing of a *promissione* that introduced serious new restrictions on the ducal power – reports coming in from the Peloponnese cast yet deeper shadows over the beginnings of his reign. But not even catastrophes like Portolungo could prevent the Venetians from enjoying the feasts of the Church; and early in 1355, on the last Thursday before Lent, we find them celebrating their *Giovedì Grasso* in the customary manner – chasing pigs round the Piazza and Piazzetta in memory of the capture of the German Patriarch of Aquileia two centuries before[1] and applauding those acrobatic performances that were already a Venetian speciality – the so-called Labours of Hercules (*Forze di Ercole*) in which a group of men climbed on each other's shoulders to form a human pyramid – or the Flight of the Turk (*Volo del Turco*), a dizzy slide down a tight-rope from the summit of the campanile to the Piazzetta.

After the public festivities were over the Doge held the usual banquet

1. See p. 102.

in the Palace. Here it was, by all accounts, that the trouble started. Among the guests was a young man – later tradition has unconvincingly identified him with Michele Steno, the future Doge – who began drunkenly forcing his attentions on one of the Dogaressa's waiting-women. Falier ordered him to be thrown out, but before leaving the Palace he somehow managed to slip into the Council Chamber and to leave a doggerel inscription on the ducal throne:

Marin Falier de la bella mujer
Lu la mantien e altri la galde.[1]

The effect on the Doge of this insult to his dignity may well be imagined; but his fury was even greater when the Quarantia, instead of pronouncing the severe sentence for which he had hoped, took the age and previous good character of the accused into consideration and let him off with a penalty so light as to be tantamount, in Falier's eyes, to a condonation of the offence. He was a cantankerous old man, with all the intolerance that old men so often show for the brashness and irreverence of the younger generation; the terms of his *promissione* continued to rankle; and as the weeks went by he began to develop an obsessive hatred of a ruling caste which could show such scant respect for the ducal authority and which apparently even protected its own kind from the proper process of law. With this hatred came a determination that somehow its members should atone for their *lèse-majesté*; if the law was powerless against them, he would take it into his own hands.

Meanwhile other incidents occurred to fortify his resolve. Two highly respectable citizens, one a sea-captain, the other a certain Stefano Ghiazza, nicknamed Gisello, director of the Arsenal, lodged separate complaints that they had been publicly insulted and had suffered bodily violence at the hands of young aristocrats. When the Doge – seemingly forgetful of his own previous treatment of the Bishop of Treviso – sympathized but pointed out the difficulty that even he himself had experienced

---

1.   Marin Falier
                Has a wife that is fair,
    He has to keep her while other men lay 'er.

The verse is quoted by Marino Sanudo in his *Vita dei Duchi di Venezia*. He is writing well over a century afterwards, and the text may well be apocryphal. It has, nevertheless, led many later chroniclers and historians to suggest that the object of the youth's attentions was the Dogaressa herself; but though she was Falier's second wife and much younger than her husband, she was none the less well over forty and there is nothing to substantiate the assumption.

in obtaining punishment for such people, Gisello murmured darkly: 'Dangerous beasts must be tied up; if they cannot be controlled they must be destroyed.'

At that moment Falier knew that he had an ally, and a powerful one; the workers at the Arsenal were a body of highly trained and trusted artisans with a para-military organization and a long tradition of personal loyalty to the Doge, whose bodyguard they always provided on ceremonial occasions. And so the conspiracy took shape. On the night of 15 April disturbances would be deliberately provoked throughout the city, and a rumour simultaneously spread of an approaching Genoese war fleet. This would bring the nobility and populace alike crowding into the Piazza where a member of the ducal family, Bertuccio Falier, would be waiting with a body of armed men – presumably the *Arsenalotti* – ready, on the pretext of protecting the person of the Doge, to massacre all the young nobles on sight. Marin Falier would then be proclaimed Prince of Venice, and his title ratified by popular acclamation.

History provides innumerable instances of aristocrats who have turned against their own class to put themselves at the head of a popular movement; few, however, have done so in their late seventies, or from a position of at least theoretical supremacy. In such circumstances, the usual motives of ambition and self-interest can be ruled out; Falier seems to have been impelled, quite simply, by hatred and rancour, by a desire for revenge magnified and distorted by advancing senility into a single overpowering obsession. It may well be that Gisello and his associates, seeing this, worked upon it further and made the old Doge a tool with which to advance their own political ends; if so, he was less an instigator of the plot than its unconscious victim. Yet it is still impossible to feel much sympathy for a man who, having attained supreme office, attempts to use that office to destroy, by force and with the maximum degree of violence and bloodshed, the government – and, incidentally, the class – that put him there. Fortunately for Venice, he succeeded only in bringing about his own downfall.

The fourteenth century had already seen two conspiracies against the Republic, both of which had collapsed because those involved had been unable to keep their mouths shut. Now once again it was the same story. One of the conspirators, a furrier from Bergamo called Beltrame, warned a rich client to keep off the streets on 15 April. The client went straight to the Doge in all innocence to pass on the warning; but Falier's reaction aroused his suspicions and induced him to confide what he knew to other, more sympathetic, ears. From the seamen's district of Castello near the Arsenal, the principal centre of disaffection, one Marco Nigro brought a similar report; and there is reason to believe that several others, including the Doge himself, were also less discreet than might have been expected. All this suggests that the Ten received their information from at least two and perhaps even three or more independent quarters. They acted with their usual formidable speed. Their first meeting, to examine the evidence and to establish whether or not the Doge was personally implicated, was held secretly in the monastery of S. Salvatore. As soon as they were certain of the facts, they called a larger council, in the Palace this time, consisting of the Signoria, the Avogadori, the Quarantia, the Signori di Notte, the Capi di Sestieri and the Cinque della Pace.[1] Significantly, two officials named Falier, one an Avogadore and one a member of the Ten, were excluded.

By the day fixed for the *coup*, strict security measures had been put into force: in every parish and *sestiere* those in authority had had orders to arm their most trusted men and to muster them on the Piazza, thus providing a militia estimated between 6,000 and 8,000 men ready to deal with any trouble. A troop of 100 horsemen stood by to deal with emergencies elsewhere in the city. Meanwhile the arrests began; and the sentences soon followed. Bertuccio Falier was lucky – he was merely imprisoned for life; but ten of the other ringleaders were condemned to be hanged in a row from the palace windows overlooking the Piazzetta.[2] Ironically enough, they included Filippo Calendario, who had succeeded Baseggio as the chief architect of the Doges' Palace and who, up to the day of his arrest, had been working on the south front.

When the time came to decide the fate of the Doge himself the Ten, considering the responsibility to be too great for them to bear alone, applied for a *zonta*[3] – an exceptional increase in their numbers specifically provided for by their constitution to deal with grave emergencies – of twenty additional noblemen. Their verdict, however, was a foregone conclusion; Falier did not attempt to deny the charges. He made a full confession, pleaded guilty and proclaimed himself both deserving

1. Rough equivalents might be the Doge's inner council of six advisers, the three public prosecutors, the judicial council of forty, the chiefs of police, the heads of the six *sestieri* or districts of the city, and the five Justices of the Peace.

2. Nicolò Trevisan, who was at that time one of the Ten and has left a valuable account of these events, notes that they were hanged between 'red marble columns', which many historians including Romanin have identified with the two such columns beneath the second window from the left on the Piazzetta side; but, as we have seen, this western façade was not built in Falier's day. If these are indeed the columns in question, they must have belonged to the old Byzantine palace of Sebastiano Ziani.

3. The Venetian dialect equivalent of the Italian *aggiunta*.

of and fully prepared for the supreme penalty. Sentence was passed on 17 April; the next morning, at the hour of tierce, the old man was brought from his private apartments to the Council Chamber and thence to the top of the marble staircase that descended from the first-floor loggia into the inner courtyard of the Palace.[1] The insignia of office were stripped from him, his ducal *corno* being replaced by a plain round cap. In a brief speech, he asked the Republic's pardon for his treachery and confirmed the justice of his sentence. Then he laid his head upon the block. It was severed with a single stroke.[2]

The doors of the Palace, which had remained shut during the execution, were now opened and the body displayed to the people. The day following, it was taken in a common boat to the family vault in the chapel of S. Maria della Pace, between SS. Giovanni e Paolo and the Scuola di S. Marco, and buried in an unmarked grave.[3] All Falier's possessions were declared confiscate, excepting only 2,000 ducats, which he had specifically bequeathed to his widow just before his execution – an indication, if such were necessary, that he still trusted her despite the slanders she had suffered. Rich rewards were voted to those who had given information leading to the plot's discovery. Marco Nigro of Castello received 100 gold ducats a year for life, with the privilege – doubtless necessary – of being allowed to carry arms at all times for his own protection. The furrier Beltrame was awarded no less than 1,000 ducats, but was foolish enough to demand in addition the Falier property at SS. Apostoli and a permanent hereditary seat in the Great Council. When these were refused he took to speaking so bitterly against the government that he was thrown into prison, whence he emerged only to be done to death by one of his former fellow-conspirators.

Meanwhile, in their minute books, the Ten could not bring themselves to record the Doge's name in the list of those condemned. Where it should have appeared there is a blank space left, followed simply by the words *non scribatur* – 'let it not be written'. A decade later, however, when the shame and shock were past, their successors were less delicate:

1. The present *Scala dei Giganti* did not yet exist. The staircase on which the execution took place was probably on the south side of the courtyard, immediately outside the wall of the Council Chamber.

2. There is a splendid portrayal of the scene by Delacroix in the Wallace Collection. Romanticized as it may be, it is probably a good deal more accurate – and certainly more dramatic – than Byron's play *Marin Falier*.

3. The grave was opened in the middle of the last century, to reveal a skeleton with the skull laid between the knees. The bones were dispersed; the sarcophagus, after some years' service as a cistern, is now rather surprisingly to be found beneath the portico of the Museum of Natural History – the former Fondaco dei Turchi.

on 16 March 1366 they decreed that the likeness of Falier should be removed from the frieze of ducal portraits that had just been painted
around the walls of the Council Chamber and replaced by a painted
black veil bearing the words, clear and uncompromising, for all to read:
'*Hic est locus Marini Faledri decapitati pro criminibus.*'[1]

1. 'Here is the place of Marin Falier, beheaded for his crimes.' What we see today, together
with all the other ducal portraits in the Chamber, is a repainting dating from after the fire
of 1574.

17

Colonies Lost and Held

[1355–1376]

It was the fourth of June – perhaps the sixth hour of the day. I was standing at my window, looking out to sea . . . when one of those long ships that they call galleys entered the harbour, all garlanded with green boughs, its oars thrusting through the water, its sails swollen by the wind. So swift was its advance that we could soon see the joyful faces of the sailors and a group of laughing young men, crowned with leaves and waving banners above their heads in greeting to their native city, victorious but still unaware of her triumph. By now the look-outs on the highest tower had signalled the arrival and, all unbidden but in universal excitement and curiosity, the citizens came flocking to the shore. As the ship came in we could see the enemy standards draped over her stern, and no shred of doubt remained in our minds that she brought news of victory . . . And when he heard it Doge Lorenzo wished with all his people to give thanks and praises to God with splendid ceremonies throughout the city, but especially at the Basilica of St Mark the Evangelist than which there is nothing, I believe, on earth more beautiful.

Petrarch, letter to Peter of Bologna,
10 August 1364 (*Epist. Sen. IV*, 3)

Giovanni Gradenigo, nicknamed *Nasone*, or Big-Nose – 'no doubt,' suggests one turn-of-the-century historian in a moment of reckless speculation, 'from some peculiarity of feature' – was elected Doge on 21 April 1355, only three days after the execution of his predecessor. It was an unusually short interregnum, possibly because of a general feeling that after the events of the past week it was important to re-establish the supreme authority with the minimum of delay. Once again, however, the Republic showed that its political institutions had flexibility and stability enough to take even the gravest domestic crisis in its stride. Any other state in Europe might have needed months, perhaps years, to recover; in Venice, by the time Doge Gradenigo ascended the newly scrubbed steps of his palace, the conspiracy of Marin Falier was nothing more than a painful memory.

The new Doge was seventy years old and a man of peace. The

Genoese war had been costly to both sides, paralysing trade and, particularly since Portolungo, confronting Venice with a serious shortage
of ships and manpower; and when the three Visconti brothers who
shared the Lordship of Milan after the death of their uncle the Archbishop offered reasonable terms on behalf of Genoa, Venice accepted
with alacrity. The treaty was signed on 1 June 1355, each Republic
undertaking – among other less important provisions – not to encroach
on the home waters of the other and to keep out of the contentious
Sea of Azov for three years. Both parties were to deposit 100,000 gold
florins in a third city as security against any violation of their commit-
ments.

The Genoese, who understandably felt that they had had the better
of the fighting, resented the strict reciprocity on which the treaty was
based. As subjects of the Visconti, they had no choice but to sign;
they did so, however, with unconcealed reluctance and a strengthened
resolve to shake off the Milanese yoke – which, in the following year,
they managed to do. The Venetians were luckier. Not only was the
peace treaty considerably more favourable to them than they had had
any right to expect, but they were free, at a time when their rival Republic
was obliged to devote all its energies to a struggle for independence,
to rebuild their fleet and re-establish their trade. While the *Arsenalotti*,
their discontent forgotten, worked overtime to keep a constant succession
of galleys, galleons, frigates and brigantines pouring down the slipways,
Venetian diplomats travelled to Barbary and Tartary, Egypt and Flanders,
reviving old agreements and cementing new ones.

If only Venice had remained the exclusively maritime power that
she had been until less than twenty years before, Giovanni Gradenigo's
short reign would have been happy indeed. But she now had a dominion
on the mainland, and her new territorial acquisitions had brought her
a new vulnerability. In former times, whenever the Hungarian Kingdom
revived its perennial claim to the towns of Dalmatia, the Venetians
could take the war straight across by sea to the enemy camp. Now all
that was changed; and they first began to understand the full significance
of that change when in 1356 King Lajos the Great of Hungary invaded
the Friuli.

This time the claim was not limited to any particular towns or islands;
Lajos demanded, quite simply, all Venetian territory on the eastern
coast of the Adriatic. He had originally done so three years before, but
had been held off by adroit diplomacy; now, on a transparently spurious
pretext, he attacked – directing the main force of his arms not even against

the area under dispute, but against the Republic itself. Sacile and Conegliano were quickly taken; Treviso was besieged. To make matters
worse, the attitude of Francesco da Carrara, Lord of Padua, was distinctly
equivocal; if Padua were to betray its allegiance, the enemy would
be on the very threshold of the Rialto.

Such was the situation when, in August 1356, Giovanni Gradenigo
died and was buried in the chapter-house of the Frari. His successor,
Giovanni Dolfin, had some initial difficulty in assuming the throne –
finding himself, at the moment of his election, under siege at Treviso;
but somehow he escaped one night and thanks to a combination of
courage, cunning and good luck, managed to slip through the Hungarian
lines. Once Doge, his first action was to clarify the position of Padua;
and no one was surprised when Carrara, emboldened by recent Hungarian successes, declared himself for Lajos. Economic sanctions were
immediately imposed on the city and a punitive expedition sent to devas-
tate the surrounding country, but such measures were of little real use;
meanwhile Serravalle and Asolo capitulated, the Bishop of Ceneda rebelled
against Venetian rule, and in beleaguered Treviso itself a plot to deliver
the city to the enemy was uncovered only hours before its implementa-
tion.

A five-month truce arranged by the Pope achieved nothing, and
when the war was resumed after Easter 1357 the Hungarian advance
continued. One or two towns successfully resisted, notably Castelfranco
and Oderzo; Treviso too held out, though its fall by now looked so imminent that its Bishop abandoned his flock and fled to Venice. Before long,
however, the Hungarians virtually controlled the shores of the lagoon
and were commandeering all the craft they could find for what was clearly
intended to be an invasion fleet. Venice replied with a ban on all lagoon
shipping. Meanwhile work began on defensive stockades, in the form of
wooden piles driven into the mud around the city.

Giovanni Dolfin was a brave man, but he was also a realist. He knew
that the Hungarians could never be turned back by defensive measures
alone, and that it was only a matter of time before the whole of Venetian
terra firma would be theirs, after which the occupation of Venice itself
must inevitably follow. Moreover the Treasury was becoming dangerously
depleted. Merchandise might still arrive in the city from the Orient,
but with the mainland in enemy hands there were no outlets for distribution. It was clear that he would have to come to terms with Lajos;
clear too that those terms would be very much more unpalatable than
those obtained from Genoa two years before.

When the Venetian envoys reached the King, they found him even more intractable than they had feared. His successes in Friuli and the Veneto had enabled him to open up a new offensive in Dalmatia, where Traù, Spalato and, most recently, Zara had all fallen, after varying degrees of resistance, to Hungarian arms. His demands were simple and sweeping: the Doge must renounce, for all time, his title of Duke of Dalmatia and Venice must surrender unconditionally all her Dalmatian possessions from the eastern corner of Istria as far south as Durazzo. In return she would be allowed to retain Istria itself, and Lajos would withdraw his forces from North Italy. There was also a vague undertaking on his part to guarantee Venetian shipping against pirates, although how Hungary, a land power, proposed to do this was not made altogether clear.

The special commission appointed by the Great Council to conduct the war – its original twenty-five members now reinforced by a *zonta* of fifty in view of the gravity of the situation – heard the Hungarian demands in a mood of rising indignation. The pine-forests of Dalmatia and its hinterland represented the chief source of timber for Venice's fleet, just as its maritime population furnished the majority of her crews. And how could her Doge, who had so recently claimed lordship over 'a quarter and a half a quarter of the Roman Empire', be expected to renounce a ducal title that had been rightfully his ever since that glorious Ascension Day three and a half centuries before?

They were strong arguments; but those on the other side were stronger still. Treviso, now on the point of collapse, and those parts of the Italian mainland that remained loyal were even more vital than was Dalmatia, which was in any case largely lost. They were the final bastion, on which the safety of the Republic itself depended. And so Lajos's terms were accepted and, on 18 February 1358, the peace treaty was signed at Zara.

The Venetians may well have felt the moral humiliation even more than the material loss; none the less, they themselves were at least partly to blame. Their tenure of Dalmatia had always been marked by a curious and, for them, most uncharacteristic vagueness. It was the one place where they never quite found their touch. From the beginning of their rule they had allowed the Dalmatians to maintain their shadowy allegiance to the Byzantine Empire; and because subject peoples inevitably prefer their distant and invisible overlords to the governors on their doorstep, the Venetians' presence along the coast had always been to a greater or a lesser extent resented. Admittedly, they tended to leave the day-to-

day tasks of government in the hands of the traditional local rulers –
princes or counts, bishops or rectors; but as time went on more and
more of these key positions came to be occupied by Venetians or their
nominees. Worst of all was their insistence on free facilities in all Dalmatian ports for Venetian shipping, and their requirement – not always
enforced – that all Dalmatian ships bound for Adriatic ports had to
offer their goods first in Venice. Local trade could not but suffer in
consequence, increasing Venetian unpopularity and making the inhabitants of the coastal towns easy game for Hungarian subversion.

Shorn of Dalmatia, Venice had saved her dominions on the Italian
mainland. She had seen, however, just how vulnerable they were to
attack – and so had her enemies, both actual and potential. Francesco da
Carrara, for example, despite a separate peace treaty and a surprisingly
lavish civic reception by the Doge later that summer, was still out for
what he could get. Before the year was over he had hired an army of
2,000 German mercenaries; and despite his assurances that they were
to be used not against Venice but the Visconti of Milan, the Venetians
felt understandable misgivings about the future. In an effort to consolidate and confirm their position, they even sent an embassy to Charles
IV to seek imperial recognition for their conquests on *terra firma*; but
Charles was his usual unsympathetic self and the only result of the
initiative was that two of the three envoys were arrested on the return
journey by Duke Rudolf of Austria – in revenge for the Venetian destruction of one of his castles in the recent Hungarian war – and spent
the next two years in captivity.

Their colleague, a certain Lorenzo Celsi, was luckier; he had decided
to stay on a little longer at the imperial court in Ratisbon. Had he not
done so, he like them would have been languishing in an Austrian
prison when Giovanni Dolfin died on 12 July 1361 – and would never
have been elected the fifty-sixth Doge of Venice.

It might be said – though perhaps a little unkindly – that nothing became
Giovanni Dolfin's dogeship like the manner of his accepting it. After
his dashing escape from besieged Treviso everything seemed to go wrong
for him. He could only preside, powerless, while the Republic he led
slowly succumbed to a foreign power and bought her deliverance by
a costly and humiliating peace. His subsequent diplomacy was no more
successful. Whether another more inspiring leader might have achieved
greater things in such circumstances is an open question. It seems unlikely.
Dolfin was not so much incapable as ill-starred. Despite his beautifully-

carved sarcophagus in the north-eastern apse chapel of SS. Giovanni e Paolo, the Venetians of today have little cause to remember him.

Lorenzo Celsi owed his elevation not only to his escape from the clutches of the Duke of Austria but also to two other strokes of luck that followed in quick succession. On his return to Venice he had been appointed 'Captain of the Gulf' – commander, in other words, of the home fleet in the Adriatic; soon afterwards he had departed on a mission; then, just as the elections were about to be held for a new Doge, a report reached the city that he had scored a signal triumph by capturing a group of Genoese privateers. The wave of jubilation caused by this news – it was the first victory that the Venetians had had to celebrate for a considerable time – was enough to tip the scales in his favour, and even when the report subsequently proved unfounded his new subjects had no real cause to regret their choice.

For the third time in the past four elections, a Doge had been chosen *in absentia* – a significant indication of the amount of time Venetian notables might expect to spend abroad. Lorenzo Celsi entered Venice in state on 21 August. He was a proud, overweening man – perhaps to compensate for his family's comparatively obscure origins – with a love of pomp and ceremonial that, anywhere else, might have been thought somewhat excessive: we are told that he had a cross fixed to his ducal cap to ensure that his old father would appear to do him adequate reverence. He also possessed a magnificent collection of stuffed animals and birds, and a stud of the finest horses in the city.

In short, he proved just the sort of Doge that the Venetians needed. Parades and processions and sumptuous display always acted on them like a tonic; and in the brief interlude of tranquillity that roughly coincided with Celsi's reign, he gave them full measure. To visiting foreign princes, too, he proved a munificent and impressive host; when Rudolf of Austria arrived in September 1361 to make his peace with the Republic (and as an earnest of his good intentions, to return in person the pair of luckless ambassadors after their two years' captivity) the Doge went out to meet him in the *Bucintoro* and later escorted him on horseback on a tour of the city, showing him the churches and palaces, the relics and priceless treasures that had made Venice famous throughout the world – though not, we may be sure, forgetting the Arsenal either. An even more splendid reception was reserved for Peter of Lusignan, King of Cyprus, during his two stays in Venice in 1362 and 1364 at the beginning and end of a European tour. He was lodged, with all the magnificence befitting his rank, in that great twelfth-century

Byzantine palace on the Grand Canal which then belonged to the Corner family and which still bears, on the cornice running along the upper loggia, the royal arms of Cyprus and of the House of Lusignan.[1]

Venice's most distinguished guest of all, however, was Petrarch, who arrived in 1362, a fugitive from the plague in Padua. His political and diplomatic life was over; in return for an offer to leave his library to the Republic he was given a fine house on the Riva, and there he lived with his daughter and her young family for the next five years until a petty insult, which he should have been able to ignore, set him off on his wanderings again.[2] What happened to the library is a question that has long puzzled scholars. An upstairs room in St Mark's was put aside for it, but the books themselves seem never to have been transferred there. It may well be that pique over the insult – four young Venetians had described him as an illiterate idiot – caused him to dispose of them elsewhere after all. Alternatively the blame may lie with the city authorities, who have been accused of simply failing to recognize the importance of the gift and allowing the books to moulder away in some forgotten repository.

In view of the reputation that Venice already enjoyed as a centre of learning and humanism, this second possibility seems unlikely. The government could well have pleaded, however, that at that particular moment it had other more pressing problems on its hands; for Petrarch's arrival in the city coincided almost precisely with a serious colonial crisis. Of all the Aegean colonies of the Republic the largest and most important was Crete; but the very size of the island had always made it something of a problem. In 160 years of Venetian domination, the Cretans had never really become reconciled to their foreign overlords, and as time went on many of the old Venetian families there also grew dissatisfied – particularly resenting the fact that whereas, had they remained in Venice, they would have enjoyed automatic membership of the Great Council, in Crete they were totally debarred from power since all local positions of authority were occupied by officials nominated by and

1. Because of their extensive sugar plantations at Piscopia (now Episkopi) in Cyprus this branch of the family took the name of Corner-Piscopia, which, according to the usual Venetian custom, was originally given to their palace as well. It is, however, more generally known by the name of Loredan, to which family it passed in the eighteenth century. One of the oldest palaces still standing in Venice – though the top two storeys are later additions – it is now joined to its contemporary neighbour, the Palazzo Farsetti, to form the modern *Municipio*, a few hundred yards down from the Rialto bridge towards St Mark's.

2. Petrarch's house in Venice was, according to long tradition and an inscription *in situ*, the former Palazzo delle due Torri just beyond the Ponte del Sepolcro on the Riva. The base of one of the two towers is still visible in the Calle del Doge adjoining.

sent out from the Republic. Flash-point was at last reached – just as in Britain's American colonies four centuries later – over the unilateral imposition of customs duties. Repeated assurances that the profit from these duties, being intended for the repair and improvement of the local harbour installations, would thus be to the colony's long-term benefit failed to impress the Cretans, who merely pointed out that they had not been consulted in advance; indeed, they were not even represented on the Great Council. They refused absolutely to pay unless they were first allowed to send a delegation of twenty wise men (*savii*) to Venice to express their grievances. Fatally perhaps, the Council could not resist a sharp retort: they were unaware, they said, that the colony possessed twenty such persons. The consequences of such an insult at such a time might have been foreseen: the standards of St Mark were lowered and those of St Titus, patron saint of Crete, hoisted in their place; the Venetian governor, Leonardo Dandolo, was deposed, narrowly escaping with his life; and the whole island rose in revolt.

Even now the Republic persisted in underestimating the gravity of the crisis. Not once but twice it dispatched official commissions to Candia – the chief city of the island – to explain to the malcontents the error of their ways. It was only after the second of these insufferably patronizing missions had had to flee back to its galleys to escape the mob that the Great Council seemed to shake off its lethargy. Letters were hurriedly sent to Pope and Emperor, and to Hungary, Naples and Genoa, urging them to refuse all support to the rebels; meanwhile a leading *condottiere*, the Veronese Luchino dal Verme, was engaged with 1,000 cavalry and 2,000 infantry to sail at once, with a fleet of thirty-three galleys, to Crete.

It was not, even by the standards of the time, a very large force, but it sufficed. The rebels were betrayed by their own lack of discipline. Their rabble army – much of it composed of hardened criminals, released from prison in return for the promise of unpaid military service – soon reverted to type and began murdering and plundering indiscriminately; soon, too, the old Venetian colonial families became alarmed at the increasing political aspirations of the far more numerous Greeks. In the rapidly changing atmosphere it began to look as though to continue the revolt might lead to open confessional strife, in which all Latins might be dispossessed and even massacred. They preferred to capitulate. Dal Verme and his men returned to Venice in triumph, and the ensuing celebrations were reported in breathless detail by Petrarch – sitting, for the occasion, at the Doge's right hand.

The size of the multitude was hard to reckon and hard to believe . . . The Doge himself, surrounded by a number of distinguished notables, occupied the loggia above the entrance to the Basilica, where stand the four horses of gilded bronze whose ancient, unknown sculptor has imbued with such a semblance of life that one can almost hear them whinnying and stamping. The loggia itself was covered with rich, multicoloured awnings to protect those present from the heat and glare of the afternoon sun . . . Below, on the Piazza, there was no room for a grain of wheat: church, towers, roofs, porches, windows, all were filled to bursting with jammed, jostling spectators . . .

On the right, in a great wooden pavilion, sat four hundred ladies magnificently dressed, the very flower of beauty and nobility . . . Nor should I omit to mention a party of English noblemen, kinsmen of the King, all exultant over their own recent victory.[1]

As things turned out, these rejoicings were a little premature. Though the Cretans of old Venetian stock had indeed capitulated – the ringleaders were beheaded and many others banished – the Greeks were to continue guerrilla activity until 1366. By that time, however, Lorenzo Celsi was dead. A certain air of mystery hangs about his death, since we find a decree by the Council of Ten, dated 30 July 1365, ordering the destruction of all written accusations levelled against the late Doge and requiring a public statement by his successor to the effect that these accusations had been thoroughly investigated and found to be without foundation. The decree was conscientiously obeyed, so that just what misdeeds had been imputed to Celsi we shall never know; some chroniclers have hinted that he was less innocent than the Ten wished it to be thought, and that had he not died so conveniently he might well have found himself arraigned on charges similar to those that had caused the downfall of Marin Falier. It may be; but there is no real evidence to support the theory. Celsi was given an honourable burial in S. Maria Celeste – now demolished – and, as we have seen, publicly exonerated. We can hardly withhold from him the benefit of the doubt.

The ducal election that followed the death of Lorenzo Celsi did not go undisputed. The name of Marco Corner – one of the ambassadors who had been imprisoned by the Duke of Austria – was put forward, but formal objections were raised to his candidature. He was too old, being well over eighty; he was too poor, and would be unable properly to meet the expenses and maintain the dignities of his office; he was

1. Presumably the Treaty of Calais of October 1360 which gave Aquitaine and much of northern France to England and brought to an end the first phase of the Hundred Years War.

too closely associated with foreign powers for his loyalty to be beyond suspicion; finally, he was married to a plebeian wife, whose numerous family would be bound to meddle in the affairs of state. But Corner rose spiritedly to his own defence. If his hair was white, he pointed out, it had gone white in the service of the Republic in which he was ready to continue; his poverty was a matter for pride rather than shame, a proof of his honesty and integrity; his ties of friendship with foreign princes were the natural results of a diplomatic career and reputation for fair dealing which had been of considerable benefit to Venice; finally, many Venetian noblemen had married ladies of humble origins, and his own wife and her family were well known and second to none in their loyalty and the love they bore their native city. His speech had precisely the desired effect: on 21 July 1365 he was elected.

His reign was short, but peaceful and prosperous. The last rebellious Cretan rumblings died away; pressure from the Count of Savoy to join in a new Crusade against the Turks was resisted, though two galleys were eventually sent off as a gesture of good will; trade with the Muslims of Alexandria was resumed and the Pope was even persuaded to give the resumption his somewhat reluctant blessing. At home, the decoration of the Doges' Palace continued, with the carving of the capitals of the south façade and Guariento's great fresco of Paradise gradually taking shape on the eastern wall of the Council Chamber, together with a long series of portraits of former Doges running around the frieze – cunningly arranged in such a way that Corner's own portrait appeared immediately above the ducal throne.

Alas, the fourteenth century was a turbulent time and Marco Corner was an old man; neither this happy breathing-space nor the Doge's life could be expected to last very long. Nor did they. On 13 January 1368 Venice once more found herself without a titular head, and within a few months of the state funeral and burial in SS. Giovanni e Paolo[1] the city was again at war.

It was not the fault of the new Doge, Andrea Contarini. He was as peacefully inclined as his predecessor and still less ambitious: he had in fact already retired to his estates near Padua, and when twelve of his most exalted countrymen arrived to inform him of his election and to escort him back in state to the Rialto, they at first met with a categorical refusal. Only after he had been threatened with banishment

---

1. Marco Corner's sarcophagus is still visible in the chancel, but has suffered badly from the treatment it received in the nineteenth century, when it was shifted and cut down to make way for the great Vendramin tomb on its transfer from the church of the Servi.

and the confiscation of his entire property did he agree to come quietly. Had he known the full measure of the tribulations that awaited him he might have shown even more reluctance; there must have been many occasions in the next fourteen years when he thought of his thwarted retirement with envious longing.

The first outbreak of trouble did not, it must be admitted, tax the strength or the resources of the Republic too severely. It took the form of an insurrection in Trieste. This was a city to which, in former years, Venice had seldom given much thought. It was smaller and, for geographical reasons, a good deal less important strategically than Zara and the other cities further along the coast. But with the loss of Dalmatia Trieste had acquired a new significance and, with it, a new susceptibility to political pressures from such dangerous neighbours as the King of Hungary, the Duke of Austria and the Patriarch of Aquileia. Whether one or more of these neighbours had a hand in stirring up the revolt we do not know; certainly the Duke was quick to send an army when the Triestines, finding themselves besieged by a Venetian fleet, appealed to him for help. But the Venetians were quicker still. They tightened the blockade and, in the summer of 1369, with a hastily gathered force composed partly of mercenaries and partly of their own fighting men, routed the Austrians utterly. Trieste withstood the siege for a few more months, but after the Austrian retreat the city's surrender could only be a matter of time. On 28 November it capitulated.

Meanwhile the behaviour of Francesco da Carrara was confirming all Venice's earlier suspicions. He was now building fort after fort along the Brenta, where he proposed to establish his own saltworks. Venice – whose monopoly of salt production in the area dated back almost as far as the Republic itself and by now probably accounted for some 10 per cent of its gross annual income[1] – sent a strongly-worded protest. Carrara instantly appealed to his old ally the King of Hungary, and was perhaps rather disappointed when Lajos, instead of supporting him, merely offered to mediate; but the ensuing discussions, which at one moment became so heated that swords were actually drawn in the council chamber, achieved nothing. Venice was not to be appeased. The salt monopoly was a cornerstone of her economy and must be protected at all costs. She hired another successful *condottiere* of the day, Renier dei Guaschi, to command her land army and declared war.

Now it was the turn of Padua to face a siege, while Venetian detachments set about the methodical destruction of Carrara's new forts and

1. We know that in 1454 it was bringing in 165,000 ducats, a still higher proportion.

the devastation of his lands. In Venice meanwhile a new plot was discovered: somehow Carrara had managed to suborn two members of the Senate and had planned with them the assassination of all his principal enemies in the government. The would-be assassins, who had been unwise enough to confide their business to a couple of patriotic prostitutes of the Merceria, were immediately arrested, drawn at a horse's tail from the Rialto to the Piazzetta and there quartered between the columns. Of the traitorous nobles, one was beheaded, the other sentenced to ten years in prison with banishment to follow. They were savage punishments, but even they did not allay the fears of the Venetian populace. New rumours flashed through the city: Carrara had poisoned the wells; he was about to set fire to the Arsenal. As much to preserve law and order as for any other reason, the Council of Ten voted special powers for the *Collegio* – to order special patrols for the streets and canals, to search all strangers entering Venice, to put suspected and accused persons to the torture. The measures were welcomed with general enthusiasm; in the popular opinion, Francesco da Carrara had become Antichrist.

The war continued almost four years, till the autumn of 1373. First Venice had the advantage; then, after a Hungarian army had arrived to supplement Carrara's already considerable force of German mercenaries – it was led by Lajos's nephew, Stephen of Transylvania – the pendulum swung and the Republic suffered a serious defeat at Narvesa on the Piave. Taddeo Giustinian, who had assumed supreme command from dei Guaschi, was taken prisoner, and the captured banner of St Mark was hung as a trophy in the great basilica of St Anthony in Padua. A second defeat followed, at Fossanuova; but soon afterwards, while the Hungarians were besieging a relatively insignificant Venetian fortress – so insignificant, indeed, that its name has not even come down to us – the Venetian army suddenly attacked. A Hungarian countercharge was broken by the unwavering stand of the Venetian pikemen, and Stephen of Transylvania taken prisoner.

Brought to Venice, he was honourably accommodated in the Doges' Palace, while the people rejoiced at the victory. They had good reason to do so. The King of Hungary, to secure his nephew's freedom, immediately withdrew from the war, and Carrara, now left without an ally, was forced to capitulate. The terms exacted were harsh: all his forts were to be destroyed, and an indemnity of no less than a quarter of a million ducats to be paid to Venice. Feltre was to be held by the Republic as security for his good behaviour. The only concession he managed to gain was that his son, rather than he himself, should come to Venice to ask pardon of the Doge, a ceremony that took place in the autumn of 1373 before the assembled Senate while Petrarch, who had accompanied the supplicant – his presence appears to have become indispensable on such occasions – pronounced one of his usual high-flown Latin orations in praise of peace.

But peace, even now, was not absolute. Another of Carrara's erstwhile allies, the Duke of Austria, continued to make trouble and for the next three years that ill-fated region of farms and hilltop towns around Treviso that had already suffered so much in the past half-century was once again torn apart by desultory and largely inconclusive warfare – in which, incidentally, the Venetians introduced a few small cannon, the first ever seen in Italy. Not until the end of 1376 did the Duke finally withdraw his army; but by then Venice had other preoccupations. Her long and bitter struggle with another, still more intractable rival was approaching its final phase.

18

The War with Genoa

[1372–1381]

'Alla fè di Dio, Signori Veneziani, non haverete mai pace dal Signore di Padova, ne dal nostro Comune di Genova, si primieramente non mettemo le briglie a quelli vostri cavalli sfrenati, che sono su la Reza del vostro Evangelista San Marco.'

'In God's name, my Venetian signors, you shall never have peace from the Lord of Padua, nor from our own Republic of Genoa, until we have put a bridle on those wild horses of yours that stand upon the Palace of St Mark your Evangelist.'

Admiral Pietro Doria (Quoted by Chinazzo,
Belli inter Venetos et Genuenses, 1378)

On 17 January 1369 Peter I of Lusignan, King of Cyprus and Jerusalem, was murdered in his palace at Famagusta. He was succeeded by his fourteen-year-old son Peter II. Owing to the new King's youth and the repeated procrastinations of his uncle the Regent, there was no immediate coronation. It was only in January 1372 that young Peter received the crown of Cyprus, and in October of the same year that of Jerusalem.

This latter kingdom was purely titular; Jerusalem had been in the hands of the Infidel for nearly two centuries[1] and Peter's second coronation therefore took place at Famagusta, in the church of St Nicholas. Already on the way to the church some dispute over precedence broke out between the Venetian and Genoese representatives. Somehow peace was restored, but at the banquet following the ceremony the contingents from the two Republics began throwing bread at each other; a brawl ensued during which, despite strict laws to the contrary, many of the Genoese were found to have been carrying swords under their cloaks. In the circumstances it is hard to believe that the Venetians were entirely guiltless of similar offences, but they were a good deal more popular on the island than their rivals and the Cypriot authorities seem to have had no hesitation in laying the blame on the Genoese. Several of the latter

1. Since Saladin captured it in 1187 after the battle of Hattin. Later, in 1229, Frederick II had talked his way into possession of the Holy Places, but had held them only ten years.

were arrested, seized and defenestrated on the spot. Meanwhile the Famagusta mob descended on the Genoese quarter, pillaging, looting and burning the warehouses to the ground.

When the news of all this reached Genoa, the reaction was much as might have been foreseen. Such an insult to the Republic could not go unpunished; moreover, unless firm measures were taken at once, there was a danger that Cyprus might fall completely under Venetian influence – a possibility, to any patriotic Genoese, almost too horrible to contemplate. Two punitive expeditions set off in quick succession; on 6 October 1373 Famagusta surrendered to a Genoese war fleet, and a few days later the whole island made its submission. The young King himself was allowed to remain on his throne, but only in recognition of a fine of over 2,000,000 gold florins and an annual payment of 40,000; his uncle, two of his cousins and sixty members of the Cypriot nobility were carried off to Genoa as hostages for his future good behaviour. Genoa kept Famagusta for herself.

It was only to be expected that Venetian property should suffer during these last upheavals, just as Genoese had done in the previous year; and though the new masters of Cyprus made no effort to evict their rivals – indeed they received the formal Venetian protests and demands for compensation with unwonted politeness and even sympathy – this abrupt reversal of fortune in one of the key areas of the eastern Mediterranean made the renewal of the war between the two republics inevitable. The fact that it was to be delayed, against all probabilities, for nearly five more years was due less to any peaceable inclinations on either side than to a sudden turn of events in Constantinople in which both were to be closely – if not altogether creditably – involved.

The Emperor John V Palaeologus had by now managed to rid himself of his father-in-law Cantacuzenus, who in 1355 had given up all hopes of founding a new dynasty and had retired to end his days writing history from a monastic cell on Mount Athos. In all other respects, however, John's problems had increased. Adrianople, and with it much of Thrace, had fallen to the Ottoman Turks, who were virtually at the walls of Constantinople. He was furthermore heavily in debt, and the imperial treasury was empty. In a desperate bid for military and financial aid he had travelled to the West in 1369 and, in return for promises of ships, cavalry and bowmen from Urban V, had actually gone so far as to acknowledge papal supremacy; but the other princes of Europe had proved less sympathetic and when John reached Venice in 1370 he had had to submit to the worst humiliation of all – confinement in a debtors' prison. His elder son Andronicus, whom he had appointed regent in his absence, seemed content that he should remain there; it was left to his second son Manuel to send his own remaining jewels to Venice and bail his father out.

Even now, however, many of the debts were still unpaid; and in the years immediately following John's return to his beleaguered capital they tended to increase. The Venetians decided once again to take a firm line with the Emperor. The five-year truce they had promised him after his release had now expired; more important still, the fall of Cyprus to Genoa had made it essential for them to find an alternative commercial base in the eastern Mediterranean. In 1375, therefore, a Venetian embassy headed for Constantinople, to be followed in March 1376 – the Emperor having shown his usual tendency to prevaricate – by a fully-armed fleet under the Captain-General of the Sea, Marco Giustinian, with an ultimatum: if John wished to continue to live on peaceful terms with Venice for the next five years, he must at once pay all his outstanding debts and mortgage to the Republic the island of Tenedos. In recognizance for this last the Venetians would pay him a substantial lump sum and return his son's jewels. If he were to refuse these terms, he must look to his throne.

To any power with trading interests in the area, the strategic importance of Tenedos could hardly be exaggerated. Lying at the gateway to the Hellespont – according to Virgil[1] the Greeks had hidden there, watching and waiting, while the Wooden Horse was sent into Troy – it controlled the entrance to the straits and the Sea of Marmara beyond them as effectively as Galata did the mouth of the Bosphorus. If Tenedos too were to fall into the hands of the Genoese, Venetian trade with Byzantium and the Black Sea would be strangled. Once before, in 1352, Venice had temporarily acquired the island to prevent just such a disaster;[2] with Genoa in her present mood and mistress of Cyprus to boot, the need to assure the freedom of the Hellespont was even more vital than it had been twenty-four years earlier.

The sight of the Venetian fleet at the very mouth of the Golden Horn was more than enough to persuade John Palaeologus to submit. He paid up, willingly surrendering Tenedos on the terms proposed, asking only that it should continue to fly the imperial standard alongside that of St Mark and that it should be allowed to maintain its ecclesiastical allegiance to the Byzantine Patriarch. He must have known that his

1. *Aeneid*, II, 21ff.
2. See p. 219.

capitulation would provoke the wrath of the Genoese; he can hardly have suspected the scale of their revenge.

The Emperor's son Andronicus had already shown himself to be untrustworthy during his father's difficulties in Venice. In 1373 he had gone further still, allying himself with the son of the Ottoman Sultan Murad in a joint conspiracy against their two fathers. The plot had been discovered; Murad had blinded and later executed his own son and had enjoined John to do the same; but John, being of gentler disposition, had left Andronicus at least partially sighted and merely imprisoned him. His throne, however, was still insecure, and he now had a new problem to contend with – unpopularity. His people, to whom their religion meant even more than imperial survival, had never forgiven him his submission to the Pope. The action taken by the Genoese after his cession of Tenedos to Venice illustrates better than anything else both the weakness of his position in Constantinople and the strength of their own: they simply deposed him. Father and son changed places; John was incarcerated in his turn while Andronicus, released, was raised to the imperial throne.

The new Emperor's first act on his accession was to make over Tenedos to the Genoese, who immediately sent a representative to the island to claim it in the name of the Republic. The attempt was a failure. Venice herself had not yet taken possession, but the local governor remained loyal to John and refused point-blank to recognize the authority of Andronicus. He had presumably received some official intimation of the agreement with Venice: for when Marco Giustinian arrived with his fleet soon afterwards he was given a ceremonial welcome, the islanders willingly – even enthusiastically – delivering themselves into his hands. By this time, however, the Genoese in Constantinople had complained to Andronicus of the rebuff they had sustained and the Emperor, terrified of losing their support, had arrested the leaders of the Venetian mercantile community, including the *bailo* himself.

Clearly the war could not be much longer postponed. Throughout 1377 the diplomatic moves between Venice, Genoa and Constantinople become ever more loaded with protests rejected, demands refused and, finally, out-and-out threats. Genoa reminds Venice that she cannot be held responsible for attacks on Venetian persons and property in the Byzantine Empire; Venice informs Genoa that their political differences in the area cannot be discussed until the rightful Emperor is restored to power; finally a second Venetian admiral, Pietro Mocenigo, is ordered to Constantinople to demand the immediate release of the *bailo* and the

other Venetians held in custody, failing which Andronicus will be forcibly deposed in his turn, if necessary with the help of the Ottoman Sultan.

But Mocenigo never reached his destination. Soon after he had left
the lagoon, word reached Venice that Genoa had sent a fleet of galleys
to sea, with the object of joining up with a Byzantine squadron and
launching a combined attack on Tenedos. Messengers overtook the
admiral with revised instructions. He and his fleet were needed in the
Mediterranean. The war had begun.

The Genoese and Byzantines did indeed try to take Tenedos by force,
and failed. But the attempt is hardly mentioned in the early histories
– understandably, because it hardly mattered. With another of those
sudden shifts of focus which make the history of the Mediterranean
so bewildering to writer and reader alike, Tenedos – and with it the
gateway to the Hellespont, the Marmara, Constantinople and the whole
Black Sea trade – fades once more into the background. The last round
of the contest between Genoa and Venice was to be fought out, more
appropriately, on Italian territory and in Italian waters: in the Tyrrhenian,
the Adriatic and, most desperately of all, in the Venetian lagoon.

Both sides had taken good care to find allies. Genoa could, as always,
count on Francesco da Carrara and that other elderly troublemaker,
the King of Hungary; Venice had the support of King Peter of Cyprus,
who had not forgiven the Genoese their recent seizure of his island
and welcomed the chance of seeing his erstwhile conquerors brought
low. Peter's support was in fact to make little difference as such; but
it had one important consequence in that it enabled Venice to secure
the alliance of the young King's prospective father-in-law, Bernabò
Visconti of Milan. The two signed a four-year treaty in November 1377,
in which it was agreed that all conquests made at sea should go to Venice,
all those on land to Milan – including, if fortune favoured their efforts,
Genoa itself. In the Doges' Palace, meanwhile, the usual steps were
taken to put the Republic on war footing: special committees of *savii*
were formed to accelerate the making of policy decisions and to raise
money; arrangements were made to hire *condottieri* and mercenaries
for fighting on the mainland, to fortify strategic points in the Treviso
region, and to form *duodene*, those twelve-man groups from which,
by that admirable and characteristically Venetian system, one or more
persons could be selected by lot for military service and paid for by
the remainder. On this occasion no less than three men from each *duodena*
were to make themselves ready for immediate departure. Finally, in

the basilica on 22 April 1378, Vettor Pisani – nephew of that Nicolò who had been deprived of command after Portolungo – was invested by Doge Contarini with the banner of St Mark and enjoined to lead the Republic to victory.

Vettor Pisani may not have been one of Venice's greatest admirals. He was, however, to prove himself one of her greatest men – a superb leader, adored by all who served under his command; and less than six weeks after his appointment his family name had recovered all its former glory. On 30 May the Venetian and Genoese fleets met off Anzio. It was a day of violent storms and a heavy sea; the battle was fought in driving rain, with winds rising to gale force so that close manoeuvring became impossible and four of Pisani's galleys were actually prevented from engaging the enemy at all. Yet somehow Venetian seamanship prevailed, and by nightfall five Genoese galleys had been captured and a sixth driven on to the rocks. The prisoners, including the Genoese commander, were brought back to the Rialto where, we are told, they were admirably looked after by the noble ladies of Venice. The people of Genoa, by contrast, were less amicably inclined: alarmed and infuriated – not so much by the news of the defeat as by the depredations of a neighbouring baron whom the Venetians had encouraged to ravage the Genoese coast while they kept the navy occupied – they stormed their own ducal palace, deposed their Doge and set up another in his stead.

Had Pisani's fleet been a little more numerous and the weather less unseasonable, he might well have advanced to Genoa itself and brought the war to a swift conclusion; but he preferred not to take the risk. Instead, he sailed to the Levant – incidentally providing an unexpected additional escort for Valentina Visconti, one of Bernabò's thirty-eight children, who was on her way to Cyprus to marry King Peter – and, after an energetic but ultimately abortive pursuit of more Genoese shipping, headed back to the Adriatic where he captured the cities of Cattaro and Sebenico.[1] Permission to return to Venice being refused, he finally settled his fleet at Pola for the winter.

This refusal on the part of the Venetian authorities was a serious error of judgement. Pisani, his captains and his sailors had already been at sea for six months and were now faced with the prospect of perhaps another year without contact with their families or friends. After their exertions and several conspicuous successes, they felt they deserved better. The ships, too, were in need of repair, and the cold, the damp and the sickness which was bound to result from a winter spent in such

1. Kotor and Sibenik.

conditions were the more intolerable for being obviously unnecessary. A renewed request to return home in the spring was again rejected; and it was a resentful and demoralized body of men that awoke in Pola on the morning of 7 May 1379 to find a Genoese fleet of twenty-five sail lying at the harbour mouth.

Pisani at first refused to fight. He knew better than anyone the condition of his men and his ships. They were outnumbered; besides, in the event of their defeat, how was Venice herself to be protected? Another Venetian fleet under his fellow-admiral Carlo Zeno was shortly expected in Pola from the East; if it were to turn up, then the two together should be able to deal with the Genoese. Meanwhile it would be better to remain in harbour, out of harm's way. He was unquestionably right; but he was overruled. Captains and crews alike, weary of inactivity, clamoured to be allowed to take the offensive and even taunted their admiral with accusations of cowardice. Pisani was no coward; at this crucial moment, however, he seems to have lacked the moral courage to stand firm. He agreed to attack and, sailing out of the harbour, bore directly down upon the Genoese flagship.

It was all over quite quickly, and with results even more calamitous, perhaps, than Pisani had feared. He himself fought heroically, and was credited with having been personally responsible for the death of the Genoese admiral, Luciano Doria; but several of his captains proved slow and irresolute, and of the entire Venetian fleet only six battered galleys escaped capture or destruction and made their way, slow and creaking, to safety in the port of Parenzo. Recalled to Venice to answer for the defeat, Pisani was charged not with cowardice but with having kept insufficient watch on the harbour approaches. He was deprived of his command, sentenced to six months' imprisonment, and debarred from all office under the Republic for five years.

It seems hard to believe that Venice, poised as she was on the brink of disaster, should have deliberately deprived herself of the services of one of her two leading admirals – at a time moreover when the other, Carlo Zeno, was away in the East and, though vaguely thought to be on his way home, beyond any possibility of immediate recall. Her only justification, sad and ironic as it might be, was that Pisani was now useless to her since, apart from the half-dozen battered hulks in Parenzo, she no longer had any ships available for him to command. Unless and until Zeno arrived with his fleet, she had only her own natural defences in which to put her trust. Fortunately she could count on a few weeks' grace. The Genoese had lost their admiral; they could hardly resume the offensive until a new one had been appointed and had had time to travel out and take up his command.

During those few weeks the Venetians worked day and night to strengthen the defences of their city. It was a gigantic effort, involving virtually the entire population, men and women, nobles and commoners alike. Many of the rich put their whole fortunes at the disposal of the Republic; others fitted out ships or undertook costly building operations at their own expense. Their task was not made easier by the presence of Francesco da Carrara – now supported by 5,000 Hungarians sent by King Lajos – on the shores of the lagoon, where they had only just succeeded in saving Mestre from his clutches. But even Carrara was now a lesser danger. Though he might do his worst on the mainland, terrifying the local populations with his cannon – still a rarity in Italy – he was powerless on water and so constituted little physical threat to the city itself. The Genoese navy was another matter. An advance squadron was already in sight – waiting just beyond the Lido port, nearer than any hostile fleet had anchored for centuries past, as if mocking the Venetians' inability to move against it.

But if Venice could not destroy the Genoese, she could at least ensure that their onward progress would be hard. Leonardo Dandolo, now given the unprecedented appointment of 'General of the Lido', set about fortifying the monastery of S. Nicolò with stout walls and a triple ditch, while three heavy hulks were chained together across the lagoon entrance and the long and sinuous rows of piles which were used, then as now, to mark the shoals and channels were taken up to baffle the invaders. Meanwhile command on land was entrusted to the *condottiere* Giacomo de' Cavalli, who appeared with 4,000 horsemen, 2,000 infantry and a considerable force of cross-bowmen. These were drawn up in strength along the *lidi* and such neighbouring areas on the mainland as remained in Venetian hands, while armed boats constantly patrolled the lagoon to block communications between Carrara and the Genoese. In the city itself it was decreed that a committee consisting of two councillors, one *capo della Quarantia* and four *savii* should be on constant twenty-four-hour call at the Doges' Palace, to be relieved weekly by another similarly constituted. Among its other duties it was to listen for the tocsin which was to be sounded, in an emergency, by the bells of S. Nicolò di Lido. This alarm would be taken up from the campanile of St Mark's and further relayed by all the churches of Venice, while each parish sent its own armed contingent to the Piazza.

The arrangements were made only just in time. On 6 August a fleet of forty-seven Genoese galleys under the newly-appointed admiral Pietro Doria appeared off Chioggia.

The town of Chioggia stands on an island at the extreme southern end of the Venetian lagoon – a region which, even by local standards, strikes one as peculiarly indecisive; where the geography fails utterly to make up its mind whether to be terrestrial or aquatic, where the contours separating land from sea, blurred enough at the best of times, are rendered still more uncertain by the multiple mouths of the two rivers, the Brenta and the Adige, which disgorge their muddy waters a mile or two beyond; and where, over the past 500 years, generation after generation of military sappers and marine engineers have built dams and breakwaters, causeways and canals, diverting here, deflecting there, to the point at which the face of the landscape as it existed in the late fourteenth century, when Venice and Genoa confronted each other across the malodorous marshes, has been lost beyond recall.

For all these reasons, and despite the display of much scholarly ingenuity on points of topographical precision, many of the details of the war of Chioggia remain obscure. The broad outlines, however, are clear enough. Doria had brought his fleet down from the north, burning Grado, Caorle and Pellestrina on his way. He had also made what appears to have been a somewhat desultory attack on Malamocco but, encountering stiffer opposition than he had expected, had not persevered; none of these places was vital to his purpose. His sights were fixed on Chioggia, where the line of *lidi* met the mainland. There he had secretly arranged to meet Carrara who, having led his army of 24,000 Italians and Hungarians down the valley of the Brenta, would provide an invaluable supply line and simultaneously establish a mainland blockade of Venice while the Genoese did the same by sea.

Chioggia was defended by a garrison of 3,000 under its *podestà*, Pietro Emo. Such a force would have been more than adequate in any normal eventuality, but it could not hope to deal with an amphibious attack on this scale. Emo appealed to Venice for help, and fifty shallow-draught lagoon boats were immediately dispatched under Leonardo Dandolo; but they would have been of little use, and anyway they arrived too late. On 16 August, after a heroic but futile defence which took an immense toll of human life both Venetian and Genoese, Chioggia fell. For the first time since the days of Pepin, a fortified city within the lagoon – and one which, incidentally, commanded a direct deep-water channel to Venice – lay in enemy hands.

As the banners of Genoa, Hungary and its new lord Francesco Carrara fluttered over Chioggia and all the bells of Venice rang out the alarm, Doge and Senate met in emergency session. Still there was no news of Carlo Zeno and his fleet, without which they could not hope to defeat the invaders in pitched battle. An initial decision to sue for terms came to nothing when Carrara refused to grant safe conduct to the Venetian ambassadors, so that Venice now found herself in a more impossible situation than ever, powerless alike to make peace or to continue the war. All she could do was look to her defences in the hopes that they might delay the enemy until Zeno's arrival. Malamocco was abandoned, to enable all available troops to be concentrated around S. Nicolò on the Lido, and – more ominously still – on S. Giorgio Maggiore. All magistrates voluntarily renounced their pay; as food shortages became more severe and prices rose, the rich were ordered to provide free meals for the poor. Finally, in deference to the people's insistent demand, Vettor Pisani was released from prison.

This last decision was taken with reluctance. There was by now general agreement among government and people alike that Venice needed, at this moment of desperate crisis, a military leader to assume supreme command; but the Senate had their own candidate for the post, Taddeo Giustinian, and were understandably reluctant to reinstate a man whom they had publicly disgraced only a few weeks before. Even now, despite Pisani's magnanimous declaration that far from bearing the Republic any grudge for his past treatment he was resolved to dedicate his life to its preservation, they tried to subordinate him to Giustinian; but the people – and, in particular, the sailors who had served with him in the past and worshipped him - protested. Pisani was their man: they would follow no other. This was no moment to risk a popular uprising. Once again the Senate gave in.

They were wise to do so. The atmosphere in Venice changed overnight. Despair and defeatism vanished. Morale came flooding back, and with it a new vigour and determination. A forced loan produced the gigantic sum of over 6,000,000 lire, not to mention quantities of gold, silver and jewels voluntarily contributed by men and women from all sections of the city. At the Arsenal, work continued day and night until forty galleys had come off the slipways. A new defensive wall, with towers at each end, was built along the Lido and completed within a fortnight; a boom, protected by armed ships – some mounted with cannon – was stretched across the western end of the Grand Canal, and another stockade was erected, running from S. Nicolò di Lido right across the lagoon, behind the islands of S. Servolo and the Giudecca, to the mainland shore. All this and much more was due, in large measure, to the infectious enthusiasm of an inspired leader, Vettor Pisani. No wonder his men loved him.

But he was also lucky. If, immediately after the capture of Chioggia, Pietro Doria had followed Carrara's advice and launched an immediate attack on Venice, it is doubtful whether Pisani or anyone else would have been able to save the city. Fortunately, Pietro stuck to his original plan, to blockade it and starve it into submission. In this he failed; instead, he gave it time to recover, while at the same time he allowed the morale of his own men to drain away. Many of them, anxious to get their hands on the fabled wealth of Venice, had been disappointed by their admiral's excessive caution and resented having to stand idly by, watching while the city erected new and formidable defences and made itself daily more impregnable. And there were other, still more disquieting signs. One day in the late summer a small squadron under Giovanni Barbarigo had fallen upon three Genoese ships guarding a mainland fort and burnt them. Meanwhile Giacomo de' Cavalli was slowly advancing southwards along the *lidi* and had regained Malamocco. Almost incredibly, it seemed, the Venetians were beginning to take the offensive.

The recapture of Malamocco was perhaps less significant than it appeared. Winter was approaching, and winter must inevitably mean, for Pietro Doria, the withdrawal of his forces into Chioggia. For Vettor Pisani, on the other hand, who had good reason to know the difficulties of keeping a large war fleet in good order when away from home throughout those bitter months, it meant the opening of the next phase of his campaign. The blockaders must themselves be blockaded. Chioggia was already almost landlocked and depended on only three narrow channels: the main harbour entrance towards Pellestrina, and, a little further south, the two entrances to the harbour of Brondolo, both of which also gave access to the lagoon. All that was necessary was to sink a large, stone-filled hulk in each of these channels; the two other lagoon outlets to the north, the Lido and Malamocco ports, could then be blocked by Venetian patrols.

On mid-winter night, 21 December 1379, the expedition set out, with the hulks in tow. Accompanying Pisani on the leading vessel was the Doge himself, Andrea Contarini, now well into his eighties. By dawn they had arrived at the approaches to Chioggia. The local lookouts quickly gave the alert, and the fighting was fierce, particularly around Brondolo, where the defence was concentrated; but the hulks were duly sunk in their appointed places, and within a few hours Chioggia was effectively closed, the Genoese and all their fleet prisoners within it.

The Venetians' work, however, was not yet done. The success of the operation depended on their continued vigilance. One of the Brondolo barricades was clearly vulnerable and needed constant defence against attempts by the Genoese to remove it; there were also the northern lagoon entrances to be watched. Ships and provisions were still woefully short, and the winter storms made the task of the Venetian patrols, unaccustomed to keeping to the open seas in such conditions, both difficult and dangerous. How long they could have continued without assistance is uncertain, but fortunately the question did not have to be put to the test. On the first day of 1380 the long-awaited fleet of Carlo Zeno appeared over the horizon.

After a quick council of war with Pisani and the Doge, Zeno sailed at once with his eighteen ships to Brondolo, still the weakest and most critical point in the blockade. In the sudden storm which coincided with his arrival he was twice nearly shipwrecked, but a day or two later he succeeded in recapturing a nearby stronghold, the tower of Londo, so opening the way for the reinforcements and provisions that Venice's ally, the Duke of Ferrara, had sent up by the lower Adige. On 6 January there was even greater rejoicing when a Venetian cannon destroyed the campanile of Brondolo and it was learnt that Pietro Doria had been struck and killed by the falling debris.[1] His successor, chosen perforce from among the officers on the spot, was one Napoleone Grimaldi who in desperation tried to cut a new channel through the Lido of Sottomarina, immediately to the east of the beleaguered port; but in mid-February Pisani took Brondolo, and the entire line of *lidi* was back in Venetian hands.

The siege continued all through the winter and into the spring. In April the Venetians suffered a serious reverse when a new Genoese fleet under Marco Maruffo captured Taddeo Giustinian and the twelve ships with which he had gone to collect grain from Sicily – famine conditions in Venice being by now almost as bad as those in Chioggia itself – and then began to harry Pisani and Zeno as they ceaselessly patrolled the entrances to the lagoon. They also had trouble with mutinous mercenaries (including a number of particularly tiresome English-

---

1. These early cannon were so unwieldy that their terrified crews dared not use them more than once a day; but they were rapidly proving their value as a weapon, being capable of firing, at a short range, stone balls weighing up to 200 pounds.

men) whom they managed to control only with promises of additional prizes and double pay. By some miracle, however, the two admirals avoided a pitched sea battle with Maruffo – in which they would almost certainly have been defeated – while successfully preventing him from making contact with his compatriots inside the lagoon and simultaneously blocking every attempt by the latter to join him. At last he gave up, and withdrew to Dalmatia; and on 24 June the 4,000 beleaguered Genoese, despairing of rescue and half-dead with hunger, made their unconditional surrender.

In Venice there was jubilation. This was not just a victory; it was deliverance. Virtually the whole population, in innumerable boats of every shape and size, accompanied the *Bucintoro* as it sailed out in state to meet the old Doge, who had remained with the fleet throughout the six-month siege. And so the triumphal procession returned to the Molo,[1] bringing in its train the seventeen battered galleys, all that was left of Pietro Doria's fleet, and their abject crews. The mercenaries were paid in full as promised, one of them – an Englishman called William Gold who was not, presumably, one of the mutineers – receiving an additional 500 ducats in recognition of his exceptional valour.

The war was not quite over. Matteo Maruffo was still in the Adriatic, from which Pisani was determined that he should not escape. After weeks of that inconsequential and profitless searching of which, until modern times, so much of naval warfare consisted, Pisani at last caught up with a dozen Genoese galleys off the coast of Apulia and engaged them. They escaped, but not before he had been gravely wounded. Brought back to Manfredonia, he died there on 13 August. His monument, formerly in the Arsenal, can now be seen in the south-east apse of SS. Giovanni e Paolo. Amid the profusion of funerary sculpture in the church, it is seldom noticed; most guide-books ignore it utterly. But of all those buried in that tremendous building, none was more generally loved or more willingly followed than Vettor Pisani, and none has a better claim to the lasting gratitude of his compatriots. It would perhaps be an exaggeration to say that he saved Venice single-handed; the fact remains that she would not have survived without him.

Carlo Zeno, now in supreme command, continued the campaign over a theatre that ranged from the coast of the Peloponnese to Genoese home waters, but achieved no more decisive victories. Meanwhile,

1. See the painting by Veronese – one of his last works – on the west wall of the Sala del Maggior Consiglio.

in the Veneto, Carrara and his friends were also keeping up the pressure. The Venetians had long suspected that these mainland territories were more trouble than they were worth; they were determined none the less not to surrender them to the detested Carrara. Their solution was to offer them to the Duke of Austria, on condition only that he should at once occupy them with an army in the Republic's name. The Duke asked nothing better: confronted with a vastly superior force, Carrara had no alternative but to withdraw.

By now the heat had gone out of the war, and in 1381 the two exhausted Republics gratefully accepted the offer of Count Amadeus VI of Savoy to mediate. The ensuing peace conference at Turin was attended by representatives not just of Venice and Genoa but of all those who had played any part in the hostilities: Hungary, Padua, Aquileia, even Ancona and Florence. Venice demanded the right, as the victorious party, to table the first proposals, but the terms eventually agreed were scarcely those that might have been expected by a conqueror. She regained from Carrara the strong-points around the lagoon that were essential to her safety; but she confirmed her renunciation of Dalmatia and also of Tenedos, the immediate *casus belli*, which was surrendered to Amadeus to dispose of as he saw fit.

The truth was that, at least in the short-term view, Venice had not won the war or anything like it. Nor had Genoa. The only victors in any real sense were those two shadowy figures on the side-lines, the King of Hungary and the Duke of Austria. The events at Chioggia, heroic and inspiring as they had been, had served only the negative purpose of averting disaster. After all the devastation and bloodshed, the two protagonists were politically very much where they had been before – a situation confirmed by the Treaty of Turin, which provided for the continuation of trade in the Mediterranean and the Levant by both republics side by side.

As time went on, however, it gradually became clear that Venice's victory had been greater than she knew. Not for the first time, she was to astonish her friends and enemies alike by the speed of her economic and material recovery. Genoa, on the other hand, went into a decline. Her governmental system began to crumble; torn asunder by factional strife, she was to depose ten Doges in five years and soon fell under a French domination which was to last a century and a half. Only in 1528, under Andrea Doria, was she finally to regain her independence; but by then the world had changed. Never again would she constitute a threat to Venice.

19

The Empire Takes Shape

[1381–1405]

The Duke cannot deny the course of law;
For the commodity that strangers have
With us in Venice, if it be denied,
Will much impeach the justice of this state;
Since that the trade and profit of this city
Consisteth of all nations.

Shakespeare, *The Merchant of Venice*

It was 4 September 1381. The Treaty of Turin had been signed the month before. Thanks had been rendered to God from every church in Venice for her deliverance from mortal danger and for her heroic victory – as the Venetians were determined to see it – over a powerful and pitiless foe. Plans were already being drawn up for the rebuilding of Chioggia. Only one more thing remained to be done before the whole epoch of Venetian–Genoese rivalries and hostilities could be regarded as closed for ever. Venice must reward, as she had promised to reward, those of her citizens who, through generosity, heroism or both, had rendered outstanding service in the hour of need. She would do so by offering them the most precious gift she had, one which many an Italian princeling had sought in vain: a place among her nobility. Even now, admission to this exclusive and exalted company was not to be taken for granted: each candidate had to submit to a proper election by secret ballot and, though in the circumstances such a procedure might have been thought to be largely a formality, it is reliably reported to have continued for the whole day and much of the night. We read with sorrow of a corn chandler named Leonardo dell' Agnello who, having offered to finance 150 mercenaries for a month, was understandably confident of election; disappointed, he died of a broken heart.

How many other candidates shared his disappointment we do not know; but on the morning of 5 September thirty new nobles, each carrying a lighted candle and followed by his family and friends, walked in pro-

cession to the Basilica for a special mass, and thence to the Palace to
be formally presented to the Doge and Signoria. The ceremony was
followed by a regatta and the usual celebrations in the Piazza; but what
must have given the greatest joy to the populace was the fact that
several of those honoured were tradesmen or artisans like themselves.
Perhaps the Venetian aristocracy was not quite such a closed circle after
all.

Despite the rigours of the Chioggia campaign, old Andrea Contarini
was still, so far as we can gather, in reasonable health when the thirty
came to do him reverence. He was to last one more winter; then, on
6 June 1382, he died. He was buried, rather surprisingly, in the cloister
of S. Stefano. The sarcophagus is simple, its surroundings nowadays
insalubrious;[1] Contarini, one feels, that reluctant Doge who served
his country so well, merited something better – something, perhaps,
more akin to that of his successor Michele Morosini who, having died
of the plague after only four and a half months in office, was accorded
a tomb – on the right-hand wall of the choir of SS. Giovanni e Paolo
– described by Ruskin as 'the richest monument of the Gothic period
in Venice'.[2]

Rich and high-principled, Morosini would have made an excellent
Doge had he had time to prove his capabilities. It was no fault of his
that he should have fallen victim, not only to one of those repeated
outbreaks of the Black Death that punctuated the second half of the
fourteenth century in Venice, but also to a contemporary misunder-
standing that continues, still today, to besmirch his name. During the
Chioggia crisis, when the future of Venice was at its bleakest, he is said
to have made immense investments in real estate. His purpose was
almost certainly to keep up property values and maintain confidence
generally; and when asked the reason for such apparently rash behaviour
he replied 'Se questa terra starà male, io non voglio aver ben' – 'If this land
is to come to grief, I do not wish to prosper.' Unfortunately the most
popular version of Sanudo's Lives of the Doges misquotes him as having
said 'io ne voglio aver ben' – 'I wish to do well out of it'; and the calumny
has stuck. Had the second version been the true one it would have
cast serious doubts on Morosini's capacity, both moral and intellectual,

1. The cloister was rebuilt in the sixteenth century, and the atmosphere has not been
improved by the offices of the Ministry of Finance to which it has now been given over.
2. Ruskin adds, as only he could have added, that the tomb furnishes 'not only the exactly
intermediate condition in style between the pure Gothic and its final Renaissance corruption,
but, at the same time, the exactly intermediate condition of feeling between the pure calmness
of early Christianity, and the boastful pomp of the Renaissance faithlessness'.

to govern; and it is unthinkable that he would have been elected Doge – particularly if, as some sources maintain, he had as a rival candidate the surviving hero of the Genoese war, Carlo Zeno.

This last suggestion has caused much puzzled speculation among modern historians, who have tended to suppose that Zeno was passed over as a result of an insignificant reversal he had suffered shortly before the end of the war. A far likelier explanation is that he was still a comparatively young man – not yet fifty – and an active one. Immured in the Doges' Palace, his time largely taken up with state ceremonial, he would have had little scope for his energies or talents. He could be of far more use to the Republic in other capacities – as indeed, for the next thirty-six years, he was.

On the death of Michele Morosini, and with Carlo Zeno still out of the running, the choice of the electors now fell on a certain Antonio Venier. The sixtieth Doge of Venice was at the time serving as *capitano* in Crete, where his family – one of the oldest in the Republic – had settled some time before; for three months the government was run by a Council of Regency until, on 13 January 1383, Venier was able to return in state to the Rialto, accompanied by the twelve noblemen who had been sent to fetch him.[1]

He was, by all accounts, a stern and austere man with a highly developed sense of justice; when his son was sentenced to a two-month prison sentence after some foolish escapade[2] and fell seriously ill almost immediately afterwards, the Doge's refusal to grant him an early release – even though the young man died as a result – earned Venier the respectful admiration both of his subjects and of later historians. For the rest, however, he seems to have devoted little time to domestic affairs. There was no real need for him to do so. Unlike Genoa, now fast relapsing into anarchy, Venice had emerged from six years of the most desperate war in her history with her political system unshaken. No other state in Italy could boast such stability, or anything approaching it. Internally, the Republic virtually ran itself; its problems all came from abroad,

---

1. A small marble statue of a kneeling Doge (Plate 25) now in the Correr Museum, is almost certainly a likeness of Antonio Venier. It is attributed to Jacobello dalle Masegne, his exact contemporary who was responsible, *inter alia*, for the superb statues along the iconostasis of St Mark's. (The museum also contains a double portrait of Venier and his successor Michele Steno; but the painter, Lazzaro Bastiani, is first heard of in 1449 and did not die till 1512, so this portrait cannot possibly have been done from life.)

2. He had, according to Horatio Brown, fastened to the front door of some distinguished patrician 'a bunch of coral charms of curious form and opprobrious significance'.

and it was to the consolidation of Venice's position in Europe and the world that Antonio Venier and his advisers now applied themselves.

First of all, there was her commercial Empire to be rebuilt. The surrender of Dalmatia had been a blow, but for the time being at least she appeared to have no choice but to accept it. Besides, Dalmatia had never been an important trading partner; its value had been above all as a source of certain raw materials – wood and stone in particular – and as a base for operations further afield, with a coast that offered any number of superb natural harbours of a kind conspicuously lacking along the Italian shore of the Adriatic. Further south, the Peloponnesian ports of Modone and Corone were still safely in Venetian hands; Crete, after the collapse of another rebellion in 1363, had been enjoying an unwonted period of peace and comparative prosperity; and now that Genoa was no longer a rival Venice could settle down, without fear of hindrance or obstruction, to the task of renewing all her old trading links and establishing new ones – in the Levant, the Black Sea, and beyond to the furthest east. Permanent agents were established in all the important ports regularly visited by her ships, with warehouses in which to amass cargoes in preparation for the next arrival – speed of turn-around time was a point to which the Venetians attached great importance – and to store those recently delivered, lest prices should be forced down by too rapid a disposal. There was a Venetian agent resident in Siam ten years before the close of the century.

Nor did the Republic stop short at purely commercial expansion. Disillusioned now as to the desirability of territorial possessions on the Italian mainland and fatalistically resigned to the loss of Dalmatia, she was eager still to expand her Empire in the eastern Mediterranean. In 1386 she acquired Corfu. Taking shrewd advantage of the internal difficulties of the Kingdom of Naples to which the island nominally belonged, she suggested to the inhabitants that they needed some major power to protect them against potential aggressors; and the Corfiots in their turn – who knew perfectly well that any list of such aggressors would begin with the name of Venice herself – had little choice but to agree. A subsequent token payment to Naples was little more than a formality. By similar methods – a combination of political opportunism, business acumen, astute diplomacy and an occasional touch of blackmail – Venice was to acquire before the end of the century Scutari and Durazzo in southern Dalmatia, Nauplia and Argos in the Morea and most of the islands of the Cyclades and the Dodecanese.

Her reasons for embarking on this impressive programme of expansion were not exclusively commercial. Despite other preoccupations, she had been watching with mounting concern the progress of the Turks in their steady westward advance. In the last twenty years of the century this advance became something more like a rout. Serres fell in 1383, followed in rapid succession by Sofia, Nish, and Salonica. Finally in 1389, at the epic battle of Kosovo, the Ottoman armies crushed Serbia and destroyed the last hopes of independence for the Balkan Slavs. Bulgaria survived only four more years. Now the days of Byzantium itself were seen to be numbered. Apart from a few islands in the Aegean, the Roman Empire of the East was virtually coterminous with its capital, Constantinople, where the Emperor reigned on Turkish sufferance, aware that his only chance of maintaining his throne lay in total submission to the will of the Sultan. The feeble old John V Palaeologus died in senile debauchery in 1391;[1] his son Manuel II was a good and gifted man who in happier circumstances might have restored the Empire to something of its former greatness, but he was powerless to stem the Ottoman tide. Before his father's death he had been forced to live at the Sultan's court as a vassal – and a hostage to ensure his father's submissive behaviour – even on occasion fighting on the Turkish side against his fellow-Greeks. As reigning Emperor in Constantinople his position was scarcely less humiliating.

In such a situation it was only to be expected that when in 1396 King Sigismund of Hungary appealed to Christian Europe to join him in a combined onslaught against the Turkish threat Venice, despite past differences with his kingdom, should have responded – at least to the extent of putting her Black Sea fleet at his disposal. Unfortunately, few other European states followed her lead. The whole continent raised only some 60,000 men, and though this figure included the flower of the French knighthood, it was the latter's over-confidence and lack of discipline which was responsible more than any other single factor for the ensuing catastrophe. They had boasted before the battle that, if heaven itself were to fall, they could support it on the points of their lances; but they were no match for Sultan Bajazet. Once again living up to his nickname of *Yilderim* – lightning – he sped to meet their advance and when they reached Nicopolis on the Danube he was ready to receive them. The battle, which took place on 28 September 1396,

---

1. Gibbon writes that 'love, or rather lust, was his only vigorous passion; and in the embraces of the wives and virgins of the city the Turkish slave forgot the dishonour of the Emperor of the *Romans*'.

was short and bloody; bloodier still was its aftermath, when 10,000 French prisoners were beheaded in the Sultan's presence. Those who escaped, including Sigismund himself, did so on Venetian ships; a German eye-witness, who had been taken captive but whose extreme youth had saved him from execution, tells how as these vessels passed through the Dardanelles he and 300 other surviving prisoners were drawn up on the banks and made to jeer at the conquered King.[1]

The part played by Venice in this unedifying story was scarcely heroic; yet the battle of Nicopolis is important in her history since it marks the point at which most of western Europe simply ceased to concern itself with the Turkish menace until it felt directly threatened more than a century later. Incredibly enough, the dying Empire was still to endure another fifty-seven years, but by now it had become less of a shield than a liability. Manuel was obliged to establish a mosque in his capital, and a court to administer the law of Islam; still the princes of Christendom remained unmoved. Venice, and Venice alone, seemed aware of the danger. Equipped neither physically nor by temperament to lead Crusades, even she could do no more than defend her interests if they were attacked. But when she did so she defended Europe too.

The same sound, if occasionally unscrupulous, statesmanship that enabled Venice to extend her domains in the eastern Mediterranean dictated her policy on the Italian mainland, and with similar success. Her old enemy Francesco da Carrara, though balked of his expected triumph in 1380 by the Genoese collapse and the surrender of Treviso to Duke Leopold of Austria rather than to himself, had lost none of his former truculence. He had not seen Venice defeated as he had hoped; but he had seen her shaken, frightened and humbled. He himself, meanwhile, had discovered just how easily he could subdue the Venetian territories on *terra firma* and had emerged from the Genoese war stronger than when he had entered it. Clearly, the sooner he returned to the offensive the better. In 1382 he laid siege to Treviso.

The result was even more successful than he had expected. Duke Leopold had been ready enough to accept Treviso when the Venetians had offered it to him, but he was not prepared to put himself to much trouble or expense defending it. He now simply sold the city to Carrara, together with Belluno, Ceneda and Feltre and, with them, the control of one of the most important trade routes through the Dolomites and into the Tyrol. The price was 100,000 ducats; the value to Carrara,

1. Johann Schiltberger, *Hakluyt Society*, Vol. 58, 1879.

now once more in possession of virtually all the Venetian mainland, was incalculable.

Without resorting again to mercenaries, which she could at that moment ill afford, Venice had no land army worthy of the name. On the other hand she knew that Carrara had no fleet – nor, with Genoa in her present state, any hope of obtaining one. She rightly guessed, therefore, that rather than risk an advance across the lagoon he would turn his attention westward, where the last of the once-great dynasty of the Scaligeri, Antonio della Scala, still kept a rather tenuous hold on Verona and Vicenza – two ripe plums ready for the plucking. And so, serious as the situation was, she made no immediate attempt to retaliate. She would wait and see.

It was not that Doge Venier and his advisers viewed with equanimity the prospect of a Paduan empire extending over the entire Veneto up to her very doorstep. But they had also foreseen something else: that easy as Carrara might find such new conquests in themselves, they would bring him in direct confrontation with Gian Galeazzo Visconti, old Bernabò's nephew, who had recently overthrown his uncle, almost certainly poisoned him, and made himself master of Milan – a *coup* for whose success he was shortly to render thanks by laying the foundations of Milan cathedral. Scheming, dissembling, driven onward by wild ambition and an insatiable lust for power, of all his remarkable family Gian Galeazzo was the most dangerous. Confrontation with such a man would inevitably, sooner or later, mean opposition; and opposition, by Gian Galeazzo Visconti, would mean defeat. Venice, then, need only bide her time. There was no cause for her to take up arms against Carrara. He could be trusted to destroy himself.

To be sure, he was not such a fool as to march against Antonio della Scala without prior consultation with Milan; and on 19 April 1387 he and Gian Galeazzo concluded an agreement to expel the Scaligeri once and for all and to share the conquered territories between them, Verona falling to Milan and Vicenza to Padua. At first everything went as planned. After putting up a token resistance, Verona surrendered; Antonio fled to Venice and thence to Florence and Rome, only to die of poison himself shortly afterwards. But it was not for nothing that the Visconti had chosen a viper as their crest; ignoring the terms of his agreement, Gian Galeazzo seized Vicenza too.

Only now did Francesco Carrara see what Venice had seen all along – that he had been made the dupe of the Milanese who intended, now that he had outlived his usefulness, to devour him in his turn. Swallowing his pride, he appealed to Doge Venier, pointing out that Visconti would prove an infinitely greater danger to the Republic than he himself had ever been, and that the only hope of Venetian salvation lay in supporting an independent Padua as a buffer state between them. Once again, however, Visconti had forestalled him – by sending ambassadors to the Rialto offering, in return for recognition of his rights to Padua, the restitution of Ceneda and Treviso and of certain strategic strongholds around the shores of the lagoon.

It cannot have been an easy decision for the Doge to take. Carrara's argument may have been dictated by self-interest, but its strength was undeniable. Twice in less than a year, Gian Galeazzo had proved how dangerous he was as a neighbour. There was no reason to believe, when the moment came, that he would show Venice any more consideration than he had shown Verona or Padua. But the recent war, if it had done nothing else, had confirmed the Venetians in their belief that their city was impregnable; they needed control of Treviso and the mountain passes, without which their trade with central Europe was crippled; finally they knew that, useful as a buffer state might be, it could never function as such under Francesco Carrara, whom they detested and were determined to destroy. On 29 May 1388, they formally accepted the Milanese proposals.

Even now Carrara did not altogether give up hope. In the understandable belief that Venice's decision might have been prompted solely by animosity to him personally, he abdicated in favour of his son Francesco, called – to distinguish him from his father – Novello. But it was no use. A Visconti army marched on Padua, a Venetian squadron sailed up the Brenta and Francesco Novello surrendered. The Carraras, father and son, were interned at Monza and Asti respectively; and Venice settled down to watch her new and deadly neighbour.

Her policy towards Gian Galeazzo Visconti was a simple one: to get rid of him as soon as possible. Obviously she could not achieve this alone; but in the endlessly shifting kaleidoscope of North Italian politics there was one pattern that recurred time and time again: that of a single state growing too large and too powerful, thus causing its sister states to unite against it and bring about its destruction. In this pattern Venice put her trust. Gian Galeazzo was by now the most powerful prince in Europe, stronger by far than Richard II of England or the mentally unstable Charles VI of France. But he was not yet satisfied. Less than a year after he had seized Padua, he turned against Florence and Bologna.

He had overreached himself. Francesco Novello, having escaped with his family from Asti, had spent the interim drumming up opposition to the Visconti, and was the principal architect of the league that now took shape. With himself, Florence and Bologna it also included Francesco Gonzaga of Mantua, Antonio della Scala's dispossessed son Can Francesco of Verona, and Duke Robert of Bavaria. What it now needed above all else was the support of Venice. This time Venice did not hesitate. Only two years before, she had been the ally of Gian Galeazzo and the implacable enemy of the Carraras; but loyalty was a luxury that no Italian state could afford. Her diplomacy depended on preserving a balance of power by playing one enemy off against another. Effortlessly and without embarrassment she changed sides, joined the league and, while carefully avoiding open warfare, willingly gave Francesco Novello and the young della Scala leave to use her reacquired territory of Treviso as a springboard for their attempt to recover Padua.

The spring of 1390 was hot and dry; and on the night of 18 June Francesco Novello led a small force silently along the almost waterless bed of the Brenta into the centre of his native city. A wooden stockade – the only defence – was quickly breached and the people of Padua, for whom two years had been more than enough time to repent of their overhasty welcome of a Milanese master, received back their hereditary lord with open arms. His triumph may well have spelt salvation for Florence; it was certainly a serious check to the progress of Gian Galeazzo, who was forced to withdraw a considerable part of his army from Tuscany to prevent the revolt spreading to Verona – which had made a similar, though in this case unsuccessful, bid for independence – and beyond. To increase his worries he also found himself hard pressed by that extraordinary soldier of fortune the Englishman Sir John Hawkwood, now in Florentine service, who pursued him as far as the river Adda and would have inflicted severe damage but for the disastrous generalship of his French colleague Jean d'Armagnac. In short, Francesco Novello's reconquest of Padua transformed a potentially dangerous military crisis into a stalemate; and it seems to have been a relief for all parties when peace was concluded at Genoa in 1392. The young Carrara, who had been careful to obtain Venice's approval to this treaty before signing it, now appeared in person to do homage to the Doge, thanking him for his support and being in return received into the ranks of the Venetian nobility.

Having played no active role in the war, Venice was not herself a signatory of the treaty; it represented, none the less, everything she could possibly have hoped for. Not only had she recovered Treviso; by her shrewd diplomacy, and without the shedding of a drop of Venetian blood, she had also curbed the growing power of Milan and, in Padua, had substituted the well-disposed, even submissive Francesco Novello for his insufferable father. She did not deceive herself, however, that the peace signified anything more than a breathing space. Gian Galeazzo Visconti might have failed to gain all he expected, but he had lost nothing either. Already he was gathering forces for a new offensive – and three years later it came.

At first it seemed as though Gian Galeazzo's enemies might be able to hold him in check. When he marched on Mantua in 1395 Venice, Florence and Bologna, with active help from Carrara in Padua, sprang to their neighbour's defence; the fighting was inconclusive and a truce was soon declared, leading in 1400 to another brief and uneasy peace. This equilibrium was however shattered early in 1402 when the new western Emperor-elect Rupert of the Palatinate, on his way – as he hoped – to his imperial coronation in Rome, was persuaded to call a halt in Lombardy and crush his dangerously ambitious vassal. His attempt met with abject failure. Equally short of men and money, he seems to have had no idea of Gian Galeazzo's strength, or of conditions in Italy. By April, after no more than minor skirmishes, he was forced to return to Germany, broken and humiliated.

This defeat of the greatest prince of the West had a tonic effect on Visconti. He smashed his way into Bologna and then turned the whole weight of his forces against Florence. With Pisa, Siena and Lucca already under his control, there seemed no hope for the city. If it fell, Tuscany would join Lombardy, Umbria and Romagna as dependencies of Milan; how long, then, could Venice hold out? Gian Galeazzo had never been stronger or better equipped. He was still only fifty years old. His coffers were full, his men seasoned and in splendid heart. The North Italian Kingdom, stretching from Genoa to the Adriatic, on which he had focused his political ambitions seemed at last to be within his grasp.

Then, without warning, on 13 August 1402, he was struck down by fever; and three weeks later he died. To the Venetians his death must have seemed like a miracle – the more so since his vast dominions now fell to his three sons, the eldest of whom was only thirteen. His widow, who was appointed regent, proved utterly incapable of controlling either them or the rapacious generals and *condottieri* who, after years of fighting for the Visconti, now saw the opportunity of helping themselves to their lands; and by the end of the year the Duchy of Milan, the strongest power in Europe only six months before, had begun to crumble away.

Now, too, other erstwhile enemies of Gian Galeazzo began to move in – among the first being Francesco Novello Carrara, who marched on Vicenza. Knowing the internal difficulties of Milan, he seems to have expected little opposition; but he had reckoned without the Vicentines themselves who, having just escaped the clutches of one political adventurer, had no wish to fall victim to another. They could not, however, stand on their own; and so, without further fuss, they offered themselves to Venice. Their embassy reached the Rialto at much the same time as one from the Duchess of Milan herself, imploring Venetian aid against Carrara and offering both Vicenza and Verona in return.

With Gian Galeazzo gone, there was no longer any reason for the Venetians to maintain their alliance with Francesco Novello. Indeed, every instinct told them that they would have no lasting peace until his whole dynasty was destroyed. The promise of Verona and Vicenza – with Padua, which would obviously revert to them once he was out of the way – meant the possession of the three key cities of north-east Italy commanding the approach to Venice on her vulnerable, landward side. A herald was dispatched forthwith to Francesco Novello, beneath the walls of Vicenza, calling on him to withdraw. Now, for the first time, the young Carrara – hitherto an obedient ally of the Republic – showed his defiance. 'Let us make a lion of St Mark of this herald,' he is alleged to have said, and gave orders that the man's nose should be slit and his ears cut off.

The action was not only inhumane; it was also foolhardy. A diplomatic retreat by Francesco Novello at that moment, depriving Venice of her *casus belli*, might still have saved his dynasty. By that action he destroyed it – and, ultimately, himself. Driven back from Vicenza, he was obliged to immure himself in his own city of Padua where, to give him his due, he put up a courageous resistance to a Venetian siege, refusing the reasonable terms which, on more than one occasion, he was offered. At last, however, a combination of famine and a renewed outbreak of plague – that continuing scourge that overshadowed Europe throughout the later fourteenth and early fifteenth centuries – compelled him to submit. On 17 November 1404 Padua fell. Francesco was brought in chains, with his son Jacopo, to Venice. Such was the popular feeling against him – aggravated by a widespread rumour that he had been plotting to poison the wells of the city – that he and Jacopo were at first held, for their own safety, on S. Giorgio Maggiore; only some days later were they transferred to that special place of captivity on the top floor of the Doges' Palace which was kept for prisoners of high rank.

By then, however, new information had come to light about Carrara's recent activities. He had had no sinister designs on the wells; he had, however, organized a vast conspiracy to overthrow the Republic from within – a conspiracy which, as more and more of its ramifications were uncovered, was seen to involve several members of the Venetian nobility. The Council of Ten, assisted by six more officers specially co-opted for the task, sat day and night opening further channels of inquiry and interrogating hundreds of suspects, many of them under torture. The more they investigated, the more evidence they found – and all led back, ineluctably, to the Carraras. Father and son were condemned to death. The story that they were suspended in an iron cage from the roof of the palace is unfounded;[1] the two were strangled in prison on 17 January 1405, Francesco Novello defending himself to the end, heroically but in vain, with a wooden stool.

The fourteenth century had been hard for Venice – the hardest century, perhaps, in her history. It had begun with two attempts at revolution, by Marin Bocconio and, more seriously, Bajamonte Tiepolo; and half-way through its course it had produced a third, when old Marin Falier brought disgrace both to the Republic and to the dogeship and paid for it with what remained of his life. Soon afterwards, suspicions surrounding the conduct of Lorenzo Celsi had still further undermined the ducal prestige. Abroad, there had been rebellions in Crete, Trieste and elsewhere, the loss of Dalmatia, and, continuing intermittently for fifty years, the fateful trial of strength with Genoa. In mainland Italy the Republic's princely neighbours, whether della Scala, Visconti or Carrara, had given her no respite; and since 1348 the Black Death, returning remorselessly every few years to cut another great swathe through the population, never allowed itself to be forgotten.

For all that, Venice had achieved much. To begin with, she had established herself once and for all on *terra firma*: with the fall of the

---

1. Romanin (Vol. IV, p. 39) says that he has found only one instance of this punishment, when, in the sixteenth century, a priest found guilty of *enormi delitti* was thus suspended from the campanile of St Mark's – and even then managed to escape. The confusion probably arose from the fact that the Venetian dialect word for a cage, *cheba* (Italian *gabbia*), was also used for the small prison in the Doges' Palace.

house of Carrara she found herself in possession of considerable mainland territories, from the Tagliamento in the east to the shores of Lake
Garda in the west, south to the Adige and north to the hills above
Bassano. These territories she was later to increase; but they would never
essentially be diminished – except for a brief period in the early sixteenth
century – until the Republic itself came to an end.

By 1400 the Venetians can have had few delusions about their status
as a European power. They had learnt, to their cost, just what it meant
in practice to have long and often imprecise land frontiers to defend
against predatory neighbours, and they knew all too well the expense
of hiring mercenaries and maintaining them in the field. On the other
hand there were obvious gains in prestige and in the influence that
they would henceforth be able to wield in the affairs not only of Italy
but of the whole continent, where their trading position would also
be immeasurably strengthened. Moreover, their confidence was but-
tressed by the one great advantage that they alone possessed over all
their rivals – an advantage that their recent tribulations had served only
to confirm: in so far as any city could ever be, theirs was impregnable.

For, despite the new terrestrial image that she presented to the world,
Venice still belonged to the sea. By it, and by the 3,300 ships and 36,000
seamen that she could boast by the close of the fourteenth century,
she was both protected and enriched. No other major Italian city
could claim to have remained inviolate for close on 1,000 years. No
other could boast such wealth or, more important still, such powers
of recuperation – powers that enabled her, when her treasury was drained
by foreign wars and her economy lay apparently in ruins, to make a
recovery so swift and so complete as to leave her enemies gasping.
The effect was almost that of a conjuring trick, and she performed
it again and again. But without her unique position it would never have
been possible. Not only was she nearer than any of her competitors
to the Eastern markets – the source of all those Oriental luxuries which
Europe, having once developed a taste for them, was demanding more
and more insistently; but the fact that the sea was, almost literally, her
home had obliged her, from her earliest beginnings, to achieve a mastery
over it that her rivals might occasionally challenge but could never
match for long. Taken as a whole, over the years, the Venetians always
remained better and faster shipbuilders, more accurate navigators and
more resourceful seamen than anyone else.

And above all – particularly after the eclipse of Genoa – more successful merchants. By the end of the fourteenth century there was scarcely

a single major commodity which was not largely transported in Venetian ships. Eastward and southward went timber from the Harz mountains and metals from the mines of Bohemia; northward and westward the spices from India and the Orient, to which had more recently been added cotton from Asia Minor and the Levant, and increasing quantities of sugar, the demand for which was now insatiable throughout Europe. The first supplies had come from Syria as early as the eleventh century, but by now Venetian entrepreneurs had introduced it in Crete and, with outstanding success, in Cyprus, when one Federico Corner established plantations on such a scale and ran them with such efficiency as to make his family within very few years the richest in Venice.[1] These two islands, together with parts of the Morea, were also the main producers of that sweet, heavy wine known as malmsey (from the port of Monemvasia whence most of it was shipped) which the English and their neighbours in northern Europe quaffed with such relish; and from the 1330s a regular and exceedingly profitable pattern had developed according to which Venetian merchant galleys carried it to English ports and there exchanged it for English wool. This they would take across to sell in Flanders, buying in return the bales of fine Flemish cloth or the finished woollen cloaks and gowns for which they could get high prices throughout Europe and even in the Levant. So lucrative did this triangular trade become that in 1349 it was nationalized and run thenceforth as a state monopoly.

Other patterns became less prosperous as the century progressed. Regular commerce with Russia, in particular, began to decline from about the 1360s, when civil war in the Mongol-occupied lands to the north and east of the Black Sea made the caravan routes unsafe. Thirty years later they were closed altogether when the cities along the Volga, which had served as essential staging posts, were destroyed by Tamburlaine. Precious furs immediately became rarer, and correspondingly more expensive, in the markets of the South. The slave trade, however, continued unabated. Despite repeated edicts by the Papacy and occasional somewhat tentative legislation by the Republic itself – going back to a law promulgated by Doge Orso Participazio in the ninth century – this had never ceased to flourish in Venice. A relatively small number of African negroes from East and West Africa and the Sahara were brought to the slave markets at S. Giorgio and the Rialto by Arab traders in gold and ivory, but the overwhelming majority of the slaves were Christians from the Caucasus – Georgians, Armenians and Circas-

1. See p. 236n.

sians – who had been taken prisoner by the Tartars and were sold by them at Black Sea ports. Most of these found their way, as domestic servants, bodyguards and concubines, to Egypt, North Africa and the Ottoman court. Occasionally, some might achieve positions of real power, as with the slave army of the Mamelukes, who were supreme in Egypt from the thirteenth century until the arrival of Napoleon, or as Janissaries or eunuchs at the Sultan's court. Others were purchased by wealthy Italian families in Tuscany and the North. The remainder, unluckiest of all, probably ended up working the vast agricultural estates in Crete and Cyprus – where Federico Corner's sugar plantations had been built up almost entirely on a slave economy.

Venice, it need hardly be said, received her full share of all these commodities; and there was another import in which she was not primarily a middleman but was herself the chief consumer. This was grain. Bitter experience had taught her that it was dangerous to rely on a single area for so vital a necessity. Drought or excessive rainfall could destroy a harvest; revolts or civil upheavals could prevent shipments; and even if both climatic and political conditions were favourable, there was always the possibility of pirates to be reckoned with. In consequence she had taken pains to diversify her sources of supply; and the Venetian grain ships that sailed up the Adriatic from the traditional cornfields of Sicily and Apulia were now joined by others coming from Anatolia and even the Black Sea.

Conversely, there was one product of her own – apart from manufactured goods – of which she was usually able to export a surplus. From the earliest days of the Republic she had jealously guarded her monopoly of the saltworks in the valley and delta of the Po and had never hesitated to fight for them when necessary. As time went on and the European demand for salt continued to increase, they became inadequate; further supplies had to be brought in from Dalmatia, Cyprus and elsewhere. But the domestic sources of production had by then come to be looked on with almost superstitious veneration and continued to enjoy a degree of protection well beyond their intrinsic worth.

There were other reasons too for her extraordinary economic resilience. Firstly she was trusted. By now she had built up a network of trading contacts half-way across the world, and a reputation for fair dealing – which did not exclude hard bargaining – that made it an easy matter to resume operations after an interruption. Secondly there was the Venetian character – tough, hardworking, determined, with an ingrained respect for wealth and a boundless ambition to acquire it. Thirdly came the firm discipline, born of long experience, imposed by the state.

For the state, where trade was concerned, left nothing to chance; and by 1400 it was taking over more and more of Venetian economic life. The days of private enterprise on the grand scale were almost gone. All the merchant galleys were built in the Arsenal and state-owned; the Republic kept the monopoly on many of the most profitable routes and cargoes. Even the ships that remained in private hands were obliged to conform to the strict specifications laid down by the Senate. The advantages were obvious. Given such conformity, all the vessels in a given convoy could be trusted to behave similarly in bad weather and so, with luck, to stay together; the convoy's speed, and consequently its arrival dates, could be more accurately estimated; standardized spares could be kept available in agencies and outposts overseas and quick convertibility to warships guaranteed in an emergency. By the end of the fourteenth century there were normally six of these major trading convoys a year, each consisting of up to 500 ships – occasionally more – and each bound for a different destination, but each sailing on appointed dates, and following specified routes, fixed months ahead. Most would be state-owned, their command – which was open to the nobility only – leased by auction to the highest bidder for the duration of the voyage; but every merchant and captain involved, whether owner or lessor, was bound by oath to obey the instructions issued by the Senate and to uphold 'the honour of St Mark'.

As always, increased public ownership led to increased taxation. A hundred years before, Venetian taxes had been among the lowest in Europe. No longer. Not only were there the soaring costs of the Arsenal and its 16,000 workers to be met; but the spread of state control had spawned hosts of civil servants, lawyers, notaries and accountants – to say nothing of a whole army of eagle-eyed tax collectors famous for their niggling accuracy – all of whom had to be paid for by the Republic. Small traders continued to be encouraged; if they could not afford, or spare, ships of their own for their ventures they always enjoyed the right – so long as they were Venetians – to demand cargo space on the state-owned convoys at fixed and reasonable rates. But for the grand old merchant adventurers like the Polos there was no longer a place. The Republic might be richer than it had ever been, and the city more beautiful; but much of the early romance had gone.

At this time, too, Venice felt herself obliged to take her first far-reaching measures against her Jewish population. These were in no sense intended as any form of racial or religious persecution, nor did the victims look upon them as such. The simple fact appears to have been that in the vastly more complicated economic system that had by now evolved, borrowing from the Jews (and, in the absence of public banks or even pawnshops, borrowing from any other source was impossible) had got seriously out of hand. In 1374 the Jews of Mestre had been encouraged to settle in Venice – technically for only five years, but this term was easily extended – and twenty years later few Venetian citizens were not, to a greater or a lesser degree, in hock. And so, after the failure of several attempts at controlling legislation, in 1395 all Jews were expelled from the city and allowed to return only for periods not exceeding fifteen days. Even then they were obliged to carry distinguishing marks – first a yellow circle on the breast, later a yellow cap, later still tall hats of prescribed colours. They were forbidden to hold real property and to keep schools; only those of them who were doctors were encouraged to continue.

Gradually, they returned, and the residence rules were again relaxed. For the next three centuries until the fall of the Republic, their fortunes would fluctuate; but their numbers remained considerable, their influence likewise. Culturally as well as economically, Venice would have been a poorer place without them.

In industry, too, the hand of the state was everywhere apparent. The most important branches were rigidly protected, with government bans on the export of certain raw materials; skilled artificers were forbidden to leave the city, while to reveal the secrets of key manufacturing processes was an offence punishable by death. (Foreign craftsmen, on the other hand, such as the German makers of looking-glasses and the silk workers from Lucca[1] were encouraged to settle in Venice and even, as an additional inducement, exempted from taxation for the first two years of their residence.) Most of the official controls on industrial standards and conditions of work[2] were imposed through the guilds, whose carefully-framed statutes were all subject to the approval of government supervisors; within broad limits, however, these organizations enjoyed a considerable measure of autonomy and proved of increasing value, as the years passed, both to their members and to the state. Unlike the guilds of other Italian towns – the *Arti* of Florence

1. See p. 202.
2. The latter, particularly those relating to children, were far in advance of any similar legislation passed in England before the nineteenth century.

for example – they never became, or attempted to become, a political force in the Republic: most of their members had been disenfranchised since the *Serrata del Gran Consiglio*, while the patricians whose power they might elsewhere have been led to oppose were, in the peculiar conditions pertaining to Venice, not feudal aristocrats but, in all probability, guild members themselves. On the other hand, the guilds provided a large number of honest, public-spirited and often wealthy tradesmen with a means of benefiting the community and so preserving their pride and self-respect. They also formed the basis for a remarkably effective system of social security, caring for their members in sickness and old age and assuming responsibility for their widows and children on their deaths. As they grew richer, their benevolence spread beyond the limits of their own membership; and of the forty-odd buildings of the Venetian *scuole* that survive today, many still testify to the wealth and importance of the organizations for which they were built.[1]

But the guilds did not have the monopoly of charitable foundations. By the end of the fourteenth century there were probably a dozen or more of these latter that had been privately endowed by wealthy citizens – sometimes, doubtless, for reasons of prestige but often for genuinely philanthropic motives. We know, for example, that old Doge Zorzi maintained a home for poor children; and similar institutions existed for the benefit of poor women, foundlings, reformed prostitutes and various other categories in need, together with free hospitals – at least one of them financed by its own chief surgeon.

Public health was, however, early accepted as a state responsibility, and to the Venetian Republic must go the honour of having founded the first national health service in Europe, if not in the world. Already in 1335 the state was paying a full-time salary to twelve doctor-surgeons who, together with all other licensed practitioners, were obliged by law to attend an annual course in anatomy, which included the dissection of corpses. After the establishment of the state-run School of Medicine in 1368, they were also required to attend monthly meetings to exchange notes on new cases and treatments. By that time any physician anywhere in Italy who achieved exceptional distinction could be sure, sooner or later, to receive an invitation to settle in Venice, accompanied by such financial inducements as would make it hard

1. Pre-eminent among these are the *Scuole* of the Carmini, of S. Giorgio degli Schiavoni, of S. Giovanni Evangelista and of S. Rocco; and, among those which have been converted to other uses, those of S. Marco (now the Civic Hospital) and of S. Maria della Carità (now the Accademia).

for him to refuse. In the field of law, on the other hand, the Republic had already become an exporter of talent, and Venetian legists were to be found in positions of authority the length and breadth of the peninsula; while as administrators – particularly in the capacity of rector and *podestà* in foreign cities – her citizens were in such demand that in 1306 it became necessary to pass a law forbidding the acceptance of these and similar posts without special permission from the Senate.

It was no wonder, therefore, that by 1400 Venice was respected and envied beyond all the cities of Europe – famed alike for her wealth, her beauty, her good government, and for a system of justice which gave impartial protection to rich and poor, aristocrat and artisan, Venetian and foreigner; for, in theory at any rate and for the most part in practice too, every man living beneath the banner of St Mark was equal in the sight of the law. It was no wonder that strangers came flocking – merchants, pilgrims bound for the Holy Land, and increasing numbers of simple travellers spurred less by commerce or piety than by curiosity and a thirst for adventure – to the point where, as a contemporary wrote, the rough accents of the Venetians were lost in the babel of strange tongues that was to be heard daily on the Piazza. Here, unlike any other sea-port on the Mediterranean, they knew that they would not be swindled – the Republic maintained a specially-trained corps of officials whose sole duty it was to look after strangers, to find them accommodation and to see that they received all the help they needed, that their wine was not watered and that they were never overcharged – and they also knew that, by the simple expedient of walking along the Riva, they could be virtually certain of finding a ship to take them on the next stage of their journey. Anyway – in the unlikely event of such a vessel not being immediately available – was Venice not a destination in herself?

Finally, it was no wonder that the native citizens of Venice accounted themselves privileged among other men, proud of the city that had given them birth and of the Empire it had won. They might, for the most part, have little or no say in the government of the Republic, but comparison of their lot with that of the populations on the mainland did not suggest that the latter were substantially better off in this or any other respect; besides, they were sensible enough to know that it was better to be well governed, even without political influence than subject to the whim of an ambitious and frequently tyrannical despot. They might feel irritated, from time to time, by the petty regulations and restrictions through which the state sought to interfere with so many aspects of their daily life; but if this was the price of living in the richest, safest, best ordered and most beautiful city in the civilized world they were prepared to pay it. In the century that was past they had worked hard, fought desperately, and suffered much. Now at last their enemies were crushed or scattered, and they looked forward to the century to come with confidence and hope.

PART THREE

❧

A Power in Europe

Wherefore if Venice *be defended from external causes of commotion, it is first, through her situation, in which respect her Subjects have no hope, (and this indeed may be attributed unto her fortune) and secondly, through her exquisite Justice, whence they have no will, to invade her: but this can be attributed to no other cause than her prudence: which will appear to be greater, as we look nearer; for the effects that proceed from fortune (if there be any such thing) are like their cause, unconstant; but there never happened unto any other Common-wealth, so undisturbed and constant a tranquillity and peace in her self, as is that of* Venice; *wherefore this must proceed from some other cause than Chance. And we see that as she is of all others the most quiet, so the most equal, Common-wealth. Her body consists of one Order, and her Senate is like a rolling stone (as was said) which never did, nor, while it continues upon that rotation, ever shall gather the mosse of a divided or ambitious interest; much lesse such an one as that which grasped the people of* Rome *in the talons of their own Eagles. And if* Machiavill, *averse from doing his Common-wealth right, had consider'd her Orders, (as his reader shall easily perceive he never did) he must have been so far from attributing the prudence of them unto Chance, that he would have touched up his admirable work unto that perfection, which, as to the civil part, hath no pattern in the universall World, but this of* Venice.

JAMES HARRINGTON, *The Common-wealth of Oceana*, 1656

20

The Empire Grows

[1405–1413]

O thou that art situate at the entry of the sea, which art a merchant of the people for many isles . . .

Thy borders are in the midst of the seas, thy builders have perfected thy beauty . . .

All the ships of the sea with their mariners were in thee to occupy thy merchandise.

Ezekiel, Chapter XXVII

Among the many and various dangers that beset the would-be writer of history, one of the most insidious is the temptation to adjust – however innocently or even subconsciously – historical events in order to fit them more neatly into a prearranged scheme; and among his bitterest causes for regret is the habitual reluctance of those events to be so adjusted. How convenient it would be, for example, to date the beginning of the Golden Age of the Venetian Republic – which did indeed roughly coincide with the fifteenth century – from the election of Doge Michele Steno on 1 December 1400; a palaeontologist, accustomed to rounding off his dates to the nearest millennium or two, would see no difficulty in doing just that. But the truth, as far as possible, must be told; and the truth is that in 1400, despite a recent uneasy peace, Doge and Senate were watching with increasing alarm while the ruler of Milan, Gian Galeazzo Visconti, extended his power further and further across Lombardy and Romagna, Umbria and Tuscany. Few Venetians, certainly, would have dared at that moment to talk of Golden Ages; to many of them the downfall of the Republic must have seemed a far likelier possibility.

Two years later, however, Gian Galeazzo was dead, stricken in his prime by a sudden fever, leaving only a widow and three sons scarcely out of their infancy; and by January 1405 those other perennial thorns in Venetian flesh, the Carraras of Padua, had been similarly – though less fortuitously – removed from the scene. Now at last, her dangers behind her, Venice could sit back and take stock of her new situation, finding the view from the Rialto a good deal more promising than it had looked before. Now at last, and properly this time, the century could begin.

One thing was clear: the Republic had become a nation. No longer could it be considered as just another North Italian city-state, to be spoken of in the same breath as Milan or Florence or Verona. The Venetians, it is true, had long since rid themselves of any such illusion – if indeed it had ever formed part of their thinking. For the best part of a thousand years already, those two or three miles of shallow water separating them from the mainland had not only protected them from invaders but had effectively isolated them from Italian political life; saved them from the internecine warfare – papalist against imperialist, Guelf against Ghibelline, town against town – that eternally plagued the peninsula; kept them untouched by feudalism and the endless territorial squabbles that it brought in its wake; and enabled them to fix their attention, except in occasional moments of crisis, resolutely eastward – to Byzantium and those rich Levantine and oriental markets on which their strength and prosperity depended. Their acquisition, after the fall of Constantinople to the Latins during the Fourth Crusade, of an immense trading empire that stretched through the eastern Mediterranean to the Black Sea and beyond had set them still further apart from their less fortunate neighbours; only two other Italian cities, Genoa and Pisa, had ever seriously rivalled them in the commercial sphere. But Pisa had quickly been eclipsed and Genoa – in 1380, after half a century of warfare – decisively crushed; and now, with the fall of the Carraras, Venice found herself mistress of a considerable area of north-east Italy, including the cities of Padua, Vicenza and Verona and continuing westward as far as the shores of Lake Garda. At last she could treat as an equal with nations like England, France and Austria – in her own right, a European power.

As her prestige grew, so too did her splendour. By 1400, though the Byzantine Empire still had half a century to run, Constantinople was a poor depleted shadow of the great metropolis it once had been, and Venice was now generally acclaimed to be the most dazzlingly beautiful city in the world. The Piazza and Piazzetta were both brick-paved – few other squares in Europe could make such a boast – and had become a meeting-place for travellers from three continents. The Basilica of St Mark, which, during the three centuries since its consecration, had been undergoing an almost continuous process of enrichment, was on the point of receiving its finishing touch, that 'Gothic Crown' of marble pinnacles and crockets that so entranced Ruskin four hundred and fifty years later.[1] The Campanile too

---

1. '. . . until at last, as if in ecstasy, the crests of the arches break into a marble foam, and toss themselves far into the blue sky in flashes and wreaths of sculptured spray, as if the breakers on the Lido shore had been frost-bound before they fell, and the sea-nymphs had inlaid them with coral and amethyst' (*The Stones of Venice*, Vol. II, Chapter IV).

was complete (although its top stage was to be remodelled in the sixteenth century), while down on the Molo the great south front of the Doges' Palace lacked only the canopied balcony at its centre, which bears the date of 1404. This new building ran northward along the Piazzetta as far as the seventh column, beyond which the last remaining wing of the old Byzantine palace of Doge Sebastiano Ziani extended to the corner of the Basilica. (Only in 1423 was the latter demolished and the new work continued along the whole Piazzetta façade.)

The Doges' Palace as we know it today is, beyond all doubt, the greatest secular Gothic building in the world; and it is hardly surprising that it should have provided new impetus and inspiration for Gothic *palazzi* all over the city. Many had already been built in the previous century, some of which still survive – the Palazzo Sagredo on the Grand Canal, for example, or, most extraordinary of all, the Palazzo Arian at S. Angelo Raffaele, with its astonishing filigree tracery of almost oriental complexity; and for the next seventy years the momentum would increase, giving rise to that glorious tradition of Gothic opulence, epitomized in the flamboyant Ca' d'Oro of 1425–30, by which Venetian palace architecture is best loved and remembered.

It was the same with churches. Those of the two great mendicant orders, the Franciscan Frari and the Dominican SS. Giovanni e Paolo, were after a century and a half still unfinished, though work was now once again proceeding apace. Meanwhile they were being joined by other Gothic buildings, slightly smaller perhaps, but often a good deal more ornate. The Madonna dell' Orto was built in the middle of the fourteenth century, as were S. Stefano and the Carmini, though their existing façades are all somewhat later elaborations. The next half-century would see, *inter alia*, S. Gregorio and S. Maria della Carità, now part of the Accademia. Then, for churches and palaces alike, came Antonio Gambello and the Lombardi and with them, belatedly, the Renaissance.

Yet Venice, for all her splendour, had not yet attained that degree of urban sophistication that the coming century would bring. Among all the coruscating architecture before which her visitors stood wide-eyed, there remained whole acres of open space – occupied, if at all, by vegetable gardens, boathouses or the cottages of fishermen. Even in the most prosperous districts, most of the *campi* and *calli* were still of beaten earth, quagmires in the winter and regularly dampened down in the summer to reduce the dust. The pigs from the monastery of S. Antonio Abbate continued to rootle freely about the city – only in 1409 was their liberty curtailed – and for the average Venetian the horse was still the principal means of transport; horses easily outnumbered gondolas, and the stables of Doge Michele Steno were reputed to be the finest in Europe.

If, however, the citizens of less fortunate nations admired Venice for her wealth and her architectural splendour, they also admired her for her system of government – an admiration that brought with it a healthy, though sometimes grudging, respect. Beyond her borders, all Italy had succumbed to the age of despotism; only Venice remained a strong, superbly ordered republic, possessed of a constitution that had almost effortlessly weathered every political storm, foreign or domestic, to which it had been exposed. The majority of her people, admittedly, had been shorn of effective power for the past hundred years, and the last vestige of that power – the general convocation or *arengo* – would be abolished by the time the century that was now beginning had run a quarter of its course; but the civil service was open to all, commerce and the craftsmanship for which the city was famous provided a source of pride and satisfaction as well as rich material rewards, and few citizens ever seriously doubted that the administration – quite apart from being outstandingly efficient – had their own best interests at heart.

Of this the government itself gave continuous and ample proof. Any attempt on the part of an individual or group to gain power or popularity outside the constitutional framework was instantly suppressed. The Church was kept rigidly in its place, its duties exclusively pastoral, barred from the slightest interference in affairs of state: bishops were elected by the Senate, their elections being only confirmed in Rome. And those institutions in which, ultimately, the political power resided were subject to exquisitely calculated systems of checks and balances that made their misuse always difficult and usually impossible. The base of the oligarchic pyramid and the fount of all authority was the Great Council – the *Maggior Consiglio*; but since it consisted by this time of some 1,500 members (a number that later increased to over 2,000), its plenary sessions were largely taken up with its many electoral duties. Day-to-day legislation was left to the *Pregadi*, now better known as the Senate, nominally 120 strong, but swollen by a considerable number of other dignitaries of state, sitting *ex officio*. At the same level as the Senate but, as it were, to one side was the Council of Ten – effectively of seventeen, since the Doge and *Signoria* were always present at its sessions – established in 1310 'to preserve the liberty and peace of the subjects of the Republic and to protect them from the abuses of personal power'. This too, despite its sinister reputation in later centuries – not entirely deserved – was subject to as much constitutional control as any other body, being elected by the Great Council for six months at a time, its three chiefs, or *Capi*, rotating monthly and confined within the Palace during their term of office.

The next stage in the political hierarchy was the *Collegio*, roughly comparable to a modern cabinet, composed of six *Savii Grandi* (among whom the chairmanship also rotated, moving at weekly intervals): three *Savii da Terra Firma* and three *Savii agli Ordini* or *da Mar*, the Ministers of War, Marine and Finance. This was the executive arm of the government, through which all state business was channelled and most legislation initiated. The chairman for the week was thus effectively Prime Minister of the Republic.

Finally, presiding over all these institutions, came the Doge himself, the embodiment of the Venetian state in all its majesty but hemmed in always by his six Councillors, the *Minor Consiglio* or Signoria. Without their supervision, approval and supporting authority he was powerless to act; a majority of the Signoria might perform his functions in his absence. Unlike them, however – and indeed unlike all other holders of exalted positions in the state – he held office for life, having been elected only at the culmination of a long and distinguished career during which he would almost certainly have held many of the subordinate government posts and have acquired a profound knowledge and experience of every facet of public life. A figurehead he might be – though possessing no less power than any other single individual in the state – but a figurehead who, even had it not been for the pomp and splendour and almost Byzantine ceremonial which attended his every public appearance, could generally expect to be revered – and listened to – both at home and abroad.

Doge Michele Steno was in every respect worthy to take his place among his fellow-princes. Even if the old improbable story were true, even if it were he whose scurrilous taunts had goaded Marin Falier into his disastrous conspiracy fifty-odd years before, an adult life spent in devoted service to the state had amply atoned for any youthful indiscretions. He had fought bravely under Vettor Pisani at Pola in 1379 and two years later had distinguished himself at Chioggia, where he had later held the rank of *podestà*. On his return he had been appointed a Procurator of St Mark, in which capacity he had been responsible for the magnificent screen, with statues by the brothers delle Masegne, which divides the nave of the Basilica from the chancel. More recently still, he had had charge of the negotiations which led to the alliance against Gian Galeazzo Visconti.

Such was the Doge who, on 4 January 1406, took his place with his Signoria beneath a splendid canopy in the Piazza, formally to receive the city of Padua into the Republic. Having already accepted Verona and Vicenza in similar style, he was by now growing accustomed to such ceremonies. On this occasion Padua was represented by sixteen of its most distinguished citizens, robed in scarlet, supported by a long procession of their families in green and accompanied by a band. Steno was presented first with the gonfalon of the city, then the mace, then the keys and finally the seals. A banquet followed, and the festivities were concluded by a tournament at which all the nobles of the city were present 'with an extra-ordinary concourse of ladies'. At nightfall the envoys returned to Padua, bearing the Venetian banner of crimson silk, with the winged lion of St Mark emblazoned in gold.

Celebration, in short, was the keynote: not submission. All three cities, in their different ways, had offered themselves to Venice of their own free will; and although the Doge may have permitted himself the occasional hint of patronage in his acceptance speeches – he is reported to have welcomed the Veronese with the words of Isaiah, 'The people that walked in darkness have seen a great light' – the arrangements agreed for their future government and administration make it clear that Venice was as usual anxious to preserve local institutions whenever possible. Certain powers – such as taxation, the maintenance of law and order and the raising of military levies – she kept, understandably enough, in her own hands through her own military and civil governors, responsible to the Senate and the Council of Ten respectively. But it is significant that in each city the civil governor, or Rector, was sworn to respect the ancient civic con-stitution: in Vicenza he was even subject to an elected committee of eigh-teen local citizens with the right to censure him if any of their traditional statutes were infringed. In Verona, where the machinery of civil govern-ment had largely crumbled away during the long years of Scaliger rule, a Great Council of fifty annually elected members was established on the Venetian model, with a twelve-man executive. There, too, Venetians and Veronese together instituted a remarkable system of education, with free primary schooling and – for more mature students – professors of canon and civil law, the humanities and medicine; all were paid out of municipal funds, exempted from personal taxation and contracted to hold public disputations during the winter months. The doctors, in addition, were bound to remain in the city during plague epidemics and even in normal times to warn every patient, on his second visit at the latest, to look to the state of his soul and his material possessions – a measure designed to reduce the number of those dying intestate without frightening patients unduly, since a warning that would previously have seemed tantamount to a sentence of death could now be seen as merely a routine precaution.

This characteristically Venetian interest in education and medicine was also reflected in the Republic's attitude to Padua, whose university – the oldest in Italy after that of Bologna – was allocated an annual subsidy of 4,000 ducats, plus a considerable share of the excise revenue. The city itself, being considerably richer than Vicenza or Verona, was obliged, unlike them, to pay half the Rector's salary; on the other hand the Republic formally undertook to levy no new taxes, protected Paduan wine and cloth, and in 1408 gave orders for the building of what can only be described as a club house on the main square of Padua, 'where Venetian and Paduan men of good will might meet and converse together to increase their mutual love and trust'. When, twelve years later, this *Palazzo Comunale* of Padua was destroyed by fire – together, tragically, with the greater part of the city archives – its larger and far more magnificent replacement was built at the sole cost of the Republic.[1]

During all these demonstrations of friendship, however, the Venetians remained on their guard. They were perfectly aware that the two younger sons of Francesco Novello Carrara had escaped to the Marches; and they knew the family too well not to suspect them of plotting a return to power. An attempt to procure their expulsion having failed, the Venetians put a price on their heads – as they had already done with the two surviving scions of the Scaligers – and then, in Padua, deliberately set to work to eliminate every outward sign of Carrara domination. Known friends and distant relations were exiled from the city, and one of the chiefs of the Ten made a special journey to Padua to examine any books and papers which might contain important or incriminating evidence. Nothing was found, but the documents in question were all brought back to Venice and carefully filed for future reference. The Republic was taking no chances.

The year 1406, which had begun in Venice with the celebrations marking the entry of Padua into the fold, ended with further festivity; for on 19 December a Venetian, Angelo Correr, was elected Pope in Rome under the name of Gregory XII. He was already nearly eighty, and so emaciated that a contemporary described him as being 'only a spirit appearing through skin and bone'; but that spirit still glowed with a deep and genuine piety, and with the single high ambition to which he was determined to dedicate what remained of his life – the healing of the Great Schism of the West.

The Church had now been in schism for almost thirty years. Pope

---

1. This building, which no longer exists, must on no account be confused with the superb Palazzo della Ragione, which by now had already been standing for the best part of a century.

Gregory XI had brought the Papacy back from Avignon to Rome in 1377, but had died a year later; and the ensuing election had been tumultuous in the extreme. The Roman populace knew full well that if the French Cardinals and their supporters had their way, they and their successful candidate would return to Avignon, probably for good. In their determination to prevent such a disaster – from which Rome might never have recovered – they had taken to the streets and even invaded the Conclave itself. Its members had met in fear of their lives, and had elected an Italian, Urban VI, who had announced his intention of remaining in Rome; unfortunately, within weeks of his coronation, he had so antagonized the Cardinals of both the French and Italian parties that in desperation they had declared the election to have taken place under duress and consequently to be null and void, and had thereupon elected a rival Pope, Clement VII, in his place. Urban, firmly entrenched in Rome, had refused to yield; and so the dispute had dragged on, with new Popes being elected on both sides as necessary. It was still as acrimonious as ever when the Venetian Gregory XII, the third successor to Urban, was called to the Throne of St Peter.

He had not occupied it a week before he was writing to the Anti-Pope, Clement's successor Benedict XIII, in Marseille: 'Let us both arise, and come together into one desire for unity.' If there was no galley to take him to the appointed meeting-place, a fishing-boat would do; if there were no horses, he would go on foot. If Benedict would resign, he would be glad to do the same. The Cardinals on both sides could then proceed to a single, undisputed election. It was a fair offer, and sincerely meant. Benedict for his part accepted – he could hardly do otherwise – and proposed a meeting at Savona. But now the difficulties began to appear. Savona was in French territory, and within Benedict's sphere of obedience. The journey from Rome would be long, costly and for an octogenarian distinctly dangerous. Ladislas of Durazzo, King of Naples, who had reasons of his own for wishing the schism to continue, tried to seize Rome and forcibly to prevent the Pope from leaving; though his attempt failed, it persuaded Gregory that the Holy City would not be safe in his absence. Finally, the strains of office were rapidly telling on the old man's strength and, as he drifted towards senility, he became less and less able to resist pressures from his family – in particular two of his nephews – who were by now digging deep into the papal coffers to gratify their own extravagant tastes and were determined to do everything in their power to prevent him from taking any step that might accelerate his resignation.

For all these reasons, the meeting at Savona never took place. In August 1407 Gregory did at last leave on his journey north, but by 1 November, the day appointed, he had got no further than Siena. The following April, when he had advanced as far as Lucca, his earlier fears were realized: Ladislas marched on Rome. The city, leaderless, impoverished and bereft of the last shreds of its morale, surrendered with scarcely a struggle. The situation was worse than ever. Both papal contenders were now in exile, each was accusing the other of bad faith and, as the stalemate continued, the chances of conciliation seemed to be fast diminishing.[1] Clearly there was nothing further to be hoped for from either of the protagonists. On 25 March 1409 a General Council of the Church some five hundred strong met at Pisa, and on 5 June it repudiated both Gregory and Benedict as contumacious, heretical schismatics. Christians throughout the world were absolved from all obedience to either of them and ordered to observe a universal holiday; the Council then went on to elect their single successor. Its choice fell on the Cardinal Archbishop of Milan, a certain Peter Philarges who, having started life as an orphan beggar-boy in Crete, was to end it as Pope Alexander V.

Now, one is tempted to reflect, would have been the time for the two rivals to retire gracefully from the scene. Yet they did not do so, and for that the Council was largely to blame. It had been summoned by neither of them, and by calling them to appear before it – and declaring them contumacious when they refused – it implied its superiority over the Papacy itself, a principle which neither could have been expected to endorse. A little more diplomacy, a little more tact and understanding for two old men who, in their very different ways, were both honest and upright and had neither of them wished to occupy their impossible positions, and the schism could have been healed. In the circumstances, they could only declare the Council's proceedings uncanonical and fight on.

It was then that Gregory took the step for which, at the time, he was more bitterly blamed than for any other. He sold the entire territory of the Papal States to Ladislas for 25,000 florins. Ostensibly, there could have been no greater betrayal of a sacred trust; seen in historical perspective, however, it becomes more comprehensible and less shocking. Much of the territory concerned was already in Ladislas's control. Gregory in his present plight had neither the means nor the money to think of reconquest; by this act, which involved little more than the acceptance of a *fait accompli*, he obtained both the funds which were vital to him if he were to

---

1. As a contemporary, Leonardo Bruni, wrote: 'If the one advances, the other retreats; the one appears an animal fearful of the land, the other a creature apprehensive of the water. And thus, for a short remnant of life and power, will these aged priests endanger the peace and salvation of the Christian world.'

continue his struggle and – equally important – a powerful Italian ally. He must have known too that Ladislas, who was fully extended elsewhere, was unlikely to be able to hold the lands for long; indeed, thanks in large measure to the activities of Florence and Siena, they were lost to Naples even before the end of the year.

On the Rialto, the joy that had greeted Gregory's election had turned all too rapidly to embarrassment. Up until the Council of Pisa, the Republic had naturally given him its fullest support; now it found itself in a quandary. In August 1409 ambassadors from England, France and Burgundy arrived in a body to seek Venetian endorsement for Pope Alexander; at the same time the Doge received a request from Gregory for safe conduct to pass through Venice on his way to Cividale, in Friuli, where he planned to settle. For several days the question was debated in the Senate, with tempers rising high on both sides. Gregory's claim, as a son of Venice, to the Republic's continued loyalty was pressed by his friends and adherents; others objected with equal vehemence that Pope Alexander, being by birth a Cretan, was also a Venetian citizen. At last Doge Steno rose to speak. It was, he declared, in the interests of the peace and unity of Christendom that the Council of Pisa and its lawfully elected Pope should be given universal recognition and endorsement. By sixty-nine votes to forty-eight, he carried the day. On his journey to Cividale, Gregory was warmly acclaimed in Chioggia, and again at Torcello; but the gates of his native city were closed to him. They never opened again.

The decision was an important one for Venice, establishing as it did a precedent which suited her collectivist philosophy and which she was careful to observe in all her subsequent dealings with the Papacy: that individual Popes were always subject to General Councils of the Church. As for Gregory, although this denial of support from the one quarter where he might above all have expected it must have wounded him deeply, it did not spell defeat. He too had his principles, and the growing weight of his years was making him, if anything, more stubborn than ever. Besides, he could still boast a few powerful adherents, including Rupert of the Palatinate, who in 1400 had been elected King of Germany,[1] and Carlo

---

1. The Holy Roman Empire had declined sadly since the death of Frederick II in 1250. It was now merely a loose federation of principalities and cities, under the honorary presidency of one of their rulers, who bore the title of King of the Romans and was traditionally entitled to an imperial coronation by the Pope; but of the eighteen Kings between 1250 and the death of Maximilian in 1519 only five actually received the Crown of Empire in Rome, the last being Frederick III in 1452. Maximilian himself was never crowned, assuming the imperial title in 1508 with no justification; Charles V was, but in Bologna – the last coronation of the Holy Roman Empire (see p. 445).

Malatesta, Lord of Rimini. Benedict, for his part, seemed also to thrive on adversity. Before long it became clear that the only real effect of the Council of Pisa had been to saddle Christendom with three Popes instead of two. But the Cardinals were unrepentant; and when Pope Alexander – the only contender unable, apparently, to stand the strain – died suddenly in May 1410 they lost no time in electing another.

Baldassare Cossa, who now joined the papal throng under the name of John XXIII,[1] was widely held at the time to have poisoned his predecessor. Whether he actually did so is open to doubt. He had, however, unquestionably begun life as a pirate; and a pirate, essentially, he had remained. Able, energetic and utterly unscrupulous, he owed his meteoric rise through the hierarchy to a genius for intrigue and extortion; morally and spiritually, he reduced the Papacy to a level of depravity unknown since the days of the 'pornocracy' in the tenth century. A contemporary chronicler, Theodoric of Niem, records in shocked amazement the rumour current in Bologna – where Cossa had been papal governor – that during the first year of his pontificate he had debauched no fewer than two hundred matrons, widows and virgins, to say nothing of a prodigious number of nuns. His score over the three following years is regrettably not recorded; he seems, however, to have maintained a high average, for on 29 May 1415 another General Council, meeting this time at Constance, deposed him and – benefiting from the lesson learned at Pisa – forced him to ratify the sentence himself. As Gibbon summed up: 'The most scandalous charges were suppressed; the vicar of Christ was only accused of piracy, murder, rape, sodomy and incest; and, after subscribing his own condemnation, he expiated in prison the imprudence of trusting his person to a free city beyond the Alps.'

Next, in early July, Gregory XII was prevailed upon to abdicate with honour, and with the promise that he would rank second in the hierarchy, immediately after the future Pope – a privilege that was granted the more easily in view of the fact that, since he was by now approaching ninety and looked a good deal older, it was not thought likely that he would enjoy it for long; indeed, two years later he was dead. By then, the Anti-Pope Benedict had been deposed in his turn; and with the election of the new, legitimate Pope Martin V in 1417, the schism was effectively at an end.

Venice's first Pope had had an unhappy, harrowing and at times humiliating pontificate. Had he been younger and stronger, had he not been encumbered with an unscrupulous and grasping family who

---

1. The circumstances of his election and subsequent deposition have denied him a place on the canonical list of Popes. It was therefore perfectly legitimate – though none the less surprising – that Angelo Roncalli should have adopted the same name on his election to the Papacy in 1958.

manipulated him for their own purposes his early hopes of healing the schism might have been fulfilled. Instead, he ended his life a failure. But he bore himself with dignity till the day of his death; his one apparently shameful action had already been recognized as a mere tactical manoeuvre; and – as the terms of his abdication clearly showed – even when deposed and dismissed, he was never discredited.

From all the upheavals and intrigues engendered by the schism, Venice had as far as possible maintained her usual position on the side-lines, committing herself to one party or another only when a decision was forced upon her and then supporting whichever side seemed most likely to bring the disruption to an end. For this reason alone she had given her full endorsement to the Council of Constance and had sent four high-ranking ambassadors to congratulate Pope Martin on his accession. To a trading republic, after all, the identity of a Pope – whether Venetian or not – was of little direct concern. Besides, during the worst years of the crisis she had had a more pressing claim to her attention: the reacquisition of the Dalmatian coast – followed, as a direct consequence, by a war with the Emperorelect of the West.

It was now almost half a century since she had been forced to cede the cities of Dalmatia to Hungary; but the loss had never ceased to rankle. Thus, when Ladislas of Naples contrived in 1403 to get himself crowned King of Hungary and shortly afterwards offered to sell back all his Dalmatian territory for 100,000 florins, she accepted with alacrity. The transaction was completed on 9 June 1409 – just four days after the deposition of Pope Gregory by the Council of Pisa. There were, however, two problems: the first was that, although some of the Dalmatian towns and islands were permanently garrisoned with Hungarian troops, several preferred the more distant overlordship of Hungary to that of Venice with her constant interference. The second was that the Hungarian throne was almost immediately reoccupied by its rightful owner, King Sigismund, who saw Dalmatia as an integral part of his dominion, besides being its only outlet to the sea. Thus, in the following year, Sigismund – having failed to foment rebellions in Padua and Verona through the last sad scions of the Carrara and the della Scala – sent an army of 20,000 men into the Friuli under the command of the most brilliant young *condottiere* of his day, the Florentine Filippo degli Scolari, better known as Pippo Spano.

Venice, meanwhile, was doing her utmost to avoid a war. She dispatched to Sigismund two of her most experienced diplomats, Giovanni Barbarigo and Tommaso Mocenigo, who argued – with some justice – that Dalmatia should remain under Venetian control since Venice alone could keep the Adriatic shores free of pirates. When this approach failed, they suggested that Venice might hold Dalmatia as a Hungarian fief, paying a token annual tribute of a white horse and a cloth of gold; they even offered on the Republic's behalf to provide Sigismund, who had just been elected Emperor of the West, with a squadron of galleys to bring him in state to Rome for his coronation. But Sigismund would not listen. Sadly the ambassadors returned to the lagoon – and Pippo Spano marched. Feltre and Belluno soon surrendered, and young Brunoro della Scala was set up, with the resonant title of Imperial Vicar, to govern them.

Hastily, Venice raised her own army – much of it conscripted, as always, from her mainland territories and commanded in succession by two Malatesta brothers, Carlo and Pandolfo – and in the course of 1411 managed to stem the Hungarian advance. Pippo was back in 1412 with substantial reinforcements, and in June of that year actually managed to land with a small force on the Lido, where he laid waste the land around S. Nicolò before being forced to retire; but two months later, at Motta in the Friuli, he met the combined forces of Pandolfo Malatesta and Nicolò Barbarigo, who had sailed up the Livenza river with three galleys and no fewer than seventy smaller craft, and suffered at their hands a serious and humiliating defeat.

These encounters seem to have convinced both sides that they had reached a stalemate. Pippo might capture much of the Venetian mainland, but he knew that he could never hope to invest the city itself. Venice for her part had experienced further proof of what she already knew only too well: that the plain of Lombardy was too vast for her to control. Her enemies might retire almost indefinitely across it; they could not, however, be expelled. As time went on, the costs escalated on both sides, until the Republic – which had already imposed a 10-per-cent property tax on all its citizens to offset the loss of mainland revenues – sent another embassy to Sigismund to seek an agreement. This time the Emperor-elect was only too happy to listen. Since he still insisted on his rights to Dalmatia, a permanent peace remained out of reach; but a five-year truce was concluded in 1413, largely through the efforts of the chief Venetian negotiator, Tommaso Mocenigo. He was still with the Imperial Court at Lodi in January of the following year when a message was brought to him that caused his immediate return: he had just been elected the sixty-second Doge of Venice.

21

The Prophetic Doge

[1413–1423]

Truth sits upon the lips of dying men.
Matthew Arnold

Michele Steno, dying the day after Christmas, 1413,[1] had left the nation considerably stronger, greater in area and – despite the temporary impoverishment resulting from the war with Hungary – inherently more prosperous than he had found it. Three years before, however, he had deliberately provoked a constitutional crisis that was to have a lasting effect on the position of the Doge within the state. The details of this crisis, which concerned his support of a motion to invalidate a decision of the Great Council, need not detain us; but it led to the Doge's being threatened with suspension and impeachment. Steno, a proud and stubborn man, refused to give way, effectively challenging his opponents to do their worst; had the latter not lost their nerve, his life might well have ended in exile or even, like that of Marin Falier, on the scaffold. Fortunately for him – and for Venice – good sense prevailed; face-saving formulas were found for those who had wished to indict him and the matter was dropped. But it was not forgotten. Before the end of Steno's reign new laws had been passed which set still more stringent limits on the Doge's power, including a measure permitting any two of the three *Avogadori di Comun* – the law-officers of the state – to arraign him if they believed him in word or deed to be bringing the constitution in jeopardy, while his successor's *promissione* – that formidable list of specific undertakings and prohibitions which every Doge was obliged to sign on his accession – removed one of the few surviving ducal rights of any real political significance: that of summoning an *arengo* at will. In future such a convocation of all Venetian citizens would be permitted only with the approval of the Great Council and the Senate, for purposes agreed in advance.

As a patriotic Venetian of seventy with a lifetime of service to the state

---

1. He was buried in the church of S. Marina – not the Servi as Ruskin maintains – with the keys of Padua hanging before his tomb. When that church was demolished in 1820, the effigy was moved to SS. Giovanni e Paolo, and placed over another sarcophagus.

already behind him, the new Doge is unlikely to have resented this further reduction of the ducal authority. We first hear of Tommaso Mocenigo in 1379, when he was given the unenviable task of bringing back to Venice the news of the destruction of her fleet at Pola by the Genoese. Later he served as Captain-General in the Black Sea, where in 1396 he succeeded in rescuing what was left of a Christian army – composed largely of French and Hungarians – under King Sigismund, after its still more disastrous defeat by the Turkish Sultan Bajazet I at Nicopolis. Since then, as we have seen, his activities had been largely confined to the diplomatic field; but scarcely was he settled upon the ducal throne than he found himself once again confronted with the growing power of the Turks. No longer, however, as an onlooker. Now – for the first time in her history – the Venetian Republic was actively involved.

It was in many respects remarkable that the clash had not come earlier. In the past half-century the Ottoman armies had overrun more than half the Balkan peninsula, until by 1410 the Byzantine historian Michael Ducas suspected – probably with good reason – that there were more Turks permanently settled in Europe than there were in Anatolia. Most Christian states, at least in the central and eastern parts of the continent, had already felt the temper of Turkish steel. Venice, however, as always preferring commerce to conquest, had hitherto contrived to remain on friendly terms, and this friendship had been confirmed in a treaty which, as recently as 1413, her special envoy Francesco Foscari had negotiated with the new Sultan Mehmet I.

By comparison with most of the Ottoman rulers of the fourteenth and fifteenth centuries, Mehmet was a man of peace. He maintained cordial relations with the Emperor Manuel Palaeologus in Constantinople and he had no quarrel with Venice. In the spring of 1416, however, an Ottoman fleet sent against the independent Christian Duke of Naxos, who had long been accustomed to harass Turkish shipping in the Aegean, suddenly turned in pursuit of some Venetian merchantmen on their way back from Trebizond, ran them into Negropont (the modern Euboea) and attacked the town. Fortunately a Venetian war squadron was close at hand. At first its commander, Pietro Loredan, tried to parley with the Turkish admiral at the latter's base at Gallipoli; but matters had already gone too far. No sooner had the discussions begun when fighting spontaneously broke out between the two fleets. The ensuing battle is best described by Loredan himself in his subsequent dispatch to the Doge and Signoria. It is dated Tenedos, 2 June 1416:

I, as commander, vigorously attacked the first galley, which put up a stout defence, being excellently manned by courageous Turks who fought like dragons. With God's help I overcame her, and cut most of the said Turks to pieces. Yet it cost me much to save her, for others of their galleys bore down upon my port quarter, raking me with their arrows. Indeed, I felt them; for one struck me in the left cheek, just below the eye, piercing the cheek and nose; and another passed through my left hand. And these were only the serious wounds; I received many others about the body and also in my right hand, though these were of comparatively little consequence. I did not retire, nor would I have retired while life remained to me; but, still fighting vigorously, I drove back the attackers, took the first galley and hoisted my flag in her ... Then, turning suddenly about, I rammed a galleot, cutting many of her crew to pieces, put some of my own men aboard and again ran up my flag ... Their fleet fought on superbly, for they were manned by the flower of the Turkish seamen; but by God's grace and the intercession of St Mark our Evangelist we at last put them to flight – many of their men, to their shame, leaping into the sea ... The battle lasted from early morning till past two o'clock; we took six of their galleys, with their crews, and nine galleots. And the Turks that were on them were all put to the sword, including the admiral and all his nephews and many other great captains ...

The battle over, we sailed beneath the walls of Gallipoli, bombarding them with missiles and calling on those within to come out and fight; but they would not. So we drew away, to allow the men to refresh themselves and dress their wounds ... And aboard the captured vessels we found Genoese, Catalans, Sicilians, Provençals, and Cretans, of whom those who had not perished in the battle I myself ordered to be cut to pieces and hanged – together with all the pilots and navigators, so the Turks have no more of those at present. Among them was Giorgio Calergi, a rebel against your Grace, whom despite his many wounds I ordered to be quartered on the poop of my own galley – a warning to any Christians base enough to take service with the infidel henceforth. We can now say that the power of the Turk in this region has been utterly destroyed, and will remain so for a long time to come. I have eleven hundred prisoners ...

It was a signal victory; and there is no indication that the subsequent savagery, reported with such nonchalance, caused any adverse comment in the Republic or elsewhere. A treaty of peace and friendship followed, and was confirmed the next year when an ambassador from Mehmet was received in Venice with much ceremony, was entertained with his entire suite at the public expense, and departed laden with honours and rich presents.

In spite of Loredan's brave words, the Venetians must have known perfectly well that they had won only a breathing-space; that the Ottoman Empire was bent on a policy of expansion which aimed not only at Constantinople but at the whole eastern and central Mediterranean and perhaps even more. Meanwhile, however, they were content to have averted the immediate danger and to have made the Middle Sea once again safe for trade. Europe, too, settled back in the comfortable belief that it had nothing to fear from the Turk: Venice, clearly, would always be able to keep him in his place.

On the other hand, she must also be kept in hers; and in the opinion of Sigismund of Hungary, King of the Romans,[1] this did not include Dalmatia. In 1418 the five-year truce negotiated by Tommaso Mocenigo came to an end, the two sides no closer to agreement. With Sigismund still refusing to consider Venice's proposals that she might hold the disputed territory in fief to him, and Venice still insisting on what she considered her historic rights to the coast – without which she could not preserve the security of the Adriatic – a renewal of the war became inevitable. And although the Republic had done its best to prepare for it by entering into treaties of mutual assistance with Filippo Maria Visconti of Milan and Joanna II, who had succeeded her brother Ladislas on the throne of Naples, there were anxious faces on the Rialto when the news arrived in the summer of 1418 that Sigismund had sent an invading force into Friuli.

This region, lying along Venice's north-eastern frontiers, had been a problem to her for centuries. Difficulties with successive Patriarchs of Aquileia had existed for almost as long as the city itself, and had become potentially still more acute after 1077 when the Emperor Henry IV had granted the entire region to the Patriarchate as a temporal fief. Since then it had constituted what was virtually an independent dukedom, more German than Italian, and several Patriarchs – aided and abetted by those other perennial trouble-makers, the Counts of Gorizia – had tried, with varying degrees of success, to use their power and wealth to the detriment of the Republic. With the Kingdom of Hungary, however, their neighbour to the east, they had normally remained on excellent terms; in particular, they had traditionally supported Hungarian claims to Dalmatia. It came as no surprise to anyone, therefore, when the reigning Patriarch, a German, not only welcomed the invading troops but put himself at their head.

Fortunately for Venice, she too had a local commander. Tristano Savorgnan was a scion of one of the oldest and most distinguished of Friulano families, whose father had been murdered by Hungarian-Patriarchal partisans and who had subsequently been driven from his city of Udine. He too was fighting on home ground, and was able to swell the modest forces that Venice had been able to put at his disposal to a very

1. See p. 288n.

considerable degree. Before long he had stolen the offensive, and it was the Patriarch who found himself fighting for survival. Sacile, Feltre and Belluno, three towns that Venice had lost in 1411, were recaptured in quick succession. In 1420 Udine was besieged, and the Patriarch, from within its walls, was obliged to send out a desperate appeal to Sigismund for reinforcements.

But by now Sigismund had other preoccupations. The previous year he had inherited the crown of Bohemia from his brother and had immediately been swept up in the religious war that had resulted from the burning, at the Council of Constance, of the reformer John Hus; the Turks were meanwhile pressing at his eastern borders. There was nothing he could do. The Patriarch escaped to Gorizia; Udine opened its gates and reinstated Savorgnan; and, seeing that further resistance was hopeless, the other towns capitulated without a fight. By the terms of the peace treaty that followed, all Friuli, apart from Aquileia itself, S. Vito and S. Daniele, was ceded to Venice. The Counts of Gorizia likewise acknowledged the Republic as their overlord. At a single stroke, the area of Venetian territory in mainland Italy was almost doubled, and for the first time given a clearly defined natural frontier to the north-east – the Alps.

Meanwhile Pietro Loredan, now responsible as Captain of the Gulf for the safety of the Adriatic, had left the lagoon in May 1420 with the intention of consolidating the Republic's hold on the cities and islands of the Dalmatian coast. Sigismund's involvement in the Hussite wars once again prevented him from sending reinforcements to the area; the only town that had maintained a substantial garrison was Traù (the present Trogir), which put up a spirited resistance for a week or two; all the others willingly made their submission, and Loredan continued in triumph as far as Corinth before returning to report that the entire Adriatic was once again in undisputed Venetian control.

There could be no doubt, during these early years of the fifteenth century, that Fortune was smiling on Venice; not, however, on Venice alone. Her neighbour to the west, Filippo Maria Visconti of Milan, had also prospered.

This second son of Gian Galeazzo – his elder brother, Giovanni Maria, a sadistic monster whose favourite pastime was to hunt down innocent subjects with his pack of wild dogs, had been murdered in 1412 – was a curious and intriguing figure, though hardly a prepossessing one. Short, swarthy, and later grotesquely fat, he harboured acute feelings of inferiority which made him shrink from all public appearances; with this he combined a degree of physical cowardice that caused him to have constructed a special sound-proofed chamber in which to take refuge during thunderstorms. Moreover, after his assumption of power, he less surprisingly developed a morbid fear of assassination, sleeping every night in a different bedroom – sometimes two or three – watched over by guards who were themselves under constant surveillance. He too could be cruel; he raised no objection when his first wife, Beatrice of Tenda, was tortured and subsequently executed for alleged adultery with her page. Normally, however, he seems to have been of a gentle disposition, kindly and devout, and deeply in love with his mistress, Agnese del Maino, to whom he remained faithful till his death.

It is hardly necessary to say that he never personally took the field in battle. Fighting was something which he left, most successfully, to professionals. He himself preferred to remain in his palace, confining himself to the two fields in which he excelled, diplomacy and intrigue. Patiently, step by step, he had regained the territories which had been snatched by rapacious generals after Gian Galeazzo's death; and with his army's reconquest of Genoa in November 1421 the process was at last complete. But Filippo Maria was not a man to rest on his laurels. He knew that in Italy – and particularly in northern Italy, where almost every city and town had its age-old tradition of independence and where there were no natural barriers by which frontiers might be fixed – empires could not remain static; they must expand or shrink. And now that his own was properly reconstituted, he began to look around him for new lands to acquire.

Foremost among the cities that felt themselves threatened by this sudden recrudescence of Visconti power was Florence. Clearly, reasoned the Florentines, if Filippo Maria was to be checked, a league must quickly be formed against him; equally clearly, any such league must include Venice. But when, in May 1422, they sent emissaries to the Doge with firm proposals to this effect, Mocenigo proved in no hurry to accept. The Republic, he pointed out, had concluded a mutual security pact with Milan only three months before, to ensure military support in the event of further trouble with Hungary. She preferred defensive agreements of this kind to aggressive alliances. Her prosperity was founded on commerce, not on warfare, and she had no quarrel with the Milanese. He would, however, lay the matter before the Senate; the noble signors of Florence would receive their reply in due course.

As a first reaction it was hardly promising, and the Florentines cannot have been surprised when their invitation was rejected. They could not, however, afford to give up. In March 1423 they were back again with a new proposal: that Florence should use her good offices to mediate with the King of Hungary and so, it was hoped, help the Venetians to reach a settlement with him. They could then safely annul their pact with Visconti, leaving themselves free to enter an alliance which would be greatly to the advantage of both Republics. Once again the Doge's reply was in the negative: Venice was grateful for this most considerate offer, but mediation had been tried before, and had failed. King Sigismund had shown himself deaf to all reasoned argument. Venice had no alternative, therefore, but to maintain her existing policy of friendship with Milan.

For the second time the ambassadors of Florence returned disappointed. They were now, however, in possession of information that gave them new hope for the future. Opinion in the Senate had been sharply divided. Doge Mocenigo had succeeded – just – in imposing his views; but he had done so only in the teeth of strong opposition from an energetic and vocal faction led by the relatively young Procurator of St Mark, Francesco Foscari, who had enthusiastically championed the Florentine alliance. There was, too, another consideration that must have given them still greater encouragement: the Doge, now eighty years old, was quite obviously dying.

The long speech which Tommaso Mocenigo is said to have made to the Senate at the close of the debate, and which is repeated in nearly all the early histories, is too riddled with anachronisms to be anything but apocryphal. Only a day or two later, however, he was to make another, predictably shorter one – to those members of the Signoria whom he had summoned to his deathbed. This, so far as we can judge, is authentic; and it is worth quoting in some detail, not only for what the old Doge has to say about the all-important questions of foreign policy and the succession but also for his summary of the economic and commercial situation in the Republic over which he had reigned for the past nine years.

During that time we have reduced our national debt, arising out of the wars of Padua, Vicenza and Verona, from ten million ducats to six ... and now our foreign trade runs at another ten millions, yielding an interest of not less than two millions. Venice now possesses 3,000 smaller transports, carrying 17,000 seamen, and 300 large ones, carrying 8,000. In addition we have 45 galleys at sea, with crews amounting to 11,000; we employ 3,000 ship's carpenters and 3,000 caulkers. Among our citizens we number 3,000 silk-workers and 16,000 manufacturers of coarser cloth. Our rent roll amounts to 7,050,000 ducats ...

If you continue in this wise, your prosperity will increase still further and all the gold of Christendom will be yours. But refrain, as you would from a fire, from taking what belongs to others or making unjust wars, for in such errors God will not support princes. Your battles with the Turk have made your valour and seamanship renowned; you have six admirals, with able commanders and trained crews enough for a hundred galleys; you have ambassadors and administrators in quantity, doctors in divers sciences, especially that of the law, to whom foreigners flock for consultations and judgements. Every year the mint strikes a million gold ducats and 200,000 in silver . . .

Beware, then, lest the city decline. Take care over the choice of my successor, for much good or much evil can result from your decision. Messer Marino Caravello is a good man, as are MM. Francesco Bembo, Giacomo Trevisan, Antonio Contarini, Faustin Michiel, and Alban Badoer. Many, however, incline towards Messer Francesco Foscari, not knowing him for a vainglorious braggart, vapid and light-headed, snatching at everything but achieving little. If he becomes Doge you will find yourselves constantly at war; he who now has ten thousand ducats will be reduced to one thousand; he who possesses two houses will no longer have one; you will waste, with your gold and silver, your honour and your reputation. Where now you are the masters, you will become the slaves of your men-at-arms and their captains.

It was, by any standards, a remarkable speech for a dying man: one, perhaps, that only a Venetian could have made. And, within a decade of his death, it was to prove more remarkable still – when Tommaso Mocenigo was seen to have been speaking not just with the voice of wisdom and experience, but with that of prophecy.

22

Carmagnola

[1423–1432]

Mercenary and auxiliary troops are both useless and dangerous; if any Prince
bases his state upon mercenaries, he will never succeed in making it stable or secure
... a point which should require little emphasis, since the present ruin of Italy is
the result of having for many years now put her trust in mercenary armies – to the
point where they have led her into slavery and ignominy.

Machiavelli, *The Prince*, Chapter XII

The undoubted respect and admiration in which Tommaso Mocenigo was
held by his subjects did not prevent the election, less than two weeks after
his burial in SS. Giovanni e Paolo,[1] of the one man against whom he
had uttered so dramatic a warning. Perhaps it should have: before the
voting began, the likeliest choice for the new Doge was Pietro Loredan,
hero of the great sea battle of Gallipoli seven years before. Francesco
Foscari's supporters among the forty-one electors were afterwards said to
have cunningly cast their votes in the earlier ballots for a candidate that
nobody wanted, thus obliging the rest to vote for Foscari, and then suddenly to have switched, taking the opposition by surprise. If the charge is true
– and it is hard to see any other satisfactory explanation for Foscari's total
having risen between the ninth and tenth ballots from seventeen to twenty-
six – it only goes to show that no electoral system, even one of such
diabolical complication as that by which the people of Venice chose their
ruler, can be completely immune from chicanery of one kind or another.[2]
But however questionable the methods employed, the election itself was
deemed to have been carried out with perfect propriety; and on the morning of 16 April 1423 the new Doge and his wife were led from their private
house to the Palace in a triumphal parade that set new standards of extravagance, even for Venice.

1. His tomb is a curious hybrid: Venetian and Florentine, Gothic and Renaissance. The nineteenth-
century critic Selvatico describes it as *'ricco, ma non bel'*; Ruskin as a 'noble image of a king's mortality',
which is fairer, though scarcely accurate.
2. The system is described on pp. 166–67.

The ceremony of Foscari's induction, however, was noteworthy for another reason, far more significant than any display of finery: the fact that, for the first time in Venetian history, the formal approval of the Doge's election by the populace was not sought. Even the relatively anodyne formula of his introduction, 'This is your Doge, if it please you', was now considered to have no place in the unashamedly oligarchic system. It may be that the splendour of the procession was part of a deliberate attempt, in the bread-and-circuses tradition, to distract the attention of the populace from this silent removal of the last vestige of their former authority; if so, it seems to have been successful. As Francesco Foscari was borne on his litter around the Piazza, scattering largesse in the approved manner – and in the approved quantities – to his cheering subjects, there is no record of a single voice being raised in protest. Scarcely ten years before, Tommaso Mocenigo's *promissione* had dealt a mortal blow to the long-moribund institution of the *arengo*, that general assembly of all adult citizens which was coeval with the Republic itself. With the accession of Francesco Foscari it was, in effect, certified as dead.

But if the corporate political rights of the masses had now dwindled to the point of non-existence, the personal power of the Doge was, as we have seen, very little greater; and the question arises why, in these circumstances, Mocenigo's last exhortation should have suggested that the future prosperity of Venice might stand or fall on the choice of his successor. Francesco Foscari was, admittedly, a forceful and self-willed man whose strength of character, allied to the dignity of his office, might have given him an influence considerably beyond that provided for by the constitution. But that cannot be the whole answer. A more likely explanation is that the dying Doge knew that the result of the forthcoming election would be a symptom of the prevailing mood; and that the choice of Foscari would reflect a new, imperialist spirit far removed from the more peaceable commercialism which had brought the Republic to greatness.

Whether he was right in this assumption is another question. It could well be held that the projected league with Florence which he so vehemently opposed was a necessary defensive measure; that Venice must destroy or be destroyed. As against that, there was the danger that such a league would provoke Filippo Maria Visconti into a similar alliance with Sigismund, threatening the Republic with a simultaneous attack on two fronts and so raising the international temperature without appreciably strengthening her comparative position. Thus, despite the well-known sympathies of the new Doge, which encouraged the Florentines to make fresh overtures, the majority in the Senate remained firmly opposed to intervention. Meanwhile, the Milanese armies began to advance through the Romagna. In February 1424 they took Imola, and five months later soundly defeated a 10,000-strong Florentine army at Zagonara, capturing its general, Carlo Malatesta, Lord of Rimini. Still the Venetians refused to budge. Further defeats followed, further embassies from Florence, further rebuffs; but with every new Milanese victory the isolationist argument was becoming increasingly hard to defend, particularly after the Florentine envoy – in a sudden outburst that probably owed more to his own frustration than to any instructions from his government – had resorted to threats:

Signors of Venice! When we refused help to Genoa, the Genoese themselves adopted Filippo as their lord; we, if we receive no support from you in this our hour of need, shall make him our king.

Now at last, the Senate was impressed – yet it still avoided any immediate open breach with Milan. Visconti for his part hastened to send all possible reassurances, and there is no telling how long he might have gone on playing for time had there not suddenly appeared, to seek urgent audience with the Doge, the magnificent figure of the most celebrated *condottiere* of his day: Francesco Bussone, called (from his Piedmontese birthplace) Carmagnola.

The son of a poor peasant farmer – some authorities describe him less flatteringly as a swineherd – Carmagnola had spent virtually all his active life in the service of the Visconti, during which time his courage, resourcefulness and military skill had won him a reputation unequalled in Italy and, perhaps, in Europe. It was he who had planned the series of brilliantly successful campaigns by which Filippo Maria had first regained his father's duchy and subsequently extended it, he who had led the Milanese armies from one victory to the next; and in doing so he had also achieved the still more remarkable feat of winning, in some modest measure, the Duke's confidence. Visconti had rewarded him handsomely, with a splendid *palazzo* – which Carmagnola lost no time in enlarging still further – an annual income of some 40,000 gold florins exempt from all taxes, a title and, in 1417, the hand of one of his cousins, Antonia Visconti, in marriage.

But Filippo Maria could never give his total trust to anyone; it was not in his nature. Nor could he forget that his general was a *condottiere* through and through – and in the language of the *condottieri* there was no word for loyalty. They did not even pretend otherwise. Their swords were sold, quite openly, to the highest bidder, to whom they belonged for just so long as he was able to pay their price. That price was high, and was further increased by their general practice of prolonging wars, and therefore the payment of their salaries, to the maximum. Victories were necessary for a *condottiere*'s name and reputation; but it was greatly in his interest to see that such victories were not too crushing, and that plenty of scope was left for further campaigns. Thus advantages once gained were seldom pressed home; and if, as frequently happened, the commanders on both sides were *condottieri*, war tended to become little more than a game of infinite skill and finesse, with real casualties reduced to a minimum and even physical discomfort avoided as far as possible. For all this we have the confirmation of no less an authority than Machiavelli himself, who, in the course of the bitter diatribe to which a whole chapter of *Il Principe* is devoted, points out that they never attacked towns by night or campaigned in winter. He omits to add that for many a *condottiere* winter began in August.

All this Filippo Maria knew perfectly well. He knew too how easily a *condottiere*'s salary, once there was no longer any gainful employment for him, could turn into protection money – little more than a blackmail payment for not transferring his allegiance elsewhere. It was undoubtedly considerations of this kind, as much as any gratitude for services rendered, that prompted him to elevate Carmagnola to a position second only to his own; if he could bind the general strongly enough to Milan, his defection to any other state would be unthinkable.

But his policy failed. Why it did so is a question still debated by historians. The trouble seems to have begun as an indirect result of Carmagnola's appointment to the governorship of Genoa in October 1422. It was a responsible, lucrative and strategically important post; but it had two dangerous consequences. First, it prevented him from assuming command of the Milanese armies in their slow but steady advance towards Florence, obliging Filippo Maria to find other, cheaper generals – among them a young man called Francesco Sforza – and suggesting to him that his magnificent *condottiere* was perhaps not quite so indispensable after all; second, it kept Carmagnola away from Milan, leaving the way clear for his enemies and rivals to intrigue against him at the ducal court. Thus, in the summer of 1424, he began to suspect that he was being quietly shelved; and when in the autumn he was suddenly removed from the governorship without explanation he knew that he was right. He hurried to Milan and demanded an immediate audience with Filippo Maria; it was refused. Now genuinely alarmed and fearful – probably with good reason – for his personal safety, he left the city and spent the winter in Piedmont, considering his new situation. By early 1425 his mind was made up; and on 23 February he reached Venice.

His arrival could scarcely have been better timed. The appearance of the most celebrated general of his age, confirming their worst fears about Visconti's ambitions, reassuring them with inside information about his weaknesses and the points at which he was most vulnerable, and finally offering to lead the Venetian land forces against his former benefactor, made a deep impression on the Senate. A week later the offer was accepted in principle, and Carmagnola made a dignified withdrawal to Treviso, there to await the negotiation of the league with Florence – and, incidentally, to survive a carefully planned (and fully documented) attempt by Filippo Maria to poison him. Even now it was to be another year before the diplomatic and military preparations were completed; but in February 1426, with the long-postponed league at last concluded and Carmagnola appointed Commander-in-Chief of the Venetian army on *terra firma* at a salary of 1,000 gold ducats a month, he received the standard of St Mark from the hands of the Doge at a solemn ceremony in the Basilica and took the field.

It was the most ambitious land war on which Venice had ever embarked, a war from which she was ultimately to emerge with the frontiers of her mainland empire extended to the furthest limits they were ever to reach. Not, however, thanks to Carmagnola. From the moment he assumed command it became clear that his old energy was gone. His first objective was Brescia. The Brescians were well known to have little love for their Milanese overlords, and it came as no surprise to anyone when the lower town gave itself up even before he arrived. The garrison withdrew to the citadel, to which he predictably laid siege; but hardly had the operation begun when he complained of a fever and retired, with the grudging permission of the Republic, to take a cure at the baths of Abano. In May he was back in Venice, fortified by the treatment and by the news of his admission to the Venetian nobility, granted to him *ut ferventius animetur* – 'that he should be inspired with greater fervour'. This fervour was, however, still not forthcoming. Indeed, he now informed the Senate with commendable frankness that while at Abano he had been approached by agents of Visconti suggesting that he himself should mediate between the two sides; with these agents, he added, he was still in almost daily touch. Surprisingly, the Senate did not at once order him to break off all such contacts; they merely counselled caution. Carmagnola returned to Brescia, only to leave again in October for reasons of health. He was still away when, on 20 November, the citadel surrendered.

By this time peace negotiations, instigated not by Carmagnola but by the Pope, were already under way; and a treaty was signed on 30 December at

S. Giorgio Maggiore. By its terms Filippo Maria was obliged to surrender not only Brescia and the Bresciano but also – and with considerably greater reluctance – Carmagnola's wife and children, whom the *condottiere* had abandoned at the time of his hasty departure. In return he gained a breathing space; for although the wording of the treaty gave no hint that it was not permanent, both sides were aware that nothing had been definitively resolved between them. The Duke was still bent on extending his power, Venice and Florence still felt threatened. Barely two months later the war broke out anew.

If, as seems probable, the Venetians had at least partly attributed their general's lacklustre performance to the continued presence of his family in Milan, and had deduced that once relieved of this domestic anxiety he would feel able to pursue the war with all his old fire, they were soon disillusioned. He left to take another cure on 2 March 1427; and a day or two later Filippo Maria Visconti launched a combined attack by a land army and his river fleet on Casalmaggiore, a strategic Venetian trading base not far from Cremona on the banks of the Po. Messengers sped to Abano, urging an immediate relief expedition, but to no avail. Carmagnola, only some sixty miles from the besieged town, first refused to budge and then, when in April he at last did so, made endless excuses for not actually engaging the enemy. He scarcely seemed even to bother to make these excuses credible. First he argued that there was not enough fodder for his horses; then that he needed more money; then that his army was inadequate, although at this time he had some 16,000 horse and 6,000 foot-soldiers on call. Casalmaggiore fell; still the Senate said nothing, allowing Carmagnola to continue at his own pace, which continued to be very slow indeed. When finally he began his advance he almost at once fell into an ambush which, with a little foresight, he could easily have avoided; and though he managed to recapture Casalmaggiore during the course of the summer this was due less to his own initiative than to a sudden flare-up with the Duke of Savoy, which obliged Filippo Maria to withdraw most of his troops from the region. By early September Carmagnola had retired again to the safety of the Bresciano and was talking about winter quarters.

It was hardly surprising, in the circumstances, that after the best part of a season's campaigning during which he had attempted little and achieved less, the people of Venice should have begun to murmur against their *condottiere* and to ask themselves not only why they were paying him such a vast salary to no purpose but where his true sympathies lay. Word of this growing dissatisfaction reached him at about this time and seems to have caused him some concern – enough, at any rate, to prompt him to send a letter of indignant expostulation to Doge Foscari. The Doge replied, assuring him that he still enjoyed the complete confidence of the Republic and privately charging his envoy, Andrea Morosini, to impress on the Venetian *provveditori* (the government representatives with Carmagnola) the importance of keeping any criticisms of his conduct strictly to themselves, 'even if they were justified'; since, as he pointed out, Carmagnola held 'the safety of our state in his hands'. There could be no clearer indication of the dilemma in which Venice now found herself, forced to pay immense sums to a well-nigh useless and quite possibly treacherous general in the constant anxiety that if she antagonized him he would have no hesitation in deserting to the enemy, taking the bulk of his army with him.

But if the Senate was anxious, so too was Carmagnola. Doubtless he possessed his own sources of information as to the state of public opinion in Venice, and he must have known that for all their assurances there was a limit to what his paymasters could be expected to tolerate. In other words, he needed a victory as much as they did. Suddenly he shook off his sloth. There was no more talk of winter quarters. Advancing into enemy territory, he met Filippo Maria's army under Carlo Malatesta near the little town of Macalo, otherwise known as Maclodio, near the Oglio river, and on 11 October 1427 virtually destroyed it. Eight thousand of the Milanese were taken prisoner, including Malatesta himself, together with huge quantities of stores and equipment.

It was the one great victory of the war, and great too was the jubilation when the reports of it were brought back to Venice. Carmagnola's popularity soared. The Doge sent him a fulsome letter of appreciation, and the Republic voted him, in token of its gratitude, a palace at S. Stae,[1] formerly the property of the Malatesta, together with a fief in the Bresciano worth another 500 ducats a year. All too soon, however, it was to have cause to regret its impulsiveness. First came the news that Carmagnola had released every one of his prisoners – the flower of Filippo Maria's army – and then that he had refused to follow up his victory with a rapid advance on the almost defenceless Cremona, whose fall would have opened the way to Milan itself. Instead he had contented himself with a few desultory skirmishes in the neighbourhood, after which, ignoring Venetian protests, he had retired for the winter.

Meanwhile the papal diplomats had returned to Venice in an effort to negotiate another peace – one that might prove more lasting than its predecessor. They had set themselves a difficult task, since the Republic

---

1. The palace was burnt down in the nineteenth century. It occupied what is now the open space immediately beyond the Palazzo Priuli-Bon, just to the west of the Campo S. Stae.

would agree to nothing less than the permanent cession of Bergamo and its entire neighbourhood, insisting also – in its determination that Carmagnola should be bound by no links, material or moral, to the Duke of Milan – on Filippo Maria's surrender of all his feudal rights over the Milanese fiefs still held by the *condottiere*. Discussions continued throughout the winter at Ferrara, the Milanese envoys reluctantly agreeing to the first demand but refusing to give way on the second; at last, however – largely because their master needed a breathing space to reconstitute his army and make good his material losses – an uneasy compromise was reached and on 19 April 1428 peace was concluded. By its terms Venice extended her dominion westward to the upper reaches of the river Adda – the furthest permanent limit she was ever to attain,[1] but one which she was to hold, with minor modifications, for the rest of her history as an independent state.

The peace lasted almost two years – longer, in all probability, than either of its principal signatories had expected – during which, in the diplomatic field, much the same pattern continued, with Filippo Maria trying to win back Carmagnola to his old allegiance, Venice struggling to maintain her increasingly tenuous hold over him, and the *condottiere* himself quietly playing one off against the other. Of the three, he was by far the most successful. His resignation in January 1429 enabled him to negotiate a new contract with the Senate on still more favourable terms than before, including a monthly salary, whether he was fighting or not, of 1,000 ducats for the next two years, plus another valuable mainland fief yielding 6,000 ducats a year. In addition he was granted supreme jurisdiction over his forces in all matters criminal and civil, except in those towns in which there was a resident Venetian governor. Meanwhile, however, he remained in almost daily contact with Filippo Maria; and though he punctiliously reported these communications back to Venice, the Senate's continual requests to break them off were ignored.

By now the direction of Carmagnola's ambitions was clear to all concerned; his sights were set on nothing less than a sovereign throne and the foundation of a dynasty. And it was a further sign of Venice's determination to humour him at all costs that, in August 1430, the Senate actually promised him the Dukedom of Milan in return for his capture of the city. Whether in the event they would ever have kept their promise is an open question; he would have made a more dangerous neighbour even than Filippo Maria. But they may well have reckoned that it would have been

---

1. Subsequent temporary acquisitions were to extend it further still, but for brief periods only.

worth the risk; at least they would have had only one potential enemy to watch.

When hostilities were resumed early in 1431, no one in Venice can seriously have thought that, promises or no promises, Carmagnola had any interests at heart but his own. He would occasionally heed the messages he received from his paymasters when it suited his book to do so; otherwise he simply brushed them aside. All this was clear enough; indeed, it was an attitude for which the Venetians, who were famous throughout Europe for the sharpness of their own eye to the main chance, might even have had some sympathy. But it still did not explain Carmagnola's behaviour. His apparent failures, in particular, left them baffled. Were they due to ineptitude? If so, how were they to be reconciled with his past record and the outstanding generalship he had shown at Maclodio? Or to apathy? Or to genuine ill health, as his continued visits to various thermal springs might suggest? Or – most sinister of all – to a secret conspiracy with Visconti? But if this last, why did he keep the Senate so minutely briefed about his Milanese contacts, reporting them – as more than one Venetian agent had been able to confirm to the Council of Ten – with such scrupulous accuracy?

But failures there were, and ones for which Carmagnola could not escape a large measure of personal responsibility. An opportunity to take Lodi without firing a shot was lost when he failed to turn up in time. At Soncino he allowed himself to be surrounded. On 26 June he ordered the Venetian river fleet on the Po to sail upstream against the Milanese, with catastrophic results. Again and again the fleet's captain, Nicolò Trevisan, appealed to him for assistance, but Carmagnola, despite strong pressure from the proveditor, Paolo Correr – the accredited representative of the Doge – and the fact that his army was encamped only a few hundred yards from the scene of the engagement, refused to move.

This time, thanks to Correr's complaints, Carmagnola was obliged to return to Venice and defend himself. Once more the Senate weakly accepted his version of the incident, even going so far as to sentence Trevisan to imprisonment and to outlaw him when he refused to give himself up. But their patience was wearing thin; and when, only a week or two later, they received word from the *condottiere* that he proposed to cease that year's campaigning at the end of August, they sent two special emissaries to his camp with orders to express their grave concern at the time he had wasted and to satisfy themselves as to the real reasons for his continued inertia, urging him at the same time to renew the pressure on Soncino and Cremona and if possible to establish a position beyond the Adda. This was followed in early September with a direct order, in itself an unprecedented step: he was forbidden to retire for the winter. The campaign must go on.

So it did, ineffectually, for another month. But in the first week of October Carmagnola, in an act which amounted to open defiance of the Senate's command, withdrew the first detachment of his troops. He himself remained in the neighbourhood of Cremona and was only three miles from the city when one of his officers – a member of the old and distinguished Cremonese family of Cavalcabò, which had been banished in a political upheaval some years before – launched a sudden night attack and captured the suburban fortress of S. Luca. With a modicum of timely support from his chief he could have taken the city by morning; but Carmagnola arrived too late. It was widely believed at the time that his delay was deliberate.

The first reports of the incident received in Venice were to the effect that Cremona had fallen – a misconception which only increased their anger and disappointment when they learnt the truth. By now, however, the Senate had already passed a special resolution to make a thorough investigation of Carmagnola's behaviour 'that we should better understand how we are to conduct our affairs and rid ourselves of this perpetual anxiety and expense.' No immediate action was taken against him; to be effective it would have to be on no less a charge than that of treachery, which was a good deal harder to prove than simple negligence or dereliction of duty. But the noose was by now being prepared; and when, early in 1432, the war was resumed with the loss of four small towns in rapid succession – one of them apparently given up on the express order of Carmagnola himself – it began to tighten.

On 27 March the evidence against Carmagnola was considered by the Council of Ten, who resolved on immediate and decisive measures. First they requested a *zonta* – a supplementary addition of co-opted members – their normal practice in matters of extreme urgency or importance; next, they decreed the death penalty for anyone who should divulge any word of their present business; finally, on the 29th, they dispatched their Chief Secretary to Carmagnola in Brescia, with a message summoning him to come with all convenient speed to Venice.

From this moment on, the actions of the Ten were obviously dominated by a single overriding consideration: that Carmagnola should not be allowed to escape, to Milan or anywhere else. Until he was safely in Venice, everything possible must be done to avoid arousing his suspicions. The ostensible reason for the summons was to decide the overall strategy for the coming campaign, various possibilities for which were set out in detail in the Secretary's brief; he was to add, for example, that the Marquis of Mantua had also been invited to Venice to take part in the talks. Instructions were meanwhile dispatched to all Venetian governors and officials in the cities and towns between Venice and Brescia, enjoining them to provide armed escorts for Carmagnola on every stage of the way, showing him all possible courtesy as befitted his rank and distinction; if, however, he were to betray any reluctance to proceed, he was to be immediately arrested and imprisoned pending further orders.

In fact these precautions proved unnecessary. Carmagnola at once agreed to come to Venice, and at no point on the journey showed the slightest misgivings. Arriving on 7 April, he was welcomed at the Palace and politely requested to wait until Doge Foscari was ready to receive him. After some time one of the *Savii*, Leonardo Mocenigo, came to apologize for the delay. The Doge, it appeared, was indisposed; the meeting must be postponed till the following morning. Carmagnola rose to leave; but when he reached the foot of the stairs and was about to emerge on to the Riva, one of the nobles stepped in front of him and indicated an open door to the left – that which led to the prisons.

'That is not the way,' objected Carmagnola.

'Your pardon, my lord, but it is,' came the reply.

Then, and then only, did the *condottiere* understand the nature of the trap into which he had fallen. '*Son perduto*,' he is said to have murmured as the door closed behind him.

Two days later the trial began. Carmagnola himself was interrogated by what the state archives describe as 'a master torturer from Padua' and, not surprisingly, confessed at once; his wife, his secretary and his servants – to say nothing of a mysterious lady known simply as *la Bella* who was reported as being seen frequently at his house – were also interrogated, rather more humanely. All his letters and papers were brought from Brescia and submitted to minute examination. Unfortunately many of the official records, including the confession itself, have disappeared; but there seems to have been evidence enough to satisfy the tribunal that the charges should be upheld. On 5 May, after a ten-day suspension during Holy Week and Easter, Carmagnola was found guilty of treason, twenty-six of his judges voting in favour and one against. On the sentence, opinion was more sharply divided. The proposal for life imprisonment, put forward by the Doge and three of his counsellors, received eight votes; nineteen, however, were cast in favour of the death penalty. That same evening the *condottiere*, dressed in crimson velvet, a gag in his mouth and his hands tied behind his back, was led out to the customary place of execution, in the

Piazzetta between the two columns. At the third blow of the axe, his head was severed from his shoulders. The body was then carried off, escorted by twenty-four torchbearers, to S. Francesco della Vigna for burial; but scarcely had the work begun when his confessor came to report that his last wish had been to lie in the Frari. Thither it was immediately transferred.[1] Carmagnola's fortune was confiscated, apart from 10,000 ducats for his widow and 5,000 for each of his two sons, provided that certain conditions of residence were met. In the circumstances, and considering where most of the wealth had come from, this was generous treatment indeed – a good deal more so, perhaps, than they could have expected in any other city in Italy.

It has seemed worthwhile to tell the story of Carmagnola in some detail, not simply in order to record the undeniably curious manner in which Venice came to extend her mainland empire to its furthest effective western limits, but because there is no more vivid illustration of the power of the *condottieri*, and of their consequent behaviour, in the early fifteenth century. He is important more for what he typifies than for his ultimate fate, which, by the standards of the time, he surely deserved. Some 400 years after his death it became fashionable to present him as an innocent victim of Venetian intrigue; but even if we reject the charges of treachery as not proven, Carmagnola still fits uneasily into a martyr's shoes. It is true that while in the service of Visconti he had suffered two severe wounds, from which he never fully recovered; and there is no reason to suppose that the ill health, of which he complained so frequently and which occasioned his numerous visits to various watering-places, was anything but genuine. Similarly it can be argued that Filippo Maria, his large and superbly or-ganized army and his team of able military leaders constituted a far more formidable foe than the motley collection of petty princes that had presen-ted the only challenge to Carmagnola before he offered his services to Venice. But partial explanations are not excuses. If he were too ill to fight he should not have accepted Venetian money to do so, driving harder and harder bargains with the implied threat that if his terms were not accepted he would return to his old allegiance. And if he were simply less good a

1. Later still it was taken to Milan, where Carmagnola had ordered a marble tomb for himself and his family in the church of S. Francesco Grande. When this was demolished at the end of the eighteenth century, his remains are said to have been returned to the Frari, and to have been placed in the wooden sarcophagus above the door in the south aisle, leading into the cloisters; but when this was opened in 1874 and the contents examined, there was no sign that the neck vertebrae had been severed. The bones could not therefore have been those of Carmagnola, whose last resting-place thus remains a mystery.

military commander than his former reputation suggested, his apathy and general reluctance to fight none the less remain unpardonable.

Venice, for her part, having accepted one demand after another and having tried again and again, by every means she knew, to galvanize her general into action, could not finally have acted otherwise than she did. Moreover, the war was not yet at an end, and the Milanese army was stronger than ever it had been. If she were successfully to defend her new conquests she would be forced to hire other *condottieri*, and she knew that any show of hesitancy or weakness would only encourage them to try to take advantage of her just as their predecessor had done. A firm stand was therefore essential; and it may well have been in consequence of the lesson she had learnt that the two other great soldiers of fortune who soon afterwards entered the lists on her behalf were to give her outstanding and devoted service – one of them, indeed, a great deal more besides.

23

The Mainland Upheaval

[1432–1455]

By numberless examples it will evidently appear, that human Affairs are as subject to Change and Fluctuation as the Waters of the Sea, agitated by the Winds. And also how pernicious, often to themselves, and even to their People, are the precipitate measures of our Rulers, when actuated only by the allurement of some vain Project, or present Pleasure and Advantage. Such Princes never allow themselves Leisure to reflect on the Instability of Fortune; but, preventing the Use of that Power which was given to them to do good, become the Authors of Disquiet and Confusion by their Misconduct and Ambition.

Guicciardini, *Storia d'Italia*
(tr. A. P. Goddard, 1763)

Despite Carmagnola's shortcomings, Venice had emerged from the first six years of the war with her land empires much increased; but although hostilities were to continue, intermittently yet often with considerable savagery, for the best part of another quarter-century, they were to yield her little more of permanent advantage. In August 1435 she concluded a treaty with the Emperor Sigismund – who, passing through Milan four years before on his way to his coronation in Rome, had been much incensed when Filippo Maria had characteristically refused to receive him – formally establishing her western frontier at the Adda river. From that time on she sought no new territories, but concentrated on defending her existing possessions and containing the power of Milan. In this latter task she was not even in any real sense the protagonist. Her initial involvement had after all been as a somewhat half-hearted supporter of Florence, which lay far more open to attack and possible capture by Milanese forces; and throughout the war she usually showed herself readier to make peace, or even a temporary truce, than her less fortunate ally.

One such peace was agreed at Ferrara as early as the spring of 1433, but was clouded from the first by a characteristic display of bad faith on the part of Visconti. It provided, naturally, for an exchange of prisoners – who included the Venetian Giorgio Corner, the former proveditor who had assumed command after Carmagnola's recall and had subsequently been captured in a skirmish. When the Milanese prisoners were delivered, however, Corner was not among them; and to Venice's specific demands for his release there came back the answer that he had died in captivity. It was a lie; and the returned prisoners confirmed it. The truth was that Corner had been subjected to appalling tortures in an attempt to make him reveal how much his masters knew about Carmagnola's contacts with Milan and who had been his accusers. He was to return to Venice only six years later, in 1439, a prematurely aged and broken man who was only just able to give an account of his sufferings before he died.

During this brief period of uneasy peace, the Republic found itself faced with a very different sort of problem. In 1431 a new ecumenical Council of the Church had been convoked at Basel to decide on further measures for reform, especially that of the upper hierarchy. Like its predecessors at Pisa and Constance, it had been called by a group of Cardinals independently of the Papacy. In such circumstances it was scarcely surprising that Pope Eugenius IV – another Venetian and indeed a nephew of Gregory XII – should have viewed it with some suspicion and done his utmost to have it dissolved; but he had failed and by 1434 the Council, despite his continued absence, had acquired a large measure of authority and prestige. That summer there suddenly appeared in Basel the Patriarch of Aquileia, still smarting over the loss of Friuli fourteen years before, to accuse Venice of being in illegal possession of his patrimony and to demand its restitution.

In itself, the incident proved to be of little lasting effect. A sentence of interdict was laid on the Republic, but since it was never ratified by the Pope (who was anyway to annul it less than two years later) its provisions were never strictly enforced; moreover the Patriarch's general bearing and intractability antagonized everyone present. It taught Venice, however, a new and valuable lesson. She saw that it was not enough for her simply to occupy conquered territory. If she were to avoid claims and counter-claims of this kind, which at best were expensive and time-consuming and at worst might well involve her in new and unnecessary hostilities, she must whenever possible obtain a legal title to her acquisitions. Fortunately Sigismund was now an anointed Emperor, invested with full imperial powers, and after the 1435 treaty Empire and Republic were once more on excellent terms. Letters were accordingly prepared for Marco Dandolo, Venetian ambassador at the Imperial court, instructing him to request a formal investiture, not only of Friuli but also of all the territories recently won from Milan.

Sigismund, still seething after his treatment by Filippo Maria, was only too pleased to agree; and on 16 August 1437 the ceremony was held in Prague. The Emperor sat, surrounded by his court, on a great canopied throne which had been erected for the occasion at one end of the Old Town Square. At the other, on a given signal, appeared Marco Dandolo, representing the Republic, magnificently arrayed in cloth of gold. He was received by two hundred noblemen of the Empire, and escorted with much pomp to the foot of the throne, where he knelt at the Emperor's feet. Sigismund stretched forth his hand and raised him up, inquiring as he did so for what purpose he had come. Dandolo replied that the Republic sought investiture of the lands it held on *terra firma*, and handed the Emperor his mandate. The assembly then proceeded in state to the Cathedral for High Mass, after which the imperial diploma was read and Dandolo swore fealty in the name of the Doge and Signoria of Venice for the territories in question. Sigismund replied with a speech in praise of the Republic and its rulers, followed by a stern summons addressed to Filippo Maria Visconti, ordering him to present himself within two months to answer for his misdeeds.

By the terms of the diploma, dated 20 July 1437, the Doge was named Duke of Treviso, Feltre, Belluno, Ceneda, Padua, Brescia, Bergamo, Casalmaggiore, Soncino, and S. Giovanni in Croce, together with all castles and strongholds in the territory of Cremona and the rest of Lombardy east of the Adda river. In return he undertook that each of his successors would renew the oath of fealty immediately after his election and, as a further pledge, that he would send the Emperor annually at Christmas a length of golden cloth to the value of not less than 1,000 ducats.

Surprisingly, the oath was not renewed by Foscari's successors; the annual tribute too was soon forgotten. The reasons for this are not entirely clear; but Venice, unlike the other cities of Italy, had never been part of the feudal system – which was in any case rapidly dying – and obligations of this kind, implying as they did a degree of subjection which with her long tradition of independence and recent history of territorial conquests she was far from feeling, doubtless went against the grain once her fundamental title had been established. In the short term, however, the investiture strengthened her legal position and gave her a firmer basis from which to continue her resistance to the Duke of Milan.

Of the changes and chances of the Milanese war the reader can be spared a detailed recital. Genoa rebelled against Filippo Maria in 1436 and joined the Venetian–Florentine alliance; after that, the story is the usual one of marches and counter-marches, of towns and castles taken and lost again, while the captains on both sides performed their indecisive (though to them highly profitable) pavane. Only occasionally does the picture sudden-

ly spring into life – above all with the attack on Brescia by a Milanese army
under Nicolò Piccinino in the autumn of 1438. By this time the Venetians
had found themselves a new *condottiere*, whose energy and brilliance, and
above all whose loyalty, must have done much to restore their faith in the
breed. He was a baker's son named Erasmo da Narni, better known by his
nom de guerre: Gattamelata.

The sudden advance of Piccinino on Brescia posed a serious threat not
only to the town itself, which was staunchly pro-Venetian and determined
to put up a stout defence, but also to Gattamelata's army there. The only
line of communication and supply open in the winter between Brescia and
Venice ran around the southern shore of Lake Garda. This was cut off by
a Milanese army of formidable strength. With Brescia facing siege, Gattamelata could not risk a pitched battle, the more so since if he were to lose
it Venice herself would be endangered. Somehow he must interpose himself between the enemy and the Veneto by falling back on Verona; and he
knew that there was only one way in which this could conceivably be done.

Lake Garda is a perfect example of what happens when a mountain
torrent completes its descent and meets even ground. Its northern end is
a long and narrow panhandle, bordered by high mountains rising almost
sheer on each side; then suddenly the mountains fall away, the lake
broadens out, and at its southern end washes the wide and level plain of
Lombardy. This southern end was now blocked by the Milanese. To take
an army of some 3,000 horse and 2,000 foot by the northern route, such as
it was, would have been a daunting prospect in midsummer; to do so in late
September, when the snow already lay deep on the mountains and the
rivers were in flood after the first autumnal rains, was to risk disaster. But
bridges were built, pathways washed away were somehow reconstructed;
armed bands sent out by the Bishop of Trento, an ally of the Visconti, were
beaten back; and after a week of forced marches Gattamelata and his
exhausted men emerged from the Val Caprino, to the east of the lake, on
to the welcome plain a few miles north of Verona.

It was an extraordinary achievement; but it was also a retreat. Brescia
was meanwhile under siege and, though fighting heroically – a local
chronicler describes how the priests and friars, the women and even the
children were mobilized to defend the walls – was suffering appalling
damage from Piccinino's eighty cannon. Without relief it could not be
expected to hold out for long. But how was such relief to be brought? Once
again the problem was the Milanese occupation of the southern shore of
Lake Garda. By now the winter had begun in earnest; there was no longer
any question of forced marches around the head of the lake, particularly
with the heavy and bulky supplies necessary for the besieged city. The

eastern shore, however, was still in Venetian hands; if the reinforcements could be ferried across in secret there was a good chance that they might get through, since any major attempt by the Milanese to block them would mean leaving the land route practically unguarded. But there was another, apparently insuperable difficulty: the only boats available on the lake were wholly inadequate for an operation on such a scale.

The course now adopted by Venice was one before which even Gattamelata might have quailed. It involved no less a task than dragging a flotilla of ships, in midwinter, over the mountains and launching them on the lake. Twenty-five barques and six galleys were sailed up the Adige to Rovereto and thence hauled on rollers, by over 2,000 oxen, up an artificial causeway to the little mountain lake of S. Andrea (now known as the Lago di Loppio). Once across this, they were dragged higher still over Monte Baldo and thence slowly lowered – a yet more perilous manoeuvre – down the flank of the mountain to Torbole, a little village at the head of Lake Garda. The few miles separating Rovereto from the lake took a fortnight to cross, and cost the Republic some 15,000 ducats. Not a vessel, however, was lost; and by the end of February 1439 all thirty-one were lying, fully rigged and loaded, in Torbole harbour.

But there they remained. Before they could sail across the lake the Milanese had brought up a flotilla of their own and Pietro Zeno, the Venetian commander, found himself bottled up in Torbole. Only a hastily constructed palisade of stakes driven into the mud saved his ships from destruction. Venice had demonstrated, magnificently, what she could do; but she might just as well not have done it.

These superhuman exertions of the Venetian engineers can scarcely have been made more congenial by the knowledge that while they were heaving their ships through the mountain snows their compatriots in Venice were enjoying a period of feasting and festivity on a scale probably unmatched since the reconciliation between Pope Alexander III and Frederick Barbarossa over two and a half centuries before. Their welcome on this occasion was for another imperial guest: John VIII Palaeologus, Emperor of Byzantium.

John was a tragic figure. His Empire, surrounded by the Turks and now reduced to little more than the city of Constantinople itself, he believed in his heart to be doomed; even if it were not, it needed a miracle to save it, and that miracle could only come about if all Christian Europe were to combine in a single-minded, selfless expedition of rescue. This in turn could be launched only by the Pope in person, and it was in a last, desperate attempt to secure the support of Eugenius IV that the Emperor had travelled to the West – prepared, if need be, to make the greatest spiritual sacrifice of which he and his subjects were capable: that of submitting his Empire to papal supremacy. With the Western Church still in conciliar mood, it was unthinkable that matters of such import could be settled by anything less than a full Council convoked for the purpose; Pope Eugenius had therefore seized the opportunity to dissolve the Council of Basel – which he believed to have grossly exceeded its mandate and which had certainly shown him scant respect – and to summon a new assembly at Ferrara, to which he had invited the Emperor. It was on his way to Ferrara that John VIII made his landfall on the Lido on 8 February 1438, together with his brother Demetrius, Despot of the Morea, the Patriarch of Constantinople and an impressive suite including over 650 Orthodox clergy.

The best description of their arrival is given by the Byzantine historian George Phrantzes, who was not an actual eye-witness but claims Demetrius himself as his authority. On the early morning of the 9th, Doge Foscari came out to greet the Emperor and, says Phrantzes with obvious gratification, showed him every mark of respect, making deep obeisance and standing bareheaded while John remained seated before him. Only after a decent interval did the Doge also take a chair, specially set for him at a slightly lower level on the Emperor's left, while the two discussed the details of their ceremonial entry into the city. Foscari then returned to prepare for the official reception.

It was the first visit ever paid to Venice by a Byzantine Emperor, and no pains or expense were spared to do full justice to the occasion. The Doge, attended as always by the Signoria, sailed out at noon from the Molo in his state barge, the *Bucintoro*, its sides sumptuously hung with scarlet damask, the golden lion of St Mark glinting from the poop, the oarsmen's jackets picked out with golden thread; as it advanced, other, smaller vessels took up their positions around it, pennants streaming from their mastheads, bands of musicians playing on their decks. Coming alongside the imperial flagship, the Doge went aboard and once again made his obeisances to the Emperor; the two then sailed back together to the Molo, where what appeared to be the entire populace was waiting to greet its exalted guest, cheering him to the echo. From there the procession slowly wound its way up the Grand Canal, beneath the Rialto bridge, where more crowds waited with banners and trumpets, and so finally at sunset to the great palace of the Marquis of Ferrara,[1] which had been put at the disposal of the imperial

---

1. This thirteenth-century palace, heavily restored with marvellous insensitivity in the 1860s and (in consequence of its later history) better known as the Fondaco dei Turchi, still stands on the upper reaches of the Grand Canal, opposite the S. Marcuola *vaporetto* station. It now serves, somewhat inappropriately, as the Natural History Museum.

party for the duration of their visit. There the Emperor stayed for three weeks, writing letters to all the princes of Europe, urging them to attend the Council or at least to send representatives. It was the end of the month before he himself left for Ferrara.

Meanwhile, in the besieged city of Brescia, the winter had brought the inhabitants to the brink of starvation. Spring promised some relief from the cold, but from little else; and as summer approached, the situation became even more desperate: 'It seems', wrote Cristoforo da Soldo, whose vividly written eye-witness account of the siege still makes compulsive reading today, 'as though the people long for death; sometimes there is no bread at all and they wander through the streets, faint with hunger. Yet they bear it without complaint rather than submit to that Duke of Milan.' Then came the heat; and with it, inevitably, the plague. By August there were between forty-five and fifty deaths a day.

If the city were to be saved, Venice saw that she would need a far larger army than that which she at present possessed; she therefore now appealed to another soldier of fortune, greater even than Gattamelata. Francesco Sforza had had a varied and eventful career since he had first entered the service of Filippo Maria Visconti some fifteen years before. He had fought for the Emperor, he had fought for Lucca, he had fought for Florence; above all, he had fought for himself. In an attempt to win him back to his former allegiance, Filippo Maria had offered him the hand of his own daughter, Bianca, but had subsequently prevaricated to such a point that Sforza, while still maintaining his claim to the greatest heiress in Italy, saw no reason to ingratiate himself with his intended father-in-law. With Filippo Maria he knew that intimidation would be a more effective argument than any other. He accepted the colours of Venice, Florence and Genoa in June 1439, on the understanding that if he were to capture Milan he would be immediately recognized by Venice as the lawful successor to the ducal throne; otherwise he might similarly claim Cremona or Mantua. Then, without any further delay, he took the field.

Once again, the importance of reaching Brescia with the minimum of losses meant a forced march through the mountains. This time, however, Sforza and Gattamelata found their passage blocked beneath the castle of Tenno, a few miles from Riva at the head of Lake Garda, which had been invested by Piccinino. A pitched battle ensued, in which the Milanese came off decidedly the worse, thanks largely to the efforts of a party of Brescians who had made a sortie from their beleaguered city to meet their deliverers, and who suddenly appeared on a crag above the castle from which they rolled huge boulders on to those below. The Venetians took many prisoners, several of whom proved to be of high rank; Piccinino himself, however, having retreated into the castle, escaped that same evening – if a contemporary account is to be believed – by having himself carried out in a sack. Riding through the night, he rejoined the bulk of his army and, only a week later, launched a surprise attack on Verona. Before the defending garrison knew what was happening, the greater part of the city was in his hands.

It was bad news for the Brescians, condemned to watch from their battered walls while the army destined for their own relief turned away from their very threshold to fling itself against the besiegers of Verona. But Sforza and Gattamelata had no choice. Of the two cities, Verona was of infinitely greater strategic importance. On the night of 19 November the two commanders led their men into the only corner of the city which remained in Venetian control, and at dawn on the 20th they attacked. After heavy fighting the Milanese were routed. So precipitous, indeed, was their flight that the bridge across the Adige collapsed and many were drowned. Piccinino was forced to return to the Bresciano, where desultory fighting continued, in the course of which the Brescians at last received the relief supplies they had awaited for so long. But their ordeal was not yet over; it was only in July 1440 that the Milanese, having suffered yet another heavy defeat at the hands of Sforza, were at last obliged to raise the siege.

That same year, Gattamelata suffered the apoplectic stroke that was to put an end to his career. He retired to Padua, where he was to die in 1443 and where a grateful Republic commissioned from Donatello the tremendous equestrian statue that still stands in the Piazza del Santo. Henceforth Sforza was in sole command of the Venetian forces; but the focus of the war now shifted back to Tuscany and need not concern us here. By late summer 1441 both sides were ready for peace – though Sforza (who was himself to act as principal mediator) wisely insisted, before any treaty was signed, on celebrating his long-promised marriage with Bianca Visconti and taking possession of the cities of Cremona and Pontremoli which she brought him as her dowry. The peace was finally announced at Cavriana on 20 November. Essentially it provided for a return to the frontiers agreed eight years before at Ferrara, and the recognition by Milan of the renewed independence of Genoa.

With the important exception of Ravenna, which had long been little more than an unofficial satellite of Venice, but which formally devolved to her by a deed of inheritance in February 1441, the Republic had reaped little material advantage during the past fourteen years of almost continuous warfare. The peace, when it came, was all the more welcome. Gattamelata was too ill to take part in the ensuing celebrations, but his house in S. Polo[1] was put at the disposal of Francesco Sforza and his bride while their own palace – on the site of the present Ca' Foscari, at the first sharp bend of the Grand Canal, which had been presented to Sforza in 1439 – was being prepared for them. They were then treated to a magnificent state reception, taken on a conducted tour of the city and loaded with presents – including, for Bianca, a jewel valued at 1,000 ducats.

Nobody, it is safe to assume, had any illusions that Venice was in fact celebrating anything more than a brief interruption in the war. With Filippo Maria Visconti still planning, plotting and intriguing from the centre of his Milanese web, with Francesco Sforza still only forty years old and at the very peak of his energy and ambition, with Cosimo de' Medici in Florence still feeling threatened by Milan but now also increasingly concerned by the spread of Venetian power in Lombardy, and with virtually every power in Italy, large or small – Genoa, Mantua, Bologna, Rimini, the Empire, the Papacy, the Kingdom of Naples, the Houses of Aragon and Anjou and countless others – by now swept up in the chain reaction that was the inevitable result of so long and turbulent a contest, all pursuing their own selfish policies, conflicting and incompatible, how could a lasting peace have been contemplated? Few of the parties concerned probably even wished for one – none, certainly, of the *condottieri*, who, though only a few have found their way into these pages, could now be counted by the score up and down the peninsula and who, even more than their paymasters, had the power to spark off a fresh round of hostilities whenever it suited them.

Indeed, perhaps the only major power at this time that genuinely wished for peace was Venice. She alone, with her mainland empire now extending almost 200 miles to the west, felt territorially secure and had no particular desire for further conquests. She hardly needed her agents in Milan to tell her that the Duke was by now ageing, sick and increasingly unstable; and that, of all those who had their eye on his throne, Francesco Sforza was not only the most probable successor but also the most friendly to herself. When, therefore, less than a year after the peace of Cavriana, Filippo Maria once more turned against his son-in-law and tried, with papal help, to rob him of the lands he had previously granted him, she promised Sforza her support – and soon found herself at war again. In September 1446 her army smashed the Milanese near Casalmaggiore, crossed the Adda, and had

1. This house, on the Campo S. Polo next to the church, was formerly the property of Giacomo da Carrara and Giacomo dal Verme before being given to Gattamelata.

advanced to within sight of the walls of Milan before the winter closed in.

Desperate now for help, Filippo Maria appealed to the Pope, to Alfonso V of Aragon – now also King of Naples and Sicily – and to the King of France. He even turned to his old enemy Cosimo de' Medici, playing on Cosimo's by now well-known – though largely unjustified – fear of Venice; but he received in return only an offer to mediate with Sforza on his behalf. Finally he was compelled to throw himself directly on the mercy of his son-in-law, offering to designate him formally as his heir and to appoint him Captain-General of the forces of Milan. This, of course, was exactly what Sforza had been waiting for; but he was by now heavily occupied on his own business in the Romagna and, despite Cosimo's urgings, was in no hurry to move. He knew that the Venetians could not capture Milan even if they had wanted to, and he doubtless calculated that the longer he waited, the more his distracted father-in-law would offer him. Only in the high summer of 1447 did he start for Milan.

But he had delayed too long. He was still on the road when, on 13 August, Filippo Maria died after a week's illness. Had Sforza been there on the spot to seize his inheritance he might have been able to face his rivals with a *fait accompli*; in his absence, all was confusion. Frederick III of Austria, the Western Emperor-elect, claimed Milan as a lapsed imperial fief; Alfonso of Aragon, blandly asserting that Filippo had named him his heir on his deathbed, had somehow managed to introduce a detachment of his own troops into the Castello and was already flying his banner from one of the towers. Meanwhile, not far away at Asti, a French army stood ready to take possession of the Duchy in the name of Charles of Orleans, who, as a nephew of Filippo Maria through the latter's half-sister Valentina Visconti, was incontestably the legitimate heir.

In the prevailing chaos the people of Milan took the law into their own hands. The Aragonese were driven from the Castello, which was razed to the ground as a symbol of outmoded despotism, and a committee of twenty-four 'Captains and Defenders of Liberty' proclaimed the new order, which, in honour of their beloved patron St Ambrose, was grandiloquently designated 'the Golden Ambrosian Republic'. It was a brave bid for popular independence; and had the Milanese been able to carry the other cities and towns of the duchy with them, they might – with Venetian support, which would have been readily given – have succeeded in achieving it. But these smaller communities were by no means unanimous. Some, such as Alessandria, Novara and Como, rallied to the Ambrosian banner; others, however, saw their long-awaited chance of shaking off Milanese domination – among them Lodi and Piacenza, which now spontaneously offered themselves to Venice.

No surer way of sowing dissension between the republics could have been found. Milan demanded the two towns' immediate restitution: Venice replied that they had a right to offer themselves to whomsoever they liked, and that to reject them would be tantamount to throwing them into the arms of Sforza, surely the last thing the Milanese would wish – an argument that was lent additional force by the news that, even while these discussions were in progress, he had seized Piacenza and Pavia. During the next two years, in an all too typical illustration of Italian politics of the time, we find Sforza taking service with Milan and fighting with conspicuous success against Venice, then changing sides and taking on the two republics single-handed. But for Venice the Milanese alliance was by now more a liability than an asset. The Ambrosian Republic was on the point of collapse, and Sforza knew it. In the autumn of 1449 he laid siege to Milan, and in the course of the winter starved it into submission. On 25 March 1450 he entered the city in triumph while his soldiers made a free distribution of bread to the people; and the following day, in the cathedral square, he was proclaimed Duke of Milan, the true and legal successor of the Visconti.

It was now nine years since Francesco Sforza and his bride had been received in Venice with all the pomp and ceremony that the city reserved for a conquering hero. For the past three, however, he had been her bitterest enemy. Venice on her side had confiscated his splendid palace in 1447 (five years later it was to be bought and demolished by Doge Foscari, to be replaced by another more splendid still) and she had striven, both by covert diplomacy and on the battlefield, to thwart his ambitions. But she had failed. Sforza had played his cards brilliantly, and had also benefited from the financial support of Cosimo de' Medici, whose fear of Venetian domination was rapidly becoming an obsession and who now saw in a strong Milan the one hope of maintaining the balance of power. Venice could only accept the inevitable, sending ambassadors to congratulate the new Duke and to wish him well. The war flared up again briefly in 1452, causing her, and her new ally the King of Naples, to expel all Florentine merchants from their respective territories; but her heart was not in it. After some secret and skilful negotiation by Sforza's confessor, Fra Simone da Camerino – who as Prior of the Augustinians at Padua chanced to be a Venetian subject – the few outstanding territorial questions were settled, with Milan confirming Venice's right to Brescia and Bergamo and throw-ing in Crema as well for good measure. In April 1454, a peace was signed at Lodi, to be followed in August by the conclusion of a twenty-five-year defensive alliance between Venice, Milan and Florence. Representatives of the three powers then travelled south, first to Naples, where they obtained the somewhat half-hearted adherence of King Alfonso, and then to Rome, where Pope Nicholas V gave the alliance his blessing. Each signatory named its lesser adherents, and the result was the emergence in 1455 of the Most Holy League, which in its final form included – with the important exceptions of Rimini and Genoa (vetoed by the King of Naples, who was quarrelling with the Genoese over Corsica) – virtually every state in the peninsula.[1]

Given the chaotic nature of the Italian political and diplomatic scene, the conflicting interests of innumerable elements, the greed of the despots, the ambitions of the *condottieri*, the lack of properly defined boundaries be-tween one state and the next, and the increasing tendency of foreign countries (particularly France) to intervene, for the sake of their own aggrandizement, in Italian affairs, it was hardly likely that the principles of the League would be invariably upheld in the years that followed. Nor were they. The princes of Italy had not yet reached the stage where they were capable of subordinating their own selfish aims to the common good. Yet the League was not forgotten. It was to remain an ever-present ideal – even if a usually unattainable one – until at least the end of the century, and though it could not prevent hostilities altogether it somehow managed to rob them of much of their sting. In the forty years between the Peace of Lodi and the French invasion there were to be six small wars fought on Italian soil; yet for nearly thirty of those years the peninsula was to be, to all intents and purposes, at peace. Not once in the entire period was a major town sacked by an Italian army.

At last Venice could turn her attention away from the mainland. Her need to do so was urgent, for less than a year before the Peace of Lodi an event had occurred which was to stand as one of the milestones of history, striking terror in the heart of all Christendom and marking, insofar as any single event could be said to mark, the end of the Middle Ages. On Tuesday, 29 May 1453, the army of the Turkish Sultan Mehmet II had taken Constantinople.

---

1. Francesco Sforza, however, continued to give trouble to Venice. In 1461 he exchanged his house in S. Polo for the site at S. Samuele on which Andrea Corner (father of the Queen of Cyprus) had just begun to construct an immense palace, meaning to continue it for his own use. Shortly afterwards, however, Venetian–Milanese relations had deteriorated to a point where this site too was confiscated. Work stopped when only one corner had been completed – still to be seen on the otherwise undistin-guished house on the Grand Canal known to this day as Ca' del Duca.

24

The Fall of Constantinople

[1453]

The spider weaves the curtains in the palace of the Caesars;
The owl calls the watches in the towers of Afrasiab.

> Lines from the thirteenth-century Persian
> poet Sa'di, said to have been quoted
> by Mehmet II on his entry into
> Constantinople

For all the city's historical significance, the fall of Constantinople had come as a surprise to no one. John VIII's visit to Italy had been, from the Byzantine point of view, a disastrous failure. The Council of Florence – whither the delegates had moved in a body from Ferrara in 1439 – had somehow managed to paper over the narrow but bottomlessly deep doctrinal gaps that separated the Eastern and the Western Churches,[1] but when the Emperor returned to Constantinople and proclaimed the union he had worked so hard to achieve, clergy and people alike simply refused to accept it. Nor had he been any more successful in inducing the princes of the West to launch a great expedition to save his Empire. Pope Eugenius had obediently preached a Crusade; but the only result was a relatively small and unimpressive army, composed mainly of Hungarians, which got no further than Varna on the Black Sea coast before being cut to pieces.

John died in 1448, to be succeeded by Constantine, his eldest surviving brother. Three years later, at the age of nineteen, Sultan Mehmet II succeeded to the Ottoman throne, and by August 1452 he had completed the construction of the huge fortress of Rumeli Hisar which still towers above the Bosphorus a mile or two north-east of the capital, where the straits are at their narrowest. Already there could be no doubt of his intentions, nor of his determination to be obeyed. Scarcely was the castle built before he issued a proclamation calling upon every ship, whatever its flag, passing up or down the Bosphorus to call there for inspection. In November, two

---

1. 'The Patriarch Joseph, after agreeing with the Latins that their formula of the Holy Ghost proceeding *from* the Son meant the same as the Greek formula of the Holy Ghost proceeding *through* the Son, fell ill and died. An unkind scholar remarked that after muddling his prepositions what else could he decently do?' (Sir Steven Runciman, *The Fall of Constantinople*, pp. 17–18).

Venetian ships successfully ran the gauntlet, despite heavy fire; but a third, hoping to follow their example, received a direct hit from a cannonball and sank. Captain and crew were taken before the Sultan. On his orders, the crew were all immediately beheaded. The captain, Antonio Rizzo, was less fortunate; he was sentenced to be impaled, and his body to be exposed by the roadside as a warning to others.

The news of this outrage was received with consternation in Venice. She had always preferred trading with the Turks to fighting them; since they now controlled much of the Eastern Mediterranean and the Black Sea, this trade was of vital importance to her continued prosperity. Sooner or later, in any case, their conquest of Constantinople was inevitable; from the commercial point of view, it might even be desirable as well. Thus she had not hesitated to renew with Mehmet the treaty of trade and friendship concluded earlier with his father. On the other hand she could scarcely ignore the interests of her own mercantile community in Constantinople, whose privileges Constantine had confirmed the previous year, nor did she have any illusions about Mehmet's strategy in the longer term. Once he had destroyed Byzantium, there was nothing to prevent him from turning his attentions against Crete and the other Venetian colonies in mainland Greece and the Aegean. Three months before the Bosphorus incident, a motion recommending that the Byzantines should be abandoned to their fate was lost in the Senate by seventy-four votes to seven; and this last act of brutal savagery on the part of the Sultan against Venetian citizens travelling on their lawful occasions surely demanded some form of retaliation.

But what? All the military resources of the Republic were fully engaged in Lombardy, where Francesco Sforza represented a far more immediate threat to Venetian security. After thirty years of almost continuous fighting on *terra firma* the Treasury was seriously depleted; manpower too was in short supply. Venice was in no position to embark on a new war, against an obviously invincible enemy, several hundred miles away in the opposite direction. If, therefore, the policy that she now adopted was something less than heroic, it was at least understandable. She would continue to make limited quantities of saltpetre and breastplates available to Constantine, in return for payment by letters of credit, and she would also permit him to recruit volunteers in Crete. Finally, she would instruct her naval commanders to afford help and protection to Christian subjects of the Empire whenever possible. On no account, however, must they antagonize the Turks by any unprovoked acts of aggression.

Early in December 1452 one of those commanders, Gabriele Trevisan,

Vice-Captain of the Gulf, arrived in Constantinople with five galleys – one of which may have also carried the young ship's surgeon Nicolò Barbaro, who was to write a day-to-day diary of the coming siege, the most detailed and accurate report of it that we possess. Trevisan was followed almost at once – purely coincidentally – by Isidore, former Metropolitan of Kiev but now a Roman Cardinal, who had been sent by the Pope to solemnize the union of the two Churches. On 14 December, the day after the service of union – which had been boycotted by nearly all the clergy and population of the city – a meeting was held on one of the ships, attended by the Venetian *bailo* (the head of the permanent Venetian trading colony in Constantinople) and all the leading Venetian merchants, at which the Cardinal made a personal appeal to the assembled captains not to abandon the city. Trevisan replied that he was under orders from the Signoria to leave within ten days of the arrival of another galley then expected from Trebizond. He would willingly take with him any merchants who wished to leave, and any merchandise; but sail he must. Back on shore, *bailo* and merchants held a second meeting, in secret. They, at any rate, were determined to stay and to fight. They therefore resolved, by twenty-one votes to one, to retain the ships by force, sending word of what had happened back to Venice by the fastest available means and explaining the reasons for their decision.

The Senate's reaction to this news is not recorded; but in February 1453 they received a further letter from the *bailo*, Girolamo Minotto, reporting the speed and scale of Turkish preparations and imploring them to send a relief force with the greatest possible urgency. This clearly had its effect; on 19 February, 'in view of the immense peril which now threatens Constantinople', they voted to dispatch a further fleet of fifteen galleys as soon as these could be refitted, together with two transports, each carrying 400 men, the expedition to be principally financed by special taxes levied on all Venetian merchants with interests in the Levant. Further letters, more urgent in tone, were sent to the Pope, King Alfonso, the Western Emperor and the King of Hungary, pointing out that unless they too immediately joined their efforts to those of Venice, Constantinople was lost.

But on the Venetian side too there were delays; and it was the second week in May before the fleet finally sailed. The city had been under siege for a month. Already in the Golden Horn, however, lay eight Venetian merchantmen – Trevisan's five from the Rialto and three from Crete. All had been hurriedly converted into men-of-war; all were ready to play their full part in the last battle.

The siege continued throughout April, the Emperor's 7,000 men defending fourteen miles of walls against the Sultan's army of 80,000 or more, and the great Turkish cannon remorselessly pounding at the triple fortifications that represented the only bulwark between the Empire and its destruction. On Sunday the 22nd, in a brillant *coup* reminiscent of the Venetian operation at Lake Garda fourteen years before, but with considerably greater success, Mehmet dragged some seventy ships from the Bosphorus over the hill of Pera and down into the Golden Horn; a few days later a Venetian attempt to destroy these ships ended – largely through the jealousy of the Genoese – in catastrophe. By now, what little hope the exhausted defenders retained of saving the city was concentrated on the long-awaited Venetian fleet.

Yet even this was problematical. Although Minotto seems to have promised the Emperor that a fleet would be sent, he had no real justification for doing so since he had not, so far as we can tell, been informed of the Senate's favourable response to his appeal. Even had he been aware of it, he would still not have known of the successive delays that had prevented the fleet's departure. None the less, there remained a strong probability that a substantial naval force was on its way, in which event it might by now be not far off. At midnight on 3 May a Venetian brigantine from inside the Golden Horn, flying the Turkish flag and with her volunteer crew of twelve disguised in Turkish dress, slipped out of the harbour and through the Marmara to the Mediterranean, in the hopes of making contact with this relief fleet and hastening its arrival.

On 23 May the brigantine returned. In the afternoon sun it had had no chance of deceiving the Turkish ships in the Marmara, and several of them were in hot pursuit. Thanks to its speed and manoeuvrability, however, it managed to avoid capture; and as evening fell the chain across the Golden Horn was lowered to let it in. But it brought no encouragement to the defenders. After nearly three weeks' thorough search of the Aegean, it had found no sign of a Venetian fleet, nor had widespread inquiries revealed so much as a rumour of any having been sent. When the mission was seen to be fruitless, one of the sailors had suggested going on to Venice, arguing that it was unthinkable that Constantinople could still be in Christian hands; that even if it were, its fall must be imminent; and thus that to return there simply to report failure would be to invite certain death or capture. But his companions would hear none of it. They had been entrusted by the Emperor on a mission. Their duty was to complete that mission, whether the city was now Greek or Turkish, whether they themselves lived or died. And so they had returned with their grim news. They were taken at once before the Emperor, who thanked them for their loyalty and courage.

Then, overcome by emotion, he broke down and wept. Only Christ and His Mother, he murmured, could save the city now.

A week later, all was over. At dawn on 29 May the Turks burst through the shattered walls and the Byzantine Empire perished. It had defended itself heroically to the last, against relentless bombardment by an enemy immeasurably stronger and better equipped, holding out for fifty-three days until it was overwhelmed. Even then, it did not surrender. Its Emperor, seeing that the end had come, had plunged into the mêlée where the battle was thickest and had died as he had always been determined to die, fighting for his Empire. It was only some time later that his body was found. It had no head; but on its legs were still the imperial purple buskins, stamped with the golden eagles of Byzantium.

What, meanwhile, had happened to the Venetian relief fleet? The explanation is to be found in the records of the Senate, from which it emerges that Giacomo Loredan, the Captain-General, received his sailing orders only on 7 May; and since these were added to on the following day he is unlikely to have left until 9 May at the earliest. He was instructed to stop at Corfu to pick up another galley there, then to take on provisions at Negropont (Euboea) before continuing to Tenedos, at the mouth of the Dardanelles. Here he would be met by another Venetian galley under a certain Alvise Longo, who had left Venice three weeks earlier in order to gather intelligence about the Turkish dispositions. They would then all sail up to Constantinople together.[1]

Given such a schedule it is hardly surprising that Loredan failed to arrive in time; it was no quick or easy matter for a large fleet to beat its way up the Dardanelles and the Marmara with the prevailing wind in the north, as it was at this season. Scarcely more mysterious is the failure of the Venetian sailors from Constantinople to make contact with Longo, who may well not have reached Tenedos by the time they returned to the city. In any case the tracking down of ships at sea without precise knowledge of their courses or sailing dates was largely a matter of luck until the present century.

But why was the Venetian fleet so seriously delayed? That is a harder question to answer. There is no doubt that, as Sir Steven Runciman has pointed out, 'no one at Venice' – or, he might have added, anywhere

---

1. At this point it may be noticed that I have departed slightly from the account given by Sir Steven Runciman (*The Fall of Constantinople*, pp. 81 and 113), according to which the fleet sailed towards the end of April under Longo – a view which seems difficult to reconcile with the Senate records. See Thiriet, *Régestes*, III, pp. 184–6.

else in the western world – 'understood as yet the tenacity of the Sultan's character nor the superb quality of his weapons of war.' Nor on the other hand can anyone, least of all the Venetians, have deceived themselves into thinking that the city was impregnable; 250 years before, old Doge Dandolo and the armies of the Fourth Crusade had proved that it was no such thing. And it is significant that Loredan was carrying on board his flagship an ambassador to the Sultan – one Bartolomeo Marcello – whose instructions, like his own, provided for the possibility of the siege being over by the time of his arrival. These instructions, to both Captain-General and ambassador, urged caution first and foremost. On the outward journey Loredan was on no account to engage any Turkish ships except in self-defence; once at Constantinople, short of a general order to put himself at the disposal of the Emperor, there was no direct injunction for him to fight; far more stress was laid on escorting back the Venetian merchantmen in good order. Marcello for his part was to emphasize to the Sultan that the Republic wished only for peace: if it had sent a fleet to Constantinople, this was only to ensure the safety of the merchantmen and to protect Venetian interests.

We are left with the conclusion that the Venetians were pursuing – though they may not fully have admitted it even to themselves – a policy of *festina lente*. They wished the world to believe that they were sending a great relief armada to save Eastern Christendom and they did their best, without much success, to encourage the princes of Europe to do likewise; but their hearts were not in it. They were realists enough to know that the Byzantine Empire was doomed, and they had no wish needlessly to antagonize its Ottoman successor. In Mehmet's friendship they saw not just the best means of assuring the continuation of profitable trading with the Orient but, in all probability, the only chance of retaining their own colonies in Greece and the Aegean. Another symptom of their lack of enthusiasm was their refusal to finance the expedition directly from public funds, or even to allow it to sail before all outstanding contributions had been paid. Such attitudes are not compatible with Crusading fire or with any true feeling of emergency. If Venice did not come to the relief of Constantinople in time, it is because she had no real desire to do so.

The Venetians and the Genoese in Constantinople, despite their mutual antipathy and distrust, had fought bravely throughout the siege. Indeed, it was a Genoese soldier of fortune, Giovanni Giustiniani Longo, who had commanded the entire four-mile length of the land walls, rallying the defenders time and time again by the sheer power of his personality and leadership, until a mortal wound in the chest during the last battle had broken his spirit; only his subsequent insistence, despite the entreaties of the Emperor himself, on being carried off to safety put a last-minute tarnish on his previously dazzling reputation. When the city finally fell, however, it was the Venetians who suffered more than their rivals. Apart from two small groups at the southern end of the walls, the bulk of the Venetian force was concentrated, under the command of the *bailo*, Girolamo Minotto, around the imperial palace of Blachernae, where the northern end of the walls curved down to the Golden Horn; and it was at this point that the Turks made their first major breach and entered the city. Many Venetians were killed in the fighting, and of those who were taken prisoner nine of the most prominent were immediately beheaded – including Minotto himself and his son.

The crews of the Venetian galleys fared better. Thanks largely to the greed of the Turkish sailors, who should have been guarding the entrance to the Golden Horn but who had deserted their posts when the looting began lest the soldiers should beat them to the best of the plunder, they managed to break through the boom; then, loaded down with refugees who had swum out to join them, they spread their sails to the strong north wind and sped off down the Marmara to safety. Several Greek and Genoese vessels were able to do the same. A few unarmed merchantmen, on the other hand, which had been anchored with two or three more Genoese galleys further up the Horn, were not quick enough to follow. They and their crews were captured.

An account of the three days of unbridled butchery, rape and pillage which followed – more terrible even than that which marked the Latin conquest of 250 years before – fortunately lies beyond the scope of this book. The news of the city's capture, however, had an immediate impact throughout Western Europe, and nowhere more than on the Rialto, where it arrived exactly a month after the event, on 29 June. Now, perhaps for the first time, as the eye-witnesses returned to tell their tales, the Venetians began to appreciate the full significance of what had occurred. It was not just the fall of the capital of Eastern Christendom; that may have been an emotional shock, but Byzantium had long since ceased to have any real political importance. Nor was it the annihilation of a valuable trading post, although Venice could by now estimate her casualties at some 550 Venetians and Cretans, killed during or immediately after the siege, and her financial losses at 300,000 ducats. There was a third consideration more serious still than these: the fact that the victorious Sultan could henceforth undertake any new conquests he might choose. Everything now depended on securing his goodwill.

On 5 July further orders were sent to Giacomo Loredan and to the ambassador-designate, Bartolomeo Marcello. The former was to take whatever steps he thought necessary for the security of Negropont, ensuring in particular that any merchandise passing through it bound for Constantinople should be redirected to Modone in the Peloponnese until further notice. As for Marcello, his orders were to emphasize to Mehmet the Republic's firm intention to respect the peace treaty concluded with his father and confirmed by himself, and to request the restitution of all the Venetian ships remaining in Turkish hands, pointing out that these were not war galleys but merchantmen. If Mehmet agreed to renew the treaty, Marcello was to ask that Venice should be allowed to maintain her trading colony in the city, with the same rights and privileges that she had enjoyed under Greek rule, and was to press for the return of all Venetians still in captivity. If on the other hand the Sultan refused or sought to impose new conditions, the ambassador should refer back to the Senate. He was also given authority to spend up to 1,200 ducats in presents for Mehmet and any of his court officials, to help negotiations along. Meanwhile the governors of other Venetian coastal cities and islands – Candia in Crete, Lepanto on the Gulf of Patras, the island of Aegina and those of Skiros, Skopelos and Skiathos, which had recently placed themselves under the Republic's protection – were all ordered to strengthen their local defences. At home, the nineteen galleys then under construction in the Arsenal were deemed hopelessly insufficient to meet the new danger, and additional funds were voted for the building of fifty more.

Marcello soon found, as many another ambassador was to find after him, that Mehmet was a hard bargainer. It was only the following spring, after the best part of a year's negotiation, that an agreement was concluded. The remaining ships and prisoners were released and the Venetian colony allowed back under its own *bailo* as before; no longer, however, would it enjoy those territorial and commercial concessions on which its former power and prosperity had depended. From this moment the Latin presence in the East began its rapid decline.

One more question remains: to what extent, if any, can Venice be blamed for the fall of Constantinople? Despite the accusations of certain contemporary writers she cannot, obviously, be said to have borne any direct responsibility. Her response may have been slow, but no other power acted any faster; Pope Nicholas V, for example, who had decided to finance five more Venetian galleys at the expense of the Holy See, did not even inform the Senate of his intentions till 5 June, by which date the city had already been in Turkish hands for a week. She may have been half-hearted, but few other Christian nations had lifted a finger to save the dying Empire. Single-handed as she virtually was, the best Venice could have done – even if her ships had arrived in time – was to have enabled Constantinople to hold out another week or two, thus prolonging the agony; and even this is questionable, since the Turkish fleet in the Marmara might well have prevented their reaching the city at all. Besides, against the dilatoriness of the Senate must be weighed the heroism of the Venetians and Cretans who fought to the end, and for the most part died, on the shattered walls – including no fewer than sixty-eight patricians, many of whom bore the oldest and most distinguished names in Venetian history: six Contarini, three Balbi, two Barbaro, two Morosini, two Mocenigo, five Trevisan.[1]

In the wider, historical perspective, however, Venice can hardly hold herself guiltless. The Byzantine Empire had been slowly dying for two and a half centuries by the time Mehmet inflicted the *coup de grâce*. The real death-blow had been struck not in 1453 but in 1205, when the Latin armies of the Fourth Crusade had ravaged and plundered their way through Constantinople and prepared the way for the pathetic succession of Frankish pseudo-Emperors who for the next sixty years had bled the city and the Empire white. For this tragedy, from which Byzantium had rallied but never recovered, the Venetians were primarily responsible. Theirs were the ships, theirs the initiative, the leadership and the driving force. Theirs too was most of the profit and much of the plunder; and theirs, at the time of the final catastrophe, must be the blame.

---

1. Nicolò Barbaro, one of their number, gives the complete list (*Giornale*, pp. 16–18).

25

The Two Foscari

[1453–1457]

There's the ducal ring,
And there's the ducal diadem. And so
The Adriatic's free to wed another.

Byron, *The Two Foscari*

When Constantinople fell to the army of Sultan Mehmet in 1453, Francesco
Foscari had already occupied the ducal throne of Venice for thirty years,
longer than any Doge had ever reigned before him. Just as the dying
Tommaso Mocenigo had predicted, those years had been marked by almost
continuous warfare – warfare which had admittedly extended the frontiers
of the Republic half-way across North Italy but had virtually emptied the
Treasury in the process. Prices were soaring; several banks had failed; many
of the great mercantile houses were on the point of collapse; Foscari's own
father-in-law, Andrea Priuli, was one of those declared bankrupt, admitting debts amounting to 24,000 ducats.

The Doge himself seems to have made little effort to curb expenditure,
either public or private. The state reception he had accorded to the Byzantine Emperor in 1438 had astonished even the Venetians, for whom lavish
displays were regular and frequent occurrences; and the festivities attendant on the wedding, three years later, of his only surviving son, Jacopo,
to Lucrezia Contarini were more extravagant still. Jacopo was one of the
leaders of the *Compagnia della Calza*, the recently formed society of young
bloods of the town which took its name from the brilliant parti-coloured
hose worn by its members, and whose constitution included special rules
for celebrating their marriages. On this occasion the bride's own brother
has described how he and his fellow-Companions, mantled in crimson
velvet with silver brocade and mounted on horses similarly caparisoned,
each attended by six liveried grooms as well as sundry attendants and men-
at-arms, rode in procession 250 strong to the Contarini palace in S. Barnabà, crossing the Grand Canal on a bridge of boats thrown across from
S. Samuele. The wedding mass was followed by a superb banquet, after
which the bridal pair, attended by 150 ladies and a company of musicians,
boarded the *Bucintoro* and were rowed in state to the palace of Francesco

Sforza, on whom they paid a formal call. They returned to S. Barnabà in time to open the dancing, which continued far into the night. Even then the celebrations were only just getting under way; the public holiday continued for several days, days given over to a wild succession of balls, masques, regattas, tournaments with jousting in the Piazza and all those other joyful manifestations that left such an indelible impression on foreign visitors to Venice.

Through it all, Doge Foscari's popularity remained undimmed. He continued, as he always had, to reflect the prevailing mood of his subjects, who – on the whole rightly – never thought of blaming him for the economic ills of the Republic any more than for his *penchant* for ostentatious display. But no man could be Doge of Venice for thirty years without making enemies, and it is the enemies of Francesco Foscari who have been accused of bringing him, when he was already over seventy years old, to his ultimate destruction.

Whether they actually did so is another matter. It is true that the allegation of sharp practice on the part of Foscari's own adherents at the time of his election may not have been altogether forgotten – least of all by the family of Pietro Loredan, whom he had so surprisingly defeated in the final ballot. In view of the tortuousness of Venetian electoral procedure, however, this was something for which Foscari could not be held personally responsible. It is also true that, thanks to one or two other subsequent incidents – among them an unhappy betrothal which, on being abruptly broken off, had aggravated the very breach it was intended to heal – relations between the houses of Foscari and Loredan had by the time of Jacopo's marriage reached a stage not far short of open vendetta. We are therefore entitled to assume that when at the beginning of 1445 Jacopo – now heavily in debt – was accused of accepting bribes as the price of his influence in the distribution of lucrative public offices, the news was received in the Loredan family with something less than unmixed dismay. But despite the fact that Pietro Loredan's close kinsman, Francesco, chanced at this moment to be one of the three *Capi* of the Council of Ten, there is no indication – at least at this point in Jacopo's career – that the course of justice ran unfairly against him. It is hard to see how it could have.

The Council's first action was to call for a supplementary *zonta* of ten members which, with the customary inclusion of the ducal Signoria and the three *Avogadori di Comun*, brought its numbers up to twenty-nine. (The Doge himself, in view of the special circumstances prevailing, was requested to absent himself from the session.) It then called for Jacopo's immediate arrest; only when he was discovered to have already fled the city did it agree to proceed without him. Interrogation of his servants brought to light several files containing irrefutable evidence of his guilt. Loredan now proposed that the investigating tribunal should be doubled and the witnesses put to the torture – in the hope, perhaps, of finding further grounds for prosecution – but he was overruled. Jacopo Foscari was sentenced to be banished for life to the colony of Modone in the Peloponnese, lesser penalties being imposed on his servants and others found to have been implicated. Neither then nor later was there any suggestion that the Doge himself had been a party to his son's misdoings, or even aware of them.

The sentence was not unduly harsh. At least by the standards of the day, young Foscari had received no more than he deserved. When, after two months, he had still made no move to present himself before the Governor of Modone, his property and goods were confiscated, but even this was no more than he might have expected under the circumstances. Two years later, by which time he had fallen seriously ill, he received still further proof of the Council's clemency when, after a moving appeal by his father, it cancelled his sentence altogether. In the autumn of 1447, 'considering the need in these troubled times that our ruler should be free of care and anxiety for the greater service of the Republic, a condition at present denied him by the knowledge that his son lies sick in body and mind; and considering also the customary humanity of this our government and the meritoriousness of this our Doge', Jacopo Foscari was allowed to return to Venice.

It seemed now as if old Francesco might have been allowed to live out his few remaining years in peace, and so indeed he probably would had not a distinguished senator, one Ermolao Donà, been struck down by an unknown assailant as he was on his way home from the Ducal Palace on 5 November 1450, to die of his wounds two days later. For several weeks, during which various suspects were arrested, interrogated and released, no suspicion fell on Jacopo Foscari; then, in the January following, a denunciation was slipped into one of the *bocche di leone*[1] accusing him of the murder. He was seized and, on this occasion, brought personally to trial.

The evidence against him was of the slightest. It was pointed out that Ermolao Donà had been one of the three *Capi* of the Ten at the time of his former sentence, and that revenge could therefore have been a possible motive; there was also the not very significant fact that a member of his

---

1. Literally, 'the Lions' Mouths': boxes placed at various places around the city into which written denunciations or accusations could be slipped. These notes were passed to the Council of Ten, who were, however, bound to ignore them if they were not signed and to act upon them only after a thorough investigation of the charges made.

household had been seen loitering around the gates of the Palace on the evening in question. Otherwise, nothing. Andrea Donà, who had been at his brother's bedside for the two days before he expired, testified that Ermolao had forgiven his unknown attacker and that he had said nothing that could possibly incriminate Jacopo. The accused himself could not be induced to admit, even under torture, that he was in any way involved. None the less he was pronounced guilty and sentenced once more to life-long exile, this time in Crete.

It must be admitted that, where this second trial is concerned, the Council of Ten moved in a somewhat mysterious way; but it remains almost impossible to attribute its actions to malice on the part of the family of Loredan – or indeed of anyone else. In the first place, there were at that moment no Loredans on the Council, and only one in the *zonta* which had as usual been summoned for the occasion. In the second, although the conviction was seemingly unjustified by the evidence, the penalty decreed was remarkably light for a charge of murder. One is tempted to conclude that Jacopo had by this time shown himself to be an inveterate troublemaker and that the Ten, regretting its former clemency, had simply taken advantage of the new opportunity to rid the state of a perennial embarrassment once and for all.

This was not, however, so easy. In the summer of 1456 the Ten received information that Jacopo Foscari had entered into secret correspondence with Mehmet II, in an effort to persuade the Sultan to send a Turkish ship in which he could escape from his Cretan exile. A motion that 'in consideration of his foolishness and the remoteness of his place of banishment' he might be let off with a severe reprimand by the Governor was rejected. Jacopo was brought back to Venice and, arriving on 21 July, was immediately arraigned before the Council. This time there was no need for torture; he confessed without hesitation that the charges were true. By now the Ten numbered once again a Loredan among its *Capi*, and it was he, perhaps significantly, who called for Jacopo's execution between the twin columns on the Piazzetta; his proposal, however, received only seven votes. The overwhelming majority – including yet another Loredan, Lorenzo – voted to send him back to Crete, with a year's imprisonment on his arrival and a solemn warning that any further intrigues with foreign powers would be paid for with his life.

Pending his departure Jacopo, pale and obviously ill, was allowed a visit from his family. An eye-witness to this last meeting, his kinsman Giorgio Dolfin, has told – in a manuscript that still survives in the Marciana Library – how the young man tearfully implored his father to use his influence to enable him to return to his home and family, and how the Doge sternly admonished him 'to obey the Republic's command, and seek nothing more'. Only after his son had been led away to his cell did the old man break down and, with a cry of 'O pietà grande!', fall back, sobbing, in his chair. The two were never to meet again. Jacopo returned to Crete, whence, some six months later, word was brought to Venice that he was dead.

Francesco Foscari had loved his son, in spite of everything, and this final blow was more than he could bear. From that moment he went into a decline, showing no further interest in government business, refusing even to attend meetings of the Senate and the Council as he was constitutionally required to do. For well over six months this state of affairs was allowed to continue – in the hope, presumably, that the Doge would recover sufficiently to fulfil at least his more important duties; but in October 1457 the Council decided that it could wait no longer. A delegation consisting of the Signoria and the three *Capi* of the Ten called on the Doge and requested him, gently and respectfully, 'as a good prince and true father of his country', to abdicate his throne.

On two occasions in the past Foscari had made determined efforts to resign and had been denied permission to do so. This time, however, it was he who refused. Perhaps he still resented the Ten's treatment of his son and held them responsible for his death; perhaps he was angered by the fact that the Council had tactlessly chosen as its spokesman that same Jacopo Loredan who, while serving a previous term as *Capo*, had been instrumental in renewing the sentence of exile. (He is unlikely to have known that Loredan had first, unsuccessfully, proposed one of execution.) Perhaps it was simply his age – he was by now eighty-four – combined with the tribulations he had endured, that had made him querulous. His reply, at all events, showed that he was by no means senile. Coldly, he pointed out that the Ten had no constitutional power to call for his resignation. Matters of such importance, as the law clearly laid down, depended on a majority decision of the Great Council, supported by the six members of the Signoria. Were he to receive a request from the proper quarter, he would naturally give it due consideration. Till then, he was staying where he was.

There is no doubt that he was technically right; but the Ten were not to be gainsaid. For reasons, one suspects, of pride as much as anything else, they made no effort to refer the question to the Great Council. Instead, in a still more flagrant breach of the constitution, they returned to Foscari with an ultimatum. Either he would resign at once and be out of the Palace within a week, in which case he would receive an annual pension of 1,500 ducats for life with full ducal honours, or he would be forcibly removed and all his property confiscated. The Doge had no longer the strength to resist. His ring of office was slipped from his finger and ceremonially broken; the *corno* was removed from his head. Giorgio Dolfin, once again an eye-witness, tells us that as the delegation was leaving the old man noticed in one of its members a look of affectionate compassion and, learning that he was the son of an old friend, murmured to him 'Tell your father that I should like him to come and visit me; we will go in a boat together and visit the monasteries.'

When he left the Palace the next morning, however, he had recovered something of his former spirit. His brother Marco suggested that he might prefer to take the small covered stair that led directly to the side door where his boat was waiting. 'No,' he replied, 'I shall descend by the same stairs as those by which I entered to assume the Dogeship.' So he did, before being rowed to the great house on the first bend of the Grand Canal that he had built and that still bears his name.

A week later his successor, Pasquale Malipiero, was attending the All Saints' Day Mass in St Mark's when word was brought to him that Francesco Foscari was dead. Dolfin writes of how the Signoria exchanged glances, 'knowing full well that it was they who had so shortened his life'; and indeed there could be little doubt that he had died of a broken heart. The feeling of guilt seems to have been general, and probably does much to explain the splendour of the state funeral which followed. Foscari's widow protested bitterly; it was a little late now, she claimed, for the Republic to seek to make amends for the wrongs it had done to one of its most distinguished and devoted servants. But her objections went unheeded. On Thursday, 3 November, the body lay in state in the Hall of the *Signori di Notte*, just inside the lower arcade of the Palace, in full ducal regalia – robes of gold brocade, sword, spurs, the *corno* back once more on the head. Thence it was carried by the traditional party of workers from the Arsenal, beneath a golden umbrella, through the Merceria and over the wooden Rialto bridge to the Frari. Among the twenty pallbearers marched Malipiero, dressed as a simple senator. The implication could hardly be missed: Foscari had died a Doge.

This fiction – for fiction it was – is maintained in his tomb, which occupies a place of honour on the wall immediately to the right of the High Altar. It deserves close inspection, first as an example of the curious transitional stage between Gothic and Renaissance and secondly since it was later to provoke Ruskin to one of his most enjoyable diatribes;[1] but a far worthier monument to Francesco Foscari is surely the west front of the Doges' Palace – that giving on to the Piazzetta – which he continued from the seventh column from the southern end up to the corner of the Basilica and which he glorified with a new formal entrance into the inner courtyard: the *Porta della Carta*.

Whatever the defects of the Frari tomb, the *Porta della Carta* is a masterpiece. There can be no more vivid expression of the spirit of Venice in her late Gothic splendour, captured just as the last of the Middle Ages was passing away; and since that period coincides precisely with the reign of Francesco Foscari, it is only fitting that this tremendous portico should carry at first-floor level a life-size statue of the Doge himself, kneeling before the winged lion of St Mark.[2] The constant warfare, the empty coffers, the personal sadness that clouded the last few years of his reign, the humiliation that marked its end – all this is forgotten. What are remembered are the triumphs: the enemies brought low, the frontiers extended, the galleys and merchantmen half-way across the world, the magnificence, the colour, the parade. This was the time when the whole Palace was given its diapered dressing of pink and white marble – one of the most inspired ideas in the history of architectural decoration; when Guariento was completing his huge 'Paradise' – now, alas, destroyed – on the wall of the new *Sala del Maggior Consiglio*; when, even before Constantinople finally fell, refugees from all over the crumbling Empire were settling in Venice, recognizing her as the most Byzantine city in the West, and bringing with them their libraries, their works of art, and a new spirit of learning and scholarship. (The most distinguished of all the immigrants, Cardinal Bessarion, who as Orthodox Archbishop of Nicaea had accompanied his Emperor to the Councils of Ferrara and Florence and had then remained

1. The inspection should ideally be carried out with Vol. III of *The Stones of Venice* in hand, open at Chapter II, Section 71: 'We shall find that the perfect Renaissance is at least pure in its insipidity, and subtle in its vice; but this monument is remarkable as showing the refuse of one style encumbering the embryo of another, and all the principles of life entangled either in the swaddling clothes or the shroud.' And so on for three pages. The actual portrait pleases Ruskin even less: 'A huge, gross, bony clown's face, with the peculiar sodden and sensual cunning in it which is seen so often in the countenances of the worst Romanist priests; a face part of iron and part of clay ...' He blames, however, the sculptor rather than the subject.

2. The existing group is an excellent late nineteenth-century copy, the original having been destroyed by French troops in 1797. Fortunately, however, the original portrait head of Foscari (by Bartolomeo Bon) has survived and can be seen in the sculpture museum of the Palace. The entire *Porta della Carta* has recently been cleaned and restored by the British Venice in Peril Fund, thanks to a munificent donation by Mr and Mrs T. A. D. Sainsbury.

in Italy to become a Prince of the Roman Church and one of the greatest ecclesiastics of his age, was soon to donate his own outstanding collection of books to Venice, where it became the nucleus of the Marciana Library.) Already the old church of S. Biagio had been given over to the Greek community – they were to transfer to the newly built S. Giorgio dei Greci only in the following century – adding still further to the city's reputation for religious tolerance, unrivalled in the civilized world.

In other respects, it must be admitted, Venice lagged behind badly. She could boast no writers comparable to Dante, Petrarch or Boccaccio, no humanists of the calibre of Leonardo Bruni, Leon Battista Alberti or Pico della Mirandola. Even in those arts in which she already excelled – painting, sculpture and, above all, secular Gothic architecture – her output in the first half of the fifteenth century must have seemed decidedly quaint to sophisticated young Florentines brought up on the works of Masaccio or Brunelleschi, Ghiberti or Donatello. In the great cities of Tuscany, the Renaissance was now approaching the fullness of its flower; in Venice it had hardly begun; such few signs of it as were yet perceptible were tentative and, for the most part, not entirely successful.

There were several reasons for this uncharacteristic sluggishness. The Venetians were not thinkers: they were doers. Empiricists *par excellence*, they mistrusted abstract theories. Their genius was essentially visual and tactile – and, later, musical; it appealed to the senses rather than to the intellect. Artists, craftsmen and merchants seldom make great poets or philosophers. Towards the end of the century they were to become pre-eminent in the new art of printing, and in the related skill of book-binding; throughout their history, however, they always remained better at producing books than at actually writing them.

Venice, too, had from her earliest beginnings shown a far greater affinity to the civilization of Byzantium than to that of the Italian mainland; and the new wave of Byzantine influences may at first have struck more sympathetic chords than the humanist ideas that had so dramatically affected the cultural development of Lombardy and Tuscany. But Byzantium was dying; and, soon enough, the seeds of the Renaissance would take root in Venice as everywhere else, yielding in their turn no less rich a harvest.

26

The Ottoman Menace

[1457–1481]

The call 'Go!' has been unheeded; perhaps the call 'Come!' will evoke a heartier response . . .

We do not intend to fight. We shall imitate Moses, who prayed on the mountain while Israel fought against Amalek. On the ship's prow or on the mountain top, we shall entreat of our Lord Jesus Christ victory for our soldiers in battle . . .

In the service of God we leave our See and the Roman Church, committing our grey hairs and our feeble body to his mercy. He will not forget us, and if he does not grant us safe return he will receive us into heaven and will preserve his See of Rome and his bride the Church in safety.

Pius II to his Cardinals, 1463

When, late in the evening of 30 October 1457, Pasquale Malipiero first assumed the insignia of his office and was borne in procession around the Piazza to the plaudits of his new subjects, he became the titular sovereign of the most splendid state of Europe. The city was dazzling in its magnificence; trade was once again beginning to flourish, and the meticulously kept exchequer accounts looked healthier than they had for many years past. Venetian political stability, never seriously shaken by the misfortunes of the two Foscari, continued to be the envy of the civilized world. A formidable land empire now stretched westward to the borders of Milan and northward to the Alps. In the Eastern Mediterranean the situation was less clear, but certainly gave no immediate cause for alarm. Constantinople had fallen four and a half years before; even before its capture, however, the Republic had concluded a treaty with the Sultan, with whom she was still on the friendliest of terms. Freedom of trade had been guaranteed for her merchants, subject to a duty of only two per cent; her consular officials had been given willing permission to reside on Turkish soil; in short, there seemed no reason why her commercial activities in the East should continue any less prosperously than they had under the last of the Palaeologi.

Had Mehmet II only been content to call a halt to his army's advance and consolidate his great conquest, such optimism might not have been misplaced. But he was not content. Still only twenty-five, he burned with a fierce missionary zeal and believed himself to be under divine guidance to spread the word of the Prophet across Europe and beyond. Subconsciously, too, he probably felt that to abandon the irresistible forward momentum that had already brought him such rewards would be fatal.[1] Offers of submission by the minor Christian princes most immediately threatened, proposing to pay tribute to him as his vassals, were rejected out of hand. He was interested in direct rule, nothing less. By the time the brief and unmemorable reign of Pasquale Malipiero came to an end in 1462,[2] the young Sultan had eliminated the last vestiges of independent Serbia – though the vital bridgehead of Belgrade had been saved through the military genius of the Hungarian warlord John Hunyadi and was to remain for another half-century in Christian hands – seized the principal islands of the northern Aegean, and then swept southward to drive out first the Florentine Dukes of Athens and then the two feckless brothers of the last Byzantine Emperor, Thomas and Demetrius Palaeologus, who had set themselves up as Despots in the Peloponnese. Two years later he was master of Bosnia, and the Venetian cities of the Dalmatian coast found themselves under serious and imminent threat.

But it was not only they who looked towards the Rialto for their salvation. Alarm was rapidly spreading across Western Europe; Venice, as the strongest naval power in Christendom and that which, through her geographical position alone, would inevitably constitute the front line in any offensive, was the obvious quarter to which to turn. Indeed, there was no alternative. Genoa, having lost to Mehmet first her colony of Galata and then her trading posts around the Black Sea – which the Sultan had now converted into an Ottoman lake – had effectively given up the struggle; Hungary, finding herself without any real leader after the death of Hunyadi, had grown feeble and demoralized; the Empire of the West seemed to be losing territory almost as fast as its new rival in the East was acquiring it.

To some extent, Venice had deliberately cultivated her role as protector of the weak against the Turkish tide, and a very successful policy she had found it. It had led to her peaceful acquisition of Corfu as early as 1356, of Nauplia and Argos in 1388, and in 1423 of Salonica, which she had been invited to take over by the local Greek despot; and although this last annexation had proved somewhat less happy – it had led two years later to a desultory war, which ended in 1430 with the fall of the city to the Sultan

---

1. If so, he was right. As subsequent Ottoman history was to show, it was precisely at the moment that its advance was halted that the decline of the Turkish Empire began.

2. His tomb, by Pietro Lombardo, will be found just outside the sacristy in SS. Giovanni e Paolo.

– she could still point to a number of profitable Aegean colonies which had voluntarily sought her protection. But, as the Turks grew stronger and more threatening, she in her turn had begun to draw in her horns. Twice in the last years of Francesco Foscari she had refused to be involved in any further hostilities; and Pasquale Malipiero had continued his predecessor's policy.[1] When in September 1459 Pope Pius II had summoned a congress of the Christian powers at Mantua to organize a European Crusade, the Republic had found it necessary to remind those present of their deplorable performance during the siege of Constantinople six years before; this time it agreed to act only if all the princes of Christendom were unanimously prepared to participate, actively and whole-heartedly, according to their respective capacities, in the enterprise – a condition which, as the marked lack of enthusiasm on the part of the delegates once again clearly indicated, was unlikely to be fulfilled. The Pope had left Mantua disappointed and disillusioned; but he had never renounced his Crusading dream. In 1462 he described to some of his Cardinals the sleepless nights he had spent, enraged by his powerlessness yet ashamed of his inactivity; then, in the following year, he publicly announced his new plan – for an expedition which despite his frailty[2] he would lead himself, jointly with the Duke of Burgundy, and for which Venice would provide a fleet.

By the time the papal invitation to join the new alliance reached the Signoria, Pasquale Malipiero was dead. He had been succeeded by a considerably more forceful character, Cristoforo Moro. Moro was already an old man, but he burned with a Crusading fervour equalled only, perhaps, by that of Pius himself; and by the stream of letters he addressed to the Pope encouraging him to action he had made his sympathies clear. These were by now shared by the large majority of his compatriots. The speed and extent of the Ottoman advance over the past decade had caused a dramatic swing in Venetian public opinion. Already the Great Council had approved an anti-Turkish alliance with Hungary; now it gave its enthusiastic blessing to the Pope's proposals. Much encouraged, Pius wrote again to Doge Moro, suggesting that he might personally join the Duke of Burgundy and himself at the head of the Crusade. 'In this event,' he wrote, 'not Greece

---

1. Her pacific inclinations, however, had not prevented the Council of Ten from approving, in 1456, a proposal for the assassination of the Sultan by a Jew from Modone in return for a rich reward payable immediately after the deed. It is also significant that, when the great gates of the Arsenal were built in 1460, the winged lion of St Mark surmounting them was given a *closed* book to hold in his paw, its usual inscription (*Pax tibi Marce* ...) being presumably considered inappropriate to the time and the place.

2. He was virtually unable to walk – a disability usually attributed to gout, but which was in fact almost certainly the result of a frostbitten pilgrimage, barefoot and in the depths of winter, from Dunbar to the shrine of the Virgin at Whitekirk while on a diplomatic mission to Scotland in 1435.

only, but Asia and all the East would be stricken with terror . . . we should be three old men, and God rejoices in trinity. Our trinity would be aided by the Trinity of Heaven, and our foes would be trampled beneath our feet.' The Council agreed – this time by a vote of 1,607 votes to eleven, with sixteen abstentions – that the Doge could indeed go; and when a few days later Moro had second thoughts about his participation, his attempts to excuse himself were angrily rejected, since, as one of the more tactless councillors put it, 'the honour and welfare of our land are dearer to us than your person.'

But the support of Venice was the last piece of good news that Pius was to receive. It had been agreed that the expedition should set off from Ancona in the summer of 1464. Early that year the acquisition of Genoa by the Duke of Milan seriously upset the balance of power in Italy, caused alarm throughout the peninsula and made it virtually certain that no mainland power would contribute forces to the Crusade; at Easter the Duke of Burgundy sent word that he could not leave for another year at the earliest. In Rome meanwhile money was short and preparations had hardly begun; the Burgundian envoys there reported that 'the dispositions were the poorest that they had ever seen, and only two galleys were ready.' The Pope, for all his enthusiasm, was devoid of any organizational ability. He had expected a mighty influx of armed and experienced soldiers of fortune, knights and men-at-arms, from all over Europe, prepared to serve for six months and perhaps longer at their own expense. Instead he found, as so many would-be Crusaders had found before him, a penniless, footloose and undisciplined rabble trickling into the city, expecting to be armed, fed and transported at no cost to themselves. Venice, who never had any time for these drifting armies of the feckless, simply refused them entry, leaving them to return home as best they could or to die of hunger or pestilence on the way; but in Rome and Ancona their presence proved a sore embarrassment.

To add still further to his misfortunes, the Pope's health was now deteriorating fast. His resolution, however, remained firm; and as if aware of the shortness of the time left to him, he resolved to brook no further delays. On 18 June he took the Cross in St Peter's and set off, first by barge up the Tiber and subsequently by litter across the Apennines. As he approached, he was passed by straggling groups of dejected Crusaders who, having reached Ancona only to find no transport available for them, were returning sadly to their homes. The sight was more than he could bear; his doctors, seeing his distress, told him that the wind was bad for him and closed the curtains of his litter. When at last the cortege reached its destination, just a month after its departure from Rome, it must have been clear to all but Pius himself that his Crusade would never be realized. The two papal galleys lay at anchor in the harbour; of the promised Venetian ships there was still no sign. Such few knights who had the money to support themselves and nothing better to do had remained in the city, waiting for something to happen; but the majority had already given up hope and gone home.

At last, on 12 August, the Venetian fleet of twenty-four sail appeared on the horizon; the Pope, who had taken up residence in the Bishop's Palace on the hill that dominates the town, next to the Cathedral of St Cyriac, had himself carried to the window from which he could watch them as they entered the harbour. He had a high fever and was by now sinking fast. The next day, when Cristoforo Moro arrived at the Palace to pay a courtesy call, he was informed that His Holiness was too ill to receive him. His first reaction was to assume that Pius had no real intention of keeping his promise by personally leading the Crusade, and that he was merely feigning sickness to avoid his obligation. Soon, however, his own doctor returned from the papal bedside with the news that the Pope was not just sick but at the point of death; and on the following day, 14 August, a delegation of cardinals came on board to announce that he was dead. Two days later the Doge sailed back with his fleet to Venice. Before it had even set out, the Crusade was over.

It was just as well. Pinturicchio's vision, on the wall of the Piccolomini Library in Siena, of Pius II at the outset of the Crusade – Ancona spread out behind him crowned by its hill-top Cathedral, the Christian fleet massing in the harbour and the roadstead, Doge Moro kneeling at his feet – has tended to obscure the truth. The modern historian Roberto Cessi comes a good deal nearer the mark when he describes the whole venture as a *miserabile parodia piccolominiana*. The Pope had died in the nick of time. Had he not done so, had the expedition set off to the East with or without him, it would have been crushed without mercy, bringing nothing but discredit, even dishonour, to the Christian cause. All this, by now, the Venetians had understood. The huge but inconclusive councils, the endless delays, the pious aspirations and expressions of intent unsupported by any effective preparations, the interminable sermons to which they had been subjected by Cardinal Bessarion as papal legate – these were no ways to halt the Turkish advance. If Mehmet the Conqueror were to be stopped, it would not be by a Crusade; it would be by an all-out, no-nonsense, secular war.

Unfortunately the war on which Venice had embarked, in alliance with Hungary, after the unprovoked seizure of Argos in 1462 was proving little more successful. At Corinth a gigantic defensive wall across the isthmus, six miles long, twelve feet high, with a double ditch and 136 towers, on which the Venetian Captain-General, Alvise Loredan, had employed 30,000 men that autumn, had been smashed like matchwood a few months later. In the immediately following years there were no real disasters; on occasion Loredan's successors – Orsato Giustinian, Giacomo Loredan and Vettor Cappello – and the commander of the land forces, Sigismondo Malatesta of Rimini, might register one or two minor conquests of islands or of coastal or mountain strongholds; but with the exception of Malvasia (Monemvasia), which placed itself under Venetian protection after the flight of its despot Thomas Palaeologus and subsequently became an important naval base for the Republic, no permanent gains were made. The story of these years is an unedifying saga of poor co-ordination between allies and jealousy between commanders; of orders not received and opportunities missed; of misunderstandings, recriminations and reproaches. Even a clumsy attempt at peace came to nothing, owing in large measure to the machinations of Florentine and Genoese agents in Constantinople, ever anxious to prolong the spectacle of their old enemy wasting her substance and draining her resources to no avail. One figure only stands out heroically above the rest, and he was neither a Hungarian nor a Venetian. For a quarter of a century already the Albanian chieftain Skanderbeg – 'Champion of Christ', as the Pope himself had dubbed him – had fought fiercely to protect his wild and mountainous homeland from the Sultan's clutches; he was still doing so with considerable success when, in 1467, he died, leaving the vital fortress of Croia to Venice.

After Skanderbeg's death the prospects looked bleaker than ever. Mehmet had fortunately turned his attentions eastward, affording the Republic some temporary breathing-space; but in the summer of 1469 disturbing reports reached the Rialto from Venetian agents in Constantinople and elsewhere. The Sultan had clearly grown impatient with this desultory and indecisive skirmishing. He had resolved to eliminate the Venetian Empire once and for all, much as he had eliminated the Byzantine; and to this end he was planning an immense combined operation, involving the war fleet which he had steadily been building up in the eighteen years since his accession and an army 80,000 strong with himself at its head. The fleet was already massed at Gallipoli, whence it was to sail westward through the Aegean; the army was gathering at Adrianople, after which it would march through Thrace and then south into Macedonia and Thessaly. The two would meet at their first major objective – the Venetian colony of Negropont.

After six years, it looked as if the crisis was approaching at last. Those years, ineffectual as they had been, had cost the Republic much – in ships and manpower, in money and morale. Venice was tired. She was also disillusioned. By now, surely, it must be evident that the Turkish threat was directed not simply against her but against all Christendom; yet the other Christian powers seemed utterly oblivious of the danger, content to let her fight their battles for them and apparently confident of her ability to do so. She did not share their confidence. None the less, fight she must. Wearily, yet with all the energy she could muster, she prepared to face the coming onslaught. The government immediately announced a new forced loan yielding 200,000 ducats – with which, in less than a month, it was able to arm twenty-nine galleys and a considerable number of lighter vessels. Over a thousand labourers set to work on a new extension of the Arsenal, almost doubling it in size. Meanwhile the mainland cities were called upon for more funds and provisions: Padua furnished 3,000 ducats and 5,000 bushels of biscuit, Gerona 2,000 ducats and 5,000 bushels, Brescia 4,000 ducats and 8,000 bushels. Ambassadors hastened to Rome with a desperate appeal to the Pope, the Venetian Pietro Barbo, who had succeeded Pius under the name of Paul II: Venice, they pleaded, had done all she could, providing men, ships and money, draining herself of her very life's blood. But it was still not enough. Christendom must come to her support – with speed, and in strength. The Pope replied by declaring a plenary indulgence for all those who took arms against the Turk or financed a substitute for four months. There was little else that he could do. Europe still refused to lift a finger. Venice, with her Empire, stood alone.

   ... At first I estimated it at 300 sail; now I would put it at 400. The whole sea appeared like a forest. This sounds incredible, but it was indeed a sight stupendous to behold ... They row magnificently, with a fast stroke; true, their galleys are less good than ours under the oar, but under sail and in every other respect they are superior, and I believe they carry larger crews. There is a vanguard and a rearguard; some fifty galleys to a squadron, each galley with its own attendant galleot. I swear that from the first ship to the last the fleet measures above six miles in length. To confront so mighty a force, I consider that we shall need not less than a hundred good galleys, and even then I would not be sure of the outcome ...

Now must our Signory show its strength. Setting aside all else, it must send at once all the ships, men, provisions and money it can raise. Otherwise Negropont is in grave danger; and if Negropont falls, all our Eastern Empire, even including our neighbour Istria, will fall with it. For next year the Turk will be half as strong again, and emboldened by this year's success.

The much longer letter from which this extract is taken was written from

Corfu by a Venetian galley commander, Geronimo Longo, to his brothers in mid-June 1470.[1] Certainly, the Republic had done all it could. Though the Venetian fleet still fell far short of the strength that Longo had prescribed, its Captain-General, Nicolò Canal, was to have at his disposal by mid-July fifty-three galleys and eighteen smaller ships, with several others imminently expected from various quarters. Sailing up from Crete, he now took up his position off Skiathos, some ten miles from the northern end of the narrow strait that separates the island of Negropont from the mainland.

Negropont was originally the name given by Venice to the ancient Greek city of Chalcis – or Khalkis, as it is once again called today – on the island of Euboea; gradually, however, it had come to denote the whole island as well, by this time the largest and most important Venetian colony in the Aegean. It had fallen to the Republic in the general share-out following the Fourth Crusade, and after the return of the Greek Emperors to Constantinople in 1261 had become the seat of the Latin Patriarch of the East; soon, too, its size and strategic position had made it the administrative and judicial centre for all the Venetian colonies of the archipelago, the seat of the Governor – who enjoyed wide powers throughout the region – and the chief base for the Aegean fleet.

Geographically it was, and is, a curious place, since although unquestionably an island it has never really been thought of as one. What has happened, as a cursory glance at the map makes clear, is that the sea has gradually encroached from both ends up a narrow coastal valley, the two prongs of its advance ultimately meeting in the middle. But only just; for although for most of its length the strait separating it from the mainland averages some ten miles across, at the point on which the city stands that distance is suddenly reduced to less than fifty yards. Perhaps because so curious a formation makes it subject to a powerful and at moments intensely dramatic tidal bore, running at great speed no less than seven times a day in each direction, this strait, which is known as the Euripos, has since 411 B.C. been spanned at its narrowest point by a bridge – presumably that after which the Venetians named their colony.[2] They had further strengthened it with a tiny turreted fort, built on a rocky outcrop in midstream, so that the channel was effectively blocked to everything but its own tumultuous waters. The city itself was protected by its own formidable walls, heavily

1. The full text can be found in Malipiero, *Annali Veneti*, pp. 49–52.

2. There is even a tradition that Aristotle, 'infuriated by his failure to explain the mystery of the Euripos, drowned himself in it' (Jan Morris, *The Venetian Empire*, p. 57). He certainly died at Chalcis, though more probably from a disease of the digestive tract than from intellectual frustration.

garrisoned, copiously provisioned and ready to face a prolonged siege.

On 14 June the vanguard of the Turkish fleet entered the Euripos from the south and landed a small advance force on the island, just outside the city. Almost simultaneously, with a co-ordination that bore witness to his ever-meticulous planning, the Sultan himself arrived at the head of his land army, which he drew up on the mainland shore. Then, ignoring the existing bridge, his engineers began to construct a new one, on pontoons, a little further to the north. Six days later, the work was complete. Mehmet crossed over with half his army to begin his siege, leaving the other half to protect his rear and ensure his supply lines.

The Venetian garrison, ably assisted by the local citizenry, defended the city stoutly for three weeks, during which they withstood no fewer than five major assaults. But Mehmet's cannon – the same, probably, that had battered down the fortifications of Constantinople itself – were pounding remorselessly, day and night, into the same stretch of wall, and by early July it was clear that a major breach could not be long postponed. A message to this effect was somehow got through to the Captain-General. Nicolò Canal was a cautious man. After all Venice's efforts to provide him with a fleet he had still not budged from the northern end of the strait; even now he seems to have been reluctant to take action. But his captains eventually persuaded him, and at last he gave the order to advance down the channel towards the Turkish bridge and the beleaguered city.

There was a fresh following breeze. The tide too was in his favour. As the ships gathered speed there seemed no reason why they should not smash the Turkish pontoons – just as Hunyadi had done at Belgrade – cutting Mehmet's lines of communication; indeed it is hard to see what other purpose there could have been in the manoeuvre. And yet, at the last moment, Canal's courage failed him. In full view of the city he had come to deliver, and despite the exhortations of his captains, he gave the order to turn about and began to beat his way up the channel to safety.

In doing so he sealed the fate of Negropont. There could have been no clearer way of indicating to its defenders that they had been abandoned. They continued to resist, but their energies were now sapped by despair. On the following day, 12 July, the Sultan's army burst through the shattered walls. Even then the struggle was not quite over; the streets were barricaded with tree-trunks and barrels, and the Turks had to face not only a hail of tiles torn from the rooftops, but deluges of quicklime and boiling water poured from the upper windows. They took a savage revenge. Men, women and children alike were violated and massacred; by evening, few of the citizens of Negropont remained alive. The Governor, Paolo Erizzo, who had taken refuge in one of the towers, gave himself up only on the condition that he might keep his head; Mehmet, true to his promise, had his body severed at the waist instead.

The news of the capture of Negropont caused, as might have been expected, consternation in Venice. With the city taken, the whole chain of castles along the 120-mile length of the island was bound to follow. One of the biggest and broadest harbours of the Aegean was denied to Venetian shipping, and could henceforth be used as a springboard for further attacks on smaller, neighbouring colonies. Merchantmen plying between mainland Greece and the Dardanelles would in future have to beat their way to the south-west corner of the Peloponnese, where Modone and Corone were now the only two available colonies capable of handling their cargoes. The island colonies of the archipelago had been deprived at a stroke of their regional government, the one authority able to exercise some control over the ever-squabbling local rulers. Most serious of all was the effect on morale, all over the Eastern Mediterranean. If Negropont, brightest pearl in Venice's imperial crown, could be plucked from it so easily and so cruelly in a single month, what chance was there for the survival of the rest?

The Senate held an emergency session; on the Rialto, the merchants tremblingly computed their losses; along the Molo, crowds awaited the arrival of every ship that might bring news of casualties or survivors. The whole city went into mourning; a court of inquiry was instituted with a view to impeaching Nicolò Canal; meanwhile a new Captain-General, Pietro Mocenigo, was appointed to succeed him and ordered to send him back, in chains, to stand trial. Canal, we are told, submitted at once. 'I am here to obey,' he murmured; 'do with me as you please.' On 19 October, with his son and his secretary, he arrived in Venice and was at once cast into prison. At the trial that followed he was found guilty of all six charges laid against him, including those of having failed to defend Negropont against the initial Turkish offensive; of having retreated from the Turkish pontoon bridge at a moment when, with his fleet making fifteen knots down the channel, he could easily have smashed it; and of having allowed the enemy fleet to withdraw unopposed after the sack of the city. Men had been executed for less; it is surprising to learn that the only penalties exacted were banishment to Portogruaro, a mere thirty miles away, together with a fine of 500 ducats and the forfeiture of his Captain-General's salary and expenses.

Clearly the Senate, by whom the sentence was passed, had taken various extenuating circumstances into account. Canal had behind him nearly thirty years' devoted service to the state, mostly in a diplomatic rather than a military capacity; anyone could see that this highly cultivated doctor and senator was no man of action. The blame lay, at least in part, with those who had appointed him in the first place to a post for which he was in no way qualified. None the less, it was lucky for him that he had not been charged – as well he might have been – with betrayal of the state. In that event he would have appeared before the *Quarantia* or the Council of Ten, and his punishment, we can be sure, would have been very different. Soon afterwards, indeed, the Ten actually put on record their dissatisfaction with the sentence. Replying to the Pope, who had appealed on Canal's behalf, they wrote that his case had been dealt with 'not according to justice, but with pity and clemency, to the point where it might be thought that he had been found innocent; considering the misfortune which, through his fault, has befallen not only Venice but all the Christian world, his sentence is one of excessive leniency with which he can be well content.'

Yet it seems unlikely that Nicolò Canal found much contentment in his place of exile. Portogruaro remains a sad and featureless town today; in the fifteenth century it was probably little more than a cluster of nondescript houses on the road to Trieste. Living there alone with his disgrace and shame, an outcast from the city he loved, in the full knowledge that but for one ironical twist of fate he might have continued the rest of his life as one of its most distinguished and respected citizens, he must often have wished that his fellow-senators had shown him less leniency rather than more. In the event, death kept him waiting another thirteen years; when it came at last, in May 1483, it cannot have been entirely unwelcome.

Doge Cristoforo Moro died on 9 November 1471, and was buried beneath a fine tombstone in the chancel of the church of S. Giobbe, which he himself had founded.[1] The nine years of his dogeship had not been happy. From the first, the shadow of the Ottoman menace had hung over them like a thundercloud. He had had to share some of the humiliation of Pope Pius's ill-starred Crusade, and still more of the national shame after the Negropont disaster. Personally, he had never been popular. Small and ill-formed, his appearance further marred by a pronounced squint, he had a reputation for vindictiveness, hypocrisy and – despite his benefactions to the Church – avarice. It was also his misfortune, even though he was almost certainly not himself responsible for the decision, to have been the first doge in whose *promissione* the traditional formula describing the state as *Communis Venetiarum* was dropped in favour of the words *Dominium* or

1. His portrait, a contemporary work by a follower of the Bellini, hangs above the door of the sacristy.

Signoria. The last vestiges of true democratic government had disappeared, it is true, long before Cristoforo Moro was born; but it was only now that the name was changed to conform with reality, and the change did not pass unnoticed among the people.

Moro's successor, Nicolò Tron, must have seemed a remarkable contrast. A gigantic man with a coarse face and a stammer, he had made a considerable fortune as a merchant in Rhodes. His long beard, unfashionable at that period in Venice, was worn in memory of a beloved son killed at Negropont. His mourning did not prevent the usual lavish entertainments to celebrate his accession; neither, however, did these entertainments conceal the fact that Venice was once again on the verge of bankruptcy. Her struggle to contain the Turkish advance was costing her nearly a million and a quarter ducats a year; and it says much for the loyalty and patriotism of her subjects that no objections were raised to a decree obliging all the more highly paid state officials – up to and including the Doge himself – to accept drastic cuts in salary: one half for those on naval service, two thirds for those on land. For those not employed by the government, the wealth tax was increased by a further twenty per cent.

Thanks to such measures, Venice was able to continue the war. The loss of Negropont had served, temporarily at least, to arouse a few of the princes of Europe from their torpor – foremost among them the new Pope, Sixtus IV, who with King Ferdinand of Naples sent a fleet of galleys to join Pietro Mocenigo's fleet. In the summer of 1472, with eighty-five vessels now under his command (they included three sent by the Knights Hospitallers in Rhodes), Mocenigo created considerable havoc in Turkish waters, sacking Antalya, Smyrna, Halicarnassus and several other ports on the coast of Asia Minor. One of Ferdinand's captains even managed to fire Mehmet's naval arsenal at Gallipoli, though he later paid for it with his life.

The reports of these minor successes, though everyone knew that they could not significantly affect the course of the war, came as a much-needed tonic to Venetian morale, still badly bruised after the Negropont disaster. Even more beneficial – and of far greater strategic importance – was the Republic's triumph in Albania two years later, when, after a heroic defence of the key city of Scutari [1] by Antonio Loredan, the Turks were eventually obliged to raise the siege and withdraw from the region. By the time they did so, the inhabitants of Scutari were, almost literally, at their last gasp: the chroniclers tell of how, the moment the enemy had disappeared into the

---

1. Not, it need hardly be said, to be confused with the other, more famous Scutari across the Bosphorus from Constantinople, where Florence Nightingale nursed during the Crimean War.

mountains, virtually the entire populace rushed through the gates to slake its thirst in the Bojana river.

The war was not yet over, but a valuable remission had been won; and that November a joint statement by the governments of Venice, Florence and Milan reaffirmed the triple alliance made twenty years before, pledging themselves for the next quarter-century to preserve and defend the States of Italy against all foreign attacks and inviting the adherence of the King of Naples and the Pope.

Doge Tron died in 1473; and on 1 December 1474, less than a fortnight after the thanksgiving mass in the Basilica for the victory of Scutari, his successor, Nicolò Marcello, followed him to the grave.[1] By some fortunate chance, Marcello's death also coincided with the return to Venice of Pietro Mocenigo after more than four years as Captain-General – the longest period of unbroken command in Venetian naval history. Small wonder it was, in view of his brilliant record of successes, that he should have been elected to fill the vacant throne.

With the pause in hostilities against the Turks and the continuing success of Venetian policy in Cyprus – for which the new Doge himself could take much of the credit[2] – the condition of the Republic over which Pietro Mocenigo now assumed sovereignty was distinctly more favourable than it had been for some time. Despite the emergency measures taken four years before, state funds were still at a disturbingly low level, but soon after Mocenigo's accession they were dramatically replenished by a bequest from an unexpected source: the last and most celebrated of Venice's *condottieri*, Bartolomeo Colleoni.

Arguably, he was also the greatest. Abler and more loyal than Carmagnola, shrewder and more subtle than Gattamelata, he had served under them both in Lombardy. His misfortune was to have been born a generation later, and thus to have had rather less opportunity to make his mark as a military leader. Of his many campaigns up and down the peninsula, few were of lasting significance or are of much interest except to specialists. For this reason he would have earned himself little more than a footnote in this history had he not, on his death in October 1475 after a quarter of a century's service as commander of the Venetian land forces, bequeathed to

---

1. In conformity with that curious Venetian law which apparently required the splendour of a ducal tomb to vary in inverse ratio to the historical importance of its occupant, both Tron and Marcello have been endowed with very magnificent memorials indeed. Tron's, in the Frari just to the left of the High Altar, is described by Lorenzetti as 'the greatest carved work of the Renaissance in Venice'; Marcello's, on the north wall of SS. Giovanni e Paolo, by the same authority as 'perhaps the most perfect and balanced of the Lombardo art'.

2. See Chapter 27.

the Republic no less than 216,000 ducats in gold and silver and more than twice that sum in land and property of various kinds. One condition only did he make – that an equestrian statue should be erected in his memory in the Piazza of St Mark.

Here was a problem indeed. To the Venetians, the idea of a statue in the Piazza was unthinkable – a privilege that they had withheld even from the Evangelist himself. Colleoni had served them loyally, but like all professional *condottieri* he had served many other masters as well and had on occasion actually fought against the Republic. Born in Bergamo, he was not even a native of their city. On the other hand they could hardly turn down such a windfall at such a time. The solution they eventually hit upon was quintessentially Venetian. Since the Piazza was impossible, they would erect the statue in front of the *Scuola* of St Mark instead, in the square of SS. Giovanni e Paolo. No one can seriously have thought that Colleoni's shade would be appeased by such a monstrous piece of casuistry; and yet, as one gazes up, five hundred years later, at Verrocchio's masterpiece – the proudest, most superb equestrian statue ever wrought – it is hard to believe that their benefactor would not, somehow, have found it in his heart to forgive them.

At the beginning of January 1475 – nine months before Colleoni's bequest – the Venetians had received, through the somewhat unlikely channel of the Sultan's stepmother, a proposal to negotiate a peace. For two days and the best part of two nights they had debated the question. Many had opposed the whole idea, pointing out that the Turkoman ruler Uzun Hasan, Mehmet's chief rival and enemy to the East, was known to be about to launch a major offensive against the Sultan at any moment; that similar action was expected from the Hungarians and the Poles, who had recently formed an alliance for that specific purpose; and that the Pope was even now planning a new pan-Italian expedition. Doge Mocenigo knew better. Much of his active life had been spent fighting the Turks; from his own first-hand experience he could speak of their strength, their courage, their firepower and their almost limitless resources of men and materials. For thirteen years now Venice had stood against them, virtually alone. The effort had cost her countless ships, many of her best fighting seamen and several of her most valuable overseas possessions. The exchequer was empty; there was by now not even enough ready money for salaries, and groups of sailors had on more than one occasion staged demonstrations on the steps of the Palace itself, loudly demanding arrears of pay. To refuse to listen to the Turkish terms would be folly.

The voice of reason narrowly won the day, and emissaries were duly dispatched to Constantinople; but negotiations broke down in October. When Mocenigo died in February 1476 – worn out, it was unkindly suggested, by the attentions of the ten beautiful Turkish slave-girls he kept as concubines[1] – the war had begun again in earnest; and by the time his successor Andrea Vendramin, stricken by the plague, was laid to rest in his turn two and a half years later in the church of the Servi,[2] both the island of Lemnos and the Albanian fortress of Croia had fallen to the Turks, who were now once again besieging Scutari. Still more alarming, bands of mounted Turkish irregulars had overrun Friuli as far as the river Livenza, laying waste the countryside, burning and pillaging as they went, so near that from the top of the Campanile of St Mark the flames of the burning villages could be plainly seen.

There had been another development too, unconnected with the Turks but no less critical for the future of Italy. On Easter Day 1478, in the Cathedral of Florence, Lorenzo de' Medici and his brother Giuliano were attacked by assassins. Giuliano was killed outright; Lorenzo, who himself escaped by little short of a miracle, took swift and savage vengeance. He knew perfectly well that the plot had been jointly engineered by his enemies the Pazzi, by the Archbishop of Pisa and by the nephews of Pope Sixtus; he also knew that it enjoyed the secret support of the Pope himself. Not only did he have the assassins publicly executed; the Archbishop was hanged from the windows of the palace, and one of the papal nephews, the eighteen-year-old Cardinal Raffaele Riario, was flung into prison. Pope Sixtus, in a fury, excommunicated Lorenzo and placed Florence under an interdict; Venice and Milan supported Florence; Ferdinand of Naples rallied to the Pope; and within weeks the peninsula was once again at war.

Seen in the perspective of history, this war, which continued for less than two years, was of no more lasting importance than most other such internecine outbreaks of which the history of Italy is so depressingly full. It did, however, make it clear to all concerned, Europeans and Turks alike,

---

1. Pietro Lombardo has portrayed him on the west inside wall of SS. Giovanni e Paolo. Fully armed and decidedly bellicose, he stands upright on his sarcophagus in an attitude more appropriate to a triumphal arch than to a memorial tomb. A more godlessly typical example of Renaissance funerary sculpture could hardly be imagined.

2 When the Servi church was suppressed at the beginning of the nineteenth century his remains and splendid memorial were transferred to SS. Giovanni e Paolo, just to the left of the High Altar. 'He died', writes Ruskin, 'leaving Venice disgraced by sea and land, with the smoke of hostile devastation rising in the blue distances of Friuli; and there was raised to him the most costly tomb ever bestowed on her monarchs.' Ruskin's contempt for the tomb is equalled only by that which he shows for the sculptor, Antonio Rizzo, who finished only those parts of the work that could be seen from below: a contempt which, he points out, was further justified by Rizzo's subsequent disgrace (see p. 363).

that there would be no combined Italian expedition to check the Ottoman advance for several years to come. Nor was there much sign of progress on the other fronts from which an early offensive had been expected. With Croia lost, Scutari doomed, Friuli devastated twice in two years and no prospects of anything but a steady deterioration of her position, Venice – where, in May 1478, Doge Vendramin had been succeeded by Pietro Mocenigo's brother Giovanni – found that she could no longer continue the Turkish war. The terms on which she at last negotiated a peace settlement with Mehmet on 24 January 1479 were considerably less favourable than those that she had refused just over three years before;[1] but this time there was no choice. She was compelled to renounce all claims to Negropont and Lemnos, to most of her holdings on the Greek mainland, and to virtually all Albania except the territory around Durazzo – which, for just a few years more, she was allowed to call her own. The Venetian Dukes of Naxos were also, rather surprisingly, permitted to continue their separate existence in the Cyclades. The Republic was given leave to re-establish a *bailo* in Constantinople with the traditional jurisdiction over his compatriots; but that privilege, together with that of trading in Turkish waters, was now accorded only in return for an annual payment of 10,000 ducats.

All this was humiliating enough; in addition Venice now had to bear the scorn and anger of her Italian and European neighbours, whose inability or unwillingness to make any significant effort themselves did not diminish their furious protests at what they called Venetian treachery. Most galling of all, she could not lift a finger when later in the same year the Turks occupied the Ionian Islands – Ithaca, Cephalonia, Zante and Leucas – and when early in 1480 they landed in Apulia and seized Otranto, treating its luckless inhabitants with the barbarism and brutality which was by now expected of them and turning it, for the next thirteen months, into a flourishing market for Christian slaves. She was even accused of complicity in this latter tragedy, which was widely interpreted as an act of savage revenge against King Ferdinand of Naples – whose kingdom extended over all South Italy – for his recent hostility towards her. Few conjectures could have been more ridiculous; it was true that had Venice not made her peace with the Turks they would probably not have launched an expedition, but it was equally undeniable that the peace was forced upon her only by the lack of any support from the western world. In the event, the news of the Turkish landings was received with as much horror in Venice

1. In the interim, too, the Genoese had been expelled from Caffa in the Crimea and the last European trading station had disappeared from the northern shores of the Black Sea.

as in Naples, and with good reason too. But any active intervention on the part of the Republic would not only have been useless; it would have led to the immediate resumption of a war which she was no longer able to sustain.

For the same reason she could take no action when in the early summer of 1480 Mehmet launched his first full-scale attack on Rhodes, that island fortress which for the past 170 years had been occupied by the Knights Hospitallers of St John. Fortunately, the Knights were able to defend themselves without foreign help. Their fortifications withstood every assault until finally, as winter approached, the besiegers drew away. They probably intended to return to the attack in the following year; but on 3 May 1481 Mehmet died, and by the time the resultant crisis in Constantinople was settled the momentum had been lost. The new Sultan, Bajazet II, had a different scheme of priorities. The Turkish force was withdrawn from Otranto, and Rhodes was left in peace for another forty years.

Venice, too, gained considerably by Bajazet's succession. As soon as she decently could, she sent him a message of congratulation, following up with a suggestion that he might like to confirm the 1479 treaty. The new Sultan, a relatively mild man – at least by the standards of his father – not only did so but made substantial modifications in Venice's favour. The annual tribute was cancelled, import duties were reduced; the Venetians even saw their position strengthened once again in the southern Adriatic – notably by the lease to them of the island of Zante, possession of which greatly facilitated the defence of Corfu.

Suddenly, it seemed, Venice had ceased to be the arch-enemy of the Turks and had become instead the object of Ottoman patronage. For her it was a welcome change. Except, perhaps, for a brief period under Cristoforo Moro, she had never sought to be in the vanguard of a Christian counter-thrust and she turned from hostility back to peaceful commerce with a relief which she made no attempt to conceal.

27

The Ferrara War and the Queen of Cyprus

[1481–1488]

You Venetians, it is certain, are very wrong to disturb the peace of other states
rather than to rest content with the most splendid state of Italy, which you already
possess. If you knew how you are universally hated, your hair would stand on end
... Do you believe that these powers in Italy, now in league together, are truly
friends among themselves? Of course they are not; it is only necessity, and the fear
which they feel for you and your power, that has bound them in this way ... You
are alone, with all the world against you, not only in Italy but beyond the Alps also.
Know then that your enemies do not sleep. Take good counsel, for, by God, you
need it ...

Galeazzo Sforza, Duke of Milan,
to Giovanni Gonnella,
Secretary of the Venetian Republic, 1467

The refreshingly undiplomatic language which Duke Galeazzo Sforza,
Francesco's son and successor, had employed to the Secretary of the
Venetian Republic in 1467 had been prompted by irritation over a relatively unimportant campaign by Colleoni. It exaggerated, perhaps, the peaceable intentions of the other states of Italy and it certainly underestimated
the influence of another emotion, more reprehensible than fear but equally
easy to understand, which informed their anti-Venetian policies: that of
envy. They were envious of her beauty, of her magnificence, of her sea-girt
invulnerability and above all of her apparently unshakeable political system
which, even after the most severe economic or military reverses, ensured
her a resilience and power of recovery that they could never hope to match.
Yet, for all that, young Sforza was speaking the truth. Venice *was* hated,
and that hatred grew steadily stronger as her neighbours watched her make
her peace with the Turks and, soon afterwards, stand idly by while Apulia
was sacked and pillaged by the Infidel. They made no attempt to understand her position; she for her part scarcely deigned to explain it, but
pursued her own policies with all that arrogance, that quiet assumption of
her own superiority, that they had long learned to expect but to which they
could never become reconciled.

None the less, as the ninth decade of the fifteenth century opened to
reveal her economy and her international reputation alike in ruins, it might
have been expected that Venice would try to ensure for herself a period of
peace and discreet diplomacy in which to restore them. Doge Giovanni
Mocenigo and his Signoria seem to have reasoned differently. The Doge
was by all accounts a gentle and modest character; but his portrait in the
Correr Museum shows a hard, determined line about the mouth which may
partially explain the action which the Republic took in the autumn of 1481
against its friend and close neighbour, Ferrara.

The two cities had been for many years on excellent terms; as recently
as 1476 Venice had even intervened to support Duke Ercole of Este against
an attempt by his nephew to usurp his throne. But now Ercole – encouraged, in all probability, by his father-in-law, King Ferdinand of Naples
– set out on a policy of deliberate provocation. First he began building salt-
pans around the mouth of the Po, in defiance of the monopoly which
Venice had jealously guarded for some seven or eight centuries; then he
raised several obscure issues of frontier delimitation which, justified or not,
were certainly not worth quarrelling over; finally, when the Venetian
consul had a local priest arrested for unpaid debts and was promptly
excommunicated by the episcopal vicar, he sided with the vicar – despite
the latter's subsequent condemnation by his own bishop. Even after the
bishop had sent Venice a fulsome apology – adding for good measure that
Pope Sixtus himself had been scandalized to hear of the excommunication
– Ercole steadfastly refused to reinstate the consul.

There could be no doubt that the Duke was spoiling for a fight; nor that
he had chosen a moment to do so when he knew that Venice was still weak
after a long and crippling war. What he may have failed to understand was
that the very humiliation she had suffered made it essential for her to prove
to herself, and to others, that she was still capable of fighting – and of
winning victories too. Once again the Doge launched an appeal for funds;
once again the Venetians responded; and once again the other states of Italy
aligned themselves as their own selfish interests dictated.

This time Venice found the scales weighted heavily against her, with
most of the stronger Italian powers – including Milan and Florence as well
as Naples – taking the side of Ferrara. Her one important ally was, surprisingly enough, Pope Sixtus, who had his own reasons for wanting to see
Naples and Ferrara humbled and who had encouraged her from the outset.
Thanks to his support her forces under Robert of Sanseverino immediately
took the offensive – with, at first, considerable success. But then, without
warning, Sixtus changed sides. His southern frontier was being seriously

threatened by the King of Naples; the smooth-tongued – and, one suspects, bountiful – diplomacy of Ludovico il Moro,[1] the most brilliant of Francesco Sforza's sons, who had recently seized power in Milan, did the rest. The Pope's first action was to appeal to Venice to lay down her arms – a request which Doge Mocenigo politely but firmly refused, taking care to point out that since those arms had but recently received His Holiness's personal blessing, their final triumph was in any case assured.

Sixtus's reply was predictable. On 25 May 1483, he laid Venice under an interdict. The Republic, however, quite simply refused to accept it. The Venetian representative in Rome declined to forward the papal Bull to his government, obliging Sixtus to have it sent by special messenger to the Patriarch, who in his turn pleaded that he was too ill to pass it on to the Doge and Senate. He did, however, immediately inform the Council of Ten, who gave orders that secrecy should be preserved at all costs and that the churches should continue to perform their sacred offices as usual. Meanwhile the Pope was informed that Venice intended to appeal to a future Council – an intention which she made public to the world by nailing a copy of her letter to the door of the church of S. Celso in Rome.

Venice had shown once again that she could defy the Pope; but she could not regain his alliance, which she desperately needed. It was at this point, with virtually the whole of Italy assembled against her, that she took a step for which she was later to be bitterly blamed; she sent envoys to the recently crowned young King of France, Charles VIII, suggesting that he should invade Italy and assert his legitimate rights over the Kingdom of Naples, while his distant kinsman the Duke of Orleans should simultaneously march to claim his own heritage of Milan.[2] There was, in fact, nothing particularly treacherous in such an action; the League was, at least temporarily, a dead letter, and it was by no means the first time, or the last, that foreign states had been invited to intervene in Italian internal wars. But the decision was, for Venice, unusually short-sighted; and it gave the King of France much dangerous encouragement for his long-term ambitions in the peninsula.

For the moment, neither he nor the Duke of Orleans accepted Venice's proposals. Fortunately, however, the King of Naples, whose ships and Apulian harbours had suffered severely from the attentions of the Venetian fleet, was himself anxious for peace; and Ludovico il Moro, who was by now finding Ferdinand a difficult and disagreeable ally, felt much the same.

1. 'The Moor' – so called for his swarthy complexion.
2. The Duke's claim to Milan, through his grandmother Valentina Visconti, was undeniable (see p. 322). For Charles VIII's rights over Naples, see p. 370 n. 2.

An agreement was reached which was honourable to both sides and which even gained for Venice the town of Rovigo and additional territory around the delta of the Po; and when the treaty was finally signed – at Bagnolo in August 1484 – there were celebrations throughout the city. For three days the bells of the churches pealed in triumph; and though to some ears the jubilation may have sounded a trifle exaggerated, the fireworks, the illuminations and the jousting on the Piazza were probably enough to persuade most of the populace that they had won some sort of victory.

One voice only, and that a feeble one, was raised against the peace. When the news was brought to Pope Sixtus, he was already on his deathbed. 'His tongue was so swollen', wrote the Florentine Ambassador to Lorenzo de' Medici, 'that he could scarcely form his words'; but form them he did, denouncing the peace as 'full of disgrace and confusion'. Never, he mumbled, would he accept it. There was little time in which this uncharitable resolution could be put to the test. When the legates tried to soothe him, he dismissed them with a gesture that they were uncertain whether to take as a blessing or as a less friendly sign of dismissal; and the next morning he died.

Doge Giovanni Mocenigo survived the Pope by little over a year – long enough, however, to see the lifting of the interdict by Sixtus's successor, Innocent VIII – before he was himself laid to rest near his brother in SS. Giovanni e Paolo. His had been another unhappy reign, largely overshadowed – like those of his five immediate predecessors – by war and, as a consequence of war, by the spectre of national bankruptcy. He had also had to contend with a major domestic catastrophe when, on the evening of 14 September 1483, a candle inadvertently left burning in the chapel of the Doges' Palace caused a fire which destroyed virtually the whole eastern range of the building, between the courtyard and the Rio di Palazzo. At the sound of the alarm, the populace came running to the blaze and managed eventually to bring it under control; but not before many priceless paintings and works of art had been destroyed. More might have been saved, writes Sanudo, if the Doge had not been so afraid of looters that he refused to open the doors of his own apartments.

When the Senate met to discuss the rebuilding, several wildly ambitious schemes were set before them. Fortunately for posterity, however, they decided to confine themselves to the existing ground plan; with more questionable wisdom, they commissioned the Veronese architect and sculptor Antonio Rizzo to take charge of the work. Whatever we may think of the results – they mark the moment at which the Palace ceased to be a purely Gothic building and began to assume the hybrid quality it has today

– the Venetians had reason to regret that they had not bestowed the commission elsewhere when, in 1498, they learnt that Rizzo had already spent 80,000 ducats and the new range was still only half built. An official inquiry revealed that at least 12,000 had found their way into the architect's own pocket; but for once the Ten were not quick enough. Rizzo had already fled to Ancona, to be succeeded by Pietro Lombardo – whose more flamboyant style, with its copious use of coloured marble inlays, must have proved almost as expensive as the peculations of his predecessor.

Ever since the constitutional reforms of Domenico Flabanico in the eleventh century, Venice had maintained a firm rule that there should never be two successive Doges from the same family; only thus, it was felt, could the Republic avoid being taken over by a ruling dynasty, as had happened in nearly all the other major Italian cities. Now, for the first time, that rule was broken when Giovanni Mocenigo's successor, Marco Barbarigo, died after less than a year in office and was succeeded by his brother Agostino in August 1486.[1] Their characters, however, could hardly have been more dissimilar. Marco was mild and gentle, well-meaning but indecisive; Agostino was self-willed and irascible, with a reputation for almost pathological meanness. Although he had been an energetic proveditor in the war with Ferrara, he owed his unexpected accession above all to a recrudescence of the long-existing rivalry between the *Longhi* and the *Curti* – the older and the newer families of the Venetian nobility. This had the effect of polarizing the forty-one electors, the majority of whom, like Barbarigo himself, represented the *Curti*; and the twenty-eight votes cast for him on the fifth ballot were more than enough to secure his victory over the candidate of the *Longhi*, Bernardo Giustinian.

The first important event in the reign of Agostino Barbarigo marked the achievement of an objective for which Venice, with that combination of shrewd diplomacy and shameless opportunism found so often in her history, had been working for over twenty years: the formal annexation of the Kingdom of Cyprus. Bestowed by Richard Cœur-de-Lion on the Knights Templar, Cyprus had been sold by them in 1192 to the Crusader Guy of Lusignan; and although it had from time to time fallen under foreign influences – notably that of Genoa in the fourteenth century and that of Cairo (to which it was still a tributary) in 1426 – the House of Lusignan had continued to reign.

1. Marco Barbarigo was the first Doge to receive his investiture at the head of Rizzo's *Scala dei Giganti* in the courtyard of the Palace – thus inaugurating a custom which was to last as long as the Republic itself.

The present crisis had had its beginnings in 1460, when James of Lusignan, bastard son of the former King John II, had seized the throne from his sister Queen Charlotte and her husband, Louis of Savoy, forcing them to take refuge in the castle of Kyrenia for three years until they escaped to Rome. Once king, however, James needed allies; and, turning to Venice, he had formally requested the hand in marriage of Caterina, the beautiful young daughter of Marco Cornaro, or Corner,[1] whose family had long been closely associated with the island. The particular branch to which she belonged, the Corner della Ca' Grande, was only remotely connected with that of the Corner-Piscopia, who as holders of the fief of Episcopi were among the richest landowners in Cyprus; but her father Marco had lived there for many years and had become an intimate friend of James, for whom he had accomplished several delicate diplomatic missions, and her uncle Andrea was shortly to become Auditor of the Kingdom. On her mother's side her lineage was still more distinguished: there she could boast as a great-grandfather no less a personage than John Comnenus, Emperor of Trebizond.

The prospect of a Venetian Queen of Cyprus was more than the Senate could resist. It gave its enthusiastic consent and, lest James should change his mind, arranged for an immediate marriage by proxy. On 10 July 1468, with all the pomp and magnificence of which Venice was capable, the fourteen-year-old Caterina was escorted by forty noble matrons from the Corner palace at S. Polo to the *Sala del Maggior Consiglio* in the Doges' Palace. There Doge Moro handed a ring to the Cypriot Ambassador, who placed it on the bride's finger in the name of his sovereign. She was then given the title of Daughter of St Mark – an unprecedented honour which caused the Bishop of Turin to observe acidly that he never knew that St Mark had been married and that, even if he had, his wife must surely be a little old to have a child of fourteen. Four years later, on 10 November 1472, Caterina sailed away, with an escort of four galleys, to her new realm.[2]

The following year, however, King James died suddenly at the age of thirty-three, leaving Caterina heavily pregnant. The inevitable suspicions of poison were probably unfounded, but the Senate, fearing a Savoyard *coup* to reinstate Charlotte, was taking no chances. Immediately it dis-

---

1. Consistency is not possible in books of this kind, nor perhaps even desirable. Although I have hitherto called Caterina's family by the Venetian dialect form of its name, 'Corner', she herself is so well known by the Italian equivalent that to have called her anything but 'Cornaro' would have been pedantic, if not actually confusing.

2. The scene of her departure is said to have provided the inspiration for Carpaccio's painting in the St Ursula series at the Accademia.

patched Pietro Mocenigo – then still Captain-General – with his fleet to Cyprus, ostensibly to protect the young Queen but in fact to watch over Venetian interests, with orders to fortify strategic strong-points round the island and to remove all persons of uncertain loyalty from positions of power and influence. The fact that Cyprus was an independent sovereign state seems to have troubled it not at all; Mocenigo would naturally act through the Queen as far as possible, but he was specifically empowered to use force if necessary.

He did his work, as always, conscientiously and well; but the measures he took served only to increase the resentment already felt by many of the local nobility at the continued growth of Venetian influence in Cypriot affairs. Soon after his departure a conspiracy was formed under the leadership of the Archbishop of Nicosia, and three hours before dawn on 13 November 1473 a small group – including the Archbishop himself – forced its way into the palace at Famagusta and cut down the Queen's Chamberlain and her doctor before her eyes. Next, after a brief search, it hunted out her uncle Andrea Corner and her cousin Marco Bembo, who both suffered a similar fate, their naked bodies being thrown into the moat beneath her windows, where they remained till they had been half eaten by the dogs of the town. Finally Caterina was forced to give her consent to the betrothal of a natural daughter of her late husband to Alfonso, the bastard son of King Ferdinand of Naples, and to recognize the latter as heir to the throne of Cyprus – despite the fact that James had specifically bequeathed his Kingdom to her and that she had by this time given birth to a son of her own.

Word of the *coup* was carried quickly to Venice, and Mocenigo was ordered to return at once to the island. He soon managed to lay hands on most of those responsible. One or two, including the Archbishop, had fled; but, of the others implicated, the ringleaders were hanged, and the remainder imprisoned. The newly promulgated arrangements for the succession were countermanded. Meanwhile the Venetian Senate sent out two trusted patricians who, under the title of Councillors, took over the effective government of the island in Caterina's name. Though shorn of all her powers, the unhappy Queen remained on the throne; but as the years went by even her position as a figurehead became increasingly difficult to maintain. Her baby son, King James III, died in 1474, almost exactly a year after his birth; thenceforth she had to contend with the intrigues of her sister-in-law Charlotte on the one hand and young Alfonso of Naples on the other, while at home the great nobles of the island, seeing her less as their queen than as a Venetian puppet, hatched plot after plot against her. Her survival, as she was well aware, was due entirely to Venetian protection; but that protection had gradually become as oppressive to her as it was to her subjects. Every important post at court or in the administration was in Venetian hands, every town and castle had its Venetian governor or seneschal. At one period she and her father had to complain to the Signoria that her protectors had become more like gaolers: she was not allowed to leave the palace, her servants were withdrawn, she was even obliged to take her meals alone, at a little wooden table. All correspondence, even with her own subjects, was forbidden. These complaints had some effect and after 1480 her life became more comfortable again; but by now she had begun to realize that, Daughter of St Mark or not, she was nothing more than an inconvenience to the Republic, which would not hesitate to get rid of her altogether when the moment came.

Venice bided her time. Since 1426 Cyprus had been held in vassalage to the Sultan of Egypt, to whom the Kingdom was bound to pay an annual tribute of 8,000 ducats, and its direct annexation might well cause her diplomatic complications in that quarter she could ill afford. But then, in 1487, the Sultan sent warning to Caterina that Bajazet was even then planning a massive expedition against him, and was likely to make an attempt on Cyprus *en route*. He begged her to take all necessary measures to strengthen her defences, in return for which he was prepared to remit two years' tribute. This development, offering as it did the prospect of Venice and Egypt allied against a common enemy, may well have encouraged the Signoria to take the plunge; what certainly did so was the discovery, in the summer of 1488, of a further plot, this time involving the marriage of Caterina to Alfonso of Naples – a plot of which the Queen was probably aware and to which she may well have been sympathetic. The principal conspirator – one Rizzo di Marino, who had also been implicated in the 1473 affair and, like his friend the Archbishop, had fled just in time – was captured, brought to Venice and strangled by order of the Council of Ten; but the possibility of Caterina's remarriage was one which could clearly not be contemplated. In October 1488 the decision was taken: Cyprus was to be formally incorporated in the Venetian Empire and its Queen brought back – in state if possible, by force if necessary – to the land of her birth.

The Captain-General, Francesco Priuli, was the man entrusted with this delicate task. Anticipating some possible reluctance on Caterina's part, the Ten had taken the precaution of secretly briefing her brother Giorgio to prepare her in advance and to persuade her that an ostensibly voluntary abdication on her own initiative would be for the good of all concerned. Cyprus, still dangerously exposed, could then be properly protected from Turkish cupidity; she herself would acquire glory and honour for bestowing such a gift upon her motherland, in return for which she would be received in state, endowed with a rich fief and an annual income of 8,000 ducats, and enabled to live in peace and luxury as the Queen that she would continue to be; finally, her family would gain immeasurably in power and prestige, whereas if she were to refuse they would all be ruined.

When Giorgio first told his sister what was expected of her, she protested bitterly. 'Are not my lords of Venice content to have their island when I am dead,' she is quoted as saying, 'that they would deprive me so soon of what my husband left me?' But she yielded at last. Early in 1489 she left Nicosia for Famagusta, where in the course of a long and solemn ceremony she formally charged the Captain-General to fly the standard of St Mark from every corner of the island; and in the first week of June she arrived with her brother at S. Nicolò di Lido. Doge Barbarigo had sailed out in his state barge to greet her, accompanied by a train of noble ladies. Unfortunately, as the *Bucintoro* approached the Lido, a sudden storm arose. The barge was forced to ride it out for several hours, much to the discomfort of the occupants; they were not at their best when Caterina was finally able to embark. There followed a stately procession up the Grand Canal to the Palace of the Dukes of Ferrara (where the Byzantine Emperor had stayed fifty-one years before[1]) while the trumpets sounded, the church bells rang, and the people of Venice cheered her to the echo. As the procession passed the Palazzo Corner,[2] Giorgio was invested by the Doge as a *Cavaliere* in recognition of his services to the Republic; later he received the additional privilege of quartering the arms of the House of Lusignan with his own.

After three days of somewhat hollow festivity at the Ferrara Palace, the Queen went through a further ceremony of abdication in St Mark's, where she formally ceded her Kingdom to Venice. In October she took possession of the little hill town of Asolo, the fief which she had been granted for the rest of her life; and there, for the next twenty years, she was to remain at the centre of a cultivated if distinctly vapid court. Only in 1509, threatened by the advancing armies of the Emperor Maximilian, was she obliged to leave this tinkling world of music, dancing and the polite

---

1. See p. 318.

2. There are no fewer than sixteen Corner palaces in Venice. This one, which stood at the junction of the Grand Canal and the Rio San Cassiano, unfortunately no longer exists. It was replaced in 1724 by the present building on the site, which, though now the premises of the Monte di Pietà, still bears the name of Palazzo Corner della Regina.

conversation of learned men, and seek refuge in her native city. There it was that she died, on 10 July 1510, aged fifty-six. On a stormy night of wind and rain her coffin was carried from the Corner Palace, across the Grand Canal on a bridge of boats to the church of the SS. Apostoli. On it rested the Crown of Cyprus; inside, however, the Queen's body was shrouded in a Franciscan habit. It was buried in the family chapel, and only later removed to S. Salvatore, where, in the south transept, her tomb bears the inscription: D.O.M. CATHARINAE CORNELIAE CYPRI HIEROSOLYMORUM AC ARMENIAE REGINAE CINERES.

28

France on the March

[1489-1500]

Me menerent au long de la grant rue qu'ilz appellent le Canal Grant: et est bien large (les gallées y passent au travers, et y ay veu navyres de quatre cens tonneaulx et plus, près des maisons), et est la plus belle rue que je croy que soit en tout le monde et la myeulx maisonnée, et va long de la ville. Les maisons sont fort grandes et haultes, et de bonne pierre, les anciennes, et toutes painctes; les aultres faictes puis cent ans, toutes ont le devant de marbre blanc, qui leur vient d'Istrie, à cent mil de là, et encores mainte grant piece de porfille et de serpentine sur le devant ... Et est la plus triumphante cité que jamais j'aye veue ...

I was conducted through the principal street, which they call the Grand Canal, and is so wide that galleys frequently pass across it; indeed I have seen vessels of four hundred tons or more ride at anchor just by the houses. It is the fairest and best-built street, I think, in the world, and goes quite through the city; the houses are very large and lofty, and built of stone; the old ones are all painted; those of about a hundred years' standing are faced with white marble from Istria (which is about a hundred miles from Venice) and inlaid with porphyry and serpentine ... It is the most triumphant city that I have ever seen ...

Philippe de Commines, *Mémoires*
(tr. A. R. Scoble)

The year 1492 marked a turning-point in the history of the West. It was the year of Columbus's discovery of the New World, and the year in which his patrons, Ferdinand of Aragon and Isabella of Castile, finally defeated the Moorish Kingdom of Granada, thus consolidating their monarchy over a united Spain. It saw, in Florence, the death of Lorenzo the Magnificent, who, despite his lifelong mistrust of Venice, had done more than any other single man to promote and whenever possible to preserve Italian solidarity against French ambitions; and in Rome, after the most corrupt election in papal history, the accession of its most immoral pontiff – if we exclude the Anti-Pope John XXIII – since the days of the 'pornocracy' nearly six centuries before: Rodrigo Borgia, henceforth to be known as Pope Alexander VI. For the twenty-two-year-old King Charles VIII of France, however, it was above all the year in which, freed at last from the control of the former regent, his sister Anne de Beaujeu, he was able to devote his energies to planning the great enterprise he had dreamt of for so long – his march into Italy.

Charles's physical appearance was hardly that of a dashing military adventurer. 'His Majesty', reported the Venetian Ambassador[1] in that same year, 'is small, ill-formed and ugly of countenance, with pale, short-sighted eyes, nose far too large and abnormally thick lips which are always apart. He makes spasmodic movements with his hands that are most unpleasant to look upon, and his speech is extremely slow ... Yet all Paris praises his skill at ball-play, jousting and the chase.' Perhaps for this last reason he was popular with his subjects. He also seems to have possessed a genuine sweetness of character that earned him his sobriquet 'the Affable' – '*si bon*', writes the chronicler Philippe de Commines, '*qu'il n'est point possible de voir meilleure créature.*' There was no doubt that, in his eyes, the expedition was to be undertaken for the highest motives. He had no wish to conquer the territory of others, only to claim such lands as belonged to him by right – a category which for him unquestionably included the Kingdom of Naples.[2] With this there had for three hundred years been united the style of King of Jerusalem, a title which would give Charles the prestige necessary, once his Italian dominions were safely confirmed, to launch and lead the long-overdue Crusade.

It was a glorious dream, and a dream it should have remained. As Commines points out, the enterprise seemed folly to all wise and experienced men. Charles had little money – he had to pawn his jewels before leaving – and still less understanding of military affairs; the prospect of leading an army to the far south of the Italian peninsula, spinning out long and fragile lines of communication and supply and leaving them at the mercy of at least half a dozen strong, wary and potentially hostile states, seemed to cause him not a moment's concern. Two only of his immediate French entourage shared his optimism: his tutor and chamberlain, Etienne de Vesc, whom Commines dismisses as '*homme de petite lignee, qui jamais n'avoit veu ne entendu nulle chose*', and his cousin, Louis of Orleans, who saw in the proposed expedition an opportunity of asserting his own claim to the Duchy of Milan through his grandmother, Valentina Visconti; but there were plenty of Italian exiles, Milanese, Genoese and Neapolitan, enemies of the Borgia from Rome and of the Medici from Florence, standing ready to give him any further encouragement he might need.

Of all the leading states of Italy Venice alone, stable and monolithic as

---

1. Venice had maintained a continuous embassy to the court of France since 1478 – the first permanent diplomatic representation outside Italy.

2. The French claim to Naples derived from Charles of Anjou, the brother of St Louis, who had accepted the throne from the Pope in 1265 and whose family had occupied it for nearly two hundred years until its seizure by the House of Aragon in 1432.

ever, had no discontented factions intriguing against her at the court of France. Her only representatives there were her properly accredited ambassadors, who, when Charles proposed a formal military alliance at the end of 1492, had shown considerably less enthusiasm than they had nine years before, smoothly pointing out that the two states were already on such friendly terms that no further demonstration of solidarity was necessary; Venice could not in any event take part in any expedition against the Turks, since she was bound by her 1482 peace treaty with Bajazet. They might have added, but did not, that she had never been on particularly good terms with Naples – from whose dismemberment, if Charles were victorious, she might moreover hope for several valuable pickings; knowing as she did that the French King was perfectly well-intentioned where she was concerned, she preferred to maintain a guarded neutrality and her favourite position on the side-lines. This policy was still unchanged in the following year, when Ludovico il Moro sent his young wife, Beatrice of Este – already an able diplomatist in her own right – to Venice at the head of a splendid embassy to ascertain the Republic's attitude to the expected invasion. She was given the usual magnificent reception, lodged at the Ferrara Palace and taken on a tour of the city; she attended a session of the Great Council, and a concert was given at the convent of the Vergini in her honour. But in answer to her questions she received nothing but expressions of pious hopes and vague generalities.

Ludovico had hoped for some rather more positive assurance of support for the French enterprise. The Orleanist claim to his Duchy does not seem to have worried him: he had other more immediate anxieties. By his usurpation of power in Milan from the rightful Duke – his nephew Gian Galeazzo, who was married to the daughter of Prince Alfonso of Naples – he had incurred the lasting hostility of the Neapolitan ruling house: and when in January 1494 Alfonso succeeded his father, Ferdinand, on the throne, that hostility assumed even more threatening proportions. Within a short time the new King had enlisted the support of Piero de' Medici – who had recently succeeded his father, Lorenzo, as effective ruler of Florence – and of Pope Alexander himself. It was a formidable combination which, if it had decided on a sudden attack, might well have brought about Ludovico's downfall. Thus, as the danger increased, the Milanese envoys in Paris had begun to encourage the King more and more openly in his Italian ambitions until they had virtually invited him to march into the peninsula – not that by then he needed an invitation. He had already bought, at an immense price, the passive acquiescence of Ferdinand and Isabella of Spain, Henry VII of England and the Emperor-elect Maximilian of Austria; and in the summer of 1494, at the head of an army of 46,000, including 11,000 cavalry, 4,000 Swiss pikemen and the King's guard of Scottish archers – by far the largest force raised in France within living memory and the first to be led by the sovereign in person since the days of St Louis two centuries before – he marched.

The speed and success of the French advance across the Alps, through Lombardy and down the Italian peninsula must have justified Charles's highest hopes. At the beginning of September he was at Asti,[1] to receive the news that a combined French, Swiss and Genoese naval and military force under his cousin the Duke of Orleans – who had set out a month earlier with an advance guard and most of the heavy artillery – had resoundingly defeated the Neapolitans at Rapallo. Despite a mild attack of smallpox he left Asti on 6 October; two months later he made his triumphal entry into Pisa and its near neighbour Lucca; and on 17 November he reached Florence, whose citizens, largely inspired by the Dominican friar Savonarola, lost no time in expelling the weak and feckless Piero de' Medici and readily opened their gates to the French forces. The last day of the year found him at Rome, where Pope Alexander, having at first locked himself up in terror within the Castel Sant' Angelo, soon understood that he too had no real choice but to come, however reluctantly, to terms.

After four weeks in Rome, the French continued their advance on Naples. The news of their approach was enough to cause King Alfonso to abdicate in favour of his son Ferdinand, known as Ferrantino, who shortly afterwards followed his example; and on 22 February 1495 the people of Naples – who had never looked on the House of Aragon as anything other than foreign oppressors – gave a rousing welcome to their new ruler. In barely six months Charles had realized all his ambitions. More remarkable still, he had done so virtually without bloodshed – without, indeed, a single serious armed encounter since Rapallo. The Italians had quite simply forgotten how to fight. For a century or more, their only major land battles had been waged by *condottieri* with assorted armies of mercenaries – men who had no high principles or feelings of patriotism for which to slay or be slain, and who thought only in terms of pay, plunder and ransom money. In consequence they had developed among themselves a kind of formalized warfare scarcely more physically dangerous to its participants than the modern art of fencing; and when faced with an enemy who showed

1. The Piedmontese city of Asti had been part of the dowry of Valentina Visconti when she married the first Duke of Orleans. Later it was regained by Filippo Maria, but on his death returned once more to the House of Orleans, making a useful Italian base for Charles's expedition.

no disposition to follow the stately rules which they had laid down but was, instead, all too obviously prepared to cut them to pieces, they fled in a mixture of panic and disgust.

Charles remained three months in his new Kingdom, where on 12 May he received his formal coronation. Already, however, his success was beginning to turn sour. The Neapolitans, delighted as they had been to get rid of the Aragonese, soon discovered that one foreign oppressor was much like another. Unrest was also growing among the populations of many smaller towns, who found themselves having to support, for no good reason that they could understand, a discontented and frequently licentious French garrison. Beyond the Kingdom of Naples, too, men were beginning to feel alarm. Even those states, Italian and foreign, who had previously looked benignly – or at least without overt hostility – upon Charles's advance were beginning to wonder whether, having achieved his initial aims with so little effort, he might not now be encouraged to go further, directing his still intact army against themselves; and nowhere was this concern felt more acutely than in Venice.

Fortunately for posterity, Charles had had the good sense to appoint as his resident ambassador to the Signoria throughout this period Philippe de Commines, Lord of Argenton, whose memoirs provide perhaps the earliest accurate account of Venetian political history, recorded by an intelligent and perceptive eye-witness, that we possess. Commines leaves us in no doubt of the mood in which the news of his master's triumph was received on the Rialto:

When the Venetians understood that several towns in Italy had surrendered, and were informed of the King's being at Naples, they sent for me to tell me the news, and pretended to be extremely pleased with it; yet they gave me to understand that the castle still held out against him; that there was a strong garrison in it, provided with everything necessary for its defence; and I could perceive they had great hopes it would never be taken.

But taken it was; and a day or two later they summoned him again:

I found about fifty or sixty of them assembled in the chamber of their Doge, who was at that time ill of the colic. The Doge, with a composed countenance, rather inclining to joy, told me the news; but there was none in all the company could counterfeit so well as himself. Some of them sat upon low seats with their elbows upon their knees, and their heads between their hands; others in other postures, but all expressing great sorrow at heart; and I believe after the battle of Cannae[1]

1. The greatest defeat in the history of ancient Rome, when the Carthaginians under Hannibal slaughtered almost the entire Roman army – some 5,000 men – in 216 B.C.

there was not more terror felt by the senators of Rome; for not one of them had courage enough to look upon me or speak to me but the Doge himself, which I thought was very strange.

Doge Barbarigo need not have bothered to dissemble as he did, for the ambassador knew perfectly well that for six weeks already the Signoria had been engaged in secret negotiations with representatives of Ferdinand of Spain, the Emperor-elect Maximilian, Alexander VI and Ludovico il Moro – who was by now as alarmed as anyone at the whirlwind he had been at least partly responsible for unleashing, and was further disconcerted by the continued presence at Asti of the Duke of Orleans, whose claims to Milan, he had finally realized, were no less strong than those of Charles VIII to Naples. It therefore came as no surprise to Commines when, on 1 April, he was officially informed of the signature of a new league.

As soon as I came thither, and had taken my seat, the Doge told me that in honour of the Holy Trinity they had entered into an alliance with our Holy Father the Pope, the Kings of the Romans[1] and of Castile, and the Duke of Milan, for three principal objects: the first, to defend Christendom against the Turk; the second, the defence of Italy; and the third, the preservation of their territories ... They were in all about a hundred or more, looked very gay and held their heads high, and there was no such sadness in their countenances as upon the day when they heard of the surrender of the castle of Naples ...

After dinner all the ambassadors of the League met together in boats upon the water (which in Venice is their chief recreation): the whole number of their boats (which are provided at the charge of the Signory, and proportioned to every man's retinue) was about forty, every one of them adorned with the arms of their respective masters; and in this pomp they passed under my windows with their trumpets and other instruments of music ... At night there were extraordinary fireworks upon the turrets, steeples and tops of the ambassadors' houses, multitudes of bonfires were lighted, and the cannon all round the city were fired.

Commines himself, whether for reasons of pique (as a contemporary observer suggests[2]) or because he was himself sick of a fever (as he subsequently maintained in a letter to his King), kept a low profile for the next few days, venturing from his lodgings on S. Giorgio Maggiore only once, incognito, to watch the festivities from a covered boat. He was present again, however, on Palm Sunday when, after an open-air High Mass in the thronged Piazza, Doge Barbarigo, the Signoria and the ambassadors of the League – the latter in magnificent new robes presented to

1. See p. 288n.
2. Marin Sanudo, *La Spedizione di Carlo VIII in Italia*, pp. 285–6.

them by the Doge himself – marched in solemn procession round the Square, ending up at the *Pietra del Bando*,[1] where the terms of the new alliance were formally proclaimed.

The Venetian scholar and diarist Marin Sanudo tells how, when Philippe de Commines was notified by the Doge of the conclusion of the new League, he immediately asked whether his King would be allowed to return unmolested to France; to which Agostino Barbarigo replied with the words: 'If he wishes to return as a friend, no one will do him any hurt; if as an enemy, the confederates will all go to each other's help and defence.' Another, better-placed authority – possibly even an eye-witness – the Senator Domenico Malipiero, records that the Doge went so far as to offer Charles up to thirty-five galleys, to transport himself and his men by sea if they feared the return journey up the peninsula. Commines himself, however, mentions no such specific exchanges.

When news of the League was brought to King Charles in Naples, he had flown into a fury; summoning the Venetian ambassador, he had threatened to form a rival alliance with England, Scotland, Portugal and Hungary. But he did not underestimate the danger with which he was now faced. Long before his Neapolitan coronation, the armies of the League were beginning to assemble against him; and a week after it, accompanied by a force of some twelve thousand French, Swiss and Gascon troops which also included a corps of German *Landsknechts* and the Scottish archers, he left his new Kingdom for ever and headed north.

His route was beset by difficulties, political as well as physical. In Rome he had hoped to confer amicably with the Pope, but arrived to find that Alexander had fled – first to Orvieto, then on to Perugia. In Tuscany there were more serious problems, arising from his having promised the Florentines that he would restore Pisa to their rule, while having given his word to the Pisans that he would do nothing of the kind. He followed the west coast as far as La Spezia, where, ill-advisedly, he split his forces. Philip of Bresse with a couple of thousand men was ordered to take the coastal route, via Genoa, while he himself with the bulk of the army branched to the right, along the mountain road that would bring him through the northern range of the Apennines and down again into Lombardy. Up to this point there had been no concerted attempt at opposition; nor, indeed, had he

1. The squat porphyry pillar which still stands at the south-west corner of the Basilica. Brought from Acre during the Crusades, it was the traditional place from which laws and decrees were promulgated from 1256 until the end of the Republic.

expected any. But he knew full well that somewhere, not far off beyond the mountains, the massed forces of the League awaited him. Would they or would they not allow him to pass?

The League, as Doge Barbarigo had so courteously explained to Commines only three months before, was purely defensive in object; it might therefore have been assumed that the allies, seeing the King of France making an orderly and peaceable withdrawal, would have been only too pleased for him to continue unhindered on his way. This prospect had been clouded, however, by a sudden act of unprovoked aggression, when in early June the Duke of Orleans, who had remained with a small rearguard in Asti while his cousin marched south, suddenly decided to press his claims to Milan and, as a first step, seized the city of Novara. From that moment armed neutrality gave way to open war. Unless terms could be negotiated and the Duke somehow persuaded to withdraw his garrison, the French had little hope of escaping without doing battle.

Even in midsummer, the task of dragging heavy artillery over a high mountain pass must have been a nightmare. The ascent was bad enough; the journey down, when it sometimes needed as many as a hundred already exhausted men, lashed together in pairs, to restrain a single heavy cannon from careering over a precipice – and, if they did not act quickly, carrying them with it – was infinitely worse. Fortunately Charles's Swiss troops, who had disgraced themselves a few days earlier by burning and sacking the town of Pontremoli after its surrender, seemed anxious to atone for their past excesses and laboured skilfully and indefatigably like the hardened mountaineers they were. At last, on Sunday, 5 July, the track began to level off and Charles was able to look down on the shallow valley of the river Taro, winding through the Lombard plain towards the Po, on the little town of Fornovo, and, deployed just behind it on the right bank, a force of some 30,000 soldiers of the League.

Most of these men were mercenaries in the pay of Venice, under the command of the Republic's specially appointed *condottiere*, Francesco Gonzaga, Marquis of Mantua. There were a few Milanese, though the bulk of Ludovico Sforza's army was occupied with the Duke of Orleans; the other three members of the League were virtually unrepresented. From the moment of his arrival at Fornovo, Charles was left in no doubt that his path to Parma had been deliberately blocked. The people of the town were friendly enough, but the two camps were pitched dangerously close together and throughout the night the French were harassed by marauding groups of *stradioti*, the awesomely ferocious light cavalry from Albania and Epirus whom Venice was by this time regularly recruiting for her mercenary forces.

The next morning, soon after first light, Charles led his army forward. He and his 10,000 men were fully arrayed for battle, but in a last tenuous hope of avoiding open conflict he resolved to cross the dangerously swollen river – there had been a tremendous thunderstorm in the night, and heavy rain was still falling–and make his way along the left bank. The crossing was successfully accomplished, but the League forces followed and charged the French rear. The vanguard, which included most of Charles's much-vaunted artillery, had advanced too far and allowed itself to get separated from the rest of the army; the King himself, however, commanding the centre, wheeled quickly round and fell upon the attackers.

Gonzaga's army had every advantage. It outnumbered the French by three – possibly even four – to one; it was fully rested and provisioned; it had had plenty of time to choose its position and prepare for the coming encounter. The French, by contrast, were exhausted, hungry – they had fought shy of the food and drink offered them at Fornovo, suspecting it of having been poisoned – and disinclined to fight. But fight they did, the King himself as bravely as any; and the battle that followed was the bloodiest that Italy had seen for 200 years. It did not last long; Commines, who was present, maintains that everything was over in a quarter of an hour; and though the number of those killed – estimated at four or five thousand – suggests that he may have been exaggerating a little, the morning was certainly not far advanced before the League army found itself hopelessly outflanked. The *stradioti* seem to have been initially to blame. At an early stage they had caught sight of the French baggage train, which was moving independently of the army some distance away from the river; the smell of plunder had proved irresistible, and the League cavalry were thus catastrophically depleted just when Gonzaga needed them most. He too had shown deplorable generalship by riding into the fray without setting up any adequate chain of command, so that half his army received no orders and were never engaged at all.

Incredibly enough, he was able to present the battle of Fornovo as a victory for himself and the League, even – on his return to Mantua – building a *Chiesetta della Vittoria* to commemorate it with a specially commissioned altarpiece by Mantegna.[1] In Venice too there were wild rejoicings; banks and shops closed in celebration; and a special edict had to be promulgated to protect the persons of French and Savoyard visitors to the city after several of their number had been pelted with fruit. Yet it is hard indeed to see just where the so-called victory lay. Charles, admittedly, lost his baggage train and all it contained – including the sword of St Louis and

---

1. The *Madonna della Vittoria*, now – ironically enough – hanging in the Louvre.

any amount of loot from Naples – to a value which one contemporary estimate puts at 30,000 ducats. The casualties among his army were, however, almost negligible compared with those of the Italians, who had utterly failed in their main objective – as was seen when Charles and his men continued their march that same night and reached Asti unmolested only a few days later.

But little comfort awaited him there. A French naval expedition against Genoa had failed, resulting only in the capture of most of his fleet and yet more of the spoils he was bringing back from the South. His cousin Orleans was being besieged in Novara by a Milanese army and was unlikely to hold out much longer. The young King of Naples, Alfonso's son Ferrantino, had landed in Calabria, supported by Spanish troops from Sicily, and was rapidly advancing on his capital. Before long, Novara fell as expected, and France and Milan made a separate peace at Vercelli. On 7 July Ferrantino reoccupied Naples. Suddenly, all the French successes of the past year had evaporated. When Charles finally crossed the Alps in mid-October he left scarcely a trace behind.

And this, surely, is one of the most extraordinary features of the whole expedition. Before it was launched there were few who thought it might succeed and many who predicted disaster. No one suspected the truth – that, for all its initial promise, it would have no long-term effect on Italy at all. Ludovico il Moro was still in Milan, the Aragonese were back in Naples. Even the great League broke up in disgust after what it rightly considered to be Ludovico's treachery in negotiating separately at Vercelli. By the end of 1496 the last French garrisons had disappeared from the peninsula. The Italians were back as they had always been. They had not even learnt the one vital lesson that Charles's invasion must, one would have imagined, inevitably have taught them: the importance of national unity, if not in their internal affairs then at least when they were faced with a foreign enemy. Their old, traditional pattern – the hotchpotch of autonomous, mutually distrustful cities and states, their allegiances and alliances constantly shifting in an endless kaleidoscope to maintain an approximate balance of power – was too deeply rooted. To them, the King of France was just another despot, to be used, manipulated, outwitted, or deceived as necessary.

More surprising still, Charles seems to have subconsciously accepted the role in which they cast him. His impact on Italy was far more akin to that of some local military adventurer or *condottiere* than to that of one of the leading princes of Europe – and correspondingly short-lived. In one re-

378

spect only did his actions reveal him for what he was: he fought like a Frenchman, and by doing so he obliged the Italians to revise their whole philosophy of warfare. In the past century, with the eclipse of the Holy Roman Empire, their land had remained virtually untrammelled by foreign invaders; in the next, it was to become one of the battlefields of Europe. No longer could they afford to look upon war as simply a tournament on a larger scale. In future they would have to learn once more to fight as their enemies fought – to kill.

Paradoxically, Charles's Italian adventure was to have its most lasting effect not in Italy, but in Northern Europe. When his heterogeneous army was paid off at Lyons in November 1495, it dispersed in every direction across the continent, carrying with it the news of a warm, sunlit land inhabited by a people who lived a life of cultivated refinement far beyond anything known in greyer, chillier climes but who – perhaps for that very reason – were too disunited to defend themselves against a determined invader. As the message spread, and as the painters, sculptors, plasterers and wood-carvers whom Charles had brought back with him from Italy began to transform his old castle at Amboise from a medieval fortress into a Renaissance palace, so Italy became more desirable in the eyes of her northern neighbours than ever before, presenting them with an invitation and a challenge which they were not slow to take up in the years to come.

But the disbanded mercenaries carried something else too – deadlier far than any dream of conquest. Columbus's three ships, returning to Spain from the Caribbean in 1493, had brought with them the first cases of syphilis known to the Old World; through the agency of the Spanish mercenaries sent by Ferdinand and Isabella to support King Alfonso against the French invasion, the disease had rapidly passed on to Naples, where it was rife by the time Charles arrived. After three months of *dolce far niente*, his men must in turn have been thoroughly infected, and all the available evidence suggests that it was they who were responsible for introducing it north of the Alps. Certainly it had reached France, Germany and Switzerland by 1495 and Holland and England by 1496; by 1497 not even Aberdeen had been spared. In that year Vasco da Gama rounded the Cape of Good Hope and reached India, where the disease is recorded in 1498; seven years later it was in Canton.

But however quick the spread of the *morbo gallico* – the French disease, as it was generally called – death came to Charles VIII more quickly still. At Amboise on the eve of Palm Sunday, 1498, while on his way to watch the *jeu de paume* being played in the castle ditch, he struck his head on a low lintel. The blow did not seem particularly severe; he walked on and saw the game. But on his way back to his apartments, just as he was passing the place where the accident had occurred, he suddenly collapsed. Although it was the most sordid and tumbledown corner of the castle – 'a place', sniffs Commines, 'where every man pissed that would' – his attendants for some reason thought it better not to move him. There he lay for nine hours on a rough pallet; and there, shortly before midnight, he died. He was twenty-eight years old.

The news of the King's death was in Venice within a week, the messenger who brought it having ridden thirteen horses to death in his haste. It occasioned no particular sorrow, but much hard thought.

Since Charles's only son had died in infancy, the throne now passed to his cousin, the Duke of Orleans, henceforth to be known as Louis XII. To the rulers of Italy, who had had plenty of experience of Louis in recent years, his succession could mean one thing only: a new invasion of the peninsula, this time to vindicate not the Angevin claim to Naples, but the far stronger Orleanist one to Milan. They were not surprised to hear that the new King had expressly assumed the title of Duke of Milan at his coronation, nor that he had almost immediately opened negotiations with potential allies: Ferdinand of Spain, Henry VII of England and the cantons of Switzerland. Meanwhile, his ambassadors flooded into Italy. Milan and Naples were pointedly ignored; but virtually all the other states, large and small, received individual approaches with requests for their alliance or at least their neutrality. Venice alone had not waited for a French initiative. She had already sent special ambassadors to Louis, to congratulate him on his accession and to assure him of the Republic's support. Serious discussions began soon afterwards, and in February 1499 there was signed at Blois a treaty providing not just for an alliance between the two powers but also for the partition, after the defeat of Ludovico Sforza, of the Duchy of Milan.

Less then four years earlier Venice had defended Lombardy almost single-handed against a French invading army, suffering heavy casualties in the process. The Pope, in consequence, had hailed her as 'Liberator of Italy'. Why had she now changed her policy so radically? Was she really so anxious to have a foreign invader on her very doorstep? Her official answer to such questions would have been that she had little choice. The superiority of French arms had been proved at Fornovo, and Louis's army bid fair to be larger, better equipped and much more efficiently organized than that of his predecessor. Little help could be expected from the King of Naples, striving as he was to avert famine in his own near-bankrupt kingdom. Florence, still uncertain of herself after the burning of Savonarola only a few months before, was hostile to Venice (with whom she was now squabbling over the independence of Pisa, on which both cities had designs) but at the same time quietly sympathetic to France. As for Pope Alexander, Louis had managed to buy him without difficulty by offering his son, Cesare – who, bored with being a cardinal, had decided to abandon the Church in favour of a life of military adventure – the rich Duchy of Valentinois and the hand in marriage of Charlotte d'Albret, sister of the King of Navarre. Ludovico il Moro, in making his separate peace with Charles VIII in 1495, had destroyed not only the League itself but the whole underlying conception of a free Italy by which alone it might have been reconstituted. Since then he had further antagonized the Republic by receiving a Turkish ambassador, openly siding with Florence on the Pisan question and refusing to allow Venetian troops to pass across his territory. Was he beginning to see himself as another Visconti? If so, it was time he was disillusioned.

All this was true enough and doubtless played an important part in persuading Venice to act as she did. But it was not the whole story. There was another, simpler incentive: territorial greed. The prospect of further extending their mainland empire towards Pisa and the Tyrrhenian ports was more than the Venetians could resist. They showed themselves, as always, hard bargainers: the length of the Blois negotiations – only a few days short of six months – is proof enough of that. But they got what they wanted. In return for 1,500 men-at-arms and 4,000 infantry they were promised, on Sforza's overthrow, the city of Cremona and its adjacent territories, and all the lands, towns and castles to the east of the Adda river as far south as its confluence with the Po.

It was in mid-August 1499 that the French army invaded. In command was a Milanese exile, Gian Giacomo Trivulzio, whose family had been dispossessed by Sforza and who consequently had everything himself to gain from a quick victory. At Annone, he massacred the garrison; then, having effortlessly occupied Valenza and Tortona, he laid siege to Alessandria, which capitulated after only four days. Already Ludovico's cause was hopeless. On 30 August there was rioting in the streets of Milan during which his treasurer was killed, and three days later he fled to Innsbruck. His trusted friend Bernardino da Corte, to whom he had confided the castle, sold it to the French as soon as his back was turned, and on 6 October King Louis formally took possession of the Duchy.

That is not quite the end of the story. From his Tyrolean refuge

Ludovico managed to collect quite a considerable army – some estimates put it as high as 20,000 men – and early in 1500 he returned to Milan and even briefly reoccupied it. But his success lasted less than two months. Abandoned by his army (whom he had proved quite unable to pay) he tried to escape in disguise but was almost immediately recognized and captured. His career, wavering and uncertain, was over. Taken to France, he remained a prisoner there for the rest of his life; and in 1508, in the castle of Loches, he died.

29

Double Disaster

[1499–1503]

Tell the Signoria that they have done with wedding the sea; it is our turn now.

Turkish Vizir to Venetian Ambassador Alvise Manenti,
28 February 1500

There could be no doubt about it: in the last two decades of the fifteenth century Venice's fortunes had taken a distinct turn for the better. After the calamitous losses sustained in the Turkish wars of the 1460s and '70s it must have seemed that her Empire was crumbling; then, with the accession of the peaceable Bajazet II in 1481, the whole outlook had suddenly changed. Rovigo and the Po delta had come to her in 1484, Cyprus in 1488; after Charles VIII's withdrawal from Naples, she had acquired three valuable ports on the Apulian coast – Brindisi, Trani and Otranto; and on 10 September 1499 her troops had entered Cremona. If only, one feels, the century could have ended there ... Alas, within days of this last triumph, news was brought to Venice that cast the whole city into mourning. In the waters off the island of Sapienza – that fateful south-west corner of the Peloponnese where she had already lost an entire fleet to Genoa in 1354 – her navy had suffered a still greater defeat, this time at the hands of the Turks. This time, too, she had to bear not only her losses but shame and humiliation as well; for the disaster, according to these first reports, had been primarily attributable to the vacillation, if not actually the cowardice, of her Captain-General.

Despite the mild temper of Bajazet – Machiavelli remarked that if there had been one more Sultan like him Europe would no longer have anything to fear from Ottoman ambitions – relations between his Empire and Venice had been worsening for some time. Turkish privateers had continued to ravage the Dalmatian coast as far north as Istria; two small towns dependent on the Venetian city of Cattaro (now Kotor) had revolted and, on Venice's refusal to allow them Rectors of their own, had sought Turkish protection; most serious of all, Bajazet had been persuaded by Milanese and Florentine agents that the recent Venetian alliance with France was ultimately to be directed against himself. By the end of 1498 matters had reached a point where Venice sent a special ambassador to the Sublime Porte in an attempt to explain matters, while at the same time gathering information about such war preparations as might be in progress.

His report was not encouraging; war, it seemed, was a certainty. In April 1499 the sixty-five-year-old Antonio Grimani was elected to the naval command, immediately offering his services without payment and a loan to the state of 16,000 ducats. Other public-spirited citizens hastened, as usual, to follow his example. And yet, as Venice herself began to prepare once again for war, there seems to have been a strange new timidity and half-heartedness on the part of her leaders. When Grimani sought instructions whether he should engage the Turks on sight, he received no reply; and the question was still unanswered when he led the fleet down the Adriatic to the East. He and his three proveditors were to sign their own orders when the conflict came.

This second battle of Sapienza was in fact not one engagement but four, occurring on the 12th, 20th, 22nd and 25th August. In each the Venetians, though outnumbered by some 260 Turkish vessels to 170 of their own, advanced bravely into the fray; and in the first and last engagements in particular, certain of their captains showed outstanding heroism – notably Andrea Loredan, the commander at Corfu, who had joined the fleet on his own initiative, Vincenzo Polani, who sailed alone into the thick of the Turkish line, where he created havoc for over two hours, and Alvise Marcello – whose example, writes Malipiero, had it been more generally followed, 'would, as surely as God is God, have delivered the whole Turkish fleet into our hands.' Repeatedly, however, 'through lack of love for Christ and our country, lack of courage, lack of discipline, and lack of reputation', the chances were thrown away. Turned to utter confusion and finally put to flight, what remained of the Venetian fleet was powerless to prevent the Turks from sailing on to Lepanto, their primary objective, besieging it by land and sea and forcing it into surrender.

How much of the Republic's shame was in fact due to the personal shortcomings of her Captain-General is hard to determine; but after the fall of Lepanto a scapegoat was clearly necessary, and immediately his compatriots began to cry for his blood. Shouts of '*Antonio Grimani, ruina de' Cristiani!*' echoed along canals; and on 29 September Melchior Trevisan was sent to assume the command, with orders to return his predecessor in chains to Venice. For one of the Republic's most respected citizens, a Procurator of St Mark who had already served his country with loyalty and distinction for over forty years, it was a cruel blow, deserved or not;

Grimani was fortunate only in his four sons, who now did everything they could to support him in his disgrace. One, Pietro, sped across the Adriatic in a fast brigantine and, finding his father at Zante, sick and half-demented by grief, told him of his recall and easily persuaded him to return at once of his own volition; another, Vincenzo, determined to be at his side when he reached the city, intercepted him at Parenzo in Istria and, knowing that the orders of the Senate must be obeyed in every particular, himself placed the shackles on his father's feet.

It was on the evening of 2 November that Antonio Grimani arrived on the Molo. There a scarlet-robed figure awaited him – another son, Domenico, a Cardinal of the Church of Rome. He too went straight to his father's side, supporting him as he passed into the prisons and holding up the fetters in his hand to spare the old man their weight. Even when he reached his cell Antonio was not left alone. The Cardinal and two other sons remained with him all night until he was arraigned the next morning before the Great Council. The trial that followed was long and exhaustive, but the speech which he made in his own defence is reported to have melted all hearts – and probably saved him from the scaffold. He was sentenced only to exile, and to confinement on the island of Cherso (the modern Cres) off the Dalmatian coast.

Encouraged by their victory, the Turks kept up the offensive. While the fate of Antonio Grimani was still in the balance, their raiding parties had again overrun Friuli and had penetrated as far as Vicenza, spreading havoc through eastern Lombardy and panic among the local populations. Before the new year was out Venice had sent yet another special ambassador to Constantinople to sue for peace. Bajazet's terms were harsh – he demanded virtually all Venetian territory in the Peloponnese – and she refused them with indignation; the following year, however, the Sultan personally led his troops to the siege of Modone. After a heroic resistance it fell at last – the garrison itself, seeing that all hope was gone, setting fire to the town and leaving nothing but its smoking embers for the conquerors to occupy. Its sister colony of Corone followed soon afterwards.

The capture by Venice – achieved only with Spanish help – of Cephalonia and Ithaca was a poor enough recompense for the loss of the two ports which had constituted the Republic's main Peloponnesian bases for two and a half centuries; and despite a good deal of subsequent naval activity through the Aegean and the Dodecanese on the part of Venice, Spain and the Knights of St John from their base in Rhodes, no further appreciable gains were made on either side. At last an uneasy peace was concluded, and was ratified in Venice in May 1503. The Turks returned nothing that they had gained; they now controlled the entire coast of the Peloponnese. Well might the banker Girolamo Priuli write sadly in his diary: 'In losing their shipping and their overseas Empire, the Venetians will also lose their reputation and renown and gradually, but within a very few years, will be consumed altogether.'

Yet the Turks were not the only cause of Venice's misfortunes, nor of Priuli's lamentations; another, Christian, state with no aggressive intent was in the long run to do the Republic more permanent harm than a whole succession of predatory sultans. On 9 September 1499, just about the time when the dreadful news of Sapienza was trickling back to the Rialto, Vasco da Gama landed at Lisbon having made the return journey to India by way of the Cape of Good Hope.

Da Gama was not the first man to have rounded the Cape; that honour had been secured by his compatriot Bartholomew Diaz thirteen years before. He was, however, the first to travel from Europe to the Indies entirely by sea; and in doing so he struck a devastating blow at the commercial supremacy of Venice – and, indeed, at the whole importance of the Mediterranean as a highway to the East. No longer would oriental merchants be obliged to unload their cargoes of silks and spices at Suez or Hormuz in the Persian Gulf, carry them overland across the isthmus or the mountains of Persia and Asia Minor and then re-embark them at Alexandria or Constantinople, Smyrna or Antioch. No longer would they have to put their trust in the slow and uncertain camel caravans that annually plodded across Central Asia to Cathay. Henceforth the same vessel that picked them up at their port of departure could deliver them to their destination. Worse still, none of those – and it was a steadily increasing proportion – that were bound for England and Northern Europe need any longer pass through the Mediterranean at all. The new international clearing-house would be Lisbon – some 2,000 sea-miles nearer London and the Hanseatic ports than was Venice, relatively safe from piracy, and offering goods which, having escaped the extortionate transit dues levied by the various oriental rulers who controlled the land routes, were available at a fraction of Venetian prices. Overnight, Venice had become a backwater.

Or so it seemed. Inevitably there were some Venetians, as Priuli records, 'who refused to believe the news, and others who averred that the King of Portugal could not continue to use the new route to Calicut, since of the thirteen caravels which he had dispatched only six had returned safely, that the losses outweighed the advantages, that few sailors would be prepared to risk their lives on such a long and dangerous voyage.' But the prophets

of doom were more numerous. 'The city was stupefied – and the wisest
men held it to be the worst news that there could possibly be.' Venice was
already in the throes of a serious financial crisis. One of her major private
banks, the Garzoni, had failed in the previous year for 200,000 ducats,
despite a personal offer of 30,000 from the Doge himself in an attempt to
save it; and since then another, the Lippomano, had gone the same way,
causing a panic-stricken run on banks throughout the city. Priuli's own was
to collapse a few years later.

But what, meanwhile, was to be done? The cutting of a Suez canal was
briefly discussed, but rejected as impracticable. At first there was some
doubt as to whether the Republic might not be well advised to accept the
invitation already extended to a Venetian emissary by King Manuel of
Portugal, and send her merchantmen to Lisbon for loading; but such a
course would have infuriated the Sultan of Egypt, who could have taken
an easy revenge by impounding or sacking the Venetian warehouses in
Cairo and Alexandria and, if he had felt like it, by taking punitive measures
against the whole Venetian trading colony. Anyway, the humiliation of
going cap in hand to Portugal was more than the Senate could bring itself
to contemplate. In 1502 it set up a special advisory committee 'to propose
measures lest the King of Portugal take the silver and gold from our hands,
to the destruction of our commerce and prosperity'; and in 1504 another
emissary, Leonardo di Ca' Masser, was sent to report on prospects for the
future and if possible to open fresh negotiations; but during the intervening years the Florentine merchants in Lisbon had been busy, and had so
poisoned the minds of the Portuguese against Venice that he narrowly
escaped a prison sentence.

Thus, within the space of a few days in the late summer of 1499, Venice
had sustained two crippling blows; and many of her citizens, watching the
two bronze Moors striking the hours on Mauro Coducci's newly completed Clock Tower, must have wondered whether those hours were not
already numbered, and whether the sound they heard was not the death-
knell of the Republic. They would have felt still more sick at heart had they
known that a third blow, more calamitous than either of the others, was
shortly to be struck – not this time by any single state but by all Europe,
united against them.

On 13 September 1501 Doge Agostino Barbarigo, now eighty-two, summoned the Signoria and told them that he had decided to resign his office.
He was old and ill; the Republic needed a younger and more energetic ruler
to steer it through the dangers and difficulties of the time. He himself

would return to his house at S. Trovaso and live out the rest of his days in peace. Pulling the ducal ring from his finger, he held it out to the senior councillor for safe keeping until his successor should be appointed.

Ring and resignation alike were refused – though not, it must be said, because of any outstanding qualities in Barbarigo's character. Proud and avaricious he had always been; during his fifteen years as Doge and despite all the safeguards provided by law to curtail the ducal power, he had laid himself open more than once to charges of corruption, perversion of justice and sale of offices – to say nothing of the smuggling of enormous quantities of wine – until by now few of his subjects had a good word to say for him. But it was plain to everyone that he was failing fast, and it seemed easier to let events take their natural course. Exactly a week later he died.[1] The populace, though no longer enjoying any legal rights where ducal elections were concerned, clamoured noisily for their own favourite, Filippo Tron, and when he died in his turn on 26 September there were the usual dark rumours of poison. Marin Sanudo's diary, however, assures us that there was no foul play: Tron was enormously fat, and one day he simply burst.[2] This misfortune seems to have slightly delayed the election: it was not until 2 October that the forty-one electors finally chose Venice's new ruler – Leonardo Loredan.

Loredan's magnificent portrait by Giovanni Bellini, which was probably painted within a year or two of his accession, shows a tall, emaciated man of about seventy with a fine and sensitive face.[3] Unlike so many of his predecessors, he could boast no glittering record as admiral or diplomat. We first hear of him in 1480 as *procuratore* for the building of S. Maria dei Miracoli,[4] then for a brief period he was *podestà* of Padua – after which he had spent virtually all his active life in Venice. Few men better understood the workings of the government machine; but it was to take more than an aristocratic civil servant, however efficient, to rescue the Republic from the desperate situation in which it now found itself.

At home, morale was low. Commercial and economic collapse was part of the trouble, but the real causes were more deeply rooted. Years of

---

1. The great Barbarigo family tomb – from the workshop, if not the actual hand, of Antonio Rizzo – was originally placed in the church of the Carità (now the Accademia) but was broken up when the church was deconsecrated. The largest section, including the figure of the kneeling Doge Agostino, is now in the ante-sacristy of S. Maria della Salute.

2. *Fo ditto per la terra esser stà tosegado, ma non fu vero, fu da graveza el crepò.*

3. Once part of the collection of William Beckford, it is now in the National Gallery, London.

4. Pietro Lombardo's masterpiece (and one of the loveliest small churches in Venice), which was consecrated on the night of 31 December 1489 – though work on the interior continued for some time afterwards.

affluence had had their usual softening effect; the old laws designed to prevent peculation and corruption were less stringently enforced than in former times, and Agostino Barbarigo was not the only patrician to have sought to feather his own personal nest at state expense. In an effort to ensure that his successors should follow a more upright code of conduct, a new system was introduced whereby, on the death of a doge, three inquisitors would be immediately elected with the task of investigating his record and examining any charges laid against him; the evil was too widespread, however, to be stamped out by *ad hoc* legislation of this kind, and the abuses continued. Nor were they the only sign of sickness in the body politic. The absence of any party structure as such meant that there was no controlled outlet for the rivalries, the clashes of personalities and opinions, that are an inevitable and necessary part of a healthy political organism; the Venetian oligarchy, enclosed and introspective, was consequently never altogether free from factional strife. In normal times this could be kept within bounds; at the beginning of the sixteenth century, however, these tensions became suddenly uncontainable, bursting out again and again into violence and bloodshed in the streets and squares. This is not to say that the Venetians were no longer capable of putting their feuds aside and uniting in the defence of the Republic when the need arose; within a very few years a new call to arms was to evoke a response as splendid and spontaneous as any in their history. They were, however, weakened, morally and physically, at a time when – more perhaps, than ever before – strength was needed.

30

The League of Cambrai

[1503–1509]

Tremblez, tremblez, bourgoys veniciens.
Vous avez trop de tresors anciens
Mal conquestez; tost desployer les fault.

Pierre Gringore (?1475–1538)

Even by Roman standards, the summer of 1503 was unusually hot. On the evening of 13 August Pope Alexander VI was dining in the garden of Cardinal Hadrian of Castello when he was attacked by a sudden fever.[1] He returned home and was bled – his doctors were much impressed by the copious flow of blood for a man of his age – but his condition rapidly worsened, and on the 18th he died. Poison, as always, was suspected; on the other hand pestilence was rife, and many others were stricken besides the Pope – including Cesare, Duke of Valentinois, who was too ill to come to his father's bedside.

Since renouncing his Cardinalate in 1498 Cesare had had two ambitions: to re-establish firm control in those parts of the Papal States – particularly the cities of Romagna and the Marches – which had fallen away over the years into semi-independence, and to carve out a permanent secular state in Italy for himself and his children. As Gonfaloniere of the papal army, he had achieved the first of these aims with brilliant success, and seemed well on the way to the second; but Alexander's sudden death threw all his plans into jeopardy. Sick as he was, he lost no time. His confidential agent was dispatched at once to the Vatican, with orders to seize the keys to the papal treasury at stiletto point and bring back the contents to his master; then, richer by 100,000 gold ducats and considerable quantities of plate, he sent his troops to occupy Rome and intimidate the Cardinals into electing a suitably complaisant successor. Their choice fell on a gently amiable nephew of Pius II, who would indeed have suited his purpose well enough;

---

1. Known throughout Rome as 'the rich Cardinal', Hadrian was also, surprisingly enough, Bishop of Hereford, a see which he was to exchange the following year for that of Bath and Wells. He too was similarly stricken, with 'a burning sensation in the intestines which brought on giddiness and stupor ... And though he in time recovered his health, it was not before his outer skin had peeled off from the whole surface of his body' (*Dictionary of National Biography*).

but Pius III died within a month of his election, and by then Cesare had already found himself confronted with a new problem – the territorial aspirations of Venice.

For Venice had seen her chance. Shorn suddenly of her commercial hegemony, bereft of friends or allies, under continual and increasing threat from the Turks in the East and the princes of Europe in the West, it seemed to her that her only long-term hope of survival lay in building up a broad mainland bulwark. Thus, when the dispossessed lords of cities that had fallen to the Duke of Valentinois sought refuge in Venetian territory, she had immediately offered them sympathy and shelter; and when, seeing Cesare facing a crisis in his fortunes, these nobles made determined and more or less simultaneous bids to reinstate themselves, she gave them her active support – always provided that they would accept her as their overlord and govern in her name. By the end of the year the banner of St Mark was already floating over Russi and Forlimpopoli, Rimini, Cervia and Faenza.

Had Pius III lived, it is possible that the Venetians might have got away with this shameless piece of rapacity. On his death, they had immediately put such influence as they could muster in the Sacred College behind the election of Cardinal Giuliano della Rovere as his successor, presumably trusting in the Cardinal's inveterate detestation of the Borgias to ensure his consent to the restoration of the dispossessed lords of the Romagna and in his well-known pro-Venetian sympathies – which had actually earned him the sobriquet of *il Veneziano* – to dispose him towards this effective extension of their dominions. If so, however, they had seriously misjudged their man. Cardinal della Rovere was duly elected, taking the name of Julius II. He made short work of the Duke of Valentinois: Cesare was first incarcerated in the Castel Sant' Angelo and then, a few months later, shipped off a prisoner to Spain, never to return.

As for the Romagna, Pope Julius had already made it clear that he found the presence of the Venetians not much more acceptable than that of the Borgias. The territory belonged, as it always had, to the Papacy; to the Papacy, therefore, it must return. In vain Venice argued that she was second to none in her devotion to the Holy See, and that she intended to hold the disputed lands only as a vicariate of the Pope, to whom she would willingly pay an annual tribute. Julius would hear none of it. 'The Venetians wish to use us as their chaplain,' he snorted to the Venetian Ambassador, Antonio Giustinian, in July 1504; 'but this they shall never do.' Venice, however, stood equally firm. Unable to persuade the Pope to acquiesce in her expansionist policy, she had no choice but to defy him.

Twenty-one years before, at the time of the Ferrara war, she had similarly defied Julius's uncle, Sixtus IV. On that occasion the Pope had placed her under an interdict – a measure which had proved singularly ineffective. Clearly, if she were to be brought to heel, more worldly methods were indicated on this occasion. Julius was equipped neither militarily nor financially to take the field himself; but Louis of France was, and so was the Emperor-elect Maximilian of Habsburg – both of whom might be expected to leap at the opportunity of recovering those territories, at present in Venetian hands, to which they had traditional claims. And so once more we have the sad spectacle of foreign armies being invited into Italy to settle what are essentially domestic differences. The Pope was later to profess his sad reluctance to take such a step: 'Venice', he remarked to Giustinian, 'makes both herself and me the slaves of everyone – she to preserve, myself to win back. Otherwise, working together, we might have found some way of freeing Italy from the tyranny of foreigners.' It was a worthy sentiment; but however real the reluctance there was little enough hesitation in the act itself, and by the autumn of 1504 Julius had succeeded in bringing France and the Empire into an alliance against Venice. The instrument was signed on 22 September, at Blois, where only five and a half years earlier Louis had signed a similar treaty with representatives of the Republic – a treaty which, at least theoretically, was still in force.

The death in November of Queen Isabella of Castile and the ensuing difficulties over the succession caused a rift between France and the Empire which soon made the Treaty of Blois a dead letter; but not before news of it had reached the Rialto. For the first time the Venetians began to understand the dangers of their expansionist policy and the calamitous consequences which, given this continued papal intransigence, it might well bring in its train. In an attempt to placate Julius they agreed to return some of the disputed Borgia territory – though not the three key towns of Rimini, Faenza and Cervia, on which they remained as adamant as ever. The Pope for his part, his hopes of a military attack now swiftly fading, accepted the offer – though he made it clear at the same time that he did not regard the cession as a final settlement, and would not be satisfied until all the Romagna had been returned to his control.

Gestures of appeasement are seldom successful. The concessions that Venice had made, important as they were, had served only to show her weakness. They certainly did not dispose the Pope any more kindly towards her; rather the reverse. Indeed, where the Republic was concerned, his whole political outlook had suffered a profound change. Only five years before, Cardinal della Rovere had been Venice's most trusted friend in the Sacred College; now, Pope Julius II was determined on her destruction.

For the moment, however, there was little that he could do about it; he occupied himself instead in the conquest of Perugia and Bologna – two cities which, like those of the Romagna, were technically vicariates of the Papacy but whose respective lords, the Baglioni and the Bentivogli, saw themselves as independent despots and ruled accordingly. But his hatred of Venice continued to smoulder until a sequence of events in the summer of 1508 once again set it ablaze. The first was when Maximilian, at the head of a sizeable army, entered Venetian territory, ostensibly on his way to Rome for his imperial coronation. He had given the Republic advance notice of his intention the year before, requesting safe conduct and provisions for the army along the way; but Venetian agents in and around his court had left their masters in no doubt that his primary objective was to expel the French from Genoa and Milan, and themselves from Verona and Vicenza, reasserting the old imperial claim to all four cities. Venice had therefore replied, politely but firmly, that His Imperial Majesty would be welcomed with all the honour and consideration due to him if he came 'without warlike tumult and the clangour of arms'; if, on the other hand, he was accompanied by a military force, her treaty obligations and her policy of neutrality unfortunately prevented her from granting his request. Meanwhile, fearing the worst, she strengthened her defences in the Friuli, taking care to reassure Maximilian – who was by this time in Trent – that these measures were not to be interpreted as any sign of hostility but were merely natural precautions which it was only prudent to take in such troubled times.

Furious at this reaction, Maximilian marched regardless. In February 1508 he advanced on Vicenza with the main body of his army while the Marquis of Brandenburg led a somewhat smaller force down the Adige valley towards Rovereto. He found the opposition, however, a good deal stiffer than he had expected. By this time Venice had secured the services of two members of the Orsini family as *condottieri*, Nicolò Count of Pitigliano and his cousin Bartolomeo d'Alviano. The former, with French help, successfully blocked Brandenburg, while the latter had no difficulty in turning back the Emperor himself. A week or two later, a third prong of the imperial attack, formed by a Tyrolese detachment who descended the valley of the Piave into the south-western corner of the Friuli, fared equally badly; Alviano, having dealt with Maximilian, made a forced march across from Vicenza, routed the Austrians utterly and then for good measure occupied Gorizia, Trieste and Fiume. By April, with his army's six-month contract expired and no money with which to extend it, Maximilian had no choice but to agree to a truce for the next three years, allowing the Venetians to keep the territory they had gained.

These victories would have been unwelcome news to Pope Julius at the best of times; coming at this moment, just as he was trying to isolate Venice completely, they resulted in a substantial strengthening of her position, which infuriated him. Already she was taking cautious soundings about the possibility of an alliance with France and Spain, neither of which seemed initially disposed to reject her advances. Then, within weeks of the truce, she took two decisions which Julius could only interpret as acts of open defiance. First she refused to surrender to him the persons of Giovanni Bentivoglio and certain of his followers, who had taken refuge in the lagoons after an unsuccessful attempt to reinstate themselves in Bologna; second, she appointed her own bishop to the vacant see of Vicenza, ignoring the Pope's official nominee.

The second act was merely the exercise of a traditional right; but Julius was in no mood to see it as such. Determined to assert his jurisdiction, 'even' – as he put it – 'if it costs me the tiara itself', he now summoned all his diplomatic strength towards his primary objective, not just the isolation but the humiliation of Venice, her deliberate reduction to a level whence she could never recover her old authority and prosperity. A new stream of emissaries was dispatched from Rome – to France and Spain, to Maximilian, to Milan, to Hungary and the Netherlands. All bore the same proposal, for a joint expedition by western Christendom against the Venetian Republic, and the consequent dismemberment of her Empire. Maximilian would regain all the lands east of the river Mincio that had ever been imperial or subject to the House of Habsburg, including Verona, Vicenza and Padua, Treviso and its neighbourhood, Friuli and Istria. To France would go Bergamo and Brescia, Crema, Cremona and all those territories that Venice had acquired by the Treaty of Blois nine years before. In the south, Trani, Brindisi and Otranto would revert to the House of Aragon. Hungary, if she joined the League, could have back Dalmatia; Cyprus would be the prize of Savoy. Ferrara and Mantua, too, would have all their former lands restored to them. There would, in fact, be something for everyone.

As for Pope Julius himself, he would naturally take back the remaining cities that formed the original *casus belli* – Cervia, Rimini and Faenza, with their dependent castles. But his long-term aim went far beyond any question of territorial boundaries. Italy as he saw it was now divided into three.

In the north was French Milan, in the south Spanish Naples. Between the two, there was room for one – but only one – powerful and prosperous state; and that state, Julius was determined, must be the Papacy. Venice might survive, if she wished, as a city; as an Empire, she must be destroyed.

The states of Europe could not be expected to feel much sympathy for such a policy; there was indeed no conceivable reason why they should. Their motive for joining the proposed league was not to support the Papacy but to help themselves. Maximilian, in fact, realizing that he would never regain his lost territories without French assistance, had already made tentative approaches to King Louis independently of the papal initiative. It was of little consequence to him or to any of the other prospective allies to whom Julius had appealed that, apart from the cities of the Romagna – which did not concern them anyway – Venice had a perfect legal right to the territories which they planned to seize, a right enshrined in treaties freely entered into by both France and Spain and, more recently still, by Maximilian himself, as part of the three-year truce signed only a few weeks before. Still less were they moved by moral misgivings as to their own behaviour. However much they might try to present their action as a blow struck on behalf of righteousness against iniquity, by which a rapacious aggressor was at last to be brought to justice, they were all fully conscious of the fact that their own conduct was more reprehensible than ever Venice's had been. But the temptation was too great, the promised rewards too high. They accepted.

So it was that the death-warrant of the Venetian Empire was signed, on 10 December 1508, at Cambrai, by Margaret of Austria, Regent of the Netherlands, on behalf of her father Maximilian and by the Cardinal Georges d'Amboise for the King of France. Julius himself, though his Legate was present at Cambrai, did not formally join the League until the following March; but, in the preamble, his voice can be heard again and again:

... to put an end to the losses, the injuries, the violations, the damages which the Venetians have inflicted, not only on the Apostolic See but on the Holy Roman Empire, on the House of Austria, on the Dukes of Milan, on the Kings of Naples and on divers other princes, occupying and tyrannically usurping their goods, their possessions, their cities and castles, as if they had deliberately conspired to do ill to all around them ...

Thus we have found it not only well-advised and honourable, but even necessary, to summon all people to take their just revenge and so to extinguish, like a great fire, the insatiable rapacity of the Venetians and their thirst for power.

Three months later, on top of all their other misfortunes, the Venetians suffered a great fire of their own, a disaster which had a still more lowering effect on the general morale. On 14 March 1509, while the *Maggior Consiglio* was in session, the Doges' Palace was shaken by the blast of a tremendous explosion. It came from the Arsenal, over a quarter of a mile distant, where a spark had ignited a gunpowder magazine. Immediately the session was suspended, and all those present hurried to see the extent of the damage. It was worse than they could have thought possible. The whole area around the Arsenal was an inferno. Many of the houses had collapsed at the moment of the detonation, countless others were already blazing. All available casual labour was summoned from every corner of the city. The Councillors threw off their robes of office and flung themselves into the work of rescue. They did all they could; but the death-toll was high and that of the wounded and homeless higher still. As was only to be expected, there were dark rumours of sabotage by the agents of King Louis; the Council of Ten ordered a thorough investigation, but to no avail. The Venetians' one consolation was the knowledge that, only twenty-four hours before, 4,000 barrels of powder had been loaded on to barges for transport to Cremona. Had they remained one more day, the explosion would have been still more violent and the Doges' Palace itself reduced to a pile of rubble. Even as things were, Venice's war potential had been dangerously diminished – and at a moment when she needed every ounce of strength to face the coming storm.

For the clouds were now gathering fast. The Pope's delay in finally committing himself seems to have been due to his initial uncertainty whether the other signatories were in earnest; he had had no wish publicly to put the whole weight of his authority behind an alliance as abortive as that which he had engineered five years before. But when, in that same month of March, the King of Spain announced his formal adherence to the League, Julius hesitated no longer; on 5 April he openly associated himself with the other members. Nine days later France declared war.

By now anxiety in the city had given way to alarm, and the Venetians were ready to make real sacrifices, even of their national pride, to deflect the League from its objectives. They welcomed proposals of mediation from Henry VII of England; they even offered to restore Rimini and Faenza to papal control – but the Pope would no longer hear of any such accommodation. 'Let the Signoria do as it wishes with its lands', he replied when he heard of the latter suggestion. Turning to the Emperor, they sent a special ambassador to assure him of the Republic's continuing devotion and to explain that their apparent discourtesy of the previous year was solely due to their treaty obligations towards France; now that they were free of any such bonds, they felt it only right to warn His Imperial Majesty of French ambitions, which could only be realized at the expense of the Empire, and to offer him their support against King Louis before it was too late.

The approach, it must be admitted, was scarcely subtle; Venetian diplomacy could – and usually did – do better than that, and Maximilian's lack of response can have occasioned the Signoria little surprise. But Venice was now confronted by an array of European powers more formidable than any Italian state had ever faced before, an array which included the four most tremendous figures in Christendom. Allies she had none. Her back was to the wall; and when the Great Council met in plenary session on Sunday, 22 April, Doge Loredan made no secret of the fact, calling on his compatriots to mend their ways, to forget their feuds and differences and to make a supreme effort to save the Republic – 'since', he concluded, 'if we lose it, we shall lose a fine state, the Great Council will be no more, and we shall no longer live in the freedom that we now enjoy.' He himself, after the state banquet traditionally given by the Doge on the Feast of St Mark – three days hence – would set an example by offering to the Treasury all his private plate and returning 5,000 ducats of his salary, keeping only 2,000 for his personal expenses; he trusted that many others would follow his lead. As he left the hall, it was seen that the old man could hardly bear himself upright in his grief.

And worse was to come. On 27 April Pope Julius issued a Bull in terms far more violent than those employed by his uncle twenty-six years before. Venice, he thundered, had become so puffed up with pride as to molest her neighbours and invade their territories, including those of the Holy See itself; she had given shelter to rebels against the Vicar of Christ; she had flouted the law of the Church and his own specific commands with regard to his bishops and clergy, imprisoning them and sending them into exile according to her whim; finally, at a time when he, the Pope, was striving to unite all Christian peoples against the Infidel, she had deliberately obstructed his efforts for her own profit and advancement. Accordingly he proposed to declare a solemn excommunication and interdict against her, permitting any other state or person to attack or despoil her or any of her subjects, to obstruct her traffic on land or sea and to do her all possible harm and hurt, if within twenty-four days she did not make full restitution.

Venice dealt with the new sentence as she had the last, refusing to accept it, forbidding its publication in her territory, and announcing – by means of a proclamation nailed by two of her agents to the door of St Peter's – her intention of appealing to a Council. But her situation now was far

graver than ever it had been in the days of Pope Sixtus; and the papal ban
was quickly followed by yet another reverse, in Rome itself. There she had
recently succeeded, in return for large financial subsidies, in securing the
support of a powerful anti-papal faction led by the Orsini, two of whom,
as we have seen, were already on her payroll as *condottieri*. Inevitably, word
of this intrigue soon reached the ear of the Pope who, thanks to the
excommunication, was able to threaten the Orsini with spiritual punishments against the entire family – the prospect of which even they could not
ignore. Not only must they at once break off all contacts with Venice; they
were also forbidden to return to her the monies they had received. It is a
lasting tribute to Orsini honour that, despite this solemn injunction, 3,000
ducats were nevertheless secretly returned to the Venetian emissary.

Desperate for allies, the Venetians made one further attempt to suborn
the Emperor, offering him, in return for his alliance, a down payment of
200,000 Rhenish florins and military help in the reconquest of Milan; but
Maximilian made no reply, and the Imperial silence was still unbroken
when the onslaught came.

On 15 April 1509, only twenty-four hours after their declaration of war,
the first French soldiers marched into Venetian territory. The Venetian
mercenaries, at this time still under the command of the Orsini cousins,
who had apparently resisted the Pope's pressures on the rest of their family
as successfully as they had repulsed Maximilian's armies the year before –
fought back fiercely, and for the first three weeks of somewhat indecisive
skirmishing probably had the balance of advantage. On 9 May, however,
they were so busy looting the town of Treviglio, which they had just
recaptured, that they failed to prevent the French from crossing the Adda
at Cassano, a mile or two to the west; and it was while discussing how best
to meet this crisis that the temperamental differences between the two
condottieri, which for some time had been threatening the efficiency of their
joint command, led them at last into open – and disastrous – disagreement.
Alviano, younger and always impetuous, favoured an early test of strength;
the cautious Pitigliano, on the other hand, pointing out with reason that
his instructions from Venice were to avoid pitched battle, counselled
patience and delay. As senior of the two, he might well have carried his
point had not Alviano, while leading his section of the army south to a
more strategic position, suddenly found himself confronted by the French
just outside the village of Agnadello.

The actual order to attack seems to have come from King Louis himself.
Whether Alviano could still at this point have avoided battle, or whether

in the circumstances he would have been well advised to do so, is an open question; at all events, he did not hesitate, and, sending an urgent appeal for help to Pitigliano, who was a mile or two further ahead, he drew up his troops and artillery on the hillside above a row of vineyards and opened fire. There was no doubt that the Venetians had the advantage of position. Twice de Chaumont,[1] the French Viceroy of Milan, tried to attack – first with his cavalry, then with his regiment of Swiss pikemen – but the vines and irrigation ditches that separated him from the Venetians prevented either attempt from gathering momentum; soon, too, it began to pour with rain, which quickly transformed the already marshy ground into a morass. Alviano, on the other hand, could charge his own cavalry down a firm and gentle slope, and thus had no trouble in repulsing both attempts, holding down his adversaries in the valley, where, despite the difficulty of lowering the elevation of his guns to the point where they could be of maximum effect, they made an easy and tempting target.

If, therefore, at this stage in the battle Pitigliano had responded to his cousin's renewed appeal and hastened to his aid, Venice might have carried the day – with far-reaching consequences for the future history of the Republic. But Pitigliano did not respond. His reply had merely re-emphasized the desirability of avoiding battle; he had then continued on his way, apparently oblivious of what was going on behind him. Even then, Alviano still had the upper hand – until, without warning, King Louis himself appeared with the main body of his army, while simultaneously the French rearguard launched a surprise attack from behind. Three-quarters surrounded, the Italians collapsed. Two of the cavalry companies fled in confusion; the infantry, unable to flee, were cut down where they stood. Alviano himself, though wounded terribly in the face, fought heroically for three hours before being captured.

The Venetian losses were about four thousand – including an entire regiment of pikemen, raised in the Romagna by another *condottiere*, Nando da Brisighella; they perished to the last man. Yet the real price of the defeat was paid, not in manpower, but in morale. Most of the cavalry remained intact, as did the several thousand troops under Pitigliano, who had taken no part in the fight. But mercenaries have ever proved untrustworthy; lacking the motivations that keep a native-born national army in the field – patriotism, protection of family, hope of glory and recognition at home, or even fear of retribution for any display of cowardice – they have tended throughout history to melt away when the prospects of rich rewards have

1. Charles d'Amboise, Seigneur de Chaumont, was the nephew of Cardinal d'Amboise, the French signatory of the League. His portrait by Leonardo da Vinci hangs in the Louvre.

grown dim or the tide of battle has turned against them. Pitigliano could only watch, helpless and – one hopes – ashamed, as unit after unit deserted him. Those few of his men who still accepted his leadership in no way constituted a fighting force with which to continue the campaign, even if he had had the stomach to do so. He had no choice but to retire, with all the speed of which he was capable, to the lagoons.

The news of the catastrophe reached Venice at ten o'clock in the evening of 15 May. Marin Sanudo the diarist chanced to be in the Senate Chamber with certain of the *Savii* when it arrived, and has left an account of the stunned silence with which they heard of the completeness of the Venetian defeat, the flight of Pitigliano, the names of the principal dead and wounded – most of whom, in a city the size of Venice, would have been well known to everyone present. Doge and Senate were immediately alerted and, despite the lateness of the hour, met in emergency session as soon as they could be assembled – the Doge, notes Sanudo, looking as usual half dead. Meanwhile rumour spread like wildfire through the city, and the ordinary citizens too hastened to the Palace until the courtyard was thronged with people, all clamouring for authoritative information in the vain hope that the truth could not be so bad as they had been led to believe.

It was worse. The French were at that moment in the course of reoccupying all those territories west of the Mincio to which they could adduce the most tenuous claim, and though Maximilian was characteristically slower off the mark, it was clear that his arrival would not be long delayed. The entire Venetian mainland, in short, was as good as lost. What was left of it lay utterly defenceless, with no armed forces worthy of the name to prevent further depredations. Most of the objectives agreed upon by the League of Cambrai had already been achieved at a single stroke, and the remainder seemed likely to be realized in the near future. But for those treacherously shallow waters with which she was surrounded, Venice herself – disillusioned, demoralized and utterly humiliated – would have stood little chance of survival.

A century earlier, the Venetians might have consoled themselves with the thought that they could manage perfectly well without the *terra firma*. In those less complicated days they were still people of the sea, living by a rich and profitable commerce largely dominated by the markets of the Levant and the further East. But times had changed. Their Levantine trade had never properly recovered from the fall of Constantinople in 1453. No longer was Venice mistress of the Eastern Mediterranean; where once her sovereignty had been virtually undisputed, her colonial empire had now been reduced to a few tenuous and uncertain toeholds in an Ottoman world. No longer, if the Turks closed their harbours to her, could she trust to the more distant Oriental markets for her salvation; the Portuguese had seen to that. No longer, in short, could she live by sea alone. Nowadays her citizens tended to look west rather than east, to the fertile plains of Lombardy and the Veneto, to the thriving industries of Verona and Brescia, Padua and Vicenza, and to the network of roads and waterways that linked them to the rich merchant cities of Europe. It was on the mainland, now, that they had invested their wealth and reposed their trust; and the mainland was theirs no more.

In the Senate and the Council of Ten there was talk of fighting on. It was agreed that an attempt should be made to raise more men and money – though no one seemed very clear where these were to be found – and that letters should be written to the Captain-General, the proveditor \Andrea Gritti and the Venetian Rector of Brescia assuring them that the government had not lost heart and encouraging them to remain steadfast. Two new proveditors, however, specially elected to supervise the regroupment and to infuse new spirit into the shattered army, declined to take up their appointments; and everyone knew in his heart that militarily, at least for the moment, the situation was hopeless. The interdict too was having its effect: on Ascension Day – 17 May – Sanudo records that the usual crowds of foreign visitors were completely absent, the Piazza forlorn and empty. The whole city seemed to be in mourning. The Venetians themselves, however, were anything but idle. Even if their enemies could not reach them across the shallows, a blockade was always a possibility; and they used this momentary breathing-space to lay in stocks of corn, and even to build emergency flour-mills on rafts along the water's edge. Vagabonds and suspicious persons were rounded up, and special committees were formed, composed equally of noblemen and ordinary citizens, to keep a twenty-four-hour watch on all entrances to the lagoon.

Further approaches had been made to Maximilian, drawing his attention once again to French ambitions, repeating the offer of 200,000 florins – or, if he preferred, 50,000 a year for ten years – in return for his agreeing to act as 'father and protector' of the Republic, and even proposing the restitution of all the territories so unexpectedly acquired the year before. But the Emperor made no reply. By the beginning of June his specially empowered representatives were already busy, receiving the submission of one city after another – Verona, Vicenza and Padua, Rovereto, Riva and Cittadella – until the Venetians had fallen back to Mestre and all Lombardy and the Veneto were lost. At the same time the Apulian ports were restored to the King of Naples; the Duke of Ferrara reoccupied Rovigo, Este, Monselice and the Polesine – that region between the Po and the lower Adige to which his Duchy had long laid a claim; the Marquis of Mantua recovered Asola and Lunato; and, on 28 May, the Pope's official Legate received back those fateful lands of the Romagna – including Rimini, Faenza, Cervia and Ravenna – with which the whole tragedy had begun. Contrary to the express terms of the agreement, all the Venetian officials in these cities were thrown into prison.

Elsewhere things went a little better. Treviso courageously defied the imperial commissioner – whose small accompanying force was intended more for ceremonial duties than for any show of strength – and hoisted the banner of St Mark on the following feast-day, 10 June. Friuli too remained for the most part firm, Udine actually appealing to the Republic for a detachment of *stradioti* with which to defend herself should the need arise. But although Venice showed her gratitude to such cities as stood by her, granting them privileges or tax concessions, their loyalty can have accorded her little real comfort in comparison with what she had lost.

31

Capitulation and Absolution

[1509–1510]

Li aricordemo stagino ben con li pontifici ... da poi questo atto arete assa' beni, e da nui non mancherà ogni bon oficio.

We recommend you to stand well with Popes ... then it will be well with you, and you will not lack favours.

> Julius II to the Venetian Ambassadors
> (Report of Domenico Trevisan,
> Sanudo X, 78)

Venice's losses were indeed immense; but as the weeks went by and her people recovered from the initial shock of Agnadello and its consequences, they soon began to ask themselves whether their first reactions had not been a little exaggerated. Where their Milanese holdings were concerned, with Louis's victorious army still in the field, they had had little option but to surrender all the territory required of them; with the Empire, however, there were signs that a more robust line might profitably have been taken. Maximilian, they suddenly realized, had achieved nothing for the League after lending it his name. He had as yet sent no army against them, and indeed had not explicitly declared war until 29 May, a fortnight after their defeat. His imperial commissioners, as the Trevisani and Friulani had demonstrated, could be defied with impunity. He was also known to be seriously short of funds. Had they been right, they asked themselves, to abandon their cities and towns so easily? They had done so because they knew that they could not defend them; but perhaps, after all, no such defence would be necessary. They had also believed that these cities and towns were the price that had to be paid to maintain their own existence as an independent state, much as a captain will jettison his cargo to save his ship – a simile which cropped up more than once during the discussions in the Senate and among the Ten. Now they were not so sure. The League members still seemed as implacable as ever in their hostility to the Republic. If at some future time they should try to eradicate it completely, then Padua and her sister-cities would be vitally important for the defence of the lagoon. Many of these, furthermore, had been perfectly content to live under Venetian rule, and within days of the transfer of power had begun to resent the heavier and far less sympathetic hand of their new imperial masters.

It was early in July, less than two months after Agnadello, that there came the first reports of spontaneous uprisings on the mainland in favour of Venice; and to Andrea Gritti, now proveditor in Treviso, were sent orders to support the insurgents with whatever forces he could muster. At about the same time there were mysterious rumours of two tall travellers in white hooded cloaks who, it was said, had been brought from the mainland under cover of darkness in the official barge of the Ten and had remained in secret consultation with the Signoria until one o'clock in the morning, when they had returned as silently as they had come. A few days later, on the 16th, a whole fleet of ships set out across the lagoon to Fusina, while other craft patrolled the waters surrounding Venice itself to ensure that no unauthorized persons left the city. In the early hours of the following morning, writes Sanudo, three heavy farm carts, laden with corn, presented themselves at the Codalunga gate at Padua. The German garrison, suspecting nothing, lowered the drawbridge. The first two carts passed over quickly enough, but the third remained half-way across, holding the bridge open. Suddenly, with a great cry of '*Marco, Marco!*' a body of horsemen appeared as if from nowhere and charged through the gates. The *Landsknechts*, once they had recovered from their initial surprise, put up a spirited defence; but after a short and bloody engagement in the main square they were forced to admit defeat.

Thus on 17 July, after just forty-two days as an imperial city, Padua returned beneath the sheltering wing of the lion of St Mark; and many smaller towns in its neighbourhood and in the Polesine followed its example. Meanwhile another *condottiere* temporarily in Venetian pay named Lucio Malvezzo had seized Legnago, a key town on the Adige, from which he was threatening Verona and Vicenza. Perhaps the situation was not quite so desperate, after all.

But although, in the high summer of 1509, some Venetians may have wondered whether the Republic might not ultimately succeed in regaining much of the mainland so hastily and thoughtlessly surrendered, not even the most optimistic among them can have supposed that they would be allowed to do so without a fight. Maximilian was known to be at Trento, only a few miles across the frontier; sooner or later he was bound to appear, and the news of the reconquest of Padua could only hasten his arrival.

And so, indeed, it did. By early August a heterogeneous and unwieldy army had started on its way towards Padua – moving even more slowly than usual because of a serious shortage of horses to drag the guns – to be joined at various stages of the journey by a force of several thousand French, both cavalry and infantry, a body of Spaniards, and smaller contingents from Mantua, Ferrara and the Pope. Maximilian himself, meanwhile, wisely decided to set up temporary headquarters at Asolo in the Palace of the Queen of Cyprus – who, with her numerous entourage, had fled to Venice at the first news of his approach.

Though light skirmishing began as soon as the first imperialist units reached the walls of Padua, it was a good month before the full army was collected and ready – during which time the defenders had plenty of time to strengthen the fortifications and lay in plentiful stocks of food, water and ammunition. By now, too, Pitigliano – who was lucky to have kept his command after his recent deplorable showing – had pulled himself and his remaining men together and had brought them, with a volunteer body of 200 young Venetian noblemen which included two sons of Doge Loredan, to supplement the existing garrison. When on 15 September the siege at last began in earnest the city was well able to defend itself against all comers.

It needed to be. For a fortnight the German and French heavy artillery pounded away at the northern walls, reducing them to rubble; and yet, somehow, thanks to the skill and discipline of those within – qualities as noticeable there as they had been lacking among Pitigliano's men three months before – every assault was beaten back. At last, on 30 September, Maximilian gave up – 'for', as he wrote a week later to his daughter Margaret, 'in consideration of the strength of guns and defenders that the Venetians have in the city, and the great works that they have done therein, such that the world has never seen their equal, and since they include more than 15,000 men fully armed, we and our captains and our counsellors have agreed that it will be more profitable to cease this siege than to prolong it further.'

There was little enough profit to be seen anywhere. The Emperor had suffered a serious loss of face and he knew it. Hurriedly, he made arrangements to leave part of his army in Italy under the Duke of Anhalt, for the garrisoning of other, less spirited cities and to provide an emergency force should the need arise; then, three weeks later, he led his shambling army back across the Alps, whence it had come.

The Venetians, meanwhile, were jubilant. To have recaptured Padua had been, in itself, a victory; but to have held it successfully against an army of some 40,000 – that was a triumph. And there was more to come. On 14 November, Pitigliano advanced on Vicenza, where the Duke of Anhalt surrendered almost at once. A similar attack on Verona failed a week later, but the disappointment was soon forgotten as more and more other towns – Cittadella, Bassano, Feltre and Belluno in the north, Este, Montagnana and Monselice in the south – all declared themselves for Venice.

These last three towns were regained as a result of a renewed Venetian offensive against the Duke of Ferrara, who had not only helped himself after Agnadello to the long-disputed region of the Polesine but whose brother, Cardinal Ippolito of Este, had given valuable, if ultimately ineffectual, assistance to Maximilian during the siege of Padua; and it was with the object of teaching the Duke a further sharp lesson that the Captain-General of the fleet, Angelo Trevisan, now received instructions to take a squadron of seventeen light galleys up the Po, causing as much devastation as he could of Ferrarese territory. Trevisan objected that the dangers involved were out of all proportion to the damage he could do; but he was overruled. Sailing up the river, he met increasingly heavy resistance until at Polesella, some ten miles from Ferrara, he decided to disembark his men, who dug themselves in behind a strong bastion, constructing a great boom of boats and chains a little further upstream to protect their ships from attack. All might have gone well had not the river, swollen by the December rains, snapped the boom just as the Duke was mounting an attack on the bastion. In the ensuing confusion the Ferrarese were able to move their heavy guns under cover of darkness right down to the water's edge – from which, at point-blank range, they proceeded to blast the defenceless Venetian ships out of the water. Two only escaped destruction. The luckless Trevisan was brought back to Venice, arraigned before the Senate and the Ten, and sentenced to three years' exile in Portogruaro.

When Pope Julius heard the news of the reconquest of Padua he flew into a towering rage; and when, after the failure of Maximilian's attempt to recover it, he learnt that Verona too was likely to declare for Venice, and that the Marquis of Mantua – who was now in the pay of the League – had been taken prisoner by the Venetians while bringing up reinforcements, he is said to have hurled his cap to the ground and blasphemed St Peter. The restitution of the papal lands had appeased him not one jot. His hatred of Venice was still as vindictive as ever, and although in response to a grovelling letter from the Doge he had agreed to accept a six-man Venetian embassy in Rome, it was soon clear that he had done so only in order to inflict still further humiliations on the Republic. On their arrival in early July, the envoys had been forbidden, as excommunicates, to enter the city until after dark, to lodge in the same house or even to go out together on official business. They enjoyed none of the privileges or courtesies normally accorded to the diplomatic representatives of foreign states. One only of them, a certain Girolamo Donà whom the Pope had known some years before, was granted an audience – which rapidly deteriorated into a furious diatribe by Julius himself. Did the Venetians really believe that the Church's ban would be lifted just because they had returned a few cities to which they had no right in the first place? Not until the provisions of the League of Cambrai had been carried out to the letter and the Venetians had knelt before him with halters round their necks would he consider giving them absolution. He finished by handing Donà a paper summarizing his demands, which Sanudo later described as a 'devilish and shameful document' and which the Senate, when they saw it, rejected out of hand. 'Rather let us send fifty envoys to the Turk', the Doge's son Lorenzo Loredan shouted in anger, 'before we accept such terms.'

It was no empty rhetoric; nor can Loredan's audience have found his words particularly shocking. They knew quite well that their recent successes on the mainland, apart from providing a much-needed boost in the general morale, had done little to improve their long-term prospects. The League was still in force, its hostility undiminished. True, the Emperor had been temporarily humiliated; but his army remained intact and he would certainly be back in the spring to redeem his honour and reputation. The French in Milan were also sharpening their swords. Meanwhile Venice continued to stand alone, her army defeated and demoralized, her treasury empty, most of her income from the *terra firma* cut off, and without a single friend to give her support. She had no choice: if no Christian power was willing to stand by her, to the Turks she would have to turn.

And so, on 11 September, the decision was taken. Venice would appeal to the Sultan, pointing out to him that the League was his declared adversary as well as her own and requesting as a matter of urgency as many troops as he could spare, together with a loan of not less than 100,000 ducats. She would even ask him to cease his purchases of Florentine and Genoese cloth, the profits from which were also being used to support the League. To the princes of the West, had they known of it, such an appeal could only have appeared as an additional proof of Venetian faithlessness, rather than as an act of desperation for which they had only themselves to blame; it is a sad reflection on European political thinking that at a time when Christendom itself was struggling for survival, its leaders, headed by the Pope himself, should have combined to destroy the one state which should have constituted their first line of defence, forcing it into an attempted alliance with the common enemy.

But the Sultan remained silent; and though the new King of England,

Henry VIII, showed unmistakable signs of sympathy with the Venetian cause, he too failed to provide any material support. The destruction of Trevisan's river fleet came as a further blow; and by the end of the year the Republic could continue no longer. On 29 December it resolved to accept the Pope's conditions for peace. They proved savage: Venice must subject herself totally to the Holy See. Gone would be her traditional right to appoint bishops and clergy within her boundaries, to try them in her courts, to tax them without papal consent. Gone, too, would be her jurisdiction over subjects of the papal states in her territory. The Pope was to receive full compensation for all his expenses in recovering his territories and for all the revenues which he had lost while those territories were in Venetian hands. The Adriatic was henceforth to be open to all, free of the customs dues which Venice had been accustomed to demand from foreign shipping. Finally, the Republic would be bound to provide not less than fifteen galleys in the event of war against the Turks.

Though they had expected no less, and despite their critical situation, the Venetians could even now scarcely bring themselves to agree to these demands. When the necessary resolution was first put to the Senate it was rejected; even on the second ballot it obtained only the bare minimum of votes required to carry it. But after a further month of negotiation they managed to wring from Pope Julius only two minor concessions: that the freedom from customs dues in the Adriatic should be accorded only to subjects of the Papacy, and that the obligation to provide the galleys, while they fully accepted it, should remain unwritten to avoid giving the Sultan unnecessary offence.

And so agreement was reached, and on 24 February 1510 Pope Julius took his seat on a specially constructed throne outside the central doors of St Peter's, twelve of his Cardinals around him. The five Venetian envoys, dressed in scarlet – the sixth had died a few days before – advanced towards him and kissed his foot, then knelt on the steps while their spokesman, Domenico Trevisan, made a formal request on behalf of the Republic for absolution and the Bishop of Ancona read out the full text of the agreement. This must have made painful listening for the envoys, not so much because it contained a compulsory confession by Venice that her manifold sins and wickedness had richly deserved the excommunication which she had suffered – the Bishop's voice was fortunately so low as to be scarcely audible – as because it lasted a full hour, during which time they were forced to remain on their knees. Rising with difficulty, they received twelve symbolic scourging rods from the twelve Cardinals – the actual scourging was mercifully omitted – swore to observe the terms of the agreement, kissed the Pope's feet again and were at last granted absolution. Only then were the doors of the Basilica opened, and the assembled company proceeded in state for prayers at the High Altar before going on to mass in the Sistine Chapel – all except the Pope, who, as one of the Venetians explained in his report, 'never attended these long services'.[1]

Venice had capitulated – but only because she had had no choice. This fact her government was determined to put on record. Thus, on the very day that her ambassadors were sent their full powers to sign the agreement on behalf of the Republic, the Council of Ten had decided, by an overwhelming vote of thirteen to two,[2] to make a formal statement to the effect that Venice had suffered grievous wrongs at the hands of the Pope and had accepted his unjust demands 'not spontaneously or of her own free will but under coercion – by force, fear and most imminent threats'; their obligations were therefore not binding, and they reserved the right to resubmit their case, as and when the opportunity offered, either to the same Pope, 'when he was better informed and not under hostile influences', or to his successors.

The Venetian envoys may not have been any more aware of the fact than were Julius and his Cardinals, but the instrument to which they set their seals with such ceremony, the terms and conditions to which they listened so long and painfully, had thus already been declared null and void by their own government, nearly three weeks before.

The news of the Pope's reconciliation with Venice had not been well received by his fellow-members of the League. The French, in particular, had done all they could to dissuade him from taking such a step, and at the absolution ceremony the French, Imperial and Spanish ambassadors to the Holy See, all of whom were in Rome at the time, were conspicuous by their absence. Although Julius had made no effort to dissociate himself formally from the alliance, he was soon afterwards heard to boast that by granting Venice absolution he had plunged a dagger into the heart of the King of France – proof enough, if proof were needed, that he now saw the French, rather than the Venetians, as the principal obstacle to his Italian policy and that he had effectively changed sides. By March 1510 we find the Venetian Senate considering how best to include the Pope in a projected alliance with England and Scotland, and Julius himself deliberately picking a quarrel with his erstwhile ally Duke Alfonso of Ferrara, whose growing identification with French interests both irritated and alarmed him.

But this did not mean that the League was a dead letter: far from it. With

---

the coming of spring the French were once again on the march, materially assisted by the Duke of Anhalt and Duke Alfonso, expecting to combine with Maximilian and then to settle the situation in the Veneto once and for all. Predictably enough, Maximilian failed to appear; but even without him, their combined armies easily outnumbered the Venetian. Venice, too, had a further problem on her hands: Pitigliano had died at Lonigo in January,[1] and a suitable successor was not easy to find. As an interim measure she could only entrust the supreme command to her proveditor, Andrea Gritti, whose integrity, courage and long experience of warfare could not alter the fact that he was, like all proveditors, essentially a civilian and consequently unable to inspire confidence in professional mercenary troops.

None the less, it is doubtful whether even the greatest of *condottiere* generals could have stemmed the advance of the French, German and Ferrarese armies which, having made their rendezvous just south of Legnago, quickly reoccupied Este and Montagnana and thrust northward against Vicenza. Andrea Gritti, unable to put up any effective resistance, withdrew to the east; and on 24 May Anhalt marched his men into the city. For the second time in a single year, the Vicentines were forced to acknowledge the Emperor as their overlord.

They did not do so willingly. Anhalt, they knew, had been enraged and humiliated by their recent defection; he would show them no quarter now that he had returned. Many of the leading citizens, in fact, had already fled with their wives, children and most precious possessions to Padua or Venice, and those that remained were quite unable to pay the savage fines that were demanded of them. When, to crown their misfortunes, they now saw the drunken German mercenaries lurching through the streets, looting and pillaging as they went, a further mass exodus took place, in the course of which well over a thousand fugitives took refuge in a huge cave, quarried deep into the heart of the nearby Monte Berico. They would have done better to stay in Vicenza: before long a band of French irregulars discovered their hiding-place and, smelling loot, called upon them to come out. They refused, whereupon the French built a huge fire in the mouth of the cave, which was soon filled with smoke. One small boy, we read, found a minute fissure in the rock, through which he managed to draw in enough fresh air to save him; all the others were asphyxiated, and the bodies were duly stripped of everything of value that was found on them.

It is only fair to add that, when news of this atrocity reached the French

---

1. He was brought back to Venice and buried with full honours in SS. Giovanni e Paolo, where his monument, which includes his equestrian statue in gilded wood, can be seen in the south transept.

camp, the punishment visited on those responsible was swift and severe. The famous knight Bayard – the original *chevalier sans peur et sans reproche*, who had taken part in all the principal French campaigns in Italy since Charles VIII's first arrival in 1494 – had two of the ringleaders hanged in front of the cave, and they were not the only ones to suffer. But the damage was done. Word of what had happened spread rapidly across North Italy, and with it a great wave of revulsion against the invaders. French prestige had sustained a grave blow, from which it would not soon recover.

But, for Venice, the loss of Vicenza – with that of Legnago, which had followed a fortnight later – was graver by far; and it augured ill for the future. The forces of the League, with or without Maximilian, were strong; their speed and momentum were formidable; their morale was high. Her own army, outnumbered and outgeneralled, was in retreat. The campaigning season had scarcely begun. What further disasters might not ensue before it ended? Padua, certainly, must expect a renewed attack; if Padua fell, what would be the chances of retaining the mainland shores of the lagoon? And if they in their turn were overrun – was Venice herself still as impregnable now as she had been in former centuries? Already, in the past twenty years, she had suffered irreparable harm. Her trade in the East, her Empire in the West, both alike were in ruins. Her honour might be intact – more or less – but her reputation was gone. Her finances were critical, with no prospect of improvement. With the enemy at her gates, what hope could she have of survival?

Yet the average, incurious visitor to the city would have noticed nothing amiss. Never had Venice looked more magnificent. The most disastrous period in her history, that anguished decade that came near to witnessing the destruction of the Republic itself, also saw the Venetian creative genius in all the fullness of its flower. Those were the years in which the seventy-year-old Giovanni Bellini worked on one of the last and loveliest of his altarpieces – that of S. Zaccaria – while his brother Gentile was engaged, with others, on the *Miracles of the True Cross*, now in the Accademia; in which Giorgione and Titian, both still in their twenties, collaborated on the Fondaco dei Tedeschi – now the Central Post Office – covering it with frescoes of which, alas, not a trace remains; in which Carpaccio produced those nine sublime paintings that have made the Scuola di S. Giorgio degli Schiavoni famous throughout the world. Meanwhile Pietro Lombardo and his sons were putting the finishing touches to S. Maria dei Miracoli, and Mauro Coducci was completing the S. Zaccaria façade, S. Maria Formosa and the *Scuole* of S. Marco and S. Giovanni Evangelista.

At this time, too, Venice had become the intellectual centre of Italy. Barely thirty years after Doge Cristoforo Moro had issued the first printer's licence in 1469, more books had been published in the city than in Rome, Milan, Florence and Naples combined; and already by 1490 its reputation as a literary centre was such that the great Roman printer and humanist Teobaldo Pio Manuzio – better known as Aldus Manutius – made it his home and, setting up his presses in the Campo S. Agostino,[1] embarked on the task which was to occupy him for the next twenty-five years: the editing, printing and publication of the whole canon of Greek classical literature. The editorial board was the so-called *Accademia di Aldo*, which numbered some of the greatest scholars of the day; it even included, for several months, Erasmus of Rotterdam, who became a firm friend of the Manuzio family (though he found their food uneatable). Such was the success of this enterprise that by the time of his death in 1515 Aldus had produced, under his famous imprint of the anchor and dolphin, no fewer than twenty-eight authoritative editions of the Greek classics. Thanks to him, moreover, books were no longer the prerogative of the rich; they were sold cheaply and in quantities undreamt of before his day, the German and Flemish merchants of the Fondaco dei Tedeschi having quickly built up a flourishing export trade to Northern Europe. In all these activities, the tribulations suffered by the Republic in the years leading up to and immediately following the formation of the League of Cambrai caused scarcely any interruption.

Nor had the Venetians, rich or poor, cultivated or philistine, forgotten how to enjoy themselves. As Girolamo Priuli notes in his diary, the carnival of 1510 was celebrated with so many festivities, fireworks and masquerades that one might have imagined the city back in its golden age. At the wedding feast of Francesco Foscari di Nicolò and the daughter of Giovanni Venier, *Capo* of the Ten, 420 guests sat down to dinner, after which there followed an elaborate masque with singers and dancers, theatrical companies, clowns and acrobats, which continued until the sun was high in the sky. Clothes, despite periodic decrees from the government forbidding excessive display, became more and more sumptuous. More than one past historian has suggested that Venice, by abandoning herself so wholeheartedly to luxury and pleasure, was merely making a desperate attempt to forget the tribulations with which she was surrounded; but such a view takes no account of the traditional character of her people. They had not

---

1. The traditional site of the original Aldine press is the small Gothic palace (No. 2311) in the Rio Terra Secondo; but there is convincing evidence that it was actually in a building on the Campo itself (see Tassini, *Curiosità Veneziane*, p. 10).

forgotten, nor were they trying to do so: when on 16 May 1510 a tremendous storm blew out a huge glass window of the *Sala del Maggior Consiglio* during a sitting of the Senate – who were meeting there because of the unseasonable heat – and simultaneously tore one of the wings off the lion of St Mark atop its Piazzetta column, many of them, including Marin Sanudo the diarist, were quick to see it as a dire portent of collapse to come. But the Venetians had always had a gift for festivity; all through their history they had loved beauty and magnificence and had never been ashamed to pursue them. The loss of their Empire, the collapse of their commerce, even the threat that their beloved Republic might be extinguished – none of these catastrophes gave them adequate reason to change the habits of centuries. On the contrary: if Venice were to die, let her die as she had lived – superbly, and in style.

32

Shifting Alliances

[1510–1513]

Questi francesi mi a tolto la fame . . . E volunta di Dio di liberar Italia di man di francesi.

These French have taken away my appetite . . . It is the will of God that Italy should be freed from the hands of the French.

Julius II, quoted in a letter from the
Venetian Ambassador (Sanudo X, 369)

But Venice did not die. Suddenly, the forces ranged against her seemed to fall apart. Maximilian, despite his promises and after endless procrastinations and prevarications, continued, as Erasmus put it, 'to doze over his stove', and simply never turned up. King Louis was thrown seriously off balance by the death in May of Cardinal d'Amboise, his closest adviser and the driving force behind his Italian policy. Yet the most important single factor was neither the German Emperor nor the French King, but the Pope. By the high summer of 1510 his *volte-face* was complete, his new dispositions made. His scores with Venice had been settled; now it was the turn of France.

By all objective standards, Pope Julius's action was despicable. Having encouraged the French to take up arms against Venice and shamelessly manipulated them for his own ends, he now refused to allow them the rewards which he himself had promised, turning against them with all the violence and venom that he had previously displayed towards the Venetians.[1] Not content with that, he also opened new negotiations with the Emperor in an effort to turn Maximilian, too, against his former ally. His claim, regularly resurrected in his defence by later apologists, that his ultimate objective was to free Italy from foreign invaders – in which, incidentally, he was singularly unsuccessful – would have been more convincing if he had not brought in these particular invaders in the first place, for no better reason than to humble the only Italian state of any size or real importance.

---

1. The Venetian envoy, writing home in July 1510, assessed the treatment of the French in Rome as being 'half as bad again': *Francesci sono tutti storniti la mita più di quello erano nostri l'anno passato.*

There was, in any case, another motive for this sudden change of policy – less idealistic perhaps, but a good deal more cogent. Having for the first time properly consolidated the Papal States, Julius was now bent on increasing them by the annexation of the Duchy of Ferrara. Duke Alfonso, during the past year, had undeniably had his uses; but by now he had become little more than an agent of the French King, with whom his ties had grown if anything closer as the Pope had moved away. His salt-works at Comacchio were in direct competition to the papal ones at Cervia; finally, as husband of Lucrezia Borgia, he was the son-in-law of Alexander VI – a fact which, in the Pope's eyes, was alone more than enough to condemn him.

And yet, however much we may argue the merits or the motives of Julius II's tortuous policies, one fact remains clear: just as he had previously been the chief architect of Venice's humiliation and impoverishment, so now he suddenly became her saviour. Not only did he step forth as the powerful champion she had so desperately sought; he took the principal initiative. The Republic could now – with what relief may well be imagined – withdraw from the centre of the stage. She was no longer a protagonist. This was a war primarily between the Pope and King Louis in which, henceforth, her task was simply to render what help she could to her unexpected new ally.

Their first joint engagement, an attempt in July by a combined naval and military force to drive the French from Genoa, was a failure; but by that time the Venetian army in the Veneto and the Polesine was already feeling the benefits of the new dispensation. Rumours that the army of 15,000 Swiss, whom the Pope had managed to hire in May, were about to invade Milanese territory on their way to an attack on Ferrara caused the hasty recall of Chaumont to Milan with the bulk of his forces; and though Anhalt and some of the French remained in the field and kept the Venetians occupied, they were no longer strong enough to prevent the reoccupation of most of the major towns in the Trevisano. Meanwhile, in no way discouraged by his failure to recapture Genoa and while waiting for the Swiss, the Pope continued the fight against his enemies in the two other fields still open to him, the diplomatic and the spiritual. First, in a blow against France that was also aimed at winning Spain over to his side, he recognized Ferdinand of Aragon as King of Naples, passing over the old Angevin claims of King Louis. A few weeks later, in a Bull which he had circulated all through Christendom, couched in language that St Peter Martyr said made his hair stand on end, he anathematized and excommunicated the Duke of Ferrara.

All this had a salutary effect on Venetian morale. In early August the Signoria at last confirmed the appointment of Lucio Malvezzo, member of a distinguished Bolognese family of *condottieri*, as military commander; that same month they succeeded in regaining a good deal of the Veneto, including Vicenza; and before the beginning of September they had pursued Anhalt – whose French contingents had by now been so reduced that he had had no choice but to beat a tactical retreat – to the gates of Verona itself. Had Malvezzo attacked the city at once, before the defenders were ready for him, he might well have taken it. Instead, he hesitated for a fortnight, and the chance was lost. A similar advance on Ferrara, this time by Venetian and papal forces together, was also checked at the walls; but a successful river expedition up the Adige largely wiped out the humiliation of the previous December and, as the autumn approached, Venice could congratulate herself on a year which, if not in every respect triumphant, had at least proved a good deal more encouraging than any of her citizens had had a right to expect.

Pope Julius, too, had high hopes for the future. The Swiss, he was forced to admit, had let him down badly; when at last they arrived in Lombardy several of their leaders, heavily bribed by Chaumont, returned almost at once across the Alps, while the remainder objected that they had been hired to defend the person of the Pope, not to fight against the Emperor and the King of France. On the other hand a joint papal and Venetian force under Julius's nephew the Duke of Urbino had effortlessly taken Modena on 17 August, and although Ferrara was strongly fortified there was good reason to believe that it would not be able indefinitely to withstand a well-conducted siege. The Pope, determined to be in at the kill, left Rome towards the end of the month and, travelling north by easy stages, reached Bologna in late September.

The Bolognese gave him a frosty welcome. Since the expulsion of the Bentivogli in 1506 they had been shamefully misgoverned and exploited by the papal representatives and were on the verge of open revolt. The governor, Cardinal Francesco Alidosi, had already once been summoned to Rome to answer charges of peculation, and had been acquitted only after the intervention of the Pope himself – whose continued fondness for a man so patently corrupt could only be explained, it was darkly whispered in Rome, in homosexual terms. But the tension inside Bologna was soon overshadowed by a yet graver anxiety. Early in October the Seigneur de Chaumont marched south from Lombardy. A feint towards Modena deceived and split the papal forces, whereupon Chaumont promptly bypassed the town and advanced at full speed on Bologna itself. By the 18th he was three miles from the city gates.

Pope Julius, confined to bed with a high fever in a fundamentally hostile city and knowing that he had less than a thousand of his own men on whom he could rely, gave himself up for lost. '*O, chè ruina è la nostra!*' he is reported to have groaned. His promises to the Bolognesi that they would be exempted from taxation in return for firm support were received without enthusiasm; and he had already opened peace negotiations with the French when, at the eleventh hour, reinforcements arrived from two quarters simultaneously – a Venetian force of light cavalry and *stradioti*, and another contingent from Naples, sent by King Ferdinand as a tribute after his recent papal recognition. The Pope's courage flooded back at once. There was no more talk of a negotiated peace. Arguing now from a position of relative strength, the foreign ambassadors to the Holy See – led by one Christopher Bainbridge, Archbishop of York – persuaded Chaumont not to press his attack; and the latter, who seems to have felt some last-minute qualms about laying hands on the papal person, agreed to withdraw – a decision which did not prevent Julius from hurling excommunications after him as he rode away.

It is hard not to feel a little sorry for the Seigneur de Chaumont. He was a good general, with occasional flashes of brilliance, but he was dogged by ill-luck. Again and again we find him on the point of a major victory, only to have it plucked from his grasp. Often, too, there is about him more than a little touch of the ridiculous. In the mid-winter campaign of January 1511, when the sixty-eight-year-old Pope personally accompanied his army through deep snow-drifts to besiege the castle of Mirandola, Chaumont's relief expedition was twice delayed – the first time when he was struck on the nose by an accurately aimed snowball which happened to have a stone lodged in it, and then again on the following day when he fell off his horse into a river and was nearly drowned by the weight of his armour. He was three days recovering, only sixteen miles from the beleaguered castle; as a result, Mirandola fell. In February, his attempt to recapture Modena failed hopelessly; and on 11 March, the victim of a sudden sickness which he – though nobody else – ascribed to poison, he died, aged thirty-eight, just seven hours before the arrival of the papal letter lifting his sentence of excommunication.

But by this time the Duke of Ferrara, on whom the ban of the Church weighed rather less heavily, had scored a brilliant victory over a papal army which was moving towards his city along the lower reaches of the Po, and Julius was once again on the defensive. In mid-May Chaumont's successor, Gian Giacomo Trivulzio, a veteran of half a century's fighting up and down the peninsula and since the days of Charles VIII a staunch adherent of the French cause, led a second march on Bologna; and on his approach, the inhabitants of the city, seeing their chance of ridding themselves once and for all of the detested Cardinal Alidosi, rose in rebellion. The Cardinal panicked and fled for his life, without even bothering to warn the Duke of Urbino, who was encamped with the papal troops in the western approaches, or the Venetians under Capello a mile or two away to the south; these two armies, taken by surprise, had thus no chance of saving a city whose gates were already locked against them, and extricated themselves only with difficulty – and some loss of baggage – from a situation that was as precarious as it was humiliating. On 23 May 1511, Trivulzio entered Bologna in triumph at the head of his army, and restored the Bentivogli to their old authority.

Cardinal Alidosi, who in default of other virtues seems at least to have possessed a reasonable sense of shame, barricaded himself in the castle of Rivo to escape the papal wrath; but the precaution proved unnecessary. Julius, who had prudently retired a few days earlier to Ravenna, bore him no grudge. Even now, in his eyes, his beloved friend could do no wrong, and he unhesitatingly laid the entire blame for the disaster on the Duke of Urbino, whom he summoned at once to his presence. The interview that followed is unlikely to have diminished the Duke's long-standing contempt for Alidosi, for whom he was now being made the scapegoat. When, therefore, on emerging into the street he found himself face to face with his old enemy – who had left his castle and had just reached Ravenna to give the Pope his own version of recent events – his pent-up anger became too much for him. Dragging the Cardinal from his mule, he attacked him with his sword; Alidosi's retinue, believing that he might be acting under papal orders, hesitated to intervene, and moved forward only when the Duke remounted his horse and rode off to Urbino, leaving their master dead in the dust.

The grief of Pope Julius at the murder of his favourite was, we read, terrible to behold. Weeping uncontrollably, waving aside all sustenance, he refused to stay any longer in Ravenna and had himself carried off at once to Rimini in a closed litter, through whose drawn curtains his sobs could be plainly heard by all whom he passed on the way. Only on the day after his arrival did he manage to recover his self-possession; but there were more blows in store. Mirandola, for whose capture he had always felt himself personally responsible, was within a week or two to be lost to Trivulzio. The papal army, confused; demoralized and now without a general, had disintegrated. With the recapture of Bologna, the way was open to the French to seize all the Church lands in the Romagna for which he had fought so hard and so long. All the work of the past eight years had gone for nothing. And now, at Rimini, the Pope found a proclamation, nailed to the door of the church of S. Francesco, signed by no fewer than nine of his own Cardinals with the support of Maximilian and Louis of France, announcing that a General Council of the Church would be held at Pisa on 1 September to investigate and reform the abuses of his pontificate.

Yet even now, for some little time at least, the most humiliating news was withheld from him. Papal agents in Bologna had reported that the jubilant citizens were not only tearing down the castle which he had built, as much for his personal glory as for his protection, in the centre of the city; they had also toppled his magnificent bronze statue, commissioned from Michelangelo, and had sold it for scrap to the Duke of Ferrara – who, in his turn, had recast it into a huge cannon which he had affectionately christened Julius.

Both as Pope and as a man, Julius II had many faults. He was impetuous – 'so impetuous', wrote Guicciardini, 'that he would have been brought to ruin had he not been helped by the reverence felt for the Church, the discord of the Princes and the condition of the times' – mercurial, vindictive, a poor organizer and administrator and a deplorable judge of character. Though an adept diplomatic tactician, he had little sense of long-term strategy. Eaten up by worldly ambition, he was utterly unscrupulous in the pursuit of his ends. Certain qualities, however, he possessed in full measure. One was courage, and another was indomitability of spirit. On his journey back to Rome, at the age of nearly seventy, he was already contemplating a new league, headed by himself and comprising Venice, Spain, England and if possible the Empire, whose combined forces would drive the French once and for all from the Italian peninsula; and by the beginning of July negotiations had begun.

They presented no serious problems. Ferdinand of Spain had already gained all he could have hoped for from the League of Cambrai and had no desire to see any further strengthening of the French position in Italy. In England, Ferdinand's son-in-law Henry VIII willingly agreed to keep his rival occupied on the north while her allies did the same in the south – although he was obliged to point out to the Pope, while accepting his proposals, that it would have been better if they had not been carried by an obvious double agent (recommended, it appears, by the late Cardinal Alidosi) who was regularly reporting all developments to King Louis. Venice, which throughout the time that the negotiations were in progress was fighting hard, and on the whole successfully, to resist French offensives in the Veneto and Friuli, asked nothing better. Maximilian, as usual, dithered; but even without him, the new League showed signs of proving a force to be reckoned with.

One reason, apart from his natural temperament, for the Emperor's ambivalent attitude was the proposed Church Council at Pisa which he and King Louis had jointly sponsored. Already Louis was beginning to regret the idea, which had been largely discredited when at least four of the nine Cardinals cited as sponsors protested that they had never even been consulted and would have nothing to do with it. Next, Pope Julius had announced that he himself would be calling a properly constituted Council for the following May, thus effectively removing the need for this uncanonical assembly, which could now be seen by everyone as nothing but a clumsy political manoeuvre. As support for it fell away, the opening date was postponed from September to November; even then, after only two short sessions, local hostility was to force its removal to Milan; and even there, under French protection, it was openly ridiculed to the point where a local chronicler forbore to record its proceedings because, he claimed, they could not be taken seriously and anyway he was short of ink.

Meanwhile the Pope, having almost miraculously recovered from an illness during which his life had been despaired of,[1] was able to proclaim his 'Holy League' on 4 October – though England did not officially announce her adhesion till 17 November – and begin preparations for war. He soon found, however, that King Louis also held an important new card in his hand – his nephew Gaston de Foix, Duc de Nemours, who at the age of twenty-two had already proved himself one of the outstanding military commanders of his day. Courageous, imaginative and resourceful, this extraordinary young man could take a decision in an instant; and, having taken it, could move an army like lightning. A dash from Milan in early February 1512 was enough to thwart a somewhat heavy-handed attempt to recapture Bologna by a papal army, consisting largely of Spanish troops and led by the Spanish viceroy in Naples, Ramón de Cardona; unfortunately, it also suggested to the citizens of Brescia and Bergamo that with the French forces away on campaign this was an opportune moment to rise in revolt and return to their old Venetian allegiance. They were quickly proved wrong. Marching night and day in the bitter weather – and, incidentally, smashing a Venetian division which tried to intercept him, in a battle fought by starlight at four o'clock in the morning – Nemours was at the walls of Brescia before the defences could be properly manned, and

1. The recovery was in fact attributed less to divine intervention than to copious draughts of wine that his doctors had forbidden him.

he and his friend Bayard led the assault, fighting barefoot to give themselves a better grip on the sloping, slippery ground. Brescia was taken by storm, the leader of the revolt was publicly beheaded in the main square, and the whole city was given over to five days' sack, during which the French and German troops fell on the local inhabitants, killing and raping with appalling savagery. It was another three days before the 15,000 corpses could be cleared from the streets. Bergamo hastily paid 60,000 ducats to escape a similar fate, and the revolt was at an end.

The campaign, however, was not. Nemours, determined to give his enemies no rest, returned to Milan to gather fresh troops and then immediately took the field again. With an army that now amounted to some 25,000 he made straight for the Romagna, whither the papalists had returned after their last reverse. Cardona was anxious to avoid a confrontation if he could, and not just because he was outnumbered and clearly outclassed; he was also expecting, in the course of the next few weeks, the arrival of 6,000 Swiss auxiliaries, and meanwhile there was good reason to believe that Henry VIII's promised invasion of France was now imminent, in which case the bulk of the French army in Italy would have to be withdrawn to deal with it. For these very same reasons, on the other hand, it was vital for Nemours to precipitate a battle quickly. Early in April he marched on Ravenna and laid siege to the town.

As a means of drawing out the papal army, the move was bound to succeed. Cardona could not allow a city of such importance to be captured under his nose without lifting a finger to save it. And so on Easter Sunday, 11 April, 1512, on the flat marshy plain below the city, the battle was joined.

Of all the encounters recorded in Italy since young Charles VIII had taken his first, fateful decision to establish a French presence in the peninsula nearly twenty years before, the battle of Ravenna was the bloodiest. On such level ground there was little opportunity for tactical skill; the two sides simply fought it out with guns and swords, pikes and lances. When at last the papalists fled from the field, they left behind them nearly 10,000 Spanish and Italian dead, to say nothing of their artillery and stores, which were immediately taken over by the French. Also in French hands were several of the leading Spanish captains, some of them seriously wounded, and the papal Legate Cardinal de' Medici. Ramón de Cardona himself, who had taken flight rather earlier in the day – he is said not to have drawn rein until he reached Ancona – was one of the few to survive unharmed.

But, as Bayard wrote a day or two afterwards to his uncle, the Bishop of Grenoble, though King Louis had won the battle of Ravenna his army felt it as a defeat. It had indeed been a Pyrrhic victory. The infantry alone had lost well over 4,000; of the fifteen German captains, twelve lay dead, while of Bayard's French companions-in-arms, who had fought at his side for the past dozen years, scarcely any remained. Worst of all, Nemours himself had fallen at the moment of victory, in a characteristically impetuous attempt to head off the Spanish retreat. His loss was irreparable, and had left his army bewildered and rudderless. His place was taken by the Seigneur de La Palice, a worthy veteran of the Italian wars, twice his age and possessed of none of the speed and *panache* that had earned his predecessor the sobriquet 'Thunderbolt of Italy'. Had the young man lived, he would probably have rallied what was left of the army and marched on Rome and Naples, forcing Pope Julius to come to terms and restoring King Louis to the Neapolitan throne; the subsequent history of Italy might then have been different indeed. But La Palice was cast in a more cautious mould. He contented himself with occupying Ravenna – where he was unable to prevent an orgy of butchery and rape which surpassed even that suffered by the Brescians a few weeks before – and then returning to Bologna to receive the submission of the Romagna cities and to await further instructions. With him he brought the body of Nemours, whose funeral service was held in the Basilica of S. Petronio.[1]

The delay proved fatal. Within two months, there suddenly occurred one of those extraordinary changes of political fortune which render Italian history as confusing to the reader as it is infuriating to the writer. When the news of the battle reached him, Pope Julius, foreseeing an immediate French advance on Rome, prepared for flight. Just before he was due to leave the city, however, he received a letter from his captive Legate – whom La Palice had unwisely permitted to correspond with his master. The French, wrote Cardinal de' Medici, had suffered losses almost as great as the League; they were tired and deeply demoralized by the death of their young leader; their general was refusing to move without receiving instructions and confirmation of his authority from France. At about the same time the Venetian Ambassador in Rome sought an audience with the Pope to assure him that, contrary to widespread rumours, the Republic had not accepted any French proposals for a separate peace, and had no intention of doing so.

At once Julius took new courage. Powerless, at least temporarily, in the military field, he flung all his energies into the Church Council he had

---

1. Later the body was sent for burial in Milan, where Bambaia's superb monumental effigy can still be seen in the Museo Civico. The rest of the tomb was, alas, dispersed – parts of it to the Victoria and Albert Museum.

summoned for the month following. This had now become more necessary than ever, since King Louis's renegade Council of Milan had taken advantage of the victory of Ravenna to declare the Pope contumacious and suspend him from office. It was true that, even in Milan itself, few people took the findings of so transparently political a body very seriously; none the less, this open split in the Church could not be allowed to go unchecked or unanswered. On 2 May, with all the state ceremonial of which the papal court was capable, the Supreme Pontiff was borne in his litter to the Lateran, followed by fifteen Cardinals, twelve Patriarchs, ten Archbishops, fifty-seven Bishops and three heads of monastic orders: a hierarchical show of strength that made the handful of rebels in Milan seem almost beneath notice – precisely as it was intended to do. At its second session this Lateran Council formally declared the proceedings of the Council of Pisa/Milan null and void and all those who had taken part in it schismatics.

From the point of view of Venice, however, the Pope's triumphs in the ecclesiastical field were overshadowed by a simultaneous achievement in the diplomatic. At last he had succeeded in stirring Maximilian to action, and on the same day that he pronounced against the schismatic Council he also announced the adhesion of the Emperor to the Holy League. An imperial safe-conduct now allowed a new army of Swiss mercenaries to make a swift descent through the Trentino, linking up with the Venetian army – which, having escaped the carnage of Ravenna, had had a chance to put itself once again on war footing – near Verona; more significant still, Maximilian now gave orders that all subjects of the Empire fighting with the French army should immediately return to their homes on pain of death.

By this time La Palice had already suffered a serious depletion of his French troops, recalled – as he had feared they would be – to deal with the impending invasion of Henry VIII; the precipitate departure of his German mercenaries now left him in the ridiculous position of being a general without an army – or at least without any force capable of holding the Swiss and Venetians whom he suddenly found ranged against him. Meanwhile the Spanish and papal forces were also back in the field and, although only a shadow of what they had been before their recent defeat, were able to advance virtually unopposed on all fronts – in Romagna, where the principal cities returned once again to papal allegiance, in Lombardy and in the region around Bologna, which once again expelled the Bentivogli and, on 13 June, opened its gates to the Duke of Urbino – now returned to his uncle's favour. By the beginning of July the Pope had not only regained all his territories but had even extended them to include Parma and Piacenza; Milan had welcomed back the Sforzas in the person of Massimiliano,

son of Ludovico il Moro; even Genoa had declared its reacquired independence and set a new doge on the throne. La Palice, with what was left of
his army, had no choice but to return to France, where Louis XII, who only
three months before might have had the entire peninsula within his power,
now saw all his hopes annihilated.

The French were gone; but it was too much to hope that the victorious
members of the League would now be able to apportion the spoils in an
atmosphere of friendly understanding. Already in early July the Pope had
caused general alarm when, not content with receiving the submission of
the Duke of Ferrara – who had ridden to Rome and prostrated himself
before the papal throne before receiving absolution – he had announced his
intention of appropriating the entire Duchy for himself. Duke Alfonso,
despite the weakness of his position, had angrily refused, and had been
supported by several of his erstwhile enemies, including the King of Spain.
'Italy', the King is reported as saying,[1] 'must not have another tyrant, nor
must the Pope govern it at his will.' Julius had been forced to abandon his
demand; but there were plenty of other questions still undecided, and it was
in an attempt to settle them that a congress of the League was held in
August, at Mantua.

For Venice, the principal problem proved to be the attitude of the
Emperor. Maximilian, as it soon became clear, was not disposed to give up
an inch of what he considered to be imperial territory – in which he
included not only the key cities of Verona and Vicenza but, it appeared,
Padua and Treviso, Cremona and Brescia as well. But Venice was no longer
the broken, demoralized republic of four years before; now, arguing once
again from a position of relative strength, her representatives declared the
imperial claims to be unacceptable. These cities, they objected, were vital
to her trade, and thus to her very survival. In the hands of a hostile power,
they could be used to close off her access to the Alpine passes and even in
some measure to western Lombardy. The Pope, in an attempt at mediation,
suggested that if the Venetians surrendered the two major cities they might
hold the remainder on payment of an annual tribute; but this proposal too
was firmly rejected, not simply because of the figures suggested – His
Holiness had mentioned 2,500 pounds of gold for the initial investiture,
and a further 300 payable annually – but because Venice refused to put
herself in the position of being a permanent tributary to anyone.

Thus, as the discussions at Mantua dragged on, the truth began to

1. By Guicciardini, who was at the time Florentine ambassador at the Spanish court.

emerge: while all the other members of the Holy League were busy carving out vast acquisitions for themselves – Parma and Piacenza for the Pope, Verona and Vicenza for the Emperor, Naples for the King of Spain – Venice, which had contributed a large share of the League expenses, was being elbowed aside, and even in danger of losing much of what she had formerly enjoyed. This too the Venetian representatives were quick to point out; but the Pope's only reaction was to lose his temper and threaten. 'If you will not accept our terms,' he shouted, 'we shall all once more combine against you.' The League of Cambrai, in other words, would be resurrected.

Pope Julius should have known better; this lack of consideration for an ally was bound to have dangerous repercussions. Venice now felt not only unfairly treated but isolated and in danger. In such circumstances it was small wonder that she turned to the one power by which she was not menaced and to which she might even have something to offer. She did not even need to take the initiative; for the last six months or more King Louis had been assiduously courting her friendship in an attempt to detach her from the Holy League. Finally, in the autumn of 1512, he succeeded in doing so. The negotiations, which were entrusted on the Venetian side to Andrea Gritti and Antonio Giustinian, continued into the beginning of 1513, during which time the Pope signed a new agreement with the Emperor in which he undertook to exclude Venice from any peace treaty that might be concluded and to take up both spiritual and temporal arms against her. He even issued a papal monitory, upbraiding the Republic for its conduct, although, to Maximilian's disappointment, he stopped short at a new excommunication. But Venice would not be intimidated. Backwards and forwards went the messengers between the Rialto and the French court at Blois – where, on 23 March 1513, a new treaty of alliance was finally signed. The two states agreed to stand together in mutual defence against any enemy who should threaten either of them, 'even if that enemy should be resplendent in the supreme dignity.' Should the King of France wish to recover Milan, or should the Republic propose to reoccupy its former dominions, both parties would move together in pursuit of these aims, with the ultimate objective of restoring the situation to what had been provided for in the treaty of 1499, whereby Venice would hold Cremona and substantial territories in Lombardy as far west as the Adda.[1]

Thus, in scarcely more than four years, the three principal protagonists in the war of the League of Cambrai had gone through every possible

1. See p. 381.

permutation in the pattern of alliances. First France and the Papacy were allied against Venice, then Venice and the Papacy ranged themselves against France; now Venice and France combined against the Papacy – and, indeed, all comers. Judged by modern standards, according to which treaties of alliance are normally – though not invariably – taken rather more seriously, such rapid tumbling within the political kaleidoscope may seem barely credible and more than a little shocking. In sixteenth-century Italy, however – the Italy of Machiavelli – such conduct was not considered particularly reprehensible. Alliances were matters, above all, of tactical convenience; when they no longer served a useful purpose they were broken off and new, more promising ones formed in their place. This was not a question of betraying friends; in international affairs, friendship did not exist. Ultimately, always, there was only one rule to be followed: that of each man for himself.

33
The New Venice

[1513–1516]

God has given us the Papacy: now let us enjoy it.

Leo X

Just a month before the signature of this last Treaty of Blois, on 21 February 1513, the seventy-year-old Julius II died of a fever in Rome; and on 4 March the Cardinals duly assembled in the small chapel that was all that was left of St Peter's[1] to elect his successor. Their deliberations were too slow for the guardians of the conclave, who in an effort to speed things up successively reduced the catering, first to a single dish per meal and later to a purely vegetarian diet; even then it was a full week before their choice was announced: Cardinal Giovanni de' Medici, who took the name of Leo X.

Whether or not the new Pope actually uttered the superbly cynical words ascribed to him at the top of this page, few Italians at the time would have shown surprise if he had. The new Pope was thirty-seven. He was immensely rich, immensely powerful – his family had been re-established in Florence by a decision of the Congress of Mantua in 1512, after an eighteen-year exile – and showed a far greater *penchant* for magnificence than his father Lorenzo had ever done; his coronation procession surpassed anything of its kind ever seen in Rome. But he was also a man of peace, who had been genuinely appalled by the carnage that he had witnessed at Ravenna; and peace was the one blessing for which the Romans now longed, clergy and laity alike. The Venetians, too, could have asked nothing better. Doge Loredan had sent at once to congratulate Leo on his accession, and soon afterwards sent him a formal invitation to adhere to the Treaty of Blois; but the Pope, however pacific his inclinations, knew that the French, once back in Milan, would insist on taking back Parma and Piacenza, which his own prestige would never allow him voluntarily to surrender so soon after their acquisition by his predecessor. Rejecting the blandishments of Blois, he prudently renewed the alliance with Maximilian and settled down with a sigh to await the new French invasion.

---

1. Pope Julius's demolition of the old basilica with virtually all it contained – one of the most shameless acts of official vandalism in all Christian history – was now virtually complete, and the new one planned by Bramante had scarcely begun to rise.

It was not long in coming. Early in May a large army entered Italy under the command of Gian Giacomo Trivulzio, now sixty-five, and of Louis, Seigneur de La Trémoïlle, both veterans of the Italian wars since the days of Charles VIII; and on the 15th of the month Bartolomeo d'Alviano, the hero of Agnadello, dressed in a superb robe of gold brocade and followed by his household in red and white checked livery, was led in state to the Doge's Palace and thence to the Basilica, where Leonardo Loredan delivered into his hands the sacred banner of St Mark. He then proceeded with his army to Lombardy, arriving more or less simultaneously with the French to find a welcome warmer than he or they had dared to hope. Massimiliano Sforza, after less than a year on the throne of Milan, had already made himself thoroughly unpopular with his subjects, who resented both his extravagance and the hordes of Swiss mercenaries on whom he relied for his protection; now, even with Swiss help, he was unable to prevent his new dominions from falling away until two towns only remained loyal – Como and Novara.

To Novara, accordingly, the French army advanced, and a garrison of 7,000 of Sforza's men moved hurriedly into the town. A siege would normally have ensued and Novara would, in all likelihood, have fallen; but on the night of 6 June, while La Trémoïlle was still making his preparations, the Swiss decided on a pre-emptive attack and fell upon the French camp, a mile or two away to the east. It was a decision of extraordinary courage; they were outnumbered by more than three to one and without horses or artillery. The French had both. Their cavalry, admittedly, was of little use – the ground was soft and marshy, and the horses were further impeded in the darkness by the ditches that the army itself had dug. Their artillery at first caused the attackers severe losses; but somehow the latter managed to keep their ranks unbroken as they flung themselves forward, and it was not long before they had occupied the gun emplacements and turned the fire in the other direction. The French, seeing that they were lost, panicked and fled, scarcely stopping till they had reached the Alps. The invasion was at an end. Massimiliano Sforza, his reputation much enhanced, returned to Milan; and the towns that had welcomed his enemies so recently and with such enthusiasm now reacclaimed him as their lord.

Venice was alone again. Alviano had been in no way responsible for the *débâcle* at Novara, which lay far beyond any territories to which the Republic laid claim; none the less, without his French allies he could not hope to pursue their joint strategy. He first withdrew to the Adige, hoping to hold the line of the river; but when reports reached him that a League army under Cardona was marching on the Veneto he hurried back to the defence of Padua. By doing so, he saved the city; but Cardona pressed forward to the very shores of the lagoon, burning Fusina, Mestre and Marghera, from which he even aimed a few threatening shots at Venice itself.

Meanwhile Doge Loredan had made another moving appeal to his subjects, calling upon them to make voluntary contributions to the exchequer for the salvation of the Republic and, if they were able-bodied males, to rally to the colours. Since he himself did neither – he was admittedly seventy-five, but it was felt that a gesture of some kind would have been appropriate – the response was initially somewhat half-hearted; as the danger increased, however, more and more young Venetians, nobles and ordinary citizens alike, crossed the lagoon and placed themselves at Alviano's disposal, ready to hurl themselves against the enemy at the first sign of any attempt to invade their city.

But no such attempt was made. Once again, as so often in the past, Venice proved impregnable. Those two and a half miles of shallow water kept her safely beyond the effective range of the Spanish guns. Cardona had no ships or invasion craft, and after a day or two found himself obliged to lead his army back whence it had come. The Venetians followed. They now felt themselves to be quite strong enough to take on the Spaniards and were loath to let them get away unscathed to their winter quarters. The two armies met on 7 October 1513 near Schio, a few miles north-west of Vicenza where the Alpine foothills begin to rise from the Lombard plain. It was a hard-fought fight, but ultimately Alviano's volunteer irregulars, for all their enthusiasm, proved no match for Cardona's professionals. First they retreated; then, suddenly, their retreat turned to precipitate flight. Some escaped; but many, overtaken by the Spaniards beneath the walls of Vicenza, were cut down as they ran. The proveditor, Andrea Loredan, a kinsman of the Doge, was captured and killed in cold blood. When the news was brought to the Rialto, the Venetians hung their heads in shame.

After so disastrous an end to the campaigning season of 1513, Venice's prospects for the year following were gloomy, particularly since her only ally, France, was far too preoccupied in dealing with a double invasion, by Henry VIII in the north and the Swiss in the east, to give much attention to Italian affairs. But though that year saw almost continual warfare, notably in the Friuli, it yielded no conclusive results. Leo X, busy on his side with the Lateran Council, provided none of the impetus in military matters that was so much a part of the style of Julius II; Maximilian, desultory and impecunious as ever, made no move; matters, in fact, had reached stalemate.

Then, on the convenient date of 1 January 1515, Louis XII died in Paris. Worn out at fifty-two and already showing signs of premature senility, he had the previous autumn married Princess Mary of England, sister of Henry VIII. She was fifteen years old, radiantly beautiful and possessed of all her brother's inexhaustible energy. Louis had done his best, but the effort had proved too great; he had lasted just three months.

His cousin, son-in-law and successor, Francis I, would have made Mary a far more suitable husband. Still aflame with youth and virility, he revealed his Italian intentions clearly enough when, at his coronation, he formally assumed the title of Duke of Milan, at the same time renewing the treaty with Venice; and by July he had already assembled an army of some 50,000 cavalry and 60,000 foot in the Dauphiné, with La Palice, Trivulzio and the Seigneur de Lautrec – a cousin of Gaston de Foix – in command. Here was a threat the League could not afford to ignore. No fewer than four armies gathered against the new invader: the papal forces, commanded by the Pope's brother, Giuliano de' Medici, the Spaniards under Cardona, Massimiliano Sforza's Milanese troops, and, finally, a strong contingent of Swiss – who were by now the effective masters of Milan. Of the four, however, the Spaniards headed for Verona to prevent the Venetians from linking up with their French allies, while the papalists advanced to the Po to protect Piacenza. Only the Swiss and Milanese moved into the mountains and took up their positions at the mouths of the two principal passes – the Mont Cenis and the Mont Genèvre – through which the French army was expected to march.

But old Trivulzio, who, despite his long years of service with the French, was himself by birth a Milanese, had not been fighting in Italy for half a century for nothing. He took neither of the obvious passes, threading his way instead through the valley of the Stura; by the time the Swiss realized what had happened, he and his army were well on their way to Milan. He did not, however, attack the city at once, preferring to take up a position at Marignano (the modern Melegnano) a few miles to the south, on the road that led to Lodi and Piacenza, in the hope that the Venetians would somehow contrive to outflank Cardona and join him.

The Swiss, who had regrouped inside Milan, decided to repeat the tactics that had served them so well at Novara. Once again they were outnumbered[1] and without artillery; once again they relied on their speed,

---

1. The authorities differ widely on the numbers of Swiss still in and around Milan at this time. Some 10,000, as a result of heavy bribes from the French, had returned to their homeland; that would probably have left not more than about 15,000 who remained loyal.

discipline and momentum to carry them through, and the sharpness of their pikes for hand-to-hand fighting. It was late in the afternoon of 13 September when they bore down upon the French camp. The French were ready and waiting, with their heavy artillery on the right wing and 12,000 Gascon bowmen on the left. Advancing through the crossfire, the Swiss – whose armour was always of the lightest for the sake of mobility – suffered fearful losses; but their line never broke, and they never halted until they were within physical reach of their adversaries. Now the advantage lay with them; but night was falling and the issue was still undecided when by mutual consent, some two hours before midnight, the fighting ceased.

It resumed at first light with a new onslaught by the Swiss. The interruption, however, was to prove decisive. Just as the French were on the point of retreat, a cloud of dust appeared on the eastern horizon. Alviano, having given the Spaniards the slip, was now advancing at full speed across the plain. The arrival of the Venetian army, fresh and determined, gave Trivulzio's men new heart as well as new strength; the Swiss, for their part, recognized that the day was lost. Ten thousand of their dead lay where they had fallen; the survivors, scarcely any of whom had escaped without serious wounds, made their painful way back to Milan.

Such was the military reputation of the Swiss mercenaries that the first reports to reach Rome of the outcome of Marignano announced their victory. The Pope personally passed the message on to Marino Zorzi, the Venetian ambassador, making no attempt to conceal his satisfaction; it was only on the following morning that Zorzi received letters from his government informing him of the true state of affairs. He at once hurried to the Vatican. Leo was still in bed, but at the ambassador's urgent request received him in a dressing-gown.

'Holy Father,' said Zorzi, 'yesterday you gave me bad news and false; today I give you good news and true: the Swiss are defeated.' He handed the letters to the Pope, who read them for himself before answering.

'What will become of us – what of you?' he murmured. Then he added as an afterthought: 'We shall put ourselves in the hands of the Most Christian King, and implore him to be merciful.'[1]

The battle of Marignano was the last significant action of the long and tedious war that resulted from the League of Cambrai. After the Swiss defeat there could be no question of Massimiliano Sforza's maintaining himself in Milan, where, on 4 October, the French formally took possession of the citadel. Two months later Leo and Francis met at Bologna

1. *Relazione di Marino Zorzi*, in Alberi, *Relazioni Venete*, 2nd series, Vol. III.

and reached an agreement by which the Pope reluctantly surrendered Parma and Piacenza – to say nothing of Modena and Reggio to the Duke of Ferrara – in return for French non-intervention in his proposed seizure of the Duchy of Urbino, which he wanted for his nephew Lorenzo. In August 1516, by the Treaty of Noyon, Ferdinand and Isabella's grandson, Charles I of Spain – soon to become the Emperor Charles V – made a separate peace with Francis, recognizing the latter's right to Milan in return for the French recognition of the Spanish claim to Naples; and in December of that same year at Brussels, old Maximilian – after one more totally abortive expedition to recover Milan, from which he turned back even before he reached the city – also came to terms, abandoning, in return for a down payment by Venice, all those lands which he had been promised at Cambrai. He hesitated only over Verona, maintaining that the honour of the Empire simply would not allow him to surrender it directly into Venetian hands; but at last even this thorny problem was resolved. He would deliver the city to his grandson Charles of Spain; Charles would transfer it to the French, and they in their turn would pass it to the Republic, together with all the other formerly Venetian territories in North Italy (except Cremona) under their own occupation.

So it came about that, eight years after the League of Cambrai had threatened Venice with extinction, those same powers who had been its original signatories came together to restore to her nearly all her former possessions and to make her once again the leading secular Italian state. During those eight years she had suffered much and made many sacrifices; but she had held firm, and with her usual combination of good diplomacy, good statesmanship and, above all, good luck she had won through. She had proved, too, that she was still impregnable. However dangerously her enemies might have threatened her from the mainland, she herself had not been touched. Her people, in short, when they heard the terms of the Treaty of Brussels, had good reason to congratulate themselves – as indeed they did.

In other respects, however, Venice could never be quite the same again. Her independence was preserved and her possessions had been returned to her, but her power was gone. Shorn of her commercial hegemony and her mastery of the seas, she would never again be able to initiate great policies and pursue them as she had done in the past. In those days of her greatness she had faced resolutely eastward, towards Byzantium, the Levant, the Black Sea and beyond, where her fortunes lay and whence her wealth had flowed. Now her about-turn was complete: she had become, in essence, an Italian state – not perhaps quite like the rest, for her history, her traditions, her extraordinary form of government and her semi-isolation would always mark her out as something individual and unique among her fellows, but an Italian state none the less; westward-facing, terrestrial rather than maritime, subject to the same political stresses and strains as the rest of the peninsula, of which, not so very long before, she would scarcely have deigned to consider herself a part.

Her confidence, too, was shattered. More than once, with what seemed like the whole of Christian Europe ranged against her, she had been brought to the brink of the abyss. She had escaped; but in this new, uncongenial, uncertain order of things, who could tell when the next crisis would come, or what results it might have? Was it enough to rely on her geographical position to protect her, or even on the generally accepted need to preserve a balance of power in Italy, which should ensure that, if any one state attempted to absorb her, the others would rally to her defence? Quite possibly, it was: yet she knew too that her future well-being, if not her actual survival, would henceforth depend not on her admirals, her merchants or her *condottieri* but on her diplomats. And so the great age of Venetian diplomacy began, an art which she pursued with the application and thoroughness that her people had always shown in matters which they considered of prime importance to the state, until her diplomatic prowess became a legend throughout the civilized world.

It was not the sort of diplomacy that makes friends. On the contrary, it tended to sow fear and distrust as much as friendship, relying as it did so heavily on spies and agents, on secrecy and intrigue, on the sinister and mysterious deliberations of the Council of Ten. No wonder that, as the century progressed, Venice came to assume – at least in the minds of many Europeans – an aura which we might associate with the more melodramatic forms of Renaissance tragedy. What was, perhaps, less generally understood was the underlying reason why the Venetian methods of diplomatic intelligence were fearsome: Venice was herself afraid.

34

The Imperial Triumph

[1516–1530]

Essendo amico dei due Re, non posso che dire coll' Apostolo: mi rallegro con chi gode e piango con chi soffre.

Being a friend of both sovereigns, I can only say, with the Apostle: I rejoice with them that do rejoice and weep with them that weep.

> Doge Andrea Gritti, on hearing of the
> capture of Francis I at Pavia

If the Treaty of Noyon did not bring permanent peace to Italy, it certainly afforded a welcome breathing-space. The year 1517 was the quietest that most of the population could remember. This is not to say that it was devoid of interest: no year that began with the capture of Cairo by the Turks and ended with Martin Luther's nailing of his Ninety-Five Theses to the church door at Wittenberg can be written off as easily as that. But the impact of these events, momentous as they were, was not immediate; and the people of Lombardy and the Veneto were able, then and in the twelve months following, to rebuild their shattered homes, resow their devastated fields, and sleep at night untroubled by dreams of marauding armies, of rape and pillage and blood.

A five-year truce signed in July 1518 between the Empire and the Republic stabilized the situation still further, and there is no telling how long the lull might not have continued if, on 12 January 1519, old Maximilian of Habsburg had not died in his castle at Wels, in Upper Austria. For some time he had been working to ensure that the Empire should pass to his grandson Charles, who, through a succession of dynastic alliances combined with a series of fortuitous deaths, found himself at the age of nineteen in possession of Spain (with Sicily, Sardinia and Naples, to say nothing of her new American colonies),[1] Austria, the Tyrol, much of South Germany, the Netherlands and the Franche-Comté. The very extent of this gigantic patrimony, however, together with the fear that the Em-

---

1. Inherited through his mother, Joanna the Mad, daughter of Ferdinand and Isabella.

pire, if allowed to remain too long in the hands of a single family, might evolve into a hereditary monarchy, inclined certain of the Electors to favour the only other serious candidate, Francis I.

As a European prince, Francis was not so outclassed as might at first appear. Territorially speaking, he could not rival Charles; on the other hand, the French throne was far more secure, its power more deeply rooted, its resources infinitely richer. Moreover, in the very year of his accession, the battle of Marignano had won him Milan and with it the control of all North Italy as far as the frontiers of Venice itself. His immense wealth seemed too to be a factor in his favour, since all seven Electors had made it clear from the outset that their votes might well be influenced by financial persuasion. Finally he enjoyed the support of Henry VIII of England and Cardinal Wolsey – who were also anxious to preserve the balance of power – and that of Leo X, for the excellent reason that the borders of Charles's Kingdom of Naples reached to within forty miles of Rome; the Pope had no desire to have an Emperor on his doorstep.

For the first two months after Maximilian's death, the contenders seemed evenly matched; but eventually the money that Charles had managed to raise in bills of exchange on the great German banking houses – notably the Fuggers of Augsburg – proved too strong. At the last moment Pope Leo transferred his support; and on 28 June 1519, at Frankfurt, Charles was elected to his grandfather's throne. To Francis, who had himself paid out considerable sums in gold coin, the defeat was a serious blow to his personal and political prestige; it was not, however, the end of the contest. The first round, fought in the chanceries and counting-houses of Europe, had been lost. Now it was time to move on – to the battlefield.

Venice, meanwhile – unlike the Pope – had remained faithful to her French alliance. Since his accession Francis had proved a good friend to her; it was he, after all, who had been primarily responsible for the restitution of her mainland territory. She had been powerless to give him much assistance in his struggle for the imperial crown, but she saw no reason to change her policy simply because that struggle had been lost. When, therefore, the ambassadors of Charles V approached her in the summer of 1521 with the request that the army of the Empire might be allowed free and unrestricted passage across her territory, they were given a courteous but firm reply. Her treaty with France made such permission impossible to give; she could only hope that His Imperial Majesty would agree to send his men by a different route, so that she would not be obliged to show opposition to those with whom she wished only to live in peace.

This reply was one of the first important pronouncements to be made by Antonio Grimani, who on 6 July had been elected seventy-fourth Doge of Venice in succession to Leonardo Loredan. Old Leonardo had not presided over Venice's destinies with any marked distinction or *éclat*, but his reign had coincided with the most agonizing chapter of her history, from which she had emerged virtually unscathed; inevitably, therefore, he was associated in the minds of his subjects with her safe deliverance. His death in his eighty-fifth year had been genuinely mourned, his obsequies and funeral procession to SS. Giovanni e Paolo marked with even more magnificent solemnity than usual; and his tomb, just to the right of the High Altar, was to be of comparable grandeur – even if he did have to wait another half-century before it was finally erected.

Antonio Grimani was, it must be said, a curious choice. To begin with, he was eighty-seven years old – the oldest Doge ever to be enthroned in Venice; secondly, his reputation had been badly stained in 1499 when, rightly or wrongly, he had been held responsible for the loss of Lepanto to the Turks.[1] After three years' exile in Dalmatia he had sought refuge in Rome, where his son's Cardinalate – purchased many years before for 30,000 ducats – doubtless stood him in good stead and gave him, together with the *entrée* into the papal court, the opportunity for performing various minor diplomatic services on the Republic's behalf. Having thus gradually won his way back into favour, he had been recalled in 1509 to Venice (by an overwhelming vote in the Great Council of 1,365 to 100) and made a Procurator of St Mark, in which capacity he had been responsible for the restoration of the Campanile, giving it for the first time its green pyramidal roof and thus the general appearance that it bears today.[2]

The real reason for old Antonio's election to the dogeship, however, seems to have been the obvious desirability of maintaining the support of a highly influential Cardinal in Rome. The Pope had formed a new alliance with the Emperor less than a month before, and although the Venetians did not feel immediately threatened they would have been foolish, at such a moment, to risk antagonizing their most valuable ally at the papal court

1. See pp. 384–5. Grimani's *promissione*, now in the British Museum, is of particular interest in that it puts an end to the venerable tradition, almost as old as the Republic itself, whereby the Doge on his accession made a present of wild birds to every member of the Magistrature. As the latter had increased dramatically in numbers over the years while the local fauna had correspondingly dwindled, this tradition had grown steadily harder to maintain; it was now established that Grimani and his successors should distribute instead specially minted coins, still to be known as *oselle* in memory of the birds they had replaced.

2. The present Campanile is not, however, the original one. This collapsed on 14 July 1902 and was replaced by a near-facsimile, inaugurated in 1912.

whom many somewhat optimistically regarded as a possible successor to Leo on the throne of St Peter.

Unfortunately for Venice, events moved too quickly for her to reap any benefits that might have accrued from her action. By early autumn, 1521, a joint papal–imperial army was on the march. In the absence of any real French opposition, it swept through Lombardy, capturing Milan on 19 November and then Lodi, Parma, Pavia and Piacenza in rapid succession, almost without firing a shot. Next, on 1 December, Leo X died of a sudden fever, contracted on his return from a hunting expedition. As a Florentine and a Medici, Leo had always maintained his family's traditional hostility towards Venice; the Venetians had cordially detested him in return; and the news of his death was greeted with rapturous rejoicing throughout the city. Sanudo described it as a *miraculosa e optime nuova*; it was, he said, as if the Republic had won a great victory or as if it was the Captain-General of the Turks who had died, for Leo had been the ruination of Christendom. But the cheering stopped soon enough when the name of his successor was known: not, as the Venetians had hoped, their own compatriot Cardinal Domenico Grimani but the one man who could not fail to be anything but an imperial puppet – the Dutchman, Adrian of Utrecht, who had been the Emperor's tutor and was even at that moment serving as his viceroy in Spain. Hope sprang anew when Adrian died in the following year; but there was still less cause for jubilation when the ensuing conclave, in November 1523, cast its vote for another Medici – Leo X's cousin Giulio, who took the name of Clement VII.

By this time Doge Antonio Grimani had also disappeared from the scene – though not before he had given his countrymen profound cause to regret that they had ever elected him in the first place. Not surprisingly, he had proved indecisive, doddering, and before long frankly senile. Unfortunately, he was also stubborn, refusing the offer of a pension of 2,000 ducats a year for life and a state funeral on his death, made by an impatient Senate in return for renouncing the throne. The only consolation was that he could not possibly last long; and it was with a general feeling of relief all round that the Venetians heard, on 7 May 1523, that he had finally expired. He was buried, as befitted his record, in the modest church of S. Antonio di Castello, which, nearly three centuries later, was destroyed by Napoleon to make room for the public gardens.[1]

1. His best remaining memorial is consequently the *Sala delle Quattro Porte* in the Doges' Palace, which contains two portraits of him. One is by Titian – though completed by another hand after the master's death and heavily restored into the bargain. The other is a signed work by Titian's pupil Giovanni Contarini.

Grimani's successor, Andrea Gritti, was a considerably more impressive figure. Tall and outstandingly handsome, he carried his sixty-eight years lightly and boasted that he had never suffered a day's illness in his life. As a young man he had accompanied his grandfather on diplomatic missions to England, France and Spain, whose languages he spoke fluently, together with Latin, Greek and Turkish. This last accomplishment was the fruit of a prolonged stay in Constantinople during which he was arrested on a well-founded charge of espionage and imprisoned, escaping impalement only through the good offices of the vizir Ahmed, a personal friend. He is said, none the less, to have been unusually popular with the Turks as well as with the European colony, several female members of which were seen standing in tearful vigil by the prison gates as he entered them. Later he had served with distinction both as a diplomat and – in a civil capacity – in the war of the League of Cambrai, and he was indeed proveditor of the army when, on 20 May 1523, he was elected Doge. Perhaps surprisingly in view of his record, he had never managed to endear himself to the people as a whole, who had hoped for the election of his principal rival, Antonio Tron, and kept up a steady chant, in the guttural Venetian dialect, of '*Um, Um, Trum, Trum*' while he made his ceremonial circuit of the Piazza; neither then nor later, however, did his lack of popular appeal occasion him the slightest concern.

It was presumably his diplomatic experience that most recommended Andrea Gritti to the electors, for his elevation came at a time when the Republic was engaged with the Empire in negotiations of considerable delicacy. Charles V was proving himself a very different ruler from his grandfather – different not just by reason of his wealth or the extent of his dominions, but in his character and political philosophy. 'God has set you on the path towards the monarchy of the world', his grand chancellor Mercurino de Gattinara had told him at the time of his accession, and he never forgot it. This was no personal ambition; it was to him a sacred trust, the fulfilment of the Divine Purpose, that Christendom should be united both politically and spiritually under the imperial standard. Then and then only could it drive back the encroaching infidel and, once the Turks were safely dealt with, turn its combined strength against Martin Luther and his company of heretics.

Such was the aim to which Charles had dedicated his life; and so far, at least, the Almighty appeared to be behind him. During his four years on the throne his position had grown steadily stronger, at the expense of his arch-rival the King of France. Not only had he regained Milan and Lombardy; by his own personal diplomacy he had managed to enlist the support of Henry VIII of England, an agreement which was to be sealed by his betrothal to Henry's daughter Mary – who, although still only six years old, had previously been affianced to Francis–and which was further confirmed at Windsor when Charles himself came to England in 1522. That same year his troops had crushed a new French offensive in Italy and captured Genoa. Meanwhile in Rome one well-disposed Pope had been succeeded by another who, being a personal friend with close imperial associations, promised to be still more amenable.

In short, it was time for Venice to reconsider her position. Her alliance with France was an increasing liability, particularly since the Emperor's recent triumphant campaign had been waged on the oft-repeated pretext of 'liberating Italy from French tyranny'. Her differences with the Empire, on the other hand, were not easily settled. Even the vacillating, procrastinating old Maximilian had found it hard enough to compromise where what he considered to be imperial territory was concerned; Charles, on his accession, had immediately resurrected several of the old issues which the Venetians hoped had been safely buried at Brussels in 1516. But negotiations had gone doggedly on, and at last, on 29 July 1523, less than three months after Gritti's election, Venice concluded at Worms a solemn treaty with the Empire whereby, in consideration of a payment of 200,000 ducats over eight years, she was to keep all the formerly imperial territories at that time in her possession. Each party agreed to come to the defence of the Italian territories of the other, unless the aggressor were the Pope; each promised to allow safe conduct to the subjects of the other, with freedom of residence and trade; and Venice further undertook to send up to twenty-five of her galleys on demand to defend Naples, provided only that she was not fully engaged at the time against the Turk. The treaty – which was also signed for good measure by Francesco II Sforza, son of Ludovico il Moro, whom the Emperor had established on the throne of Milan – was to be jointly guaranteed by the Pope and Henry VIII, both of whom were invited to accede to it themselves.

Not, perhaps, without some embarrassment, the Doge then wrote to the King of France. The treaty, he explained, had been forced upon Venice by the non-arrival of French troops and reinforcements, without which she could not hope to maintain herself alone. She had also wished to respect the Pope's repeated wishes for a general peace in Europe. Francis was therefore on no account to interpret this new development as a hostile act; on the contrary, the friendship between the two countries remained, so far as Venice was concerned, unaltered. The very last thing the Republic would wish was any resumption of hostilities among the forces of Christendom, at a time when the infidel host was growing even stronger and its threat to Western Europe increasing every hour.

Here at least Andrea Gritti spoke no more than the truth. During the forty-two years since the death of Mehmet the Conqueror, Venice had been at war with the Ottoman Empire for only four – from 1499 to 1503 – and then largely because the peace-loving Sultan Bajazet had felt himself to be threatened. Even after Bajazet had yielded the throne to his son Selim the Grim in 1512, the lull had continued – so far as Europe was concerned – since the new Sultan had fortunately devoted most of his considerable energies to the task of consolidating his Islamic dominions in the East. Eight years later, however, Selim in his turn had been succeeded by his own first-born, Suleiman – soon to be known as 'the Magnificent' – and immediately the situation had changed. Suleiman had lost no time. In 1521 he had successfully besieged the great Hungarian frontier fortress of Belgrade, and in the following year had launched an immense amphibious attack on Rhodes, where for over two centuries the Knights of St John had maintained their own independent state and whence they had kept up a steady offensive against Turkish shipping. Once already, forty years before, the Knights had faced such an onslaught and after a heroic resistance had finally driven the invaders back to the mainland; but this time their old enemies had been too strong for them. On 21 December 1522, after many weeks of siege, and even then only out of consideration for the civilian population, they surrendered in return for a promise that they would be allowed to withdraw from the island unmolested – a promise which Suleiman later had cause to regret since it enabled them, within a decade, to set up a new state in Malta – and by the end of the year they were gone.

Politically and strategically, the fall of Rhodes was of little enough significance to Europe as a whole. The Knights had at no time constituted a major power in the Mediterranean. Operating from so small a base, they had never been able to equip or support a navy on a scale that could rival the mighty fleets of Venice, or Genoa, or the Sultan. Most of their energy and resources they anyway devoted to their medical work – for a century and more the hospital at Rhodes was generally accounted the best in Christendom – and their military operations had been for the most part limited to raids on Turkish ports and the harassment of Turkish shipping: a mild irritant rather than a serious threat. Had it not been for their near-impregnable island defences, they would not have lasted anything like so long as they did. None the less they were pious, resolute and awesomely brave; they were drawn from every corner of Europe; and the news of their collapse was everywhere received with a dismay quite disproportionate to their political significance. Only, perhaps, among the Venetians was the reaction other than purely emotional. For them, the defeat of the Knights was a portent. With Rhodes gone, how much longer could the Republic hope to keep its remaining colonies in the Dodecanese? Or Crete, or Cyprus? For how long, indeed, would the Aegean mark the limit of Suleiman's ambitions? Soon, they knew, it must be the turn of the Adriatic.

But Venice could not fight the Turks alone, and Charles V could not fight them either while his contest with the King of France was unresolved. That contest was to last until 1529, though henceforth Venice and the other states of Italy were to play only a relatively minor part in it. The European situation had by now become polarized: there was room only for the two protagonists at the centre of the stage. No Venetian forces were present at the great battle of Pavia in February 1525, when Francis I was taken prisoner and sent off to captivity in Spain; and when, after his release in the year following, Pope Clement formed the pro-French Holy League of Cognac in an attempt to check the growing Spanish-imperial power, Venice lent her signature but little else. In May 1527, when the vengeful Charles sent some 20,000 troops, mostly Germans and Spaniards, against Rome itself and the city was subjected to three days of butchery and pillage and the wholesale destruction of its works of art, all carried out with a ferocity unmatched since the barbarian invasions, Venice did not lift a finger to assist her papal ally. Such indeed was her apparent apathy that she could hardly complain when Francis, following the defection of the Genoese, under their famous admiral Andrea Doria, to the imperial cause, agreed to a separate peace. By terms of the treaty, which was concluded at Cambrai in August 1529 and, having been negotiated by the Queen Mother of France and Margaret of Austria, the Emperor's aunt, was ever afterward known as the *Paix des Dames*, the French King formally renounced all claims in Italy, as well as his rights of suzerainty in Artois and Flanders. In return he received a promise from Charles not to press the imperial claims to Burgundy; but France's allies in the League of Cognac were left entirely out of the reckoning and were thus subsequently forced to accept the terms that Charles was to impose at the end of the year – terms which included, for Venice, the surrender of all her remaining possessions in Apulia to the Spanish Kingdom of Naples.

It was a sad and – to those who felt that the King of France had betrayed them – a shameful settlement. But at least it restored peace to Italy and put an end to a long and unedifying chapter of her history – a chapter which had effectively begun with Charles VIII's invasion of 1494 and had brought the Italians nothing but devastation and destruction. Twice more, briefly, in 1536–7 and 1542–4, the two great rivals were to find themselves in conflict; but by then the heat had gone out of the struggle, and already there could be no doubt that the Emperor had emerged the victor.

But not the only one. Suleiman the Magnificent had taken full advantage of his enemies' disarray to continue his relentless advance into Europe. In 1526, while Pope Clement was threatening Charles V with his League of Cognac and Francis I was negotiating his release from his Spanish prison, a huge Turkish army was on the march against Hungary; and on 29 August of that year, at Mohács, it inflicted on the Hungarians the most devastating defeat of their history. The twenty-three-year-old King, Lájos II, died on the field of battle, and a contemporary writer describes how, for a day and a night afterwards, the waters of the Danube were swollen with the bodies of men and horses. Further resistance was impossible; within days, the crescent was fluttering over Buda. The Archduke Ferdinand, Charles's brother and his imperial viceroy in Austria, acted quickly: elected king by the Magyar nobility, he was able to save perhaps a third of Hungary's former territory. The rest was lost to Suleiman.

Now Vienna was seriously threatened; and three years later, on 10 May 1529, Suleiman resumed the offensive at the head of a still larger force. Ferdinand, meanwhile, was preparing the city to face the most terrible siege in its history. Walls were strengthened, veterans recalled to the colours to reinforce the garrisons; a constant stream of wagons and carts, loaded with corn, weapons and ammunition, threaded its way into the city from every corner of Austria and Germany. And yet, as the Turks advanced further into Europe, there were few men in Christendom who believed that even these measures would be of any avail, or that anything could now be done to stem the Ottoman tide.

But Vienna was saved – by, of all things, the weather. The summer of 1529 in Central Europe proved to be the worst in living memory. Relentless rain swelled the rivers, washed away roads and bridges, destroyed the crops on which the Turks had relied for sustenance during their long march. As a result, the journey from Constantinople took some six weeks longer than had been foreseen, and it was not until 27 September that the Sultan finally pitched his camp beneath the city walls. At best, this left him only a month of the campaigning season – a month in which to enforce the surrender of one of the most strongly defended cities in Europe. As things turned out, he had less time even than that. Instead of mellowing into an Indian summer, the weather grew steadily worse; in the second week of October the rain gave way to blizzards of snow; and on 14 October Suleiman issued the order to retreat to winter quarters at Belgrade. The following spring he decided, against all expectation, not to renew the attack and returned instead to the Bosphorus.

While the Sultan was marching on Vienna, Charles V was on his way to Italy, to conclude the necessary formal treaties of peace following on the *Paix des Dames* and to arrange his imperial coronation. The latter was not an indispensable ceremony; several of his predecessors, including his grandfather Maximilian, had done without it altogether, and Charles himself had already been ten years on the throne without this final confirmation of his authority. The fact remained, none the less, that until the Pope had laid the crown on his head he could not technically call himself Emperor, and, to one possessing so strong a sense of divine mission, both the title and the sacrament were important.

By tradition, imperial coronations were performed in Rome; on landing at Genoa in mid-August, however, Charles received reports of the Turkish advance and at once decided that a journey so far down the peninsula at such a time would be folly. Not only would it take too long; it would also leave him dangerously cut off in the event of a crisis. Messengers sped to Pope Clement, and it was agreed that in the circumstances the ceremony might be held in Bologna, a considerably more accessible city which yet remained firmly under papal control. Even then the uncertainty was not over: while on his way to Bologna in September Charles received an urgent appeal from Ferdinand and almost cancelled his coronation plans there and then to ride to his brother's relief. Only after long consideration did he finally decide that to do so would be pointless. By the time he reached Vienna the city would either have fallen or Suleiman would have retired for the winter; and in any case the small force he had with him in Italy would be insufficient to tip the scales.

And so, on 5 November 1529, Charles V made his formal entry into Bologna, where, in front of the Basilica of S. Petronio, Pope Clement waited to receive him. After a brief ceremony of welcome, the two retired to the *Palazzo del Podestà* across the square. Neighbouring apartments had been prepared for them; there was much to be done, many outstanding problems to be discussed and resolved, before the coronation could take place. It was, after all, only two years since papal Rome had been sacked by imperial troops, with Clement himself a virtual prisoner of

Charles in the Castel Sant' Angelo; somehow friendly relations had to be re-established. Next there were the individual peace treaties to be drawn up with all the Italian ex-enemies of the Empire, the most important of which, apart from Clement himself, were Venice, Florence and Milan. Only then, when peace had been finally consolidated throughout the peninsula, would Charles feel justified in kneeling before the Pope to receive his imperial crown. Coronation Day was fixed for 24 February 1530, and invitations were dispatched to all the rulers of Christendom. Charles and Clement had given themselves a little under four months to settle the future of Italy.

The Emperor had the whip hand. None of the Italian states was in a position categorically to reject any terms he liked to impose. His object, however, was to establish not just a patched-up peace but a lasting one, if only to be able to concentrate his attention, and that of Christendom, on the Turkish threat; and he was determined to show no bitterness, making concessions wherever possible. In the agreement which he concluded with Venice on 23 December, the Republic was obliged – not surprisingly – to return Trani, Monopoli and her other towns and territories in Apulia to Charles's own Kingdom of Naples; and, as a sop to Pope Clement, the formerly papal cities of Ravenna and Cervia to the Holy See. These territorial losses were not, however, seriously prejudicial to her prosperity or well-being. In the areas that really counted – Lombardy, Friuli and the Veneto – all her possessions were confirmed; and when she protested, with some vehemence, against Charles's proposal to place Alessandro de' Medici on the throne of Milan he actually agreed to reinstate Francesco Sforza, despite the fact that the latter had fought stoutly for the French – insisting only that the castle in the centre of the city continue to be garrisoned by Spanish troops.

Similarly successful agreements were concluded with all the other states of Italy with which the Empire had differences outstanding – except one. Two years before, in 1527, the Florentines had once again risen in revolt against the Medici and expelled them from their city. It was a brave, not to say foolhardy, step to take at a moment when one of this by now generally detested family occupied the papal throne, and Pope Clement, determined that it should not go unpunished, had left Charles in no doubt that without a firm commitment to send troops to restore the city to Medici control he could renounce all his plans for an imperial coronation. At first he had hoped to persuade the Florentines by peaceful means to capitulate; but memories of Savonarola were still fresh in their minds, Michelangelo was in charge of their defences and they were determined to fight. With a sigh Charles accepted the inevitable; if the success of his Italian policy necessitated the sacrifice of Florence, then sacrificed Florence would have to be.

No other problems proved insuperable, and well before the day appointed for the great ceremony Charles had laid the foundations of a pan-Italian league – a league, moreover, which testified to a spread of imperial power across the length and breadth of Italy unparalleled for centuries past. Admittedly it was based on free diplomatic association rather than feudal law; but it was none the less real for that. And so the peace was signed;[1] Clement's League of Cognac and Charles's sack of Rome were alike forgotten, or at least dismissed from memory; and on 24 February 1530, in S. Petronio, Charles was first anointed and then received from the papal hands the sword, orb, sceptre and finally the crown of the Holy Roman Empire. Something of a cloud was cast over the proceedings when a makeshift wooden bridge linking the church with the Palace of the Podestà collapsed just as the Emperor's suite was passing across it; but when it was established that the many casualties included no one of serious importance spirits quickly revived, and celebrations continued long into the night.

It had been a splendid ceremony, but it might have been more solemn still had any of its participants been aware that it was the last of its kind. The Holy Roman Empire had been established when, on Christmas Day, A.D. 800, Pope Leo III had laid the imperial crown on the head of Charlemagne. Since that day, the concept of a papal coronation had been an integral part of that of the Empire itself, and many a King of the Romans had risked his life to obtain this ultimate confirmation of his claims. For a few of them, the journey involved had proved too hazardous in the prevailing political conditions; but these, though occupying the throne *de facto*, could never properly call themselves Emperor. Now, with the coronation of Charles V, the seven-hundred-year tradition was brought to an end. The Empire was not yet finished; but never again would it be received, even symbolically, from the hands of the Vicar of Christ on earth.

1. The event is commemorated, surprisingly enough, in a painting by Marco Vecellio in the Hall of the Council of Ten in the Doges' Palace.

PART FOUR

Decline and Fall

And what if she had seen those glories fade,
  Those titles vanish, and that strength decay;
Yet shall some tribute of regret be paid
  When her long life hath reached its final day:
Men are we, and must grieve when even the Shade
  Of that which once was great, is passed away.

WORDSWORTH

35
Peace

[1530-1564]

Ces vieux coquz vont espouser la mer,
Dont ils sont les maris et le Turc l'adultère.

Du Bellay

The peninsula was at peace – at least by Italian standards; and though that peace had been brought about by imperial-papal agency and all Italy still lay under the shadow of the Eagle's wing, Venice had managed to safeguard not only her political independence but even the integrity of her mainland dominions. More remarkable still, she had done so by diplomacy alone. For the past fourteen years, despite several treaties and alliances into which the circumstances prevailing at the time had obliged her to enter, she had steered clear of actual fighting. Peace had served her interests better than war, and she was determined to preserve that peace by every means within her power.

The task was obviously not going to be easy. Francis I, back at Blois licking his wounds, was still young and vigorous and had not by any means renounced his Italian ambitions. He was now watching with interest the rapid spread of Protestantism in Germany, weighing the likelihood of religious wars within the Empire which might keep the imperial armies tied down and allow him free rein to recapture those lands beyond the Alps which he still considered his birthright. Suleiman the Magnificent, meanwhile, was advancing on all fronts – the islands of the Mediterranean, the coast of North Africa, the Balkans and Central Europe. With a grand alliance of the Christian powers manifestly out of the question, there would be no hope of effective military resistance to him at present. Appeasement seemed the only alternative, and by the time Venice was selecting her representatives to attend the imperial coronation another of her envoys, Tommaso Mocenigo, was already on his way to Constantinople to assure the Sultan once again of the Republic's continued esteem and to shower him with gifts on the occasion of his son's circumcision.

But good relations with Suleiman were never easy to maintain, least of all for Venice. The Ottoman navy was assuming more formidable proportions than ever; the Eastern Mediterranean was thick with Turkish shipping; and since much of it was under the command of corsairs like the notorious Khaireddin Barbarossa, who cared little for treaties and truces and tended simply to attack Christian vessels wherever he saw them, incidents were unavoidable. There was one particularly embarrassing one in November 1533 – only eight months after Venice had categorically refused to join an anti-Turkish alliance with the Pope, the Emperor and certain other Italian states, knowing full well that with the forces at its disposal it could only infuriate Suleiman unnecessarily – when a young Venetian commander, Girolamo da Canale, spying a potentially hostile Turkish squadron in Cretan waters, sank two of its ships and captured five others. In former times that would have been the end of the affair, but things were different now. Venice, panic-stricken, at once dispatched further ambassadors to the Porte to present her excuses and offer reparations. The problem of what to do with Canale himself was a difficult one, since he was being widely acclaimed as a hero. It was perhaps fortunate that he chose just that moment to die, with suspicious suddenness, at Zante.[1]

This same policy of appeasement led Venice to refuse her support to other small-scale operations launched against the Turks, such as the short-lived seizure of Tunis by an imperial fleet under the Genoese admiral Andrea Doria in 1535. It was all very well for Charles V to embark on adventures of this kind; he could always withdraw at will, retiring to his land-locked fastnesses. He was not, as she was, in the front line, still possessor of a few Mediterranean trading-posts vital to her interests, whose continued preservation depended entirely on the maintenance of the Sultan's good-will.

Perhaps so, Charles might have replied; but how was that good-will to be maintained in its turn? Here, as the Venetians well knew, was something utterly beyond their control. Suleiman would move against them precisely when it suited him to do so; and sooner or later they would have to resist.

Two years later, in 1537, the moment came. Much had happened in the interim. In October 1535 Francesco II Sforza of Milan had died without issue; the King of France had immediately claimed the Duchy on behalf of his son, Henry of Orleans; the Emperor's brother Ferdinand, King of the Romans, had done likewise for one of his own offspring; and by the following summer the two old enemies were once again at war. An army led by the Emperor himself crossed the French border and penetrated deep into Provence, besieging Arles and Marseille and laying waste the country

---

1. After a discreet interval, his son erected a monument to him in SS. Giovanni e Paolo – high on the wall in the north-west corner.

as it went – a trail of devastation equalled only by that left by the retreating French. But then the tide turned. Dysentery broke out in the imperial ranks and continued until over half their number were dead or incapacitated. The remainder, continually harassed by French cavalry, dragged themselves back as best they could, and by the end of September, only two months after it began, the first phase of the war had ended in a resounding victory for France.

Venice had done her best to mediate and, when her efforts failed, had taken no part in the fighting. Francis's next move, however, was to draw her inescapably back into the theatre of war. He came to a secret agreement with Suleiman, according to which the French would launch a new campaign against the Empire in Flanders, holding down a large proportion of the imperial troops, while Ottoman forces simultaneously pressed deeper into Hungary and a French fleet joined with a Turkish one under Barbarossa in a combined operation against the Kingdom of Naples. For the Venetians, the prospect of war at the mouth of the Adriatic was unwelcome enough; they were still more dismayed by the arrival of an ambassador from the Sultan, suggesting that the Republic might like to lend its support to this new alliance.

Suleiman's invitation was nicely calculated. If Venice were to accept it, he would have her active help in acquiring an insuperable position in the central Mediterranean from which he could subsequently bring her to her knees; if she were to refuse, it would give him a useful pretext for immediate action against her. On balance, her acceptance must have seemed to him a more likely possibility; but after the dramatic proof he had recently received of the division of Christendom, she might decide either way. In any event, he could hardly lose.

Doge Gritti and his advisers, on the other hand, were now in a serious quandary. To embroil themselves once again with the Empire was clearly unthinkable; yet to refuse the Sultan's offer would invite measures of revenge for which Suleiman was at that moment particularly well placed and which they preferred not to contemplate. They accordingly returned as polite, but non-committal, a reply as they could devise; meanwhile the Captain-General, Girolamo Pesaro, was sent urgent instructions to avoid all encounters with French or foreign shipping, especially Turkish, unless the safety of the Adriatic itself was threatened.

The Sultan's answer was not long in coming. The first to suffer were Venetian merchants in Syria, on whom he imposed a new 10-per-cent tax on all goods. Next came the Republic's ships at sea, which were systematically harassed by every Turkish vessel they chanced to meet. Some, inevitably, resisted; and it was not long before Suleiman, claiming that he had been unjustly attacked, declared war. Soon afterwards – towards the end of August 1537 – the Ottoman fleet appeared off Corfu. Now it was Venice's turn to appeal for help. The island had been a Venetian colony since 1386 and, especially after her loss of the twin ports of Modone and Corone in 1499, had served as her principal naval and commercial base in the southern Adriatic. In view of its proximity to the Kingdom of Naples, its strategic value to Spain and the Empire was almost as great. Yet not only did Venice's appeal to these powers go unanswered; an imperial fleet under the famous *condottiere*-admiral Andrea Doria, which had been cruising nearby, actually sailed away to Genoa. Doria's excuse, that he could not give battle without the Emperor's instructions, was believed by no one; the Venetians knew perfectly well that as a Genoese he had always hated them and would never offer them help if he could possibly avoid it. They were left to face the enemy alone.

Fortunately, Corfu's defences were strong. The town, half-way up the eastern coast of the island, lay, as it still lies today, behind and below the high citadel crowning the rocky peninsula that juts out further eastward still towards the shores of Albania, commanding the approaches from both land and sea. Within this citadel was a garrison of some 2,000 Italians and roughly the same number of Corfiots, together with the crews of such Venetian vessels as happened to be in port at the time. Food and ammunition were in plentiful supply; morale was excellent. It needed to be; for the defenders now found to their dismay that they were faced not just with an attack from the sea but with a combined naval and military operation, carefully planned and on a considerable scale. On 25 August the Turks landed 25,000 men and thirty cannon in the village of Patara, some three miles from the town, and these were joined five days later by substantial reinforcements. The devastation suffered by the local peasantry and ordinary citizens was appalling; but the citadel, despite constant battering from Turkish cannon on land and sea and several attempts to take it by storm, somehow stood firm. Then, mercifully, came the rain. Corfu has always been famous for the ferocity of its storms, and those which burst upon it in the early days of September 1537 seem to have been exceptional even by local standards. The cannon became immovable in the mud; dysentery and malaria ran through the Turkish camp. After barely three weeks' siege, the Ottoman army re-embarked on 15 September leaving a triumphant if still somewhat incredulous garrison to celebrate its victory.

But the war was not over. Barbarossa's fleet was still active, and the other Mediterranean harbours and islands that remained in Venetian hands

31. The Porta della Carta –
Doge Francesco Foscari and the Lion of St Mark

32. Colleoni (Verrocchio)

33. Gattamelata (Donatello)

34. Francesco Sforza (Gian Cristoforo Romano)

35. Mehmet II (Gentile Bellini)

36. Pius II arrives in Ancona for his Crusade (Pinturicchio)

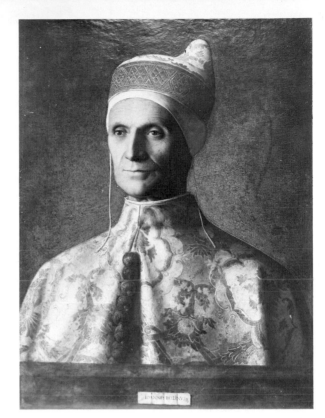

37 (*Left*). The Rialto in 1500
(Carpaccio)

38 (*Right*). Doge Leonardo Loredan
(Giovanni Bellini)

39 (*Below*). Caterina Cornaro and
her ladies (Gentile Bellini)

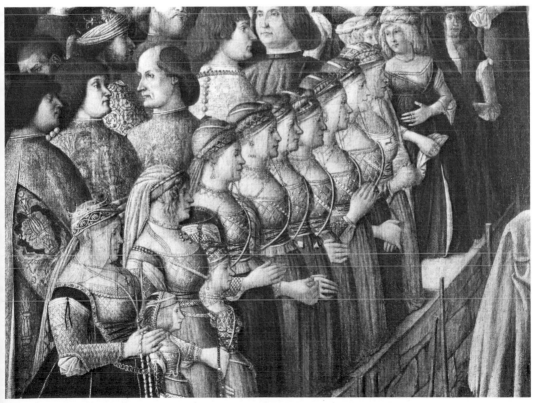

40. The Battle of Lepanto

41. King Henry III of France arrives in Venice, 1574

42. Doge Alvise Mocenigo I (Tintoretto)

43. Suleiman the Magnificent

44. Pope Julius II (Raphael)

45. Pope Leo X (Raphael)

46. Sir Henry Wotton

Sʳ Henry Wotton Kᵗ

47. Paolo Sarpi

FATHER PAUL.

Engraved for the Encyclopædia Londinensis April 1803.

48. The courtyard of the Doges' Palace in the seventeenth century

49. The Arsenal in the seventeenth century

CANEA.

The White Mountains

50 (*Top*). Corfu   51 (*Bottom*). Canea

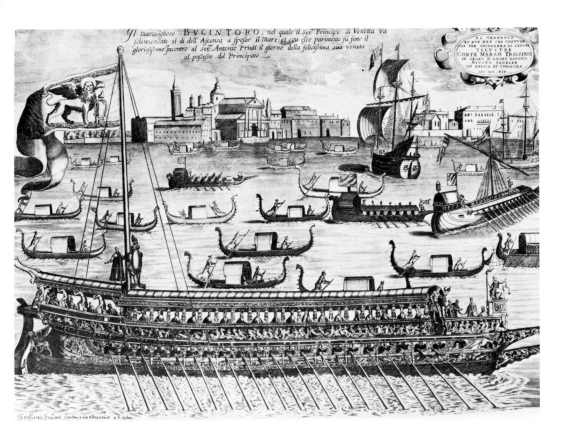

52 (*Top*). The Bucintoro 53 (*Bottom*). A naval battle against the Turks, 1661

54 (*Above*). The Ridotto (Longhi)

55 (*Opposite, above*). The *Sala del Collegio* in the Doges' Palace (Malombra)

56 (*Opposite, below*). The Piazzetta (Canaletto)

57. The *Bacino* of St Mark (Canaletto)

58. The horses of St Mark removed by the French, 1797

59. A Venetian torture chamber, as imagined by French propagandists

were not as defensible as Corfu had been. Many of them, though theoretically under the protection of the Republic, were in fact ruled by private Venetian families who had no means of staving off any sustained attack. One by one they fell: Nauplia and Malvasia on the east coast of the Peloponnese, then the islands – Skiros, Patmos, Aegina, Ios, Paros, Astipalaia – all considerably nearer to the Turkish mainland than to Venice, whose fleet was by now largely blocked by the throng of Turkish ships in the Adriatic narrows.

The victory of Corfu had already gone sour; every week was now bringing reports of new defeats, new losses. Suleiman was again on the offensive; and the European powers, for all their plans and promises, seemed incapable of forming alliances that existed otherwise than on paper or that were not poisoned by mutual suspicions and petty bickering before they even took shape. In the summer of 1538 one such attempt, embarked upon by Venice, the Pope, the Emperor and the King of the Romans with all the fervour of a Crusade and a degree of wild optimism such that the participants actually made advance plans for the division of the Ottoman Empire between them, ended not as they had imagined with the capture of Constantinople but with a further miserable defeat off Preveza, a Turkish stronghold on the coast of Epirus where the battle of Actium had been fought 1,569 years before. It was here that Andrea Doria, reluctantly persuaded to return to the theatre of war, delayed and prevaricated, obstructing his Venetian colleague at every turn, until the battle was as good as lost. Since he was neither a coward nor a fool, treachery or deliberate malice are the only other possible explanations. Whichever is the true one, he was indirectly responsible for the seven Venetian galleys lost. The Turks, by contrast, sustained no damage of any kind.

Venetian fortunes were thus at a low ebb when, late in the night of 28 December 1538, Doge Andrea Gritti died in his eighty-fourth year – it is said of a surfeit of grilled eels, unwisely consumed on Christmas Eve. He had always been a sensualist; already before his election his fellow-senator Alvise Priuli had been heard muttering 'We cannot make a Doge of a man with three bastards in Turkey', and if contemporary records are to be trusted he was subsequently to produce at least two more, one by a nun named Celestina. Perhaps this was one reason why he never gained his subjects' true affection. Yet they owed him much – both for his youthful heroism on the battlefield and for his later diplomatic achievements which brought them many years of peace. Even near the end of his life, in 1537, he had argued for three days in the Senate against going to war with the

Sultan, losing his motion by a single vote. Shortly before this he had sought formal permission to abdicate, and to retire quietly to the magnificent *palazzo* that he had built at S. Francesco della Vigna;[1] but when he saw that war was inevitable he had withdrawn his request. He was buried, with the pomp and ceremony that he had loved all his life, in the church of S. Francesco, which had been completed by Sansovino only four years previously, and where his tomb can still be seen just to the left of the main altar.[2]

It was by now clear that Venice must negotiate a peace with the Sultan on whatever terms she could; and one of the first actions of Doge Gritti's successor, the seventy-seven-year-old Pietro Lando, was to send a plenipotentiary to Constantinople. Of all her recent losses those which crippled her most were Nauplia and Malvasia, her last trading posts in the Peloponnese; and the ambassador, Tommaso Contarini, was given as his highest priority the task of negotiating, as part of the peace settlement, the return of these two ports, for which the Republic was prepared to pay a stiff ransom – 150,000 ducats in the first instance, rising to 300,000 should the Sultan prove particularly intractable. This last sum was by any standards enormous, and it was thought that Suleiman – who had new preoccupations in the east and was known to be not averse to the idea of at least a truce in western waters – would be only too happy to accept it. He proved, however, to be nothing of the kind, and Venice at last found herself obliged, in October 1540, to agree to a treaty on terms far harsher than she had ever contemplated. The 300,000 ducats that she had offered were exacted from her as general reparations, but there was to be no question of the return of Nauplia, or of Malvasia, or indeed of any other of the territories lost to her in the last three years. In future, too, Venetian ships would not be permitted to enter *or leave* Turkish ports without permission. There followed a score or more of minor items, each of which seemed calculated to cause the Republic the maximum of inconvenience and humiliation. But by now Venice had no choice; and so it was the sad fate of Pietro Lando, who a quarter of a century before had distinguished himself as one of the most dashing Captains-General of his day, to sign away yet another slice of his city's Levantine Empire.

At this point in her history it has become all too evident that Venice has

1. It still stands, on the west side of the *campo*. In 1564 it was bought by the state and presented to the Pope as a residence for the Apostolic Nuncios; later, in the nineteenth century, it passed to the Franciscans, who built the overhead gallery on columns to link it with their monastery.

2. Although the body of the church is Sansovino's, the façade is based on a design by Palladio and is a later addition of 1568–72.

entered upon her decline – a decline from which there can be no lasting recovery. The days of expansion are gone; those of retrenchment have set in. The patterns of trade are changing fast, and even though the adverse economic effects have not yet proved as bad as the pessimists feared, there are few long-term grounds for optimism. The Turk is at the gates, his advance relentless, his appetite apparently insatiable; and the Christian west has shown itself incapable of offering him any concerted resistance.

The government, meanwhile, is on the verge of bankruptcy, forever debating methods of raising funds yet somehow always lacking the courage to take the decisive action required. In 1537 the number of outstanding debts by private citizens to the Treasury was such that it was proposed to select twenty-five of the worst offenders and confiscate all their property without more ado; but no action was taken, and Venice embarked upon a new and ruinous war with her debts still uncollected. Two years later, her financial situation graver than ever, we find the Senate debating no fewer than five different emergency measures to replenish her coffers: forced loans, a poll tax, a tithe on all incomes, a wealth tax and a tax on land. All were carefully considered; not one was systematically put into practice. The conclusion is inescapable; the administration had grown lazy and inefficient, and lacked the courage to propose any legislation that it feared might be unpopular. Worse still, it was showing signs of corruption; two years after the peace of 1540, the real reason was discovered for Suleiman's intransigence over Nauplia and Malvasia. The brothers Nicolò and Costantino Cavazza, two highly placed and trusted state secretaries, one of the Senate and one of the Council of Ten, were found to have been in the pay of the King of France and to have revealed to him the secret orders of Contarini and his successor – orders which included the authority to renounce all claims on the two ports if this were absolutely necessary to achieve a treaty; and the Most Christian King had lost no time in passing the information to his new ally the Sultan.

This general breakdown of morale seems to have infected the whole population. The old public spirit had evaporated. The Venetians were growing soft. Wealth had led to luxury, luxury to idleness, and idleness to inertia, even when the state itself was threatened. Nor is this a latter-day judgement; it was recognized, and admitted, by many of them at the time. 'Formerly,' wrote Cristoforo da Canale in 1539, 'the Republic, single-handed, had raised many a powerful fleet – something of which she would now be incapable; for although our people are united and law-abiding, such is their present comfort and prosperity that nothing short of imperious necessity would induce them to embark in a galley.'

Comfort and prosperity of the people; indecisiveness and insolvency of the state: this was the paradox of sixteenth-century Venice. The Republic was out of tune with itself. Even during the famine years of 1527 and 1528, when the crops were ruined for two summers in succession – the first by incessant rain, the second by prolonged drought – when a serious outbreak of plague was followed by a still worse epidemic of typhus, and when the city's problems were further aggravated by the influx of refugees fleeing from the path of the imperial army as it plunged murderously down the peninsula towards Rome, the carnival was celebrated with undiminished gaiety, the balls and masques and marriage-feasts were more sumptuous than ever they had been. Was there, one wonders, an element of desperation in this wild spending, a touch of hysteria in this frenzied pursuit of pleasure? Or was there, alternatively, a cold and fatalistic logic, whispering that the Republic was doomed and that its citizens might as well enjoy themselves in the little time they had left?

However we may answer this question, the fact is that the Venetians were perfectly right. Whenever the law of the jungle prevails – and certainly no other law prevailed in Renaissance Europe – weakness must be concealed and full use must be made of any special gifts that providence has been pleased to bestow. If Venice had allowed any obvious signs of her economic or moral sickness to become evident to the outside world, her chances of survival would have been dangerously reduced; she took care not to do so. As for her special gifts, she possessed three. The first, her birthright, was her unrivalled position in her lagoon, isolated and impregnable. The second, to some extent a corollary, was her innate knowledge and understanding of the sea and all that pertained to it. The third was her genius for splendour and parade.

It was her good fortune that as the closing in of her commercial horizons gradually diminished the importance of her second gift, so she was able to derive increased advantages from her third. Thus, throughout the middle years of the sixteenth century, work continued unabated on that great unwritten programme of sumptuous building which we noted as the century opened, and regular visitors marvelled at the way in which, after even the briefest absence, they would always return to find the city more dazzlingly opulent than when they had left it. The Piazza in particular was in the process of transformation. Although it had long been considered a wonder of the world, it had only been cleared of its last remaining trees and bushes – vestiges of the days when it had been part of a monastic garden – in 1504, a year or two after the completion of Mauro Coducci's Clock Tower and a decade before the finishing touches were put to the rebuilt campanile. By this time Coducci had begun work on the *Procuratie Vecchie*, the single continuous range that forms the north side of the Square, which was inaugurated in its turn in 1532. Five years later, in 1537, while the Turks were vainly pounding against the defences of Corfu, Jacopo Sansovino was planning his lovely little *Loggetta* against the east side of the Campanile, which was to take shape simultaneously with his tremendous Library giving on to the Piazzetta behind; and no sooner was this latter masterpiece completed than he turned his attention to the Doges' Palace, where teams of masons had already been engaged for nearly half a century on the eastern extension along the Rio di Palazzo and to which he now contributed the *Scala d'Oro* and the two colossal statues of Mercury and Neptune flanking the *Scala dei Giganti*. By 1586, when Vincenzo Scamozzi completed his *Procuratie Nuove* along the south side of the Piazza, the view from the western end was almost precisely that which we know today. Elsewhere in the city the transformations were no less dramatic. Along the Grand Canal, the first Renaissance palaces, such as Pietro Lombardo's ravishing little Palazzo Dario or Coducci's more imposing Palazzo Vendramin-Calergi,[1] were now joined by others grander still like Sansovino's Palazzo Corner and Palazzo Manin[2] or Michele Sanmicheli's immense Palazzo Grimani. Meanwhile, on Venice's two principal off-shore islands to the south there arose the church of the Redentore and the monastery of S. Giorgio Maggiore, the two ecclesiastical masterpieces of Andrea Palladio.

When we remember that this was also the Venice of Titian, Tintoretto and Veronese, that the splendour of the art and architecture was reflected in the richness of the costumes of nobility and bourgeoisie alike – a richness on which none of the occasional sumptuary laws seemed to have any but the most temporary and barely perceptible effect – and that scarcely a day went by without some magnificent procession, public or private, religious or secular, we begin perhaps to get some idea of the impact that this coruscating city had on all who saw it. Cynical foreign ambassadors might ask themselves what lay behind all the glitter and the pomp; stern Lutheran pastors might avert their eyes in revulsion at such a shameless display of luxury and mammon; but none could fail to be impressed. And it was vital for Venice that they should be. To maintain her position in the changing world about her, she could no longer rely on her commercial wealth, nor on her navy, nor on the proud, swaggering *condottieri* of the previous century. If she were now to survive, she must have peace; and peace, in its

1. The winter Casino where, incidentally, Richard Wagner died in 1883.
2. Now the Prefecture and the Banca d'Italia respectively.

turn, depended on neutrality in the struggles which continued, as they always had, to tear Europe apart. But neutrality itself was hard to preserve against the pressures to which she was increasingly subjected – from Emperor and Pope, Frenchman and Spaniard, Austrian and Turk. It could be maintained only by the most subtle diplomacy; and diplomats must always speak, or appear to speak, from a position of strength.

Thus, more than ever before, Venice needed the respect of her more powerful neighbours; and none knew better than she the importance, in this regard, of the face which she presented to the world. This is not to say that she would not always have decked herself out as gorgeously as she was able, or that she would ever have resented money spent on her own self-glorification; far from it. The splendour of Venice can never be dismissed as a confidence trick. But like any great beauty, she was acutely conscious of the effect that that beauty had on others; and she used it to the full.

The neutrality which Doge Pietro Lando and his successors strove so hard to preserve was twofold: in the continuing, if by now unequal, struggle between the Habsburgs and the Valois, and in the losing battle against the Turk. There was, however, a third great issue which was causing an ever-widening rift across Europe, the more serious in that it had revealed itself to be no respecter of national frontiers. Already the teachings of Martin Luther and his followers had split England, France, Germany and those parts of central Europe which had formerly owed allegiance to Rome, spreading out in a shock-wave of violence and persecution on a scale unknown in Europe since the days of the Albigensian Crusade three centuries before.

Natural barriers, on the other hand, seemed to have proved rather more efficacious. Protestant doctrines had so far generally failed to recommend themselves to the populations of those lands beyond the Alps or the Pyrenees, and certainly the Venetians, who had never had any need of a Luther as defence against papal pretensions, showed for the most part little interest in the theological issues involved. Pope Paul III, however, was not convinced. Like all Romans of his day, he deeply mistrusted Venice; he knew that Vicenza, which was under Venetian rule, possessed a small but vocal Protestant minority; he was alarmed, too, by the number of young German students at the University of Padua who, he believed, would spread the contagion whenever and wherever they could. Nor could he forget that Venice was still one of the principal centres of printing and book production in all Christendom, and thus uniquely placed to subvert – if she wished or were otherwise persuaded – the minds of the faithful.

His suspicions were not entirely well founded. The Venetians had crossed swords with the Papacy often enough on political matters, and they had never allowed religion to dominate their conduct of affairs. None the less they were good Catholics according to their lights, and they were perfectly prepared to take such active measures against Lutheranism as they thought necessary, just as they had against other heresies in the past. Savage or unbridled persecution, however, they abhorred. Already in 1289, when they had first accepted a representative of the Holy Inquisition on Venetian territory, they had done so only on the understanding that his duties should be those of an examining magistrate rather than of a judge, and that his findings should always be subject to the secular authority. This principle they continued to uphold against ever stronger papal pressure, firmly rejecting all suggestions that suspected heretics should be sent to Rome for trial or punishment. If such persons were found on Venetian soil, they should be dealt with in Venice and judged by Venetian judges; thus, and only thus, could justice be ensured.

Still less, it need hardly be said, could there be any question of the Republic allowing itself to be dragged into a religious war, any more than a political one. When the Council of Trent opened in December 1545 in an endeavour to settle the policy of the Roman Church towards the Reformation, Venice like most of the other states of Europe sent ambassadors to report on the proceedings but otherwise played no active part; and when, in the war which followed, the Pope sought her alliance in his league with the Emperor against the Protestant states of Germany, she refused outright and indeed obstructed the League in every way she could. Requests to break off relations with the Protestants were also refused 'not on religious grounds, but for reasons of state', since, she maintained, those concerned were acting 'more in the interests of personal liberty than of religion'.

There is no reason to suspect, here, that the Venetians were being more than usually disingenuous. The Pope had a duty to protect the purity of the Faith; no one disputed that. The Emperor, on the other hand, for all his genuine piety, was, they knew, deeply worried by one of the Reformation's most ominous side-effects – its tendency to strengthen individual national feelings within the Empire; and with these feelings – having themselves fought so long and hard against imperial pretensions – they had every sympathy. Besides, Charles V remained their principal potential threat among the western powers; any weakening of his position was hardly likely to cause them much regret.

Thus it was that, thanks to a combination of painstaking diplomacy and good luck, Venice was able to settle down to one of the longest periods of peace she could ever remember – a period in which, in the words of one of her principal French historians,[1] 'the history of the Venetians flows on without being marked by any events worthy of the attention of posterity.' Doge succeeded doge in swift and largely unmemorable succession: the art-loving Francesco Donà in 1545, the pious Marcantonio Trevisan in 1553, the learned Francesco Venier in 1554, and, in July 1556, Lorenzo Priuli, whose distinction it was, after a long line of widowers or bachelors, to give Venice a *dogaressa* for the first time since the days of Marco Barbarigo seventy years before.

Priuli's dogeship, though overshadowed by a year of famine – the effects of which were only partly mitigated by a serious epidemic of measles[2] which took a heavy toll of the population – was, so far as internal politics were concerned, as uneventful as those of his immediate predecessors; but, on the European stage, his brief occupation of the ducal throne marked the end of an epoch: only two months after his accession Charles V, having resigned the Empire to his brother Ferdinand but all his dominions in Spain, Naples, Milan, the Franche-Comté, the Netherlands and the Americas to his son Philip, embarked at Flushing on his last voyage – that which was to take him back to Spain and, ultimately, to the small house attached to the monastery of Yuste in Estremadura where he was to die early in 1558. He left behind him an Italy as strife-torn as ever. Even as he sailed down the Channel, a Spanish army under the Duke of Alba was driving up through papal territory: an invasion soon to be answered by a French force of 10,000 under the Duc de Guise, marching to the Pope's rescue. In all this, despite inducements from Paul IV which included the restitution of her old territories in Apulia and even the grant of the entire island of Sicily – where she had never possessed so much as a trading-post – Venice refused to be involved. Thus, when Guise was suddenly recalled to deal with another Spanish-backed invasion, this time of France itself, the Pope was left without allies and forced to sue for peace.

But the age-old struggle between the Valois and the Habsburgs was nearing its close. It was finally fought out, surprisingly enough, not in Italy but in France; and there, at Cateau-Cambrésis on 5 April 1559, was signed the permanent treaty of friendship and alliance which brought to an end Italy's sixty-year martyrdom. Honour was saved on both sides, the treaty being further cemented by the marriage in June of Philip of Spain, a widower since the death of Queen Mary Tudor seven months earlier, to

1. Daru, Vol. IV, p. 118.
2. This, at least, seems the most probable diagnosis on the basis of the symptoms recorded.

Elizabeth, the fourteen-year-old daughter of Henry II of France.[1] But, at least where Italy was concerned, there was no doubt to which side the victory belonged. France had retired, beaten from the field. Less than three weeks after his daughter's wedding, Henry II was dead – struck in the eye while jousting at a tournament - and in August Pope Paul IV, whose violently anti-Spanish views had brought about Alba's invasion three years before, followed him to the grave. The Habsburgs had won; theirs, henceforth, was to be the dominant influence in the peninsula. But beyond the Alps, too, Charles's abdication marked a major turning-point: henceforth the Empire and Germany lose their prestige and fade into the background; Europe's centre of gravity shifts to Spain.

Thanks to the settlement of Franco-Spanish differences, Doge Girolamo Priuli, Lorenzo's elder brother who succeeded him in November 1559, found that many of the Republic's perennial problems of foreign policy had melted away. Not, however, all of them. The Ottoman Turks remained as always a long-term threat; fortunately, Suleiman was seriously preoccupied with a civil war at home caused by a dispute among his sons over the eventual succession, while much of his navy was kept fully engaged preventing the Portuguese from establishing themselves along the shores of the Red Sea and the Persian Gulf. He was not likely to cause Venice any major difficulties for some time. A more serious problem in the short term was that posed by the piratical Uskoks, a heterogeneous but exceedingly troublesome community largely – but by no means entirely – composed of Christian fugitives from the Turkish advance, who had settled at Segna (now Senj) and elsewhere along the Dalmatian coast and given themselves over to the traditional occupation of the inhabitants of those regions.[2] As readers of this history will be aware, the problem was hardly new; sporadic outbursts of piracy based on the innumerable islands

1. The Duke of Alba stood proxy for Philip, not only at the marriage ceremony but also at the consummation the same night. The Venetian ambassador, Giovanni Michiel, reported the details to his government:

'The Queen retired to bed, and after her there entered, by the light of many torches, the King her father in company with the Duke of Alba. That Duke, having one of his feet bare, lifted the coverlet of the Queen's bed on one side, and, having inserted his foot beneath the sheet, advanced it until it touched the naked flesh of the Queen; and in such manner the marriage was understood to have been consummated in the name of King Philip through the agency of a third person – that which was never afterwards to be understood by anyone.'

2. This is a grossly over-simplified description of a people who, historically, ethnically, politically and socially, are notoriously hard to define. Readers who wish to know more about these unlovely folk should see Philip Longworth, 'The Senj Uskoks Reconsidered', in the *Slavonic and East European Review*, Vol. 57, No. 3, July 1979.

and hidden creeks along the eastern shores of the Adriatic had constituted a threat to – and an occasional disruption of – Venetian commerce for almost as long as the Republic itself had lasted. With the Uskoks, however, there was an additional complication in that such outbursts called down the wrath of the Turks, who, after every Uskok attack on their own shipping, would make formal complaints to Venice, pointing out that as the power who claimed dominion over the Gulf it was her duty to keep it efficiently policed. The corollary to this proposition was not spelt out, but the implication to the Signoria was clear enough. Since Dalmatia was now the territory of the Empire and the offenders technically imperial subjects, Venice would in her turn make ever more pressing representations to Ferdinand for effective measures to be taken against them; but despite repeated promises he did nothing, and the Uskoks were to remain a perennial thorn in the Venetian flesh for many years to come.

A third problem, though a lesser one, was that posed by the Reformation. Its teachings continued to spread, and with them, through much of Europe, the persecutions and burnings at the stake of those who, whether Catholic or Protestant, had the misfortune to find themselves among the dissenting minority. Against excesses of this nature the Venetians felt, as they always had, an instinctive revulsion. As befitted the most cosmopolitan city of Europe, they were proud of their long tradition of tolerance – apart from higher considerations, they knew that anything else was disastrous to trade – and were now more than ever determined to maintain it. Since, however, this depended on simultaneously maintaining their freedom of action in matters of faith, it was clearly vital for them to preserve good relations with the Pope as far as possible, and to avoid giving him unnecessary cause for alarm. When therefore Paul's successor, Pius IV, reopened the Council of Trent in January 1563, Venice – no longer as chary of imperial influence as she had been at the Council's earlier sessions – showed herself both helpful and sympathetic, to such an extent that, when the Council finally closed at the end of the year, the grateful Pope made her a present of the Palazzo S. Marco in Rome, to serve as a perpetual embassy for the Republic and the residence of the Cardinal of S. Marco who was always to be a Venetian.[1]

The Council of Trent was the first clear answer by the Church of Rome to the Reformation. It defined the essential Catholic doctrines, carefully distinguishing them from those other theological issues which were con-

---

1. The Palazzo Venezia, as it later came to be called, remained the Venetian Embassy till the fall of the Republic; thereafter – when the Veneto became part of Austria – it served as the Austrian Embassy till after the First World War. Later Mussolini used it as his offices. It is now a museum.

sidered legitimate subjects for discussion; it exerted a moderating influence on the more extreme reactionaries; and it instituted many reforms, urgently needed and often long overdue. From the Venetian point of view, however, the Council was at least as important for what it left undone – a negative aspect for which Venice may have been at least partly responsible. While reaffirming the general supremacy of the Church over Christendom, it did not overtly challenge the right of sovereign states to apply their own laws in religious as in secular affairs. Thus, when in January 1564 its decrees and decisions were printed and published – by the Venetian Paolo Manuzio, third son of Aldus, whom Pius had persuaded in 1561 to set up a pontifical press in Rome – the Republic had good reason to be satisfied.

36
The Loss of Cyprus

[1564–1570]

Selim, Ottoman Sultan, Emperor of the Turks, Lord of Lords, King of Kings, Shadow of God, Lord of the Earthly Paradise and of Jerusalem, to the Signory of Venice:

We demand of you Cyprus, which you shall give us willingly or perforce; and do not awake our horrible sword, for we shall wage most cruel war against you everywhere; neither put your trust in your treasure, for we shall cause it suddenly to run from you like a torrent.

Beware, therefore, lest you arouse our wrath . . .

Venice had now been at peace with the Turks for almost a quarter of a century: twenty-five years in which she had had a chance to restore her finances, build up her fleet, and erect ever more sumptuous monuments with which to dazzle friend and foe alike. She well knew, however, that that peace could not last indefinitely. Suleiman the Magnificent was not yet satisfied with his conquests. Recently, it was true, domestic affairs had claimed much of his attention; but since 1559 Turkish naval activity in the Mediterranean had been noticeably – and ominously – on the increase, and though much of it was centred on the North African coast and so somewhat outside Venice's direct sphere of interest, it was nevertheless near enough to cause her misgivings. The great Khaireddin Barbarossa, at whose name all the maritime states of Europe had once trembled, was dead – though not before he had sacked and briefly occupied Nice and actually had the audacity to winter his fleet in Toulon; but his mantle had fallen on another freebooting captain, Torghud Ra'is, known to most Christians as Dragut, who had already proved himself more than worthy of it – capturing Tripoli from the Knights of St John in 1551 and utterly routing, nine years later, a Spanish fleet sent by Philip II to dislodge him.

It was, as likely as not, these two successes that now decided Suleiman to launch a major attack against Malta, with the object of expelling the Knights from the island just as he had expelled them from their earlier base at Rhodes some forty years before. He had no reason to think that the operation would prove any harder than its predecessor. Malta might possess one of the finest natural harbours in the world, but it was not a natural stronghold, and the Knights had only their own man-made defences in which to put their trust. Moreover their resources were quite unusually poor. Compared with the greenness and fertility of Rhodes, Malta was almost a desert island, rocky and treeless, possessed of no lakes or rivers and manifestly incapable of withstanding a prolonged siege through one of its long, rainless summers.

If, however, the Knights could expect little sustenance from their scanty, stony soil, that soil would show itself still more inhospitable to a besieging army. It followed that the force which the Sultan was to hurl against them in May 1565 had from the first to be largely self-supporting. And whereas Rhodes was only ten miles from the Turkish coast, Malta was nearly a thousand. Small wonder that Suleiman's invasion fleet, carrying as it did not only the entire army with its horses, cannon and ammunition but all its food and water too, was said to be one of the largest ever seen on the high seas.

The story of the siege, with the heroic and ultimately successful resistance of some 600 knights – many of them, like the Grand Master Jean de la Valette, already old men – and rather fewer than 7,000 soldiers, including mercenaries and local militia, is one of the great epics of history: but it has no place in this book. Since their settlement in Malta in 1530 – the island having been leased to them by Charles V at the nominal rental of a single falcon, payable annually on All Souls' Day – the Knights of St John had lost what little strategic importance they had once possessed. As hospitallers they still had a useful duty to perform; their Great Hospital, open to all, was famous throughout Christendom. As an aggressive fighting force against the Turk, they were negligible.

Malta itself, on the other hand, occupied a key position in the central Mediterranean, being a natural stepping-stone between Turkish-held Tripoli and Sicily – which latter formed part of the dominions of Philip of Spain. Had it fallen, with its superb harbour, into the hands of Suleiman, the consequent danger to Sicily would have been real and immediate, and that to South Italy scarcely less so. In the circumstances it was only surprising that the *Gran Soccorso* – the 9,000-strong Spanish force which ultimately came to the relief of the by now desperate Knights in September – was not more numerous, and that it had delayed so long. None the less, its appearance was decisive. The Sultan's army, well over half of it incapacitated by dysentery and fever, raised the siege and re-embarked; and Christendom rejoiced. After five centuries of almost unbroken advance, the Turks had been halted at last. And a year later, almost to the day, came more, equally welcome news: Suleiman the Magnificent was dead.

The Turks had been halted; but there was no indication that they had been finally stopped. Indeed, by the time the eighty-five-year-old Pietro Loredan succeeded Girolamo Priuli as Doge[1] in November 1567, there was already reason to suspect that the new Sultan, Selim II, was contemplating a major expedition of conquest. This time, however, he had his eye not on Malta but on Cyprus.

It was always said of Selim – nicknamed 'the Sot' – that his much-publicized determination to seize the island was due to an equally well-known *penchant* for its unusually potent wines. In fact its strategic value was as obvious as the wealth and fertility of its soil; the wonder is that his father Suleiman had not acted years before to rid himself of an unwanted Christian presence less than fifty miles from his own southern shores. In February 1568 reports reached the Rialto of various Turkish-inspired intrigues among the local inhabitants, many of whom were known to have no love for their Venetian overlords: there were ominous tales of Turkish ships taking clandestine soundings in Cypriot harbours, even of a huge mine being secretly prepared at Famagusta, ready to be detonated at the approach of the Turkish fleet. At the same time there arrived the more reliable but equally unwelcome intelligence that Selim, who had hitherto been continuing his father's campaigns in Hungary, had concluded an eight-year truce with the new Emperor Maximilian II and was consequently free to devote all his resources to his new enterprise.

In the face of these reports, the Venetian Senate remained indecisive. Clearly some preparations must be made to meet the expected onslaught; on the other hand, Selim had willingly signed a peace treaty with the Republic on his accession. Besides, there had been similar alarms before, and quiet diplomacy – helped, on occasion, by a discreet and well-placed bribe – had usually done the trick. In any case nothing must be done that risked annoying the Sultan, who was as yet unused to power and whose character was known to be somewhat unstable. All through 1569 the argument went on, firm decisions being made even harder to reach by the disastrous harvest of that year, which caused a famine all through Italy, and – at midnight on 13 September – by a mysterious explosion at the Arsenal, which burnt out much of the area between it and the church of S. Francesco della Vigna, destroying the convent of the Celestia and three other churches besides. Inevitably, foul play was suspected, but was never proved.

---

1. Loredan had been elected only after fourteen days and seventy-seven ballots, a compromise candidate to break the deadlock. His career had been notably undistinguished, and when he was overtaken, on his way home to lunch, with the news of his election, for a long time he flatly refused to believe it.

Towards the end of January 1570, however, news reached Venice which impelled the Senate to action. The Venetian *bailo* in Constantinople had been sent for by the Grand Vizir, Sokollu Mehmet, who informed him in so many words that the Sultan considered Cyprus to be historically part of the Ottoman Empire and was determined that it should be his. A day or two later there followed mass arrests of Venetian merchants and seizures of Venetian ships in harbour. Immediate orders were given to take similar steps against all subjects of the Sultan and Turkish vessels in Venice. Appeals for help were dispatched to the Pope, Philip of Spain and various other Princes of Europe. The Captain of the Gulf, Marco Querini, hastened to Crete with twenty-five galleys and orders to fit out twenty more which were lying, unmanned and unvictualled, at Candia.

Although there was a party in the Senate that was reluctant to see the end of the long peace and that still believed that some accommodation with the Sultan might be possible, the chances of avoiding open war seemed to be diminishing fast. Then, in mid-March, came further, still more ominous reports from Constantinople. An ambassador from Selim was actually on his way with an ultimatum: either Venice must surrender Cyprus of her own free will or it would be taken from her by force. No longer could the Venetians doubt where they stood. According to a centuries-old custom, when the Doge and Signoria marched in formal procession to the various churches in the city, six banners would be carried – two white, two blue and two red. In time of peace, the white went first; during periods of truce, the blue; in war, the red. That Easter – which fell on 26 March, still two days before the arrival of the Sultan's envoy – in the annual progress to the church of S. Zaccaria for vespers, it was the red banners that led the way; and on Easter Monday a certain Girolamo Zane was appointed Captain-General of the Venetian fleet, receiving his baton and standard from Doge Loredan at a special mass in the Basilica. Zane was seventy-nine years old, the Doge by now eighty-eight; already more than one observer of the ceremony must have asked himself whether, at this crucial moment in its history, the fate of the Republic was in entirely the right hands.

Less than six weeks later Pietro Loredan was dead, his place being taken by a former ambassador to both Charles V – who had loaded him with imperial honours – and to Pius IV, by name Alvise Mocenigo.[1] Girolamo Zane, meanwhile, had sailed with seventy galleys as far as Zara, on the first stage of an expedition which was to end in fiasco and bring upon him humiliation and disgrace.

1. It was indicative of the general state of emergency that members of the Collegio and all those officials connected with the Arsenal or the rearmament programme were excused attendance at the election.

The original letter which the Sultan's envoy delivered to the Collegio[1] on 28 March has not come down to us. If, however – as seems likely – the version given at the head of this chapter[2] is a reasonably accurate rendering, Selim's ultimatum could hardly have been more clearly, or more offensively, presented. The Venetian reply was equally to the point: Venice was astonished that the Sultan should already wish to break the treaty he had so recently concluded; she was, however, the mistress of Cyprus and would, by the grace of Jesus Christ, have the courage to defend it. The envoy was then let out by a side door to escape the attentions of the furious crowd which had gathered outside the Doges' Palace, and escorted back to his waiting ship.

As if in an attempt to make up for so much lost time, war preparations in Venice now proceeded apace. The Arsenal, its fire damage hastily repaired, was once again working flat out; to raise funds, meanwhile, the government was adopting ever more desperate measures, even going so far as to increase the number of Procurators of St Mark – the highest dignitaries in the state apart from the Doge himself – by eight, disposing of the new titles in return for loans of 20,000 ducats. Neighbouring towns and cities contributed according to their means, and, just as in the old days, rich citizens undertook to build or equip ships, or enlist private militias – sometimes of several thousand men – at their own expense. From the other Christian states to which appeals had been sent, the response was less enthusiastic. The Emperor Maximilian pointed out that his formal truce with the Turk still had five more years to run. The King of Poland was equally reluctant in view of his own exposed position. From France Catherine de' Medici, now effectively the Regent, was quarrelling with Spain over Flanders and pleaded her nation's old alliance with the Sultan, though she offered the services of her son, Charles IX, as mediator – an offer which was politely declined. The King of Portugal pointed out that he was fully engaged in the Orient, and that anyway his country was being ravaged by plague. The Knights of St John – who were, incidentally, the biggest landowners in Cyprus – offered five ships, but four of them were to be captured by the Turks soon after they left Malta. A letter had even gone off to the Tsar of Muscovy, but it seems unlikely that it ever reached him; in any event Ivan the Terrible was at war with Poland and it is hard to see what assistance he could have given. No appeal was addressed to

---

1. At this time the Collegio consisted of the Doge with his six Councillors, the *Savii*, the Heads of the Council of Ten and the Grand Councillor.
2. Quoted by Sir George Hill, *History of Cyprus*, Vol. III, p. 888.

Queen Elizabeth of England, who had been under sentence of excommunication since February.

That left Pope Pius V and Philip II of Spain. The Pope had agreed to
equip a dozen vessels if Venice would provide the hulls. Philip, for his part,
had offered a fleet of fifty ships, under the command of Gian Andrea Doria,
great-nephew and heir of that Andrea whose hatred of Venice had twice
led him to betray the Republic's trust, at Corfu and Preveza, some thirty
years before.[1] Even this was a niggardly enough contribution; Venice had
produced a fleet of 144 ships, including 126 war galleys. But Philip had
always mistrusted the Venetians, whom he suspected (not without some
cause) of holding themselves ready to make terms with the Sultan if the
opportunity offered; and, as events were to show, he had given Doria –
whose feelings against the Republic were no whit less hostile than those of
his great-uncle – secret instructions to keep out of trouble, to let the
Venetians do the fighting, and to bring the Spanish fleet safely home again
as soon as possible.

From the start, the expedition seemed to be ill-fated. The Captain-
General, who had understood that the Spanish and papal squadrons were
to join him at Zara, waited there in vain for two months during which time
his fleet was ravaged by some unidentified epidemic, causing not only
many deaths but a general demoralization which in turn led to scores of
desertions. On 12 June he sailed to Corfu, where he picked up Sebastiano
Venier, the erstwhile Proveditor-General of the island who had recently
been appointed to the same position in Cyprus. Here he heard that the papal
squadron under Marcantonio Colonna was awaiting the Spaniards at
Otranto – but of Philip's promised fleet there was still no sign. Not till July
was it learnt that Gian Andrea Doria had simply remained in Sicily, on the
pretext that he had received no instructions to go further. After urgent
protestations from the Pope, Philip finally sent his admiral sailing orders,
which arrived on 8 August; even then, it was another four days before the
fleet set forth from Messina and a further eight before it reached Otranto
– a journey which, in the perfect weather conditions prevailing, should
have taken no more than two.

Having at last joined his papal allies, Doria made no effort to call on
Colonna or even to communicate with him; and, when Colonna decided to
ignore this studied piece of discourtesy and take the initiative himself, he
was answered with a long speech implicitly recommending that the whole
expedition should be called off. The season was late; the Spanish ships were

---

1. See pp. 452 and 453.

not in fighting condition; and, as Doria was at pains to point out, though his instructions were to sail under the papal flag, he was also under the orders of his sovereign to keep his fleet intact. Colonna somehow forbore to remind him who was to blame for the first two misfortunes, merely pointing out that both King and Pope expected their fleets to sail with the Venetians to Cyprus; accordingly, sail they must. Finally, and with ill grace, Doria agreed.

Girolamo Zane had by now moved on to Crete, where the papal and Spanish fleets joined him on 1 September – almost exactly five months since his departure from Venice. A council was called, at which Doria at once began raising new difficulties. This time it was the Venetian galleys that were unfit for war: if the allied fleet were to come to grips with the enemy, it would be either destroyed or ignominiously put to flight. More-over, once they had left Crete there were no harbours in which to take refuge. Now, too, he revealed a fact that he had not, apparently, thought necessary to mention before: he must return to the West by the end of the month at the latest.

Colonna remained firm. The season, though advanced, was not yet prohibitively so; there were still two clear months before the onset of win-ter. Cyprus was rich in admirable harbours. The Venetian ships had admittedly been undermanned, but their long wait had given them plenty of time to find replacements and their crews were all once again up to strength. Altogether the combined fleets now comprised 205 sail; the Turks were thought to number 150 at the most. Why, therefore, should they fear an armed encounter? Flight would indeed be ignominious, but to retire now, before even sighting the enemy, would be more dishonourable still.

At this point Zane – who at Colonna's discreet suggestion had remained absent from the opening discussion – joined his colleagues and immediate-ly tabled a written request that the expedition should be allowed to proceed. Doria still prevaricated, finally agreeing only on condition that the Spanish ships should be given preferential treatment: that they should be exempt from rearguard duty and that they should sail in a group apart, in such a way as to be able to disengage completely if they felt so inclined. It was no wonder that, by 7 September, while discussions were still drag-ging on, Zane addressed an almost desperate letter to the Council of Ten, complaining that Doria was obviously determined not to fight, that he was continually raising new objections and resuscitating old ones, and that although with patience and tact it had so far been possible to overcome these objections, he was throwing all their plans into confusion and dis-rupting the whole enterprise.

On the 13th, the fleet moved on to Sitia, at the eastern end of the island; and there, at Doria's insistence, there was a general review at which it was revealed, to his ill-concealed satisfaction, that the Venetian galleys were indeed below strength, with only some eighty fighting men per vessel as compared with the hundred-odd in the papal and Spanish squadrons. Once again he advised withdrawal, and although once again ultimately overruled he managed to delay departure three full days, long enough for Zane to sustain another severe blow: a report that the Turks had landed in Cyprus. It was now or never. On the night of 17 September the fleet sailed for the beleaguered island.

But off Castellorizo there came worse news still. Nicosia had fallen. Another council was called, at which Doria predictably redoubled his protestations. And now, for the first time, the Marquis of Santa Cruz, who as commander of the Neapolitan contingent was technically a subordinate of Doria's but who had hitherto taken a considerably more robust line than his chief, also advised turning back. The capture of Nicosia, he pointed out, would mean a vast increase in the number of fighting men available for the Turkish fleet, and a corresponding upsurge in enemy morale – at the worst possible time, when the allied crews were becoming more and more dispirited. Colonna agreed with him; so, sadly and reluctantly, did old Girolamo Zane. One voice only was raised in favour of a continued advance: that of Sebastiano Venier, who argued that, however strong the Turks might be, they would almost certainly be a good deal stronger next year – when, incidentally, the allies were most unlikely to have a fleet of over 200 sail to throw against them.

They were brave words, but they failed to convince; and the mighty fleet, flying the banners of Christendom, turned about and sailed for home without having once sighted the enemy. In an almost pathetic attempt to salvage the last shreds of his reputation, poor Zane proposed that the allies should at least try to inflict some damage on enemy territory during their return journey; but once again his hopes were sabotaged by Doria's impatience to get home. By the time he reached Corfu on 17 November – having stopped in Crete on the way – a new epidemic had broken out in his ships and he himself was, mentally and physically, a broken man. Lacking even the heart to return home, he wrote to the Senate asking to be relieved of his post. His request was granted, and on 13 December Sebastiano Venier was appointed Captain-General in his stead.

So ended one of the most humiliating episodes in the history of Venice. Unless it were argued that, having provided some three quarters of the combined fleet, she should not have lost time waiting for her allies but should have pressed on alone in June, she could not in fairness be held responsible; but neither could she escape her share of the disgrace, much of which fell on the undeserving head of old Girolamo Zane himself. Ordered back to Venice early in 1571, in the following year – the cause of the delay is unknown – he was summoned by the Council of Ten to answer several grave charges relating to his conduct during the expedition. After a long inquiry he was acquitted – but too late. In September 1572 he had died in prison.

The fate of Gian Andrea Doria was somewhat different. Philip II had been left in no doubt of the bitter feelings his admiral had aroused; Pope Pius, indeed, on receiving Colonna's report, had sent the King a formal letter of complaint. But Philip chose to ignore it. Doria had obeyed his instructions to the letter, and was rewarded by immediate promotion to the rank of General, with seniority over all the commanders of the fleets of Spain, Naples and Sicily – in which capacity he was to do still further damage to the Christian cause before his unedifying career was over.

In 1570 Venice had held Cyprus for eighty-one years. Queen Caterina had been replaced by a Venetian governor, with the title of Lieutenant: in him and his two Counsellors – the three together, known as the Rectors, were the Cypriot equivalent of the Signoria – rested in effect virtually all the civil power. There was in addition a Great Council, comprising all the nobility of the island over the age of twenty-five, plus certain of those resident Venetians who had settled there; of these latter, the nobles were immediately eligible, the rest – provided they were not members of the 'mechanical' trades – could purchase their seats after a five-year residence. But its functions were largely electoral, and even then its decisions were subject to the Rectors' confirmation.

While the civil government was established at Nicosia, the military headquarters were at Famagusta. There the standing garrison of cavalry and infantry, and the Cyprus-based fleet, were under the command of a Venetian Captain – though in time of war he might expect a Proveditor-General to be sent specially out from Venice to assume supreme authority. Famagusta, unlike Nicosia, was superbly fortified: *omnium urbium fortissima,* as an astonished traveller described it. Historically, too, it was the island's principal harbour, although by 1570 Salines (the modern Larnaca) had overtaken it in terms of commercial traffic.

The total population was about 160,000, still living under an anachronistically feudal system which the Republic had made little or no effort to change. At the top were the nobility, partly Venetian but for the most part still of old French Crusader stock like the former royal house of Lusignan. Much of the land was in their hands, but under the prevailing law of primogeniture there was an ever-increasing number of unpropertied younger sons who frequently constituted a problem to the government. At the bottom was the peasantry, many of whom were still effectively serfs, owing their masters two days' service a week. For them, despite the extreme fertility of the island, life was a struggle and oppression an integral part of it. Between the two was the merchant class and the urban bourgeoisie – a Levantine melting pot of Greeks, Venetians, Armenians, Syrians, Copts and Jews.

Cyprus, in short, cannot have been an easy place to govern; it must be admitted, however, that the Venetians – whose own domestic administration was the wonder and envy of the civilized world – should have governed it a great deal better than they did. Perhaps the very strictness of the standards demanded of them at home increased the temptation to feather their nests once they were a safe distance away; probably, too, they were infected by the general atmosphere of venality which, we are told, prevailed in the island long before they took power. What is certain is that by the time the Turks landed in the summer of 1570 Venice had acquired a grim record of maladministration and corruption, and had made herself thoroughly unpopular with her Cypriot subjects. Even the rich nobility, however much they might oppress their own peasantry, objected to the way in which, as they saw it, the Republic was enriching itself at the island's expense, and its official representatives, by less overt methods, following suit. They resented, too, their lack of any real power. The other, humbler, sections of the population felt much the same. Many indeed believed that any change of government could only be for the better – a sentiment which was not without significance when the moment of crisis came.

The joint expedition for the relief of Cyprus had been an unmitigated disaster; and yet, even if it had safely arrived at its destination, disembarked its fighting men and obeyed all its instructions to the letter, it could scarcely have saved the island. A major victory at sea might perhaps have proved temporarily effective, delaying the inevitable for a year or two; but since the Turkish invasion fleet that dropped anchor on 3 July at Larnaca numbered not less than 350 sail – more than double Colonna's estimate – such a victory would have been, to say the least, unlikely. The truth is that, from the moment that Selim II decided to incorporate the island in his Empire, Cyprus was doomed.

It was doomed for the same fundamental reason that Malta, five years before, had been saved: the inescapable fact that the strength of any army in the field varies inversely with the length of its lines of communication and supply. Since Cyprus had neither the means, the ability, nor – probably – the will to defend itself, it could only be defended by Venice, from which all military supplies, arms and ammunition, and the bulk of the fighting men and horses would have to come. But Venice lay over 1,500 miles away across the Mediterranean, much of which was now dominated by the Turks. They, on the other hand, had only fifty miles to sail from ports on the southern Anatolian coast, where they could count on an almost limitless supply of manpower and materials.

Their success seemed the more assured in that the Cypriot defences, apart from those of Famagusta, were hopelessly inadequate. Nicosia, it is true, boasted a nine-mile circuit of medieval walls; but they enclosed an area considerably larger than the town and needed a huge force to defend them. They were moreover far too thin – the siege techniques of the sixteenth century were vastly different from those of the fourteenth – and despite the feverish last-minute efforts of Venetian engineers to strengthen them they stood a poor chance of survival against the massive artillery which had long been a speciality of the Turks. Kyrenia had once been a splendid fortress, but it had fallen long since into ruin; and though there too some work had recently been done to repair and strengthen the existing walls, it was unlikely to hold out for long. The fortifications of all other Cypriot towns were either negligible or non-existent; from the first it was understood that only in Nicosia and Famagusta was there any hope of prolonged resistance. Manpower too was in short supply. Accurate estimates of numbers are never easy, but it is unlikely that there were more than 20,000 fighting men – including some 500 cavalry – in Nicosia when the siege began, and of these little more than half were fully effective. Fra Angelo Calepio, who was present throughout, tells us that there were 1,040 arquebuses in the magazines, but that they were not properly distributed nor were any instructions given as to their use, with the result that many soldiers found it impossible to fire them without setting light to their beards.

For this and many other shortcomings in the defences of the capital, the principal blame must fall on the Lieutenant, Nicolò Dandolo. Uncertain, timid, forever vacillating between bouts of almost hysterical activity and periods of apathetic inertia, he was obviously unsuited to the supreme command – which would not have been his if Sebastiano Venier, the Proveditor-General designate who had sailed with Girolamo Zane's expedition, had managed to reach the island. Through the agonizing months which were to follow, Dandolo was to prove a constant liability, his lack of judgement and immoderate caution occasionally giving rise to suspicions – as it happened, unfounded – that he was in enemy pay. Fortunately there were better men at Famagusta: the Perugian general Astorre Baglioni, who had been sent out from Venice in April as Commander-in-Chief, and the Captain, Marcantonio Bragadin, whose appalling fate when the siege was over was to earn him a permanent niche in the Venetian Hall of Fame – and his conqueror lasting infamy.

The Turkish invasion force had appeared off the coast of Cyprus on 1 July. Sultan Selim – the memory of his father's humiliation in Malta still fresh in his mind – had spared no pains in its preparation, and had entrusted it to two of his ablest and most experienced commanders: Lala Mustafa Pasha for the land forces and Piale Pasha – a Croat who, with Dragut, had trounced a Spanish fleet under Gian Andrea Doria ten years before – for the fleet. After a lightning raid on Limassol, where it did considerable damage, sacking the town and a neighbouring monastery before being repulsed, it continued along the south coast to Larnaca. Here, owing to Dandolo's timidity, Mustafa was able to land his entire force without opposition, settling in his men while he awaited further troops from the mainland. From Larnaca he then dispatched a blind Greek monk to Nicosia with the usual ultimatum: since Venice had no chance of successfully resisting his superbly equipped force of 200,000 men, let her now cede the island peaceably, thus retaining the friendship and favour of the Sultan. If she did not, it would be the worse for her. To this missive the Rectors in Nicosia sent no reply; they did, however, send an urgent appeal to Famagusta, asking for the return of Baglioni with reinforcements. The request was refused, on the grounds that the threat to Nicosia might well be a feint: the weight of the Turkish attack was still expected at Famagusta.

But Mustafa was not dissembling. When his reinforcements arrived on 22 July he set off that same evening for Nicosia; and two days later his immense army was encamped outside the walls of the city. Now once again a chance was lost: the Italian commander of infantry begged for permission to mount an immediate attack, while the enemy were still tired by their march of thirty miles through the heat of a Cyprus summer, and their artillery and heavy cavalry were still unprepared. Once again Dandolo and his fellow-Rectors declined to take the risk, and the Turks were allowed to dig themselves in undisturbed.

And so the siege began. The Turkish army, though not perhaps quite as numerous as its commander had claimed, must have been a good 100,000 strong; its cannon and light artillery were formidable and, in contrast to the pathetic firing-pieces of the defenders along the walls, were employed with deadly accuracy and expertise. Meanwhile Dandolo, fearing a shortage of gunpowder, had rationed its use to the point where even those of his soldiers who had fire-arms and knew how to use them were forbidden to shoot at any group of Turks numbering fewer than ten. Yet, however weak-spirited the Lieutenant, there were others around him who did not lack courage. Somehow the city held out, all through a sweltering August; and it was only on 9 September, after Mustafa's men had given the noisiest and most jubilant welcome of which they were capable to a further 20,000 troops freshly arrived from the mainland, that the defenders finally yielded to the fifteenth major assault. Thus, after forty-five days, Nicosia fell. Even as the triumphant Turks swarmed through the city, the resistance continued, a final stand being made in the main square, in front of the Lieutenant's Palace. Dandolo, who had taken refuge inside it some hours before while his men were still fighting on the ramparts, now appeared in his crimson velvet robes, hoping to receive the favoured treatment due to his rank. Scarcely had he reached the foot of the steps when a Turkish officer struck his head from his shoulders.

It was customary, when a besieged town had defended itself to the last, for the victorious commander to allow his men a three-day period of rapine and plunder. The usual atrocities followed, the usual massacres, quarterings and impalements, the usual desecration of churches and violation of the youth of both sexes; what was unusual was the sheer extent of the looting. Nicosia was a rich city, generously endowed with treasures ecclesiastical and secular, western and Byzantine. It was a full week before all the gold and silver, the precious stones and enamelled reliquaries, the jewelled vestments, the velvets and brocades had been loaded on to the carts and trundled away – the richest spoils to fall into Turkish hands since the capture of Constantinople itself, well over a century before.

As he and his army returned to the coast, Mustafa left a garrison of 4,000 janissaries to refortify the city. He still expected a Venetian relief expedition; if it came, an attempt to recapture Nicosia could not be discounted. Meanwhile, however, he had no intention of abandoning the offensive himself. Already on 11 September, two days after the fall of Nicosia, he had sent a messenger to the commanders at Famagusta, calling upon them to surrender and bearing, as an additional inducement, the head of Nicolò Dandolo in a basin. It would be their turn next.

Although Mustafa Pasha can hardly have expected that his ultimatum would have the desired effect and that Famagusta would capitulate without a fight, he must nevertheless have cursed its commanders for their stubbornness. Even Nicosia had given him more trouble than he had expected; but Famagusta promised to be a really formidable challenge. The old fortifications had been torn down at the end of the previous century and replaced with a completely new *enceinte*, incorporating all the latest advances in military architecture; and the town was now, to all appearances, as near impregnable as any town could be. Behind those tremendous walls the defenders were admittedly few: some 8,000 as compared with a Turkish force which, with new contingents arriving every few weeks from the mainland, probably by now fell not far short of the 200,000 of which Mustafa had boasted to Dandolo. On the other hand they had in Bragadin and Baglioni two first-rate leaders whom they already respected and for whom their love and admiration were to grow during the trials that lay ahead.

The army and the fleet, loaded to the gunwales with Nicosia loot, arrived at Famagusta on the same day, 17 September; and the siege began at once. Thanks to the courage and enterprise of the two commanders, it was from the first a far more dynamic affair than that of Nicosia, with the defenders making frequent sorties outside the walls and sometimes even carrying the battle right into the Turkish camp. All through the winter it continued, the Venetians showing no signs of weakening; in January, indeed, they were considerably strengthened, both materially and morally, by the arrival of a fifteen-hundred-man relief force, with arms and munitions, under the command of Marco and Marcantonio Querini, who had managed to break through the depleted Turkish blockade. In April the level of food supplies began to give some cause for concern; but Bragadin dealt with the problem efficiently enough by evicting over 5,000 'useless mouths' from among the civil population and sending them out to seek shelter in the neighbouring villages. Towards the end of that same month Mustafa changed his tactics, ordering his corps of Armenian sappers to dig a huge network of trenches to the south. As the corps numbered some 40,000 and was further supplemented by forced labour from the local peasantry, work progressed rapidly: by the middle of May the whole region was honeycombed for a distance of three miles from the walls, the trenches numerous enough to accommodate the whole besieging army and so deep that mounted cavalry could ride along them with only the tips of their lances visible to the watchers on the ramparts. The Turks also constructed a total of ten siege towers, progressively closer to the town, from which they could fire downwards on to the defenders. From there, on 15 May, the final bombardment began.

The Venetians fought back with courage and determination. Again and again their own artillery would destroy whole sections of the Turkish siege towers, but to no avail; a few hundred sappers would get to work, and the towers would be as good as new by morning. Slowly, as the weeks dragged by, they began to lose heart. Hopes of the great Venetian-Spanish relief expedition, which had kept their spirits up through the winter and spring, had faded; powder was running short; food was even shorter. By July all the horses, donkeys and cats in the town had been eaten; nothing was left but bread and beans. Of the defenders, only 500 were still capable of bearing arms, and they were dropping through lack of sleep. On the 29th the Turks unleashed a new general assault, their fifth. The Christians held them back, but at the cost of two thirds of their number killed or wounded. On the 30th came another, on the 31st another still. Even then, Mustafa failed to break in; but that night the Venetian generals inspected their defences and their remaining stocks of food and ammunition and realized that they could hold out no longer. By a voluntary surrender they might still, according to the accepted rules of warfare, avoid the massacres and the looting that were otherwise inevitable. Dawn broke on 1 August to reveal a white flag fluttering on the ramparts of Famagusta.

The peace terms were surprisingly generous. All Italians were to be allowed to embark, with colours flying, for Crete, together with any Greeks, Albanians or Turks who wished to accompany them. On their journey they would not be molested by Turkish shipping, which would on the contrary furnish them with all the assistance they required. Greeks who elected to stay behind would be guaranteed their personal liberty and property, and would be given two years in which to decide whether they would remain permanently or not; those who then elected to leave would be given safe conduct to the country of their choice. The document setting out these terms was signed personally by Mustafa and sealed with the Sultan's seal; it was then returned to Baglioni and Bragadin with a covering letter complimenting them on their courage and their magnificent defence of the city.

For the next four days arrangements for the departure went smoothly enough. Food supplies were sent in and, apart from a few minor incidents, relations between the Europeans and the Turks were friendly. On 5 August Bragadin sent word to Mustafa proposing to call and formally to present him with the keys of Famagusta; back came the reply that the general would be delighted to receive him. Donning his purple robe of office, he set off that evening accompanied by Baglioni and a number of his senior officers, escorted by a mixed company of Italian, Greek and Albanian soldiers. Mustafa received them with every courtesy; then, without warning, his face clouded and his manner changed. In a mounting fury, he began hurling baseless accusations at the Christians standing before him. They had murdered Turkish prisoners; they had concealed munitions instead of handing them over according to the terms of surrender. Suddenly, he whipped out a knife and cut off Bragadin's right ear, ordering an attendant to cut off the other and his nose. Then, turning to his guards, he ordered them to execute the whole party. Astorre Baglioni was beheaded; so too was the commander of artillery, Luigi Martinengo. One or two managed to escape; but most were massacred, together with a number of other Christians who chanced to be within reach. Finally the heads of all those that had been murdered were piled in front of Mustafa's pavilion. They are said to have numbered 350.

Now that the killing had begun it was very hard to stop. Mustafa himself, who seemed at last to have regained his composure, forbade his howling soldiery to enter Famagusta on pain of death; many, however, disobeyed his orders and ran amok through the city, killing any citizen they chanced to meet, burning and pillaging in a frenzy of blood-lust. Others headed for the port, where they found victims in plenty among the Christians preparing to embark for the West.

But the worst fate had been reserved for Marcantonio Bragadin. He was held in prison for nearly a fortnight, by which time his untreated wounds were festering and he was already seriously ill. First he was dragged round the walls, with sacks of earth and stones on his back; next, tied into a chair, he was hoisted to the yardarm of the Turkish flagship and exposed to the taunts of the sailors. Finally he was taken to the place of execution in the main square, tied naked to a column and, literally, flayed alive. Even this torture he is said to have borne in silence for half an hour until, as the executioner reached his waist, he finally expired. After the grim task was completed, his head was cut off, his body quartered, and his skin, stuffed with straw and cotton and mounted on a cow, was paraded through the streets.

When, on 22 September, Mustafa sailed for home, he took with him as trophies the heads of his principal victims and the skin of Marcantonio Bragadin, which he proudly presented to the Sultan. The fate of the heads is unknown; but nine years later a certain Girolamo Polidoro, one of the few survivors of the siege, managed to steal the skin from the Arsenal of Constantinople and to return it to Bragadin's sons, who deposited it in the church of S. Gregorio. From here, on 18 May 1596, it was transferred to SS. Giovanni e Paolo, and placed in a niche behind the urn which forms part of the hero's memorial. Here it still remains today.[1]

1. In the south aisle, on the right soon after you enter the west door. The niche was opened on 24 November 1961 at the instigation of the leading authority on Bragadin – and his direct descendant – Signora Maria Grazia Siliato. It was found to contain a leaden casket in which were several pieces of tanned human skin. They were replaced in March 1962, after a restoration of the monument. The bust is by a follower of Vittoria – good, but not inspired. There is also a distinctly disappointing fresco in monochrome depicting the martyrdom.

37

Lepanto

[1570–1571]

Sembrose por la corte como negocio venido de la mano de Dios, y á todos nos parescia un sueño, por ser cosa que no se ha jamas visto oido esta batalla y victoria naval.

There is no man at the court who does not discern in it the hand of the Lord, and it seems to us all like a dream, in that never before has such a battle and victory at sea been seen or heard of.

Letter from State Secretary Juan Luis de Alzamora
to Don John of Austria, 11 November 1571

The failure of the 1570 expedition had been, for Venice and the Papacy, a humiliating blow; already, however, negotiations were well under way for a firmer and more effective alliance. The prime mover of this new initiative was the Pope. Pius V had thought long and hard about the Turkish threat, and had realized that the principal obstacle to any close understanding between Spain and Venice was that Venice saw the problem in terms of her colonies in the Levant, while Spain was a good deal more anxious about the danger presented by the Sultan's Moorish vassals to her own possessions in North Africa. To Pius, therefore, the primary aim of Christendom should be to re-establish control of the central Mediterranean, cutting off the Sultan's African territories from those in Europe and Asia and thus effectively splitting his Empire into two. In July 1570 the Pope had accordingly called a conference to draft the charter of a new Christian League, and over the following months, by patient argument and with active Venetian help, had gradually won King Philip round. It was a hard struggle. After eight months, just when the last obstacles seemed on the point of being overcome, the Spaniards had second thoughts and threatened to renege on all that they had so far agreed. It was only after Venice, her patience exhausted, had actually dispatched an envoy to Constantinople to try and make a separate peace that they changed their attitude once again and allowed the remaining points to be settled.

The resulting treaty was formally proclaimed on 25 May 1571 in St

Peter's. It was to be perpetual, offensive as well as defensive, and directed not only against the Ottoman Turks themselves but also against their Moorish vassals and co-religionists along the North African coast. The signatories – Spain, Venice and the Papacy (the way was left open for the Emperor and the Kings of France and Poland to join if they so wished) – were together to furnish 200 galleys, 100 transports, 50,000 foot soldiers and 4,500 cavalry, with the requisite artillery and ammunition. These forces were to foregather every year, in the month of April at the latest, for a summer's campaign wherever they thought fit. Every autumn there would be consultations in Rome to determine the next year's activity. If either Spain or Venice were attacked, the other would go to her assistance, and both undertook to defend papal territory with all their strength. All fighting would be under the banner of the League; important decisions would be taken by a majority vote of the three generals commanding – Sebastiano Venier for Venice, Marcantonio Colonna for the Papacy, and for Spain the Captain-General of the combined fleet, the King's half-brother, Don John of Austria.

Don John was the bastard son of Charles V by a German lady called Barbara Blomberg. Twenty-six years old, outstandingly good-looking and a natural leader of men, he had already distinguished himself the previous year by putting down the Morisco rising in Spain. The Venetians expressed themselves delighted at the appointment – as well they might have been, since the King's first choice, about which he had luckily had second thoughts, had been Gian Andrea Doria. They would have expressed rather less pleasure had they known that Philip, who suspected that the young prince's courage was apt to override his judgement, had told him that he must on no account give battle without Doria's express consent.

Although it was clearly too late to observe the timetable stipulated in the treaty, the allies had agreed that the summer of 1571 should not be wasted, and that the forces for the first year's campaign should muster as soon as possible at Messina. By August all had arrived, and Don John drew up his sailing orders. He himself, with Venier and Colonna, would take the centre, with sixty-four galleys. The right wing, with fifty-four galleys, would be under Doria; the left, with fifty-three, under the Venetian Augustino Barbarigo. In addition there was to be a small vanguard of eight galleys and a rearguard of six, to be respectively commanded by Don Juan de Cardona and the Marquis of Santa Cruz. To each group were allotted six galleasses. The galleons and heavy transports, which – not being oared like the galleys – were considerably less manoeuvrable, were to form a separate convoy.[1]

Emboldened by the fall of Famagusta and by the departure of virtually the entire Venetian fleet for Messina, the Turks had by now entered the Adriatic in strength; landings in Corfu and in Dalmatia had aroused increasing fears in Venice of a sudden invasion which would find the city almost without defence. At the approach of the combined fleet, however, the Turks rapidly withdrew to their bases in Greece; they had no wish to be blockaded within the narrow sea with the enemy all round them. Thus it was from Lepanto (the modern Naupactos on the Gulf of Patras) that they sailed out, on 6 October, to meet the advancing Christians.

The Christians were in a fighting mood. Two days before, at Cephalonia, they had heard of the fall of Famagusta and, in particular, of the death of Marcantonio Bragadin; rage and vengeance were in their hearts. On the same day, however, there occurred an incident which almost proved disastrous. A Spanish officer and a few of his men on Sebastiano Venier's galley insulted some Venetians, and in the ensuing fight several men were killed; Venier, without consultation and on his own initiative, had the culprits hanged at the masthead. When this was reported to Don John, he flew into a rage and ordered the captain's arrest – a command which, had it been obeyed, might well have torn the whole fleet apart. Fortunately wiser counsels – probably those of Colonna – prevailed and John was persuaded to revoke his order; but he never forgave Venier. Henceforth all his communications with the Venetian contingent were addressed to the second-in-command.

The two fleets met at dawn on 7 October, a mile or two east of Cape Scropha, at the entrance to the Gulf of Patras. The galleons had not yet arrived, but Don John was determined to engage the enemy at once. Only slightly revising his order of battle – Barbarigo and Doria receiving ten more galleys each – he drew his ships up into formation and sailed to the attack. The Turks were ready for him, with a fleet that almost precisely matched his own, describing a huge crescent that extended from one shore

1. Brief descriptions of these vessels may not come amiss.

Galley: single deck, 120–180 ft long, 20 ft beam. Normally moved under sail, but always propelled by oars when in battle. Five guns mounted in bow, several smaller ones amidships. A metal beak of 10–20ft was used for ramming.

Galleon: far heavier than galley, two decks, both thickly mounted with guns. No oars. Tall, unwieldy, a floating fortress.

Galleass: half-way between the two. High poop and forecastle (providing cover for oarsmen); 50–70 guns, lateen rigged.

of the Gulf to the other. The admiral, Ali Pasha, commanded the central squadron, with eighty-seven galleys; on his right was Mehmet Saulak, governor of Alexandria, with fifty-four; and on his left, opposite Doria, was Uluch Ali with sixty-one.

It was about half-past ten when the battle opened, at the north end of the battle lines, where Don John's left wing under Barbarigo engaged Ali's right under Saulak. The fighting was fierce, Barbarigo's own flagship being at one moment set upon by five Turkish vessels which simultaneously let loose a hail of arrows, one of them wounding the Venetian admiral mortally in the eye. His nephew, Marco Contarini, took over the command, but within five minutes he too was dead. Yet the engagement ended in total victory for the Christians, who, under the leadership of Federico Nani and Marco Querini, eventually succeeded in driving the entire Turkish right wing into the shore. The Turks abandoned their ships and tried to escape in the surrounding hills, but the Venetians pursued them and cut them down as they ran. Saulak was taken prisoner, but he was already seriously wounded and did not long survive.

Now the focus of the battle shifted to the centre, where at eleven o'clock or thereabouts Don John's galleys, advancing in line abreast at a steady, even stroke, closed on those of Ali Pasha, the two flagships making deliberately straight for each other. They met, and entangled; to each side of them along the line, the other galleys did the same, simultaneously closing in towards the middle until the sea was scarcely visible and men were leaping and scrambling from ship to ship, fighting hand to hand with swords, cutlasses and scimitars. Twice Ali's force of 400 picked janissaries boarded Don John's flagship, the *Real*; three times the Spaniards returned the attack, the last time under heavy covering fire from Colonna, who had just set fire to the galley of Pertau Pasha, Ali's second-in-command. It was on this third occasion that Ali was struck on the forehead by a cannon-ball. Scarcely had he fallen before his head was sliced off by a soldier from Malaga, who stuck it on a pike and waved it aloft to give courage to his comrades. With their admiral killed and their flagship captured, the Turks rapidly lost heart. Many of their ships were destroyed in the *mêlée*; those that managed to extricate themselves turned and fled.

To the south, meanwhile, things were going less well. From the very beginning of the advance, at about ten o'clock that morning, Gian Andrea Doria had been uneasy about his position. The Turkish left wing under Uluch Ali which confronted him was longer and stronger – ninety-three vessels to his own sixty-four – and, extending as it did further southward, threatened to outflank him. It was to avoid this danger that he had altered his course towards the south-east, a decision which left an ever-widening gap between Don John and himself. He should have known better. Uluch Ali saw the gap, and instantly changed his plans, altering his own direction towards the north-west with the object of cutting straight through the Christian line and falling upon it from the rear. This new course led him against the southern end of Don John's squadron, which consisted of a few ships contributed by the Knights of Malta. They fought bravely, but they had no chance against the overwhelming odds and were massacred to a man. Their flagship was taken in tow, and Uluch Ali raised their captured standard on his own.

By now Don Juan de Cardona, whose eight galleys had been held in reserve, was hurrying to the relief of the Knights. As he approached, sixteen Turkish galleys fell on him. There followed the fiercest and bloodiest encounter of the whole day. When it was over, 450 of the 500 fighting men of Cardona's galleys had been killed or wounded, and Cardona himself was on the point of death. Several ships, when boarded later, were found to be manned entirely by corpses. Meanwhile others were hurrying to the rescue: the second reserve force under Santa Cruz and – as soon as he could leave his own area of the battle – Don John himself. Uluch Ali stayed no longer, ordered thirteen of his galleys to quicken their stroke and headed with them north-west at full speed towards Santa Maura (the modern Leucas) and Preveza. The remainder broke away in the other direction and returned to Lepanto.

Despite the confusion and the appalling losses sustained as a result of the cowardice, treachery and sheer bad seamanship of Gian Andrea Doria – and there were plenty of his colleagues after the battle to accuse him of all three – the battle of Lepanto had been an overwhelming victory for the Christians. According to the most reliable estimates, they lost only twelve galleys sunk and one captured; Turkish losses were 113 and 117 respectively. Casualties were heavy on both sides, as was inevitable when much of the fighting was hand-to-hand; but, whereas the Christian losses are unlikely to have exceeded 15,000, the Turks are believed to have lost double that number, excluding the 8,000 who were taken prisoner.[1] In addition there was enormous plunder; Ali Pasha's flagship alone was found to contain

1. Among the Christian wounded was Miguel de Cervantes, aboard the *Marquesa*. He was struck twice in the chest, a third shot permanently maiming his left hand – 'to the greater glory', as he put it, 'of the right.' He was to describe Lepanto as 'the greatest occasion that past or present ages have witnessed or that the future can hope to witness', and to remain prouder of his part in it than of anything else in his life.

150,000 sequins. Finally comes the most gratifying figure of all: that of the 15,000 Christian galley slaves set at liberty. For all this the lion's share of the credit must go to Don John himself, whose handling of his unwieldy and heterogeneous fleet was masterly and whose brilliant use of his fire-power was to have a lasting effect on the development of naval warfare. In future, sea battles would be decided by guns rather than by swordsman-ship. This in turn would mean bigger, heavier ships, which could only be propelled by sail. Lepanto was the last great naval engagement to be fought with oared galleys, ramming each other head-on. The age of the broadside had begun.

It was 18 October before one Giuffredo Giustinian, aboard the galley *Angelo*, reached Venice with the news. The city was still mourning the loss of Cyprus, raging against the bestial treatment of Marcantonio Bragadin, and fearful as to what further reverses the future might have in store. Within an hour of the *Angelo*'s appearance, trailing the Turkish banners in the water behind her stern, her deck piled high with trophies, the whole mood had changed. Venice had had her revenge; nor had she had long to wait for it. Suddenly the *campi*, the *calli* and the canals were filled with sounds of jubilation, as everyone hurried to the Piazza to hear the details, find their friends and celebrate. Total strangers were falling on each other's necks, laughing and kissing each other; the gates of the debtors' prison were opened in an act of spontaneous amnesty, while the Turkish mer-chants, with a contrary motion, barricaded themselves for safety inside the Fondaco dei Turchi until the excitement was over. In St Mark's, specially illuminated for the occasion, a *Te Deum* was followed by a High Mass of thanksgiving; around the Rialto the cloth merchants decked the shops and houses with sky-blue draperies spangled with golden stars, while over the bridge itself there was erected a great triumphal arch bearing the arms of Venice and her gallant allies. That night there was scarcely a building in the city that was not illuminated by candles and torches inside and out, while bands played, the people danced and – in order that no one need fear to join the general rejoicing – the wearing of masks was permitted by a special dispensation. In more permanent commemoration of the event, Gam-bello's great entrance portal to the Arsenal was enlarged and adorned by the addition of the winged lion (with appropriate inscription) and the two winged victories. A year or two later the pediment was to be surmounted with a statue of St Justina, on whose day the great battle had been fought and won; and from 1572 to the fall of the Republic that day was annually celebrated with a procession by the Doge and Signoria to the church of that same fortunate patron, outside which the captured Turkish standards were displayed to the populace.[1] At SS. Giovanni e Paolo a votive chapel was dedicated to the Madonna of the Rosary, its ceiling painted by Veronese. Finally, in the Doges' Palace, the great victory was twice represented – on a heroic, if ultimately uninspired, canvas by Andrea Vicentino in the Hall of the Scrutinio and, in that of the Collegio, by Veronese's radiant painting of Sebastiano Venier and Augustino Barbarigo giving thanks, while St Mark and St Justina look on.

And so Lepanto is remembered as one of the decisive battles of the world, and the greatest naval engagement between Actium and Trafalgar. In England and America, admittedly, its continued fame rests largely on G. K. Chesterton's thunderous poem; but in the Catholic countries of the Mediterranean it has broken the barriers of history and passed, like Roncesvalles, into legend. Does it, however, altogether deserve its reputation? Technically and tactically, yes; after 1571 sea battles were never the same again. Strategically, no. Lepanto did not, as its victors hoped, mark the end of the pendulum's swing, the point when Christian fortunes suddenly turned, gathering momentum until the Turks were swept back into the Asian heartland whence they had come. Venice did not regain Cyprus; only two years later, as we shall see, she was to conclude a separate peace with the Sultan relinquishing all her claims to the island. Nor did Lepanto mean the end of her losses; in the following century, Crete was to go the same way. As for Spain, she did not appreciably increase her control of the central Mediterranean; and only seventeen years afterwards the defeat of the Armada was to deal her sea power a blow from which it would not quickly recover. Nor was she able to break the links between Constantinople and the Moorish princes of North Africa; within three years, the Turks were to drive the Spaniards from Tunis, make vassals of the local rulers, and reduce the area – as they had already reduced most of Algeria to the west and Tripolitania to the east – to the status of an Ottoman province.

But for all the Christians – and particularly the people of Venice – who rejoiced in those exultant October days, the real importance of Lepanto was neither strategic nor tactical; it was moral. The heavy black cloud which had overshadowed them for two centuries and which since 1453 had grown steadily more threatening, to the point where they felt that their days were numbered – that cloud had suddenly lifted. From one moment to the next,

---

1. Goethe chanced to see the procession arrive at the church in 1786, and described it in his *Italian Journey*. He did not, however, attend the mass which followed.

hope had been reborn. It was, perhaps, the Venetian historian Paolo Paruta who best summed up the popular feeling in the course of his funeral oration in St Mark's on those who had been killed in the battle:

They have taught us by their example that the Turks are not insuperable, as we had previously believed them to be . . . Thus it can be said that as the beginning of this war was for us a time of sunset, leaving us in perpetual night, now the courage of these men, like a true, life-giving sun, has bestowed upon us the most beautiful and most joyful day that this city, in all her history, has ever seen.

38

The Twilight of the Century

[1571-1595]

To have been leagued with allies has wrought the greatest injury to the
Republic, from which experience we may draw certain useful conclusions. In war,
promptness and a ready capture of occasions is all-important, and for naval war
it is essential to put to sea at the beginning of April ... It is injurious to act in
concert with princes so powerful that we are obliged to consider their wishes ...
we should rely on our own forces rather than on those of our allies, since allies
consult their own interests instead of those of the League as a whole. Nor should
the commander-in-chief be a prince, but a man amenable to reward and
punishment ... Finally, he who has not good prospect of totally or in large
measure destroying the enemy will be better advised to seek peace with him; but
if war is inevitable, let him carry the war into the enemy camp rather than remain
on the defensive.

Giacomo Foscarini, Captain-General,
to the Senate, autumn 1572

'Promptness and a ready capture of occasions': for Venice in the aftermath
of Lepanto, that could mean but one thing. Their glorious victory must be
followed up at once. The Turk must be given no rest, no time to catch his
breath; he must be pursued and brought to battle again before he had had
a chance to repair his shattered forces and while the allies still had their
forward impetus. This was the message that the Venetians now propoun-
ded to their Spanish and papal allies; but their arguments fell on deaf ears.
Don John himself, one suspects, secretly agreed and would have been only
too happy to press forward through the winter; but he had orders from
Philip which could not be disobeyed. By the terms of the League, the allied
forces would meet again in spring; till then, he must bid them farewell. He
and his fleet returned to Messina, where they arrived on 1 November.

By the spring of 1572 it was plain to the Venetians that their instincts had
been right. Spain was, as usual, prevaricating and procrastinating, raising
one objection after another. The Pope did his utmost to spur them to
action, but he was already a sick man and on 1 May he died. With his death
the spirit went out of the League. At last, despairing of Spanish help,
Venice decided to launch an expedition of her own, which Marcantonio
Colonna willingly joined with his squadron of papal galleys. Only then

were the Spaniards goaded into action. They had no wish to be left out if there was indeed another victory to be won. Philip's objections fell away and in June Don John was finally given permission to join his allies.

The fleet met at Corfu and sailed south in search of the enemy. They had learnt with some dismay that in the eight months since Lepanto Selim had managed to build a new fleet of 150 galleys and eight galleasses – these latter being an innovation for the Turks, who had obviously been impressed by the brilliant use Don John had made of them at Lepanto. Rumour had it, however, that the shipwrights, aware of the fate that awaited them if they failed to meet the Sultan's deadlines, had been obliged to use green timber; that the guns had been so hurriedly cast that many of them were useless; and that the crews, press-ganged into service after the appalling losses of Lepanto, were scarcely trained. It was unlikely, in short, that they would give the allies much trouble. The principal problem would be to bring them to battle.

And so indeed it was. The fleets met off Modone – for 250 years one of Venice's principal trading posts in the Peloponnese, until it had fallen to the Sultan in 1500 – and immediately the Turks ran for harbour. The allies followed them, took up their positions just outside, at Navarino (the modern Pylos), and settled down to wait. Modone, they knew, could not maintain a fleet of such a size for long. The mountainous hinterland was barren and without roads; all supplies must come in by sea. It was only a question of time before the enemy would be forced to emerge, and a second Lepanto would follow.

But once again Venice saw her hopes dashed; and once again the Spaniards were the cause. On 6 October Don John suddenly announced that he could no longer remain in Greek waters and was returning to the West. Foscarini, dumbfounded, asked why and, when the Prince unconvincingly replied that his provisions were running low, at once offered to supply him from his own stock and to order more from Venice as necessary. But Don John, clearly acting on new orders from Spain, could not be shaken. Colonna took his side. Foscarini had to admit to himself that his fleet was not big enough to challenge the Turks alone; fuming at the thought of the opportunity lost, he had no choice but to give the order to return.

All that winter the Venetian Ambassador in Madrid worked on King Philip. The Turks, he argued, were bent on world domination; they had been constantly extending their dominions for some 500 years and were continuing to do so; the longer they were allowed to advance, the stronger and more irresistible they would become; it was the King's duty to Christendom – and to himself, if he wished to keep his throne – to take up arms against them and not to lay them down until the work that had been so gloriously begun at Lepanto were thoroughly finished. But Philip refused to listen. He hated and mistrusted Venice; he had done his duty as far as the Turks were concerned the previous year, and with considerable success; after such a *débâcle* it would be some time before they raised their heads again. Meanwhile he was fully occupied with William the Silent's revolt in the Low Countries. He did not go whining to Venice to help him with his problems; he saw no reason why he should assist her any further with hers.

But in those same winter months, Charles IX of France was also busy, intriguing against Philip on three separate fronts. In the Low Countries, he was giving all possible support to the rebellion; in the Mediterranean, he was manoeuvring to gain control of Algiers, where his machinations may well have been responsible for Philip's recall of Don John from Navarino; in Venice and Constantinople, his ambassadors were working hard to bring about a peace between the Sultan and the Republic. By the spring they had succeeded. Venice had not wished for peace. Particularly since Lepanto, she had done everything in her power to hold the League together and persuade her fellow-members to join her in an out-and-out offensive, stopping, with God's help, only at Constantinople itself. But she had failed. Philip was frankly not interested, the new Pope Gregory XIII scarcely more so. Deserted by her allies, knowing full well that to continue the war alone would be to invite new Turkish invasions of the Adriatic and, in all probability, the seizure of Crete and her last stronghold in the Levant, she had no choice but to accept the terms which were offered her. On 3 March 1573 the treaty was signed. Venice undertook, *inter alia*, to pay the Sultan 300,000 ducats over three years, and to renounce all her claims to Cyprus.

In the dominions of the Most Catholic King, there were cries of horror and disgust. In Messina, a furious Don John tore the League banner from his masthead and ran up that of Spain. How right Philip had been, said his subjects, not to trust those Venetians; they were bound to betray him sooner or later. It was as if the battle of Lepanto had never been won.

It was indeed. In spite of all the jubilation, the cheering and the shouting, and the building up of the great Lepanto legend that still persists today, the truth is that one of the most celebrated naval battles ever fought proved to be of no long-term strategic importance whatever. But those who lamented the loudest had only themselves to blame.

The dogeship of Alvise Mocenigo had begun with another double disaster:

the failure of the 1570 expedition and the loss of Cyprus. It had continued with the triumph of Lepanto, which had instantaneously lifted Venetian spirits from their nadir to a pitch of exaltation perhaps unparalleled in the Republic's history. The old Doge was to preside over another burst of popular rejoicing, and another catastrophe even greater than its predecessor, before his brief but eventful reign came to an end.

The first of these occasions was the visit, in July 1574, of the twenty-three-year-old King Henry III of France. The circumstances were, to say the least, unusual. It was only in February of that same year that – thanks to the machinations of his mother, Catherine de' Medici – Henry had been crowned King of Poland. In May, however, the unexpected death of his elder brother, Charles IX, had brought him an urgent summons to Paris, where the crown of France awaited him. Fearing the displeasure of his Polish subjects – to whose service he had dedicated his life only three months before – he had fled his unwanted kingdom in disguise and under cover of darkness (taking with him, in case of need, diamonds from the Polish crown which were valued at 300,000 *écus*) and had not stopped until he reached imperial territory. Thence, after a short stay with the Emperor Maximilian in Vienna, he had come on to Venice.

Since her separate peace with the Sultan and consequent estrangement from Spain and the Empire, Venice's relations with France had become of prime importance; and the Venetians, never reluctant to put on a show, had decided to give Henry a reception that he would long remember. At Marghera on the mainland the King was greeted by sixty senators in crimson velvet; thence he was conducted in a fleet of gilded gondolas to Murano, where a guard of honour of sixty halberdiers awaited him, in specially designed uniforms featuring the national colours of France, together with forty young scions of the leading Venetian families, who were to form his personal suite for the duration of his visit. His state entry to the city was planned for the next day; that same evening, however, he managed to slip out in a black cloak, unobserved, for a silent, secret journey through the canals.

The following morning, Doge Mocenigo arrived in state at Murano and the two rulers were rowed together to the Lido, where they passed under a triumphal arch (designed for the occasion by Palladio and painted by Veronese and Tintoretto) and entered the church of S. Nicolò for a solemn *Te Deum*.[1] The service over, they stepped again into the state barge and proceeded across the Bacino and up the Grand Canal to the Palazzo Foscari,

---

1. There is a painting of the scene by Vicentino in the *Sala delle Quattro Porte* in the Doges' Palace.

which, with the adjoining Palazzo Giustinian, had been hung with cloth of gold, crimson velvet and pale blue silk embroidered with fleurs-de-lis in the young King's honour.

During the next week, for every moment of the day and most of the night, Henry was kept enthralled. All sumptuary laws were suspended; the Venetian nobility were encouraged to wear their most magnificent clothes, to deck themselves with their most precious jewels. There were banquets and parades, performances by actors, dancers and acrobats. He was made an honorary member of the Senate and attended one of its sessions. The glass-blowers of Murano came and gave exhibitions of their craft under his window. He called on Titian – then aged ninety-seven – and posed for Tintoretto. He even found time, in one of his few spare moments, to enjoy the favours of Venice's most sought-after courtesan, Veronica Franco – selected, we are told, after diligent perusal of an album of miniatures shown to him by the Signoria for the purpose. But the Venetians were determined, too, to prove to him that they lived for other things besides beauty and pleasure. Early one morning they took him along to the Arsenal, to show him the keel of a ship being laid. That same evening at sunset, they took him back: there was the same ship being launched down the slipway ready for action – fully rigged, fully armed and fully provisioned.

It was only towards the end of the visit that Doge Mocenigo, calling on the King ostensibly to make him a present of some rare book, began to speak of political matters. Lepanto, he said, had indeed been a glorious victory; but it had resulted in a still further increase in the already overbearing power of Spain; and this must be, to all right-thinking nations of Europe, a matter for regret. He sincerely trusted that France, now deservedly restored to her former greatness, would do her utmost to restrain King Philip's ambitions. As to the religious question in France – the massacre of St Bartholomew had taken place only two years before – this was naturally no concern of Venice; he hoped, however, that His Majesty would permit him to express the wish that France would return, under her new sovereign, to the ways of clemency and a reasonable degree of tolerance. Such a policy had served his own Republic well; only thus, he ventured to suggest, could peace and stability be assured.

Henry was non-committal; as the former head of the Catholic party in France, he could hardly be anything else. Shortly afterwards, after a farewell banquet of surpassing opulence, he left the city, the Doge personally accompanying him as far as Fusina. But he never forgot Venice, the welcome he had received there, the uniquely Venetian combination of beauty and efficiency, of elegance and wisdom. As he bade his new friends farewell, giving them rich presents in gratitude for their hospitality – a huge diamond for the Doge, a heavy gold chain for his host Luigi Foscari – they and their fellow-citizens knew, beyond all doubt, that their money had been well spent.

And yet, if King Henry could have revisited Venice towards the end of the following year, or in 1576 or 1577, he would have seen a very different city – a city in which the cheering and the shouting had died, giving place to a strange and sinister silence. The crowds were gone from the Piazza; around the Rialto and the Merceria the shops were closed and shuttered. The plague had struck.

It was a visitation as dramatic and as terrifying as the Black Death over two centuries before, spreading to every corner of the city and every class of society. The two distinguished doctors from Padua called in by the official *Provveditori di Sanità* proved useless. Before long the old Lazzaretto was filled to overflowing with the sick, the new one with suspects; some superannuated galleons were towed out to the middle of the lagoon and hastily converted into supplementary isolation hospitals, provisioned with food, medicines, fresh water, doctors and priests. As the population succumbed or fled, Venice began to take on the air of a deserted city. The inns and hostelries shut their doors; the law courts, too, ceased to function, while judges, lawyers and litigants alike sought refuge on the mainland. In the prisons, few were left alive. Only the Doge, his Signoria and the Senate continued to perform their duties, though the number of active senators was declining at an alarming rate. In the autumn of 1576, in a desperate attempt to prevent any further dissemination of the pestilence, all the surviving inhabitants of the city were confined to their houses for a full week; but the measure had no effect. At last, with the onset of winter, the incidence of disease began to show faint signs of slackening; but it was only the following summer, on Sunday, 21 July 1577, that the government dared to proclaim officially that the epidemic was over.

It had accounted for some 51,000 Venetian lives, including that of Titian. The population of the city, which was assessed at 168,000 in 1563 and by 1575 had probably risen to some 175,000, in 1581 stood at a mere 124,000. There was scarcely a Venetian who had not lost one or more of his close relations; many families, indeed, had been wiped out altogether. Even now it was feared that a formal proclamation was tempting fate and that any moment might bring news of a further outbreak. But Venice was not slow to give thanks for her deliverance: already, on the island of the Giudecca, a great new church was beginning to rise, commissioned by the state from its greatest living architect, Andrea Palladio – the church of the Redeemer, the Redentore. There, every year until the end of the Republic, on that same third Sunday in July, Doge and Signoria would attend High Mass; even now, the occasion is still annually celebrated.[1]

Alvise Mocenigo himself never lived to see the church's completion. He died – of natural causes – on 4 June 1577, and was buried in SS. Giovanni e Paolo, where his tomb can be seen in the middle of the west wall between those of two earlier Mocenigo Doges, Pietro and Giovanni. A week after his death, his successor was elected – the eighty-one-year-old hero of Lepanto and most distinguished living Venetian, Sebastiano Venier. Testy, unbending and acutely conscious of his distinguished record – one of his first acts as Doge was to decree that all nobles who had fought at Lepanto should wear red robes for a week – Venier was to reign for only a year; but that year was to bring another catastrophe, more tragic in its long-term effects than even the plague itself. Already in 1574, soon after the departure of Henry III, there had been a serious fire in the Doges' Palace, destroying the rooms of the Collegio and the Senate and some of the Private Apartments. Now, on 20 December, there followed a second conflagration, far worse than before. The *Sala del Maggior Consiglio* and the *Sala dello Scrutinio* were both completely gutted. Works by Guariento and Bellini, and other contemporary masters such as Titian, Tintoretto and Veronese all perished in the flames; and although the last two were able to supply new works for the rebuilt rooms, the loss was permanent and irremediable. So great was the damage, indeed, that several of the foremost architects of the time, among them Palladio himself, strongly urged that the whole building should be demolished and replaced by a new palace of more classical design; we can only be thankful that saner counsels prevailed and that, in the space of only eight months, the greatest secular Gothic building in the world was carefully reconstructed, its old elevations lovingly restored.[2]

When Doge Venier, who throughout the blaze had refused to leave the Palace, died less than three months later,[3] the Great Council – meeting,

1. Until the middle 1970s the celebrations included a bridge of boats, thrown across the Giudecca Canal from the Redentore to the Zattere opposite; alas, this splendid tradition has now been discontinued in deference to the requirements of the *zona industriale*.

2. As can be seen on the waterfront façade, however, the new *Sala del Maggior Consiglio* was given windows on a somewhat higher level, without the lovely fourteenth-century tracery still existing on the two older windows – which escaped the flames – to the right.

3. He was buried, rather surprisingly, in the church of S. Maria degli Angeli in Murano. Only in 1907 was his body brought back to Venice and deposited in the north transept of SS. Giovanni e Paolo, near the tomb of his forebear, Doge Antonio Venier.

according to the curious Venetian practice, to elect the electors – was forced to hold its session in the Arsenal. Only when the forty-one had been appointed could they repair to one of the undamaged rooms in the Doges' Palace for their conclave. Their choice fell, on 18 March 1578, on a certain Nicolò da Ponte, who, at eighty-seven, was considerably older even than his predecessor. He could look back on a blameless career in the service of the Republic, having represented it not only at the Council of Trent but also in Rome, where he had had the unenviable task of justifying to the Pope Venice's separate peace treaty with the Sultan. Fortunately, the seven years of his dogeship presented no diplomatic problems of similar magnitude, and only one which – by reason of its curious human interest rather than for any real historical importance – is worth recording here. It concerns one of Venice's few romantic heroines whose name is still remembered: Bianca Cappello.

Bianca was the outstandingly beautiful daughter of an old Venetian family who, in 1563 at the age of fifteen, had eloped with a penniless Florentine bank-clerk, Pietro Bonaventuri, her neighbour in the parish of S. Aponal. Her father, outraged, had preferred charges, the Council of Ten had ordered an official inquiry and the *Avogadori di Comun* had declared the young couple *banditi*, with a price on their heads. Safe in Florence, however, Bianca had quickly begun to regret her impulsiveness. Pietro's parents, with whom the two were forced to live, could not afford servants and she had no taste for the domestic chores – including the nursing of her mother-in-law, a chronic invalid – which now dominated her life. It was therefore not altogether surprising that, having fortuitously caught the eye of Francesco, the reprobate son of Grand Duke Cosimo de' Medici, she should have yielded to his blandishments and embarked on an affair which promised to be incomparably more enjoyable – and rewarding – than life with the Bonaventuri.

Since her lover was already married – to the morosely pious Archduchess Joanna of Austria – Bianca soon became the centre of a scandal even greater than that which she had caused in Venice. Meanwhile, ignoring his father's fury, Francesco appointed her husband a member of his household and even unsuccessfully tried, through the good offices of the Florentine Resident in Venice and the Papal Nuncio, to arrange an amnesty for her and a reconciliation with her parents. Then, in 1574, Cosimo died; and so, at about the same time but in rather less exalted circumstances – being killed in a street brawl, probably with Francesco's knowledge but not on his direct orders – did Pietro Bonaventuri. Francesco was now Grand Duke of Tuscany. He immediately installed Bianca in a palace next to his own and for the next four years paraded her about Florence as his *maîtresse en titre*, to the deep humiliation of the melancholy Joanna, who sought refuge in ever longer and more frequent devotions.

Yet the Grand Duchess cannot have been completely ignored; in the spring of 1578 she died in childbirth. Less than two months later, on 5 June, Francesco and Bianca were married – although, owing partly to the need to observe the customary period of mourning, another year was allowed to pass before the marriage was publicly proclaimed. Thus it was not until June 1579 that the Grand Duke sent a special ambassador to Doge da Ponte informing him of the event and adding a special request: that Venice should signify her pleasure and gratification at the match by declaring his wife a Daughter of the Republic. This request was repeated in a second letter from Bianca herself, expressing her joy in the closer ties between Venice and Tuscany that the marriage would undoubtedly bring, and her determination to do full justice to those two roles in which she took an equal pride: the loving consort of the Grand Duke and the loyal daughter of the *Serenissima*.

To promote, at a single stroke, a declared outlaw to the highest title the Republic could confer on any woman might have been thought a lot to ask. Almost without hesitation, however, the Senate gave its approval, simultaneously appointing Bianca's father and brother to the rank of *Cavaliere* and to membership of the distinguished delegation, led by the Patriarch of Aquileia, which was to represent the Republic at the long-deferred public celebrations of the marriage in Florence the following October. In return, the young Grand Duchess was as good as her word, for the next eight years never forgetting her Venetian origins and letting no opportunity slip for furthering the interests of her native city.

But she and her husband had enemies in Florence, none of them more dangerous than her brother-in-law Ferdinando de' Medici, a Cardinal since the age of fourteen, who, in default of any male children of Francesco, found himself heir to the throne. Bianca's continued inability to present her husband with a son was a source of perpetual anxiety to her. Once already, in 1576, she had contrived a mock pregnancy and birth, claiming as her own a baby who had been secretly introduced into her apartments, but her husband had discovered the deception; now, ten years later, she tried the same trick but with no greater success. It was her last attempt: before the end of the following year both she and her husband were dead.

The fact that Francesco and Bianca died suddenly in their prime within two days of each other, and that, despite the mutual mistrust between the brothers, Cardinal Ferdinando was actually paying them a visit at the time, inevitably led to the usual speculations and suspicions. There were dark whispers of a poisoned tart, which some believed to have been prepared by Ferdinando but others maintained had been a concoction of Bianca herself for her brother-in-law. According to this latter theory, the suspicious Cardinal had deliberately tried it out on Francesco, whereat the horror-stricken Bianca, seeing her husband in his death agony, had seized a slice of her own and swallowed it in a gesture of suicidal despair. One would dearly like to believe in so Shakespearean a *dénouement*; it must, however, be admitted that at the post-mortem which Ferdinando immediately ordered to be performed, in the presence of members of Bianca's family as well as all the court doctors, no trace of poison was discovered. The cause of both deaths is now believed almost certainly to have been malaria.

Although the new Grand Duke was quick to inform the Venetians of the 'most tragic double loss' that he had sustained, he refused to allow his sister-in-law to be buried with her husband. Instead, her body was wrapped in a shroud and flung into the common ditch. He also decreed that her family crest should be obliterated wherever it appeared and replaced by that of Francesco's first wife Joanna. All mourning was forbidden – as, in deference to Ferdinando's feelings, it also was in Venice.

In Florence such a petty-minded act of vengeance, however much it might be deplored, would at least be understood; in her own city it was unforgivable. Bianca had deserved better than that. But her fellow-Venetians never forgot her; and it is pleasant to record that the house where she was born and spent her childhood, next to the Ponte Storto in the parish of S. Aponal – one of the prettiest corners of Venice – still bears a plaque to her memory.

When Bianca Cappello died in October 1587, Doge Nicolò da Ponte had already been two years in his grave. We should not leave him to his rest, however, without mentioning another incident in his reign which, though relatively minor in itself, was symptomatic of a significant and sinister feature of Venetian political life at this period: the increasing power – and increasing unpopularity – of the Council of Ten.

The Council of Ten, as the reader may remember, had originally been established as a temporary Committee of Public Safety to deal with the aftermath of the unsuccessful conspiracy of Bajamonte Tiepolo in July 1310.[1] Its intended life-span had been two and a half months; at the time of which we are speaking it had been in existence for as many centuries,

1. See pp. 197–9.

during which time it had become an important component of the Venetian governmental machine. Important, and yet somehow not quite integral: from the beginning, it had refused to fit tidily into the pattern of the constitution. This pattern took the usual form of a pyramid – the Doge at its apex, then the Signoria, then downward through the Collegio and the Senate to the Great Council. The Ten, however, had always remained apart – an illogical, anomalous body with extraordinary powers which, in an emergency, it could use to cut red tape, to by-pass the slow-moving deliberations of the Senate, to take its own decisions and put them immediately into effect. Normal business, political or military, financial or diplomatic, passed through normal channels and was subject to normal reservations and delays; urgent matters, or those demanding extreme secrecy or delicacy of handling, could be passed by the Collegio direct to the Ten, which was authorized to act on its own initiative, to make payments out of clandestine funds, and even to give covert instructions to Venetian diplomats proceeding abroad. Its field of competence covered 'all things concerning the security of the state and the preservation of morals' – limits so nebulous as to be practically without meaning.

In such circumstances, it might at first sight be thought surprising that, for most of the time at least, the Ten wielded its immense power so wisely and so well – particularly since it seldom needed to account for its actions to any higher authority. In practice, however, abuses were largely avoided by its own built-in checks and balances. Election was for a single year, with no eligibility for re-election till another year had passed. Two members of the same family could never sit at the same time. Leadership of the Council was never vested in one person, but in a triumvirate – the *Capi* – which changed every month and whose members, during their period of office, were forbidden all social intercourse with the outside world, lest they be exposed to rumours or bribes. Venality or corruption was punishable by death. Finally – a vital point which is all too often forgotten – the Council, as well as its ten elected members, also included the Doge and Signoria, bringing its effective strength to seventeen.

But, as time went on, it gradually became clear that even seventeen was not always enough. We have already seen[1] how, when really important decisions had to be taken, the Ten would ask the Great Council to elect a *zonta* – a supplementary body of Senators who would join it for the specific issue under discussion. These *zonte* strengthened its hand considerably, diminishing the likelihood of opposition in other councils; but as the Ten

1. See p. 335.

grew stronger, arrogating more and more state business to itself, so the other, constitutionally more orthodox bodies tended to dwindle in importance – and, inevitably, to resent it. The first signs of this resentment had appeared as early as 1457, when the Ten was accused, rightly, of having overstepped its authority in ordering the deposition of Doge Francesco Foscari. Eleven years later, its authority was explicitly limited to 'most delicate matters' only – *cose segretissime*. This definition, however, still left plenty of scope for argument, and its activities were not appreciably curtailed.

Rather, indeed, the reverse. Venice's troubled history during the last years of the fifteenth century and the first quarter of the sixteenth had led to more and more frequent requests for *zonte*, until in 1529 what had started as an occasional and exceptional measure became an established institution, and a permanent *zonta* was proclaimed, to consist of fifteen of the leading functionaries of state. Eight years later there followed a new and still more unconstitutional departure: the enlarged Ten began to appoint subcommittees, directly responsible to itself only. The first of them had been a body known as the *Esecutori contra la Bestemmia*, which concerned itself specifically with the suppression of vice – in which it was no more successful than any other organization of its kind has ever been; but this had been followed in 1539 by the introduction of three *Inquisitori di Stato*, a development which, in the minds of many thoughtful Venetians, awoke serious misgivings. Its declared aim – to tighten state security – was understandable enough. The Kings of France and Spain both maintained a veritable army of agents throughout the Republic, to whom the sale of secrets had become a regular and profitable occupation; Venice relied on diplomacy for her very survival; plainly, therefore, so dangerous a traffic must be stopped. But when it was learnt that the Three, though technically responsible to the Ten, had been specifically invested with the same authority that the Ten itself possessed and, in particular, had the right to try and condemn without prior reference to their parent body, men began to ask whether the cure might not be worse than the disease.

It was a pertinent enough question, but it remained unanswered and the Council of Ten continued effectively to govern Venice, apparently heedless of its by now almost universal unpopularity. Then, in 1582, two incidents occurred which, if they did not break its power, certainly shook its confidence. The first concerned a certain Andrea da Lazza, a Procurator of St Mark, whom the Ten particularly wished to be included in the fifteen-man *zonta*, but whom the Great Council obstinately refused to elect. Furious at this reverse, the Ten countered by increasing by one the number of

Procurators who sat with it by right and co-opting da Lazza *ex officio*, but this step too was vetoed by the Great Council. The second incident concerned a brawl on the Lido, when a party of young nobles insulted a local girl and were promptly set on by the local *bravi*. The *bravi*, emerging victorious from the fray, promptly lodged a complaint with the Ten, who listened sympathetically; so sympathetically indeed that when on the following day the young nobles, after a day in which to recover, lodged a complaint in their turn, they were given short shrift. They thereupon appealed to the *Quarantia*, who upheld their cause, reversing the Ten's decision.

At the next elections to the *zonta*, the Great Council showed its disapproval of the attitude of the Ten by refusing to approve more than twelve candidates in place of the usual fifteen, and in December it made a determined effort to define, once and for all, the precise nature of the *cose segretissime* referred to in the law of 1468. It was no use: the more the matter was argued, the more impossible it became to resolve. On 1 January 1583 the three unapproved members came up again for election, but with no greater success, and the whole principle of the *zonta* was abandoned by tacit consent. This had the effect of diminishing the powers of the Ten to some degree, but it could not obviously resolve the fundamental problem: the Ten was an anomalous body, it had always been so, and therein lay its strength. No amount of trimming would ever allow it to fit comfortably into a constitution which had no room for it. Reduced to its normal size, it drew in its horns and, for the time being, confined its activities to those limits within which its authority was beyond question. It continued to be feared; but much of the respect it had formerly enjoyed had been lost, and was never entirely to be regained.

It is doubtful whether old Nicolò da Ponte, now well over ninety, was able to exert much influence during this trial of strength between the *Maggior Consiglio* and the Council of Ten. He was failing fast. Owing to his embarrassing tendency to doze off during discussions in the Collegio, it had already proved necessary to build a sort of shelf across the front of his throne to prevent him from sliding to the ground. On 15 April 1585 he suffered a stroke which robbed him of his speech. He continued as best he could, but soon afterwards he fell asleep again during a state reception in the Hall of the Senate; this time his ducal cap – the *corno* – is said to have fallen off and rolled across the floor, stopping at the feet of one of the Procurators, Pasquale Cicogna; and it may well have been in deference to so blatant a manifestation of the divine will that, when da Ponte mercifully breathed his last on 30 July, Cicogna was elected as his successor.[1] It was not the first time, either, that the new Doge had been miraculously singled out: some years before, in Corfu while he was attending Mass, a sudden puff of wind had blown the sacrament out of the hands of the officiating priest and straight into his own. Thus Pasquale Cicogna already had about him, if not actually an odour of sanctity, at least an aura of being one of God's elect.

His elevation to the supreme power had not, however, taken place without a struggle. It was only on the nineteenth day of the deliberations, and after the fifty-third ballot, that he acquired the necessary majority, and even then his success was due only to the sudden decision of his rival, Vincenzo Morosini, to stand down. When the result was proclaimed, the populace, who had already staged noisy demonstrations in support of Morosini outside the Doges' Palace, were furious. Their favourite was immensely rich and renowned for his generosity; both qualities, they knew, would have been fully demonstrated during his inaugural procession round the Piazza, when the Doge traditionally scattered coins to his scrambling subjects. Cicogna, on the other hand, was notoriously mean: a fact which he proved by scattering not the usual golden ducats but small silver coins of five *soldi* – and, we are told, not very many of those. (For years afterwards, they were contemptuously referred to as *cicognini*.)

In spite of this somewhat shaky start, however, Pasquale Cicogna had a quiet and peaceful reign, during which he gradually built up a considerable measure of popularity. The unspeakable Uskoks, admittedly, continued to give trouble as they always did, but such other major problems as he encountered were all diplomatic and were tackled with quite remarkable success. The most important were those arising from the assassination, on 1 August 1589 by a fanatical Dominican friar, of King Henry III of France. Henry, who had long since forsaken his wife's bed for the company of his somewhat spicier *mignons*, had not surprisingly failed to produce any offspring; and with him the Valois line became extinct. The legitimate heir to the throne was the Protestant Henry of Bourbon, King of Navarre, but, although Henry had proclaimed himself ready to adopt the Roman faith, he was nevertheless violently opposed by the French Catholic party, the hugely powerful house of Guise, Philip of Spain and Pope Sixtus V.

Venice, on the other hand, welcomed his succession. Always tolerant in

---

1. Da Ponte was buried in the church of the Carità but his tomb was destroyed when the church was suppressed and converted into the Accademia in 1807. Only the bust was saved, and is now in the museum of the Venice Seminary.

matters of religion, she was also fully aware that, among the leading powers of Europe, France was her only buttress against the ambitions of Spain. All she wanted was that the country should be strong, united and well-disposed to herself. The moment that the report of the assassination reached the city, instructions were sent to the Venetian ambassador in France, Giovanni Mocenigo, to seek an immediate audience with the new King, to offer him her congratulations, and to assure him of her continued friendship and goodwill. She was rewarded by a fulsome reply – brought to Venice by a special ambassador, François de Luxembourg – thanking her for these friendly sentiments, which, Henry cheerfully admitted, he appreciated all the more for the fact that Venice was the only state in Italy to have granted him recognition.

Such an initiative could not fail to arouse the wrath of the Pope, who was not slow to react. If, he thundered, Venice wished to preserve her good name as a loyal daughter of the Church, she would do well to abstain from dealings with heretics. Did she consider herself the greatest nation in the world, that she should be so eager to set an example to all others? The Republic's answer was respectful, but firm: Henry of Navarre was the legitimate successor to the throne of France. He was a prudent and virtuous prince – besides being, incidentally, an extremely strong one – who showed every sign of willingness to adopt the True Faith; he had already decreed that the Catholic Church in France, and all its members, should remain free, respected and undisturbed. Moreover, no one else was capable of holding the country together after the agonies it had suffered. At this point the argument took on a new edge: must France continue to suffer subversion and ruination at the hands of foreign intriguers? Did the Pope genuinely believe that the foreign armies whom she had been obliged to admit on her soil were prompted by a selfless devotion to the Faith, rather than personal ambition and a lust for power?

It was a strong case, persistently and convincingly argued by the Venetian ambassador in Rome, Alberto Badoer; and it had its effect. The Pope expressed his agreement that de Luxembourg should remain in Venice – provided that he did not appear at state ceremonies – and, more important, agreed to receive a representative from Henry at the Vatican to begin discussions on the King's conversion.

Now it was Philip's turn to fume, to remonstrate, even to threaten; but his Spanish troops and the forces of French Catholicism were slowly retreating before Henry's armies. On 25 July 1593 the triumphant King embraced the Catholic faith, remarking as he did so that Paris was well worth a Mass; in March 1594 he entered his capital, and eighteen months later Pope Clement VIII gave him absolution and formally welcomed him into the Christian fold.

Venice, clearly, could take no credit for Henry's military success in winning his rightful crown. In the diplomatic field, however, by her open and courageous example as well as by her advocacy with five successive Popes,[1] she did much to enable him to consolidate his hold on it, breaking down the Catholic opposition and gradually winning for him the political and religious respectability that he needed. This consolidation, and Henry's recognition by the Pope, finally broke the spirit of Philip II. He continued his struggle a little longer with ever-diminishing success, but in May 1598 he was forced to come to terms. In September he was dead.

So, indeed, was Pasquale Cicogna. He had succumbed to a short but virulent fever in April 1595. He was buried in the church of S. Maria Assunta;[2] but his best memorial is to be found in one of the most familiar of all Venetian monuments – the Rialto bridge.

This was still the only bridge over the Grand Canal. There had been a crossing at that point, on pontoons, since the twelfth century; but it was only in 1264 that the first true bridge had been constructed, on wooden piles. This was twice destroyed – the first time deliberately, by Bajamonte Tiepolo after his unsuccessful rising in 1310, the second time inadvertently, by the weight of the populace crowding on to it to watch the passage of the Marquis of Ferrara in 1444. After this latter disaster it was rebuilt yet again, still in wood but on a much grander scale, with shops and a central drawbridge – as, indeed, it was painted by Carpaccio in one of the *Miracles of the Relic of the True Cross*, now in the Accademia. By the middle of the sixteenth century the structure was obviously nearing the end of its natural life, and the decision was taken to rebuild it in stone. A competition was declared – perhaps, by the quality of those who entered it, the most distinguished architectural competition ever held, with Michelangelo, Sansovino, Vignola, Scamozzi and Palladio (whose plans for a five-arched bridge with pedimented colonnade still exist) all submitting designs. Faced with such an *embarras de richesse*, the authorities were for a long time unable to make up their minds; and they were still hesitating when the two successive fires in the Doges' Palace and the consequent demand for all the best

---

1. Incredibly enough, Rome had three Popes between the death of Sixtus V in August 1590 and the accession of Clement VIII in January 1592. Urban VII reigned for a fortnight in September 1590; Gregory XIV for ten months from December 1590 to October 1591; and Innocent IX for sixty-two days from October to December of the same year.

2. Rebuilt in the eighteenth century, it is now known as the Gesuiti, but Cicogna's tomb was preserved from the earlier church and now frames the sacristy door.

available skilled workmen caused yet further delays. When at last they were able to turn their attention back to the Rialto, the contract was given not to any of the competing giants, but to the somewhat humbler architect who had been in charge of the Palace rebuilding, the aptly-named Antonio da Ponte. It was he and his nephew, Antonio Contin – architect of Venice's other best-loved bridge, the Bridge of Sighs – who together designed and built, between 1588 and 1591, the Rialto bridge as we know it today, suitably inscribed with a memorial inscription to Doge Pasquale Cicogna.

As a work of art, we must frankly admit, the bridge lacks distinction. Most people by now are vaguely fond of it, as they would be of any other well-known landmark, and there would – rightly – be a general outcry if any alteration were suggested. Somehow, therefore, it gets by. Its very familiarity blinds us to its faults – the poor proportions, the curious air of topheaviness, the coarseness of the detail. So much the better. Only very occasionally do we suddenly, unexpectedly and momentarily see it for the mediocrity it is; but it is difficult, at such times, not to feel a quick stab of regret for the masterpiece that Venice might have had, if genius had been allowed its way.

39

The Last Interdict

[1595–1607]

We cannot understand how it is possible to pretend that a free principality like our Republic, born such, and as such by the grace of God preserved for 1,200 years, should not be permitted to take such steps as it may deem necessary for the preservation of the State when these in no way prejudice the government of other princes.

The Venetian Senate to their
Ambassador in Rome, 26 November 1605

Some two hundred yards down from the Rialto bridge on the eastern side of the Grand Canal, utterly dwarfing its neighbours on each side, rises the immense bulk of the Palazzo Grimani. Begun by Michele Sanmicheli in 1556, it is not by any means the most beautiful of Venetian palaces, but in its size and scale, and in the sheer magnificence of its High Renaissance façade, it is undeniably one of the most impressive. It was from this tremendous pile that its owner, Marino Grimani – Venice's eighty-seventh Doge,[1] whose reign was to usher in the seventeenth century – was rowed in state, on 26 April 1595, to his enthronement.

As was obvious from the style in which he lived, Marino Grimani was one of the richest men in Venice. Rich men, so long as they were generous as well, always made popular doges; and though Grimani's election was quite phenomenally protracted, needing seventy-one ballots over a period of three and a half weeks, it was accordingly greeted with much jubilation by the people. Nor were they disappointed: in striking contrast to his predecessor, the new Doge on his ceremonial tour of the Piazza positively deluged them in gold pieces, his wife and sons simultaneously flinging down copious handfuls from the windows of the Palace. The usual flowery orations followed, one of which, it is recorded, was delivered by a certain Dioniso Lazzari, aged six. Free bread and wine were distributed to all the poor of the city in apparently limitless profusion. The celebrations continued far into the night, and no wonder.

Yet even all this extravagance was as nothing to what Grimani spent two

---

1. By traditional reckoning he was the eighty-ninth; it has, however, now been established beyond reasonable doubt that the first two names generally listed were not Doges at all, but a Byzantine Exarch of Ravenna and his *magister militum*. See pp. 13–14.

years later – the interval seems to have been due only to the time necessary for adequate preparations to be made – on the coronation of his wife. Such an honour was rare in Venice; it had been accorded only twice before, to the consorts of Pasquale Malipiero in 1457 and of Lorenzo Priuli in 1556. Neither of these ceremonies, however, could approach in splendour that which took place on 4 May 1597. First the Dogaressa, in cloth of gold and attended by upwards of 200 ladies in superb dresses specially designed for the occasion, was formally inducted into the Basilica for a joyful *Te Deum*, after which she mounted to the balcony of the Palace to witness a grand procession of all the nineteen guilds of the city. There followed a prodigious banquet in the *Sala del Maggior Consiglio*. For three days the festivities continued; more banquets, more processions, dancing by torch-light in the Piazza and on rafts in the Grand Canal – the latter somewhat spoilt by bad weather – and even a naval review, with the participation of ships from England, Holland and Flanders, ending with a regatta. There was much giving of costly presents, the Dogaressa distributing special *oselle*[1] bearing her likeness, and receiving, *inter alia*, a golden rose from Pope Clement VIII.

Before long, however, the Pope was to appear in a somewhat different light, causing Doge Grimani and his subjects a good deal of anxiety. The crisis had begun with the death of Alfonso Duke of Ferrara a short while before. Having no sons of his own, the Duke had named as his heir his cousin, Don Cesare of Este; but the Pope refused to recognize the legality of this succession – on the grounds that Don Cesare, though subsequently legitimatized, had been born out of wedlock – and maintained that the Duchy should now revert to the Church. This claim was, not surprisingly, contested with some vigour by the new Duke, whereupon Clement dispatched an army under the command of one of his more bellicose cardinals to take Ferrara by force, simultaneously calling on Venice for help.

Here, now, was a problem. The Dukes of Ferrara were not strong enough to cause Venice any serious trouble, but a powerful Pope on her very doorstep, controlling the all-important delta of the Po – that was another matter. On the other hand, if she followed her instincts, preserved her present neutrality and refused Clement the military aid he wanted, he might well turn his arms against her; Spain, always watchful for an oppor-tunity to do her down, would then come in on the papal side, and the ensuing war might have still more dangerous consequences. She decided to prevaricate, pointing out to the Pope's envoy that the prime necessity was always peace in Italy, and that problems of the kind that had now arisen

1. See p. 436n.

should always be settled by negotiation rather than force. If mediation were required, she would be happy to offer her services.

The situation quickly resolved itself. In January 1598, before Venice was obliged to come to a definite decision on intervention, Don Cesare – his morale shattered by the news that the Pope had excommunicated him – surrendered to the papal forces, agreeing to cede Ferrara and all the territory of the Duchy in return for his readmission to a state of grace and one or two other minor concessions which cost Clement virtually nothing. Overjoyed at his success, the Pope came in person to take possession of his new dominion and made a triumphal entry into Ferrara – whither Venice, forced to make the best of what she was unable to prevent, sent four ambassadors to offer him her congratulations.

Unfortunately, her difficulties with the Pope were not over; indeed, they had scarcely begun. First, Clement made new attempts to diminish the Republic's authority over the local clergy; then he protested against Venice's employment of one Marco Sciarra, an excommunicate, in her continuing struggle against the Uskoks; next came an argument over frontiers and navigation on the Po; next, indignation when Venice proposed to tax the clergy of Brescia, together with their fellow-citizens, for the restoration of the ramparts; and in 1600 there followed another, more serious quarrel, once again over the question of jurisdiction. This time it related to the little town of Ceneda,[1] which, although Venetian for the past two hundred years, had been effectively ruled by its local bishop since the early Middle Ages – a fact which encouraged the Pope to send the Bishop a monitory letter denying the authority of Venice and demanding that all appeals should in future be addressed to Rome, on pain of excommunication. In the dispute that followed, Venice, believing that an important point of principle was involved, refused to budge an inch. Clement realized that he had overreached himself and partially backed down, but the affair rumbled on – heralding, could the Venetians but know it, the far more furious storm that lay ahead.

As the new century opened, it was plain that Venice's instinctive tendency towards religious toleration was becoming more and more unacceptable to Rome. This worsening state of affairs was the fault of Rome, and not of Venice. With the spread of the Reformation across Europe and, in particular, the promulgation in 1598 of the Edict of Nantes, in which Henry IV had confirmed the Pope's worst suspicions by granting to French

1. The name of Ceneda will not be found on modern maps. It now forms part of the modern town of Vittorio Veneto, some twenty kilometres south-east of Belluno.

Protestants freedom of worship and equal political rights with Catholics, the Roman rein was being steadily tightened and increasing pressure brought to bear on Catholic governments to submit to papal control. This Venice refused to do. In taking her stand she believed herself guilty of no religious insubordination; as her Doge was soon to expostulate when charged with Calvinism, 'What is a Calvinist? We are Christians, as good as the Pope himself, and Christians we shall die, whether others like it or not'.[1] The difficulty was that what the Pope saw as a religious problem the Republic saw as a purely political one. Her duty of doctrinal obedience she did not question; her political independence, on the other hand, was sacrosanct to her, and could not be set at risk. Besides, as a cosmopolitan city whose very existence was founded on international commerce, how could she discriminate against heretics, any more than in the past she had discriminated against infidels?

Though Clement VIII never relaxed his efforts, Venice did score a few victories. The question of Ceneda was one; there had been another in 1596, when a special Concordat actually granted to Venetian booksellers and printers the right – under certain conditions – to handle works figuring on the *Index Expurgatorius*. (In the event they very seldom did so, but the principle was at least admitted.) The Republic defied papal protests in allowing Protestant merchants and craftsmen from the Swiss canton of the Grisons to settle in her territory. She also staunchly defended the religious freedom of foreign diplomats. When reproached in 1604 for allowing Sir Henry Wotton to import Protestant prayer-books and to hold Anglican services in his private chapel, she sent Rome a firm reply: 'The Republic can in no wise search the baggage of the English ambassador,[2] of whom it is known that he is living a quiet and blameless life, causing no scandal whatever.' The Pope did not insist, and Sir Henry continued to perform his devotions undisturbed throughout the fourteen years of his Venetian embassy.[3]

But in March 1605 Pope Clement died, and was succeeded – after the reign of Leo XI, which lasted only twenty-six days and is memorable for no other reason – by Paul V. Camillo Borghese, despite a distinguished ecclesiastical career, seems to have been genuinely astonished by his elec-

---

1. *Che vuol dir Calvinista? Siamo Cristiani quanto il Papa, e Cristiani moriremo, a dispetto di chi non lo vorria.*

2. In fact, it almost certainly had. See the next chapter.

3. Those fourteen years were not continuous. Wotton's first term of office lasted from 1604 to 1612, his second from 1616 to 1619 and his third from 1621 to 1624. Much of his time was spent buying pictures for the King and the Duke of Buckingham. To Eton College, of which he later became Provost, he gave the huge painting, depicting the entire city of Venice, which still hangs there.

tion, which he could only interpret as a sign that he had been divinely appointed to stamp out heresy and to impose the supremacy of the Church, down to the very letter of the canon law. Papal legates sought even more frequent audience with the Doge, to remonstrate and protest. Why had the Senate recently prohibited the erection of any more religious buildings in the city without special licence? Why had it even more recently forbidden the alienation of secular real property to the Church, thereby depriving the latter of profitable bequests from pious Venetian testators? Venice protested in vain that it was becoming impossible to maintain even the existing churches and monasteries, which already occupied half the area of the city; or that, since Pope Clement had decreed that no church property might be sold to laymen, some reciprocal law was necessary to prevent more and more land passing out of the hands of the Republic. Such arguments were simply not accepted, and the papal communications began to acquire a new edge – of menace.

The two parties were thus, from the very beginning of Paul's reign, set on a collision course from which the one would not, the other could not be deflected. Venice did her best to maintain friendly relations, even going so far as to enrol the Borghese family among the ranks of the nobility – a gesture which delighted the Pope, who sent a fulsome and flattering letter of appreciation; but the polite veil could not be maintained for long, and it so chanced that even before Paul had been a year on his throne there had occurred three events, any one of which might have precipitated the coming crisis.

The first of these was the death of the Venetian Patriarch, Matteo Zane, and the appointment by the Senate of Francesco Vendramin as his successor. On such occasions it had long been Venetian practice, as a matter of courtesy, to request Vatican approval. At the time of Zane's appointment, however, Clement VIII had replied that such approval could no longer be considered automatic, and had insisted that the new Patriarch should personally present himself in Rome to be examined. Venice had at first refused, and then agreed that Zane might make the journey on condition that it was not for examination, but merely that the Pope might honour him with a special audience. Now, with the appointment of Vendramin, Paul replied as his predecessor had done, in terms still more abrupt. Again Venice was ready to compromise as she had before, but this time the Pope was adamant. The matter was still unsettled when the next storm broke.

Or, more accurately, two storms; but storms so similar, and occurring in such swift succession, that they can virtually be considered as one. They centred on two professed clerics, Scipio Saraceni (who was subsequently found never to have taken holy orders) and Marcantonio Brandolin, who, in August and September respectively, were denounced to the Council of Ten: the first for persistent attempts on the honour of his niece, which, when they proved unsuccessful, he followed up with publicly slandering her, abusing her and plastering her front door with filth, the second – in the words of the noble uncle who laid the charges – for 'murders, frauds, rapes and every kind of violence against his dependants.' In each case the Ten ordered an immediate inquiry and, when both of these seemed to confirm the justice of the charges, arrogated to itself the responsibility for the trial and punishment of the two offenders. Instantly the Pope forgot his Venetian ennoblement and reverted to the attack. These two prisoners, as members of the clergy, were outside the jurisdiction of the Republic, which had no right to hold them in distraint. They must be handed over at once to the ecclesiastical authorities, who would then take whatever action they deemed appropriate.

All through the autumn of 1605 the argument went on, in an atmosphere that grew steadily more tense as the year drew to its end. Then, in mid-December, with relations rapidly reaching breaking-point, Venice appointed as her spokesman in Rome one Leonardo Donà, an experienced diplomat who had represented his country in Spain and Constantinople and was a veteran of many former missions to the papal court. It was too late. Donà was still on his way through the Apennines when the Pope ordered the dispatch of two briefs to Venice. One dealt with the question of Church property, the other with the cases of Saraceni and Brandolin. If Venice did not forthwith annul her decrees in the first instance and surrender her two prisoners in the second, the ban of the Church would be laid upon her.

The missive was presented on Christmas morning, and was consequently not opened at once. It was still unread when, that same evening, the old Doge died;[1] and so it remained until his successor could be elected. That successor was Leonardo Donà himself. Hastily recalled from his mission, it was he who finally broke the seals of the papal ultimatum. This grim communication had now been in Venice for the best part of a month, and the attitude of the Papal Nuncio in the interim had left no one in doubt of the general tenor of its contents. Apart, therefore, from the discovery that a careless secretary in the Curia had omitted to send the second of the two briefs, inadvertently enclosing in its place an additional copy of the first,

1. Marino Grimani and his wife, who survived him another seven years, share a tomb in the distant church of S. Giuseppe di Castello – their family church, but a curiously remote and obscure resting-place for one of the most self-consciously magnificent ducal couples that the Republic ever produced.

the new Doge can have felt little surprise. The inevitable crisis had come. That being so, since capitulation was out of the question, the Republic must prepare to resist. But with what weapons? The time for diplomacy was past; the battle must now be carried into the enemy camp. Paul V, as was well known, fancied himself as a legist; what Venice now required, to present, argue and defend her case before the world, was an expert on canon law who was also a theologian, a dialectician and a political philosopher, a man deeply versed in ecclesiastical history and a polemicist who could argue with clarity and pitiless logic, turning all the Pope's own arguments back against himself.

The Senate did not hesitate. It sent for Paolo Sarpi.

It is a misfortune, both for the historian of Venice and for his readers, that the tale he has to tell should be so lacking in great personalities. Doges apart – and even those appear a fairly dim lot when viewed in the mass, if only because they had little opportunity to express themselves once they had reached the supreme office – few indeed are the figures who stand out as creatures of flesh and blood, worthy of our reverence, hatred or even contempt, and who were none the less permitted to influence the turn of events. Paolo Sarpi was such a man; but, however grateful we may feel to him for giving a little human warmth to these pages, our debt is as nothing compared to that of Venice, whose course he guided through the last and gravest religious crisis in her history.

At the time of his summons Sarpi was fifty-three, and had been a Servite friar since the age of fourteen. After a period in his youth as court theologian to the Duke of Mantua, he had returned to Venice in 1575 and four years later was appointed Provincial of his Order. Already he was renowned for his learning, which extended far beyond the field of the spirit; indeed, the whole cast of his mind seems to have been scientific rather than philosophical. As an anatomist, he has been credited with the discovery of the circulation of the blood, a quarter of a century or more before Harvey; he certainly discovered the valves in the veins. As an optician, he earned the gratitude of Galileo himself, who was teaching in the University of Padua between 1592 and 1610 and who acknowledges the help of *mio padre e maestro Sarpi* in the construction of his telescope.[1] Possibly because of the austerity of his eating habits, he suffered terribly from the cold: Sir Henry

1. The two used to meet regularly in Venice in the palace now known as the Corner-Martinengo on the Grand Canal. At that time it was the property of the brothers Andrea and Nicolò Morosini, who had made of it a sort of scientific academy. Leonardo Donà and Nicolò Contarini (the future Doge) were also *habitués*.

Wotton, who knew him well, has left an unforgettable picture of him in his cell, 'fenced with a castle of paper about his chair and over his head when he was either reading or writing alone, for he was of our Lord of St Albans' opinion that all air is predatory, and especially hurtful when the spirits are most employed.' Though he was 'one of the humblest things that could be seen within the bounds of humanity', Sir Henry's admiration for him was boundless:

Excellent in positive, excellent in scholastical and polemical divinity; a rare mathematician even in the most abstruse parts thereof, and yet withal so expert in the history of plants as if he had never perused any book but Nature. Lastly a great canonist, which was the title of his ordinary service with the state, and certainly in the time of the Pope's interdict they had their principal light from him.

It was Sarpi, now appointed official counsellor to the Senate, who drafted the Republic's reply to the Pope's first brief – that which related to Church property. The tone was respectful but utterly unyielding, the style concise and unadorned, with every word pulling its weight. 'Princes,' it ran, 'by divine law which no human power can abrogate, have authority to legislate on matters temporal within their jurisdictions; there is no occasion for the admonitions of Your Holiness, for the matters under discussion are not spiritual but temporal.'

The second papal brief, concerning the two miscreant clerics, arrived at the end of February; to this too Sarpi produced a similarly reasoned and measured reply. But the Pope had no patience with arguments which, as he put it, 'reeked of heresy'. On 16 April he announced at a consistory that unless Venice made full submission within twenty-four days, the sentence of excommunication and interdict would come into force; on the 17th, a monitory to this effect was published to the world. Venice, however, did not bother to wait until her time expired. On 6 May Leonardo Donà set his seal on an edict addressed to all patriarchs, archbishops, bishops, vicars, abbots and priors throughout the territory of the Republic. He, Doge of Venice, who in temporal affairs recognized no superior power except the Divine Majesty itself and whose duty it was to ensure the peace and tranquillity of the State, made solemn protest before Almighty God and all the world that he had striven by every means possible to bring His Holiness the Pope to an understanding of the Republic's most legitimate rights. Since, however, His Holiness had closed his ears and had instead issued a public monitory 'against all reason and against the teachings of the Holy Scriptures, the Fathers of the Church and the sacred canons, with prejudice to the secular authority conferred by God and to the liberty of the State, and to the detriment of that undisturbed possession of their life and goods enjoyed, with God's blessing, by his loyal subjects', that monitory was formally declared to be worthless. The clergy were therefore adjured to continue as before with the cure of the souls of the faithful and the celebration of the Mass, since it was the Republic's 'most firm intention to continue in the Holy Catholic and Apostolic Faith and the observance of the Holy Roman Church.' The protest ended with the prayer that God would lead the Pope to the knowledge of the vanity of his action, the wrong he had done to the Republic and the justice of the Venetian cause.

Next, the Doge on Sarpi's advice banished all Jesuits (whose Spanish orientation had led them to take a strongly papalist line from the outset), Theatines and Capuchins from the territory of the Republic and dismissed the Papal Nuncio with the words:

'Monsignor! You must know that we are, every one of us, resolute and ardent to the last degree, not merely the Government but the whole nobility and people of our State. We ignore your excommunication: it is nothing to us. *Think now where this resolution would lead, if our example were to be followed by others.*'

This was no empty bravado. In their unshakeable conviction that they were in the right, the Venetians were not unduly overawed. Nor were most of their clergy. The story is told of one parish priest who had declined to say vespers awaking in the morning to find a gibbet erected outside his church; he took the hint. Another, better-documented case is that of the capitular vicar in Padua who, on being ordered to surrender certain letters from Rome, replied that he would act as the Holy Spirit moved him. The Venetian Governor replied that the Council of Ten had already been moved by the Holy Spirit to hang all who disobeyed; and the letters were duly handed over.

This was not, after all, the first interdict that the Republic had suffered; there had been one in 1284, one in 1309 and yet another in 1483. What distinguished the present issue from the rest was that Venice was specifically restricting her defiance to the temporal sphere. In the spiritual, she wished only to remain a loyal daughter of the Church. If the Pope insisted on expelling her from the fold, it would not be her fault; the loss, moreover, would be his. Here was something new: the old problem of what things are Caesar's and what are God's, now presented in a new form to the eyes of post-Reformation Europe. Thus, whereas the three previous interdicts had aroused little enough interest in the outside world, the present controversy was taken up in all the states of the Christian West. In books and pamphlets, from pulpits and public squares, Venice was enthusiastically defended or venomously reviled.

As the dispute grew in strength and ferocity, Paolo Sarpi remained at the centre of the stage, writing countless letters and polemics, preaching, disputing, debating, striving ever more clearly to define the boundary between the celestial paths of the Church and the terrestrial paths of temporal princes. To some he was an Archangel; to others, Antichrist. In Venice, people prostrated themselves to kiss his feet; in Rome and Madrid, his writings were publicly burned. Inevitably, he was cited before the Inquisition; predictably, he refused to appear. Meanwhile he achieved a fame – or notoriety – far beyond anything that his scientific, historical or earlier theological works had ever earned him, or that he himself had ever desired or dreamed.

It soon became obvious that so vital an issue could not remain on the theoretical plane. Nations, as well as polemicists, were taking sides. Spain, naturally, was hostile; England and Holland offered their active support. In France, Henry IV was already treading a dangerous tightrope; he could not declare himself as openly as he would have wished. Nevertheless he left Venice in no doubt where his sympathies lay, and offered his services as a mediator. But Venice, by now, was in no particular mood to make concessions. Thanks to Sarpi's brilliant advocacy, her stand had been endorsed far more widely than she had expected. Her religious life was continuing as it always had; her churches were if anything fuller than before. Her cause was just, her conscience clear. As the weeks and months went by, she began to feel a growing pride and exhilaration: this was a great moral battle, and she was winning it. A single anxiety remained: that the Pope might try to impose his authority by force of arms, with Spain as his willing ally. For that reason only, she might consider coming to an agreement; but it would have to be on her terms.

For Pope Paul and his Curia, there was a terrible truth to be faced. The interdict had failed. The most dreaded weapon in the papal armoury – that same weapon the very threat of which, in the Middle Ages, had been enough to bring kings and emperors to their knees – had lost its power. Worse, its failure had been revealed to the world. The effect on papal prestige, already incalculable, was growing with every day that this farcical sentence continued in operation. It must be lifted, and quickly. To do so would not be easy, but somehow a formula would have to be found.

Thus the Curia argued. For some time Paul was unable even to contemplate so crushing a blow to his pride, but at last even he was obliged to agree. The French offer of mediation was accepted and negotiations began. Venice, advised as always by Sarpi, drove a hard bargain. She refused outright, for example, to petition for the removal of the ban. Any such request must come from the King of France, in which case she would allow her name to be associated with his; further than that she would not go. As for the two prisoners, once the ban was lifted, she would consign them to the French Ambassador as a token of her regard for the King, but without prejudice to her right to judge and punish them. On no account would she readmit the Jesuits; the other banished orders, save for certain individuals, might be permitted to return, but she declined to put this in writing. Finally, a carefully drafted decree was prepared stating that in view of the Pope's change of heart and the lifting of the sentence, Venice in return rescinded her solemn protest; it contained, however, no word to suggest that she had at any time been in the wrong or regretted her actions.

And so, in April 1607, after almost exactly a year during which it had succeeded only in bringing discredit on its instigators, the interdict was lifted. It was the last in the history of the Church; with the example set by Venice as an eternal warning before him, no Pope ever dared risk another, and papal authority over Catholic Europe was never quite the same again. But the end of the interdict did not mean reconciliation in any but the most formal sense. Paul V had been publicly humiliated; there were, moreover, several issues which remained unsettled – church property, the examination of bishops and patriarchs, the future of Ceneda – and which he had no intention of allowing to be forgotten. Foremost in his mind, however, was a determination to be revenged on those clergy who had defied his edict and above all on the architect of his defeat, Paolo Sarpi.

Sarpi did not immediately give up his office on the resumption of normal relations with Rome. There was still work for him to do, and he continued to make the daily journey on foot from the Servite monastery to the Doges' Palace, waving aside all suggestions that his life might be in danger. Returning to the monastery in the late afternoon of 25 October 1607, he was descending the steps of the S. Fosca bridge when he was set upon by assassins who stabbed him three times before making their escape – twice in the neck and once in the side of the head, where the knife, entering the right ear, was left deeply embedded in the cheek-bone. Miraculously, he recovered; later, on being shown the weapon, he tested its point, smiled painfully and was able to pun that he recognized the 'style' of the Roman Curia. Naturally, there is no proof that he was right; but the fact that the would-be assassins – who had by this time been identified – fled at once to Rome, where they flaunted themselves, fully armed, in the streets and where no charges were ever preferred against them, suggests that the attack, if it were not actually instigated by the papal authorities, at least did not incur their disapproval.

After this incident Sarpi refused the Republic's offer of a house on the

Piazza, but agreed to make his daily journey by gondola and to allow the construction of a covered way through which he could pass in safety from the door of his monastery to the landing-stage. Despite these precautions, he was to suffer two more attempts on his life, one from within his own cloister. These too he survived, finally dying in his bed in the early hours of 15 January 1623. His last words were '*Esto perpetua*' – 'may she endure for ever' – which his hearers took to apply to the Republic he had served so well. But papal rancour followed him beyond the grave; when the Senate proposed a monument in his honour the Nuncio raised violent objection, threatening that if anything of the sort occurred the Holy Office would declare the friar an impenitent heretic. This time Venice gave in; and it was only in 1892 that the present bronze statue was erected in the middle of the Campo S. Fosca, a few yards from the spot where he so narrowly escaped martyrdom.[1]

1. Sarpi was buried in the monastery church, whence his remains were transferred in 1828 to the church of S. Michele. There is a portrait of him in the Marciana Library, painted when he was an old man and clearly showing the scar on his face. The dagger itself has survived, and is now in the possession of the Giustinian family. Of the Servite monastery, alas, only a few vestiges remain; it was suppressed at the beginning of the nineteenth century, and the fine fourteenth-century buildings were demolished some years later. The ruins were offered for sale to Ruskin – 'ground and all, or stone by stone' – in 1852.

40
Treason and Plot

[1607–1622]

Mix with hir'd slaves, bravoes, and common stabbers,
Nose-slitters, alley-lurking villains! Join
With such a crew, and take a ruffian's wages
To cut the throats of wretches as they sleep.

Thomas Otway, *Venice Preserved*

Great victories, whether military, diplomatic or moral, almost invariably have a tonic effect on the popularity of the leader of the victorious side. To this rule, however, Leonardo Donà was an exception. The leadership of Venice during the interdict had passed, in fact if not in theory, to Paolo Sarpi, and though Donà was to reign over Venice for another five years, he was never loved by his people. The reason is all too clear. Again and again, especially at this period of Venetian history, the same melancholy fact is demonstrated: the Venetians judged their Doges by a single standard – their generosity. It is recorded that Donà scattered scarcely any of the expected largesse on his inaugural tour of the Piazza, and that the three nephews who accompanied him were still more parsimonious, to the point where the indignant populace began to pelt them with snowballs. The same austerity characterized his whole reign. Processions were shortened, public spending ruthlessly cut; state banquets, which were traditionally attended with so much pomp and parade that they often gave more pleasure to the uninvited masses than to the guests themselves, were reduced both in number and in magnificence. Just at the time it was most needed, much of the colour went out of Venetian life. The citizens looked wistfully back to the days of their previous Doge, open-handed old Marino Grimani, and were sad.

In all other respects, Donà was an excellent ruler. He was outstandingly intelligent – a close friend, incidentally, of Galileo – hard-working and deeply conscientious; it is said that he never missed a meeting of the Great Council, the Senate or the Council of Ten except on those rare occasions when illness prevented him, and that no detail was too small for his attention. The strange thing is that this tall, severe, unsmiling man with the curiously brilliant, penetrating eyes seems to have desperately minded his unpopularity. In February 1612, during the annual Purification Day visit to the church of S. Maria Formosa, he was actually greeted by the crowd with jeers and shouts of '*Viva il Doge Grimani!*' – an experience which shook him so severely that he refused to make any more public processions. And he never did. Five months later, on 16 July, after an unusually heated debate in the Collegio, he suddenly collapsed. He was dead within the hour.[1]

Donà's three successors, Marcantonio Memmo, Giovanni Bembo and his own distant kinsman Nicolò Donà, made little impact on history – though Bembo had fought with distinction at Lepanto, where he had accounted for three Turkish galleys and sustained two serious wounds whose scars he bore to the end of his life. Their reigns were short – the first two occupying the throne for three years each, the last dying of apoplexy after only thirty-four days – and, perhaps for that reason alone, undistinguished; but the Republic over whose fortunes they presided was passing through one of the most strangely unreal periods of its history.

It was a period in which all Italy was overshadowed by the looming spectre of Spain. For a century or more, Spanish ambitions had been held in check by France; but France had renounced her last Italian possession in the peninsula at the beginning of the century,[2] and the assassination of Henry IV in 1610, leaving the throne to his nine-year-old son, Louis XIII, and the regency to his determinedly pro-Spanish widow, Marie de' Medici, had ensured that the Most Catholic King would encounter no further opposition in that quarter. Spain was now supreme in Milan and Naples; in Florence, Marie's cousin, Grand Duke Cosimo II, was largely under Spanish control; so too, thanks to the joint influence of the Spanish Cardinals in the Curia and of the Jesuits, was the Pope in Rome. Only two Italian states were determined to resist the growing threat. One was the Duchy of Savoy, where Duke Charles Emmanuel II had amassed an army of over 20,000 and – with the help of the French Marshal Lesdiguières, who had joined him on his own initiative – was perfectly ready to take on any force that the Spanish Governor of Milan might send against him. The other was Venice.

1. He was buried in S. Giorgio Maggiore, where his tomb can be seen on the west wall. There is also a fine portrait of him by Marco Vecellio (Titian's son) in the Hall of the Bussola in the Doges' Palace.
2. Saluzzo, ceded to Savoy by the Treaty of Lyons in 1601.

While Milan made trouble for Savoy, Venice – whence Charles Emmanuel was by now drawing considerable financial subsidies – was facing even greater difficulties from the other, eastern, arm of the Spanish pincers: the Habsburg Archduke Ferdinand of Austria. The underlying cause, as usual, was the Uskok pirates, whose continuing depredations had culminated in 1613 with the beheading of a Venetian admiral, Cristoforo Venier. Again and again Venice had protested to Ferdinand, demanding that he take effective measures to keep his intolerable subjects in order; but as Venetian–Spanish relations grew worse the Archduke began to view the Uskoks with a steadily more sympathetic eye and, while feigning a few gentle remonstrations, gave them secret encouragement in every way he could. Venice, not for the first time, took the law into her own hands and launched a punitive expedition; Ferdinand in his turn protested; and the resulting war, while it remained on a fairly desultory level, grumbled on in Istria and the Friuli until the autumn of 1617, when Venice, Savoy and Spain came to an uneasy peace by which – though it achieved little else – the fate of the Uskoks was settled once and for all. Their harbours and fortresses were destroyed; their ships were burnt; and all those who escaped a more disagreeable fate were transported with their families to the Croatian interior, where, gradually over the years, they intermarried with the local populations and lost their separate identity.

Spain, however, was not looking primarily either to armed force or to peaceful diplomacy to advance her interests. There were other, darker methods at her disposal. The late sixteenth and early seventeenth centuries were above all the Age of Intrigue. Intrigue in itself, of course, was nothing new: in the Florence of the Medici, in the Milan of the Visconti, above all (if the legends are to be believed) in the Rome of the Borgias, there were instances aplenty of plots and poisonings, of spies and counterspies, of the secret meeting and the stiletto beneath the cloak. Nor was it peculiar to Italy; in France, within the memory of men barely approaching middle age, there had been the massacre of St Bartholomew, the assassinations of Coligny and of Henry IV himself; in Scotland, the numberless conspiracies that twined themselves through the sad, violent life of Mary Queen of Scots; in England, the Gunpowder Plot. Only Venice, until the attempted murder of Paolo Sarpi, had remained relatively free of the contagion. But by then Venice too was changing fast. As always, her streets were full of footloose adventurers, Italian and foreign; but whereas in days gone by most of these would have found employment as mercenaries or seamen, now they were more likely to join the little groups of *bravi* who could be seen loitering around the Piazza or the Rialto, supporting themselves as best they could while they sought to attach themselves to any potential patron for whom there was dirty work to be done.

Usually, they would not have long to wait. In the past few decades a new sort of visitor had begun to make his appearance in Venice – the foreign gentleman of quality. Though the Grand Tour as such was still unknown, by 1600 the whole of Western Europe had become thoroughly permeated with Renaissance ideas, one of the most central of which was the value of foreign travel – and above all travel to Italy – as part of a cultivated gentleman's education. In the Middle Ages few such men would have ventured abroad unless for war or pilgrimage or the occasional diplomatic mission. Travelling for pleasure was a new conception; and Venice, with her beauty, her splendour, her cosmopolitanism, her pageantry and her rapidly growing reputation as the known world's foremost purveyor of delights both innocent and corrupt, was the favourite destination. Venice welcomed these early tourists, accommodated them in every way possible and took pains to see that no unfair advantage was taken of them; nevertheless, what could be more natural for the new arrival than to accept the smooth blandishments of one or more of these *bravi*, who knew their way around, spoke the language, understood the money and the local customs and could provide entertainment, protection and any other more specialized services of which their clients might feel the need?

But there were other, more sinister employments. Venice's superb communications and the almost legendary stability of her government had made her Europe's principal centre of espionage, an international clearing-house for secrets of state. By now all the principal nations of the world were represented there, by embassies, agencies, banks, trading centres or other more clandestine associations, and for many of them the gathering of intelligence was a primary function. For such purposes extra pairs of eyes and ears were always useful; nor did a skilful hand with a knife or a none-too-sensitive conscience invariably come amiss.

It would have been odd if Venice, with an intelligence system of her own far more highly developed than that of any foreign power, had not maintained a close eye on all these covert activities and, where possible, used them for her own ends. Every embassy, every foreign household even, was thoroughly penetrated by Venetian agents, reporting directly back to the Ten details of comings and goings, of letters received and conversations overheard. A special watch was kept on the leading courtesans, several of whom were paid by the state to pass on any information that might prove useful, for blackmail or otherwise. There was also an active network of double agents whose task was to feed false or misleading information into the foreign systems. Yet even the Ten, with all its expertise and its unseen army of informers – to say nothing of the notorious *bocche di leone*[1] – could not be everywhere at once; and the very geography of Venice – the labyrinth of narrow *calli*, the dark *sottoportici*, even the proximity of the lagoon for the ready disposal of bodies – made their task a hard one.

The greatest of their triumphs culminated on 18 May 1618. Venice was even more crowded than usual, not only because the greatest of the Republic's annual celebrations, the Ascension Day Wedding of the Sea, had been held four days previously, but because on the 17th, following the untimely death of Nicolò Donà, a new Doge, Antonio Priuli, had been elected and would shortly arrive from Dalmatia, where he had been serving on a commission to regulate the Venetian–Austrian frontier. Priuli was a rich man with a reputation for generosity, and great things were expected from his tour of the Piazza.[2] Venice, however, was still technically without a Doge on the 18th, when early risers passing across the Piazzetta were astonished to see the bodies of two men, each dangling by a single leg from a hastily erected gallows between the two columns. Though this had always been the traditional place of execution in past centuries, in more recent years the Ten had been accustomed to perform its more distasteful duties in secret; such a departure from its usual practice could only mean that it wished to issue a public warning. And yet, as the days passed, although another corpse appeared in the same place, no proclamation was made, no pronouncement of any kind to identify the unfortunates or to explain the reason for their fate. Inevitably, rumours spread, and were encouraged by the numbers of *bravi* making hasty departures from the city; inevitably, too, these rumours presupposed a major conspiracy against the Republic, of which there could only be one instigator – Spain. Hostile demonstrations were held outside the Spanish Embassy, to the point where the Ambassador, the Marquis of Bedmar, was obliged to ask the authorities for official police protection. 'The name of the Most Catholic King,' he reported to his government, 'and that of the Spanish nation, is in Venice the most odious that can be pronounced. Among the people, the very word *Spanish* is an insult . . . They seem to thirst for our blood. It is all the fault of their rulers, who have always taught them to hate us.'

This was not strictly true. For years the Spanish Embassy had been the

---

1. See p. 336n.
2. He did not disappoint, scattering 2,000 ducats in small coin and a further 1,000 in gold. His daughter, Adriana Corner, flung a good deal more out of the Palace windows.

busiest centre of intrigue in the whole of Venice, its basements, anterooms and corridors teeming with sinister, slouch-hatted figures whispering together in groups while they awaited audiences with the Ambassador. And when, the following October, the Council of Ten finally disclosed in a full report to the Senate the details of what had taken place, the Marquis of Bedmar was revealed – as everyone had known he would be – as one of the leading figures in what has gone down in history as the Spanish Conspiracy.

It is entirely appropriate that the Spanish Conspiracy should have indirectly furnished Thomas Otway with the plot for his best and most celebrated play, *Venice Preserved*.[1] Although it did not actually end in tragedy (except for those who met their deserts) and although sadly deficient in sex (an element which Otway was well able to supply from his own imagination) the story has all the elements of seventeenth-century melodrama. Here is the arch-villain Don Pedro, Duke of Osuna, Spanish Viceroy of Naples, determined to destroy the power of Venice in the Mediterranean but also to betray his own country by assuming the crown of an independent Neapolitan Kingdom. Here is the Marquis of Bedmar, Spanish Ambassador, cultivated and charming in society but in reality 'one of the most potent and dangerous spirits Spain ever produced', filled with an implacable hostility towards Venice and the Venetians and fully approving of the first of Osuna's objectives, though unaware of the second. Here is Gasparo Spinelli, Venetian Resident in Naples, a loyal servant of the Republic but innocent, gullible and none too bright, certainly no match for the diabolical wits of those who are plotting its overthrow. And here are the two chief instruments of the conspirators, the men who execute the orders and take the pay: Jacques Pierre, Norman adventurer and corsair, practically illiterate but one of the most brilliant seamen of his day, and his inseparable antithesis Nicolas Regnault, educated, plausible but equally unscrupulous, with his mellifluous Italian and exquisite handwriting. Finally the hero: Balthasar Juven, a young Frenchman, nephew of Marshal Lesdiguières, who has come to Venice in order to enter the service of the Republic.

Like all of its kind, the plot was complicated and convoluted in the extreme, both in its conception and its attempted execution. A full account of it would be long and insufferably tedious, and has no place in this book.[2]

1. Otway's direct source was the Abbé de Saint-Réal's novel, *La Conjuration des Espagnols contre la Venise en 1618*.
2. Readers perverse enough to want one will be best advised to turn to Vol. II of Horatio Brown's *Studies in the History of Venice*, pp. 245–95, where the whole story is set out in remorseless detail.

The general scheme, however, was ambitious enough to satisfy the most demanding dramatist. For some weeks before the appointed day, Spanish soldiers in civilian clothes would be infiltrated in twos and threes into Venice, where they would be secretly armed by Bedmar. Then, when all was in readiness, Osuna's ships, flying his own personal standard, would advance up the Adriatic and land an expeditionary force on the Lido, together with a fleet of flat-bottomed barges in which that force would be rowed across the lagoon to the city. The Piazza and Rialto would be seized and barricaded, and special groups would take possession of the Arsenal and the Doges' Palace, forcing a way into their respective armouries and distributing the contents to the conspirators and to those citizens who were prepared to give them support. At the same time a force of Dutch mercenaries who had recently been hired by the Republic in case of need and were at present being lodged, together with the crews of the eleven ships that had brought them, at the Lazzaretto would be persuaded to mutiny and join in the attack. The leading Venetian nobles would be killed or held to ransom. As a separate operation, the Venetian garrison at Crema would be betrayed from within and the town handed over to the Spanish Governor of Milan. Venice itself would pass into the possession of Osuna; the loot and the ransom money would go to the other conspirators to share among themselves.

Whether so wild an enterprise could ever have succeeded seems, to say the least, highly improbable. Fortunately, its originators never had a chance to put it to the test. The discovery of the plot was due to Juven, who was approached in his hostelry – the *Trombetta* – by a compatriot, Gabriel Moncassin, informed of what was afoot and invited to participate. What Moncassin had foolishly failed to find out in advance was that Juven was a Huguenot, who shared all his famous uncle's hatred of Spain. Introduced to Pierre and Regnault, he agreed to join them and gradually elicited the full details, with the names of all those principally implicated. A day or two later, on some innocent pretext, he went to the Palace, taking Moncassin with him, and made his way straight to the Doge's antechamber. Suddenly – so the story goes – Moncassin began to feel alarm.

'But what do you want with the Doge?' he asked.

'Nothing, really,' replied Juven. 'I am merely going to ask him for permission to blow up the Arsenal and the Mint, and to hand over Crema to the Spaniards.'

'You'll ruin us all!' cried Moncassin, turning pale.

'Not you,' said Juven, and leaving his friend in charge of a Venetian nobleman, Marco Bollani, whom he had already taken into his confidence, entered the audience chamber. Having explained the matter in outline to the Doge, he then brought in Moncassin, who immediately made a full confession – thereby almost certainly saving his own life.

Once in possession of the facts, the Council of Ten acted, as usual, swiftly and in secret. Jacques Pierre, who was with the Venetian fleet, was summarily dispatched, sewn into a sack and dropped overboard. Regnault, together with two minor conspirators, the brothers Desbouleaux, were seized, tortured and then, after confession, hung upside-down from the gibbet in the Piazzetta. As many as 300 minor participants were discreetly liquidated.

Osuna and Bedmar, foiled again and inwardly fuming, were too powerful to be touched and continued their villainies from behind the walls of their respective palaces. But their grand opportunity had been missed. Venice was preserved.

The Venetian Republic has often been described as a police state, and so in a way it was. There are, however, certain points that its accusers tend to forget. The first is that so was virtually every other state in sixteenth- and seventeenth-century Europe – the principal difference being that Venice was considerably more efficient. Moreover, although like the rest she often used methods which would nowadays be considered reprehensible (at the time they were accepted as quite normal) against those who overstepped the permitted limits, such limits were usually drawn a good deal more generously than elsewhere. This was especially true where freedom of speech was concerned – a department in which modern police states are notoriously sensitive – and also on the at that time all-important question of religion. Finally it is worth remembering that Venice was an exception in another way: she was never a despotism. Every one of her rulers owed his position to free election, and with the possible exception of the Swiss cantons no state in contemporary Europe governed itself more democratically. On occasion, however – and particularly when she allowed her justifiable suspicions of Spain to warp her better judgement – Venice was capable of tragic mistakes; and of these perhaps the most celebrated is that which concerned Antonio Foscarini and Alatheia, Countess of Arundel.

Foscarini's career had started well. He had served with distinction as Venetian Ambassador to France in the days of Henry IV, and subsequently in the same capacity in London, where he had favourably impressed King James I and made many friends. While there, however, he had aroused the enmity of one of his secretaries, who made several more or less hysterical accusations against him – principally concerning the sale of state secrets – finally denouncing him to the Council of Ten. Summoned back to Venice to answer the charges, Foscarini was immediately clapped into prison, remaining there throughout a three-year inquiry (during which, it is only fair to say, much apparently convincing evidence was given on both sides) until at last, on 30 July 1618, he was found not guilty and released without a stain on his character. By 1620 he had been made a Senator and the whole unfortunate incident seemed well on the way to being forgotten.

In the summer of 1621 the Countess of Arundel arrived in Italy. Granddaughter of Bess of Hardwick, god-daughter of Queen Elizabeth herself, she was now about thirty-five, the wife of Thomas Howard, second Earl of Arundel, one of the leading figures at the court of King James. Like her husband she was a passionate lover of art, and was using her boundless wealth to amass one of the first great private collections in England. This was one reason for her journey; the other was the education of her two young sons, to whom she was determined – in a manner well in advance of her time – to give an Italian humanist education. These, however, she had left to spend the summer in a villa at Dolo, on the Brenta, while she herself continued to the city and settled with her extensive suite in the Palazzo Mocenigo on the Grand Canal.

She was still there the following spring when a second blow fell on Antonio Foscarini: on the evening of 8 April, on leaving the Senate, he was arrested and charged with 'having secretly and frequently been in the company of ministers of foreign powers, by day and by night, in their houses and elsewhere, in this city and outside it, in disguise and in normal dress, and having divulged to them, both orally and in writing, the most intimate secrets of the Republic, and having received money from them in return.' This time the machinery of the law moved fast. Less than a fortnight later, on 20 April, the Ten unanimously found him guilty. The sentence of death by strangulation was carried out the same night.

By now the Venetians were all too accustomed to the sight of the exposed corpses of malefactors swinging by a leg from the Piazzetta gibbet; but this time was different. Here was no anonymous cut-throat but a Senator of Venice – a man well-known to all, of noble and distinguished family, one who had received general sympathy from all sections of the population for the gross slanders that had been levelled against him in the past and for the physical and mental sufferings he had endured during his long and undeserved imprisonment. Could it be, men wondered, that there was truth in those first allegations after all? As usual, the rumours began to spread, and it gradually came to be believed that the majority of Foscarini's secret meetings had taken place in the Palazzo Mocenigo, under the auspices of the *nobilissima inglese* herself – who must logically be the arch-villainess, the huge mother-spider at the centre of the web.

It was not long before word of all this reached the English Ambassador, Sir Henry Wotton; and Sir Henry, uncharacteristically, lost his head. Had he sought an immediate audience with the Doge to discuss the affair, all would have been well. Instead, he sent Lady Arundel an urgent letter informing her that sentence of banishment was in preparation and would be served within three days. He accordingly advised her to leave the territory of the Republic with all possible speed. In doing so, however, he gravely underestimated her spirit. Lady Arundel was not Bess of Hardwick's grand-daughter for nothing. Going straight to Wotton, she denied that Foscarini had ever met the Papal Nuncio or the Secretary of Emperor Ferdinand[1] – the two foreign diplomats whom the Ambassador had specifically mentioned – in her house; moreover, she added, as this concerned the reputation of England as well as her own, she herself would seek a ducal audience the following morning. She naturally hoped he would accompany her. If not, she would go alone.

This was not at all what Wotton had expected. He was now deeply embarrassed, for the fact was that he had had no official notification of any banishment; he had merely heard the rumours and had probably seen no reason to disbelieve them. There may too have been in his conduct more than an element of wishful thinking. Lady Arundel was rich and powerful; he himself had no money of his own, and his meagre salary and allowances scarcely enabled him to keep up the minimum dignity his position required. That he managed to do so at all was largely due to the commissions he received from the Duke of Buckingham, for whose art collection he was trying to buy pictures; but Lady Arundel was now snatching all the best ones away – even though she was paying grotesquely inflated prices for them. The fact that her husband was Buckingham's chief rival at court was a further complication. Finally there was the matter of religion. The Countess, unlike her lord, had remained firm in her Catholic faith. Wotton was an equally staunch Protestant, who had worked hard for years to secure for his religion those rights in Venice that it now enjoyed. For all these reasons she was a thorn in his flesh, and he would have been glad to see the last of her.

1. The former Archduke had succeeded to the Empire in 1619.

At the audience the next morning the Doge welcomed Lady Arundel warmly and paid her the unusual honour of bidding her sit by his side. He listened in silence to her case and then assured her categorically that there had never been the slightest question of her banishment, or even of her implication in the recent distressing affair. On the contrary, she was more than welcome in Venice and always would be. She graciously accepted his assurances and thanked him; she had, however, one further request: that she should receive a public exoneration in writing, the terms of which should be made known in Venice and London. Here, too, she received full satisfaction: a few days later, when she and Sir Henry returned to the Collegio, a formal declaration by the Senate was read aloud to her, together with the relevant dispatch to the Venetian Ambassador in London, instructing him to give the most unequivocal assurances of her innocence first to Lord Arundel and then to any other persons at the Court who might express interest. As further tokens of the Republic's esteem, the Doge extended to her a special invitation to attend the forthcoming Wedding of the Sea in a special state barge, escorted by two of the *Savii agli Ordini*, and dispatched to her house fifteen bowls of 'wax and confections' to the value of a hundred ducats.[1]

Lady Arundel had good reason to be pleased with the outcome of events – though she made it abundantly clear to poor Sir Henry that she held him entirely to blame, to the point where he began to fear that she might be planning his dismissal. But he was still in Venice six months later when his formidable compatriot finally took her leave and, followed by a train of thirty-four horses and seventy sealed bales of goods – all specifically exempted from customs duty by personal order of the Doge – trundled off northwards with her little sons.

By then, it is pleasant to record, another restitution had been made, however tragically belated. Precisely what information came to light to suggest that Antonio Foscarini had been for the second time falsely accused is unknown, but on 22 August 1622 those who had laid the charges against him were arraigned before the Three,[2] found guilty and in their turn put to death. The Ten then made a full, public confession of its error, copies of which were handed to his family and distributed to all Venetian em-

1. It should perhaps be noted at this point that there is no suggestion anywhere made that gives support to the popular story that Lady Arundel, while admitting that Foscarini made regular nocturnal visits to her house, assured the Doge that they were not political, merely adulterous. On the contrary, there is every reason to believe that, despite Foscarini's English past, the two were not particularly close friends and in fact seldom met.

2. The Inquisitors of State (see p. 500).

bassies abroad. Others were passed about the streets of the city. Foscarini's coffin was exhumed and he was given a state funeral at public expense. In the church of S. Stae the Foscarini chapel contains a bust of him and an inscription:

ANTONIO FOSCARENO EQUITI
BINIS LEGATIONIBUS
AD ANGLIAE, GALLIAEQUE REGES FUNCTO
FALSAQUE MAJESTATIS DAMNATO
CALUMNIA INDICII DEJECTA
HONOR SEPULCRI ET FAMAE INNOCENTIA
X VIRUM DECRETO RESTITUTA
MDCXXII

41

Zen against the Ten

[1623–1631]

Pronto di lingua, di popolare eloquenza, di buon zelo, generoso e di conosciuta integrità, ma di pensieri torbidi, facile ad intraprendere le controversie e atto a sostenerle con l'apparenza delle leggi e del pubblico bene, fatto vago degli applausi della piazza aspirava alla gloria di rendersi autore di deliberazioni cospicue.

Ready of tongue, a good popular speaker, zealous, generous and of well-known integrity, but troubled in his thoughts, ready to enter controversy and adept at supporting his arguments with reference to law and the public weal; ever desirous of the applause of the market-place, he always longed to foment some public debate in which to shine.

Michele Foscarini on Renier Zen

The death of Antonio Priuli caused his subjects few tears. He had promised well, but had proved something of a disappointment. Admittedly, his reign had not been easy, beginning as it had in the middle of the Spanish Conspiracy and ending with the exoneration of Foscarini, one of whose judges he had been; but there was more to it than that. While not actually dissolute – indeed it is hard to see how he could have been, given the circumstances in which a Doge was obliged to live – he somehow gave the impression of never taking his duties quite seriously enough, of failing to maintain that last ounce of ducal dignity; and when he died at the age of seventy-five on 12 August 1623, shortly after returning from his villa on the Brenta, it was murmured that he might have lasted several years longer if he had led a more regular life. He was buried in S. Lorenzo, but there is no memorial, or even an inscription, to mark the spot.

Francesco Contarini, his successor, reigned for fifteen months, which were largely – if not, perhaps, very deeply – overshadowed by another of those minor wars which, though frequently reflecting far grander conflagrations elsewhere, could usually be contained within fairly narrow limits and made little impact on the European scene. Such a war was that of the Valtelline – the name given to the long mountain valley which follows the course of the river Adda from its source in the south-west Tyrol to where it debouches into Lake Como, and which at that time marked, for some seventy miles of its length, the north-western frontier of the

Republic. With the outbreak of the Thirty Years' War in 1618 the valley, which formed part of the predominantly Protestant Swiss canton of Grisons, had become of vital importance to Spain as the only direct means of communication between Spanish-occupied Milan and Habsburg Austria; two years later it had been occupied by Spanish troops.

This development had been viewed with understandable alarm by France, Savoy and Venice, who had concluded an alliance in 1623 with the object of driving out the invaders and restoring the *status quo*; but before they could do so the Spaniards transferred all the strong places in the valley to the hands of the Pope. It was – or should have been – a brilliant move, based on the supposition that Cardinal Richelieu, who had just assumed power in France, would defer to the papal authority; but they had misjudged their man. In November 1624, 3,000 French and 4,000 Swiss infantry, with 500 horse, marched into the Valtelline with strong Venetian support, and by the end of the year had driven out the papal garrisons – whose captured standards were promptly returned, with every show of respect, to Rome. This short and completely successful campaign was followed early in 1626 by a Franco-Spanish treaty, signed at Monzon in Aragon, by which it was agreed that the Valtelline should be made a self-governing, Roman Catholic state whose independence would be jointly guaranteed by both France and Spain, all its fortresses being permanently demolished.

Venice and Savoy were furious. What right had Richelieu to make a separate peace without even consulting them, taking it upon himself to agree with their former enemy on the disposition of an area of primary strategic importance? Venice, in particular, complained bitterly over the destruction of the fortresses, which she considered essential for the continuance of free communications.

The Cardinal was profuse in his apologies: it was all the fault of the French Ambassador in Madrid, who had exceeded his instructions; King Louis himself was displeased with certain aspects of the treaty. But the damage was done and he felt sure that the Republic would not wish to risk a possibly long and expensive war by reopening the whole affair. The Venetians shrugged sulkily, and accepted the inevitable.

By this time Doge Contarini was dead. He had been succeeded in January 1625 by Giovanni Corner, a member of the senior branch of that vast clan and a direct descendant of Doge Marco Corner who had occupied the same throne nearly three centuries before. The news of his election was received with general surprise in Venice, by no one more than himself, since his career had not been especially distinguished. As the papal Nuncio reported to Rome, he was more given to his devotions than to affairs of business or of state; and though he had always lived in the considerable style that befitted his rank and station, dispensing alms with a free and pious hand from his splendid palace next to the church of S. Polo, [1] he had never shown the faintest ambition for high office. Paradoxically, therefore, it may have been a sort of naive unworldliness rather than the reverse that led him to attract the fire of a certain Renier Zen, perhaps the most zealous reformer that Venice has ever produced and certainly the most uncomfortable.

Zen had already caused the Republic some embarrassment when, as Ambassador to the Pope in 1621, he had openly accused the Venetian Cardinal Dolfin – with whom he was sharing the Palazzo di S. Marco – of being in the pay of France. On his return he had been given a senior government post, but his arrogance and inflexibility on what he – sometimes alone – considered to be matters of principle had led to his dismissal and even to a brief period of exile on a charge of contempt. There were, however, many people in Venice who were worried by a general decline in moral standards and who believed that, insufferable as he was, Zen might be just what the Republic needed; he was therefore pardoned and recalled in 1627, and almost immediately found himself elected to the Council of Ten. Now at last his reforming zeal could be given free rein; and its first object was the Doge himself.

Giovanni Corner was in a distinctly vulnerable position – a position which, even if it were not entirely of his own making, he should at least have been able to avoid. First, his son Federico, Bishop of Bergamo, had been appointed a cardinal by Pope Urban VIII. There was a long-established Venetian law by which the sons and nephews of reigning Doges were forbidden to accept ecclesiastical benefices; but Federico was unwilling to refuse his elevation and, rather than order him to do so, the Doge had chosen to uphold the appointment, arguing that the cardinalate was a rank rather than a benefice. This argument failed to impress the Senate; it was, however, eventually agreed that, in view of the exceptional distinction of the Corner family and the danger that, if Federico declined, the Pope might be offended and refuse to appoint any more Venetian Cardinals, the law might on this one occasion be overlooked.

Unfortunately the matter did not end here. Within a short time the new Cardinal had been offered, and had unhesitatingly accepted, a new

1. Now No. 2128a. Built by Sanmicheli in the 1550s, its main front gives on to the canal and can best be seen from the bridge. Early in the present century it was briefly inhabited by Fr Rolfe, Baron Corvo.

bishopric – that of Vicenza; and soon after that, in the summer of 1627, two of the Doge's other sons had somehow managed to get themselves elected, by an extremely irregular ballot, to a senatorial *zonta* – once again in flagrant contravention of existing law.

It was at this precise moment that Renier Zen returned to Venice and took up his duties with the Ten. By October he was one of the three *Capi*.[1] Immediately he sent for the *Avogadori di Comun* – the state prosecutors – showed them the relevant laws and demanded that the *zonta* elections be declared null and void. Weakly, the *Avogadori* agreed – they could hardly do anything else – but before they had time to act they were pre-empted by the Doge himself, who made a similar demand, claiming that neither he nor his councillors had fully understood the scope of the law; had they done so, they would never have permitted the election in the first place. On 27 October the elections were annulled. At this point most other men might have been content to let the matter rest; not Renier Zen. That same afternoon, shortly before the Senate was to convene, he sent word to the Doge requesting, in his capacity as a *Capo* of the Ten, some minutes with him in private. Corner agreed, but very properly insisted on the presence of the Signoria. Zen then, with every show of courtesy and deference, pointed out that as a *Capo* he had a particular duty to ensure the correct observance of the ducal *promissione*, and went on to read a formal admonition in which he set out full details of the relevant laws and of the precise manner in which they had been contravened, adding for good measure particulars of one or two other minor infractions which had come to light during his investigations.

Giovanni Corner was a patient man. He listened in silence, made a short but equally courteous reply and passed on to the Senate Chamber, where two new members were to be elected in place of his sons. But Zen, still unsatisfied, now demanded before the Senate that his admonition be form- ally entered in the records of the ducal Chancery – a step which would have been effectively tantamount to its publication. The demand was angrily refused. Doge Corner might have acted unwisely in the past; but he was nearly seventy-seven and universally respected, and he himself had rectified what was, after all, a very minor transgression. Not only would the demand put an ineradicable and undeserved stain on his reputation; it would have a serious, even dangerous effect on the ducal prestige. But by this time Zen had mounted the rostrum, from which he launched into a determined defence of his proposal. In no other way, he claimed, could similar abuses

1. The speed of his apparent promotion is explained by the fact that the *Capi* held office for only a month at a time. See p. 283.

be prevented in future. No longer could Venice be exposed to these nefarious intrigues on the part of Rome, which sought to suborn even her most influential citizens with dignities and benefices. The law existed to protect the state: why else had ecclesiastics been made the subjects of special legislation? Why, similarly, should there be checks on the activities of a Doge's kinsmen? It was because of their potential exposure to foreign influences that they were excluded from the Senate, just as – he paused – just as it was because of their special opportunities of gain that they were excluded from commercial pursuits.

For a moment there was silence. All present knew that several members of the Corner family were accustomed to making protracted visits to Rome, and that at least one – the Doge's son Giorgio – had amassed a considerable fortune in the past two years by importing cattle from Dalmatia. Family friends were also fully aware that the palace in S. Polo was stuffed with Florentine luxuries whose importation was forbidden. A hundred years before, such flagrant – if relatively minor – abuses of the law and of a Doge's *promissione* would never have been tolerated and Renier Zen's diatribe, in the unlikely event of its having been necessary at all, would have met with quiet nods of approval. Now, there was uproar. If certain members of the Corner family were quietly feathering their nests, that was no doubt reprehensible; but it was no excuse for allowing the Doge of Venice to be insulted before the whole Senate by a self-righteous prig who had been serving a richly deserved sentence of exile only three months before. Zen's two fellow-*Capi* called on him to descend from the rostrum, announcing to the Senate that they had annulled his admonition altogether. He refused to leave, and claimed that they had no power to do any such thing. Finally the Ten were summoned and formally upheld the annulment. Still Zen fought on. At the next meeting of the Great Council he obtained a ruling that the two other *Capi* had indeed acted unconstitutionally and were liable to a fine of 2,000 ducats each; but this too was overruled by the Ten, and it was only when the end of his term of office made it impossible for him to continue his campaign that he let the matter drop. Even then he continued to speak out against virtually every proposal made by the Doge and Signoria.

At about five o'clock in the evening of 30 December 1627, Renier Zen was set upon by a party of masked assassins outside the *Porta della Carta*. Though badly wounded, he managed to stagger to his feet and raise the alarm. The day being a Sunday, the Council of Ten were not in the Palace; but they were hastily summoned from their homes to an extraordinary session, at which three special inquisitors were appointed to investigate the case and a reward of 10,000 ducats proclaimed for information leading to the arrest of the would-be assassins. Anyone found guilty of harbouring them or assisting in their escape would be put to death.

Soon it was established that the assailants had been seen to take refuge in the Palace itself; and all the available evidence pointed to the Doge's son Giorgio as the principal culprit. When it was discovered that he and two close kinsmen had fled to Ferrara, together with their private gondoliers, the suspicion became a certainty. On 7 January 1628 the three were formally sentenced to exile from Venice, deprivation of their nobility, and confiscation of their goods; and the traditional *nota d'infamia* was inscribed at the scene of the crime.

The general populace, however, was still unsatisfied. Self-appointed scourges of the rich and powerful are always popular, and they had taken Renier Zen to their hearts. They had not failed to notice that the confiscation order against Giorgio Corner had not come into force until his family had had plenty of time to spirit a good deal of his property away; nor that several other members of that same family who were suspected of complicity had not even been interrogated, but were still strutting about the city as arrogantly as ever. Finally there was the evidence of recent arrivals from Ferrara, who reported that the three suspects were living there quite openly and with every appearance of comfort. Why was the Republic taking no action to bring them personally to justice? Obviously because the Ten had been corrupted, and was unwilling – or afraid – to act against the interests of the Doge.

Renier Zen, meanwhile, was rapidly regaining strength, and in the following July found himself again elected one of the *Capi* of the Ten. Arriving on his first day of office with a substantial bodyguard, he was coldly informed that the latter could on no account be admitted; he discovered also that steps had been taken to reduce his powers to a minimum. A newly drafted memorandum informed him that, according to recent decisions of the Ten, no question that had already been fully discussed by them could be brought up for reconsideration, nor could any accusations be levelled against holders of public office. For some days he held his peace; then, early on 23 July, he gave notice that at the meeting that morning of the Great Council he intended to raise the question of the ducal *promissione*; this advance notification, he emphasized, was given in order that the Doge and his family might be requested to stay away from the Chamber in accordance with the law. But no such request was made; and it was consequently in the presence of Giovanni Corner and several of his kinsmen that Renier Zen once more mounted the rostrum.

He believed, he said, that his recovery had been granted him solely in order that he might continue his long fight against the corruption of the State. In the past month the Council of Ten had done its best to muzzle him, in defiance of the law which permitted every citizen freedom of speech in what he considered the Republic's good. Now another law was being broken: that which demanded the absence of all members of the ducal family when that family's affairs were under discussion. At this point an old counsellor, Paolo Basadonna, interrupted him, accusing him of trying to overthrow the government, to rush the assembly into hasty decisions, and to set himself up as a Caesar. On the contrary, Zen retorted: Caesar had wanted power for himself, whereas he, as a loyal Venetian, sought only to persuade the legitimate organs of the State to accept their responsibilities.

Before he could continue further, the Doge himself rose and launched into an impassioned protestation of his innocence. These accusations were, he had no doubt, simply a form of revenge for an attack in which he himself had played no part. Those responsible had been punished as they deserved; the remainder of his family was blameless. He had never broken the terms of his *promissione*; the Signoria had agreed to his sons' election; his son the Cardinal had received the bishopric of Bergamo in the days of a previous Doge, when there was consequently no reason to refuse it; while as for that of Vicenza, he had merely accepted it in substitution for the first. He had attended the present session of the *Consiglio* as usual, because the Signoria had told him he could; if it was the assembly's will, he would immediately withdraw. These final words were almost lost, since Zen, unable to contain himself any longer, was loudly calling on the *Avogadori di Comun* to do their duty and see that the laws were obeyed. 'What now?' shouted the Doge, 'are we no longer to be allowed to speak?' Pandemonium followed, with shouting on all sides and much banging of benches as some sought to silence Zen, others to encourage him, others to applaud the Doge while he vainly tried to make himself heard above the hubbub. Finally he gave up, Zen tried to table a document without success, and the session ended in anger and confusion.

That afternoon the Ten, in a specially called meeting in the Doge's private apartments to which Zen was not invited, decided on his arrest. An officer dispatched to his house having failed to find him, a proclamation was issued ordering him to present himself at the Palace within three days. Zen made no effort to obey the summons. He was forthwith sentenced to ten years' exile with a fine of 2,000 *lire*, and left Venice the next day. But the Council of Ten had not solved its problems; rather had it aggravated them, for to many people the sentence against Zen merely confirmed what he had always said – that the Ten were in reality just so many puppets, and that the Corner family pulled the strings. His supporters grew more and more numerous, and not just among the disenfranchised populace; among the nobility too, particularly its lower echelons, a party of reform began to take shape – though precisely what reforms were required was a more difficult question. Should the Ten's range of authority be restricted? Should the Doge be excluded from it, and perhaps his kinsmen also? Should it be forbidden to delegate its powers to powerful sub-committees like the Three? Should it draw its members from a broader section of society? And what about its servants – those secretaries who were appointed for an indefinite period, often for life, and who gradually managed to arrogate to themselves immense power; should they not have limited terms of office, just as their superiors did?

These and similar questions became the major issues of the day, but it took one further incident to spur the government to action. This occurred on 4 August, less than a week after Zen's banishment, when yet another close relative of the Doge, Angelo Corner, fired an arquebus at a respectable citizen, Benedetto Soranzo; the Ten showed itself unwilling to take any action against him and only did so, nearly a month later, in response to continued protests. Now at last the party of reform had its way; and on 3 September a committee of five 'Correctors' was appointed to report on the terms of reference of the Ten and on the members and staffs of all the various Councils of State. Two weeks later, while they were still preparing their report, one of the *Avogadori*, Bertucci Contarini, addressed the Great Council for two hours on the Zen affair, during which he showed that the memorandum addressed to Zen on 8 July – from which, he maintained, the warrant for the arrest and the exile had both directly resulted – was illegal. On the conclusion of his speech a vote was taken; by a majority of 848 to 298, the memorandum, warrant and sentence were all declared null and void, as if they had never occurred.

Thus, on 19 September, Renier Zen returned to Venice from his second exile, and was welcomed at his house at S. Marcuola by a cheering crowd; but disappointments were to follow. At the next meeting of the Great Council, by delivering yet another harangue, he antagonized everyone by his complacency and self-righteousness; finally he was called to order and warned that he must content himself with the victory he had won, for he could expect no more. A few days later the Correctors published their report. On the working of the Council of Ten they had a few reforms to suggest: *zonte* would be discontinued, secretaries would serve in future for a specified term only, and there would be one or two other minor administrative changes. In the really important section, however, concerning the overall powers of the Ten, its authority was confirmed in virtually every respect, except that it lost the right to revise decisions of the Great Council. Otherwise its terms of reference remained as wide as ever they had been.

This was a sad day for Venice, since the Ten was encouraged to behave in ever more dictatorial fashion, to consider itself ever more immune from outside control and – not least important – to make itself ever more unpopular both with the citizens as a whole and with other organs of government, on whose territory it trespassed and whose jealousies and animosities it could not fail to arouse. Renier Zen, it seemed, had achieved little after all. He had not even succeeded in bringing the Corner family to book; old Giovanni, who had been much grieved by the harsh accusations made against him and had begged that he might be allowed to abdicate and retire to a monastery, had been wisely discouraged from such a course – which would certainly have been taken by his enemies as an admission of guilt – and still occupied the ducal throne, from which his family continued to derive considerable surreptitious profit. Meanwhile his accuser gradually withdrew from political life, enjoying the respect of many but the friendship of none: a perfect example of that most unpleasant of breeds – the reformer who, beginning with a worthy cause sincerely pursued, gains such fame and universal admiration that he allows it to go to his head and finally sees his once-sacred cause as little more than a means of his own self-glorification.

He had, however, one last moment of satisfaction – when news came from Ferrara that Giorgio Corner had died at the hand of an unknown assassin. Whether Zen was implicated has never been established; it seems unlikely. Corner was a villain who must have had many enemies; it is hard to imagine Zen, insufferable as he was, descending to murder. On the other hand he was a fanatical lover of justice, which he frequently interpreted in his own idiosyncratic fashion. We can imagine him, guilty or not, smiling a thin, triumphant smile.

Four days before Renier Zen was struck down outside the Doges' Palace, Duke Vincenzo Gonzaga died in Mantua. Death came to him peacefully, in his bed; but it led to a short and bitter war that must have caused the rulers of Venice far more real anxiety than any of Zen's accusations. The *casus belli*, as so often when a prince dies leaving no issue, was the succession. Vincenzo had designated as his heir his first cousin, Charles, Duke of Nevers; but Spain, already deeply embroiled with France in the Thirty Years' War, and determined not to allow a French prince to take possession of an important Italian duchy, was backing – on far shakier genealogical grounds – a rival claimant in the person of the Duke of Guastalla. Here already were the makings of a nasty confrontation; but the position was further complicated by the fact that Duke Vincenzo possessed a second, equally strategic dominion: the Marquisate of Montferrat, a large if somewhat formless area covering the upper Po valley to the east and south of Turin. This had long been coveted by Charles Emmanuel of Savoy; but in order to keep the two territories under one ruler Vincenzo had taken the precaution of marrying the heiress of Montferrat, his niece Maria, to the Duke of Nevers's son, Charles, Count of Rethel.

Venice's foreign policy was at this time based on two principles: the preservation of peace in Italy and the curbing, whenever possible, of the power of Spain and the Empire. Her frontier marched with that of Mantua; the last thing she wanted was a Spanish or Imperial puppet on her doorstep. Unhesitatingly she gave her support to Nevers and accordingly, on 8 April 1629, joined with France, Mantua and the Pope in a six-year treaty of mutual defence, undertaking to put 12,000 infantry and 1,200 horse into the field should the need arise. By this time, in fact, the war had already begun; the Spanish Governor of Milan and the Duke of Savoy had jointly occupied Montferrat, in answer to which the French had also crossed the frontier in support of Nevers and taken the town of Susa. But it was only in August that the appearance of Imperial troops in the Valtelline made it clear that Mantua itself was in danger and that active Venetian participation could no longer be delayed. As these troops advanced southward, so Venetian money, men, arms and equipment poured into the threatened town; by March 1630 it was calculated that Venice had spent 638,000 ducats to help the new Duke maintain his position.

But it was not enough. On 25 May 1630 a badly organized and poorly led army of Venetians, Mantuans and a few French were routed at Valeggio with serious losses – the Venetian Proveditor-General, Zaccaria Sagredo, being subsequently impeached and sentenced to ten years' imprisonment for dereliction of duty – and on 18 July, after nearly ten months' siege, Mantua finally surrendered to the Imperialists and was put to the sack. And yet, surprisingly, even as the conquerors entered the starving, plague-ridden city, some 200 miles away to the west the French were winning the war. At the end of March a new French army had entered Savoy under the command of Richelieu himself, his Cardinal's hat discarded in favour of a helmet and plume, his pectoral cross covered by a cuirass. The army of Savoy was destroyed at Vegliana, and on 6 April 1631 a treaty of peace was signed at Cherasco in Piedmont. By its terms the Emperor Ferdinand agreed to invest Nevers with Mantua and Montferrat, Nevers ceding in return part of the latter to the Duke of Savoy.

So Mantua was saved after all – or what was left of it, for when Nevers returned on 20 September to resume possession he entered a ghost city, its treasures and works of art looted, its beauty destroyed, its population reduced by three-quarters in less than a year. For the survivors, there was only one consolation: that the plague, having done its worst within the city, had spread to the German invaders, relatively few of whom returned to their homeland alive.

But it did not, alas, stop there. Sweeping across Lombardy, leaving behind it a trail of devastation far wider and more calamitous than any barbarian army could have achieved, it reached Venice in the month that Mantua fell, and sixteen months later it had accounted for 46,490 deaths in the city alone, among a population that had not yet recovered its numbers since the previous visitation. In 1633 the population, according to official registers, was down to 102,243 – smaller than at any time since the fifteenth century. By then, work had begun on what was to become one of the city's best-known landmarks. Just as after the plague of 1575 the Venetians had built the church of the Redentore, so in 1630 they decided to raise – this time more as a prayer for deliverance than as a thank-offering – a still grander edifice, on the site of the old Ospizio della Trinità at the entrance to the Grand Canal. It was to be dedicated to the Virgin – S. Maria della Salute.[1] A competition was opened, and of the eleven projects thought worthy of serious consideration the winner was that submitted by a young Venetian architect of thirty-two, Baldassare Longhena. The foundation stone was due to be laid by Doge Nicolò Contarini – who had succeeded Giovanni Corner in January 1630 – on Ascension Day, 1631, but was postponed a week in the hopes that he might recover from an indisposition (not the plague, though this was still claiming several victims a day) from which he had been suffering for some time. On 1 April he was no better, but dragged himself from his sick-bed to perform the ceremony; at seven o'clock on the following morning he died.

It is an ironical fact indeed that the very first result of the building of the Salute – as the church is generally called – should have been the death of a Doge; but even Longhena himself – though he was forty-five years younger than Contarini and lived to be eighty-four – never saw it completed. Only in November 1687 was the scaffolding removed and the Venetians given their first unimpeded view of that splendid, extrovert

---

1. No literal rendering is possible, since the Italian word *salute* means both 'health' and 'salvation'.

proclamation of self-confidence and strength – sentiments that they were far from feeling when that first stone was laid, with such fatal results, over half a century before.

42

The Cretan War

[1631–1670]

Il regno di Candia è antemurale dell' Italia, e porta per dove l' insidiosa forza turchesca può spingersi all' oppressione della maggior parte d' Europa.

The dominion of Crete is Italy's outer defence, the gate whereby the insidious force of the Turk may penetrate, to the great hurt of the major part of Europe.

The Venetian Ambassador, Giovanni
Sagredo, to Oliver Cromwell

When the forty-one electors met on 10 April 1631 to choose a successor to Nicolò Contarini the result was, most unusually, a foregone conclusion. Francesco Erizzo, at sixty-five, was young for a Doge; but as Proveditor-General of the army – a post he had taken over after the disaster of Valeggio from the disgraced Zaccaria Sagredo – he had deeply impressed his superiors by the way in which, in the space of a few months, he had managed to breathe new life and spirit into the shattered and demoralized troops. So sure, indeed, were the Signoria that he would be elected that they actually summoned him from Vicenza – where he was supervising the construction of new fortifications – before the election took place; and in the event their confidence proved fully justified. Only one other, somewhat controversial, candidate was even considered, but in the very first ballot the electors made their preference clear. The result was: Francesco Erizzo, 40; Renier Zen, 1.

The new Doge was delayed on his journey to Venice by abnormally high water on the Brenta – one of the bridges had to be dismantled to allow his barge to pass – and arrived in the city only on 11 April; but he could not have timed it better. Two hours after his arrival there arrived the news from Cherasco that his subjects had long been awaiting: the treaty had been signed, and Italy was once again at peace. Being a man of comparatively modest means, he must have been almost as relieved to learn that all unnecessary public assemblies had been banned by reason of the plague, and that he was therefore excused the traditional tour of the Piazza which, for him, would have been as embarrassing as it was expensive.

His good luck continued to hold. As the weather grew warmer the plague figures increased just as everyone knew they would; but the summer had not even reached its height when, quite suddenly, they began to fall. Soon it was clear, even to the most pessimistic, that the epidemic was dying out; and on 28 November the Doge was authorized by the *Magistrato della Sanità* to issue the long-awaited proclamation that Venice was once again free of contagion. For the first time since the disease had struck, the Piazza was thronged; then all the citizens followed the ducal procession as it wound slowly past S. Moisè to a bridge of boats, leading across the Grand Canal to where Longhena's great church was just beginning to rise on the opposite bank. A service of thanksgiving was held in a temporary wooden structure erected for the occasion; and the whole ceremony became yet another of those annual events of which the Venetian calendar was – and indeed is still today – so agreeably full.

Moreover, for the next twelve years there was peace. This was the more remarkable in that the Thirty Years' War was still raging and Venice was under relentless pressure from several sides to involve herself. Her diplomats were busier than they had ever been, and in the city itself the Senate, the Collegio and the Ten seemed to be in almost permanent session. Somehow, nevertheless, they managed to steer a middle course, and while the rest of the continent continued to tear itself apart around her, Venice remained at the still centre of the hurricane. In 1642 there was a brief flurry when – as a result of a purely local quarrel which need not concern us here – the Pope sent an army of occupation into the Duchy of Parma and Venice was forced into a defensive alliance with Tuscany and Modena. In the following year the three allies were actually forced into war, during which they inflicted considerable damage on the land forces of the Papacy as well as on its commercial shipping. But the hostilities lasted less than a year, and in March 1644 a peace treaty was signed at Ferrara, based on a compromise that gave reasonable satisfaction to all parties.

From Venice's point of view, however, the peace came only just in time. In October of that same year there occurred an incident which, though she bore no part of the responsibility for it, was to involve her in a quarter of a century of war and to result in the loss of her most valuable colony – the island of Crete. Sooner or later, as she must have known, that war was inevitable; Crete was too tempting a prize, the Turks too covetous an adversary, for her possession of it to go much longer uncontested. It seems ironical, all the same, that the initial Turkish attack should have been the result of a piece of deliberate provocation on the part of a minor power which, after Venice itself, stood to lose more than any other from the surrender of the last important Christian outpost in the Eastern Mediterranean.

Although the Knights of St John possessed a church and a priory in Venice – inherited from rhe Templars after their dissolution in 1312 – they and the Venetians had for centuries cordially disliked one another. It was hardly surprising. Since their order was immensely rich in property held all over Christian Europe, the Knights despised trade and commerce. As men of God, bound by the monkish vows of personal poverty, chastity and obedience, they disapproved of Venetian worldliness and love of pleasure. Finally, as men of the sword and children of the Crusades, their avowed object – apart from the cure of the sick – was to fight the Infidel wherever they found him; and they deplored Venice's reiterated desire for peace with the Sultan, an attitude which they considered a shameless betrayal of the Christian cause.

By the middle of the seventeenth century the Knights were but a frail and feeble reflection of what they had been in those heroic days only eighty years before when they had successfully defended their island against Suleiman the Magnificent. They continued to run their famous hospital, where they still maintained standards of nursing and hygiene far in advance of any to be found elsewhere; but their Crusading spirit was beginning to evaporate, and their naval operations tended all too often to savour less of honourable warfare than of common piracy. Nor, even, did they invariably confine their depredations to Muslim shipping; unprovoked attacks, launched on the flimsiest of pretexts, against Venetian and other Christian merchantmen were becoming increasingly frequent.

To the Venetians, in short, the Knights of Malta had become a nuisance only slightly less appalling than the Uskoks had been in former days. Worst of all, they had adopted the old Uskok habit of harassing Turkish vessels in the Adriatic, a practice for which the Sultan invariably held Venice responsible – with much consequent damage to the all-important friendly relations between the Rialto and the Sublime Porte. More than once, the Doge had been obliged to send for the local representative of the order to make a vehement protest – never more forcefully than in September 1644, when he went so far as to threaten the sequestration of all the Knights' property on the territory of the Republic if they did not improve their behaviour. But the Knights as usual took no notice. Instead, barely a month later, they thoughtlessly provoked that final incident that put a spark to the fuse and ended in the greatest Venetian military disaster of the century.

Cruising in the Aegean at the beginning of October, a squadron of six ships of the order fell upon and captured a rich Turkish galleon laden with distinguished pilgrims bound for Mecca, among them the Chief of the Black Eunuchs at the Sultan's court, the Cadi of Mecca, some thirty ladies of the harem and about fifty Greek slaves. They then sailed on with their prize to Crete, where, landing at some unguarded point on the southern coast, they took on water and disembarked the slaves, together with a number of horses. Soon the local Venetian governor arrived and, not wishing to be implicated even after the event in what was, after all, an act of sheer piracy, ordered them away. Having made several attempts to put in at various ports of the island, where on each occasion they met with the same point-blank refusal, they finally abandoned the Turkish vessel (which was no longer seaworthy) to its fate and returned to Malta.

Occupying the Ottoman throne at this time was the half-mad Sultan Ibrahim, who until his accession in 1640 had spent his entire life a virtual prisoner in the seraglio and who, after a brief reign marked only by cruelty, frivolity and vice, was destined to be executed in 1648 by his own exasperated subjects. When the news was brought to him he exploded with rage, and ordered the immediate massacre of all Christians in his Empire. This order, fortunately, he was later persuaded to countermand; but it soon became clear that punitive action on an alarming scale was being contemplated, as Venetian agents brought news of an immense war fleet being prepared in the Bosphorus. At first it was automatically assumed that this fleet was to be directed against Malta, an assumption that was confirmed by an official proclamation in March 1645; but dispatches received in Venice from the Venetian *bailo* in Constantinople contained increasingly urgent warnings that this was a feint. The Sultan, he reported, was convinced that the Venetians had been behind the whole incident – why otherwise would the raiders have made straight for Crete? Venice, not the Knights, was his true enemy; Crete, not Malta, his immediate objective.

It was not long before the *bailo* was proved right. On 30 April a Turkish fleet of 400 sail, carrying an estimated 50,000 fighting men, passed through the Dardanelles. At first it headed towards Malta as announced, sailing straight past Crete and putting in at Navarino (the modern Pylos, in the south-west corner of the Peloponnese) for reinforcements and supplies. Only on its departure from there on 21 June was it seen to have changed course. Three days later it was sighted off Cape Spatha, and on the 25th the invading army landed a little to the west of Canea and advanced on the town. The first round of the battle had begun.

Crete – or, as the Venetians called it after its capital city, Candia – had been Venice's first properly constituted overseas colony, dating from the year 1211 and the sharing out of the Byzantine Empire after the Frankish capture of Constantinople. Its government was based on that of the mother-city, with a governor who bore the title of Doge (serving, however, only a two-year term), a Signoria and a Great Council; but it had never worked as easily or as well. The most fertile parts of the island had been largely swallowed up in vast feudal estates owned by prominent Venetian families, whose limitless wealth and overbearing ways did little to endear them to the indigenous Greek population; these families in turn grumbled over their lack of any real political power, all the principal officials being sent out from Venice, where all major decisions were taken. Defence was in normal times entrusted to feudal levies, raised and maintained at the expense of the great landowners, and to local militias of townsfolk and peasants; but both sides tended to shrug off their obligations, and discipline varied between the poor and the non-existent. Bribery and venality were endemic, and the colony, its own treasury always empty, was a constant drain on Venetian resources. In 1574 things had reached the point where a certain Giacomo Foscarini was sent out with special powers to institute reforms. He achieved considerable temporary success, introducing more accurate accounting systems and fairer methods of taxation, stamping out corruption, reanimating the levies and militias and repairing the crumbling fortifications; but after his departure the Cretans soon began to slip back into their old ways. Now, faced with the imminent danger of Turkish attack, the Venetian government ordered a new and vigorous defensive programme, sending out to their Proveditor-General, Andrea Corner, an army of 2,500 men, including military architects and engineers, and a fleet of thirty galleys and two galleasses, to supplement those already in the island. A further fleet was in preparation and would sail as soon as possible. All this was followed on 10 February 1645 with a special additional remittance of 100,000 ducats and orders to Corner to take whatever further measures might seem necessary to meet the expected onslaught. Corner, like Foscarini before him, worked conscientiously and efficiently; but his resources were still inadequate for the magnitude of his task, and the time allowed him far too short. Already as he hurried to the beachhead on that fateful June day, he must have known that the colony's chances of survival were slim.

Much depended on the speed of the promised Venetian fleet; if it could only arrive within a week or two, Canea might yet be saved. But it did not arrive. Corner would have been horrified to learn that it had orders to wait at Zante until it should be joined by a further combined fleet of twenty-five sail, comprising ships from Tuscany, Naples, the Order of Malta and the Pope; time was what counted now, not numerical strength. The Turks were entrenching themselves more deeply with every day that passed. The island fortress of St Theodore fell to them, though only after its commander, Biagio Zuliani, seeing that further resistance was hopeless, waited until it was overrun and then set light to the powder magazine, blowing up himself, his men, the attacking Turks and the building itself in a single epic explosion which must have been clearly audible in Canea. The town was weakening fast, its ammunition and supplies running out, its defences steadily undermined by Turkish sappers. On 22 August it surrendered. The Turks, doubtless hoping by a well-timed show of magnanimity to encourage further surrenders as they advanced, promised to respect the lives, honour and property of the local population. Then they allowed the garrison to leave the town with its colours flying and to embark unmolested for Suda.

Now more than ever, fortune seemed to favour the invaders. At Suda the Venetian admiral, Antonio Cappello, suddenly lost his head and abandoned the town; the combined fleet, at last arrived in Cretan waters, made two attempts to recapture Canea by surprise attack but was each time driven back by equinoctial storms. Then, in mid-October, its non-Venetian element, under the command of the papal admiral Nicolò Ludovisi, Prince of Piombino – who from the start had shown extreme distaste for the whole expedition – announced its intention of returning home. Not for the first time, Venice's allies had done her nothing but harm. As her own *Provveditore del Mar*, Girolamo Morosini, was not slow to point out, she would have been better off alone.

Her government, meanwhile, was on full war footing. Having no reason to believe that Ibrahim intended to confine himself to a single theatre of operations, it sent additional garrisons to Dalmatia and Corfu and even began strengthening the lagoon defences along the Lido and at Malamocco. But the top priority was naturally given to Crete. Galleys and transports were now sailing for the island almost daily, laden with munitions and supplies of every kind. One need, however, remained unfulfilled: what was now required was a supreme commander, a man whose seniority and reputation would set him above the petty jealousies and rivalries which – particularly where Venetian Cretans were involved – were an ever-present danger. The appointment was long debated in the Senate, and in the ensuing vote the name that emerged with an overwhelming majority was that of the Doge himself, Francesco Erizzo. One voice only was raised against the proposal. Giovanni Pesaro – later to assume the ducal throne on his own account – very reasonably argued that the Doge was now only two months short of his eightieth birthday; that the cost of sending him out, with the Signoria and an adequate staff and secretariat, was quite unjustifiable at a moment when the Republic needed every penny to pursue the war; and that such a step would probably encourage the Sultan similarly to take the field in person, and thus greatly intensify the Turkish war effort. But no one listened: all attention was fixed on the old Doge who, in a speech which brought tears to the eyes of all who heard it, declared himself ready to assume the formidable task that had been laid upon him.

Fortunately, perhaps, for Venice, he never did so. The preparations alone proved too much for him, and just three weeks later, on 3 January 1646, he died. He was buried in the church of S. Martino, where stands the tomb which he had ordered during his lifetime; but his heart, in recognition of his unhesitating acceptance of his last commission, was interred beneath the pavement of St Mark's itself.[1] He was succeeded by Francesco Molin, another veteran of many campaigns who, however, having recently been prevented by severe gout from taking up an appointment as Proveditor-General, was not called upon to assume command of Cretan operations. There being no one else available in Venice of sufficient stature, the whole idea of the supreme generalissimo was shelved, and is heard of no more.

The other pressing need was money. In the spring of 1646 all heads of households in Venice were assembled in their respective parish churches and implored to save the Republic in this moment of crisis by contributing all they could spare; but by then the government had already resorted to methods which, though in the short term they may have been more success-ful, were ultimately a good deal more dangerous. Three more procurator-ships of St Mark were instituted and sold at 20,000 ducats apiece; these proved so popular that their total number was later increased to forty and the price to 80,000 ducats. Even then they were quickly snapped up. Young nobles, on payment of a mere 200 ducats, were permitted to take their seats in the Great Council at the age of eighteen instead of the statutory twenty-five; and finally, in February, it was proposed to put the patriciate itself up for sale. Any citizen offering to support 1,000 soldiers on campaign for a year – a cost assessed at not less than 60,000 ducats – would be immediately

---

1. Just to the right of the High Altar at the entrance to the choir. The precise spot is marked by a small slab of white marble, inlaid with a heart-shaped piece of porphyry bearing the ducal *corno*. The heart itself, in its glass container, was recently unearthed during restorations to the pavement and found to be in remarkably good condition.

admitted among the ranks of the nobility, with all its honours and privileges for himself and his descendants for ever. This proposal, though approved by the Senate, was, not surprisingly, rejected by a large majority in the Great Council, who had no wish to open their doors to a crowd of upstart *nouveaux riches*; but in the years following, a large number of individual applicants were nevertheless admitted by special decree – subject to suitability as well as to a substantial payment.

At the same time the new Doge addressed another round of appeals to Christian Europe – not only in the predictable directions of England, France and Spain, but to Sweden and Denmark, Poland and Muscovy. She even appealed to Safavid Persia, which, though firmly Islamic, was equally threatened by Ottoman expansion. But nowhere was there any response. France, in fact, where Cardinal Mazarin had succeeded Richelieu in 1642, continued to pursue her traditional policy of friendship towards the Porte; she merely advised the Republic – through her Ambassador to the Sultan, La Varenne, passing through Venice on his return from Constantinople – to come to terms as quickly as she could if she wished to avoid total destruction. The Doge retorted that he would do nothing of the kind; nevertheless, as the new campaigning season opened, it was more than ever plain that Venice would have to carry her burden alone.

Everything depended on containing the Turks in Canea, still the only Cretan port they held. If they could be blockaded there while Venice built up her military strength in all the other strong-points along the coast, it should not be impossible eventually to dislodge them. To this end Girolamo Morosini, captain of the relief fleet, now applied all his energy and skill. The fact that he failed was not his fault. His kinsman Tommaso Morosini, sent with a fleet of twenty-three sail in an attempt to close off the Dardanelles and thus to pen up the Turkish fleet in the Marmara, managed at least to delay it considerably; this delay so enraged the Sultan that he ordered his admiral to be beheaded forthwith. But the admiral's successor, doubtless impelled as much by the fear of a similar fate as by a favourable wind behind him, finally smashed his way through the Venetian line and swept down through the archipelago to Canea, where the Captain-General, the seventy-five-year-old Giovanni Cappello, was too slow and indecisive to stop him entering the harbour. It was a bad beginning; and as the summer came and then the autumn, the situation grew steadily worse. Though Venice somehow retained Suda – whose superb natural position and recently renewed fortifications made it almost impregnable by sea – her ships were effectively driven from the bay, and fell back on

Rettimo (the modern Rethymnon), which, after a prolonged struggle, was driven to surrender on 13 November.

The fall of Rettimo had one beneficial effect, in that it brought about the dismissal of Giovanni Cappello – sentenced on his return to a year's imprisonment – and his replacement as Captain-General by Gian Battista Grimani, a respected and popular commander whose arrival instilled new life into the fleet. Early in 1647, too, young Tommaso Morosini was given an opportunity to take his revenge for his failure the previous year when, while pursuing some Barbary pirates, he suddenly found himself surrounded by no fewer than forty-five Turkish ships. In the unequal battle that followed he and his crew fought heroically, holding their fire till the enemy was almost upon them and then blasting out at point-blank range. Before long the Venetians were grappled by three of the Turkish vessels simultaneously and the fighting was hand-to-hand, Morosini himself continuing in the thick of it until a Turkish *arquebusier* managed to steal up behind him and blew his head off. At just about the same time the Turkish admiral also fell mortally wounded, but still the battle continued. Suddenly the exhausted Venetians saw three more ships approaching in close order, the banner of St Mark fluttering at their mastheads; Grimani, hearing the firing, had come to investigate. They too now plunged into the *mêlée*, forcing the Turks to disengage. Four Ottoman vessels had gone to the bottom, the rest fled. Of the Turkish sailors who had boarded the galley, the few survivors quickly gave themselves up. Battered but still afloat, Morosini's ship was towed back to Candia, whence the remains of its courageous young captain were returned to Venice for a hero's funeral.

Great, once again, was the Sultan's rage when the news was brought to him. He could not execute his admiral this time, the unfortunate man being dead already; he merely confiscated all his worldly goods, and gave orders that more men, more ships and more arms should be sent against Crete and that these should be followed by more, and yet more still, until Venice were taught the lesson she deserved.

Meanwhile among the Venetians in Crete it was recognized that the heroism of Tommaso Morosini, inspiring as it had undoubtedly been, had in no way improved their basic position. Of the four principal strongholds ranged along the northern coast of the island – the fifth, Sitia, was so far away to the east that it could be for the moment ignored – two were already in enemy hands; of the other two, Suda had been blockaded from the sea for well over a year and was desperately short of food, and both it and the town of Candia itself had now been struck by the plague, which not only destroyed morale but made adequate garrisoning impossible. The Turks, however, outside the walls, remained free of disease; and it was in the summer of 1647 that they first laid serious siege to Candia – on which, as the capital, the whole future of the colony depended.

The siege of Candia lasted for twenty-two years, during which Venice, virtually single-handed, defended the small town – its civilian population numbering only some ten or twelve thousand – against the combined military and naval force of the Ottoman Empire. In former times so long a resistance would have been inconceivable – if only because the inter-dependence of Turks and Venetians in commercial matters demanded that all hostilities between them should be short and sharp. But now that most of the carrying trade was in English or Dutch hands, such considerations no longer applied: the Sultan could afford to take his time. That Venice was able to hold out for so long was due less to the determination of the defenders within the walls – though that was considerable – than to her fleet, which by maintaining an almost continuous patrol of the Eastern Mediterranean not only frustrated every Turkish effort to blockade Candia from the sea; it actually increased its control over the Aegean to the point where, for the last ten years of the siege, the Turks were doing everything they could to avoid any direct naval confrontation. This is not to say that such confrontation never occurred; the story of the war is a national epic in every sense of the word, a story of countless battles, large and small, deliberate and unsought, ranging from the mouth of the Dardanelles, where the Venetian fleet gathered every spring in the hope of blockading the enemy within the narrows, right through the archipelago to the road-stead of Candia itself. It is rich, too, in tales of heroism: of Giacomo Riva in 1649, pursuing a Turkish fleet into a small harbour on the Ionian coast and smashing it to pieces; of Lazzaro Mocenigo in 1651 off Paros, sailing in defiance of his admiral's orders to attack a whole enemy squadron and, though severely wounded by several arrows and a musket-shot through the arm, putting it to flight; of Lorenzo Marcello leading his ships right into the Dardanelles in 1656, but not surviving to witness one of the most complete and overwhelming victories of the entire war; and in 1657, of Lazzaro Mocenigo again, now Captain-General, his squadron of twelve vessels driving thirty-three of the enemy still further up the narrow straits and pressing on through the Marmara towards the walls of Constantinople itself. (He might well have reached the city had not one of the shore batteries scored a direct hit on his powder magazine; the ensuing explosion brought down the mast and a falling yard struck him on the head, killing him instantly.) And yet, however glorious the victories, however superb the seamanship and the courage, one feels, as one works through the long, grim record of the war, that somehow there was always lacking an overall plan; that a more organized defence of the immediate approaches to the besieged town might have been more successful in cutting off the assailants from their supplies and reinforcements. For, despite all Venetian efforts, these continued to get through; and even in their most triumphant moments, the defenders must have known in their hearts that the fall of Candia could only be a question of time.

One thing only could have saved it – the unstinting and enthusiastic support of the European powers. But this was not given. It is arguable that the whole history of Ottoman expansion in Europe can be attributed to the perennial inability of the Christian princes to unite in the defence of their continent and their Faith. They had not done so, in all the fullness of heart and soul, since the Third Crusade nearly 500 years before; and they did not do so now. Again and again Venice appealed to them, emphasizing always that it was not the future of an obscure Venetian colony, but the security of Christendom itself, that hung in the balance; that if Crete were lost, so too was half the Mediterranean. Again and again they refused to listen, just as they always had. From Germany the Emperor pointed out that he had recently signed a twenty-year truce with the Porte; from Spain, to the astonishment of all, His Most Catholic Majesty was actually sending an ambassador to infidel Constantinople; France, true to her double game, passed occasional small and secret subsidies to Venice with one hand but continued to extend the other in friendship to the Sultan. England – whence little was expected, since she was not yet a power in the Mediterranean – was prodigal with promises, but with little else. Successive Popes, seeing Venice's plight as a useful means of gaining some advantage for themselves, offered assistance only in return for concessions – Innocent X, for the control of Venetian bishoprics, his successor Alexander VII for the readmission of the Jesuits, banned from the territory of the Republic since the days of the interdict.

Admittedly, as the years went by, and the continuing resistance of Candia became the talk of Europe, foreign aid in the form of men, money or ships was a little more forthcoming; but such aid was invariably too little and too late. A typical example was the force of 4,000, under Prince Almerigo of Este, sent out from France in 1660. It arrived not in the spring, when it would have been most useful, but at the end of August; its first sortie against the enemy, over terrain which it had not troubled to reconnoitre, ended in panic and flight; a week or two later, laid low by dysentery, it had to be sent *en masse* to other more restful islands to recover its strength;

after which the survivors – whose numbers did not, regrettably, include the Prince[1] – returned to their homes having achieved nothing. With 2,000 Germans, dispatched at about the same time by the Emperor, it was a similar story. They in their turn arrived far too late to be of any use, and left without anything to show for their involvement except a further depletion of the rations in the besieged town.

So many, and so memorable, were the exploits of the Venetian commanders at sea that one all too easily forgets the still more heroic defence of Candia by the garrison itself, doomed to face twenty-two years of attrition – of all forms of warfare the most hopelessly discouraging – and to suffer constant disappointment when promised reinforcements from their so-called allies proved time and again to be worthless. Such forces as did appear always seemed intent either on saving their skins or – what was almost as bad – gaining personal glory for themselves, thus risking not only their own lives but also many others that, with the chronic shortage of manpower, could ill be afforded. This latter phenomenon became more and more frequent in the last stages of the siege. By now the name of Candia was famous across Europe, and among the French in particular the young scions of noble families flocked to the island, determined to make proof of their valour on so glorious a field of battle. The most remarkable influx came in 1668, when Louis XIV was at last persuaded to take an interest in the siege. Even now he did not enter the war, or even break off diplomatic relations with the Sultan; French merchants in the Levant had taken full advantage of the sudden departure of their Venetian rivals, and were doing far too well for Louis to dream of any open rupture. He did, however, compromise his principles to the point of allowing Venice to raise troops from within his dominions, under the overall command of the Lieutenant-General of his Armies, the Marquis de Saint-André Montbrun; and the result of this was a 500-strong volunteer force, the list of which sounds less like a serious professional army than the roll-call at the Field of the Cloth of Gold. Foremost under Montbrun was the Duc de la Feuillade, who, though by no means a rich man, had insisted on personally bearing the lion's share of the cost; then there were two more Dukes, of Château-Thierry and of Caderousse, the Marquis of Aubusson, the Counts of Villemor and Tavanes, the Prince of Neuchâtel (who was barely seventeen) and a quantity of other young noblemen bearing names which numbered them among the proudest families of France.

1. His body was brought back to Venice, where the Senate ordered him an imposing tomb in the Frari; it is hard to see exactly why.

The party arrived at the beginning of December, to find the Venetians in a situation more desparate than ever before. The Sultan was losing patience and his Grand Vizir, Ahmed Koprülü, understandably anxious to keep his head on his shoulders, had poured new troops into the island and assumed personal command, telling them that they would have no rest until Candia was theirs. Heavy rain was fortunately delaying their siege operations, filling up the trenches almost as fast as they could be dug, but they had now begun to build a long mole only just beyond the harbour mouth which threatened to cut the Venetians' principal lifeline. Francesco Morosini, the new Captain-General, had during the summer's campaign lost 600 officers and 7,000 men, while the auxiliaries from the allies had been even more useless than in previous years; the few vessels sent by the Pope and various other states of Italy had sailed away at the first sign of autumn, and on their journey home had chanced to meet a small Spanish squadron which, promised for the summer, had not even left its home port until September. Hearing from the Italians – who were anxious to justify their early departure – that the campaign was over for the year (it was in fact nothing of the kind) they had immediately and with much relief turned about and headed back to Spain.

On their arrival in Crete the young French nobles were entrusted by Morosini with the defence of one of the outer ramparts on the landward side. They refused. They had not, they pointed out, made the long and uncomfortable journey to Crete only to be told to crawl through the mud to some advanced outpost, there to wait, patiently and in silence, until the Turks should decide to launch their next attack. Instead, they demanded a general sortie which would, in the words of one of their number, 'oblige the enemy to raise the siege'. Morosini very sensibly forbade any such thing. He had already made dozens of sorties, none of which had produced lasting results. His remaining men – there were by now fewer than 5,000 – would be barely enough to defend the breaches in the walls that the Turkish sappers were regularly opening up. But his arguments went unheard. As one of France's own historians[1] was to put it:

Monsieur de la Feuillade sought only vigorous action and glory for himself; he would have concerned himself little over the loss of seven or eight hundred of the Republic's men so long as he could enjoy, on his return to France, the honour of having made a valiant sortie in Crete. Once out of the place, its subsequent loss through want of men to defend it would have occasioned him little distress.

When he saw that the Captain-General would not be moved, La

1. Philibert de Jarry, *Histoire du Siège de Candie*, quoted by Daru.

Feuillade, complaining loudly of Venetian timidity, announced his intention of making an unsupported attack on his own; and this he did on 16 December, symbolically armed with a whip, at the head of a force whose numbers, we are told, had already been reduced from the original 500 to 280. The Turks resisted fiercely; but the Frenchmen, for all their foolhardiness, showed an almost superhuman courage and drove them back a full 200 yards, holding the conquered territory for two hours and accounting for some 800 of the enemy before the arrival of a fresh battalion of janissaries finally forced them to retire. The Counts of Villemor and Tavanes and some forty others were killed and over sixty badly injured, including the Marquis of Aubusson. La Feuillade himself, streaming with blood from three separate wounds, was the last to return to safety.

It was magnificent, but it was no help to Venice or to Crete. When it was over, the young heroes could not get out quickly enough. They were gone within a week, though many of them – even those who had somehow escaped unscathed – never saw France again. They had taken the plague bacillus with them.

Soon after the survivors landed at Toulon, another force, far larger, more professional and better equipped, set off from France for Candia. At last, Louis XIV had been persuaded by the Venetian Ambassador – Giovanni Morosini, a kinsman of the Captain-General – to take his Most Christian responsibilities seriously; and in the spring of 1669 his first important contribution was ready – 6,000 men, 300 horses and fifteen cannon, all carried in a fleet of twenty-seven transports, with fifteen warships as an escort. But even now Louis tried to conceal his breach of faith from his Turkish friends: the fleet sailed under the banner, not of the fleur-de-lis, but of the crossed keys of the Papacy.

The bulk of the army, some 4,000 strong and commanded jointly by the Dukes de Beaufort and de Noailles, arrived on 19 June. They were appalled at what they saw. One of the officers[1] wrote:

The state of the town was terrible to behold: the streets were covered with bullets and cannonballs, and shrapnel from mines and grenades. There was not a church, not a building even, whose walls were not holed and almost reduced to rubble by the enemy cannon. The houses were no longer anything more than miserable hovels. Everywhere the stench was nauseating; at every turn one came upon the dead, the wounded or the maimed.

At once, the story of La Feuillade began to repeat itself; so eager were

1. Desreaux de la Richardière, *Voyage en Candie*, quoted by Daru.

the new arrivals for the fray that, refusing even to wait for the remainder of the army, they launched their own attack at dawn on 25 June. It began badly: the first body of troops on whom they opened fire proved to be a recently arrived detachment of Germans, marching up to give them support. Once order had been re-established, they charged the Turkish emplacements, with considerable initial success. Then, suddenly, a stray shot ignited the powder barrels in one of the hastily abandoned batteries. The prowess of the Turkish sappers was renowned; indeed, their mining operations had been a feature of the siege, and much of the damage to the defences of the town had been the result of subterranean explosions. The word now suddenly spread through the ranks of the French that the whole terrain on which they stood was mined, that the battery was a concealed blast-hole and that the detonation they had just heard was the first of a chain of similar explosions that would blow them all to smithereens. With the rumour went panic. The soldiers fled in terror, tripping over each other as they ran. Seeing this sudden and to them utterly unaccountable flight, the Turks regrouped themselves and counter-attacked. Five hundred Frenchmen lost their lives, and within minutes their heads, impaled on pikes, were being paraded in triumph before the Grand Vizir. They included those of the Duc de Beaufort, the Comte de Rosan – nephew of the great Turenne – and a Capuchin monk who had accompanied the army as almoner.

Five hundred men out of 6,000 is not an intolerable loss; four days later the rest of King Louis's army arrived and Morosini started planning a fresh attack on Canea. But the spirit of his new allies was already broken. On 24 July a French man-of-war of seventy guns approached too near a Turkish shore battery and was blown out of the water; and a few days later de Noailles coldly informed the Captain-General that he was re-embarking the army and returning home. Protestations, entreaties and threats, appeals from the surviving civilian population, even thunderings from pulpits were of no avail: on 21 August the French fleet weighed anchor. In the general despair that followed, the few auxiliaries from the Papacy, the Empire and the Knights of Malta likewise set their sails for the West. Morosini and his garrison were left alone – and the Grand Vizir Ahmed ordered a general attack.

Somehow, it was repelled; but the Captain-General knew that he was beaten at last. His garrison was reduced to a mere 3,600 men. No more reinforcements could be expected that year, the defences were in ruins and he knew that he could not hope to hold Candia for another winter. By surrendering now, on the other hand, rather than waiting for the inevitable taking of the town by storm, he might be able to secure favourable, even honourable, terms. Admittedly, he had no powers to parley on behalf of the Republic; but he was aware that on at least three occasions in the past – the first as early as 1647, and then again in 1657 and 1662 – the question of a negotiated peace had been hotly debated in the Senate and on every occasion had found a measure of support. In any case, he had little real choice.

The treaty was agreed on 6 September 1669. The Grand Vizir, who had much personal admiration for Morosini, proved generous. The Venetians would leave the town, freely and without molestation, within twelve days, though this term could be prolonged in the event of bad weather. All the artillery that had already been there before the beginning of the siege must be left in place; the remainder they could take with them. The Turks would be left as masters, but Venice could retain the Grabousa islands at the north-western extremity, Suda – which had never surrendered – and their island fortress of Spinalunga, off the modern village of Elounda.

And so, on 26 September, after 465 years of occupation and twenty-two of siege, the banner of St Mark was finally lowered from what was left of the citadel of Candia, and the last official representatives of the Republic – including the colony's last Doge, Zaccaria Mocenigo, who appears to have played little if any part in the negotiations – returned to their mother city. With them went virtually all the civilian population of the town, none of whom had any desire to remain under their new masters. For Venice it was the end of an epoch. She had retained her three outposts, and there were still one or two pinpoints on the map of the Aegean archipelago where the winged lion still ruled, though his roar was gone and even his growl was barely audible; but Crete had been her last major possession outside the Adriatic, and with its loss not only her power but even her effective presence in the Eastern Mediterranean was dead for ever.

It had at least died magnificently. Never had Venetians fought longer or more heroically on land and sea; never had they faced more determined adversaries. The financial cost had been enormous – 4,392,000 ducats in 1668 alone – and that in lives greater still. Moreover, for nearly a quarter of a century, they had fought virtually alone. The assistance of their allies, on the comparatively rare occasions when it was given at all, was grudging, half-hearted, inadequate or self-seeking; occasionally – as for example when it caused long and inactive delays, or when it was suddenly withdrawn without warning – it was positively detrimental to the interests of the Republic. Even in those last two or three years, when the former policy of attrition gave way to a frenzy of destruction and blood-letting, foreign interventions served only to demoralize and to discourage.

Yet it was neither demoralization nor discouragement that drove Francesco Morosini to his surrender. It was the cold realization that the loss of Candia was inevitable, that no amount of help from Venice or anywhere else could do anything but prolong the agony of the town and its inhabitants, and that the only choice was between departure on honourable terms now or wholesale massacre and pillage a very little later. Few accusations in Venetian history have been more unfair than those which were flung against him by the *Avogador di Comun* Antonio Correr on his return. The charges were not only those of having exceeded his legitimate powers by treating with the enemy in the Republic's name; for those he was ready with his reply. There were others, however, as unexpected as they were undeserved – cowardice, treason, even peculation and corruption. Fortunately Morosini had no lack of champions who were quick to defend him; and when, after impassioned speeches on both sides, the question was finally put to the Great Council, the vote was overwhelmingly in his favour. He emerged from the affair without a stain on his honour and, as we shall see, was to avenge himself many times over on his old enemies when the moment came.

This account of the long struggle for Crete has of necessity been short and episodic. Out of consideration for the average reader, to whom one battle, military or naval, seems very like another, there are many incidents and engagements, many acts of courage and heroism, to which – even if they have been mentioned at all – less than justice has been done. For the same reason, a period of forty years has been covered in what must be accounted, even by the standards of this avowedly superficial survey, a very few pages. Before passing on to the next chapter, therefore, we must briefly retrace our steps in time and turn our eyes back to Venice.

The Cretan war covers the reigns of no fewer than seven Doges. Francesco Molin died in 1655; his successor, Carlo Contarini, barely fourteen months later; and the next, Francesco Corner, enjoyed the shortest reign of record, from 17 May to 5 June 1656. These three had all been in their seventies, and when Bertucci Valier, Venice's hundredth Doge,[1] was elected on 15 June at the age of only fifty-nine, it was hoped that with the energy of his comparative youth he might be able to resolve what appeared to be a stalemate in Crete. Alas for Venice: he proved a spiritless invalid,

---

1. But see p. 506n.

and in March 1658 the forty-one electors found themselves at work again. Giovanni Pesaro was ten years older than Valier, but still possessed plenty of inward fire; indeed, he probably owed his election to the vigour with which he had attacked his predecessor some months before over the question of whether to accept Turkish peace offers. Valier had been in favour, and several others in the Collegio had shared his opinion; but Pesaro's indignant oratory had carried the day. He, perhaps, might have given Venice the leadership she so badly needed; but in the mere seventeen months of life that were left to him he too achieved little. He was succeeded in September 1659 by Domenico Contarini, in whose reign Candia fell at last and peace with the Turk was finally restored.

During these short and undistinguished reigns the attention of the Venetian government was fixed principally on Crete, but not exclusively so. Venice had always accepted the possibility of an extension of the war to other fronts and, as we have seen, had taken defensive measures as and where these seemed necessary; by the same token, once hostilities had begun in earnest, she had never hesitated to attack if there seemed an opportunity for a quick and easy victory, even at the risk of opening up new theatres of operations. Whether this policy was wise for a state whose forces were overwhelmingly outnumbered by those of the enemy is, to say the least, questionable; but it cannot be denied that it worked. Between 1645 and 1648 a Venetian fleet under Leonardo Foscolo executed a series of raids up and down the coast of Dalmatia, beating off several land-based attacks by the Turks on Venetian-held towns. This campaign culminated in 1648 with Venice's capture of Clissa, a Turkish fortress a few miles south-east of Spalato.[1] Similarly in 1659 Francesco Morosini, during his first period as Captain-General in Crete, after repeated unsuccessful attempts to bring the Turkish fleet to battle, had relieved his frustration with a sudden attack on Kalamata in the southern Peloponnese. Both the town and citadel surrendered at once – the first step in Morosini's reconquest of the Morea a quarter of a century later.

Throughout the period of the Cretan war, however, Venice enjoyed one inestimable blessing. The rest of Europe left her alone. The Peace of Westphalia had brought the Thirty Years' War to an end in 1648; Spanish Catholic zeal and Venetian civic spirit had alike burnt themselves out; and though various other relatively minor outbreaks of hostilities among the princes of Europe continued to mark the years that followed, none of these had much political impact on the Republic or on any of the other secular

1. Or, to use their modern Yugoslav names, Klis and Split.

states of Italy. Indeed, if one reads a general European history of the time, one cannot fail to be struck by the way the spotlight has shifted northward, leaving the peninsula in dark and quiet shadow. Only the Turk threatened it now, and – as the next twenty years were to show – even he was past his prime.

43
Morosini and the Morea

[1670–1700]

Il ne s'ébranlait jamais pour quoi que ce fût; il avait toujours un visage riant et égal, qui témoignait néanmoins beaucoup d'assurance et de fierté. Pour conclusion, ce qui se peut dire de lui avec vérité, est, que c'était un galant-homme, et que la république n'en a jamais eu ni n'en aura peut-être un autre de sa force.

Philibert de Jarry
on Francesco Morosini

The fifteen years that followed the fall of Candia were years of peace for Venice – years during which she could put her house once again in order and do her best to restore her shattered finances. It was no easy task. French and German – and even a few English – merchants had largely supplanted her in the Levant; Venetian goods, meanwhile, had suffered disastrous rises in price, since the war at sea had obliged her either to hire foreign ships to transport them or, if she could spare any of her own, to have them escorted by armed convoys. She was also heavily in debt, with interest rates soaring in some instances as high as fourteen per cent. Slowly, however, through carefully contrived combinations of taxes, incentives, tariffs, new protection laws and a major programme for the reanimation of old river traffic on the Adige, she worked her way back towards recovery; and by the time old Domenico Contarini died in January 1675 – he was ninety-four and had been virtually bedridden for eighteen months after a stroke[1] – her treasury was once again beginning to fill.

Contarini's successor, Nicolò Sagredo, reigned over an economically renascent Venice for a year and a half – during which, appropriately enough, the Merceria was paved in stone for the first time; and on his death the forty-one ducal electors were chosen as usual by the same almost unbelievably convoluted system that had been in force since 1268.[2] Clumsy

---

1. He was buried in his family tomb in S. Benedetto, '*La nature l'avait doué d'une si grande douceur d'esprit, d'une affabilité si charmante et d'un extérieur si noble et si maiestueux, qu'il s'attiroit également l'amour et la vénération de la noblesse et du peuple: les ieunes gentilshommes étoient surtout si touchéz de son mérite que je leur ay plusjours ouy dire tout haut en le considérant dans les fonctions publiques: "L'è adorabile quel vechio",*' (Limojon de Saint-Didier, *La Ville et la République de Venise*, 1680).

2. The system is described in detail on p. 166. Briefly, the Great Council chose thirty of their number, then reduced them by lot to nine; these would vote for forty, who were reduced to twelve, who would vote for twenty-five, who were reduced by lot to nine again, who voted for forty-five, who were reduced to eleven, who finally voted for the forty-one.

as it was, it had worked well enough for over 400 years; on this occasion, however, it became known that at least twenty-eight of the electors favoured Giovanni Sagredo, the former ambassador to Oliver Cromwell and a distant cousin of the dead Doge Nicolò. Indeed, so certain was the outcome of their deliberations that the Sagredo palace had already begun to fill with the family and friends arriving to celebrate, when one of the arrivals brought disturbing news: some sixty gondoliers had gathered beneath the windows of the Doges' Palace and were expressing vehement disapproval of Sagredo – even threatening to stone him on his *giro di Piazza*.

The gondoliers do not seem to have levelled any precise accusations, and it is virtually certain that they had been paid to demonstrate in this way by one or more of Sagredo's rivals for the Dogeship. However that may be, the Council members were not prepared to ignore the danger signals. They refused to confirm the forty-one electors and called upon the eleven who had elected them to vote again. The upshot of all this was that Giovanni Sagredo did not, after all, assume the *corno*, which went instead to Alvise Contarini, a former diplomat and member of the Collegio, under whom Venice continued on her peaceful path towards prosperity.

But peace was not always easily preserved. When in 1683 the Emperor Leopold's Hungarian subjects rose in revolt and, inviting the Sultan to support them, brought a vast Turkish army to the gates of Vienna, Venice's diplomats must have needed all their skill to explain why she declined to take any active part in the defence of one of the foremost capitals of Christendom. (It is doubtful whether they reminded the Emperor of how little, and how useless, had been the support that he had offered to her during the Cretan struggle.) But this was a land war; the Republic had no military might at her disposal that could have made a useful contribution. Leopold in any case had plenty of allies – among them the Electors of Saxony and Bavaria and, more valuable than either, the Polish King John Sobieski. Her confidence in the Emperor's success proved amply justified. The Turks were badly led, and without heavy artillery; caught in murderous cross-fire between the superbly defended city and Sobieski's relief force, they fled in panic, leaving 10,000 dead behind them on the field. Their prestige was shattered, their legend was destroyed, their decline now patent for all to see. Never again would they constitute a serious threat to Christendom.

But the war was not over; and as the Christian armies continued to advance on all fronts, the Emperor, supported by the Pope and Sobieski, sent renewed and still more urgent appeals to Venice. The momentum of victory, they argued, must be maintained; with a new offensive league, in which Venice's sea power would be combined with their own on land, the Sultan could be swept from Europe for ever – an expulsion from which no nation would derive more benefit than the Republic itself.

To this invitation Venice sent no immediate reply. She had taken well over a decade to recover from the effects of the Cretan war. Her recovery had been achieved only after much sacrifice and suffering, and even now she had barely begun to enjoy the fruits of peace. Was she really to stake everything, yet again, on the fortunes of another confrontation? On the other hand, since the Turkish defeat at the walls of Vienna the situation had undoubtedly changed. The next phase of the war might well be fought at least partially at sea; did not both Venice's interests and her good name require that she should now adopt a more active policy? Even in the past few years, she had suffered in silence countless minor irritations and humiliations from the Porte, which had cost her dearly in honour and, sometimes, in good Venetian ducats. Was she not paying too high a price for what was really little more than an uneasy truce which the Sultan might break from one moment to the next? Besides, what if he were to make some accommodation with the Emperor and his friends; would he not then turn against the Republic in all the fury of his wounded pride? And if he did, what support could she hope to receive from a quarter to which she had just refused her own? The Turks were weak and demoralized; their Grand Vizir and Commander-in-Chief, the abominable Kara Mustafa, had been executed on the Sultan's orders; their army was in shreds. Venice, by contrast, was restored to comparative strength: was this not the time to take the offensive, not only to avenge the loss of Candia but to recapture it and perhaps her other former colonies as well? The question was long debated; at last on 19 January 1684, the Emperor's ambassador was summoned before the Collegio. Venice, he was informed, would join the league.

So historic a decision would normally have been announced by the Doge himself. On this occasion, however, the ducal throne stood empty. Doge Alvise Contarini had died four days before and his successor had not yet been elected. Francesco Morosini, now once again Captain-General, had already put his name forward as a candidate and was known to be longing for the opportunity to sail, as the head of his nation as well as of his fleet, against his old enemy; much to his disappointment, however, it was decided that his military responsibilities would be better left uninhibited by the cares of state, and he was passed over by the electors in favour of one Marcantonio Giustinian, an elderly scholar who had been an outstandingly successful ambassador to Louis XIV and was rumoured throughout Venice to be not only a bachelor but a virgin to boot.

It was, therefore, under these vaguely incongruous auspices that Venice embarked on what was to be her most successful military campaign for 200 years. Preparations for a summer expedition were immediately put in hand, while in Constantinople Giovanni Cappello, the secretary to the hastily departed *bailo*, delivered a formal declaration of war to the Sultan – wisely fleeing the capital, disguised as a sailor, the same evening.

Francesco Morosini was now sixty-four. Though deprived of the hoped-for *corno*, he assumed command of his sixty-eight fighting ships, including six galleasses, with enthusiasm and determination. So considerable a fleet had taken some time to make ready and he had been unable to sail before July; but the delay had at least enabled a few auxiliary vessels from the Pope, the Grand Duke of Tuscany and the Knights of Malta to join him before his departure. Once out of harbour he headed straight for his first objective, the island of Santa Maura (the modern Leucas) and captured it, after a sixteen-day siege, on 6 August. Few quick conquests could have had a more strategic value; from its situation between Corfu and Cephalonia, Santa Maura commanded the entrances into both the Adriatic and the Gulf of Corinth; it also provided a bridgehead from which, a month or so later, a small land force crossed to the mainland and forced the surrender of the castle of Preveza. Meanwhile, further north along the coast, the Christian Vlachs of Bosnia and Herzegovina rose in simultaneous revolt against their Turkish overlords and drove south into Albania and Epirus. Further north again, the armies of the Emperor and John Sobieski continued their advance through Hungary. By the time winter set in to put an end to the first campaigning season, Venice and her allies had good reason to be proud of their success.

With the coming of the spring, 1685, Morosini sailed against the old Venetian port of Corone – lost to the Turks in 1500 – landing some 9,500 men, including (as well as 3,000 Venetians) German, papal and Tuscan troops and 120 Knights of St John. This time the Ottoman garrison put up a desperate defence; it was not until August that the white flag was raised on the citadel. Then, while the terms of surrender were being discussed, a Turkish cannon opened fire, killing several of the Venetians. Negotiations were broken off immediately; the allied troops burst into the town in fury and gave it over to massacre. A whole series of other fortresses followed; within another two or three months much of the south of the Morea was under allied control, and a Swedish general, Count Otto William von Königsmark, had arrived – hired by the Republic at a salary of 18,000 ducats – to take overall command of the land forces.

Early in 1686, Morosini and Königsmark met on Santa Maura for a council of war. There were four main objectives from which to choose: Chios, Negropont, Crete or the rest of the Morea; and, largely, it seems, on the pressing insistence of Königsmark, the last of these targets was selected. It was not, ultimately, to prove a wise choice; but it certainly gave the attackers no trouble. In the next two summers' campaigning the League forces accepted the submissions of Modone and Navarino, Argos and Nauplia, Lepanto, Patras and Corinth.

It was on the morning of 11 August 1687 that the news of these last three victories was brought to Venice. The whole city went wild with joy. Candia was avenged at last. The Great Council at once suspended its session to enable its members to attend a spontaneous service of thanksgiving in the Basilica, and the Senate ordered a bronze bust of Morosini to be placed in the Armoury of the Council of Ten in the Doges' Palace bearing the inscription:

FRANCISCO MAUROCENO
PELOPONNESIACO ADHUC VIVENTI
SENATUS.[1]

Meanwhile the conquest of the Morea was proceeding apace. Königsmark was now mopping up such pockets of resistance as remained in the interior – notably in the region of Mistra and Sparta. Morosini and his fleet, on the other hand, had sailed around to Attica and had begun to lay siege to Athens.

There now occurred the second of the two great tragedies of history the blame for which must, alas, be laid at Venice's door. The miserable story of the Fourth Crusade has already been told;[2] we now have sadly to record that on Monday, 26 September 1687, at about seven o'clock in the evening, a mortar placed by Morosini on the Mouseion Hill opposite the Acropolis was fired by a German lieutenant at the Parthenon – which, by a further curse of fate, the Turks were using as a powder magazine. He scored a direct hit. The consequent explosion almost completely demolished the *cella* and its frieze, eight columns on the north side and six on the south, with their entablatures.

1. The bust, by Parodi, was later presented to its subject, and remained in the Morosini Palace in S. Stefano (on the east side of the square, overlooking the Rio di S. Maurizio, No. 2802) until the death of the last of the line, Contessa Loredana Morosini Gattenburg, in 1884. It is now back in its original position in the Armoury; a marble copy will be found in the Correr Museum.
2. See Chapter 10.

Nor was this the end of the destruction. After the capture of the city, Morosini – doubtless remembering the carrying off of the four bronze horses from the Hippodrome of Constantinople in 1205 – tried to remove the horses and chariot of Athena that formed part of the west pediment of the temple. In the process the whole group fell to the ground and was smashed to pieces. The determined conqueror had to content himself with lesser souvenirs: the two flanking lions of the four now standing in front of the Arsenal.[1]

It is doubtful that many tears were shed in Venice over the fate of the Parthenon. The Venetians were too busy celebrating. They had forgotten what major victories felt like – their last, Lepanto, had been well over a hundred years before – while a series of actual territorial conquests like those which Morosini was now making was unparalleled since the fifteenth century. More important still, they seemed to point towards a final lifting of that black Ottoman cloud that had overshadowed the Republic for so long, and perhaps even a return to those far-off days of commercial imperialism. No wonder they rejoiced; no wonder that their victorious admiral was acclaimed as the greatest military hero in Venetian history; and no wonder that when Marcantonio Giustinian died in March 1688 Francesco Morosini was elected, unanimously and at the first ballot, as his successor.[2]

His highest ambition realized at last, Morosini had no intention of giving up his command. On 8 July 1688 he led his fleet of some 200 sail out of the Gulf of Athens and headed for his next objective – the island of Negropont. Like Crete, Negropont had first come into Venetian hands as a result of the partition of the Byzantine Empire after the Fourth Crusade, and although Venice had forfeited it to the Turks two centuries before, in 1470, its loss had never ceased to rankle. It was known to be heavily fortified, and the Turkish garrison of 6,000, even if it were to receive no reinforcements, was expected to put up a spirited resistance. But the League forces numbered more than twice that many, and neither the Admiral-Doge nor Count

1. The one on the right comes from the Sacred Way; that on the left, which bears the famous runic inscription (now barely discernible) thought to have been carved by Vikings from the Varangian Guard of the Byzantine Emperors, from the Piraeus. The bronze column in the middle of the square and the great copper doors of the entrance are also memorials to Morosini's victories.

2. Despite the jubilation that attended Morosini's election as Doge, Marcantonio Giustinian had been genuinely loved and was much missed. The Venetian poor worshipped him almost as a saint, and Pope Innocent XI was said never to have let a week go by without exclaiming 'Would to God that the other sovereigns of the earth were like him!' He was buried in the family chapel – the so-called *Cappella dei Profeti* – in S. Francesco della Vigna.

Königsmark had any serious doubts that the island would soon be theirs. They had reckoned, unfortunately, without acts of God. Suddenly their luck changed, and no sooner had the siege begun than an appalling epidemic struck the Christian camp. What it was we do not know: dysentery, or possibly malaria, seems the most likely suggestion. Within a few weeks, the army had lost a third of its men, including Königsmark himself. In mid-August the arrival of a 4,000-strong relief force from Venice encouraged Morosini to continue; but almost immediately he found a mutiny on his hands. The imperial troops from Brunswick-Hanover flatly refused to fight any longer. With disaffection spreading almost as fast as disease, he had no choice but to order a general re-embarkation.

Yet even now he could not reconcile himself to the humiliation of a direct return to Venice. One more victory, however modest, would be enough to redeem his honour and enable his subjects to greet him as a hero after all. The fortress of Malvasia (Monemvasia) in the south-eastern corner of the Peloponnese, one of the few mainland strongholds left to the Turks, would serve the purpose admirably. Alas, the good fortune that had smiled upon the admiral frowned upon the Doge. The castle, set high on its virtually impregnable rock, could be approached only by a narrow path measuring for the most part less than a yard across – useless for a besieging army. Bombardment was the only hope, and Morosini ordered the construction of two gun emplacements; but even before they were completed he himself was struck down by illness. Leaving the command to his Proveditor-General, Girolamo Cornaro, he sailed home in January 1690, sick and disconsolate, to a stirring welcome which he was scarcely able to enjoy and an extended period of convalescence in his villa on the mainland.

Cornaro proved a worthy successor, and a luckier one. He took Malvasia, where the standard of St Mark was hoisted on the battlements for the first time for 150 years; then, hearing that an Ottoman fleet was heading through the archipelago, sailed north again to meet it and scattered it off Mytilene, inflicting considerable damage in the process. Returning once more to the Adriatic, he launched a surprise attack on Valona, seized it and dismantled its defences. He was still there when the fever struck him; a day or two later he was dead. Here was a loss indeed – a loss all the greater in that Domenico Mocenigo, who now assumed the supreme command, soon showed himself to be a broken reed, attempting the recapture of Canea in 1692 and then, on hearing the mere rumour – unfounded – of the arrival of a Turkish relief fleet off the Morea, abandoning the entire enterprise.

With the prospect of the Turkish war, which had begun so magnificently, now grinding to an ignominious halt, the Venetians looked once again to their Doge for active leadership. Morosini, now seventy-four, had never properly recovered his health; none the less, when he was invited to resume command he did not hesitate. The day before he was due to embark, Wednesday, 24 May 1693, he marched in solemn procession to the Basilica, splendidly robed in the gold-embroidered mantle of Captain-General, baton in hand. Many of his subjects, we are told, objected to the baton 'as too manifest a sign of authority in a free and republican city'; even so, it did not prevent them from cheering him to the echo from every window when he emerged after mass to make a ceremonial tour of the Piazza, passing through a number of triumphal arches specially erected for the occasion.

On the following day, escorted as before by his carabiniers and halber-diers, his standard-bearers, military band and trumpeters, the Patriarch and clergy, the Signoria, the Procurators of St Mark, the Papal Nuncio and foreign ambassadors, the Senate and finally his family and friends, he proceeded in state from the Zecca at the corner of the Piazzetta, along the Riva to the furthest extremity of Castello, where the *Bucintoro* waited to carry him across the lagoon, through a dense throng of exuberantly decorated gondolas, first to S. Nicolò on the Lido for a last prayer before departure and thence to his galley. Scarcely was he on board when the anchor was weighed and the ship, with her sails set and the Lion of St Mark at her prow, headed out through the Lido port towards Malvasia, where the main body of the fleet was already gathered.[1]

After so glorious an embarkation, this last campaign of Francesco Morosini proved something of an anti-climax. The Turks had taken advan-tage of the winter and spring to strengthen the defences of both Canea and Negropont. Contrary winds persuaded him against another attempt on the Dardanelles; the Turkish fleet, meanwhile, kept well out of the way. He reinforced the garrison in Corinth and one or two other strong-points in the Morea; chased a few Algerian pirates; finally – in order not to return entirely empty-handed – he occupied Salamis, Hydra and Spetsai before putting in to Nauplia for the winter. But by then it was clear that his exertions had taken their toll. Throughout December he was in constant pain from gallstones, and on 6 January 1694 he died.

1. It seems to have generally escaped the notice of historians that this tremendous departure occurred on Ascension Day, on which the Doge would normally have officiated at the traditional Wedding of the Sea. There seems no reason why this ceremony should not have been included among the rest; curiously, however, the Venetians seem to have missed their opportunity.

He received, as might have been expected, a tremendous funeral: first at Nauplia, where his heart and viscera were consigned to the Venetian church of S. Antonio, and later in Venice at SS. Giovanni e Paolo, whence the body was taken to S. Stefano for burial. Here a carved ledger-slab marks its final resting-place; but Morosini's greatest memorial is not there but in the Doges' Palace itself where, at the far end of the *Sala dello Scrutinio*, there rises a huge marble triumphal arch, reaching almost to the roof and adorned with six symbolic paintings by Gregorio Lazzarini. Neither architecturally nor artistically is it particularly distinguished,[1] and it looks moreover curiously out of place in its unexpected setting; but few memorials could better illustrate the respect in which Venice held the last of her great warrior-doges, or the gratitude which she felt to him for having restored, at least for a few years, some of her old self-confidence.

The unenviable task of following Francesco Morosini on the ducal throne fell to one Silvestro Valier, son of that Bertucci Valier who had briefly occupied it forty-odd years before. From the moment of his election it was made clear that he was not expected to assume his predecessor's military command; many Venetians of sternly republican sentiments, however great their personal admiration for Morosini, had been troubled by what they considered the potentially dangerous concentration of civil and military power in one man and were anxious lest it should start a precedent. In the new Doge's *promissione* it was accordingly laid down that the separate election of a Captain-General could in future be suspended only with the consent of four of the six ducal Councillors or two of the three heads of the *Quarantia*; even then it must be approved by the Senate and two thirds of the Great Council, for which the quorum would be not less than 800. These precautions were to prove more than adequate; never again in the Republic's history was a Doge to go to war.

Meanwhile the supreme command was entrusted to Antonio Zen, who sailed out the following summer and on 7 September 1694 landed some 9,000 men on the island of Chios. The island already boasted a large Christian population, both Catholic and Orthodox; each community had its own bishop, both of whom hastened to greet the Venetians and to assure them of their support against the Turkish garrison, which consisted of only 2,000 soldiers, concentrated in the citadel above the town. The bombard-

---

1. Far more interesting are the paintings in the Morosini rooms of the Correr Museum (Nos. XIX–XXIV), which contain several fascinating items of Morosiniana, including the embalmed body of his cat, of which he is said to have been inordinately fond.

ment began at once; the harbour, including three Turkish vessels that chanced to be lying at anchor, was captured without a fight and the garrison surrendered on the 15th in return for a guarantee of safe conduct to the mainland.

So far all had gone well; and when reports now reached Chios of the approach of a Turkish fleet of some fifty sail, Venetian spirits rose higher still. For years now the Turks had done their utmost to avoid naval engagements, and Zen's captains had little admiration for their seamanship or indeed their courage. Unfortunately, just as the Captain-General was about to emerge from the narrow straits that separate Chios from the mainland and to make for the open sea, the wind dropped; in the flat calm that followed, no confrontation was possible; and when on the 20th a very faint breeze sprang up, it favoured the Turks, who, seeing their danger, quickly made for home and reached the harbour of Smyrna before the Venetians could catch up with them. Zen, still ready to fight, anchored in the roadstead outside the harbour; but no sooner had he done so than he was visited on board his flagship by the local consuls representing the three European powers outside the League – England, France and the Netherlands – who implored him not to risk Christian lives and property in the city by any unprovoked attack, backing up their entreaties, we are told, with 'a considerable sum of money'. He agreed, probably as much because of his own shortage of supplies as for any other reason, and returned to Chios.[1]

But the great sea battle that most of the Venetian captains so eagerly awaited was not to be much longer delayed. The Sultan, furious at the loss of one of his most valuable off-shore islands, had given orders for its immediate recapture at all costs, and early in February 1695 a new Ottoman fleet was signalled, consisting of twenty of their heaviest capital ships – *sultanas*, as they were called – supported by twenty-four galleys and a few galleots. Antonio Zen once again sailed out to meet it with a roughly comparable fleet, which included a sizeable squadron from the Knights of Malta, and at about ten o'clock on the morning of the 9th, battle was finally joined off the Spalmatori islands at the north end of the straits. It was long and violent, marked by several deeds of outstanding courage among the Venetians (and probably among the Turks too, though they are not recor-

---

1. Several historians, among them Daru and Romanin, follow the contemporary Venetian historian, Pietro Garzoni, who was to be one of Zen's chief accusers, in repeating a story to the effect that at one moment during the calm the Venetians had the Turkish ships in their power but that the Captain-General refused to allow his captains to attack them. This seems on the face of it improbable, and the reports are so conflicting that the truth can never be known. For the whole Chios episode the most accurate, detailed and thoughtful account is that of Philip Argenti, *The Occupation of Chios by the Venetians, 1694* (London, 1935).

ded in the Venetian reports); but when the two fleets separated at nightfall, despite heavy casualties on both sides – for the Venetians, 465 dead and 603 wounded – the result was inconclusive.

This proved, however, to be only the first phase. The fleets anchored just out of range from each other's guns and waited for ten full days, watching. Then, on 19 February, with a strong north wind behind them, the Turks once again bore down upon their adversaries. As they fought, the wind rose to gale force; the sea grew rougher, until close manoeuvring became impossible. The Venetians fought desperately to get to windward, but gradually they were forced down the narrow channel to the harbour walls. In such weather, entry into port, at least for the heavy galleasses, was impossible; they could only lie to in the roadstead, where they were raked again and again by the pursuing Turks. It was a disaster; the Venetian losses were immense, the Turkish comparatively slight. The Captain-General called a council of war, but the outcome seems to have been a virtually foregone conclusion. There were no longer enough men available for the adequate manning of the fortress; the defences were in deplorable condition; the treasury was empty and supplies were running low. Long before any help could be expected, the Turks were bound to attack again; if they did, the consequences could not be anything but catastrophic. Only the commander of the land forces, Baron von Steinau, believed that Chios could still be held, but he was over-ruled. By this time, according to a letter written at the time, almost certainly by one of those present,[1] 'the Captain-General was weeping like a child; his spirit was quite gone, and he could only repeat the words "Do as you like: it is in your hands!" '

So it was that the island of Chios was won and, within less than six months, lost again. On the night of 20 February all the war material that could be carried away was loaded on to the ships, the defences destroyed or dismantled – wherever, at least, it was worth while doing so. Then, on the morning of the 21st, the fleet sailed out of the harbour; with it, to escape the revenge of the Turks, went most of the leading Catholic families of the island, who were granted new estates in the Morea to compensate them for what they had left behind. Even on her departure, Venice's ill fortune went with her. Scarcely was the last ship round the mole when one of Zen's most important remaining vessels, the *Abbondanza Ricchezza*, laden with arms and ammunition, struck a hidden rock. All endeavours to free her failed, and she finally had to be abandoned, with most of her cargo still intact on board.

1. Quoted by P. Argenti, op. cit.

To the Venetians, who has so recently been celebrating the capture of Chios, the news of its loss was a matter less for sorrow than for anger. There was no lack of ships' captains to testify to the shortcomings of the Captain-General – his indecision, his timidity, his improvidence, his lack of initiative or any qualities of leadership. The Senate demanded an immediate inquiry, pending which the unfortunate Zen, together with his two proveditors and several other senior officers, were brought back to Venice in chains. He himself died in prison on 6 July 1697 while the inquiry was still in progress, though not before he had defended himself with a long written apologia; this was subsequently published by the Venetian government, a gesture which was considered by informed opinion to be tantamount to an acquittal; but no formal results of the inquiry were ever made known.

By this time, fortunately for Venetian morale, Zen's successor, Alessandro Molin – seconded on land by the admirable Baron von Steinau – had scored several notable successes. A Turkish landing in the Argolid was repulsed, and another sea battle off Chios did much to wipe out the humiliation of the previous year. This was followed by a further naval victory for Venice near Andros in 1697 and yet another in September 1698 at the entry of the Dardanelles by which Venice regained effective, if temporary, control of the Aegean; but the loss of Chios still rankled, and was to continue to do so for many years to come.

While Venice had thus been fighting the League's battles in the Mediterranean, her allies to the north had been anything but idle. In 1686 Duke Charles of Lorraine had reconquered Buda, which thus returned to the Empire after 145 years of Turkish rule, and in 1688 the fall of Belgrade had restored much of Bosnia, Serbia and Walachia to Christian control. This all-important fortress had been recaptured in 1690, but its loss was to some extent mitigated by the conquest of Transylvania in the following year. The death of John Sobieski in 1696 had been a grievous blow; the League had, however, received a valuable new adherent in the person of Peter the Great of Russia – at whose request, in the same year, the Venetians had sent a team of thirteen shipwrights to Moscow. Finally, in 1697, Prince Eugene of Savoy had practically annihilated the Ottoman army at Zenta, leaving some 20,000 Turkish dead on the battlefield.

The Turks were not beaten; but they were undeniably battered, and seemed likely to welcome the opportunity for a negotiated peace. The Emperor Leopold for his part was anxious that they should, for he knew that a fresh crisis was approaching – not on his eastern border this time but in the west, where the half-mad and childless King Charles II of Spain obviously had not long to live. There were two principal contenders for his throne – the Emperor himself and Louis XIV of France, both grandsons of Philip III and sons-in-law of Philip IV; and Leopold understandably wished to have his hands free to deal with the struggle ahead. England and Holland, horrified at the prospect of seeing France and Spain united under Louis, offered their mediation with the Sultan; Poland and Venice, on the assumption that they would retain the territories they had conquered, were only too pleased to lay down their arms after fifteen years of war, while Peter the Great had more than enough to do to drag his country out of the Middle Ages. The arrangements were quickly made, and on 13 November 1698 the various powers concerned met at Karlowitz in Hungary (now the Yugoslav town of Sremski Karlovci).

The negotiations did not run as smoothly as had been expected, the representatives of the Sultan pointing out that their master, not having surrendered, saw no reason why he should be required to abandon all the territories now in Christian hands. In particular he had in mind certain of his Mediterranean possessions. Venice could have the Morea: he would make no difficulty about that. She could also retain Santa Maura on one side and Aegina on the other, and a number of fortresses on the Dalmatian coast. He himself, however, was determined to keep Athens, Attica and all Greek territory north of the Gulf of Corinth. The Venetian representative, Carlo Ruzzini, objected vehemently; but he received little support. The Emperor, once he had been assured of Hungary and Transylvania, was anxious to get home as quickly as possible and let it be known to the Venetians that if they insisted on making difficulties, he would have no hesitation in concluding a separate peace. For a time the Republic continued to argue, and when the treaty was signed on 26 January 1699, she was not among the signatories. But at last wisdom triumphed over pride, and on 7 February Doge Valier appended his seal.

It was as well that he did so, for the Treaty of Karlowitz is the one diplomatic instrument above all others that marks the decline of Ottoman power; and Venice, which had directly confronted that power for longer than any other Christian state, had more right than any to be a party to it. On the other hand, her forced renunciation of an important part of her conquests was not just a blow to her self-respect; it made it considerably more difficult for her adequately to defend that part which remained. The Turks, it was true, had undertaken to demolish the fortifications of Lepanto and Preveza; but there was nothing to prevent them invading the Morea from Attica, or indeed anywhere along the northern shore of the Gulf of Corinth – a point which they were to prove all too soon.

Less than a year later, on the morning of Saturday, 7 July 1700, Doge Silvestro Valier died of a sudden apoplexy following an argument with his wife; and it was perhaps a feeling of partial responsibility for his death that led her to commission from the architect Andrea Tirali the immense baroque tomb which occupies the entire fourth bay on the south side of SS. Giovanni e Paolo and in which he, she and his father, Doge Bertucci, are now enshrined. It is somehow fitting that this, the last and perhaps the most sumptuous of the great ducal tombs in all Venice, should have been reserved for the last doge of the seventeenth century; for with Silvestro Valier's successor, Alvise Mocenigo II, there begins a new age, of elegance and restraint rather than grandiloquence and pomposity – a new age to match the opening of the new century, before whose close the Republic itself was to pass into history.

44

Passarowitz and Peace

[1700–1718]

Il n'y a plus de Pyrénées!

Louis XIV, on hearing of his grandson's
inheritance of the Spanish crown

The year 1700 saw the deaths of two reigning princes of Europe. That of
the immensely able and intelligent Doge Silvestro Valier passed virtually
unnoticed outside Italy; that of the half-wit Charles II of Spain, on the other
hand, flung the whole continent into chaos. Charles had first bequeathed
his kingdom to 'the illustrious House of Austria'; then, a month before his
death, he had suddenly changed his will, leaving it instead to Philip of
Anjou, grandson of Louis XIV. Louis lost no time in packing the young
claimant off to Madrid to assume his throne without delay; he was right to
do so, for he was well aware that the Emperor Leopold would not accept
this new dispensation without protest. What he could not have known was
how long and how desperate the ensuing war would be, and what a price
he would have to pay for his grandson's throne.

The Emperor had two valuable allies – England and the Netherlands,
where memories of Spanish oppression were still fresh. France for the
moment had none; so King Louis hastily sent one of his most trusted
advisers, Cardinal César d'Estrées, to Venice. Already, the Cardinal pointed out, imperial troops were marching through the Tyrol into Italy, bent
on seizing the Milanese from Spain. If they were allowed to continue
unchecked, all North Italy would be overrun, the territory of the Republic
included. The only solution was an immediate Franco-Spanish-Venetian
league. Venice could then block the passage of the Emperor, while France
and Spain in return would protect Venetian interests wherever they were
threatened, in the east – Dalmatia, Friuli or the archipelago – or in the west,
where 30,000 men were already drawn up in the Dauphiné, ready to march.
Meanwhile an ambassador from Leopold, Count Lamberg, was describing
in similarly horrific terms the consequences of allowing the French and
Spanish crowns to be united in all but name, and painting an equally rosy
picture of the blessings that could not but ensue from an imperial alliance.

In the Senate, the Council of Ten, the Collegio, even in the Great Council, the Republic's proper line of action at so critical a moment was long and hotly debated. The final consensus of opinion was that neither of the two giants who were so assiduously cultivating her friendship could be trusted an inch.[1] A plague, Venice decided, on both their houses: she would opt for a position of armed neutrality. And so she did – somehow managing to maintain it, in the face of immense pressure from both sides, throughout the war which now broke out in all its fury. Whether she was right to do so is another of those questions that still divide historians today. The disadvantages were plain enough. She could not prevent the belligerents entering her mainland dominions or her home waters; indeed, for the next few years the whole of the Venetian mainland was one huge battlefield. Through the Vicentino, the Veronese and the Bresciano, along the Adige, the Adda and the Mincio, the imperial armies of Prince Eugene of Savoy and the French forces under the Marshal de Catinat or, later, the Dukes of Villeroi[2] and Vendôme marched and countermarched. In vain Venice addressed protests, admonitions and claims for compensation to Paris and Vienna, while herself facing continuous accusations from each side that she was favouring the other. In vain she sought to prevent the Austrians from shipping war material across from Trieste and other imperial ports to the Po delta; or the French from sailing in strength up the Gulf, to attack and destroy the offending vessels at Chioggia and Malamocco and the gates of the lagoon itself; or the Anglo-Dutch fleet from presuming to police those waters which she still claimed as her own but was plainly unable to control.

All these trials and humiliations were the inevitable consequences of the policy that Venice had freely chosen for herself; and several commentators, Venetian and foreign, have suggested that she would have done better to take a more positive line from the outset: not, perhaps, to declare categorically for one side or the other, for in the event of an out-and-out victory of either of the two protagonists she could only have been the loser; but rather to have followed the example of Duke Victor Amadeus of Savoy,

---

1. It was said of Leopold that throughout his life he invariably referred to Verona as '*my* Verona', although it had been Venetian for 300 years.

2. Villeroi, who lost through sheer incompetence virtually every battle he ever fought, did not last long in Italy, where he soon became a universal laughing-stock. In 1702 he was surprised by an imperial army in Cremona and taken prisoner, though his captors failed to hold the town; for the rest of the war French soldiers on the march would sing:

> *Parsembleu! la nouvelle est bonne*
> *Et notre bonheur sans égal:*
> *Nous avons conservé Crémone*
> *Et perdu notre général.*

who fought for himself, supporting first the French – to avoid expulsion – and subsequently the Empire, changing sides when he felt like it and ending the war with his dominions actually increased. The French Napoleonic historian Daru goes even further, maintaining that the Republic 'should have taken a more dominant attitude, inspiring all the princes of Italy with a noble resolution, placing itself at their head in such a way as to prevent the ravaging of that beautiful land by foreign intruders.' But this, surely, is to misread the character of the time. Most of the peninsula was under foreign occupation. The Risorgimento, or anything remotely like it, was still far away. Even had it not been, Venice was the last quarter from which the necessary impetus would have come. She had never felt herself to be altogether a part of Italy. Although her feeling of *Italianità* had naturally been strengthened by the acquisition of an empire on *terra firma*, it was still by no means fully consolidated. (Perhaps, indeed, it never would be.) And in any case, the sort of man required to focus Italian ambitions – colourful, magnetic, fiery, a born orator and leader – was hardly likely to spring from the cautious and committee-ridden bosom of the Most Serene Republic.

As it happened, Venice was to emerge from the War of the Spanish Succession remarkably unscathed. A series of French defeats, together with a shift of the epicentre of the war towards the North, where Marlborough was rapidly creating his own legend, meant that after the first four or five years the Veneto was left in comparative peace. Venice was consequently able in March 1709 – in a way that no other European state could have considered at such a time – to give a characteristically lavish welcome to King Frederick IV of Denmark, despite being in the grip of the most savage winter in her history, when the whole lagoon froze over and people walked to Mestre and Fusina over the ice.

The excitement – or perhaps the winter – seems to have been too much for the Doge, who died two months later.[1] One of his last official acts was to inform the French Ambassador that the Republic would be happy to accept King Louis's invitation to mediate between France and her enemies, and one of the first decisions of his successor, Giovanni Corner II, was to send a shrewd and experienced diplomatist, Sebastiano Foscarini, to the Hague, where he did his best to negotiate a peace. But the Coalition, with

---

1. Alvise Mocenigo's chief memorial is the façade of S. Stae, a magnificent baroque extravaganza by the architect Domenico Rossi (and a whole bevy of exuberant sculptors), made possible by the Doge's bequest of 20,000 ducats for that specific purpose. He himself lies beneath a large ledger-slab in the middle of the floor bearing no precise identification: only the ducal *corno* and a Latin inscription recording that 'name and ashes have been buried together'.

a succession of splendid victories behind it, offered terms so humiliating that Louis rejected them out of hand and resolved to continue the struggle; only after another three years – years which saw the bitterest fighting of the entire war and, at Malplaquet, the bloodiest battle – did the exhausted combatants, together with Venice and Savoy, finally assemble at Utrecht, where the map of Europe was redrawn. The territory of Venice, as a neutral power, was preserved intact, without gains or losses; but her ambassador, Carlo Ruzzini, was much impressed by the honours accorded him, not least by the other Italian powers – who, though they had no seat at the conference table, had all sent observers and, he proudly reported, unanimously recognized Venice as *la principale potenza e protettrice d'Italia* – 'the principal power and protectress of Italy'.

When that whole series of international agreements collectively known as the Treaty of Utrecht was signed during the first four months of 1713, Venice had been in possession of the Morea for just over a quarter of a century. Her new experiment in empire had not been a success. The years of Turkish occupation that had preceded the reconquest had reduced a once prosperous land to a place of poverty and desolation; all too soon the Venetians had realized that the task of administration would be not only expensive but largely thankless. The downtrodden local populations, their patriotism nurtured and sanctified as always by the Orthodox clergy, dreamed of a nationhood of their own and saw little advantage in having their infidel overlords replaced by Christian schismatics who showed no greater sympathy with their aspirations. The establishment of Latin bishoprics aroused still further resentment. Finally, there was the question of defence. In former days, when the Venetian presence was confined to a few important commercial colonies and garrison towns, this presented few problems; but how could nearly a thousand miles of serrated coastline be made safe from invaders? Even such new defences as were deemed indispensable, like the lowering fortress of Acrocorinth – still today one of the most impressive examples of Venetian military architecture – served only to antagonize still further the local inhabitants, by whose taxes it was paid for and by whose conscript labour it was built. No wonder that when Turkish troops appeared once again on the soil of the Peloponnese, they were welcomed as liberators.

The fact remained that, to every Venetian, the Morea stood as a monument to the Republic's last great burst of military glory, and there was consternation on the Rialto when, in December 1714, the Ottoman Grand Vizir summoned the Venetian *bailo* at Constantinople, Andrea Memmo, to inform him that, in consequence of certain recent incidents in Montenegro and the interception of a Turkish ship in the Adriatic, his master had decided to declare war. The transparency of the excuse served only to confirm suspicions that the real object of the Sultan – or, more accurately, of the Grand Vizir himself, whose belligerent disposition appeared in marked contrast to that of the peace-loving Ahmed III – was to regain the Morea. Once again Venice appealed to the states of Europe for assistance; once again she obtained the usual dusty answer, apart from the offer of a galley or two from the Pope and the Knights of Malta.

The Vizir, Damad Ali, had planned a combined operation in which a land force would march down through Thessaly while a fleet would sail simultaneously south-west through the Aegean; and in the course of the summer of 1715 both prongs of the attack scored success after success. By the time the fleet reached its destination it had already forced the surrender of Tinos – whose craven commander, Bernardo Balbi, was condemned to life imprisonment when he returned to Venice – and of Aegina, while the army captured Corinth after a five-day siege. Nauplia followed; then Modone and Corone; then Malvasia; then the island of Cythera. Meanwhile the Turks in Crete, encouraged by reports of their compatriots' success, had attacked and seized the last remaining Venetian outposts at Suda and Spinalunga,[1] whose inhabitants, relying as they did on Turkish treaty obligations for their survival, had no alternative to surrender. By the end of 1715, with Crete and the Morea both lost and all the great victories of Francesco Morosini set at naught after a few disastrous months, the Turks were once again at the gates of the Adriatic. For Venice, only one bulwark remained: Corfu.

The Turkish army which, early in 1716, the Grand Vizir flung against the citadel of Corfu consisted of 30,000 infantry and some 3,000 horse. For the Venetians, estimates differ: they were certainly outnumbered. But in siege warfare comparative strengths are less important; what counts is the sophistication of offensive and defensive techniques. And here Venice could count on the knowledge and skill of one of the leading soldiers of his day, Marshal Matthias Johann von der Schulenburg. He had fought under Marlborough at Oudenarde and Malplaquet, then after the peace had sought service with the Republic. He had spent much of the winter improving the fortifications of Corfu, and though he was unable to prevent the Turkish army from disembarking, he was now able to confront it with a defensive system far superior to anything it had previously encountered.

1. The Grabousa islands had been relinquished by Venice in 1692.

All through the heat of the summer the siege continued. Early in August, however, there arrived reports that gave new encouragement to the defenders and must have struck gloom into Turkish hearts. Venice had concluded an alliance with the Empire; the latter had entered the war. The almost legendary Prince Eugene was once again on the march. He had routed a Turkish army, appropriately enough at Karlowitz – the very town where, eighteen years before, the Turks had signed that treaty which they had now so shamefully broken – and shortly afterwards had gained a still more crushing victory at Peterwardein, where he had killed 20,000 of the enemy and seized 200 of their guns at the expense of fewer than 3,000 of his own men.

This unexpected necessity of fighting on two fronts at once probably suggested to the Turkish commander that if he could not take Corfu quickly he would be unlikely to take it at all. On the night of 18 August he ordered a general assault, to the accompaniment, as always, of an ear-splitting din of drums, trumpets, rifle and cannon fire and hideous shrieks and war-cries – psychological warfare of a primitive but by no means ineffectual kind. Schulenburg and his Proveditor-General Antonio Loredan were instantly at their posts, summoning every able-bodied Corfiot – women and children, the old and infirm, priests and monks alike – to the defences. After six hours the fighting was still desperate, with neither side gaining an obvious advantage; and Schulenburg decided to stake all on a sudden sortie. At the head of 800 picked men, he slipped out of a small postern and fell on the Turkish flank from the rear. The success was immediate – and decisive. The Turks were taken utterly by surprise and fled, leaving rifles and ammunition behind them, while their colleagues along other sections of the wall, bewildered and mystified, saw that the assault had failed and also retired, though in better order. The next night, as if to consolidate the Venetian triumph, a storm broke – a storm of such violence and fury that within hours the Turkish camp was reduced to a quagmire, the trenches turned to canals, the tents torn to ribbons or, their guy-ropes snapped like thread, lifted bodily into the air and carried off by the gale. In the roadstead, many of the Turkish ships, similarly driven from their moorings, crashed into each other, splintering like matchwood.

When dawn broke and the full extent of the damage was revealed, there were few indeed of the erstwhile besiegers who wished to remain another moment on an island where the very gods seemed to be against them; and indeed within a matter of days orders reached the Turkish camp to return at once. Corfu was saved; Schulenburg was awarded a jewelled sword, a life pension of 5,000 ducats, and the honour of a statue erected in his lifetime in the old fortress;[1] and the Turks withdrew, never again to seek to enlarge their empire at the expense of Christian Europe.

It had been more than the raising of a siege; it had been a victory, and its effect on Venetian morale was enormous. That winter the *Arsenalotti* worked night and day, and early the following spring a new fleet of twenty-seven sail set out from Zante for the Dardanelles under the command of a brilliant young admiral, Ludovico Flangini. On 12 June 1717 it met the Turks head-on, and after a battle that lasted several days it won a splendid victory, marred only by the death of Flangini, who, mortally wounded by an arrow, insisted on being carried up on to his quarterdeck to watch, through glazing eyes, the last stages of the conflict. A month later, off Cape Matapan, the Ottoman fleet was again beaten and put to flight, this time by Andrea Pisani, who, turning northward, was able to recapture both Preveza and Vonitsa before the coming of winter. In Dalmatia, Alvise Mocenigo was reporting similar victories. By then, too, Prince Eugene had reoccupied the all-important river fortress of Belgrade and the Turks were retreating on all fronts.

Had the war continued another season and the Venetians managed to sustain their momentum, the Morea might well have been theirs once more – though whether this would have been in their long-term interest is open to doubt. But the Turks, predictably enough, decided to sue for peace; and it was now that Venice was to discover how ill-advised she had been to conclude her Austrian alliance. The Empire, faced with new threats from Spain, was anxious to reach a quick settlement and paid little heed to Venice's territorial claims on the entirely spurious grounds that the victory of Corfu and the subsequent upsurge of Venetian fortunes were the direct results of Prince Eugene's victory at Peterwardein. When, therefore, the parties met in May 1718 at Passarowitz – together with representatives of England and Holland as mediators – the Venetian envoy, Carlo Ruzzini, despite his diplomatic experience at Karlowitz and Utrecht, found that he could make little impression on his colleagues. For six hours he pleaded, calling for the restitution to Venice of Suda and Spinalunga, of Tinos, Cythera and the Morea, or, in default of this last, an extension of Venetian territory in Albania as far south as Scutari and Dulcigno, a pirate stronghold which she was eager to eliminate. Unfortunately, however, his speech coincided with the arrival of a report that 18,000 Spanish troops had just

---

1. It was transferred during the British occupation of the island to its present position on the Esplanade. Another, more modest, monument by Morlaiter will be found in the courtyard of the Arsenal in Venice.

landed on the Austrian-held island of Sardinia, and he was overruled. Venice had to be content with Cythera, Butrinto, Preveza and Vonitsa, together with a few additional frontier fortresses in Dalmatia – where, however, she was obliged to allow free Turkish communications with Ragusa. It was a meagre reward indeed for the effort and expense of the past four years, for the heroism of Schulenburg, Flangini and the rest.

At Passarowitz the frontiers of the Venetian Empire, such as it was, were drawn for the last time. There would be no more gains, or losses, or exchanges. It may therefore be a good moment to outline those frontiers here. Apart from the historic city and the towns and islands of the lagoon, the Empire included, on *terra firma*, the provinces of Bergamo, Brescia, Cremona, Verona, Vicenza, the Polesine of Rovigo and the March of Treviso, including Feltre, Belluno and Cadore. Around the Gulf, it embraced Friuli, then Istria and Dalmatia with its dependent islands, then Northern Albania, including Cattaro (Kotor), Butrinto, Parga, Preveza and Vonitsa; then the Ionian islands of Corfu, Paxos and Antipaxos, Santa Maura (Leucas), Cephalonia, Ithaca, Zante and the Strophades; and finally, south of the Morea, the island of Cythera. That was all.

The treaty was signed on 21 July 1718. Two months later to the day, in another of those terrifying summer storms, a bolt of lightning struck the powder magazine in the old fortress of Corfu. The explosion ignited three other smaller ammunition stores, and the citadel was virtually destroyed. The Governor's Palace in particular was reduced to rubble, killing the Captain-General and several of his staff. Nature, in the space of a split second, had achieved more than the combined Turkish forces in several months; the futility of the recent war was more than ever underlined. And yet, amid all the lamentations when the news reached Venice, there could also be heard the still, small voice of the optimist: what if that other great tempest of two years before had had the same result? Perhaps, despite outward appearances, the Almighty was on the side of Venice after all.

Before long, moreover, the optimist had been joined by another – the political realist, who saw that the age of imperial greatness was past; that Morosini's conquests had given Venice nothing but trouble and that she was better off without them. The Treaty of Passarowitz, inglorious as it may have appeared, settled her differences with the Turks and proclaimed eternal friendship with Habsburg Austria, the only other power which might have posed a serious political threat. The result was peace – peace which was to last the best part of a century, until the coming of Napoleon brought the Republic itself to an end.

45

The Eighteenth Century

[1718–1789]

As for Venice and its people, merely born to bloom and drop,
Here on earth they bore their fruitage, mirth and folly were the crop:
What of soul was left, I wonder, when the kissing had to stop?

Browning, A Toccata of Galuppi's

'*Ici finit l'histoire de Venise*', wrote Count Paul Daru, when he reached this point in his own monumental work on the subject, completed in 1821; and, despite the three massive volumes still to come, he was not very far wrong.

> She is reduced [he continued] to a passive existence. She has no more wars to sustain, peaces to conclude, or desires to express. A mere spectator of events, in her determination to take no part in events, she pretends to take no interest in them ... Isolated amid her fellow-nations, imperturbable in her indifference, blind to her own interests, insensible to insults, she sacrifices all to the single object of giving no offence to other states, and to preserve a lasting peace.

Daru, an old companion-in-arms of Napoleon who had distinguished himself in the retreat from Moscow before becoming a pillar of the Académie Française, makes little effort to conceal his disgust at so craven a policy. Nowadays, one suspects, most of us would be inclined to take a more favourable view; and readers of this book finding no fewer than seventy years covered in a single chapter, will doubtless be swift to rejoice. Yet there is always something sad in the spectacle of departed greatness, and entrancing as we may find all the paintings of the *vedutisti* and the descriptions that have come down to us of Venice in the *settecento*, it is impossible to close our eyes to the fact that a city that was once the unchallenged mistress of the Mediterranean – to say nothing of 'a quarter and half a quarter of the Roman Empire' – could now no longer control the approaches to her own lagoon; or that a people famous for centuries as the most skilful seamen, the shrewdest and most courageous merchant adventurers of their time, were now better known for their prowess as cheapskates and intriguers, gamblers and pimps.

The political history of the Most Serene Republic after the Peace of

Passarowitz can consequently be told in a very few pages. Doges come and go; but the salient features of their reigns tend to be less often things that they did than things that they managed not to do – the wars they avoided, the alliances they escaped, the responsibilities they ignored. The historian is thus constrained, in sheer self-defence, to alter his technique: to abandon, at least in part, the strictly chronological approach in favour of something more episodic, and to try to analyse Venice's political and moral decline by examining its symptoms rather than by recording any day-to-day progress of events. He also finds himself able, more than in any previous chapters, to confine his attention to the domestic front, since for Venice in the eighteenth century, just as for Switzerland throughout the ages, foreign affairs scarcely seem to exist. On the other hand, he can afford to stray a little more widely into fields other than the strictly political; and, as he does so, he comes upon a curious and unexpected phenomenon – that for the greater part of the century, so generally castigated as one of demoralization and decay on all fronts, Venice was enjoying a period of unusual commercial prosperity and economic growth.

Suddenly, he pulls himself up short. Perhaps, after all, he has been over-hasty in his judgement. How important is it to be a Great Power of Europe, or even a capital of Empire? Is the pursuit of pleasure, which creates much that is beautiful and harms nobody, really more reprehensible than the pursuit of wealth, territory or military glory, which kills thousands and devastates and destroys wholesale? Eighty years of peace is, in itself, no small tribute to wise government and successful diplomacy. It was a period, moreover, when the average citizen seems to have been no less happy or contented than in former times; when, if the economy was not invariably booming, there were at least no wars to pay for; when the arts flourished – painting in particular having risen up from its *seicento* nadir to celebrate once again the age-old Venetian love of colour and light – and a city of some 160,000 inhabitants could boast no fewer than seven full-time opera houses, to say nothing of the theatres, where the *commedia dell'arte* was slowly giving place to the more sophisticated comedies of Venice's best-loved writer, Carlo Goldoni. Throughout the century hundreds – perhaps thousands – of the most cultivated and civilized men and women of Europe poured into the city every year; they cannot all have been wrong.

On Ascension Day, Thursday, 3 May 1722, just as Doge Giovanni Corner was stepping aboard the *Bucintoro* for the annual Marriage of the Sea, he stumbled and the *corno* slipped from his head. The incident was made light of by those around him, but he himself was much distressed; it was, he said, a sign from heaven. He died on 12 August, and was buried in his family chapel in S. Nicolò da Tolentino; and on the 24th he was succeeded, confusingly enough, by yet another Alvise Mocenigo, the third of that name to rise to the supreme dignity.[1] Mocenigo had distinguished himself both as a soldier in Dalmatia and as a diplomat, in which capacity he had spent two years in those long, involved discussions on infinitesimal points of interpretation which were part and parcel of any peace treaty with the Turks. On his accession to the Dogeship he made the city a charming present – the two porphyry lions that give their name to the Piazzetta dei Leoncini just to the north of the Basilica, and have afforded endless pleasure to the children of Venice for over 250 years.

By now Venice had acquired that aspect familiar to us through the paintings of the great *vedutisti* – Antonio Canal, called Canaletto, his successor Francesco Guardi, his nephew Bernardo Bellotto and their followers – and the masters of *genre* like Pietro Longhi and Domenico Tiepolo. It was the age of the Grand Tour – the age, indeed, when tourism might be said to have been invented, when not only young English noblemen but the whole aristocracy of Europe was, at some time or another, to be seen in the loveliest and most magical of all cities. It was the age, too, of the carnival – still the most protracted and abandoned in Europe, the mandatory masks providing all the anonymity that could be desired. The Council of Ten, the Inquisitors of State and the secret police were no longer feared as they had been a century before. To give but one example, in 1718 the Inquisitors employed a staff of only three; half a century later that figure had been reduced to one. Meanwhile, the gambling was the most smoothly organized, the stakes the highest anywhere; the courtesans were the loveliest and the most elegant, catering for every taste, able to satisfy the most fastidious and exacting of clients. For those visitors of more intellectual proclivities, there were books, pictures and sculptures to be bought, churches and palaces to be wondered at, and the music and opera for which Venice was famous throughout the civilized world.

By the early eighteenth century the centre of Venetian musical life had moved from St Mark's, where both Giovanni Gabrieli and Claudio Monteverdi had been organists a hundred years before, to four orphanages for female foundlings – the Pietà, the Incurabili, the Mendicanti and the Os-

---

1. Readers may derive a little *Schadenfreude* from the reflection that Doge Alvise Mocenigo II was the youngest of nine brothers, *all* of whom were given the Christian name of Alvise. Until his elevation he was therefore known as Alvise IX. His nephew, Doge Alvise III, was the fourth of six sons of his elder brother Alvise IV, and – since these six sons were also Alvises to a man – had also previously been known as Alvise IV. We must be grateful that Venetian genealogists do not panic easily.

pedaletto. At the first of these, from 1703 until shortly before his death in 1741, the *maestro di cappella* was Antonio Vivaldi.[1] At the second, orchestra and choir were under the direction of Baldassare Galuppi – immortalized by Browning even if his own music is nowadays largely forgotten.[2] But not all of the foremost Venetian musicians of the age were even full-time professionals. Tommaso Albinoni was a rich paper-merchant of the city; Benedetto Marcello was a lawyer, a member of the *Quarantia* and a one-time proveditor in Pola.

In all branches of the arts except music, the foremost collector and connoisseur was an Englishman, Joseph Smith. He had settled in Venice in 1700, and remained one of its most distinguished foreign residents until his death, at the age of eighty-eight, seventy years later. For the last thirty of those years he lived in the palace on the corner of the Grand Canal and the Rio dei Santi Apostoli which he had had specially redesigned and rebuilt for him by the architect Antonio Visentini;[3] this rapidly became a treasure-house, filled to overflowing with Smith's ever-increasing collections of paintings and sculptures, coins and medals, drawings and cameos, books and prints. Apart from these personal collections, there were always additional works by his principal protégés – Antonio Canaletto, the brothers Marco and Sebastiano Ricci, Francesco Zuccarelli and that superb portraitist in pastel, Rosalba Carriera – for all of whom he acted as chief agent and go-between with their patrons among the English nobility. Of these by far the most important was Canaletto, whom Smith probably first met through Visentini in the early 1720s. Every rich English visitor longed for at least one picture of the city to remind him of one of the most remarkable experiences of his lifetime; no other painter was so well able to provide what he wanted; and Smith soon made himself indispensable to the artist and his patrons alike. It is largely thanks to him that virtually all the master's best work is in England – Venice possesses scarcely a single canvas – and that Canaletto's ten-year stay in London should have been so conspicuously successful. No wonder that, when he himself briefly took up the art of engraving, he should have dedicated his only published collection of prints to Joseph Smith.

But we are indebted to Consul Smith – he was appointed British Consul

---

1. Such was its reputation that a plaque was placed in the south outer wall of the church, threatening 'fulmination', excommunication and other dire penalties on any parents who attempted to pass off their legitimate offspring as orphans to gain them admission. It is still there today.

2. He wrote upward of a hundred operas and some thirty sonatas for harpsichord – but, so far as we know, no toccatas.

3. Now better known as the Palazzo Mangilli-Valmarana. Visentini had, incidentally, been Canaletto's engraver.

in the city in 1744 – for a good deal more than Canalettos. In 1762 he sold his complete collections to George III for £20,000 – 'the most spectacular acquisition by an English royal collector', writes Sir Oliver Millar,[1] 'since Charles I's agent had brought off his coup in Mantua in the 1620's.' Three years later the King followed this tremendous purchase with another – that of Smith's entire library, bought *en bloc* for £10,000; it forms the nucleus of the King's Library, now in the British Museum. Even this did not, however, mark the end of Smith's collecting career; he immediately began amassing new treasures, and after his death in 1770 the sale of his new library alone occupied thirteen days.

Doge Alvise Mocenigo III – he is sometimes called by his middle name of Sebastiano, to distinguish him from his innumerable namesakes – was succeeded in 1732 by the seventy-eight-year-old veteran diplomat Carlo Ruzzini; and his death three years later left the throne free for Alvise Pisani, a member of what was by now the richest family of Venice, owner not only of the immense and sumptuous Palazzo Pisani – now the Conservatory of Music – at S. Stefano but also of the still grander Villa Pisani at Strà on the Brenta. The new Doge, brother of that Andrea Pisani who had distinguished himself at Preveza and elsewhere in the last phase of the Turkish war, had himself served as Venetian Ambassador to the Court of Queen Anne, where he had impressed all London by the splendour of his retinue; on his election as Doge on 17 January 1735 he and his family financed, despite the season, three days of celebrations on a scale which was generally held to be unprecedented, even in Venice. The *Arsenalotti* who by tradition carried him round the Piazza were ordered to go especially slowly, to allow more time for the scattering of largesse; during the three following nights, the entire square was illuminated *all ' inglese*, with set pieces that changed every night; and on the last night of the three, on every column of the *Procuratie* buildings along each side, outsize wax candles revealed huge representations of the Pisani coat of arms, while at the ends the entire façades of the Basilica and the church of S. Geminiano[2] were lit with thousands of flaming torches.

And yet, however dazzling his outward magnificence, Alvise Pisani strove, just as his two immediate predecessors had striven before him, to maintain for the Republic the lowest possible profile on the international stage. Their task was far from easy: Europe was still a battleground. In Italy

1. *Italian Drawings and Paintings in the Queen's Collection* (London, 1965).
2. Demolished, alas, by Napoleon and replaced by the early nineteenth-century range which bears his name.

alone, the extinction of two ruling houses in quick succession – the Farnese in Parma and the Medici in Tuscany – brought about a new confrontation between Spain and Austria, and the tension was still further increased by the dispute over the claim of Louis XV's father-in-law, Stanislaus Leszczynski, to the throne of Poland. By 1733 most of the continent was again at war; and though an uneasy peace was re-established in 1735, it was only another six years before the succession of Maria Theresa to the throne of Austria, on the death of her father Charles VI, once again set the princes of Europe at each other's throats.

That Venice somehow contrived to preserve her neutrality through all these upheavals, successfully withstanding the formidable pressures – diplomatic, economic and even military – which were brought to bear in efforts to persuade her to declare herself on one side or another, was an extraordinary achievement: every bit as remarkable as many more glorious aspects of her past on which she looked back with justifiable pride. Around her, the face of Italy was changing as quickly and as kaleidoscopically as ever it had; yet there she remained, the still centre of the whirlpool, seeming barely conscious of the turmoil. There was, inevitably, the occasional heavy price to be paid; warring armies are poor respecters of national frontiers, especially when they know that those frontiers will not be active-ly defended, and more than once the Republic had to suffer the indignity of invasion, with the consequent devastation of farms and villages unfor-tunate enough to stand along the line of advance of one army or another. In the city itself, however, pleasure continued to reign supreme; and it took more than a European war to stop that ceaseless flow of visitors that had by now become Venice's life-blood.

This determined neutrality had another serious consequence: it encouraged Venice to neglect her war fleet. Perhaps, indeed, it might be more true to say that the state of this fleet was at least a contributory cause of her neutrality, for the appearance of ships from northern nations in the Adriatic during the War of the Spanish Succession had at last brought her face to face with a disagreeable fact that she had long been trying, with increasing lack of success, to ignore. In the art of ship-building, in which she had once led the world, she was by now hopelessly out of date.

Already in the first half of the fifteenth century, Venice had abandoned the old oared galley in her merchant fleet. The new, foreign-built 'round' (i.e. broader-beamed) sailing ships were not only more economical, since they had far larger capacity and did not require huge crews of rowers – in those days always free men – who, in their turn, needed food, water and regular periods of rest ashore; they were also more easily defended, since weight was a secondary consideration and they could mount heavy cannon on board. Unlike the northern and Atlantic nations, however, Venice continued to favour the galley as the basis of her war navy, confining her own ship-building activities entirely to the old models. On the face of it, there were good reasons for this decision: the galleys were more manoeuvrable, especially in shallow Adriatic waters; since they were not at the mercy of the weather, their speed and performance could be more accurately predicted; as for their shortness of range, this was of little importance at a time when the Republic still possessed any number of supply bases in the eastern Mediterranean. Round ships, on the other hand, were infinitely more expensive to build and to equip, particularly for Venice, suffering as she did from a chronic shortage of timber, both for the ships themselves and as fuel for the cannon-foundries. Ship's cannon, she told herself, was anyway of less value in the narrow waters of the Mediterranean; inaccurate at the best of times, it was no match for stable shore batteries. If the supply of heavy fire-power was limited, it was to these batteries that priority should be given.

Fortunately for her, the Turks felt much the same way; and for as long as she had no other serious adversary to fight at sea, there was little incentive for her to revolutionize the Arsenal, to throw out all the old machinery and equipment, the old skills and techniques, to embark on new and prodigiously expensive programmes fraught with problems and difficulties of which she had no clear understanding or certainty of solution. (This explains how, as late as 1571, a battle on the scale of Lepanto could still be fought between oared galleys – a battle inconceivable at such a date in northern waters, relying as it did on vessels and tactics a good deal closer to those used at Salamis, 2,000 years before, than to those of Drake and the Spanish Armada seventeen years later.)

Meanwhile, however, the shipwrights of England, France, Holland and Spain were moving rapidly ahead, developing new galleons whose improved systems of sails and rigging enabled them to beat against the wind and whose heavy cannon—now sunk well below decks – increased their stability rather than the reverse. Equally well suited for military or commercial use, these were the ships that had dominated the Mediterranean from the beginning of the seventeenth century, capturing more and more of the carrying trade from Venice. Thus it was that the old-fashioned round merchantmen of the Republic, slower and far more vulnerable, became the preferred targets of the Barbary pirates and, obliged to sail only under escort and to pay hideous sums for insurance, effectively priced themselves out of the market.

From about 1650 onwards Venice had done her best to catch up. At first she had tended to buy or hire English or Dutch ships as the need arose; several galleons had been used in the later stages of the Cretan war, though they had still been treated – like the galleasses that had succeeded so well at Lepanto – as little more than floating gun platforms, being towed into position by one or more galleys before letting off their broadsides. But it was only in 1667 that she began building her own ships-of-the-line in the Arsenal, using an imported English vessel as a model; and as late as 1695, when a Venetian Captain-General suggested using one of the new-type galleons as his flagship, he was refused permission. The fact of the matter was that although by the turn of the century Venice had amassed a small fleet of relatively modern warships of her own manufacture, she never felt really happy or confident with them. Even in the victories of Flangini and Andrea Pisani of 1717, oared galleys constituted at least half her fleet.

And by then there was yet another unpalatable truth to be faced. Venice had lost her lordship of the Adriatic: a loss perfectly – and poignantly – symbolized in 1702 when the activities of the French around the borders of the lagoon caused the cancellation of the annual Ascension Day Wedding of the Sea. From that time on English, French, Dutch, Austrian and even Russian warships made free of the entire Gulf, ignoring Venetian protests – which, indeed, grew fewer and fewer as the Republic gradually came to terms with reality. Where commercial shipping was concerned, the position was, if anything, more humiliating still. In the Middle Ages all foreign merchantmen entering the Adriatic had been obliged to bring their cargoes to Venice, where they would then be trans-shipped as necessary. Later these rules had been relaxed; instead, Venetian patrols had levied customs dues on all cargoes bound for other ports, and had ensured that other regulations concerning tariffs, quarantine and – most important – the traditional state monopoly on salt were properly observed. Now those merchantmen, faster and better equipped than the patrols, could afford to laugh at such attempts to control their activities, sailing unmolested to imperial Trieste, to papal Ancona, or indeed to any other port they chose.

It was only in 1736, under Alvise Pisani, that Venice took active steps to remedy the situation. By then the government's insistence that all Venetian merchantmen in the eastern Mediterranean should sail in convoys to protect themselves from the Barbary pirates had proved a failure. Shipowners often had to wait months before a convoy could be gathered together; when it did leave, its speed was restricted to that of its slowest ship; and when it arrived the resultant sudden glut of goods had a disastrous effect on prices. Henceforth, any ship more than seventy feet in length with a minimum number of forty men on board and twenty-four guns was permitted to sail unescorted. This proved reasonably successful, leading to an immediate ship-building boom at the Arsenal in response to the demand for more vessels of the required design. In consequence, trade expanded to the east and – especially during those periods of European war when Venice could offer the advantage of a neutral flag – to the west also; but the Barbary pirates, themselves no sluggards where developments in ship design were concerned, remained a threat for another twenty years until the Republic swallowed still more of her pride and frankly bought them off. Even then, as we shall see, the problem was not entirely solved; the Republic none the less succeeded, in the last thirty years of its existence, in almost doubling its commercial tonnage; in 1794 there were no fewer than 309 Venetian merchantmen listed on the state register.

Simultaneously with the increase in ship-building there was a dramatic upsurge in the transit trade. In the early years of the century this had declined sharply, particularly after the Emperor declared Trieste a free port in 1719 and the Pope did the same for Ancona thirteen years later. But as part of the reform of 1736 Venice abandoned her old protectionist policy and before long the Rialto was as popular with foreign merchants as it had ever been. True, the cargoes tended to be less exotic than in former days. The spice trade had been lost to the Dutch as early as 1600, with the founding of the Dutch East India Company; Venice now dealt mainly in domestic, or at least local Adriatic, commodities – wine, olive oil, sulphur, salt, raisins and currants from the Ionian Islands. But the money flowed in; in 1782 it was found necessary to broaden the Riva eastward from the Prisons to allow more space for the unloading of merchandise;[1] and according to the leading modern authority on the Venetian economy[2] 'it seems likely that the total tonnage moving through the port of Venice was larger in 1783 ... than ever before in the thousand years of the city's history.'

On 17 June 1741, a few months after the outbreak of the War of the Austrian Succession, Doge Alvise Pisani was being treated by his doctor for an infected sore on his leg when he suffered a sudden stroke and died almost at once. He was succeeded by Pietro Grimani, a man of wide learning and, incidentally, the only Doge who was also a Fellow of the Royal Society, having been proposed for membership while Ambassador to London in 1712 by the Society's President, Sir Isaac Newton.[3] Like those

1. A white marble strip in the paving marks the original breadth.
2. F. C. Lane, *Venice, a Maritime Republic*.
3. His speciality was astronomy, on which subject his address to the Society is said by his biographer to have been *applauditissimo*.

of his three predecessors, his reign too was peaceful and politically uneventful – which is a good deal more than can be said of any of his contemporary rulers. It was, however, marked by the final disappearance of an institution that had been part of Venetian history longer even than the Dogeship itself – the Patriarchate of Aquileia.

Although during recent centuries the Patriarch of Aquileia had no longer been the pest that he was in earlier times, he had remained something of a problem since his Friuline see was more or less bisected by the Venetian –Austrian frontier. It had accordingly long ago been agreed that successive Patriarchs should be appointed by each state alternately, but Venice had chosen to ignore this ruling from the first: the Venetian Patriarch at the time had named a Coadjutor, who had automatically succeeded him on his death, and the practice had continued unchecked with the Patriarchal throne passing smoothly and uninterruptedly from one Venetian to the next, despite occasional protests on the part of Austria. But now Maria Theresa put her foot down and appealed to Pope Benedict XIV, who thereupon proposed that the old system be discontinued and that the see should be divided; the Patriarch would have authority only over the part which lay within the frontiers of the Republic, which he would administer from a new residence at Udine; the rest, which fell within Austrian territory, would be placed under the jurisdiction of an Apostolic Vicar. It was a sensible enough suggestion; but Venice, reluctant to accept the loss of the ecclesiastical authority she had formerly enjoyed in Austrian territory, voiced strong objections. The Pope mildly replied that he had only been trying to satisfy both parties in the dispute; if the solution he had recommended was not acceptable, they had better argue one out for themselves.

For a while the question threatened to have serious consequences for the relations between Empire and Republic; at last, however, both agreed to accept the mediation of the Court of Turin; and it was King Charles Emmanuel III of Sardinia[1] who decided the final dispensation: the Patriarchate would be suppressed altogether and replaced by two separate bishoprics – one Venetian and one Austrian, at Udine and Gorizia respectively. Venice saw that she would have done better to accept Pope Benedict's proposal, but it was too late now. She could only bow to the inevitable; and the Patriarchate of Aquileia, after 1,200 years, passed into history – a problem to the last.

The Pope had shown himself to be reasonably accommodating in the matter of Aquileia; he proved a good deal less so in 1754 when Francesco Loredan, who had succeeded Pietro Grimani as Doge two years before,

---

1. The ruling family of Savoy had held the title of King of Sardinia since 1718.

appended his seal to a strongly worded edict which condemned the ease and frequency with which Venetian citizens, 'through ignorance, without discernment and perhaps even for reasons of malice', were making application to Rome for indulgences, special dispensations and privileges, with prejudice to the interests of the state. In future, the edict continued, such documents would be considered null and void unless they were obtained in the approved manner and officially confirmed by the Government of the Republic. To Pope Benedict, the tone of this proclamation was as objectionable as its content. He sent the Doge an indignant message of protest, refusing to accept the somewhat half-hearted attempts by the Senate in Venice and the Venetian Ambassador in Rome to placate him. As relations grew steadily more tense, Maria Theresa and Louis XV both intervened on the papal side, and there is no telling how the dispute might have ended if Benedict had not died in 1758 – to be succeeded, through a stroke of rare good fortune, by a Venetian, Carlo Rezzonico, who took the name of Clement XIII.

With the accession of this fifth – and last – citizen of the Republic to the throne of St Peter[1] the difficulties faded away as if by magic. The event was marked with characteristically splendid celebrations throughout the city, and no fewer than eight special ambassadors were nominated to carry official congratulations to the new pontiff, who immediately sat down and wrote a letter in his own hand, beseeching the *Serenissima* 'by its own sovereign authority' to withdraw the offending edict; 'anyone,' he added, 'would be doing us a grave injustice were he to suppose that we should make any request of our motherland the granting of which would do it anything but honour.' Such conciliatory terms as these offered the Senate a perfect opportunity to yield without loss of face, and the seal was set on the new friendship when, in 1759, Pope Clement sent Doge Loredan that most precious token of his special favour, the Golden Rose.

If, however, the Pope intended this coruscating award to be an encouragement to tread the paths of righteousness in future, he was due for a disappointment. In 1767 a special commission reported that the total revenue of the Church within the territory of the Republic, excluding casual contributions, amounted to over eight and a half million ducats. It had received in addition, over the previous ten years alone, bequests totalling nearly two and a half million. The government did not hesitate. On 10 September of that same year it decreed the suppression of 127 monasteries and convents, and the sale of their property for the benefit of the state. Thus, at a single stroke, the exchequer was enriched by some three

---

1. The previous four were Gregory XII (Correr) in 1406, Eugenius IV (Condulmer) in 1431, Paul II (Barbo) in 1464 and Alexander VIII (Ottobon) in 1689.

million ducats and the monastic population reduced from 5,798 to 3,270.

It would have been pleasant to record, at this point, that the Rose was returned to Rome; but such gestures are not the way of governments, and the *Serenissima* was, alas, no exception.

The people of Venice, following their rulers' example, were now enjoying the most godless age in all their history. The Republic, to be sure, had never shown the degree of spiritual fervour – not to say fanaticism – manifested at one period or another by most of its neighbours, in Italy and beyond. Alone of all the states of Catholic Europe, it had never burnt a heretic. We have seen how, even in the two previous centuries when much of Europe was torn to shreds by religious strife, Venice had alone maintained that moderate, humanist outlook which had sprung from the Renaissance and which must have seemed oddly out of place, even old-fashioned, in the world of the Counter-Reformation. She had allowed the Greek Orthodox community a church of their own (S. Giorgio dei Greci, consecrated in 1561), the Jews their synagogues in the Ghetto, the Muslims their mosque in the Fondaco dei Turchi. In 1707 the Armenians had established their monastery on the island of S. Lazzaro. Thus she had acquired a reputation for tolerance which had in its turn made her a centre both for enlightened liberal thought and – through her printing houses – for its dissemination, and giving her university at Padua (for there was none within the lagoon) a prestige unrivalled in Europe.

Now the wheel had come full circle. The religious wars had burnt themselves out, western civilization had returned once again to its senses, and most of those values for which the Republic had always stood were enthusiastically adopted by the Age of Reason. But by this time Venice had gone further still. If we examine the list of doges who reigned during the hundred years from 1675 to 1775, we cannot help noticing an extraordinary fact: out of a total of fourteen, only four were ever married.[1] And there is something else, more extraordinary still: that if we then turn our attention not just to the doges but to the Venetian aristocracy as a whole, much the same pattern is revealed. There was nothing new in this strange tendency towards celibacy. It has been calculated that, as early as the sixteenth century, 51 per cent of noble Venetians remained unmarried; in the seventeenth century this figure rose to 60 per cent; in the eighteenth to 66 per cent.[2] The underlying philosophy is clear. The family must continue; and

1. Silvestro Valier, Giovanni Corner, Alvise Pisani and Alvise Mocenigo IV.
2. E. Rodenwalt, *Untersuchungen über die Biologie des venezianischen Adels*, quoted in McNeill, *Venice, the Hinge of Europe*.

it must continue rich. One son – often the youngest – was therefore required to marry, and to beget enough legitimate male heirs to ensure the first of these requirements; the other sons would remain single – or at least childless – thus, by preventing the dispersal of wealth, fulfilling the second. This enforced bachelorhood may well have accounted for the number of professional courtesans in Venice – as opposed to the regiments of whores that are part and parcel of any flourishing sea-port – long before its emergence as the pleasure capital of Europe. It certainly explains the quantity of 'orphanages' – and of convents, since it was on the upper-class girlhood of the city that the blow fell hardest. To the two noble girls in every three who failed to find husbands – the proportion was actually rather higher, since impoverished aristocrats often took their wives from the wealthier bourgeoisie – no other way of life was open but to take the veil. It is small wonder that many of these convents enjoyed a reputation for licentiousness barely surpassed by that of the gambling-houses and *ridotti*; though it is less often remembered that, like the orphanages, they were often centres of Venetian musical life as well.

For a lady fortunate enough to marry, life was agreeable indeed. Before long she would have acquired for herself a *cicisbeo* – that specifically Venetian breed, a *cavaliere servente* but with more than a touch of the gigolo – from whom she would appear practically inseparable, while her older and busier husband would make only comparatively rare appearances at her side. The *cicisbeo* might or might not be her lover; he would have plenty of opportunities to be, if so required, but this was by no means an invariable rule. Affairs in Venice did not always end up in bed. Casanova's memoirs give that impression, admittedly; but Casanova was an inveterate boaster. Besides, he records a similar measure of success in Vienna, Paris and London. In any case, the *cicisbeo* possessed, from his lady's point of view, the great advantage of disposability; husbands might be in short supply, but with so many young bachelors to choose from, the alternative was cheap indeed.

Yet husbands – and wives – were disposable too. One of the aspects of Venetian life that most shocked visitors to the city was the frequency with which marriages were annulled, and the apparent simplicity of the operation. The French *chargé d'affaires* reported in shocked tones to his government in 1782 that the Patriarch sometimes had as many as 900 applications before him at one time; and when in that same year it was decided that firm steps must be taken to check the practice, it was the Council of Ten who acted – not the ecclesiastical establishment, who merely complained, yet again, of the encroachment on their authority.

This reluctance to marry had two dangerous consequences. The first was that sometimes a carefully laid plan would go wrong; several old and distinguished families became extinct in this way. The second, more serious still, was that the Venetian nobility suffered from an ever-widening split between rich and poor. Already in the preceding century, an ominous feature of social life in the city was the growing class of impoverished nobles who, tending as they did to live in or near the parish of S. Barnabà, were popularly known as the *barnabotti*. As official members of the Venetian aristocracy, they were required to dress in silk and continued to be entitled to their seats in the Great Council; many, however, were too poor or too uneducated to occupy any but the lowest administrative positions, and since they were debarred by their rank from working as craftsmen or shopkeepers, increasing numbers drifted into corrupt practices such as the rigging of minor elections or the selling of votes. Others simply gave up the struggle and lived on poor relief. Special arrangements (including free housing) had been made for them by the state – on the condition, however, that they remained single, bringing no more young *barnabotti*, unwanted and unemployable, into the world. Meanwhile, even among the relatively rich, a number of families were beginning to feel the strain of keeping up the appearances expected of them – appearances indeed which were absolutely required of all aspirants to high office. Throughout the eighteenth century (and much of the seventeenth) the Republic was thus effectively run by only forty-two families, from whom all holders of key governmental positions were drawn.

It was in an effort to attract new blood, to instil new life into this shrinking aristocracy, that seats on the Great Council were offered for sale to approved – and suitably affluent – outsiders even on occasions when funds were not urgently needed for the Turkish wars. By 1718, 127 Venetians had bought themselves and their descendants into the patriciate in this way, at a price of 100,000 ducats each; but though nearly two thirds of these had previously been merchants, it is significant that all of them abandoned their former life immediately on being ennobled. Trade, despite the part it had played in the Republic's history, was no longer considered a fit occupation for a gentleman. Nowadays, like his counterparts across Europe, he would draw his wealth from his mainland estate, which he would visit at least twice a year on *villeggiatura*, moving his entire household – family and servants, furniture, books and pictures – to his Palladian or baroque villa, there to escape the heat of the summer and the *ennui* of early autumn until the reopening of the Great Council and the new social season called him back to Venice. Commercial matters were, it was felt, far better left to foreigners: to Jews and Greeks and Dalmatians, who, it seemed, were good at that sort of thing and even actually liked it.

It was perhaps inevitable, in so prolonged a period of peace as that which Venice was now enjoying, that her more politically conscious citizens should have turned their attention towards matters affecting her constitution; and that they should not always have liked what they saw. As to the basic structure of the Republic, few people – at least of the governing class – had any complaint. It had now lasted, largely unchanged, for over a thousand years – a record unmatched by any other state in Europe, perhaps in the whole world; and a comparison of the condition of Venice with that of the rest of the continent, swept up in the Seven Years' War less than a decade after the Treaty of Aix-la-Chapelle had ended that of the Austrian Succession, scarcely suggested that any major changes were necessary. But there remained one feature of the governmental machine which had never found universal favour: the Council of Ten with its still more sinister offshoot, the three Inquisitors of State, whose very *raison d'être* – to work swiftly and in secret, without the need for consultation outside their own number – became increasingly repugnant to eighteenth-century liberal minds.

We have seen how, in the seventeenth century, reformers like Renier Zen had attempted – unsuccessfully – to strip the Council of its powers. Now, 140 years later, neither the Ten nor the Three were seen as the ogres that they had appeared during the dark and violent days of the Spanish Conspiracy or the Arundel affair; among the general populace, to whom they seldom gave any reason for fear, they even enjoyed a large measure of support. Yet they were still hated by a large number of those nobles – and particularly the *barnabotti* – who, though members of the Great Council, were not rich or influential enough to be themselves eligible for more exalted bodies and whose discontent made them liable to constant surveillance.

The attack that was launched by a discontented and embittered *Avogador di Comun* named Angelo Querini in 1761, and that was to be revived at regular intervals throughout the 1770s, followed a course so uncannily similar to that of Renier Zen – up to and including its completely negative result – that there is no point in retracing the story here. Tempers, however, ran high; impassioned, and often immoderate, speeches were made on both sides; and when, in 1762, Francesco Loredan was succeeded on the ducal throne by the most outspoken champion of the Ten and the Inquisitors, there were many in Venice who viewed the new Doge with profound misgiving.

Marco Foscarini was indeed no radical. He was, however, a scholar and a man of letters, probably – with Andrea Dandolo – the most cultivated of all the doges of Venice. He was the author of a long poem, *Il Corallo*, written in an attempt to inspire a revival of the Venetian coral industry, and – more important – a major work of literary history, *Letteratura Veneziana*. Of this latter work, only the first volume was ever published; the second was still incomplete when he died, aged only sixty-seven, in March 1763, having reigned for only ten months. He was buried in his family chapel at S. Stae.

His successor was yet another Alvise Mocenigo – the fourth, and mercifully the last, of that name to be elected to the supreme office. Himself a man of respectable, but in no way remarkable, attainments, he began his reign by concluding four treaties which, in earlier times, the Republic would have been ashamed even to consider. All had the same object: to put an end to the increasing harassment of Venetian shipping by the pirates of the Barbary coast, in return for a regular payment of protection money. Within six months of his accession, agreements had been reached with the rulers of Algiers and Tunis; similar ones followed with Tripoli in 1764 and Morocco in 1765, by which time Venice had committed herself to an annual expenditure of some 60,000 ducats for the right to sail unmolested through those seas that she had once commanded. For the former mistress of the Mediterranean, here was a humiliation indeed; but her shame must have been even greater when, within a very few years, it became evident that the money was being paid in vain. The rulers concerned, despite their assurances, were soon revealed to be either unable to control the corsair captains who sailed under their flags, or else simply disposed to turn a blind eye to their operations. Acts of piracy, though slightly less frequent, still presented a problem that could not be ignored; and Venice was fortunate that in these last years of her life she still possessed one admiral of the old school, capable of making a show of what little strength remained to her.

Angelo Emo, from the time he reached manhood, had dedicated himself to a single ideal – the complete remodelling of the Venetian navy on Anglo-French lines. He had not been altogether successful, but his skill in seamanship and knowledge of modern naval tactics – qualities by then rare among the Venetian nobility – had marked him out among his fellows, so that when in 1768 the government at last decided to take active measures against the pirates he was, though still under forty, the obvious choice for the command. In the years immediately following, he was to make frequent raids on their bases along the North African coast; and between 1784 and 1786, with a handful of ships which Venice now called a fleet but which in former days would scarcely have been accounted a squadron, he waged an intermittent small-scale naval war against the Bey of Tunis, forcing him, after three seasons' bombardment, into submission on very favourable terms. Thus, although none of these campaigns was of such a nature as to lead to any pitched battle or decisive victory, this last of the great Venetian admirals was able to make the Mediterranean safer for European shipping than it had been for decades, while proving to the world that the lion of St Mark, though old now and enfeebled, could still occasionally make his presence felt.

On 22 July 1769 the young Emperor Joseph II arrived in Venice. He was travelling incognito and stayed, not in any of the great palaces that would have been willingly put at his disposal, but at the *Leon Bianco* at SS. Apostoli, probably the best of the score of hotels and inns which now existed for the reception of the wealthier foreign visitors.[1] This did not, however, prevent the drawing up of a full and varied programme of entertainments in his honour; it was only when he heard of the government's proposal to construct a representation of the Gardens of the Hesperides, 300 yards across, on rafts between the mouth of the Giudecca Canal and S. Giorgio Maggiore, complete with flowers, trees of variously coloured crystal and an artificial lake stocked with fish, in which he and his fellow-guests were to take their pleasure before passing on to a banquet on the island of S. Giorgio itself, that he put his foot down.

To any student of Venetian social history – any reader, perhaps, of this book – such a proposal, which was planned in far more elaborate detail than is suggested by the above comparatively stark description, should occasion no surprise. What is more remarkable, and perhaps more ominous, is the reaction it provoked among the Venetians. Perhaps, if the festivity had been allowed to materialize as planned, the sheer magnificence of it might have disarmed opposition; but it did not materialize, and the rumours of the hundreds, even thousands, of ducats that had already been spent to no purpose on its preparation triggered off a wave of anti-government feeling, particularly among the discontented *barnabotti* and many of the younger intellectuals, inside and outside the nobility, on whom the new, revolutionary ideas gradually seeping in from France were beginning to have their effect. How, they demanded, could such sums be authorized on meaningless frivolities for the delectation of foreigners who did not even

---

1. One of the oldest of the buildings on the Grand Canal, it has now reverted to its former name of the Ca' da Mosto.

want them, at a time when the Republic was known to be in debt? How, for that matter, after more than half a century of peace, did it come to *be* in debt? Was it right that the potential rulers of Venice should be steadily decreasing in numbers, that the membership of the Great Council should be down to less than a thousand and that on some days it should have difficulty even in raising a quorum? That the highest offices of the State should now be the perquisite of a few immensely rich families? That many members of these families, both male and female, should gamble away their days and nights in the *ridotti*, masked and pomaded, while others, un-masked, sat at the head of the tables in their crimson state robes, impassive-ly holding the banks and dealing out the cards?

During the early years of the next decade this dissatisfaction became more and more vocal, finding its most effective spokesman in one Giorgio Pisani, a young and more than usually embittered *barnabotto* who reani-mated the long-existing, if intermittent, campaign against the Council of Ten and the State Inquisitors and soon made himself the unofficial leader of the party of reform. It was not, however, till 1774 that it scored its first major success; on 27 November of that year a new law was approved by the Great Council, whereby the Republic, 'determined to preserve the piety, sound discipline and moderate behaviour so necessary for the well-being of society, and to restrain the spread of every vice tending to the corruption and dissolution of the social order', decreed that 'the Casino of the *Ridotto* at S. Moisè,[1] the centre of gambling in the city, shall be closed for ever and turned over to some public purpose; and that all games of hazard shall be strictly prohibited in Venice as in her Provinces, the In-quisitors being charged to see that there be no infraction.' The law, it is credibly reported, was received with jubilation by the populace, who ran through the streets spreading the news to everyone they met; but Venice's passion for gambling was stronger than her respect for the law, and though the S. Moisè *ridotto* remained closed there were plenty of other more discreet houses, where, within a few weeks, the tables were as crowded as ever.

Two months later, in January 1775, it was proposed once again to offer seats in the Great Council for sale, this time to forty families from the mainland, provided that each could claim membership of its own local nobility for four or more generations and show a minimum annual income of 10,000 ducats. The proposal was hotly debated against strong op-

1. This, the original '*Ridotto*' of the city, still stands at No. 1362 in the Calle del Ridotto, and runs right through to the Calle Vallaresso (No. 1332). Thousands of visitors a day walk past it unconscious-ly, on their way to the *vaporetto* stop or to Harry's Bar.

position, and adopted by the most slender of majorities; its adherents, however, were in for a sad disappointment. A century before, there had been three times that number of families for whom 100,000 ducats was a small price to pay for a place among the patriciate; now, out of the forty approached, only ten were willing to accept – several, even of these, showing a marked lack of enthusiasm.

When Doge Mocenigo died on 31 December 1778 Venice's morale was at a frighteningly low ebb; nor was it appreciably raised by the election, on 14 January following, of Paolo Renier. The new Doge was a classical scholar, a translator of Homer, Pindar and Plato into the Venetian dialect; he had been a senator and a *Savio*, ambassador in Vienna and *bailo* in Constantinople. But he had a reputation for sharp practice and corruption, and even if he had not, as was widely rumoured, bought the Dogeship by bribing 300 members of the Great Council, the populace mistrusted him from the start. He also seems to have been sadly deficient in physical courage; his election address in St Mark's was barely audible, and the consequent shouts from the congregation to speak up frightened him to such a degree that on leaving the Basilica he could hardly climb into the *pozzo* for his tour of the Piazza, and several times asked his entourage if he were not seriously in danger of his life. The most sympathetic thing we know about him is that he married, as his second wife, a Greek tightrope walker he had met in Constantinople; but even this did not endear him to his people's hearts. She was never recognized socially, and throughout his reign the offices of dogaressa were performed by his niece.

Whatever his personal shortcomings, Doge Renier seems to have worked hard and conscientiously to halt the Republic's decline, but it was clear that Venice was becoming less and less governable. The year after his accession Giorgio Pisani was elected Procurator of St Mark; this was a major victory for the *barnabotti* and the radicals, if only beause it placed their champion on the same level as that occupied by the most powerful member of the reactionary opposition, Andrea Tron. For a decade and more, Tron – *il Paron*, as he was generally called in the Venetian dialect[1] – had dominated the Venetian political scene, wielding, thanks more to the sheer force of his personality than to any actual offices he held, considerably more real power than the Doge himself. The son of one of Venice's few genuine industrialists (his father, Nicolò, had established highly profitable textile mills near Vicenza) he had been a vociferous upholder of the old Venetian values, and was forever calling upon his fellow-nobles to leave

1. *Il Padrone, le Patron*, the Boss.

their country estates and return to their old commercial ways – declining, however, to set any such example himself. He made no secret of his contempt for all those foreigners or 'new men' who, he felt, had been allowed to take the Republic's economy into their own hands; and he had a particular detestation of the Jews, against whom he had managed to put through savage new legislation in 1777, forbidding them to employ Christians, barring them from manufacturing and ownership of property, and so reducing a once prosperous and useful community to the status of rag-and-bone merchants.

Now, in Giorgio Pisani and his equally vehement colleague Carlo Contarini, it seemed for a brief moment that Andrea Tron had found his match. Day after day they thundered against the government, its criminal mismanagement of the affairs of state, its irresponsible handling of the economy, its decadence and its corruption. And their oratory had its effect; before long they could command a majority in the Great Council. In vain Doge Renier appealed for unity, pointing out that the Republic could no longer defend itself in the event of foreign aggression, and that without internal solidarity it was as good as lost. 'The Princes of Europe', he reminded his hearers, 'are watching us closely in our present turmoil and judging how best to turn it to their advantage.' But Pisani and Contarini had no intention of moderating their language to oblige a political establishment for which they felt nothing but contempt.

It would have been better for them if they had; a quieter, more measured approach might have achieved at least some of their ends. As it was, their constant agitation, public speeches and secret meetings ultimately forced the authorities to move against them. On the night of 31 May Giorgio Pisani was arrested in his house at S. Moisè; the next ten years he was to pass in prison on the mainland. Contarini, for his part, was consigned to the fortress of Cattaro, where he died soon afterwards. The Council of Ten and the Inquisitors had won again, just as they always did. But the long, traumatic debates in the Great Council – debates during which Venice seemed, as never before in all her history, to be tearing her very soul apart – were not forgotten; the bitterness of the *barnabotti* continued to increase; and, for the seventeen years that the Republic had still to live, certain words of Paolo Renier rang ominously in the ears of his more thoughtful compatriots:

If any state has need of unity, it is ours. We have no forces, neither on land nor at sea. We have no alliances. We live by good fortune, by accident, putting our trust solely in that reputation for prudence that the government of Venice has always enjoyed. Here, and here only, lies our strength.

It was true – though, as the Doge had admitted earlier, Venice's reputation was no longer enough where the chanceries of Europe were concerned. However rapidly the *Serenissima* was declining, her diplomatic service was as alert as ever; and Renier knew full well that Austria had already initiated discussions with other governments to consider a future in which Venice would have ceased to exist. Yet somehow, despite all her tribulations, she contrived to put on a brave, even a united, front to the world: to project the by now traditional image of a frivolous and brittle society with elegance and taste and money to burn, but invisibly supported by a monolithic infrastructure composed of grave and experienced men whose wisdom was infinite and whose touch was sure. Nor was it only the mindless pleasure-seekers whom she deceived. In January 1782 there arrived the Hereditary Grand Duke of Russia – the future Tsar Paul I – and his wife, travelling under the romantic aliases of Count and Countess of the North. The usual magnificent festivities were held in their honour, in the course of which, at a touch from the Countess's hand, an outsize artificial dove sped round the Piazza sparking off a hundred torches as it went, finally coming to rest on an eighty-foot high replica of the Arch of Titus in Rome; but what really impressed her husband, we are told, was the quiet discipline shown by the crowds, who needed no soldiers to control them or any other authority but five ushers from the Ten, led by their red-robed *Capitan-Grande*. '*Voilà*', he exclaimed, '*l'effet du sage gouvernement de la République. Ce peuple est une famille.*' He could not, one suspects, have said anything that would have given his host more pleasure.[1]

The Grand Duke was not an intelligent man – he was insane by the time he ascended the throne and was very properly assassinated in 1801 – but there were many visitors far more perceptive than he who failed to discern any division or dissatisfaction in the city. They would not, in any case, have found it among the populace. The average working-class Venetian was well content with his lot. Given a modicum of bread and plenty of circuses – and neither were in short supply – he had nothing to grumble about. Taxation was light, or non-existent. Being born outside the governing élite, it seldom occurred to him to have political ambitions. He gave no trouble to the Ten or the Three; on the contrary, he believed them to be a useful, even a necessary, element in the state, and cheered lustily whenever they uncovered a conspiracy or moved against some discontented *barnabotto*. They in their turn bothered him not a jot, allowing him far more

---

1. In other respects, the imperial couple seem to have been less of a success. 'They paid only half their bill for lodgings, left no tips at the Arsenal banquet, and gave nothing for the orphanage girls as was the custom' (Philip Longworth, *The Rise and Fall of Venice*).

freedom than they allowed the nobility, whose every movement was watched and who were forbidden to leave the city, let alone the Republic, without special permission. Thus he had shed no tears for Pisani or Contarini; they spoke only for their own disaffected class; they were not, and never pretended to be, men of the people. The sooner they were put away in a safe place, and the longer they stayed there, the better.

The remaining seven years of Paolo Renier's dogeship were uneventful. In May 1782 he entertained Pope Pius VI on his way to Vienna – the first visit to Venice by a reigning Pope since Alexander III's triumph over Frederick Barbarossa in 1177; in the following year he and the Senate rejected, for reasons not altogether clear, proposals from three plenipotentiaries – John Adams, Benjamin Franklin and Thomas Jefferson – for a treaty of trade and friendship with the young United States of America. Meanwhile his venality was growing more and more shameless with advancing age, and most of his subjects cordially despised him. By far his greatest monument (for which he can take none of the credit) must unquestionably be the *murazzi* – the gigantic sea walls of irregular blocks of stone, fourteen metres thick at the base, that stretch some four kilometres along the littoral of the island of Pellestrina. This tremendous bulwark, started in 1744, had been thirty-eight years a-building and still stands in impressive – though, alas, increasingly ineffectual – testimony to the fact that even the sea, for so long Venice's refuge, was beginning to turn against her. And yet, among those who attended its inauguration, there must have been many who reflected sadly that she was now facing other, still greater dangers, both internal and external, against which she had no defence. All she could do was to keep up the charade; and it was in this cause that Paolo Renier, dying unlamented in February 1789, made his last unconscious sacrifice for the Republic.

Instead of receiving the usual state obsequies, he was buried in the church of the Tolentini secretly and at night, so as not to interrupt the Carnival.

46
The Fall

[1789–1797]

La raison du plus fort est toujours la meilleure;
Nous l'allons montrer tout à l'heure.

La Fontaine, *Le Loup et l'Agnea*

When Lodovico Manin, the 118th Doge of Venice and the last, was elected by twenty-eight votes to thirteen on 9 May 1789, he and his subjects were still unaware that, only four days previously, the States General of France had met at Versailles, and that the chain of events had already begun that was to bring France to revolution. It is not likely, however, even if the news had reached the Rialto, that the Venetians would have paid it much heed. For over seventy years now, they had lived in an ivory tower, secure in the belief that their by now traditional policy of neutrality would save them from all ills and that their determination to live at peace with their neighbours would be universally respected. Their mistake – the most tragic mistake in all their history – was to cling to this belief long after they should have seen it to be untenable; and for this disastrous piece of self-deception Lodovico Manin must bear much of the responsibility.

He was, in many respects, a surprising choice. For one thing, unlike any other doges of the past few centuries, he was not a member of the old Venetian aristocracy. The Manins were a powerful family from the Friuli who had bought their place in the Golden Book for 100,000 ducats in 1651, only seventy-four years before Lodovico's birth. To most of his senior colleagues, therefore, he was an upstart; one of his defeated rivals for the dogeship, the Procurator Pietro Gradenigo, was heard to murmur, during the post-electoral celebrations, 'With a *Friulano* Doge, the Republic is dead!' Eight years later, his words were to be remembered all too well.

Manin's career in public life had been distinguished enough, but not unusually impressive; he was principally remembered for the efficiency with which, when *podestà* of Verona, he had dealt with the catastrophic floods of 1757. In marked contrast to his predecessor, he was honest; even in the worst of the days that lay ahead, his integrity was never questioned. But in the years during which he was called upon to guide the Republic, there were other qualities more important even than honesty: strength, vision, courage, firmness of will – in a word, leadership. Of these qualities Lodovico Manin seems to have possessed scarcely a trace; indeed, as one reads through the last painful records of the dying Republic, one is tempted to wonder whether they had not disappeared altogether from Venice. One man only, Francesco Pesaro, saw the danger from the start and did his utmost to waken his colleagues to a realization of what lay ahead: but he failed, and when the end came he revealed that he too had feet of clay.

The French Third Estate, which on 17 June proclaimed itself the National Assembly, emphasized its peaceable intentions from the start; the attitude of the European monarchies, however, soon made it clear that peace was not to be. The philosophy of revolution was heady stuff. Already it had spread throughout western Europe; if the contagion were allowed to continue unchecked, other thrones would totter as well as the French, and the thousand-year-old political foundations of the whole continent would be in jeopardy. By June 1790, the Venetian representative at Turin was writing to warn the Senate of a French secret organization that had sent agents the length and breadth of Italy with the express purpose of disseminating revolutionary propaganda and organizing disaffection; and three months later a long dispatch from Antonio Cappello, the Ambassador in Paris, confirmed that this was no alarmist rumour. The organization, he wrote, included some of the most prominent members of the Assembly: men like Mirabeau, Lafayette and the Abbé Sieyès.

Now Venice might be a Republic, but she had never pretended to be radical or egalitarian. Indeed, her whole constitution was élitist through and through; and even though in recent years her nobility had occasionally been allowed limited transfusions of new blood, it remained considerably harder for the ordinary citizen to penetrate than the peerages of Britain or even of France, both of which were always open to those who, by their wealth, talent or qualities of person or character, gained the favour of the king. To her ruling families, the doctrines of the Revolution were every bit as repugnant as they were to the most reactionary of feudal aristocrats in Austria, England or Prussia. The European monarchies, in short, saw no reason why the *Serenissima* should not prove an enthusiastic, even if a not very effectual, ally in the struggle against the godlessness and chaos that they saw ahead.

They were soon to be disillusioned. It was not that the Republic underestimated the dangers of subversion. Giorgio Pisani and Carlo Contarini might be safely out of the way; but there were plenty of others, among *barnabotti* and *cittadini* alike, who made little or no secret of their sympathy for the radical cause. The Ten and the Three tightened their grip. Censorship became stricter; political public meetings were forbidden; all foreigners and many Venetians were put under surveillance. But when, in November 1791, King Victor Emmanuel of Sardinia suggested that Venice should join in a League of Italian Princes to resist the Jacobin threat, she replied that she did not consider such measures necessary; the threat had been greatly exaggerated; such precautions as might be considered advisable she was perfectly capable of taking on her own.

Six months later, the war had begun; Austria was first to enter the lists, to be followed shortly afterwards by Prussia and Sardinia. Then, on 10 August 1792, the Paris mob invaded the Tuileries, massacring the Swiss Guard, seeking out the royal family – who took refuge, not a moment too soon, in the National Assembly building – and, incidentally, giving the Venetian Ambassador, Alvise Pisani, a most unpleasant shock. He wrote to a friend:

Never in my life shall I witness such a scene of horror, bloodshed and fear ... The mob burst into the palace at noon, armed to the teeth, and dragging heavy cannon behind them, shouting 'We want the King, where is the King?' They did not find him ... There were many casualties among the hussars and the palace guards; the dead are estimated at between one and three thousand. Such was my confusion and terror that I simply cannot describe the picture that lay before my eyes, enough to daunt the strongest spirit. From the windows of my house, shaking as it was from the crashing of the guns, I could see the blood flowing in rivers. Just imagine my situation!

A few wounded hussars were brought into the house, only to be followed by a hundred or more of the mob. I had the doors closed, when up came armed troops, shouting: 'Ambassador, you are sheltering the King in your house; we want him.' I then showed unusual courage: first I sent my terrified children upstairs with the chaplain, then I myself opened the door, presented myself before that diabolical crowd, and swore that there was no one taking refuge in the house but a few wounded men. 'Come, friends,' I cried to them, 'come, see for yourselves!' At that moment the Lord himself protected me. They believed me. No one entered, but all turned away, still shouting 'We want the King!' ... Now the tumult has a little subsided, but for how long? There are fears of still more terrible and tragic happenings; danger is everywhere ... Only consider my position, and that of my trembling family ...

The shock had indeed proved too much for him. Leaving his secretary in charge of the Embassy, he and his family fled to London and remained there for the next three years.

In September 1792 the King of Sardinia made a further effort to enlist

Venetian aid. This time the invitation was to join with himself and the Kingdom of Naples in a neutral defensive league, to which it was hoped that all the other states of Italy would ultimately adhere. Once again, however, the Republic refused point-blank – the Collegio taking the decision themselves without even bothering to submit the question to the Senate. Venice, they pointed out, had formally declared herself neutral; how could she therefore join any alliance, even one specifically dedicated to the preservation of her neutrality? As an argument, it seemed distinctly thin; but the minds of the decision-makers were made up. Even when, four months later, King Louis XVI met his death at the guillotine they refused to be shaken. In Venice, as in every other capital in Europe – including Paris – men were shocked and horrified by the news; but the demand that diplomatic relations with France should be broken off – a mild enough reaction, in the circumstances – was rejected by the Senate, and Alvise Pisani continued to enjoy his rank and title, and to draw his salary, from the safety of London. Meanwhile the French representative in Venice was authorized to fly the Republican flag from his palace. In February 1793 the monarchies made their last attempt: Great Britain, Austria, Prussia, Holland, Spain and Sardinia had formed a coalition to protect Europe from atheists and regicides. Would Venice not join them in this sacred mission? Venice would not.

Neutrality is – or can be – a perfectly respectable policy; but, as Francesco Pesaro strove to impress upon his fellow-countrymen, it must be backed by strength. Wars between France and Austria had almost invariably been fought out on Italian soil; it could not now be long before Lombardy and the Veneto were once again a battleground. When that moment came Venice, however peaceably inclined, must show herself ready, and able, to fight. If she were not, what hope was there that her territorial integrity would be preserved? In her present condition, her very existence as an independent state was in danger.

So, in debate after debate, Pesaro argued; but he argued in vain. Once again, the opposing arguments were thin; they could hardly have been anything else. Armed neutrality of the kind that he advocated would necessitate a major reorganization, even a reconstruction, of both the army and navy. How could the Republic possibly afford such a measure, except by a swingeing and totally unacceptable levy on private wealth? The army of the Revolution had already turned back the invading Prussians at Valmy and inflicted a crushing defeat on the Austrians at Jemappes; was Pesaro seriously suggesting that Venice should measure herself against so formidable a fighting force? As for the idea of a Venetian army on her western frontier, what purpose could that possibly serve except to antagonize the French unnecessarily and encourage them to attack?

These arguments may well have been advanced in all sincerity; but they bore no relation to the real reason for the Republic's inertia. The fact of the matter was that Venice was utterly demoralized. It was so long since she had been obliged to make a serious military effort that she had lost the will that makes such efforts possible. Peace, the pursuit of pleasure, the love of luxury, the whole spirit of *dolce far niente* had sapped her strength. She was old and tired; she was also spoilt. Even her much-vaunted constitution, once the envy of all her neighbours, seemed to be crumbling: votes were bought and sold, the effective oligarchy was shrinking steadily, the Senate was reduced to little more than a rubber stamp. In this last decade of her existence as a state, almost every political decision she made seemed calculated to hasten her end. Did she, one wonders, have a death wish? If so, it was to be granted sooner than she knew.

For nearly two years after the execution of King Louis, relations between France and Venice remained correct, at times almost cordial. No amount of pious professions of neutrality could conceal the fact that the Venetian oligarchy was pro-Austrian and monarchist at heart, and the new French minister, Lallement, knew perfectly well that his every movement was watched and reported to the Inquisitors; he had no reason, on the other hand, to believe that his fellow-diplomats in the city fared any better, and even if he could not hope to gain the friendship of those in power he did at least succeed in winning a certain degree of grudging respect. France, after all, now possessed no friends in Europe; a strategically placed neutral was worth cultivating.

Late in November 1795, however, a French army won its first victory over the Austrians on Italian soil – at Loano, a small seaside town about half-way between San Remo and Genoa. Almost at once, the French attitude to Venice hardened, and the first sign of that hardening was a peremptory demand to expel from her territory the Comte de Lille, the brother of the dead King. He had settled in Verona the previous year and, after the death of the young Dauphin in July, had issued a proclamation in which, under the name of Louis XVIII, he laid formal claim to the throne of France. Thus, in the past four months, he had made Verona the centre of French émigré activity.

Now Venice, as a neutral, had a perfect right to offer refuge to anyone she liked, and the French Republic never produced any concrete evidence that Louis, from the safety of Venetian soil, was actually plotting its overthrow. The Emperor, meanwhile, although he himself had refused to accept the pretender on Austrian territory, was putting heavy pressure on Venice to allow him to stay in Verona. But at last the French demands became so threatening that the Signoria dared resist them no longer; on 31 March 1796 Louis was politely requested to leave, and shortly afterwards did so, demanding – in an understandable show of pique – that the House of Bourbon be formally expunged from the Golden Book. The affair was not, perhaps, of primary importance, but it perfectly illustrated Francesco Pesaro's argument. If Venice had been strong, she could have afforded to ignore the French threats or, alternatively, to expel Louis and his followers in defiance of Austria; in either event, she would have retained the friendship of one of the parties. In her weakness, she had hesitated and havered, and succeeded only in antagonizing both.

By now, too, a more serious dispute had arisen. The French had complained – quite justifiably, on this occasion – that Venice had allowed an Austrian army to cross her territory on its march from the Tyrol to Mantua. The Venetians replied lamely that the Empire had been specifically authorized to use the road through Goito by an ancient treaty which could not be abrogated. They may well have believed this themselves up to a point, since the Austrians had certainly been passing backwards and forwards along the Goito road without let or hindrance since their acquisition of the Duchy of Mantua in 1708; but despite repeated French demands Venice was never able to produce a copy of the treaty concerned. So far as the French were concerned, therefore, this was a clear breach of her proclaimed neutrality – a point which Napoleon Bonaparte was to turn to good account in the months ahead.

Bonaparte was now twenty-six years old. He had first distinguished himself when only twenty-four, at the siege of Toulon, after which his general, Dugommier, had sent urgent advice to the Minister for War in Paris: '*Récompensez, avancez ce jeune homme; car, si l'on était ingrat envers lui, il s'avancerait de lui-même*' ('Reward that young man, promote him; for if his services are not recognized, he will promote himself'). That advice had been taken. In the following year, having saved the Convention virtually single-handed from the royalist insurrection of 13 Vendémiaire, he had been made second-in-command of the Army of the Interior; and five months later, in March 1796, when the newly established Directory resolved to launch a new campaign against Austria through Italy, the slim, solemn young Corsican, bilingual in Italian, seemed the obvious choice to lead it. No one, however – except possibly Bonaparte himself – could have foreseen the measure and speed of his success. Montenotte, Millesimo, Dego, Ceva, Mondovi: almost every day brought news of another victory. Before the end of April, Austria's ally Sardinia was forced to sign a separate peace, by which she surrendered Savoy and Nice to France. On 8 May the French crossed the Po and, two days later, forced the bridge over the Adda at Lodi. On the 15th Bonaparte made his formal entry into Milan.

All Lombardy was now in his hands, saving only Mantua; Mantua, however, could wait. The way was effectively clear to the imperial frontier. True, it lay across the neutral territory of Venice, but that could not be helped. Such considerations were certainly unheeded by the Austrians, who were no longer even sticking to the Goito road: only a few days before, the Austrian general Kerpen, now in full flight with the remnants of his army, had sought permission to pass through Crema – permission which, since the fortress was in a ruinous condition and utterly indefensible, the Venetian *podestà* had not felt able to refuse.

On learning of this further instance of Venice's imperialist sympathies, Bonaparte had at once ridden personally to Crema to ask the *podestà*, a certain Gian Battista Contarini, for an explanation. The ensuing meeting was of no special importance; its interest lies chiefly in the fact that Contarini's report of it to the Senate gives us the first account of Bonaparte by a Venetian. Contarini was struck by his evident physical frailty, and by the fact that he made no effort to conceal his fatigue. Here was no arrogant young conqueror, angrily pacing up and down the room, berating Venice for her duplicity and threatening dire retribution – merely an exhausted young man lying back in an armchair with his eyes closed. 'He seemed', wrote Contarini, 'serious and thoughtful; and to the direct question "Are you tired?" the General answered "Yes, I am very tired."' At no time during the conversation did he express any friendly sentiments towards Venice; but when his only companion and fellow-Corsican, General Saliceti, launched into a violent tirade against the Republic he took no part, and indeed on several occasions smiled his approval of the spirited retorts with which – if Contarini's account is to be believed – the indignant *podestà* gave as good as he got. His own protests were couched in mild, almost courteous language; he seemed more interested in establishing precisely which route the Austrians had taken, and in satisfying himself that it was in fact the only route open to them that could save them from capture by his own forces.

The next Venetian report on Bonaparte – from *podestà* Alvise Mocenigo in Brescia on 26 May – shows him, however, in a stormier mood. The retreating Austrians had been allowed to occupy the fortress of Peschiera on Lake Garda; the Venetian authorities, apart from the gentlest of protests, had made no effort to prevent them, and he wished to know why. Mocenigo might well have pointed out that since the French were by now in Brescia, similarly without leave or opposition, they were hardly in a position to complain; but, given the General's attitude, he seems to have thought this argument inadvisable. Instead, he reported to the Senate that he had finally been able to pacify him, and that on his departure Bonaparte had actually declared his friendship for Venice; but, the report added, 'he feels in the highest degree the passion of pride. Every occurrence, no matter how innocent, that seems to him to create the slightest opposition to his plans arouses him instantly to anger and to threats.'

What the poor *podestà* did not know was that most of Napoleon Bonaparte's anger on these occasions was nothing but a simulated display, and that most of his threats were empty. His plans were working beautifully. A final battle – on 5 August at Castiglione – in which the Austrians lost 2,000 men and all their artillery was a fitting climax to one of the most extraordinary campaigns of modern military history; after it Peschiera was rapidly evacuated and the surrender of Mantua, the Empire's last remaining toe-hold in Italy, could only be a matter of time. Bonaparte's real purpose in his dealings with Venice at this period was not to enlist her aid or even to persuade her to take a more firmly neutral line; he knew just how powerless she really was, equally unable effectively to help or seriously to hinder him. Rather it was to frighten her, to put her in the wrong, to make her feel guilty and inadequate, to erode her pride, confidence and self-respect to the point where her moral resistance would be reduced to the same level as her physical. Simultaneously he could claim, in her alleged misdeeds, justification for his own. And the success of this technique was never more perfectly illustrated than in his dealings with Nicolò Foscarini.

Early in May 1796 the Collegio, worried by the growing sympathy being .shown in the Senate for Francesco Pesaro's ever more insistent calls to rearm, had suggested as a compromise the appointment of a *Provveditor-Generale in Terra Firma*, with headquarters at Verona. It was an office which normally carried near-dictatorial powers; on this occasion, however, the proveditor's were clear. They were 'to ascertain the state of public opinion, to preserve tranquillity and to give to the subjects of Venice that consolation and reassurance to which they are accustomed, going promptly wherever he is required, keeping the Senate constantly informed of developments and carrying out its orders.' Had Nicolò Foscarini, who as *Savio di Settimana*[1] had piloted the relevant resolution through the Senate, known

1. The six *Savii Grandi* assumed the chairmanship in rotation, for a week (*settimana*) at a time. The *Savio di Settimana* was thus roughly equivalent to Prime Minister for the week.

that he would himself be elected to the post, he might perhaps have framed these terms of reference slightly differently; largely responsible for them though he was, it is impossible not to feel sorry for him. How could he reassure his fellow-citizens in the face of an advancing and apparently irresistible army commanded by an obvious military genius, when the entire Venetian land forces consisted of perhaps 5,000 men, scattered across the country in small garrisons, ill-armed, ill-equipped, and destitute of artillery or munitions? How could he carry out the Senate's orders when it never sent any – answering his repeated requests, if at all, with deliberately ambiguous and evasive generalizations? In such circumstances his only sensible course would have been to act on his own initiative; but initiative was not, alas, his *forte*.

From the start, Foscarini's attitude to Bonaparte, like that of his government, might have been expressly designed to irritate. On 31 May, within a few days of taking up his appointment, he sent his *aide-de-camp* to the French headquarters at Valeggio to congratulate the General on his successes but, simultaneously, to submit a bill for all the damages reportedly caused by the army of the Revolution on Venetian territory. This time Bonaparte's rage, real or simulated, was fearful to behold. What, he demanded, were these paltry complaints compared with the harm Venice had done to the French cause? Had she not opened her territory to his enemies, even granting them the fortress of Peschiera? Now France would have her revenge: first he would march on Verona and burn it to the ground, then he would deal with Venice as she deserved. When at last the tirade subsided, the trembling *aide-de-camp* was dismissed with a message to the proveditor to present himself in person that same evening at Peschiera to justify his conduct and that of his government.

Foscarini was terrified, and made no secret of the fact. Before leaving, he wrote to the Senate what sounds almost like a farewell letter, calling God's blessings on what he describes as 'my *holocaust* for the good of my country', and in his subsequent report of the interview he sounds grateful to have emerged alive. Bonaparte, seeing the state he was in, took full advantage. The Directory, he thundered, had given him authority to demolish Verona, and he was dispatching General Masséna there that very night with enough troops and artillery to ensure that the task would be properly done. He himself would declare war on all the princes of Italy at the next sign of pro-Austrian sympathies on the part of any of them; meanwhile he had already written to Paris for authority to march against Venice. He ended by pointing out that Foscarini was at that moment on French territory, since Peschiera had been treacherously passed by Venice into the hands of Austria from whom he had taken it by right of conquest.

For the same reason he had also decided to annex all the previously Venetian strong-places along the Adige.

The luckless proveditor could only plead for mercy. For a long time he could make no impression; at last, however, Bonaparte agreed to spare Verona, on condition that Masséna and his army were guaranteed free and unimpeded entry into the city, all three bridges on the Adige being given over unconditionally into his control. Venice must also undertake to supply provisions and even certain items of military equipment on credit. When Foscarini was finally allowed to withdraw, he had given away to the French everything they wanted, without a shot being fired or a penny paid. It seemed to him a cheap price to pay for saving Verona from the flames.

And so, perhaps, it might have been – if Bonaparte had had the faintest intention of burning it. The truth was that he had never dreamt of doing so, nor had he ever given Masséna orders to that effect. A week later he admitted as much to the Directory:

I have purposely engineered this quarrel, in case you wish to get five or six millions out of Venice ... If you have more decided intentions, I think it will be in our interest to continue the *brouillerie*; just let me know what you wish to do, and we will await the favourable moment, which I will make use of according to the circumstances ...

The truth about the Peschiera affair is that Beaulieu [the Austrian commander] basely deceived them; he requested passage for fifty men, then seized the town.

In other words the Republic, until recently world-renowned for the shrewdness of her diplomacy, had been the victim, not of a double-bluff, but of two single bluffs in quick succession; the first by the Austrians, the second by the French. Impotent, indecisive and afraid, she had now shown herself to be gullible as well.

In Venice, the Senate continued to dither. At last they had learnt how to deal with the urgings of Francesco Pesaro and his supporters; rather than attempt to silence them, it was better to propose some hopeful-sounding compromise and then, by withholding funds or erecting a sort of bureaucratic blockade, to render it nugatory and allow it to be gently forgotten. It was this policy which had led to the appointment of the proveditor, a measure which had had the added advantage that henceforth they had a scapegoat as the situation on *terra firma* continued to worsen. Admittedly, Nicolò Foscarini had not taken easily to the rôle; his incessant requests for instructions revealed a marked reluctance to assume the slightest responsibility for anything. This ploy, however, was simple enough to counter; the requests were ignored, the letters went unanswered.

At the beginning of June – once again, it seems, with the sole purpose of placating Pesaro – the Senate ordered the fleet up from Corfu, then quietly revoked the order a few days later. Next they appointed a *Provveditor alle Lagune* – an admiral for home waters – in the person of seventy-six-year-old Giacomo Nani. Despite his age, Nani was an able and conscientious officer who had produced a plan forty years before for the defence of Venice, and he and his equally efficient lieutenant, Tommaso Condulmer, set to work with a will; but his report on the state of the navy proved so discouraging – only four galleys and seven galleots, all obsolete, were even partially ready for service – that it was decided to shelve it. No further funds were voted, and when Nani died the following April he was not replaced. A half-hearted attempt to strengthen the army was equally abortive. An invitation to Prince William of Nassau to take over its command gave rise to a strong protest from Austria and was immediately withdrawn; almost simultaneously, Napoleon objected that since Venice had made no attempt to rearm when Austria had invaded her territory, he would consider it a hostile act if she were to do so merely because her frontier had now been crossed by the French. At this the Signoria decided that the army, like the navy, had better be left untouched. Never again was the question of rearmament or mobilization publicly discussed.

In fact, it scarcely mattered. The time was long since past when Venice might have built up her forces. Five – even two or three – years earlier, strong, determined action, followed by a firm defensive alliance with Austria, might have saved the day; but not now. By the summer of 1796 she had only one chance left: to throw in her lot with the French and trust that by bending to the storm she might somehow survive it. Against all probabilities, that chance was now offered her; and she turned it down.

We do not know how long Bonaparte had been seriously considering the idea of a Venetian alliance. It is quite possible that it had been in his mind from the first, but that he had deliberately delayed making any proposals until he felt that there was a good chance of their being accepted. On the other hand it is not immediately easy to understand what advantage he saw in wooing the friendship of a state which he already knew to be entirely at his mercy, incurring obligations and responsibilities towards it which might well inhibit his freedom of action after his certain victory. But woo it he did, and assiduously: in less than two and a half months Venice received three separate offers of alliance – the first on 21 August from Bonaparte himself in Brescia, the second on 19 September through the French minister, Lallement, and the third, most formal of all, on 31 October, from Jean-François Rewbell, the member of the five-man Directory responsible for foreign affairs, through her Venetian envoy in Paris, Angelo Querini. She was to discuss the possibility in the Senate as late as the following March, but the decision, reached almost unanimously, was still the same. No.

Why did Venice refuse? A probable reason – and almost certainly a contributory one – is that the whole concept of revolutionary France was repugnant to those who guided her destiny. At other levels of society, both on *terra firma* and within the city itself, support for radical principles might be spreading fast; but to the handful of rich families who now constituted the permanent government of the *Serenissima*, France was a nation of anarchists and regicides; they could no more contemplate a treaty of friendship and alliance with such a power than, let us say, King George V of England would have contemplated a similar pact with Soviet Russia in the 1920s. Perhaps they allowed their disgust to blind them to political realities; perhaps, on the other hand, they were fully aware of the dangers they incurred by rejecting Bonaparte's overtures, but were determined none the less to make a stand on a point of principle. If so, their courage – however misguided – does them credit. But there is another explanation too: more likely and, alas, less honourable. It is that even now, with the Napoleonic tide already threatening to engulf them, they were so terrified by the thought of war that any other prospect – even annihilation itself – was preferable. One can argue for ever whether, if Venice had accepted Bonaparte's offer, she could have retained her independence; he might well have sacrificed her anyway, once she had served his purpose. But one thing is sure. By rejecting him, she not only convinced him of her instinctive hostility to all he stood for; more dangerous still, she inflicted a dangerous blow to his pride. The decision was suicidal: the moment she took it, her death warrant was sealed.

Mantua fell on 2 February 1797, and with it the last outpost of Austrian power in Italy. Six weeks later, Bonaparte led his army over the Brenner Pass into imperial territory. He left behind him only such forces as he thought necessary to maintain order in the towns he had already occupied: light garrisons in Bergamo and Brescia, where he was on friendly terms with the local Venetian *podestà* – and where, incidentally, there were strong radical factions among the people – but a considerable force in Verona. This was the one city in which he could take no chances, for as well as being Venice's largest and most important mainland possession it controlled the approaches to the Brenner, over which he might well wish to return to Italy in due course.

Unfortunately, Verona was also the city in which anti-French feeling was strongest. The massive garrison had long since given up paying for its provisions in cash, and was now forcing local tradesmen to accept tokens and vouchers which everybody knew would never be redeemed. Moreover its commander, General Antoine Balland, saw his duties as those of a military governor; he showed no consideration for the people of the city and ordered about the recently appointed proveditor Giuseppe Giovanelli and the vice-*podestà* Alvise Contarini as if they were his own sergeant-majors. Even so, the Veronesi would probably have borne their tribulations in silence but for a totally unexpected development that occurred in mid-March: both Bergamo and Brescia rose in rebellion against Venice.

We now know that these revolts were deliberately engineered by a small group of French officers, without the knowledge of Bonaparte. Given the political climate in the two towns, in both of which the radical and anti-clerical influence of the freemasons was particularly strong, the task had not been difficult; a far greater problem was, however, to subvert the surrounding country, where the peasants, having no interest in political ideologies, remained determinedly loyal to the Republic. They poured down from the mountains with staves, pitchforks and any other weapons they had ready to hand, and at one town in the province of Brescia – Salo on Lake Garda – they actually overcame the rebels and restored Venetian rule, taking some 300 prisoners, including 200 Poles fighting with Napoleon's army and a few French soldiers. From that moment there was a limited guerrilla war between the peasants of the mountain valleys and the revolutionaries on the plain below.

Despite the prisoners at Salò, the French had from the first played no ostensible part in these uprisings, for which they disclaimed all responsibility. There was, however, a third city in which the same group of agitators had tried to stir up a similar rebellion, and failed. That city was Crema, about twenty miles south of Bergamo. Here they were obliged to resort to another, more shameless technique, much the same as that used so successfully by the Austrians at Peschiera. On 27 March a small detachment of French troops asked to be admitted, explaining. to the *podestà* that they wished only to pass through and would be on their way the following morning. Permission was reluctantly given; but the next day, instead of keeping their promise, they opened the gates to two more detachments, then seized the *podestà* and his fellow-officials and abducted them. Crema was declared free and the French, together with a group of rebels from Bergamo who had accompanied them, performed the traditional dance round a liberty pole erected in the main square, while the local population looked on in amazement.

The news of these defections, when it reached Venice, caused something akin to panic. All the *terra firma* west of the Mincio was effectively lost; the new frontier formed by that river must be defended at any price, and since Venice's regular army was obviously inadequate, armed militias raised from the local peasantry were the only alternative. General Balland was informed of the Republic's intentions, it being emphasized to him that the measures proposed were to be purely defensive, and directed not against the French but against rebellious citizens of the Republic; every volunteer was to be given the clearest possible instructions in this sense. Then the recruiting drive began. The number of those enrolled is uncertain, but seems to have been limited only by the quantity of arms available for distribution. They were probably not fewer than 10,000; there may have been more.

What nobody seems to have properly foreseen is that these tatterdemalion forces, suddenly finding themselves for the first time with weapons in their hands, might not be over-conscientious in the matter of obeying orders. They had no quarrel with the rebels of Bergamo and Brescia, who indeed made no attempt to cross the Mincio or even to approach it; they did, however, have plenty of outstanding scores to settle with the French, whose foraging parties regularly made free of their crops, their livestock and, as often as not, their wives and daughters into the bargain. Thus, as bands of trigger-happy youths, blue and yellow cockades in their hats, multiplied in the streets of Verona and the neighbouring towns, their shouts of '*Viva San Marco!*' were increasingly mingled with another, more ominous, war-cry: '*A basso i francesi!*' And it was not long before the serious sniping began. A couple of French soldiers, loitering at a street corner, would be picked off where they stood; a whole platoon, out in the countryside on a foraging expedition, might suddenly find themselves surrounded and mercilessly cut down. Balland's reprisals were swift and predictably savage, but they had no effect. By early April every pretence of civility between French and Italians was gone.

Bonaparte, on the road to Vienna, was kept fully informed of the worsening situation; and on 9 April he decided to send an ultimatum to the Doge, to be delivered at once and in person by the hand of a special emissary, his *aide-de-camp* General Junot. Junot arrived in Venice on the evening of Good Friday, 14 April, and immediately demanded an audience with the Doge early the following morning. The reply was polite but firm. Such an appointment was impossible. Holy Saturday was a day traditionally set aside for religious observances, and neither then nor on Easter Sunday itself could any government business be transacted. The Doge and his full Collegio would, however, be happy to receive the General early on Monday morning.

This was not the sort of answer that Junot was prepared to tolerate. He was not interested in religious observances and said so. His orders were to see the Doge within twenty-four hours, and he intended to obey them. If he were not given an audience within that time, he would leave and Venice would have to take the consequences. They would not, he suggested, be pleasant.

Thus, when the Collegio reluctantly received Bonaparte's representative, as he desired, early on the Saturday morning, its dignity was already bruised. Ignoring the seat to which he was shown – that normally reserved for ambassadors, on the Doge's right hand – Junot remained standing; then without preliminary, he pulled Bonaparte's letter from his pocket and began to read. It is a memorable letter – one can almost hear the young General's voice as he dictated it – and it is worth quoting in full:

Judenberg, 20 germinal, year V.

All the mainland of the Most Serene Republic is in arms. On every side, the rallying-cry of the peasants whom you have armed is 'Death to the French!' They have already claimed as their victims several hundred soldiers of the Army of Italy. In vain do you try to shuffle off responsibility for the militias that you have brought into being. Do you think that just because I am in the heart of Germany I am powerless to ensure respect for the foremost people of the universe? Do you expect the legions of Italy to tolerate the massacres that you have stirred up? The blood of my brothers-in-arms shall be avenged, and there is not one French battalion that, if charged with such a duty, would not feel the doubling of its courage, the trebling of its powers.

The Venetian Senate has answered the generosity we have always shown with the blackest perfidy. I send you my principal *aide-de-camp* as bearer of this letter. Is it to be war, or peace? If you do not take immediate measures to disperse these militias, if you do not arrest and deliver up to me those responsible for the recent murders, war is declared.

The Turk is not at your gates. No enemy threatens you. You have deliberately fabricated pretexts in order to pretend to justify a rally of the people against my army. It shall be dissolved within twenty-four hours.

We are no longer in the days of Charles VIII. If, against the clearly stated wishes of the French government, you impel me to wage war, do not think that the French soldiers will follow the example of your own militias, ravaging the countryside of the innocent and unfortunate inhabitants of the *terra firma*. I shall protect those people, and the day will come when they will bless the crimes that obliged the Army of France to deliver them from your tyranny.

BONAPARTE

In the shocked silence that followed, Junot flung the letter on the table in front of him, then turned on his heel and strode from the room to where, on the waterfront below, a boat was waiting to take him back to the French Legation.

The meeting of the Collegio was not the only extraordinary session to interrupt the Republic's official devotions on that last agonizing Easter Saturday of its existence. The same evening the Senate was summoned, and approved by a vote of 156 to forty-two a letter of cringing apology. Bonaparte was assured that the peasant activities to which he objected were nothing but spontaneous expressions of loyalty, whose sole object was that of restraining the rebels beyond the Mincio; the occasional unfortunate incidents had been due to the confusion of the moment and were in no wise the fault of the government, which had always stressed the need for moderation. Every effort would be made to apprehend those guilty of violence against the French and to bring them to justice. As an additional and unsolicited token of its good faith, the Republic was also arranging to release all political prisoners taken at Salò. The letter was entrusted to two special emissaries, Francesco Donà and Lunardo Giustinian, and dispatched at once.

The emissaries had hardly had time to leave the lagoon, however, before reports arrived from the mainland which caused even greater consternation than the appearance of Junot. All Verona had risen, spontaneously, against the French. Throughout Holy Week, placards and posters had been mysteriously appearing all over the city, calling upon the populace for a massed uprising; torn down by Venetians or French, they would be replaced almost at once. The priests, too – always prominent in anti-revolutionary agitation – had profited by the seasonal opportunities to inflame their congregations against the invaders; besides which there had been the usual influx of peasants, who had come in from the country the better to celebrate the feast and who, by the afternoon of Easter Monday (17 April), having duly celebrated it, were wandering noisily and somewhat unsteadily around the streets, more than ready for a fight. In such circumstances, and given the already explosive situation, it was not long before individual acts of violence gave place to general rioting. Before nightfall some 400 Frenchmen had been taken prisoner, and the rest had been driven to seek refuge in the city's three strong-places, the Castel Vecchio, the Castel S. Pietro and the citadel of S. Felice. There they were penned in and forced to withstand what was effectively a siege, until on 20 April the arrival of a new detachment of French troops secured their release. Even then it was another three days before order was fully restored throughout the city.

Bonaparte's retribution for what came to be called the *Pasque Veronesi* – the Veronese Easter – was harsh. An indemnity was demanded of 120,000 ducats. Verona was systematically despoiled of her pictures, sculptures and works of art. Silver was seized from the churches, the Monte di Pietà mercilessly looted. Forty thousand pairs of boots were demanded – without payment – for the army, and other clothing in similar quantities. Scarcely a single horse was left anywhere in the city. Of the leaders of the rising, eight – including a Capuchin monk, Luigi Collaredo – were executed by firing squad.

And what part, it may appropriately be asked, had Venice played in all this? A surprisingly small one, since at the earliest possible moment her two senior officials, Giovanelli and Contarini, disguised themselves as peasants and fled from the city. On the following day they were briefly persuaded to return, but disappeared again almost at once. Meanwhile the Veronese Count Francesco Emili hastened to Venice to implore, even at this late stage, the support of the *Serenissima* for the rising. His request, it is hardly necessary to record, was turned down flat. Venice – how many times did she have to say so? – was neutral, and neutral she proposed to remain.

To Napoleon Bonaparte in Austria, long before he heard the news of the Easter rising, the situation in the Veneto was causing considerable anxiety. He had never deluded himself as to the extent of anti-French feelings there, and he knew that the longer the war was allowed to continue the more dangerous this hostility would grow. Meanwhile reports were coming in of similar insurrections over large areas of the Tyrol. He had no doubts, for the moment, that the forces he had left behind him could keep the situation in hand, maintaining his lines of supply, communication and, if necessary, retreat; but there was no indication that they would be able to do so indefinitely.

All this was worrying enough; but he was also receiving daily information from another sector that gave him still more serious grounds for concern. His army formed only one prong of the French attack on Austria; there was also the Army of the Rhine, commanded by his brilliant young contemporary and chief rival, Lazare Hoche, which was now advancing eastwards through Germany at terrifying speed and threatening to reach Vienna before him. This was a possibility that he refused to contemplate. He, and no one else, must be the conqueror of the Habsburg Empire – his whole future career depended on it. He could not allow Hoche to steal his triumph.

For both these reasons, Bonaparte had decided that France must make an immediate peace with Austria. Already as early as 31 March he had written to the imperial commander-in-chief, the Archduke Charles, one of the most hypocritical letters of his life, suggesting that the war should be ended on humanitarian grounds:[1] Charles had responded favourably and a week later an armistice was agreed upon as a preliminary to peace negotiations.

Thus it came about that on 18 April 1797, at the castle of Eckenwald, just outside Leoben, a provisional peace was signed between Napoleon Bonaparte, acting in the name of the French Directory (although in fact he had never bothered to consult it) and the Austrian Empire. By its terms – details of which remained secret until they were confirmed six months later at Campo Formio – Austria was to renounce all claims to Belgium and to Lombardy, in return for which she would receive Istria, Dalmatia and all the Venetian *terra firma* bounded by the Oglio, the Po and the Adriatic. Venice was to be compensated – most inadequately – by the formerly papal territories of Romagna, Ferrara and Bologna.

Bonaparte, it need hardly be said, had no conceivable right to dispose in such a way of the territory of a neutral state. He would probably have argued, however, that in his eyes Venice was a neutral state no longer. He could not accept her continued protestations of good-will when, by her every action, she blatantly betrayed her pro-Austrian sympathies. Again and again he had offered her his friendship and invited her to join him in an alliance, but she had always refused. Those that were not with him were against him, and had no more claim on his consideration. On the other hand, there was no escaping the fact that the laws of international diplomacy did not look kindly on the arbitrary carving up of neutrals. However hollow Venice's professed neutrality might be, she would still have to be shaken out of it; and if, during the process, she could be made to appear in an unfavourable or even aggressive light, so much the better.

At this point one might have expected the Republic – which was well aware of the possible consequences of a Franco-Austrian peace and was still trembling at the prospect of Bonaparte's wrath over the *Pasque Veronesi* – to have leant over backwards to avoid giving him any further offence. Instead, just two days after the signing of the Leoben agreement, Venice committed an act of such supreme foolishness as to be – even in the context of this whole miserable saga of blundering ineptitude – almost beyond belief. In doing so, moreover, she played straight into Napoleon's hands.

1. '*Avons-nous assez tué de monde et commis assez de maux à la triste humanité ... Si l'ouverture que j'ai l'honneur de vous faire peut sauver la vie à un seul homme, je m'estimerai plus fier de la couronne civique que je me trouverais avoir méritée, que de la triste gloire qui peut revenir des succès militaires ...*'

On the morning of Thursday, 20 April, three French luggers appeared off the Lido port. At their head was the somewhat provocatively named *Libérateur d'Italie*, commanded by Citizen Ensign Jean-Baptiste Laugier, carrying four guns and a total complement of fifty-two which included twenty Italian volunteers recently recruited from Ancona. They were on patrol duty, their principal task being to protect French shipping in the Adriatic, and to harass such Austrian vessels as might come their way. Laugier and his fellow-captains obviously knew nothing of the Leoben agreement of two days before; nor, in all probability, were they aware that on 17 April the Council of Ten had issued a decree closing the harbour of Venice to all foreign ships of war. There is no reason to believe that their intentions were aggressive.

But the commander of the fortress of S. Andrea, Domenico Pizzamano, was taking no chances. The moment the *Libérateur* entered the channel he fired two warning shots across her bows. At this the two other ships immediately went about and were not seen again; Laugier, however, continued on his way until two armed pinnaces from S. Andrea came out to intercept him and block his path. What happened after that is uncertain; French and Venetian testimonies, not surprisingly, conflict. At some point, however, the *Libérateur*, hove to but carried by a strong tide, collided with a Venetian galleot; its crew immediately boarded her, as did the crews of the two pinnaces; meanwhile Pizzamano opened fire again and continued his bombardment despite Laugier's repeated signals of surrender. By the time the firing eventually ceased, Laugier and four of his crew were dead and another eight were wounded, as were five Venetians – one of whom, a fisherman from Chioggia who had been taken on by the *Libérateur* as pilot, subsequently died. The surviving Frenchmen were put in irons, while their ship – or what was left of it – was towed to the Arsenal.

The French minister, Lallement, at once lodged a strong protest. The *Libérateur*, he maintained, was being pursued by two Austrian ships and had simply sought refuge from them and from the weather in a neutral port, as she had every right to do. When a Venetian officer had come on board and demanded her immediate withdrawal, Laugier had had no alternative but to comply, but before he could do so the guns had opened up both from the fortress and from the neighbouring ships. Caught in the crossfire, he had ordered all his men below and himself remained alone on deck, protesting through his megaphone his readiness to submit. He had been killed almost instantly; the other casualties had been sustained only after the arrival of the Venetian boarding-party, who had cut down any crew member who made the slightest resistance. Lallement accordingly demanded the arrest of Pizzamano – whose own account of the affair he condemned as a tissue of lies – the imprisonment of all others concerned and their eventual handing over to Bonaparte for punishment, the restitution of all the impounded property and the immediate return of the survivors to Ancona.

The Venetians must have known that they were in the wrong. They cannot have seriously believed that a single small French lugger intended to attack their city, or that – even if it had – it could have done much serious harm. Laugier might have been a little cavalier in his behaviour, but that was no excuse for Pizzamano's apparent determination to blow him out of the water. Their only sensible course, to minimize the consequences of this disastrous incident, would have been to apologize to the French, make reasonable reparations – which would have cost them very little – and institute an inquiry, which could have been allowed to drag on until the French had returned to France or the whole thing had been forgotten. Instead, on 22 April, the Senate passed a resolution thanking Pizzamano, congratulating him on his courage and patriotism, and voting an extra month's pay to the crews of the pinnaces and all others concerned. If Venice had deliberately set out to convince Napoleon of her hostility – not that he needed convincing – she could hardly have made a better job of it.

Among all the unhappy characters who play their part in this last act of the Venetian drama there are few more deserving of our sympathy than Francesco Donà and Lunardo Giustinian, the two deputies sent off to Bonaparte with the reply to his letter and instructions to placate him as best they could. Even the physical aspect of their task was disagreeable enough; throughout his career, Napoleon was famous for the speed at which he travelled; and for two middle-aged Venetians, those gruelling days and nights spent trying to catch up with him, the endless jolting over some of the worst mountain roads in Europe only occasionally interrupted by a few hours' rest snatched at some verminous and evil-smelling inn, must have been a nightmare. Nor can their spirits have been improved by the prospect of the stormy scenes that they knew lay ahead of them when they finally ran their quarry to earth. And even that was not all: in every town and village at which they stopped, either to rest or to seek information, the same rumours besieged their ears. France had made peace with Austria; and on the altar of that peace Venice was to be sacrificed.

The pursuit lasted over a week; it was not until 25 April, at Graz, that the two exhausted deputies finally drew up before the French camp. Bonaparte received them at once, courteously enough, and listened in silence to their protestations of friendship and good-will. Suddenly his expression changed.

'Have the prisoners been freed?'

Giustinian had started to reply that all the French and Poles, and even certain of the Brescians, were now at liberty when he was angrily interrupted.

'No, no – I insist on the release of *all* prisoners, all those who have been arrested for their political opinions since I arrived in Italy ... If not, I myself shall come and break your prisons open, for I shall tolerate none of your Inquisitions, your medieval barbarities. Every man must be free to express his opinions ... And what of all my men, whom you Venetians have murdered? My soldiers cry for vengeance; I cannot deny it to them ... The murderers must be dealt with – any government unable to restrain its own subjects is an imbecile government and has no right to survive.'

Throughout this outburst the deputies were doing their utmost to appease Bonaparte's mounting fury. Those guilty of violence against the French, they assured him, had already been brought to justice. If he knew of any further evidence of crimes still unpunished, he had only to inform them; all such matters would be immediately investigated. But by now he was past listening. Striding backwards and forwards across the room, the speed and volume of his heavily accented Corsican Italian increasing with every step, he launched into a searing diatribe against Venice, her government and her people, accusing them of perfidy, hypocrisy, incompetence, injustice and – most serious of all in his eyes – hostility to himself and to France, ending with the words that were soon to echo in the heart of every Venetian:

'I will have no more Inquisition, no more Senate. *Io sarò un Attila per lo Stato veneto* – I shall be an Attila to the State of Venice.'

By now the two deputies – from whose detailed report of the interview, in the Venetian state archives, this account has been taken – were longing only to escape; but Bonaparte had not yet finished with them. His anger subsided; he now insisted that they remain and dine with him, and throughout the meal – which they credibly describe in their report as *incommodissimo* – submitted them to an interrogation, sometimes teasing, sometimes openly hostile, about the Council of Ten, the Inquisitors of State, the prisons, the tortures, the Orfano Canal (where, in the Middle Ages, the Republic used secretly to dispose of its undesirables) and, as they put it, 'other fabrications by French authors seeking to defame or discredit our government – from which, we protested, the righteous had nothing to fear and which was genuinely beloved by our people.' After dinner came yet another tirade before the miserable pair were finally allowed to withdraw.

The following morning they left for Venice, only to be intercepted by a courier with a further dispatch from the Signoria – a dispatch as unwelcome as anything they could possibly have imagined. It began with a detailed, if somewhat tendentious, account of the *Libérateur* incident – the first they had heard of it – and ended with instructions to seek another immediate interview with Bonaparte in order to give him the approved Venetian version of the story. Still shaken from their experience of the previous day, the deputies can perhaps be forgiven for interpreting these instructions a little freely and deciding to break the news, in the first instance, by letter. Two hours later they received a reply:

Gentlemen,

I have read with indignation your letter concerning the murder of Laugier, which event – without parallel in the annals of the nations of our time – you have made still more outrageous by the tissue of lies by which your government has sought to justify itself.

I cannot receive you, gentlemen, since you and your Senate reek with French blood. When you have delivered into my hands the admiral who gave the order to fire, the commander of the fortress and the Inquisitors who direct the police of Venice, I will hear your justification. You will meanwhile be good enough to evacuate, with the shortest possible delay, the mainland of Italy.

However, gentlemen, if the dispatch that you have just received concerns the Laugier incident, you may present yourselves before me.

Bonaparte

Tremblingly, they did so; there followed another stream of invective, the General shouting that, just as he had already brought liberty to other subject peoples, he was now coming to break the chains of the people of Venice. The government, he knew, was now in the hands of a mere handful of nobles; the Council of Eight Hundred (*sic*) had not been summoned for the past three weeks. (Both Donà and Giustinian seem to have been genuinely astonished by his ignorance, or misinformation, about Venetian affairs.) If the Republic wished to avoid destruction, he continued, those few men who were using their power to stir up hostility to France must be proscribed at once. In their despair, the deputies were unwise enough to hint that Venice might offer 'another kind of satisfaction'; but this only aroused Bonaparte to a fresh outburst of rage. All the riches of Peru, he thundered, would not deter him from avenging his men.

The two Venetians saw that there was no more to be said. Collecting the few shreds of dignity left to them, sorrowfully and in fear, they took their leave.

When the report by Donà and Giustinian of their first meeting with Bonaparte reached Venice, Doge Manin and the Signoria already knew that the Republic was doomed. War was imminent; further negotiation was impossible; the *terra firma* was as good as lost; and the only hope of saving the city itself from destruction lay in capitulation to the conqueror's demands. These demands were terrible indeed – nothing less than the abdication of the entire oligarchy, the abandonment of a constitution that had lasted more than a thousand years, and its replacement by a democracy. A revolution, in fact: but a revolution initiated from above, by those who were to be its principal victims – the suicide of the State.

But how was this suicide to be accomplished? It could not come to pass constitutionally, through the Senate, where such a proposal would meet with violent opposition; the resulting debates would drag on for days, and long before they were resolved the French would be within the lagoon. In any case, what use was discussion when the issue was inevitable, and why respect a constitution in the very act of abolishing it? The Senate gathered on 29 April to conduct some formal business of no particular interest or importance. When that business was over it broke up as usual. It never met again.

The following day, towards evening, the Doge summoned a special meeting. Present, apart from himself and his six Councillors, were the three chiefs of the *Quarantia*, all the *Savii* including the three outgoing *Savii del Consiglio*, the three *Capi* of the Council of Ten and the three *Avogadori di Comun*. Although such a grouping was wholly unconstitutional, its forty-two members included representatives of all the principal executive organs in the government; its moral authority was therefore considerable. Robes of office were set aside. The members all wore informal black clothes, and the *Consulta Nera*, as it came to be called, was the only effective decision-making body in the Republic's last days.

The Great Council, however, was still in existence, its 1,169 members still constituting the fount of political authority in the Republic. It could not be cast aside as the Senate had been, and the first decision of the *Consulta Nera* was that it should be summoned to an extraordinary session the next morning, when the Doge in person should officially inform it of Bonaparte's ultimatum and seek its approval for the measures proposed. The *Consulta* was still discussing the precise terms of the resolution when there suddenly arrived a dispatch from Tommaso Condulmer, written from his flagship off Fusina, reporting that the first French soldiers had already arrived on the shores of the lagoon and were even now positioning their heavy guns well within range of the city. The effect of this news was electric. In the general consternation some members panicked, others broke down and wept. Francesco Pesaro – hitherto one of the most courageous and robust advocates of a strong line against the French – openly declared his intention of taking flight to Switzerland. The Doge himself set an example only slightly more edifying, walking up and down the room wringing his hands and repeating those words which, for the rest of his life, he was never able to live down: '*Sta notte no semo sicuri nè anche nel nostro letto*' ('Tonight there will be no safety for us, not even in our own beds').

But the night passed uneventfully enough, and the next morning, 1 May, the Great Council met as arranged, in a Doges' Palace now heavily guarded by *Arsenalotti* and Dalmatian troops. Doge Manin, 'his face deathly pale and with tears streaming down his cheeks',[1] took his place at the rostrum, warning his audience at the outset that his emotional and physical state might prevent him from finishing even the short allocution he had prepared. Then, simply and sadly, he described the circumstances in which the Republic now found itself, and proposed a resolution instructing the two deputies, Donà and Giustinian, to inform Bonaparte that all political prisoners would be freed at once and all those who had taken up arms against Frenchmen punished. The deputies were also empowered to discuss and elucidate the constitutional changes the General required.

The Doge was not to know that, by the time this resolution was approved – by 598 to seven, with fourteen abstentions – the deputies were already on their way back to Venice; nor that on that very same day Bonaparte was issuing a manifesto adducing fifteen separate proofs of Venetian hostility – most of them travesties of the truth – and formally declaring war on the Republic. Simultaneously he sent instructions to his representative in Venice, Lallement, to leave the city forthwith – his sinister and intrigue-loving secretary, Villetard, remaining as *chargé d'affaires*. Other directives were sent to the French commanders in Italy, ordering them to treat all Venetians as enemies and to pull down or efface the Lion of St Mark wherever it appeared.

Henceforth the collapse was swift. On 9 May Villetard produced an

---

1. '*Squallido in viso, e grondante di lagrime*': such at least is the description of the Abbate Tentori, who may or may not have been an eye-witness, but who has left the only reliable account of the dealings of the *Consulta Nera*, and of much else besides, during this chaotic time.

ultimatum, spelling out Bonaparte's requirements in considerably greater detail than before. These were the following:

The Comte d'Antraigues – the self-styled Ambassador of Louis XVIII, but never recognized as such by Venice – to be arrested, and freed only after the seizure of all his papers and their transmission to the Directory in Paris.

The *pozzi* and *piombi* – respectively the cells on the ground floor (above the water level) of the *prigioni* and those immediately under the leads of the Doges' Palace roof – to be opened for inspection by the people, after the release of the last three political prisoners from the latter.[1]

The cases of all other prisoners to be reviewed and the death penalty abolished.

The Dalmatian troops to be disbanded and discharged.

The policing of the city to be entrusted to patrols under the authority of a specially constituted committee headed by General Salimbeni, the former Venetian commander-in-chief on *terra firma*, and others of known democratic sympathies.

A Tree of Liberty to be erected on the Piazza.

A provisional *Municipalità* to be established of twenty-four Venetians, later to be supplemented by delegates from the cities of *terra firma*, Istria, Dalmatia and the Levant.

A manifesto to be issued announcing the creation of a democracy, inviting the populace to choose its representatives.

The insignia of the former government to be burnt at the foot of the Tree of Liberty, a general amnesty to be proclaimed for all political offenders and the freedom of the press to be decreed, 'with the proviso that there should be no discussion about the past, either of personalities or government.'

Services of thanksgiving to be held in St Mark's.

Three thousand French troops to be invited into Venice, to take over the Arsenal, the fortress of S. Andrea, Chioggia and any other strategic points that the French general might designate.

The Doges' Palace, the *Zecca* and other important buildings to be entrusted to the Civic Guard for protection.

The Venetian fleet (such as it was) to be recalled to the lagoon and to be placed under the joint command of the French and of the Municipality, of which Manin and the democratic leader Andrea Spada were to be co-Presidents.

All Venetian ambassadors abroad to be replaced by 'democrats'.

1. But see p. 638.

The credit of the mint and the national bank to be guaranteed by the state.

To approve these demands – there was no longer any influential voice to advocate resistance, or even argument – the Great Council was called for Friday, 12 May. From soon after sunrise the people of Venice had been congregating in the Piazza and Piazzetta, just as they had done countless times before in the city's history. In the past, however, they had usually assembled for purposes of celebration or – on rare occasions – to express their dissatisfaction or concern. Never before had they gathered together out of fear. By now all were aware that the end had come; but none had any clear idea of what form that end would take. The atmosphere was an unfamiliar one in Venice – an atmosphere of uncertainty, bewilderment, and ill-defined apprehension. Among the working population there were many who, in contrast to their enfranchised superiors, believed that the Republic, doomed or not, could and should have fought for her survival; for them, there was anger mingled with their shame, and they were in no mood to conceal it. Bands of these rough loyalists were roaming the streets, crying '*Viva San Marco!*' and hurling abuse at any patricians they chanced to encounter on their path. Partly, perhaps, for this reason – though many of the nobles seemed already to have fled the city, or to have hurried to their mainland estates in an effort to save them from the French soldiery – the Council fell short, by sixty-three members, of its constitutional quorum of 600.

But the time for such niceties was past. The Doge called the meeting to order, apprised it of Bonaparte's terms and proposed a motion by which, 'with the most high object of preserving unharmed the Religion, life and property of all these most beloved inhabitants', the oligarchy surrendered all its powers to a provisional democratic government. When he had finished, one of the members mounted the rostrum to open the debate; even though the conclusion was foregone, the Council had to be given the chance to express its views. Scarcely had he begun to speak, however, when the sound of firing was heard just outside the Palace.

At once, all was confusion. To the terrified members of the Council, such sounds could mean one thing only: the popular uprising that they had so long dreaded had begun. Some saw themselves being torn to pieces by the mob as they left the Palace; others had visions of days and weeks in the *pozzi* or *piombi*, so recently vacated by their former occupants, while the guillotine was set up in the Piazza. All had one single object in view: to escape from the Palace, in disguise if necessary, while there was still time. Within minutes, the true source of the firing had been established: some of the Dalmatian troops, who were being removed from Venice on Bonaparte's orders, had simply discharged their muskets into the air as a parting salute to the city. But the panic had begun; reassurances were useless. To urgent cries of 'Vote! Vote!' the debate was abandoned and the remaining legislators of the Venetian Republic rushed to the ballot boxes to perform their last hurried duty to the state they had claimed to govern. The final count was 512 in favour of the resolution, twenty against, and five abstentions; but few of those who voted remained to hear it. Leaving their all-too-distinctive robes of office behind them, they were already slipping discreetly away out of side entrances to the Palace when, to an almost empty chamber, the Doge declared the resolution adopted. The Republic of Venice was no more.

Lodovico Manin himself made no attempt to flee. Almost alone among his fellow-nobles, he had maintained a quiet calm amid the hubbub – a calm born, perhaps, of fatalism or even of despair, but a calm none the less that enabled him to keep his dignity, even while the last frail structure of the Republic crumbled about him. In the sudden stillness that followed the break-up of the meeting he slowly gathered up his papers and withdrew to his private apartments. There, having laid aside his ducal *corno*, he carefully untied the ribbons of the close-fitting cap of white linen worn beneath it, the *cuffietta*, and handed it to his valet, Bernardo Trevisan, with those sad words which, more than any others, seem to symbolize the fall of Venice: '*Tolè, questa no la dopero più*' ('Take it, I shall not be needing it again').

Epilogue

It was Sunday, 4 June – Whit Sunday, a day which in former years the Venetians had been accustomed to celebrate with all the pomp and parade appropriate to one of the great feasts of the Church. But this year, 1797, was different. Shocked and stunned to find their city occupied by foreign troops for the first time in its thousand years of history, the people were in no mood for rejoicing. Nevertheless, General Louis Baraguey d'Hilliers, the French commander, had decided that some form of celebration would be desirable, if only to give a much-needed boost to local morale. He had discussed the form it should take with the leaders of the Provisional Municipality, in whom, under his own watchful eye, the supreme political power of the new Republic was now entrusted; and plans had been accordingly drawn up for a *Festa Nazionale*, at which the citizens were to be given their first full-scale public opportunity to salute their 'Democracy' and the resonant revolutionary principles that inspired it.

Those who, prompted more by curiosity than by enthusiasm, made their way to the Piazza that Sunday morning had grown accustomed to the 'Tree of Liberty' – that huge wooden pole, surmounted by the symbolic scarlet Phrygian cap which bore more than a passing resemblance to the ducal *corno* – rising incongruously from its centre. This they now found to have been supplemented by three large tribunes, ranged along the north, south and west sides. The western one, which was intended for the sixty members of the Municipality, carried the inscription LIBERTY IS PRESERVED BY OBEDIENCE TO THE LAW; the other two, destined for the French and other less distinguished Italian authorities, respectively proclaimed that DAWNING LIBERTY IS PROTECTED BY FORCE OF ARMS and ESTABLISHED LIBERTY LEADS TO UNIVERSAL PEACE. The

Piazzetta was similarly bedecked, with a banner in praise of Bonaparte stretched between the two columns by the Molo, one of which was draped in black in memory of those brave Frenchmen who had perished victims of the Venetian aristocracy – the name of Jean-Baptiste Laugier heading the list.

After Baraguey d'Hilliers and the Municipality had taken their places, the bands began to play – there were four of them, disposed at intervals around the Piazza, comprising a total of well over 300 musicians – and the procession began. First came a group of Italian soldiers, followed by two small children carrying lighted torches and another banner with the words GROW UP, HOPE OF THE FATHERLAND. Behind them marched a betrothed couple (DEMOCRATIC FECUNDITY) and finally an aged pair staggering under the weight of agricultural implements, bearing words 'referring to their advanced age, at which time liberty was instituted'.

The procession over, the President of the Municipality advanced to the Tree of Liberty, where, after a brief ceremony in the Basilica, he proceeded to the most dramatic business of the day: the symbolic burning of a *corno* and other emblems of ducal dignity (all obligingly provided for the purpose by Lodovico Manin himself) and a copy of the Golden Book. He and his fellow-*municipalisti*, together with the General and the senior members of his staff, then led off the dancing round the Liberty Tree, while the guns fired repeated salutes, the church bells rang and the bands played *La Carmagnole*. The celebrations ended with a gala performance of opera at the Fenice Theatre, completed less than five years before.

This was the level to which Venice had sunk within a month of the Republic's end – the level of tasteless allegory and those empty, flatulent slogans so beloved of totalitarian governments of today: a demoralization so complete as to allow her citizens, many of whom had been crying '*Viva San Marco!*' beneath the windows of the Great Council as it met for the last time, to stand by and applaud while all their proud past was symbolically consigned to the flames. Not long afterwards one Giacomo Gallini, head of the stone-masons' guild, signed a contract to remove or efface every winged lion in the city, as had already been done by the French, with horrible thoroughness, throughout the *terra firma*. We can only be thankful that he proved less conscientious: though he accepted his pay – 982 ducats – relatively few lions were touched.[1] But the fact that such an action was even contemplated is indication enough of the mentality of French and Venetians alike through that nightmare summer.

1. The most serious casualty was the sculptural group of Doge Francesco Foscari kneeling before the lion which forms the centrepiece of the *Porta della Carta* (see p.340n. 2).

There is, or seems to be, a law of politics whereby the degree of freedom and democracy actually enjoyed by a given state varies in inverse ratio to the vehemence and volume with which it is proclaimed. The so-called 'Democratic' government that wielded power in Venice for the next eight months was, for all its crude trumpetings, nothing of the kind. The sixty members of the Municipality did not even have the pretence of a popular mandate. They were appointed under the direction of the French *chargé d'affaires*, Villetard; the people of Venice were neither consulted in advance nor called upon to ratify the appointments later. During the government's short life, no election was ever held; indeed after 17 October, when Bonaparte treacherously handed over the city, together with Istria and Dalmatia, to Austria by the Treaty of Campo Formio, there was very little point in holding one.

The Austrians took formal possession of Venice on 18 January 1798. They did not keep it for long on that occasion; in 1805, after Austerlitz, Napoleon seized it back to incorporate it in his new Italian Kingdom. But only ten years later the Congress of Vienna returned it once more, together with the provinces of Venetia and Lombardy, to the Habsburg Empire; and Austrian it remained – apart from those seventeen heroic, hopeless months in 1848–9 during which the Venetians rose up in arms against their masters and declared a new independent republic – until 1866, when the imperial army was destroyed by the Prussians at Sadowa. Then, and only then, was Venice at long last allowed to take her place in Cavour's united Italy, by that time almost complete.

The purpose of this book, however, has been to tell the story of the Most Serene Republic; and that story is now told. How much more pleasant it would have been to record a less ignominious end; history – to echo the lament expressed on the first page of Part Three – seldom behaves exactly as the historian would wish, yet as one reads through the chronicle of·the Republic's dying agony one cannot help reflecting on how easily events might have taken a different and more favourable turn. If, for example, there had arisen one strong leader of the stamp of Enrico Dandolo or Francesco Foscari or Leonardo Donà, able to focus Venetian energies and to stand firm against Bonaparte's bullying; if Venice had been able, in the summer of 1796, to throw into the field a properly equipped army of perhaps as few as 25,000 determined men under a competent general, she and Austria together – aided, as they would have been, by the Kings of Naples and Sardinia – could almost certainly have saved the situation and driven the French from Italy.

Alas, none of these things occurred; yet, even so, the story need not have been quite so unedifying as it is. The Venetians might still have showed, as the Republic began to totter, some spark of that courage and endurance that they had shown often enough in defending their colonies against the Turks – or that their own grandchildren were to show against the Austrians half a century later. One would not have asked for – and certainly not have expected – a heroic resistance such as was seen on the walls of Constantinople in 1453; merely a flash of the old Venetian spirit which would have allowed the *Serenissima* to pass into history with some semblance of honour. But that too was lacking. The real tragedy of Venice was not her death; it was the manner in which she died.

One thing only can be said of Lodovico Manin and those sad, feckless men who presided with him over her downfall. By their craven surrender they did at least ensure the preservation of their city. Had the French artillery been induced to open fire from its emplacements on the mainland shore, had French warships found it necessary to enter the lagoon and bombard Venice from the water, one dares not imagine what the consequences might have been. Even as things turned out, much was lost. On the flimsiest of pretexts,[1] Bonaparte gave orders for the seizure of pictures, sculptures, manuscripts, church plate and all the priceless works of art his specially appointed Commissioners could lay their hands on, including even the four bronze horses of St Mark, which were shipped off to Paris to adorn the Arc du Carrousel in the Tuileries gardens. The horses, as we know, were later restored to the gallery of the Basilica;[2] but much of the conqueror's loot, including Veronese's tremendous *Marriage of Cana* from the Refectory of S. Giorgio Maggiore, and his central panel from the ceiling of the Hall of the Council of Ten in the Doges' Palace, is still in the Louvre – and likely to remain there. We can only be thankful that Bonaparte himself, astonishingly enough, never set foot in Venice. Had he done so, there is no telling how much more thoroughly he would have despoiled the most opulent of all cities, or how much deeper would have been the scar that even his shadow was able to leave behind.

And yet, whether or not we accept the view that Venice could – given courage, determination and good leadership – have saved herself from extinction, we must still feel mildly surprised that she lasted as long as she did. Of the three greatest blows she sustained in all her history – the opening up of the Cape route to the Indies in 1499, the steady spread of

1. The terms of the worthless 'Treaty of Milan', signed on 16 May by Venetian deputies in the name of a Republic that had four days before ceased to exist, and never ratified by the Directory in Paris.

2. At the time of writing they are in the course of being removed inside, victims of the atmospheric pollution that is taking a more terrible toll of Venetian sculpture than Napoleon ever did.

Turkish power for the two centuries following the fall of Constantinople in 1453 and the combined onslaught launched against her by virtually the whole of Europe, united in the League of Cambrai – she was to blame for none; yet any one of them might have caused her downfall. To have survived all three was no small achievement.

From the beginning of the sixteenth century, however, her *dégringolade* was slowly gathering momentum; and though, just occasionally, it seemed to be checked by some spectacular victory or success, by the time the smoke dispersed and the cheering died away her triumphs were always revealed as illusory, and what had at first been hailed as a turning-point in Venetian fortunes was seen to be merely another milestone on the downward path. Her much-vaunted defeat of the Turks at Lepanto in 1571 did her no good at all; Francesco Morosini's Peloponnesian conquests of 1685 lasted barely thirty years; and the jubilation with which the Venetians greeted the successful skirmishes of Angelo Emo against the Barbary pirates in the 1770s and '80s proved only how desperately they needed encouragement and how far their standards had declined.

By then, too, another fact was becoming evident. Though cultural life might continue to flourish, though the economy might still have its ups and downs, the body politic was sick unto death. It was as if the constitution – that miraculous constitution which had preserved the Republic until it could boast a longer period of unbroken authority than any other state in Europe – had worn out at last, all its former flexibility and resilience gone. The degree of influence wielded, for example, by Andrea Tron, who for a whole generation was virtual dictator of Venice by virtue not of any offices he held but of his character and personality alone, would have been unthinkable in former times – a betrayal of the one key principle for which the Republic had always striven, that too much power should never be concentrated in the hands of a single individual. Even after Tron's death, Paolo Renier and his friends tended to govern through small, semi-official groups and caucuses, some members of which might from time to time hold positions of responsibility in the Collegio or elsewhere but would not appreciably lose influence even when their terms of office expired. Such a system, whatever its faults, did not necessarily result in weak government, at least in the short term; with a firm hand at the helm, it might have even made for quicker decisions and more determined action at the moment of crisis. But in the hands of mediocrities it could not fail to sap the constitutional strength of the state, rendering it powerless to resist the combined ideological and military threat posed by the philosophy of revolution on the one hand and Napoleon Bonaparte on the other. Thus Bonaparte, for all his bluster, cannot be held uniquely responsible for the fall of Venice. He it was who administered the *coup de grâce*; but the *Serenissima* was already doomed. Exhausted, demoralized and no longer able to keep pace with the changing world, she had, quite simply, lost the will to live.

Her death was lamented by no one except her own citizens and by no means all of those. Where Europe and even the rest of Italy was concerned, she died without a single friend. Dilettanti admired her for her beauty; libertines flocked to her for the pleasures she might afford; but few foreigners, if any, loved her for herself. There was nothing surprising about this, and nothing new. To the outside world she had never been very lovable. In the days of her greatness, part of her unpopularity was due to envy – of her wealth, her magnificence, and her superb geographical position which rendered her impregnable from invasion or attack; but this was not the whole story. Particularly by their fellow-Italians, Venetians tended to be thought of as arrogant and overbearing. Their merchants, though not in general dishonest, drove mercilessly hard bargains. Their diplomatists were suave, yet somehow always seemed a little sinister as well. As a people, they lacked warmth and passion. They did not even seem to care whether they were liked or not. They were, in short, cold fish.

Such, at least, was their reputation; nor was it altogether unjustified. Where Venice was genuinely misjudged – and continues to be so today – was in the way she chose to govern herself. For well over half a millennium she was universally considered a police state, a tyrannical oligarchy that arrested without charge, imprisoned without trial and condemned without appeal, permitting her citizens – apart from the chosen few – no voice in the administration, no liberty of speech or action. That such an idea of the Venetian constitution is a travesty of the truth should long have been clear to all readers of this book. If the Republic was an oligarchy, it was a remarkably broadly based one, with a Great Council frequently exceeding 2,000 members; within this circle, democratic principles were observed with almost exaggerated respect – until the last few decades, more so than in any other country of the western world, in no part of which was universal suffrage dreamt of, or even thought desirable. Far from being tyrants, her doges enjoyed less real power than any European ruler, while those to whom power was entrusted could exert it only through councils and committees whose stringent electoral rules and constantly changing memberships frustrated the most determined ambitions.

It was this system of collective responsibility more than any inherent injustice that gave Venice her reputation as a police state. Committees, particularly those whose composition never remains the same for more than a month or two together, are bound to have a faceless quality about them, which in turn imbues them with a largely spurious air of mystery and secrecy. There is no denying that the Ten and the Three both used spies and informers, just as every security service has since the world began; but such bodies must be judged less by their methods (unless these involve violence or the threat of it) than by the ends to which they use them. In Venice arrests were normally made only after the fullest inquiries, and sentences – except those on conspirators against the state – were seldom harsh. They were also surprisingly few. Napoleon Bonaparte was not the only one to imagine Venetian dungeons swarming with political prisoners whose only crime had been the love of liberty. He must have been astonished to learn that, at the fall of the Republic, there was not a single prisoner anywhere on Venetian territory whose captivity was due to his political opinions.[1]

And so, the more one studies the domestic history of Venice, the more inescapable does the conclusion become: by whatever political standards she is judged, she compares favourably with any nation in Christendom – except, arguably, in the days of her final dotage. Nowhere did men live more happily, nowhere did they enjoy more freedom from fear. The Venetians were fortunate indeed. Disenfranchised they might be; they were never downtrodden. Although, being human, they might occasionally complain of their government, not once in all their history did they ever rise up against it; such few attempts as there were at rebellion were inspired by discontented nobles, never by the populace. They worked hard, an unusually high proportion of them as artists and craftsmen; they knew, better than any other people in the world, how to enjoy themselves with style and *panache*; and they lived out their lives in a city even more beautiful – though such a thing seems scarcely possible – than that which we know today. They loved that city passionately, and for a thousand years they remained fiercely loyal to the Republic that had built it, enriched it and kept it safe. And when the end came, with all its hopelessness and humiliation, when the *corno* and the Golden Book were cast alike into the flames, when all Europe was beginning to tremble at the advance of Napoleon Bonaparte – then, and only then, did that loyalty waver. But not for long. Today, though the *Serenissima* has been dead for nearly two hundred years, it is commemorated with pride in every corner of the city – where, painted on

1. Giorgio Pisani had been released from the fortress of Brescia a short time before. When the French entered the *piombi*, they were found to be empty; the *pozzi* had three prisoners, all murderers. Venice's third major prison, popularly known as the *Quattro*, had a complement of twenty-four criminals of various kinds.

wood or canvas, carved in marble or stone, moulded in plaster or cast in bronze, Venice's ever-faithful protector, the great winged lion of St Mark, still points proudly and majestically at the word of God.

PAX TIBI MARCE EVANGELISTA MEUS

List of Doges

726–1797

Orso Ipato	726–737	Otto Orseolo	1008–1026
Interregnum	737–742	Pietro Centranico	1026–1032
Teodato Ipato	742–755	Domenico Flabanico	1032–1043
Galla Gaulo	755–756	Domenico Contarini	1043–1071
Domenico Monegario	756–764	Domenico Selvo	1071–1084
Maurizio Galbaio	764–775	Vitale Falier	1084–1096
Giovanni Galbaio	775–804	Vitale Michiel I	1096–1102
Obelario degli Antenori	804–811	Ordelafo Falier	1102–1118
Agnello Participazio	811–827	Domenico Michiel	1118–1130
Giustiniano Participazio	827–829	Pietro Polani	1130–1148
Giovanni Participazio I	829–836	Domenico Morosini	1148–1156
Pietro Tradonico	836–864	Vitale Michiel II	1156–1172
Orso Participazio I	864–881	Sebastiano Ziani	1172–1178
Giovanni Participazio II	881–887	Orio Mastropiero	1178–1192
Pietro Candiano I	887	Enrico Dandolo	1192–1205
Pietro Tribuno	888–912	Pietro Ziani	1205–1229
Orso Participazio II	912–932	Giacomo Tiepolo	1229–1249
Pietro Candiano II	932–939	Marin Morosini	1249–1253
Pietro Participazio	939–942	Renier Zeno	1253–1268
Pietro Candiano III	942–959	Lorenzo Tiepolo	1268–1275
Pietro Candiano IV	959–976	Jacopo Contarini	1275–1280
Pietro Orseolo I	976–978	Giovanni Dandolo	1280–1289
Vitale Candiano	978–979	Pietro Gradenigo	1289–1311
Tribuno Memmo	979–991	Marino Zorzi	1311–1312
Pietro Orseolo II	991–1008	Giovanni Soranzo	1312–1328

Francesco Dandolo	1329–1339	Nicolò da Ponte	1578–1585
Bartolomeo Gradenigo	1339–1342	Pasquale Cicogna	1585–1595
Andrea Dandolo	1343–1354	Marino Grimani	1595–1605
Marin Falier	1354–1355	Leonardo Donà	1606–1612
Giovanni Gradenigo	1355–1356	Marcantonio Memmo	1612–1615
Giovanni Dolfin	1356–1361	Giovanni Bembo	1615–1618
Lorenzo Celsi	1361–1365	Nicolò Donà	1618
Marco Corner	1365–1368	Antonio Priuli	1618–1623
Andrea Contarini	1368–1382	Francesco Contarini	1623–1624
Michele Morosini	1382	Giovanni Corner I	1625–1629
Antonio Venier	1382–1400	Nicolò Contarini	1630–1631
Michele Steno	1400–1413	Francesco Erizzo	1631–1646
Tommaso Mocenigo	1414–1423	Francesco Molin	1646–1655
Francesco Foscari	1423–1457	Carlo Contarini	1655–1656
Pasquale Malipiero	1457–1462	Francesco Corner	1656
Cristoforo Moro	1462–1471	Bertucci Valier	1656–1658
Nicolò Tron	1471–1473	Giovanni Pesaro	1658–1659
Nicolò Marcello	1473–1474	Domenico Contarini	1659–1675
Pietro Mocenigo	1474–1476	Nicolò Sagredo	1675–1676
Andrea Vendramin	1476–1478	Alvise Contarini	1676–1684
Giovanni Mocenigo	1478–1485	Marcantonio Giustinian	1684–1688
Marco Barbarigo	1485–1486	Francesco Morosini	1688–1694
Agostino Barbarigo	1486–1501	Silvestro Valier	1694–1700
Leonardo Loredan	1501–1521	Alvise Mocenigo II	1700–1709
Antonio Grimani	1521–1523	Giovanni Corner II	1709–1722
Andrea Gritti	1523–1538	Alvise Mocenigo III	1722–1732
Pietro Lando	1539–1545	Carlo Ruzzini	1732–1735
Francesco Donà	1545–1553	Alvise Pisani	1735–1741
Marcantonio Trevisan	1553–1554	Pietro Grimani	1741–1752
Francesco Venier	1554–1556	Francesco Loredan	1752–1762
Lorenzo Priuli	1556–1559	Marco Foscarini	1762–1763
Girolamo Priuli	1559–1567	Alvise Mocenigo IV	1763–1778
Pietro Loredan	1567–1570	Paolo Renier	1779–1789
Alvise Mocenigo I	1570–1577	Lodovico Manin	1789–1797
Sebastiano Venier	1577–1578		

Bibliography

I. ORIGINAL SOURCES

1. Collections of Sources

(The abbreviations used elsewhere in this Bibliography and in the footnotes follow each entry in parentheses.)

ALBERI, E., *Relazioni degli Ambasciatori Veneti al Senato*, 15 vols. (Florence, 1846–59). (Sixteenth century only.)

Archivio Storico Italiano. 1st series (Florence, various dates). (A.S.I.)

BAROZZI, N. and BERCHET, G., *Relazioni degli Stati Europei lette al Senato dagli Ambasciatori Veneti nel secolo decimosettimo*, 5 series (Venice, various dates).

Calendar of State Papers, Venetian, 38 vols., edited and translated by Rawdon Brown (London, 1864–1940). (C.S.P.V.)

CESSI, R., *Documenti Relativi alla Storia di Venezia anteriori al Mille. Cura di Roberto Cessi* (Padua, 1942). (C.D.R.S.V.)

Corpus Scriptorum Historiae Byzantinae (Bonn, 1828–97). (C.S.H.B.)

Cronache Veneziane Antichissime, ed. G. Monticolo (Rome, 1890). (C.V.A.)

Documenti del Commercio Veneziano, XI–XIII sec. (Rome, 1940). (D.C.V.)

GRAEVIUS, J. C., *Thesaurus Antiquitatum et Historiarum Italiae, etc.*, 10 vols. in 45 fol. (Leyden, 1704–25). (G.T.A.)

MIGNE, J. P., *Patrologia Latina*, 221 vols. (Paris, 1844–55). (M.P.L.)

MOSCATI, R., *Relazioni degli Ambasciatori Veneti al Senato* (Milan, 1943). (Reports from France in eighteenth century only.)

MURATORI, L. A., *Rerum Italicarum Scriptores*, 25 vols. (Milan, 1723–51). (M.R.I.S.)

Recueil des Historiens des Croisades, Publ. Académie des Inscriptions et des Belles Lettres (Paris, 1841–1906). Historiens Occidentaux, 5 vols. (R.H.C.Occ.)

SEGARIZZI, A., *Relazioni degli Ambasciatori Veneti al Senato* (Bari, 1912). (Report from other Italian states, sixteenth to eighteenth centuries.)

TENTORI, B. M., *Raccolta Cronologico-Regionata di Documenti Inediti della Rivoluzione e Caduta della Repubblica di Venezia* (Florence, 1800).

2. Individual Sources

Altino Chronicle, in A.S.I., Vol. 8.

BARBARO, N., *Giornale dell' Assedio di Costantinopoli*, ed. E. Cornet (Vienna, 1856).

BROSSES, Président Charles des, *Lettres sur l'Italie*, 2 vols. (Paris, 1885).

CHINAZZO, D., *Belli inter Venetos et Genuenses, 1378*, in M.R.I.S., Vol. 15.

COMMINES (COMMYNES), Philippe de, *Mémoires*, ed. B. de Mandrot (Paris, 1901–3). (Tr. A. R. Scoble, London, 1901–4.)

CORYATE, T., *Coryate's Crudities, 1611*, 3 vols. (London, 1776).

CRISTOFORO DA SOLDO, *Cronaca*, in M.R.I.S., XXI, iii.

Cronica de singulis patriarchis Nove Aquileie, in C.V.A.

DANDOLO, Andrea, *Chronicon Venetum*, in M.R.I.S., Vol. 12 (new edn. by E. Pastorello, Bologna, 1938–42).

FABRI, F., *The Book of the Wanderings of Brother Felix Fabri*, ed. A. Stewart (Palestine Pilgrims Texts Society, London, 1892–3).

GIUSTINIAN, A. (Venetian Ambassador in Rome, 1502–5) *Dispacci*, ed. P. Villari (Florence, 1876).

GIUSTINIANI, Bernardo, *De Marci vita, ejus translatione et sepulturae loco*, in G.T.A., Vol. 5, i.

GIUSTINIANI, Bernardo, *Historia dell' origine di Venetia*, in G.T.A., Vol. 5, i.

Grado Chronicle, in C.V.A.

GUICCIARDINI, F., *Storia d'Italia*, tr. and ed. S. Alexander (New York, 1969).

INNOCENT III, Pope, *Letters*, in M.P.L., Vol. 215.

JOHN THE DEACON, *Cronaca Veneziana*, in C.V.A., and M.P.L., Vol. 139.

LORENZO DE MONACIS, *Chron. de rebus Venetis*, ed. F. Cornelius, Venice, 1758 (also in M.R.I.S.), Vol. 8.

MALIPIERO, D., *Annali Veneti, 1457–1500*, ed. T. Gar and A. Sagredo, in A.S.I., VII, 1843.

MANIN, L., *Memorie del Dogado di Lodovico Manin* (Venice, 1886).

MARTIN DA CANALE, *Chron. des Veniciens*, ed. F. L. Polidori, in A.S.I., Vol. 8.

MORYSON, F., *An Itinerary* (Glasgow, 1907).

NICETAS CHONIATES, *Historia*, in C.S.H.B. (French trans. by L. Cousin in *Histoire de Constantinople*, Vol. 5, Paris, 1685).

PETER DAMIAN, St, *Vita Sancti Romualdi*, in M.P.L., Vol. 144.

PETER DAMIAN, St, *Opuscula*, in M.P.L., Vol. 145.

PETRARCH, Francesco, *Epistolae de rebus familiaribus et variae*, ed. G. Fracassetti, 3 vols. (Florence, 1859–63). (Italian trans. by G. Fracassetti, 5 vols., Florence, 1863–7).

PHRANTZES G., *Chronicon*, ed. E. Bekker, in C.S.H.B., 1838.

PIUS II, Pope, *Memoirs of a Renaissance Pope* (London, 1958).

POLO, Marco, *The Travels of Marco Polo*, tr. R. Latham (Harmondsworth, 1958).

PRIULI, G., *Diarii*, ed. R. Cessi, in *Rerum Italicarum Scriptores*, xxiv, part iii (Bologna, 1933–7).

ROBERT OF CLARY, *La Conquête de Constantinople*, ed. Lauer (Paris, 1924).

SANSOVINO, F., *Delle Cose Notabili della Città di Venezia* (Venice, 1596).

SANUDO, M., *Diarii*, 58 vols. (Venice, 1879–1903). (Diaries run from January 1496 to March 1533.)

SANUDO, M., *Le Vite dei Dogi di Venezia*, in M.R.I.S., VIII.

SANUDO, M., *La Spedizione di Carlo VIII in Italia*, ed. R. Fulin (Venice, 1873).

SANUDO, M., *Itinerario per la Terrafirma nell' Anno 1483*, ed. R. Brown (Padua, 1847).

SANUTO (or SANUDO), Marino (the elder), *Liber secretorum fidelium crucis super Terrae Sanctae recuperatione*, in Bongars, *Gesta Dei per Francos*, Vol. II, Hanover, 1611.

SARPI, P., *Advice Given to the Government of Venice*, tr. Dr. Aglionby (London, 1693).

STELLA, Georgius, *Annales Genuenses, 1298–1409*, in M.R.I.S., Vol. 17.

TAFUR, P., *Travels and Adventures, 1435–9*, tr. M. Letts (London, 1926).

TREVISAN, Nicolò, *Chronicle*, in Biblioteca Marciana, Cl. xi, Ital. Codex xxxii.

VILLEHARDOUIN, Geoffrey of, *La Conquête de Constantinople*, ed. E. Faral, 2 vols. (Paris, 1938–9).

WILLIAM OF TYRE, *Belli sacri historia*, and *Historia rerum in partibus transmarinis gestarum*, in R.H.C.Occ., Vol. I.

WILLIAM OF TYRE, *A History of Deeds Done Beyond the Sea*, tr. with notes by E. A. Babcock and A. C. Krey (New York, 1943).

II. MODERN HISTORICAL WORKS

ALZARD, J., *La Venise de la Renaissance* (Paris, 1956).

ARSLAN, E., *Gothic Architecture in Venice*, tr. A. Engel (London, 1971).

BASCHET, A., *Histoire de la Chancellerie Secrète* (Paris, 1870).

BASCHET, A., *Les Archives de Venise* (Venice, 1857).

BASCHET, A., *Les Princes de l'Europe au XVIe Siècle, d'après les Rapports des Ambassadeurs Vénitiens* (Paris, 1862).

BATTISTELLA, A., *La Repubblica di Venezia nei suoi Undici Secoli di Storia* (Venice, 1921).

BATTISTELLA, A., *Il Conte Carmagnola* (Genoa, 1889).

BERENGO, M., *La Società Veneta alla Fine del Settecento* (Florence, 1956).

BERLAN, F., *I Due Foscari* (Turin, 1852).

BLANC, A., *Il dominio veneziano a Creta nel Trecento* (Naples, 1968).

BRAGADIN, M. A., *Repubbliche Italiane sul Mare* (Milan, 1951).

BRAUDEL, F., *La Méditerranée et le Monde Méditerranéen à l'Epoque de Philippe II* (Paris, 1949). (Tr. Siân Reynolds, 2 vols., London and New York, 1973).

BRAVETTA, E., *Enrico Dandolo* (Milan, 1919).

BROWN, Horatio, *Studies in the History of Venice*, 2 vols. (London, 1907).

BROWN, Horatio, *Venice: An Historical Sketch of the Republic* (London, 1893).

BROWN, Horatio, *The Venetians and the Venetian Quarter in Constantinople to the Close of the Twelfth Century* (London, 1893).

BROWN, Rawdon, *L'Archivio di Venezia con riguardo speciale alla storia inglese* (Venice and Turin, 1865).

CAMBRIDGE MEDIEVAL HISTORY, esp. Vol. V, Venetian chapters by R. Cessi. (Contains excellent and comprehensive bibliography.)

CAMBRIDGE MODERN HISTORY, Vols. I, II.

CARILE, A., *La Cronachistica Veneziana (Secoli XIII–XVI) di Fronte all' Apartizione dei Romani nel 1204* (Florence, 1969).

CECCHETTI, B., *La Repubblica di Venezia e la Corte di Roma nei Rapporti della Religione*, 2 vols. (Venice, 1874).

CECCHETTI, Bartolomeo, *La Vita dei veneziani fino al 1200* (Venice, 1870).

CESSI, Roberto, *Venezia Ducale*, 2 vols. (Padua, 1927).

CESSI, Roberto, *Le Colonie medioevali italiani in Oriente*, Part I, *La Conquista* (Bologna, 1942).

CESSI, Roberto, *Storia della Repubblica di Venezia*, 2nd edn, 2 vols. (Still without sources, bibliography or index!) (Milan, 1968).

CHAMBERS, D. S., *The Imperial Age of Venice, 1380–1580* (London, 1970).

COZZI, G., *Il Doge Nicolò Contarini* (Venice and Rome, 1958).

CRAWFORD, F. M., *Gleanings in Venetian History*, 2 vols. (London, 1905).

CREIGHTON, M., *History of the Papacy*, 5 vols. (London, 1882–94).

DARU, P., *Histoire de la République de Venise*, 9 vols. (Paris, 1821).

DAVIS, J. C., *The Decline of the Venetian Nobility as a Ruling Class* (Baltimore, 1962).

DEMUS, Otto, *The Church of S. Marco in Venice: History, Architecture, Sculpture*, Dumbarton Oaks Studies, 6 (Washington, D.C., 1960).

DIEHL, Charles, *Venise: une République Patricienne* (Paris, 1915).

FILIASI, Giacomo, *Memorie storiche dei Veneti*, 11 vols. (Venice, 1796).

FILIASI, G., *Ricerche Storico-critiche sull' Opportunità della Laguna Veneta, nel Commercio, sull' Arti e sulla Marina* (Venice, 1803).

FONDAZIONE GIORGIO CINI, *Storia della Civiltà Veneziana*, 10 vols. (Florence, 1955–66).

FULLER, J. F. C., *The Decisive Battles of the Western World and Their Influence upon History* (London, 1954).

GACHARD, M., *Relations des Ambassadeurs Vénetiens sur Charles–Quint et Philippe II* (Brussels, 1855).

GALLICCIOLLI, G. B., *Delle Memorie Venete antiche profane ed ecclesiastiche . . . libri tre*, 7 vols. (Venice, 1795).

GEANAKOPLOS, D. J., *Byzantine East and Latin West* (Oxford, 1966).

GEANAKOPLOS, D. J., *Greek Scholars in Venice* (Cambridge, 1962).

GFRÖRER, A. F., *Byzantinische Geschichten*, ed. J. B. Weiss, 3 vols. (Graz, 1872–7).

HALE, J. R. (ed.), *Renaissance Venice* (London, 1973).

HAZLITT, W. C., *History of the Origin and Rise of the Venetian Republic*, 2 vols. (London, 1900).

HEYD, W., *Geschichte des Levantehandels im Mittelalter* (Stuttgart, 1879). (French translation by F. Raynaud, *Histoire du commerce du Levant au Moyen Âge*, 2 vols. Leipzig, 1936.)

HILL, Sir G., *History of Cyprus*, 4 vols. (Cambridge, 1948).

HODGKIN, Thomas, *Italy and Her Invaders*, 11 vols. (Oxford, 1880).

HODGSON, F. C., *The Early History of Venice* (London, 1901).

HODGSON, F. C., *Venice in the Thirteenth and Fourteenth Centuries* (London, 1914).

HOPF, K., *Geschichte Griechenlands vom Beginne des Mittlealters bis auf die Neuere Zeit* (Leipzig, 1867–8).

KRETSCHMAYR, H., *Geschichte von Venedig* (Gotha, 1905–20; Stuttgart, 1934).

LAMANSKY, V., *Secrets d'Etat de Venise* (St Petersburg, 1884).

LANE, F. C., *Venetian Ships and Shipbuilders of the Renaissance* (Baltimore, 1934).

LANE, F. C., *Recent Studies on the Economic History of Venice* (*Journal of Economic History*, XXIII, 1963).

LANE, F. C., *Venice and History* (Baltimore, 1966).

LANE, F. C., *Venice, a Maritime Republic* (Baltimore, 1973).

LAURITZEN, P. L., *The Palaces of Venice* (London, 1978).

LAURITZEN, P. L., *Venice* (London, 1978).

LONGWORTH, P., *The Rise and Fall of Venice* (London, 1974).

LOPEZ, R. S., and RAYMOND, I. W., *Medieval Trade in the Mediterranean World* (New York and London, 1955).

LUZZATO, G., *Storia Economica di Venezia dall' XI al XVI Secolo* (Venice, 1961).

MACCHI, M., *Storia del Consiglio dei Dieci* (Turin, 1848).

McCLELLAN, G. B., *Venice and Bonaparte* (Princeton, 1931).

McNEILL, W. H., *Venice, the Hinge of Europe, 1081–1797* (Chicago, 1974).

MALAGOLA, C., *Le Lido de Venise à travers l'Histoire* (Venice, 1909).

MALAMANI, V., *Il Settecento a Venezia*, 2 vols. (Turin and Rome, 1891).

MARANINI, G., *La Costituzione di Venezia*, 2 vols. (Venice, 1927–31).

MARIN, C. A., *Storia Civile e Politica del Commercio de' Veneziani*, 8 vols. (Venice, 1798–1808).

MARZEMIN, G., *Le Origini romane di Venezia* (Venice, 1938).

MILLER, W., *The Latins in the Levant* (London, 1908).

MILLER, W., *Essays on the Latin Orient* (Cambridge, 1921).

MOLMENTI, P., *La Storia di Venezia nella Vita Privata*, 6th edn, 3 vols. (Bergamo, 1923). (English translation by H. F. Brown, *Venice: Its Individual Growth from the Earliest Beginnings to the Fall of the Republic*, 6 vols., London, 1906–8).

MOLMENTI, P. G., *I Banditi della Repubblica Veneta* (Florence, 1898).

Morris, J., *The Venetian Empire* (London, 1980).

Muir, D., *A History of Milan under the Visconti* (London, 1924).

Musatti, E., *Storia di Venezia*, 2 vols. (Milan, 1936).

Mutinelli, F., *Annali Urbani di Venezia, 810–1797* (Venice, 1841).

Newett, Margaret, 'The Sumptuary Laws of Venice in the Fourteenth and Fifteenth Centuries.' In *Historical Essays by Members of Owens College, Manchester*, ed. T. H. Tout and J. Tait (London, 1902).

Nystazapoulou-Pelekidis, Marie, 'Venise et la Mer Noire du XIe au XVe Siècles, in *Thesaurismata: bolletino dell' Istituto Ellenico di Studi Bizantini e Post-Bizantini* (1970).

Okey, Thomas, *Venice and its Story* (London, 1930).

Oliphant, Mrs, *The Makers of Venice* (London, 1893).

Perocco, G., and Salvadori, A., *Civiltà di Venezia*, 3 vols. (Venice, 1973–6).

Pirri, P., *L'Interdito di Venezia del 1606 e i Gesuiti* (Rome, 1959).

Pullan, B. (ed.), *Crisis and Change in the Venetian Economy in the 16th and 17th Centuries* (London, 1968).

Pullan, B., *Rich and Poor in Renaissance Venice* (London, 1971).

Pullan, B., *A History of Early Renaissance Italy* (London, 1973).

Quadri, A., *Abrégé de l'Histoire de la République de Venise* (Venice, 1847).

Ragg, L. M., *Crises in Venetian History* (London, 1928).

Romanin, S., *Storia Documentata di Venezia*, 2nd edn, 10 vols. (Venice, 1912–21).

Romanin, S., *Gli Inquisitori di Stato* (Venice, 1858).

Roth, C., *History of the Jews in Venice* (Philadelphia, 1930).

Rowdon, M., *The Fall of Venice* (London, 1970).

Rubin de Cervin, G. B., *Bateaux et Batellerie de Venise* (Paris, 1978).

Runciman, Steven, *A History of the Crusades*, 3 vols. (Cambridge, 1951–4).

Runciman, S., *The Fall of Constantinople* (Cambridge, 1965).

Ruskin, J., *The Stones of Venice*, 3 vols. (London, 1851–3).

Ruskin, J., *St Mark's Rest* (London, 1877).

Sansovino, F., *Venetia, città nobilissima et singolare descritta in XIII libri* (Venice, 1658).

Sella, D., *Commerci e Industrie a Venezia nel Secolo XVII* (Venice and Rome, 1961).

Seneca, F., *Il Doge Leonardo Donà* (Padua, 1959).

Simonsfeld, H., *Andreas Dandolo und seine Geschichtswerke* (Munich, 1876).

Sismondi, J. C. L., *History of the Italian Republics in the Middle Ages* (London, 1906).

Sottas, J., *Les Messageries maritimes de Venise aux XIV et XV siècles* (Paris, 1938).

Tamaro, A., *La Vénétie Julienne et la Dalmatie*, 3 vols. (Rome, 1918–19).

Tassini, G., *Curiosità Veneziane*, 8th edn (Venice, 1970).

Tenenti, A., *Piracy and the Decline of Venice, 1580–1615*, tr. J. and B. Pullan (London, 1967).

THAYER, W. R., *A Short History of Venice* (New York, 1905).

THIRIET, F., *Histoire de Venise* (Paris, 1952).

THIRIET, F., 'La Romanie Vénitienne au Moyen Âge. Le Développement et l'Exploitation du Domaine Colonial Vénitien' (XII–XV siècles), *Écoles françaises d'Athènes et de Rome*, 193 (Paris, 1959).

THIRIET, F., *Régestes des délibérations du Sénat de Venise concernant la Roumanie, 1329–1463*, 3 vols. (Paris, 1959–61).

TIEPOLO, C. D., *Discorsi sulla Storia Veneta* (Udine, 1828).

WIEL, A., *Venice* (London, 1894).

YRIARTE, C., *La Vie d'un Patricien de Venise au Seizième Siècle* (Paris, 1874).

III. GUIDE-BOOKS AND OTHERS

BLUE GUIDE, *Venice* (London, Chicago, New York, San Francisco, 1980). The most comprehensive English guide-book, serious and scholarly in the house tradition.

GRUNDY, M., *Venice, an Anthology Guide* (London, 1976). Extracts from past writers grouped under individual monuments; beautifully produced.

HONOUR, H., *The Companion Guide to Venice* (London, 1965). By far the most useful general-purpose guide-book to the monuments of Venice for the informed visitor.

LINKS, J. G., *Venice for Pleasure* (London, 1966). Four long walks through the city described by one who knows and loves every stone of it. A little gem of a book, which contains, incidentally, a much fuller bibliography of Venetian guide-books than there is space for here.

LORENZETTI, G., *Venice and Its Lagoon* (Rome, 1961). An English translation by John Guthrie of one of the most comprehensive and encyclopedic guide-books to a single city ever written. Indispensable for real lovers of Venice; but the average visitor will find it overwhelming and hard to handle, and will be happier with Honour's *Companion Guide*.

McCARTHY, M., *Venice Observed* (London, 1956). A brilliantly written coffee-table book. Intelligent and informative, but not a guide.

MORRIS, J., *Venice* (London, 1960). Surely the best full-length essay on Venice ever written. Once again, in no sense a guide-book; but as a portrait of the city, incomparable.

PIGNATTI, T., *Venice* (tr. J. Landry, London, 1971). A superbly produced and illustrated guide-book by one of Venice's leading art historians.

SHAW-KENNEDY, R., *Art and Architecture in Venice. The Venice in Peril Guide* (London, 1972). Particularly useful for those as interested in the contents of the buildings of Venice as in the buildings themselves, since it contains lists of all the principal works of Venetian painters, sculptors and architects with their locations.

Index

READ MORE IN PENGUIN

In every corner of the world, on every subject under the sun, Penguin represents quality and variety – the very best in publishing today.

For complete information about books available from Penguin – including Puffins, Penguin Classics and Arkana – and how to order them, write to us at the appropriate address below. Please note that for copyright reasons the selection of books varies from country to country.

In the United Kingdom: Please write to *Dept. EP, Penguin Books Ltd, Bath Road, Harmondsworth, West Drayton, Middlesex UB7 0DA*

In the United States: Please write to *Consumer Sales, Penguin Putnam Inc., P.O. Box 12289 Dept. B, Newark, New Jersey 07101-5289*. VISA and MasterCard holders call 1-800-788-6262 to order Penguin titles

In Canada: Please write to *Penguin Books Canada Ltd, 10 Alcorn Avenue, Suite 300, Toronto, Ontario M4V 3B2*

In Australia: Please write to *Penguin Books Australia Ltd, P.O. Box 257, Ringwood, Victoria 3134*

In New Zealand: Please write to *Penguin Books (NZ) Ltd, Private Bag 102902, North Shore Mail Centre, Auckland 10*

In India: Please write to *Penguin Books India Pvt Ltd, 11 Community Centre, Panchsheel Park, New Delhi 110017*

In the Netherlands: Please write to *Penguin Books Netherlands bv, Postbus 3507, NL-1001 AH Amsterdam*

In Germany: Please write to *Penguin Books Deutschland GmbH, Metzlerstrasse 26, 60594 Frankfurt am Main*

In Spain: Please write to *Penguin Books S. A., Bravo Murillo 19, 1° B, 28015 Madrid*

In Italy: Please write to *Penguin Italia s.r.l., Via Benedetto Croce 2, 20094 Corsico, Milano*

In France: Please write to *Penguin France, Le Carré Wilson, 62 rue Benjamin Baillaud, 31500 Toulouse*

In Japan: Please write to *Penguin Books Japan Ltd, Kaneko Building, 2-3-25 Koraku, Bunkyo-Ku, Tokyo 112*

In South Africa: Please write to *Penguin Books South Africa (Pty) Ltd, Private Bag X14, Parkview, 2122 Johannesburg*

BY THE SAME AUTHOR

Byzantium: The Early Centuries

In this exciting narrative history, John Julius Norwich tells of the five formative centuries of an empire that would enthral the western world for more than eleven hundred years. 'He is brilliant . . . He writes like the most cultivated modern diplomat attached by a freak of time to the Byzantine court, with intimate knowledge, tactful judgement and a consciousness of the surviving monuments' – *Independent*

Byzantium: The Apogee

Although surrounded by hostile Turks, Bulgars, Russians and barbarian tribes, and controlled by an extraordinary sequence of adventurers, lustful emperors, sinister eunuchs and unworldly scholars, the Byzantine Empire somehow managed to survive. Here, Lord Norwich continues his compelling chronicle up to the coronation of the heroic Alexius Comnenbus in 1081. 'Eminently readable' – *Spectator*

Byzantium: The Decline and Fall

'[He] tells this dark, intricate and tragic story in a fluent and accessible way. His Byzantine trilogy is a superb achievement, rescuing the Eastern Empire from the contempt of Edward Gibbon and other historians' – Joan Smith in the *Independent on Sunday*

The Normans in Sicily

When first published, *The Normans in Sicily* was acclaimed for its 'diligence, narrative skill, and a scholarship fired by enthusiasm' (*Sunday Telegraph*) which made it 'instructive throughout, as well as consistently entertaining' (*The New York Times Book Review*). In this volume it is published with its sequel, *The Kingdom in the Sun*, and a comprehensive Appendix, which lists all Sicily's surviving Norman monuments. The result is both a superb traveller's companion and a masterpiece of the historian's art.

also published:

Christmas Crackers
More Christmas Crackers